THE PENTATEUCH

—AS—

NARRATIVE

A Biblical-Theological Commentary

JOHN H. SAILHAMER

ZondervanPublishingHouse
Grand Rapids, Michigan

A Division of HarperCollinsPublishers

Edited by Gary Lee

Library of Congress Cataloging-in-Publication Data

Sailhamer, John.
    The Pentateuch as narrative : a biblical-theological commentary / John H. Sailhamer.
      p.   cm.
    Includes bibliographical references and index.
    ISBN 0-310-57421-8
    1. Bible. O.T.–Pentateuch—Commentaries. 2. Narration in the Bible. I. Title.
BS1225.3.S235   1992
222'.1'07–dc20   91-47604
                                              CIP

Printed in the United States of America

13 14 /QG/ 30 29

CONTENTS

CONTENTS

DETAILED OUTLINE
OF THE PENTATEUCH

EXODUS

LEVITICUS

NUMBERS

ABBREVIATIONS

ad loc. In a commentary, under the verse discussed
BZAW *Beiheft zur Zeitschrift für die alttestamentliche Wissenschaft*
EBC *The Expositor's Bible Commentary*
EvT *Evangelische Theologie*
EVV English versions of the Bible
GKC Gesenius, Kautzsch , and Cowley, *Hebrew Grammar*
HALAT *Hebräisches und Aramäisches Lexikon zum Alten Testament*
ICC International Critical Commentary
IDBS *Interpreter's Dictionary of the Bible: Supplement*
KAT Kommentar zum alten Testament
KJV King James Version
LSJ Liddell, Scott, Jones *Greek-English Lexicon*
LXX The Greek Septuagint
M. Maimonides' interpretation
MT The Hebrew Masoretic Text
NASB New American Standard Bible
NICOT New International Commentary on the Old Testament
NIV New International Version
(N)JPS The (New) Jewish Publication Society
(N)RSV (New) Revised Standard Version
OTL Old Testament Library
RB *Revue Biblique*
RE *Realencyclopädie*
RGG *Die Religion in Geschichte und Gegenwart*
SBL Society of Biblical Literature
THAT *Theologisches Handwörterbuch zum alten Testament*
TrinJ *The Trinity Journal*
VT *Vetus Testamentum*
VTSup *Supplements to Vetus Testamentum*
WTJ *Westminster Theological Journal*
ZAW *Zeitschrift für die alttestamentliche Wissenschaft*
ZDMG *Zeitschrift der deutschen morgenländischen Gesellschaft*

PREFACE

The aim of this commentary is to trace the narrative strategy of the Pentateuch. Taking seriously the literary and historical claim that the Pentateuch was originally composed as a single book, we have attempted to analyze and describe its structure from the beginning of Genesis to the end of Deuteronomy. We believe it is evident in reading the Pentateuch that its broad stretches of narrative, spanning the time from the Creation to the covenant at Sinai and, further, to the conquest of Canaan, cannot conveniently be broken down into the "books" of Genesis, Exodus, Leviticus, Numbers, and Deuteronomy as we now have them in our Bibles. There is an appreciable loss of sense when we view the Genesis narratives without following them all the way to Sinai and the conquest. There is an even greater loss when we attempt to read the exodus, wilderness, and conquest narratives apart from those in Genesis. By reading the narratives in Exodus in isolation from those in Genesis, for example, we can easily overlook the author's attempts to link God's work of Creation in the beginning with his work of covenant at Sinai. We fail to see the tabernacle as the author's view of a return to the Garden of Eden, or the crossing of the Red Sea as a retelling of God's great work of judgment and redemption in the Flood. Moreover, if we read the collections of laws in Leviticus, Numbers, and Deuteronomy apart from their context within the overall pentateuchal narrative, we can easily fail to appreciate the many and varied links between these laws and their narrative framework. For example, a comparison of the arrangement of laws in Leviticus 11–16 suggests that the author of the Pentateuch intentionally linked the spread of sin in God's good creation and the measures Israel was to take to prevent the spread of sin and defilement within their camp. We may also miss the author's argument that the purpose of the Sinai covenant was the redemption and blessing of "all the families of the earth" (Ge 12:3).

It is of utmost importance to view this present commentary in the light of its overall purpose stated above. In writing this book, we were faced with three unavoidable constraints. First, we sensed the need for a commentary on the entire Pentateuch published in a single volume. To accomplish this goal for a book as large as the Pentateuch meant severe space limitations. Second, we felt it was necessary to trace the Pentateuch's literary structure throughout the whole of the work in a way that gave proper attention to each and every part. We did not want to offer mere summaries of large sections of laws, for example, or to omit discussion of parallel sections. It was important to treat each section of the Pentateuch as it occurs in the present shape of the book. For example, it was not enough to treat the Ten Commandments in Exodus 20 and omit a discussion of them in Deuteronomy 5. Nor was it enough in Deuteronomy 5 merely to repeat what had been said about them in Exodus 20. It was necessary in such parallel cases to raise the question of why the author had included two versions of the Ten Commandments within the one literary work of the Pentateuch. Third, in writing this book we believed it was important to keep a constant eye on the central ideas and themes of the whole Pentateuch. Therefore, in our discussion of the various details of the laws, for example, we were not intent on raising the question of the particular role this or that law might have played within ancient Israelite society. Rather, we were concerned about the role that a particular law or group of laws played in the strategy of the author's composition of the Pentateuch. For example, rather than attempt to explain what role the slaughter of the red heifer may have played in the religious life of ancient Israel, we were concerned about the question of why the author included that ritual and why he put it where he did in the Pentateuch. More importantly, what literary relationship exists, if any, between the account of that ritual and the earlier pentateuchal narratives? To give another example, from the viewpoint of the author's strategy it was important to attempt to explain the well-known fact that the "judgments" in Exodus 21:1–23:12 described a form of worship quite different from the prescriptions for the tabernacle in Exodus 25–31, although within the narrative itself both sets of instructions were given to Israel while Moses was on Mount Sinai.

When faced with such differences, biblical scholars have traditionally responded in at least three ways. First, classical biblical scholarship has tried to harmonize the differences. We confess sympathy with that approach, but we want to stress that we will not take that course. We are concerned in this book not with explaining these kinds of differences away but in explaining why they are there. Second, modern evangelical scholarship has often responded to such difficulties in the text by looking beyond the text to the historical events recorded in the text. By explaining the historical events in a coherent and meaningful way, evangelical scholars feel they have alleviated the difficulty in the text. Though we are also in sympathy with the attempt to explain the coherence of the historical events recorded in the text and the attempt to show that they are, in fact, reliably recorded, in our view such an approach misses the real question. What must be explained is the text and its meaning. Third, modern biblical criticism has consistently focused on the various literary strata reflected in such differences within the Pentateuch. These scholars attribute such differences to various oral or literary documents used in the process of the Pentateuch's composition. We believe that this approach also leaves unanswered the real question. In attempting to explain the text as we now have it, our focus will not be on the literary *strata* that may or may not lie behind such differences. Rather, our focus will be on the literary *strategy* reflected in these differences.

We do not claim any originality in the approach we have taken. We do recognize, however, that there is a need for further explanation and justification for it. We have attempted to meet that need in the introduction to this work. The purpose of the introduction is to describe and defend an approach to the Pentateuch that focuses on the narrative and literary continuity of Scripture rather than on its historical background and setting. As will be apparent to the reader, the introduction is written at a different level than the commentary itself. Whether we have adequately defended our approach to the Pentateuch and whether we have adequately carried out our approach throughout the commentary, we leave to the reader to decide.

Because this commentary is based on a close reading of the Hebrew text, we often rely on our own translation in order to reflect a particular interpretation. In doing so, we are not suggesting that standard English versions (e.g., the NIV) are inadequate or do not reflect our understanding, though that may at times be the case. In giving our own translation we are merely attempting to make our point more clearly and with some emphasis. Moreover, this commentary is based on the Masoretic text (MT) as represented in Biblia Hebraica (Stuttgart edition). We are not assuming that this is the best text in every instance, but it is the text before us and thus its interpretation is our primary goal.

I wish to acknowledge my gratitude to those who have helped and encouraged the writing of this book. First, the students in the courses on the Pentateuch I have taught as well as my colleagues in both Old Testament and New Testament have both listened to and questioned my reading of the Pentateuch. I would like to make special mention of my colleague and dean, Dr. Walter C. Kaiser, Jr. Second, the editors, specifically Ed M. van der Maas, Verlyn D. Verbrugge, and Stanley N. Gundry of Zondervan Publishing House, and Gary Lee, have made many helpful suggestions along the way.

Lastly, I wish to thank my wife and friend, Patty, and our four children, David, Betsy, John, and Peter.

INTRODUCTION

INTERPRETING THE PENTATEUCH

A. The Pentateuch Is a Book

We begin our exposition of the Pentateuch with the simple observation that the Pentateuch is a book—that is, a written text. This observation may appear too obvious to warrant consideration, but it is often overlooked. Throughout the course of these introductory sections we will frequently return to this point. Here at the beginning, however, we shall note a few important implications of the fact that the Pentateuch is a book.

1. The Pentateuch Is a *Single* Book

Though we often think of the Pentateuch as a collection of five books, viz., Genesis, Exodus, Leviticus, Numbers, and Deuteronomy, it was originally intended to be read as a single book. References to the Pentateuch within the OT itself show that from the earliest times it was considered a single book. For example, subsequent OT writers call the whole of the Pentateuch a "book" (2Ch 25:4; 35:12; Ezr 6:18; Ne 13:1). The NT also considered the Pentateuch a single book. For example, in Mark 12:26, the Pentateuch is called "the book of Moses."

The name "Pentateuch,"[1] which means simply "five-part book," came into use in the second century A.D.,[2] apparently as a translation of the

---

[1]The word is Greek, ἡ πεντάτευχος, meaning "the [book] consisting of five parts." It was rendered into Latin as *pentateuchus*.

[2]The first use of the Greek term ἡ (ὁ) πεντάτευχος is found in an epistle (to Flora) by the Valentinian Ptolemaeus (c. A.D. 160). Ptolemaeus is cited in Epiphanius's (c. 315–403) *Refutation of All the Heresies* (33.4): "that whole law which passes around in the

Hebrew expression "the five-fifths of the Law."[3] Though this Hebrew expression is known only from the later talmudic period,[4] the division of the Pentateuch into five parts is known already by the time of Josephus (c. A.D. 37–100) and Philo (c. 20 B.C.–A.D. 50).[5] It is commonly held that the five-part division of the Pentateuch is as early as the Greek (Septuagint, or LXX) translation (3d century B.C.).[6]

The case for this assumption, however, is inconclusive, since we do not have early evidence concerning the structure of the Greek Pentateuch, and the shape of existing manuscripts reflects a much later period.[7] Moreover, the earliest references to the Greek Pentateuch clearly regard it as a single book.[8] In any event, it is safe to conclude that the five-part division is early and no doubt reflects a custom of writing large works on multiple scrolls.[9] It is equally certain, however, that this division was not original. The original work was written as a single book.

---

pentateuch of Moses." Tertullian (c. 160–220) used the Latin Pentateuchus in Against Marcion, 1.10 (Realencyklopädie für protestantische Theologie und Kirche, 3d ed., 24 vols. [Leipzig: J. C. Hinrichs'sche, 1904], 15:114). Since Jerome, Pentateuchus has become common usage in the Western church.

[3]Otto Eissfeldt, The Old Testament: An Introduction, trans. P. R. Ackroyd (New York: Harper & Row, 1965), 156.

[4]Bereshit (Genesis) Rabba, 3.5. The date of Bereshit Rabba is c. 400 or after (H. L. Strack and G. Stemberger, Introduction to the Talmud and Midrash, trans. M. Bockmuehl [Edinburgh: T. & T. Clark, 1991], 304). See Bab. Talm. Sanhedrin 44a, "Achan transgressed the five-fifths of the Law [the whole Law] because 'also' is mentioned five times." See also Eissfeldt, Introduction, 156.

[5]See Josephus, Contra Apion, i.8, "Our books, those which are justly accredited, are but two and twenty, and contain the record of all time. Of these, five are the books of Moses" (Josephus, 9 vols., trans. H. St. J. Thackeray, Loeb Classical Library, [Cambridge: Harvard Univ. Press, repr. 1966], 1:178–79). See Philo, De Abrahamo, "The first of the five books in which the holy laws are written bears the name and inscription Genesis" (Philo, 10 vols., trans. F. H. Colson, Loeb Classical Library [Cambridge: Harvard Univ. Press, repr. 1966], 6:4–5).

[6]Eissfeldt, Introduction, 156. See Georg Fohrer, Introduction to the Old Testament, trans. D. E. Green (Nashville: Abingdon, 1968), 103, "This division took place in the fourth century B.C. at the latest; the LXX is already familiar with it."

[7]The basis for the assumption that the Septuagint translators knew of a five-part division is the fact that existing manuscripts contain titles for the five sections of the Pentateuch, viz., Genesis, etc. It is not certain, however, when the titles were added to the manuscript tradition: "The Greek titles are probably of Alexandrian origin and pre-Christian use. Not only were they familiar to Origen (Eus. H.E. vi. 25), but they are used in Melito's [d. c. 190] list. . . . Philo uses γένεσις. . . ."(Henry Barclay Swete, An Introduction to the Old Testament in Greek [New York: KTAV, 1968], 215).

[8]Prologue to Ben Sirach (Ecclesiasticus), "For things originally spoken in Hebrew have not the same force in them when they are translated into another tongue: and not only these, but the Law itself, and the Prophecies, and the rest of the books, have no small difference when they are spoken in their original form" (The Apocrypha and Pseudepigrapha of the Old Testament in English, ed. R. H. Charles, 2 vols. [Oxford: Clarendon, 1913], 1:316–17). The Letter of Aristeas, 15, "Since the law [νομοθεσία] which we wish not only to transcribe but also to translate belongs to the whole Jewish race. . . ." (ibid., 2:96). But see also, "Their laws are written on leather parchments [ἐν διφθέραις] in Jewish characters," (ibid., 94).

[9]Werner H. Schmidt, Old Testament Introduction, trans. Matthew J. O'Connell (New York: Crossroad, 1984), 43.

2. The Pentateuch Has an Author

Another important implication of the fact that the Pentateuch is a written text is that it has an author. Somebody wrote it. Furthermore, its author had a purpose in mind and intended to accomplish that purpose by writing the Pentateuch. A large part of our task in seeking to understand the Pentateuch will be to pay close attention to the intention of its author. By the nature of the case, the meaning of the Pentateuch consists in what the author set out to accomplish in this book. To understand it, we must understand the meaning that the author intended.

When we speak of the authors of Scripture we are thinking of the individual prophets and godly persons who wrote each of the books that is contained in the OT. But is it not also true that God is the author of Scripture? It is surely correct to say that the whole Bible, including the OT, had only one Author—God (see 2Ti 3:16). But, though God was the Author of Scripture as a whole, including the OT, we are still faced with the reality that each book of the Bible also had a human author. God inspired the human authors, but that did not rule out the fact that each author wrote using his own talents and skills. What we now have as the OT comes ultimately from God, but it also comes directly from its human authors.

The fact that the OT, or rather each book of the OT, has both a human and a divine author raises an important question: Whose message are we seeking to understand in reading Scripture, God's or the human author's? Might it not be the case that God intended many things in the writings of the OT that its human authors did not understand or intend?

That the Bible has both a divine and a human origin does not mean that it has both a divine and a human purpose or intention. It does not mean that though the human authors may have meant one thing, God intended another. When the Bible speaks about its own origin as "inspired" Scripture (2Ti 3:16), it does not pit its human authors against its divine Author. On the contrary, its view is that the human authors were so moved by God to write that what they wrote was what God intended. As Peter puts it, "Men spoke from God as they were carried along by the Holy Spirit" (2Pe 1:21).

3. The Pentateuch Is Literature

Still another implication of the fact that the Pentateuch is a book is that it is literature. The biblical books are not hastily written documents or mere historical records. These books are carefully constructed works of literature. They are not merely the literature of a bygone era and people—they have, in fact, proved themselves to be classic works of literature.

A great deal of attention will be devoted to this aspect of the Pentateuch throughout this book. For now, however, it is sufficient to make the point that as one studies the Pentateuch and attempts to understand the meaning of its author, one must pay close attention to its literary dimensions. A sensitivity to the author's literary skill and techniques goes a long way in helping to elucidate his purpose in writing the book.

B. The Historical Background of the Pentateuch

An understanding of the historical background of a work has always played an important part in its interpretation. The Pentateuch is no different.

We must, however, distinguish at least two forms of historical background material in the study of the Pentateuch: first, the historical background or context within which the book was written, second, the historical background or context of the events recorded in the book. In the former, we have in mind a specific time and place in which the book was composed. We look for the occasion of the writing of the book, who wrote it, and for whom it was written. In the latter, we must look over a wide array of settings for the events of the book itself: from the Garden of Eden to the Flood, to the building of the city of Babylon, to the land of the patriarchs, and, finally, to the land of Egypt and the Sinai wilderness.

Both of these settings are important in understanding the events in the Pentateuch. For example, the travels of Abraham after he left Ur of the Chaldeans show that he rested at three locations: Shechem, Bethel, and the Negev. From the perspective of the historical setting of this event, it is significant that Abraham stopped at places which were sparsely occupied during the early second millennium B.C., namely, the central mountains and southern deserts in Canaan. Thus we can see that at that time Abraham was not in possession of the land and had to dwell on the outskirts. He was an "outsider," and, as some have suggested, he may even have derived his name as a "Hebrew" from the fact that he lived on the fringes of his society (the word *Hebrew* can be interpreted as "outsider').

These three locations are also important from the perspective of the period during which the Pentateuch was written, the period just prior to Israel's conquest of the land of Canaan. We know from the book of Joshua that Israel took the land in three campaigns: one central (at Bethel), one southern (in the Negev), and one northern (at Shechem). Thus, if we read the account from the point of view of the first readers, we see that Abraham was claiming each of these three areas by moving into the land and establishing a place of worship there. It is as if the Pentateuch was telling its readers that just as God had given the land to Abraham, so also he would give the land to the "seed" of Abraham as they were about to go in to take the land under the leadership of Joshua.

Thus looking at the book from the point of view of the time and place of its composition can help us understand some of the main features and purposes of the book.

1. Background of the Author

If we assume Mosaic authorship of the Pentateuch, then it was written during the general period of the Exodus and the initials stages of the conquest of the land. During this time Moses was engaged in his task of forming Israel into a nation. Before God called Moses, Israel had found itself in bondage to the house of Pharaoh in Egypt (Ex 1:8–14). When the proper time came and Israel cried out to God from their bondage, God heard their cry and remembered his covenant with Abraham (Ex 2:23–24). A strong link then connects the events of Moses' life with those of the earlier patriarchs, Abraham, Isaac, and Jacob. The key to that link is the covenant which God made with Abraham.

God's covenant with Abraham was a promise to make a great nation out of Abraham's descendants and to give them the land of Canaan. This covenant was the basis of all God's further dealings with Israel, including the event of the Exodus. It provided a key link between God's covenant with Israel at Mount Sinai and the earlier promise of God, as well as the central link to the new covenant promised through the prophets (Jer 31:31–34) and fulfilled in Christ's death and resurrection (Matt 26:28).

When God began his work of bringing about the fulfillment of the promise to Abraham, he chose Moses to carry out the task (Ex 3). Most readers of the Bible are familiar with the way in which Moses carried out this task. He first went before the king of Egypt and through a series of ten signs (plagues), the Egyptian king was persuaded to release the Israelites, the seed of Abraham.

Moses then led the people out of the land and through the Red Sea. When they had left the land of Egypt, he began the task of organizing and shaping the people into a nation. He gave them God's laws; he established their worship of God; he organized them into administrative units necessary to maintain order and survival in the wilderness and in the land of Canaan. In other words, Moses gave the people the kinds of laws and instructions that we find throughout the books of Exodus, Leviticus, Numbers, and Deuteronomy.

But this was not all Moses did to complete the task that God had given him. No sooner had this band of people been established as a nation living under God's covenant promises than they fell away from serving him and broke his commandments. God had said, "You shall have no other gods before me" (Ex 20:3), and "You shall not make for yourself an idol" (Ex 20:4). But even while God was speaking these words to Moses on Mount Sinai, Aaron and the people were making images and worshiping them at the foot of the mountain. The great promises of God which were on the verge of fulfillment at Sinai were now being threatened by the failure and faithlessness of the people. Moses would have to warn the people of their failure and encourage them in their faith and trust in God.

Thus the people for whom Moses wrote the Pentateuch needed to know more fully what was about to happen to them. They needed to know who they were and the great purpose God had for them in his covenant. Thus, as part of the overall task of forming this people into a nation obedient to God, Moses wrote a history of the "children of Israel." In this history he explained to Israel who they were and why they had come to Egypt. Moreover, he showed them that they were not an ordinary people. They were descendants of a promised seed—heirs to the great covenant promises that God had made to their forefathers. Moses wanted Israel to know that what was happening to them was not simply a liberation from a particularly bad period of enslavement. Rather, God was beginning to work in their lives and they were now becoming a major part of his program to redeem the world to himself. They were being called into fellowship with a God who wanted nothing short of their perfect obedience and trust.

Moses also warned the people of the danger of unbelief and failure to trust God. Many of the pentateuchal narratives seem directed to just this end. The lives of characters such as Adam, Noah, Abraham, Sarah, Isaac, and Jacob are often used as examples of a failure to trust in God and of the consequences of such failure.

Moses set out to recount other things as well in the Pentateuch. For example, a central concern was his view of God. He seemed especially intent on portraying God as the Creator of the universe. We should make special note that Moses began his history of God's promises with an account of the creation of the universe and the beginning of world history. For Moses, the God of the Sinai covenant was the Creator of the universe and Lord of history. When first chosen by God to be the deliverer of his people, Moses had asked, "Suppose I go to the Israelites and say to them, 'The God of your fathers has sent me to you,' and they ask me, 'What is his name?' Then what shall I tell them?" (Ex 3:13). The short answer he was to give them was simply, "I AM has sent me to you" (Ex 3:14). The long answer was the Pentateuch.

Thus, as a part of the Pentateuch as a whole, the main thrusts of the book of Genesis from the point of view of Moses its writer are: (1) The God of the covenant is our Creator; (2) Israel is heir to a divine covenant promise; (3) Israel's failure to live up to God's promises was preceded by a long list of similar human failures; (4) God's promises remain certain in spite of Israel's failure. In other words, God's relationship with his people has a future, even though they have proven faithless in the past.

Through the writing of this book, then, Moses told his readers that the Creator God had entered into a covenant promise with his people Israel. The implication of this message is clear enough. For Moses, the author of the Pentateuch, biblical Israel was not an ordinary people and Israel's history was not an ordinary history. The history which is recounted in the Pentateuch is a history of God's redemption of his people and through them the redemption of the world.

One further observation should be made regarding the setting of the Pentateuch's composition. It becomes clear as one reads through the second half of the Pentateuch that it was not written primarily to the generation that came out of Egypt. Its readership was specifically the generation of Israelites that was about to go into the Promised Land. All the events of the Exodus and the wilderness journey as well as the giving of the Law at Mount Sinai were cast as something that happened in the past. From the perspective of the Pentateuch as a whole, the events of Sinai and the wilderness were as much in the past as those of the patriarchs. Those events had already become a part of the lessons Israel was to learn from. The focus of the writer was on the future, the next generation. They were the particular readers he had in mind.

2. Background of the Events

For purposes of historical background, the events of the Pentateuch can be divided into three types. First, events are recorded which happened on a global or even cosmic scale (e.g., the Creation account and the account of the Flood). Second, events are recorded throughout the book that happened only in a very isolated, localized way (e.g., Noah's drunkenness, Ge 9; Abraham's vision, Ge 15; or Moses' encounter with God at the burning bush, Ex 3). Third, events are recorded that fall within the scope of what we normally think of as world history—that is, major events in the life of a nation (e.g., Israel's exodus from Egypt, Ex 12–14), or events involving the conflict of nations (e.g., the invasion of Canaan by the four kings from the East (Ge 14).

By far the greatest majority of events recorded in the Pentateuch follow the second of these three types, events happening within a limited sphere of time and location; they can best be described simply as family or tribal matters. The narratives of the book turn from full-scale global catastrophies, such as the Flood or the destruction of the cities of Sodom and Gomorrah, to seemingly incidental encounters between private individuals. Of course, it is just these types of events, both the global and the individual, which prove to be the most difficult of all historical events to reconstruct by modern historical methods. On the whole, events recounted in the Creation and Flood accounts do not belong to the field of historical research at all. Rather, they fall in the domain of the natural sciences—astronomy, geology, and biology. Thus, on the one hand, investigation of the biblical Flood, which on the face of it appears to have been global in scope, would be the task of the science of geology, not history. On the other hand, isolated events in the lives of a few individuals, like Abraham and his family, or even a great number of people, such as the tribes of Israel in the wilderness, can be studied only in the general terms of historical and cultural anthropology.

C. Historical Background and the Meaning of the Text of the Pentateuch

How does the study of historical background material affect our understanding of the text of Scripture? Do we look for the meaning or sense of the Pentateuch in the text of Scripture itself, or is the text primarily a witness to the act of God's self-revelation in the events recorded by Scripture?

For many evangelicals the choice between these two alternatives is not a happy one. Their desire and inclination is to remain open to both options. Recognizing the importance of the inspired text of Scripture, they want to affirm that an interpretation of the OT, or the Pentateuch, should look to the text itself as its source. However, wanting also to affirm the importance of history and God's revelation of his will in historical events, they do not wish to minimize the importance of the historical events recounted in Scripture.

In fact, as evangelicals, we do not have to choose between Scripture and history. Evangelicals should and do affirm the absolute importance of both. For an evangelical, the question should not be whether God has acted in history. The historical basis of biblical faith is fundamentally important and will always remain so. The real issue is our commitment to an inspired *written* Word of God as the locus of God's special revelation. How does our commitment to the written Word of God relate to our use of historical background material in interpretation?

In 2 Timothy 3:16 Paul writes, "All Scripture is inspired by God." As evangelicals we are accustomed to directing our attention to the second part of Paul's statement, that Scripture "is inspired." We often insist either that our interpretive methods be adjusted to our view of inspiration or that our view of inspiration conform to our methods. Methodologically, however, it is equally appropriate to begin by focusing on the first part of Paul's statement, that "all Scripture" is inspired. In calling Scripture "inspired," Paul gives the written text the highest claim to authority. It is specifically "Scripture" that Paul points to as the locus of God's revelation.

The older theologians emphasized this point by stressing that Scripture (*sacra scriptura*) and God's Word (*verbum dei*) are one.[10] Although such an understanding of the nature of Scripture cannot claim universal acceptance among modern theologians, it remains the hallmark of theologians who call themselves evangelical.

1. The Old Testament Is a Text

To say, with Paul, that the OT is Scripture is to acknowledge that the OT is a text. As a text the OT has certain properties that distinguish it from nontexts. For example, texts are made of words, phrases, clauses, sentences, paragraphs, and the like—that is, texts are composed of language. They are structured utterances. They represent the work of an author.

A commitment to an understanding of the OT as Scripture, then, implies an exegetical method and biblical theology that is a direct function of the meaning of a text. Exegesis and theology must ask: How does a text have meaning? One must seek to discover the way in which the authors of Scripture have construed their words, phrases, clauses, and the like into whole texts.

Before we go any further, it is important to have clearly in mind what a narrative text is. We often take for granted that we know what a text is, and for the most part we do. We have had enough experience with various kinds of texts to recognize one when we see it. It is helpful, however, to review some of the basic features that make up a text, if for no other reason than that it may help us take them more seriously in the process of reading the Bible.

By its very nature a narrative text is something that does not project itself on us as such. When reading a text we are not constantly reminded of the fact that we are looking at words on a page. The function of a historical narrative text is not to reflect on its role as a text but to be a vehicle for telling a historical story. An important part of becoming a sensitive reader, however, is developing an awareness of the biblical narratives as texts. No matter how self-evident the following characteristics may seem, it is not uncommon to find one or more of them overlooked in the process of reading and interpreting biblical narrative.

---

[10]"Unicum Theologiae principium esse Verbum Dei in Scripturis sacris propositum," Johann Gerhard, *Locorum Theologicorum cum pro adstruenda veritate, tum pro destruends quorumuis contradicentium falsitate, per theses nervose, solide et copiose explicatorum*, 1. *De Scriptura sacra* (Geneva, 1639), 1. According to Benedict Pictet, "God, taking pity on the human race, was pleased to commit his word to writing. 1. By this means the truth could be more easily preserved, and transmitted to later generations, for 'this wonderful gift of letters is truly divine so that they might watch over the words and give them to those not present as a sort of trust,' as Quintilian remarks, 2. and the truth could also not so easily be corrupted, or at least could be more easily and successfully rescued from corruptions. By this means also, there was no necessity for the truth to be repeated and restored by continually new revelations, and thus a certain and fixed rule of faith was established. Thus it pleased God to help the feebleness of man and to oppose diabolical plots by inscribing his enduring word in raw figures" (*Theologia Christiana Ex puris S. S. Literarum Fontibus hausta* [Langerak, 1723], 16–17.

2. The Old Testament Text Is a Written Document

Some would not want to restrict the idea of a text simply to that of a written document, but since our primary interest is in Scripture, the inspired written Word, we can safely stay within such a limited definition.[11] Thus the first requirement of a text is that it be written and that it can be read. That is, a text is composed of a written language, biblical Hebrew in our case. Meir Sternberg has put it well when he speaks of a text as a "web of words."[12]

This basic feature of a text has two important implications. First, since it is composed of language, a text must follow the rules of the language in which it is written. The author of a text is not free to do or say what he or she pleases when composing a text. One cannot invent new rules of grammar and add new words to the lexicon. If it is to be understood, the OT text must be composed within the constraints of Hebrew vocabulary, grammar, and syntax. Such things are the given part of the text, the raw material with which the author must work. They form the common ground between the author of a text and the readers, thus enhancing the possibility of the text being understood.

By the same token, a reader is not free to do or say whatever he or she pleases about the meaning of a text. The reader must understand the text in terms dictated by the grammatical and syntactical constraints of the language in which it is written. The same is to be said for translations of the Bible. The importance of this point is not difficult to appreciate. The reading of biblical narrative texts cannot dispense with the necessity to pay close attention to the grammar, syntax and lexicography of Hebrew (or English, in the case of a translation). While it is true that reading a biblical text is more than merely a grammatical, syntactical and lexical study of the Hebrew Bible (or of a translation), it is certainly not less than that.

The second implication that a text is a written document is not as immediately self-evident as the first, but it is equally important. It has to do with historical narrative texts which render a realistic depiction of the world. As far as the reader is concerned, the world of historical events (*eventus*) in the Bible comes to the reader mediated through the textual world (*dicta*).[13] The biblical text gives the reader an account of those historical events. The reader, as a reader, stands always before the text (*textus*). Thus the world that one stands before as a reader is never more than a *representation* of the real world. In the case of the Bible, the text is a true and accurate representation, but though true and accurate, the text is still a representation of those actual events.

A photograph of a tree is an accurate and realistic representation of a tree. Yet the photograph does not have bark and leaves, nor is the sky

---

[11]We would not want to deny that the concept of a "text" can be extended far beyond the present definition. Much insight can be gained from the study of "non-written texts" and sign systems in general, that is, semiotics. As a guide to understanding biblical texts, however, it seems best to limit the range of our terms to that which corresponds directly to biblical texts, namely, *written* texts.

[12]Meir Sternberg, *The Poetics of Biblical Narrative, Ideological Literature and the Drama of Reading* (Bloomington: Indiana Univ. Press, 1985).

[13]Masao Sekine, "Vom Verstehen der Heilsgeschichte: Das Grundproblem der alttestamentlichen Theologie," *ZAW* 75 (1963): 145–54.

behind the tree in the photograph a real sky. Nevertheless, the actual bark
and leaves of the real tree are represented in the photograph and so is the
real sky. We can readily understand that the whole of the photograph is a
representation of its subject matter, which in this case is the real tree.[14]

To say that a photograph only represents the tree but is not actually the
tree does not mean that the tree never existed or that the photograph is
inaccurate because it shows only one side of the tree. The same can be said of
the biblical narrative texts. To say that they represent real events but are not
those events themselves merely recognizes a very obvious fact about
historical texts.[15] As readers of these biblical texts we stand before them as
their authors have construed them, and we look to them, the texts
themselves, for our understanding of the world they depict.

3. The Old Testament Text Represents an Author's Intention

Thus far our description of a text has focused on elements of the written
document itself. But it is also necessary to look beyond the document to its
author to get a complete picture of what a text is. Texts do not originate out
of thin air. Texts have authors—real persons who write with a sense in mind
of what the text is about. Biblical texts are no exception, whatever one's view
of inspiration and revelation. A text is an embodiment of an author's
intention—that is, a strategy designed to carry out an author's intention.[16]

4. The Old Testament Text and Its Communication Situation

One of the developments of recent text theory is the emergence of the
idea that a text is a system of signs that can be understood as an act of
communication and thus implies a communication situation.[17] A typical

---

[14]I wish to thank a student, Drew Moen, for the following quote: "Somebody was
saying to Picasso that he ought to make pictures of things the way they are—
objective pictures. He mumbled he wasn't quite sure what that would be. The person
who was bullying him produced a photograph of his wife from his wallet and said,
'There, you see, that is a picture of how she *really* is.' Picasso looked at it and said,
'She is rather small isn't she? And flat?'" (Bradford P. Keeney, *Aesthetics of Change*,
[New York: Guilford, 1983], 79).

[15]The question raised here is not that of the accuracy of the depiction in the textual
world. That question should be raised in the context of the relationship between the
reader and the real world. Though the importance of that question cannot be
overlooked, it is a question of the *historical accuracy* of the biblical narratives and as
such belongs to the task of apologetics. That question should not be allowed to cloud
the issue at hand, which is that the biblical narratives present themselves to their
readers as *representations* of the real world.

[16]Closely akin to the notion of intentionality in texts is that which de Beaugrande
and Dressler call "acceptability," i.e., the notion that the reader's own cooperation in
receiving a text as a cohesive and coherent unit plays a major role in textuality
(*Introduction to Text Linguistics* [London: Longman, 1981]). The notion can already be
seen in Flacius's comment on *Anacoluthon:* "Saepissime enim sit, ut vel verba, vel
construction, seu forma orationis, vel denique etiam sententiae aut res, si ad Latinum
morem examinentur, parum respondeant praecedentibus: aut plane non adsint; sed
tantum intelligi debeant" (Matthias Flacius, *Clavis Scripturae seu de Sermone Sacrarum
Literarum, plurimas generales Regulas continentis, Altera Pars* [Leipzig, 1695 (1st ed.,
1567)], 4).

[17]Siegfried J. Schmidt, *Text Theorie, Probleme einer Linguistik der sprachlichen Kommunikation,* Uni-Taschenbücher 202 (Munich: Wilhelm Fink, 1976), 9ff.

communication situation consists of a speaker who transmits information[18] to a hearer via a shared mode of communication or sign system:

SPEAKER ─────────▶ SIGN SYSTEM ─────────▶ HEARER

Seen within such a context, a text can be understood as the sign system bearing the information in an act of communication. Thus, if we replace the general notion of information in the diagram above with the specific idea of a text and put the author and reader in the place of speaker and hearer, we can construct the following diagram to show the role of a text within a communication situation:

AUTHOR ─────────▶ TEXT ─────────▶ READER

On the basis of the diagram above, it is possible to formulate a view of a text as a written linguistic communication between an author and a reader.[19]

Viewing a text within such a model of communication acts enables us to understand various features of a text in terms familiar from other acts of communication in everyday life. In other words, the features of a text, which are primarily linguistic, can be related to familiar functions in ordinary conversations. For example, in an ordinary conversation, a speaker often has to adjust his or her words to what he or she perceives to be the level of understanding and comprehension of the hearer. The speaker gains clues from the hearer's immediate response (feedback) to what he or she has said. The hearer may interrupt the speaker to ask a question of clarification; he or she may simply have a puzzled look on his or her face. In any case, the speaker can pick up such feedback and adjust his or her information accordingly. The message is, then, constantly being adjusted to suit the new level of the hearer's "information awareness."

In a text, however, the author does not have access to such immediate responses of the readers. Rather, the author must anticipate the reader's questions and construct the text in such a way that responses which a reader is likely to have will be satisfied as the text is read or reread. The author must anticipate legitimate reader responses and satisfy them within the course of the text.

An example of a textual device for interacting with a reader is repetition. In a conversation, a speaker is often asked to repeat or restate what he or she has said. This repetition not only serves the purpose of memory but also helps clarify ideas and correlate them with other ideas developed within a speech act. In a text, such repetitions often become an essential part of an author's strategy. For one reading the biblical text, such repetitions are helpful guides to the author's purpose and intention.

---

[18]The term *information* is used here in a very general sense. It stands for any "message" which the speaker intends to transmit to the hearer. The use of the term does not mean that only information in a quantitative sense is transmitted in texts.

[19]More technically, we can say that through a text a "deficiency" of information between the two communication partners is overcome. See Robert Oberforcher, *Die Flutprologe als Kompositions-schlüssel der biblischen Urgeschichte* (Innsbruck: Tyrolia, 1981).

5. The Old Testament Text Has a Literary Form

It is not difficult to see a difference between the kind of literature that makes up the biblical narratives and that which is found, for example, in the book of Psalms. Whatever terms we may use to distinguish the two types of texts, the important point is that there is a recognizable difference between them. Compare, for example, the literary types represented in the sections below from Genesis 1 and Psalm 33.

> *Genesis 1:1:* In the beginning God created the heavens and the earth. Now the earth was formless and empty, darkness was over the surface of the deep, and the Spirit of God was hovering over the waters. And God said, "Let there be light," and there was light.

> *Psalm 33:6:* By the word of the LORD were the heavens made, their starry host by the breath of his mouth.

The two texts clearly differ. The differences are not so much related to the subject matter, since both texts speak of God's creation of the universe. The differences lie rather in the *way* the two texts present their subject matter. Genesis 1 sets out to tell a story, a history of Israel's beginnings. The author recounts events from the past in a straightforward, realistic manner. He describes events as they happened in the real world. Such a literary type is akin to the literary type used in everyday language, newspapers, books, and conversation.

In the psalm, we can recognize a quite different literary type. One does not need to be an expert in poetic analysis to recognize that Psalm 33:6 differs from the narrative of Genesis 1 in that it is a kind of poetry. We recognize it as poetry because, like most poetry we are familiar with, it is written in distinguishable lines, having a sense of proportion and rhythm. Our understanding may stop there, but we can at least sense a difference between the two literary types at this level. Our ability to distinguish these two types is part of what makes us literate. Certainly not everyone possesses the same degree of literacy, but no one would get very far in understanding texts without at least a rudimentary ability to distinguish between these two basic types.

One of the assumptions of the present study is that, along with this ability to distinguish basic literary types, readers as a rule also possess the ability to respond appropriately to the various types. When a reader recognizes a text as a narrative story, he or she is able to draw on a reservoir of expectations which has been acquired through reading other stories. These expectations give one a sense of what to look for in a story and what a story may be setting out to do. To a large extent one's enjoyment and appreciation of a story stem from the expectation brought to the story in the process of reading. The same is true of poetry. Such expectations are by and large acquired through reading and hearing stories or poems, and thus they vary greatly among individuals. Those who are well-read have a greater, more refined reservoir of expectations. Knowing what to expect, they often come away from a story with a greater understanding and appreciation than one who has little idea of what stories are about.

Historical narrative is a convenient label for a general category or type of literature found in the Hebrew Bible. It is the literary type representative of the large stretches of texts that range from the book of Genesis through the book of Kings. There are also smaller narrative works, such as the books of Ruth, Esther, and Jonah, as well as narrative in the *framework* for many other books, for example, the prologue and epilogue to the book of Job.[20] A nearly equivalent term is *prose*, though the usual connotations of that term do not do full justice to this type of biblical literature. In order to maintain the similarity between historical narrative in biblical texts and the notion of prose in English, we can propose a preliminary definition of historical narrative as a proselike literature which seeks to render a *realistic* picture of the world.

Such a preliminary definition focuses on one of the most characteristic features of narrative, namely, its attempt to mimic the real world—that is, to reproduce the real world in linguistic terms. In the study of narrative texts, it is easy to overlook this essential characteristic of historical narrative by simply taking it for granted. In going about the task of exegesis, however, it is helpful to pay particularly close attention to this feature of narrative. The biblical writers did not necessarily want their narrative depictions of reality to be noticed as such. They intended their audience to read their narratives as versions of the events themselves, and to a large extent they succeeded. Nevertheless, it is important to keep an eye on the text and the particular way it represents the great acts of God in history.

A biblical narrative text takes the raw material of language and shapes it into a version of the world of empirical reality. Its essentially linguistic structures are adapted to conform to events in real life.[21] The constraints that shape real life (for example, the limitations of time and space and perspective) are the constraints to which historical narrative texts must strive to conform in their imitation of real life. The more conformity a text shows to such real-life constraints, the more realistic the historical narrative will prove to be. Events and characters are put before the reader as happening just as they happen in real life. The reader looks at the events in the narrative in much the same way as he or she would look at events in real life. They happen in the text before one's eyes. As Benveniste has put it, "The events are chronologically recorded as they appear on the horizon of the story. . . . The events seem to tell themselves."[22]

---

[20]In Job the historical narrative texts are a kind of shelving on which is laid the poetic discourses that make up the body of the work. The same is true for many of the prophetic books. The poetic discourses of the prophets are arranged within the framework of a historical narrative. This same procedure can be found within the Pentateuch, where the large blocks of legal discourses are set within the very thinly built narratives of the wilderness wanderings.

[21]"Linguistic structure" refers to the simple fact that languages have their own sets of rules by which they operate. In learning to use a language, one must master such rules in the form of a grammar and syntax. All or most languages may follow some general rules, but for the most part each specific language has its own unique set. Historical narrative texts written in classical Hebrew, then, must follow the rules of grammar and syntax that govern that language. The linguistic features of biblical Hebrew include such verbal patterns as WĀYYIQTOL, which provides the effect of sequence in time, and $\emptyset + X + QATAL$ clauses, which appear to break into time. See John Sailhamer, "A Database Approach to the Analysis of Hebrew Narrative," *MAARAV* 5–6 (Spring 1990): 319–35.

[22]Emile Benveniste, quoted by Hayden White, "The Value of Narrativity in the Representation of Reality," *Critical Inquiry* 7 (1980): 7.

The following chart illustrates the relationships at play in historical narrative texts.

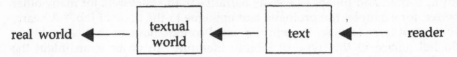

As the diagram above shows, in historical narrative, the text bears an important relationship to the real world which it depicts. It must conform to the requirements of that real world. If, for example, in the real world depicted in the text, birds fly and fish swim, so also in the narrative birds will fly and fish will swim. In such a historical narrative, however, a fish would not fly. That would not conform to the way things are in the real world.

The diagram above also shows that, as a narrative, the text bears an important relationship to the reader. It must be written in a language that is known to the reader, and it must follow the normal rules of that language. Moreover, if the author expects the general reader to understand the text, the author will represent the text as the central focus of the reader—that is, the author will not always assume that the reader will be looking elsewhere for the information the text is meant to transmit. While it is possible for texts to do this sort of thing and virtually abandon their readers, narrative texts are known for their steady supply of information to the reader regarding the events they are depicting. Biblical narratives, in particular, are noticeably reader conscious. In reading them, one rarely has the impression of being left alone. The authors have their way of guiding the reader along, even though in most cases the reader is unaware of their presences.

Still another important relationship exists within a historical narrative that is not shown in the diagram. Though the reader approaches the real world through a text, if it is a historical narrative, the real world also exists independently of the text as its subject matter. In other words, historical narratives make ostensive reference to the real world outside the text itself.[23] As important as the text is for our purposes here, we should not overlook that it is only one of several avenues through which the reader may gain information about the real world that lies outside the text.[24] In making this point, however, we should be clear that other avenues through which information can be rightly gained about the real world events beyond the text are not a part of the text and are not controlled by the author of the text. Whatever one may say about the world behind the narratives, one should not identify that world with that which is depicted in the text itself. The text is a version of the events it depicts. It should not be taken as their replacement.

We have briefly discussed the essential nature of narrative texts and have distinguished them from their subject matter, historical events in time

---

[23]"Ostensive reference" is "the spatiotemporal occurrence or state of affairs to which it (the text) refers," according to Hans W. Frei, *The Eclipse of Biblical Narrative: A Study in Eighteenth and Nineteenth Century Hermeneutics* (New Haven: Yale Univ. Press, 1974), 78.

[24]For example, the reconstructions of the sciences of history, archaeology, sociology, and sociolinguistics.

and space. We will now attempt to describe more carefully the nature of those historical events themselves. Our primary purpose will be to clarify the point made earlier in this chapter, that events are quite different from texts. Our ultimate purpose is to turn our attention to the texts themselves and their unique depiction of the events of biblical history.

6. The Old Testament Is About Events

Put simply, an event is something that happens in time and space. It is an occurrence. A history is an accumulation of connected events. The word *history*, however, is ambiguous. We will see in the next section that the term *history* can denote not only a flow of events in time and space but also the written record of the flow of events. Thus the term *event* offers a more precise way of speaking about history when we want to distinguish it from a written record about history.

The study of historical events is as old as the earliest civilizations. In most early attempts to uncover the past, historians relied heavily on tradition, accounts handed down from earlier ages. Modern historiography not only relies on tradition but also has developed more sophisticated tools for reconstructing the way things were. Its primary procedure is to reconstruct past events by means of the two principles of causality and analogy.

The principle of causality starts with the assumption that every historical event is best understood as the result of a series of earlier events. The historian can understand an event from the past by attempting to describe what caused an event or the series of events in which it occurred. Various factors or causes have been suggested for the general flow of historical events. Some have suggested that human events are determined by invariable laws, such as economic or political determinism. The specifically Christian view of historical events is that they are determined ultimately by God's providence.[25] This is not the place to discuss the merits of the one view of history over the other. Whatever one's particular view, it is agreed that human events are interrelated and can be understood best by describing the nature of their causal interdependence.

The principle of analogy is the code by which the historian describes a past event. According to this principle, the set of causes used to describe past events must be similar to or analogous to causes of events in the present. We should not expect human affairs to have been any different in the past than they are in the present.

Some have objected to the principle of analogy on the grounds that it can be too rigidly applied. For example, biblical critics used the principle to rule out the miraculous events recorded in the Bible. They argued that since the category of miracle is not used in writing modern history, it should not be used in describing events from the past. The resolution of this problem

---

[25]See Heinrich Heppe, *Die Dogmatik der evangelisch-reformierten Kirche* (Neukirchen, 1935), 199ff.; Heinrich Schmid, *The Doctrinal Theology of the Evangelical Lutheran Church* (Minneapolis: Augsburg, n.d.), 170ff.; also Johann Coccejus, *De Providentia Dei, etiam circa mala, Summa Theologiae ex Scripturis repetita, Opera Omnia* (Amsterdam, 1701), 217, par. 2: "Mundum non creavit Deus, ut per se ac sua ipsius virtute, manu Dei subducta, subsisteret: quod somniavit Taurellus. sed eum perpetuo fert."

goes far beyond our purposes here. However the question is decided, the fact remains that for the historian the principle of analogy is indispensable as a tool for reconstructing the past.

This brings us to the events recorded in the OT. If we are to understand these events, we will certainly need to employ the tools of causality and analogy. An evangelical approach to the events recorded in the OT almost surely would employ not only the notion of God's providence in explaining the causes of the biblical events but also knowledge of the events gained from ancient records and archaeology. In doing so we would simply be following the lead of the biblical writers, whose purpose was to show the hand of God in all human affairs. An evangelical approach, as in classical orthodoxy, would also not hesitate to use the principle of analogy. To be sure, one would not rule out the possibility of miracles, for the past or the present; nevertheless, there is no reason why we would not also seek an explanation for biblical events in the reconstructions of modern archaeologists and historians who used analogy.

Enough has been said to show the nature of historical events and the procedures for understanding them. What should be clear is that events are things (*res*) quite different from texts (*verba*). We have seen this point from the side of texts, which are written documents (a "web of words") *about* events, and from the side of events, which are single acts or series of actions in a web of causes and effects.

D. Revelation in Scripture (Text) and in History (Event)

An emphasis on Scripture as an inspired text has a direct bearing on the problem of revelation. How has God revealed himself in the Bible? Has he revealed himself only in Scripture or has he also revealed himself in history? To a large extent the OT texts are historical narrative texts.[26] In other words, the texts are about events in the real world. In speaking of historical narrative, however, one must make important distinctions in the use of the term *history*. It is not enough to say that the biblical narratives are only "history-like" and to relegate them to the level of "realistic narrative."[27] Much has yet to be investigated regarding the categories of "history" and "fictionality,"[28] but one can say with reasonable certainty that the authors of the biblical narratives give every indication of intending their works to be taken as history rather than fiction.[29] Their aim, they imply throughout, is to record what actually happened in human history. One can also say today with confidence that there is reasonable evidence that the history recorded in these narratives corresponds to the events themselves.

The point at stake, however, is that in ordinary language the term

---

[26]See John Sailhamer, "Exegetical Notes: Genesis 1:1–2:4a," *TrinJ* 5, no. 1 (1984): 73–82.

[27]Frei, *Eclipse of Biblical Narrative*, 10.

[28]See Manfred Oeming, "Bedeutung und Funktionen von 'Fiktionen' in der alttestamentlichen Geschichtsschreibung," *EvT* 44 (1984): 254–66; Siegfried J. Schmidt, "Towards a Pragmatic Interpretation of 'Fictionality,'" in *Pragmatics of Language and Literature*, ed. T. A. van Dijk (Amsterdam: North-Holland Publishing Co., 1976), 161–78; Sternberg, *Poetics*, 23–35; Hayden White, "The Value of Narrativity in the Representation of Reality," *Critical Inquiry* 7 (1980): 5–27.

[29]Sternberg, *Poetics*, 32–33.

history can have two very different senses. On the one hand, *history* can refer to the kind of text we suppose the narrative to be—namely, a nonfiction text that intends to recount actual events from the past. As such the term fits the biblical narratives well. On the other hand, *history* can refer to the actual events from the past. In this sense the term refers to that which the biblical texts are about: events in the real world.

This distinction is of some importance when attempting to develop an approach to the OT that is text-centered. We should recognize that in only one of the above senses does *history* actually refer to a text, the recording of past events. In the other sense *history* refers to an actual event in the real world. This distinction becomes important in using the expression "revelation in history." Which of the above senses of *history* is meant? Does this expression refer to revelation in a text or revelation in an event as such?[30]

A text-oriented approach to the OT would insist that the locus of God's revelation is in the Scriptures themselves, in the text. There is no reason to discount the fact that God has made known his will in other ways at other times. But, given the theological priority of an inspired text (2Ti 3:16), one must see in the text of Scripture itself the locus of God's revelation today. Thus, on the question of God's revelation in history, the sense of *history* in a text-oriented approach would be that of the record of past events. The history in which God makes known his will is the recorded history in the text of Scripture. When formulated this way, evangelical biblical theology is based on a revelation that consists of the meaning of a text, with its focus on Scripture as a written document. Even the formula "revelation in history" then concerns the meaning of a text.

Evangelical biblical scholars have not always been clear on this point. Although holding to a view of Scripture as God's revelation, they have tended to interpret the formula "revelation in history" in such a way that the term *history* refers not to the text of Scripture but rather to the past events themselves. In other words, the locus of revelation is taken to lie not in the text of Scripture but in the events witnessed by the text. In such an approach the events lying behind the text of Scripture are read as a salvation history within which God makes known his will to humanity.

Though subtle, the distinction is real. The effect of overlooking the text of Scripture in favor of a focus on the events of Israel's history can often be a "biblical" theology that is little more than a philosophy of history, an exegetical method that is set on expounding the meaning of the events lying behind Scripture rather than those depicted in Scripture itself. Meir Sternberg has aptly described such an approach: "The theologian, qua

---

[30]As we have stressed earlier, the issue here is not whether a text is historically accurate. In both senses of the term *history* the accuracy of the text is without question. Fictionalized history or historical fiction, both legitimate literary categories, are not here in view. Both categories are anachronistic when applied to the biblical narratives. One cannot overemphasize the importance of the apologetic task of demonstrating the accuracy of Scripture, but that is no reason to push the hermeneutical question of the meaning of the text aside. Both questions are of utmost importance. At this point, our focus is on the second. Nor is the issue raised here that which the neo-orthodox (more precisely the "pneumatischen Schriftausleger") would call the distinction between *Historie* and *Geschichte*, where two kinds of history are posited: that which actually happened, and that which Israel believed.

theologian, dreams of piecing together a full picture of ancient Israelite religion, mutations and conflicts included. The historian wants to know what happened in Israelite history, the linguist what the language system (phonology, grammar, semantics) underlying the Bible was like. And the geneticist concentrates on the real-life processes that generated and shaped the biblical text."[31]

Even when one has clearly in view the goal to be "biblical" in the textual sense of the term—that is, to get at the meaning of the text of Scripture—it is all too easy to blur the boundaries between the text and the event and to handle the text as if one were dealing with the event represented in the text. Therein lies a fundamental threat among evangelicals to a theology based genuinely on Scripture.[32] The biblical message has been encoded in a text. Insofar as we say that this text is inspired and thus is the locus of God's revelation, then the meaning or content of that revelation is understood as the meaning of a text. To say that the text is an accurate portrayal of what actually happened is an important part of the evangelical view of Scripture, but it does not alter the fact that God's revelation has come to us through an inspired text, and thus no amount of delving into the history of Israel as an event apart from the text can take the place of the meaning of the scriptural text. Our task is to understand

> the text itself as a pattern of meaning and effect. What does this piece of language—metaphor, epigram, dialogue, tale, cycle, book—signify in context? What are the rules governing the transaction between story teller or poet and reader? . . . What image of a world does the narrative project? Why does it unfold the action in this particular order and from this particular viewpoint? What is the part played by the omissions, redundancies, ambiguities, alternations between scene and summary or elevated and colloquial language? How does the work hang together?[33]

It may be helpful to give an example of where evangelical biblical scholarship has apparently failed to see as clearly as it should this aspect of its commitment to an inspired text of Scripture and has looked beyond the scriptural text in its exegesis to expound on the events behind the text. The most obvious example is the salvation-history school, an approach to biblical studies that was thoroughly evangelical in its origins and continues to play an important role in evangelical theology.[34] It cannot be said that everyone

---

[31]Sternberg, *Poetics*, 15.

[32]Emanuel Hirsch points to the influence of Sigmund Jakob Baumgarten at the University of Halle in the mid-eighteenth century as the decisive turning point from a view of Scripture as revelation to a view of Scripture as a record of a revelation in events: "All and all it may well be said that with Baumgarten German Protestant theology entered the decisive stage in its transition from a Bible-faith to that of a revelation-faith in which the Bible in reality is nothing more than a document of revelation given at a specific moment in time" (*Geschichte der neuern evangelischen Theologie im Zusammenhang mit den allgemeinen Bewegungen des europäischen Denkens*, 5 vols. [Gütersloh: Bertelsmann, 1949], 2:378).

[33]Sternberg, *Poetics*, 15.

[34]See Hans-Joachim Kraus, *Die Biblische Theologie: Ihre Geschichte und Problematik* (Neukirchen: Neukirchener, 1970), 240. "Die Bibel ist der literarische Niederschlag der Offenbarung Gottes in der Heilsgeschichte. Sie is nicht monolithisch in einem Nu

taking a salvation-history approach to the OT necessarily overlooks the message of Scripture itself in favor of the meaning of events. From the beginning, however, that tendency can be seen within their writings. In an unusually perceptive article Benjamin Warfield has focused on what appears to be an equivocation of the meaning of the phrase *salvation history*.[35] At times the notion of salvation history was taken to refer to the work of God in history, specific acts of redemption by which God has brought about his promised salvation. Thus salvation history is the history of what God did to effect salvation and not revelatory as such. This has been a common position in historical evangelicalism and was that of Warfield himself. It is because of such a position that evangelicals have rightly stressed the importance of the historicity of biblical narratives in the face of the challenge of historical criticism.[36]

At the same time, however, some evangelicals understood the notion of salvation history to refer to the revelation of the will of God in history, God's making known his will to humanity through concrete historical events.[37] According to one early history-of-salvation theologian, Richard Rothe, "revelation consists fundamentally in the 'manifestation' of God in the series of redemptive acts, by which God enters into natural history by means of an unambiguously supernatural and peculiarly divine history, and which man is enabled to understand and rightly to interpret by virtue of an inward work of the Divine Spirit."[38]

In this sense salvation history is revelation history. It is true that when God works in history he inevitably makes himself known, and thus revelation in history is a natural consequence of God's working in history. But the category of revelation alone is not sufficient to deal with the problems raised by the idea of salvation history. In order to show the limits of the revelation that comes from salvation history, Warfield argued, one must point to the work of inspiration. The important distinction lies in the final evaluation of the status of the text of Scripture as revelation. Here Scripture, as a text, is more than a mere record of God's revelatory acts—it is itself revelation.

Scripture records the direct revelations which God gave to men in days past, so far as those revelations were intended for permanent and

---

als dogmatisches Kompendium entstanden, sondern dokumentiert uns das geschichtliche Handeln Gottes mit seinem Volk durch die Jahrhunderte und lässt uns die Offenbarungsgeschichte Gottes durch die Zeitalter von der Schöpfung bis zur Vollendung transparent werden" (Helge Stadelmann, *Grundlinien eines bibeltreuen Schriftverständnisses* [Wuppertal: R. Brockhaus, 1985], 122. See also *Epochen der Heilsgeschichte, Beiträge zur Förderung heilsgeschichtlicher Theologie*, ed. Helge Stadelmann (Wuppertal: R. Brockhaus, 1984); *Glaube und Geschichte, Heilsgeschichte als Thema der Theologie*, ed. Helge Stadelmann (Giessen: Brunnen, 1986).

[35]Benjamin B. Warfield, "The Idea of Revelation and Theories of Revelation," in *Revelation and Inspiration* (Oxford: Oxford Univ. Press, 1927; repr. Grand Rapids: Baker, 1981), 41–48.

[36]"Seit jeher war heilsgeschichtliches Denken der Feind geschichtsloser theologischer Systeme" (Stadelmann, *Grundlinien*, 123).

[37]A recent example is Stadelmann's apparent identification of *Heilsgeschichtliche* and *Offenbarungsgeschichte* (*Grundlinien*, 122).

[38]Richard Rothe, *Zur Dogmatik* (Gotha, 1863), quoted in Warfield, "Idea," 43.

universal use. But it is much more than a record of past revelations. It is
itself the final revelation of God, completing the whole disclosure of his
unfathomable love to lost sinners, the whole proclamation of his purposes
of grace, and the whole exhibition of his gracious provisions for the
salvation.[39]

Such a view of Scripture in Warfield's own day was regarded as sheer
biblicism and continually faced the unjust charge of being merely a
"repristination" of the outmoded dictation theory of inspiration. Warfield
was, of course, fully aware of the charge and in the face of it offered his
critique of the early and influential history-of-salvation theologians J. C. K.
von Hofmann, Richard Rothe, and A. B. Bruce.[40]

The confusion between reading the text as revelation and as a witness
to revelation continues today among evangelical OT theologians. The OT,
which is clearly and simply a text and as such gives a representation of the
events of God's work in history, is often treated as if it were the event itself.
Through earlier history-of-salvation theologians such as Rothe and von
Hofmann were aware of their looking past the text of Scripture to God's
revelation in history itself, contemporary evangelicals often give the appearance of doing so unwittingly. Both Rothe and von Hofmann saw themselves
as theologians of the history of salvation, whereas today evangelicals,
wanting to remain faithful to the orthodox view of Scripture as revelation,
attempt to identify salvation history with the text itself. In what can only be
described as a collapse of the genre category "text," biblical revelation is
made synonymous with that which happened in the history of Israel, and
revelation is posited in an event.

The Biblical Theology of Geerhardus Vos is a classic evangelical work and
exhibits clearly the kind of mixture of text and event that characterizes many
more recent evangelical salvation-history approaches to the OT. For example, in his definition of biblical theology Vos lays out its task as "to exhibit
the organic growth or development of the truths of Special Revelation from
the primitive pre-redemptive Special Revelation given in Eden to the close of
the New Testament canon."[41] Inasmuch as this is his definition of "biblical
theology," what else can Vos mean than that it is possible to speak of a
biblical theology already in the Garden of Eden? Can the word biblical here be

---

[39]Warfield, "Idea," 48.

[40]Warfield was not alone in his opposition to the views of Rothe and von Hofmann,
however. At least two other noted evangelical theologians entered the debate:
Friedrich A. Philippi (Kirchliche Glaubenslehre, 5 vols. [Gütersloh: C. Bertelsmann,
1883], 282ff.) and W. Rohnert (Die Dogmatik der evangelisch-lutherischen Kirche [Leipzig:
Hellmuth Wollermann, 1902], 41ff.). Both of these theologians argued strenuously
against the tendency to reduce Scripture to the role of witness to revelation, rather
than a source of revelation, by defending the orthodox identification of "revelation"
and "Scripture." Even such representative evangelical theologians as Karl F. A.
Kahnis (Die lutherische Dogmatik historisch-genetisch dargestellt [Leipzig: Dorffling and
Franke, 1874], 256ff.), Friedrich A. G. Tholuck, and E. Ernst Luthardt had moved
significantly away from the orthodox notion that revelation rests in the written words
of Scripture, largely under the influence of the prevailing interest in Heilsgeschichte
(Rohnert, Dogmatik, 103–5; Kahnis, Dogmatik, 256).

[41]G. Vos, Biblical Theology: Old and New Testaments (Grand Rapids: Eerdmans, 1948,
repr. 1980), v–vi.

related to the sense of the word *biblical* as it is used of the Bible as Scripture (text)? When he speaks of a biblical theology in the days of Adam and Eve, Vos shows that he has not made a distinction between any kind of special revelation in history and God's revelation of his will in the inspired Scriptures. Indeed, Vos is clear that this is his understanding of the sense of "biblical theology": it is any form of special revelation from the time before the Fall to the time of Christ.

The point here is not to criticize Vos's approach to biblical theology or his view of revelation. The point is to show how his salvation-historical approach has blurred his distinction between the Bible as a record of revelation and the Bible as that revelation itself. For Vos, revelation may go far beyond the scope of the text of Scripture. The category of "salvation history," which he had apparently inherited from earlier theologians such as von Hofmann, allowed him to see revelation in events quite apart from the text. At the same time his deep roots in Protestant orthodoxy kept him from severing completely his ties to the biblical text as revelation.

Thus both forms of revelation found their way into his biblical theology but with two quite different bases: the one focused on the revelation of God recorded in the Bible; the other focused on the revelation of God that is the Bible itself. For example, Vos discusses the patriarchs not in categories derived from the Pentateuch as a text and its author but rather from an historical orientation. The section is entitled "Revelation in the Patriarchal Period." The focus of his interest is not the author's representation of Abraham in the Pentateuch as such but rather the revelation of God during the patriarchal period. Vos was interested in the religion that had been revealed to Abraham. Thus, when it is necessary to explain Abraham's role in God's revelation during this period, Vos is just as comfortable calling to his aid recent archaeological material to show that God brought Abraham to Canaan because "it was actually a land where the lines of intercourse crossed. In the fulness of time its strategic position proved of supreme importance for the spreading abroad of the Gospel unto the whole earth."[42] Vos may be correct in his assessment of God's plan for Abraham and for Israel, but it cannot be disputed that Vos did not get such information from the text of Genesis. Such ideas about Canaan's strategic position in the ancient Near East were gathered from a knowledge of the geography of the ancient world. They were not mediated through the words of Scripture, and Vos appears fully aware of this. From his perspective it matters little whether we have gathered our understanding from Scripture alone or from both Scripture and archaeology, as long as the information is not incompatible.

Vos's approach, which I take to be characteristic of many evangelical approaches to Scripture, is not one that has neglected Scripture in favor of a "revelation in history." Rather, it is an approach that can only be described as a curious lack of distinction between or awareness of the way in which texts and events have meaning. At the same time that he can recall recent archaeological evidence as a means of explaining God's actions with Abraham at the end of the third millennium B.C., Vos can appeal to the text of Genesis 15:6 to show the centrality of faith in the life of Abraham.[43]

---

[42]Vos, *Biblical Theology*, 77.
[43]Ibid., 83.

However, Genesis 15:6 is a text that Vos himself takes to be written by Moses hundreds of years later. The only way such a treatment of the patriarchs can hold together is to say that Vos's idea of revelation includes but goes far beyond what we now have as the text of Scripture.[44]

The hermeneutical consequences of a mixture of text and event can be seen in the point discussed above that the process of construing the meaning of an event is not the same as that of construing the meaning of a text. An obvious difference concerns the matter of perspective. Events stand open to multiple perspectives. The meaning or sense of an event lies in the ability of the onlooker to gather the appropriate data and evaluate it from a certain vantage point. In narrative texts, however, readers are given a privileged perspective on an event. They have the advantage of the author's guidance and perspective on the event. Thus the world of the event "reaches us through the mediation of the words, selected and combined to form their own logic. . . . More generally, the narrator's mediation offers the reader a pre-interpreted image of reality," whereas those who attempt to interpret an event find only the "raw materials on their hands."[45] For the evangelical the privileged perspective of the reader does not so much rest in the fact that one has only the perspective of the author to go on. That would be only making a virtue of necessity. Rather, it lies more importantly in the theological fact that the text, which gives the privileged perspective, is inspired.

In sum, behind texts stand authors who have rendered their intentions in texts, inspired texts in the case of the Bible. This simple fact makes a text-oriented approach to exegesis and biblical theology crucial for the evangelical. Our task is not to explain what happened to Israel in OT times. Though worthy of our efforts, archaeology and history must not be confused with exegesis and biblical theology. We must recognize that the authors of Scripture have already made it their task to tell us in their texts what happened to Israel. The task that remains for us is to explain and proclaim what they have written. The goal of a text-oriented approach is not revelation in history in the sense of an event that must be given meaning. Rather, the goal is a revelation in the history as it is recounted in the text of Scripture.

---

[44]There is precedent for Vos's view in the Protestant position that the recording of revelation in Scripture did not materially effect the revelation itself. Roman Catholic theologians held along with the Protestants that before the time of the writing of Scripture, God's revelation was maintained by oral tradition (*viva voce*). Catholic theologians, however, went on to argue that this oral tradition was not and could not be replaced by Scripture because it was of a fundamentally different kind of revelation than that of a written text. They held that oral and written revelation were different as two distinct species of a similar genus. By means of this argument, the necessity of a continuing oral tradition alongside Scripture found apparent support in the prehistory of the text. The Protestant response was to argue that divine revelation did not differ in essence (*non differt realiter*) whether in oral form (ἄγραφον, *viva voce*) or written (ἔγγραφον, *scriptum*). Though a sound argument, this radical and polemical identification of oral tradition with Scripture left little room for appreciating the nature of a written text as such (see J. A. Quenstedt, *Theologia Didactico-polemica sive Systema Theologicum* [Wittenberg, 1685], chap. 4, sect. 1; A. Rivetus, *Isagoge* [Lugdunus, 1627], 4:2; Franciscus Turrettini, *Institutio Theologiae Elencticae* [New York, 1847], 1:55).

[45]Sternberg, *Poetics*, 162.

E. Authorship and Sources

1. Authorship

The question naturally arises as to who wrote or composed the final account. Who was responsible for putting all the narratives together into the larger picture? Like most biblical books, however, the Pentateuch does not state the name of its author. While we may concur with later biblical authors in ascribing the authorship of the Pentateuch to Moses, we should not lose sight of the fact that the Pentateuch itself comes to us as an anonymous work and was apparently intended to be read as such.

Very little is known today about the origin and authorship of the Pentateuch. Jewish tradition and the NT have attributed it to Moses (cf. Jn 5:46). Though many modern biblical scholars doubt the possibility of Mosaic authorship for most of the book, there is little evidence within the book itself to warrant such skepticism. In most cases the question of the authorship of the Pentateuch has been taken up within the context of theories regarding the literary history of the narratives.[46] In the same way, questions of the authorship of the Pentateuch have been bound up with doubts regarding the historicity of many of the narratives as well as varying assessments of the nature and purpose of the narratives themselves. Fortunately, an understanding and appreciation of the book is not dependent on a definite answer to these and other introductory questions. In the final analysis, an understanding of the book and its message comes from reading the book itself. No amount of historical and literary scholarship can replace the simple reading of the text as the primary means for determining its nature and purpose.

2. The Sources of the Composition of the Pentateuch

Both conservative biblical scholarship and critical scholarship have attempted to discover the various sources that may have been used in the composition of the Pentateuch. Critical scholarship supposes that writers of a date later than Moses composed the Pentateuch, using various sources that had been preserved among the diverse groups within ancient Israel. Some conservative scholars suppose Moses used a collection of clay tablets which had preserved the accounts of creation, the flood, and the lives of the patriarchs.[47] Thus, Moses would have written the Pentateuch in much the same way as Luke says he wrote his gospel (cf. Lk 1:1–4).

However Moses may have obtained his information, one thing is certain: the Pentateuch depicts accurately the age and historical period of the patriarchs and the Exodus, which is a period about which our knowledge has considerably increased in modern times from archaeological discoveries. Many of the historical details and customs in the lives of the patriarchs are

---

[46] The work of H. Holzinger, *Einleitung in den Hexateuch* (Freiburg: Mohr [Siebeck], 1893), which remains the primary source for the question of the Mosaic authorship of the Pentateuch, is a good example of how the question of authorship is wrapped up in the question of the literary history or sources of the narratives. In most cases, Holzinger's arguments against the Mosaic authorship of the Pentateuch are arguments against the unity of its composition ("der Mangel an Einheitlichkeit").

[47] Cf. R. K. Harrison, *Introduction to the Old Testament* (Grand Rapids: Eerdmans, 1969), 547–53.

now known to us from contemporary documents. In the case of the patriarchs, Moses or someone later than him would not have known such details. Thus, although we cannot say precisely how Moses obtained his information about the events and persons in the book of Genesis, the account of those events and persons exhibits all the traits of historical trustworthiness.

We will say more about the author's use of historical sources in the section below on the composition of the Pentateuch.

3. Unity

The Pentateuch is characterized by both an easily discernible unity and a noticeable lack of uniformity. The history of the study of the book is often marked by the tendency to stress one of these characteristics over against the other. On the one hand, critical scholarship has tended to see the lack of uniformity of style and vocabulary as a sign of the lack of unity in the structure and message of the book. On the other hand, conservatives have often ignored the rough edges in the narratives, thinking that in so doing they were safeguarding the unity of the book. To sustain a realistic understanding of the book's unity, an appreciation of the nature of its composition and an understanding of its structure are necessary.

Much like the writers of the NT Gospels and the later historical books of the OT (e.g., Kings and Chronicles), the writer of the Pentateuch appears to have composed his work from archival records of God's great deeds in the past. We know from references within the early historical books that such records were maintained at an early stage in Israel's history (Ex 17:14; Nu 21:14; Jos 10:13), and it is not unlikely that similar records were kept at far earlier stages within the individual households of the patriarchs and their tribal ancestors. We know from Exodus 17:14 that contemporary written records of important events were kept "for remembrance." In any event, most of the narratives within the Pentateuch appear to be made up of small, self-contained stories spun together into larger units by means of various geographical and genealogical tables. Within the center section of the Pentateuch, these narratives in turn provide the framework for incorporating large collections of laws into the text.

If such is, in fact, the case, one should no more expect to find absolute uniformity among all the individual narratives than in the later historical books, such as Kings and Chronicles or the Gospels. Indeed, we would more likely expect the writer to have preserved his records just as he had received them, to have sacrificed a lack of uniformity for the sake of historical faithfulness.

We should thus look for the unity of the Pentateuch in the compositional strategy of the book as a whole rather than in an absolutely smooth and uniform narrative. For example, the brief narrative about the building of the city of Babylon (Ge 11:1–9) is almost entirely self-contained and shows little external relationship with other narratives within its immediate context. Yet the narrative plays a strategic role in the development of one of the major themes in the book: the restoration of the primeval blessing through the call of Abraham. How does the author bring about this theme using the Babylon narrative? By placing the narrative between two genealogies of "Shem," the author establishes a relationship between the central point of the narrative—

"Let us make a name ['Shem'] for ourselves" (11:4a)—and the central point of the patriarchal narratives—"and God said, 'I will make your name ['Shem'] great'" (12:2a). Thus, the genealogies of "Shem" provide a narrative link between the story of Babylon and the account of the call of Abraham. The picture of the pentateuchal narratives that emerges from such observations is one of a carefully wrought account of Israel's early history fashioned from the narratives and genealogical tables of Israel's own ancestral archives.

F. Literary Form of Historical Narrative

1. What Is Historical Narrative?

Historical narrative is the re-presentation of past events for the purpose of instruction. Two dimensions are always at work in shaping such narratives: (1) the course of the historical event itself and (2) the viewpoint of the author who recounts the events. This dual aspect of historical narrative means that one must look not only at the course of the event in its historical setting but also for the purpose and intention of the author in recounting the event. In what follows, we will outline briefly some general principles on how we will find the author's intent and purpose in recounting the events of the Pentateuch in historical narrative.

2. Assessing the Structure of the Narrative Account

The most influential yet subtle feature of an author's work in relating historical events is the overall framework within which he arranges his account. Some call this the literary context. Perhaps a more usable term would be *structure*. What this means is that each segment of a narrative always has an internal relationship to the other segments of that narrative and to the narrative viewed as a whole. When we speak of structure we are speaking of the total set of relationships within a narrative unit.

General structural elements to look for in every historical narrative are simple but nonetheless important. They include an introduction, a conclusion, sequence, disjuncture, repetition, deletion, description, and dialogue. These elements combine to form the building blocks of the larger narrative units. For example, Genesis 1:1–2:4a is clearly recognizable as a unit of historical narrative. It has an introduction (1:1), a body (1:2–2:3), and a conclusion (2:4a). These three segments form a unit. Within this unit several structural elements combine to tie this passage (1:1–2:4a) together and give it a specific meaning. One of the more obvious elements is the repetition of the phrase "evening and morning," which divides the passage into a seven-day scheme. Creation forms a period of one work week concluding with a rest day. Already in this simple structural framework the tilting of the account betrays the interests of the author—Creation is viewed in terms of the human work week.

Another structural element, more subtle than the previous one, tying the passage together is the tight sentence pattern (or sequence) within which the events of Creation are recorded. This is apparent in the almost monotonous string of "ands" in the English versions of chapter 1. In contrast to this smooth sequence, an abrupt disjuncture at 1:2 in effect shoves this verse outside the regular sequence of the chapter. A study of the author's style in the Pentateuch shows that when he begins a specific topic much narrower than the preceding subject matter, he uses this technique of disjuncture.[48]

Here, then, at the beginning of the account the structure reveals the aim of the author: to narrow the scope of his narrative from the universe (1:1) to that of the land (1:2–31). This is quite a remarkable turning point in the account of Creation and should not be overlooked by anyone attempting to follow the author's intent in this chapter. Structure implies purpose, which in turn suggests a central concern or integration point that gives a passage its meaning and direction.

The two examples just cited suggest that the central concern of Genesis 1 is on the human and the land. Certainly we need more than these two examples to be convinced that this is the central concern, but the cumulative effect of further observations confirms that this is the direction or purpose behind the framework of the account. When we have observed the internal structure of a passage, as we have briefly done with Genesis 1:1–2:4a, we have not completed the task of assessing the total structural relationship of the passage to the broader context within which it is found. Indeed, a whole series of further structural ties between the passage and its literary environment may exist.

Here we face the problem of where to fix the outside limits to a passage within a historical narrative. Very often in the OT the division of the narratives into "books" cuts across tightly constructed segments (e.g., Ge 1:1–Ex 1:7 is a structurally complete unit not recognized by those who divided the Pentateuch into five parts). Beyond these literary units lie the larger borders of the OT canon and the subsequent canon of the Old and New Testaments.

In working with Genesis 1:1–2:4a, we can safely set out perimeters around the Pentateuch (Genesis–Deuteronomy) as the largest meaningful unit (literarily speaking). Since it comes first, one may safely consider Genesis 1:1–2:4a an introduction to the Pentateuch. Once the largest unit of historical narrative has been drawn, a twofold task remains: (1) to determine the central concern of this unit and (2) to develop the contribution of the smaller unit (Ge 1:2–4a) to the concern of the whole.

The central concern of the large narrative unit is not always immediately apparent but usually becomes clearer with trial-and-error efforts to relate the parts to the whole. This amounts, in practice, to reading through the entire unit and formulating a general statement of the overall theme. This theme is then checked against further readings of the text. Each reading should produce a clearer idea of the whole, which in turn should cast more light on the parts or segments.

Since we have drawn the Pentateuch as the largest unit with a meaningful structural relationship to Genesis 1:1–2:4a, the question we should now ask is whether the Pentateuch has a center. In the present commentary we will suggest that the central concern of the Pentateuch should be described in the following way.

---

[48]See Ge 3:1; see also W. Gross, "Syntaktische Erscheinungen am Anfang althebräischer Erzählungen: Hintergrund und Vordergrund," *VTSup* 32 (Leiden: Brill, 1981), 131–45.

First, the most prominent event and the most far-reaching theme in the Pentateuch, viewed entirely on its own, is the covenant between God and Israel established at Mount Sinai. The meaning of this event as it is described in the Pentateuch can be summarized in the following cluster of themes: (a) God comes to dwell with Israel; (b) Israel is a chosen people; (c) God gives Israel the land; (d) Israel must obey God's will; and (e) salvation or judgment is contingent on Israel's obedience.

If we leave these ideas in their original dress, we find that they are clothed in the metaphor of the ancient Near Eastern monarch: God, the Great King, grants to his obedient vassal-prince the right to dwell in his land and promises protection from his enemies. Somewhat more generally, this cluster of ideas may go by the name "theocracy," or the kingdom of God. However we may state it, this rule of God among his people Israel is the central concern of the Pentateuch.

We can say even more about the intention of the author of the Pentateuch—namely, what he is telling his readers about the covenant at Sinai. This can be summarized in the following three points:

1. The author wants to link God's original plan of blessing for humanity with his establishment of the covenant with Israel at Sinai. Put simply, the author sees the covenant at Sinai as God's plan to restore his blessing to humanity through the descendants of Abraham (Ge 12:1–3; Ex 2:24).

2. The author wants to show that the covenant at Sinai failed to restore God's blessing to humanity because Israel failed to trust God and obey his will.

3. The author wants to show that God's promise to restore the blessing would ultimately succeed because God himself would one day give to Israel a heart to trust and obey him (Dt 30:1–10). The outlook of the Pentateuch, then, might be described as eschatological, in that it looks to the future as the time when God's faithful promise (blessing) would be fulfilled. The past, Mount Sinai, had ended in failure from the author's perspective. The message of the Pentateuch, however, is hope: God's people should trust and obey him and, like Abraham, have faith in his promises. Thus the primary subject matter of the Pentateuch is the Sinai covenant. The author sees God's election of Israel and the establishment of a covenant at Sinai as a central religious and theological concern. The Pentateuch is his answer to the concern raised by the covenant in the same way that Galatians is Paul's answer to the same concern. The Pentateuch is both the author's explanation of the place Sinai occupied in God's plan and his explication of the lessons to be drawn from the experience.

It is important to see that while the Pentateuch is about the Sinai covenant, it is not the document of that covenant. To be sure, the Pentateuch does contain documents that were part of the Sinai covenant (e.g., the Ten Commandments, Ex 20; the covenant code, Ex 21–23; the tabernacle instruction, Ex 25–31; and the law of sacrifice, Lev 1–7); but the Pentateuch, as a literary document, is fundamentally different from a document of the Sinai covenant. The Pentateuch is a document that looks at the Sinai covenant as an object under consideration. It attempts to evaluate the Sinai covenant from a perspective that was not the same as that of the covenant itself. Like the other OT historical books, the Prophets, and the NT, the

Pentateuch represents a look back at the failure of Sinai and a look forward to a time of fulfillment (e.g., Dt 30).

It now remains to develop the contribution of the smaller narrative unit (Ge 1:1–2:4a) to the central concern of the whole (Pentateuch). In other words, if we are right in saying that Genesis 1 is an introduction to the Pentateuch, then we should ask what it introduces about the Pentateuch's central concern, the covenant at Sinai. The following principles are intended to show how a segment of historical narrative can contribute to the central concern of the larger narrative of which it is a part.

3. The Principle of Selectivity

No historical narrative is a complete account of all that occurred in a given event or series of events. The author must select those events that most effectively relate not only what happened but also the meaning and significance of what happened. We can formulate a working description of this principle of selection in this way: The author selects and arranges those features of a historical event that most characteristically portray the meaning of the event as he or she conceives it.

A close reading of Genesis 1:1–2:4a shows that the author made a careful and purposeful selection in composing the Creation account and that the features he selected do, in fact, provide an introduction to the Sinai covenant—that is, the Creation account tells the reader information that makes the author's view of the Sinai covenant understandable. One way to grasp this notion of selection is to ask: What general features of Creation (the subject matter) that I would expect to find in Genesis 1:1–2:4a are lacking? For example, where is the account of the creation of the angels? Where, for that matter, is the account of the creation of the stars and the galaxies? Verse 1 certainly stated the creation of these bodies as a brute fact, and verse 16 editorially alluded to them; but relative to the detail of the rest of the account in chapter 1, we could almost say that the author has passed them by. He has chosen rather to concentrate on the creation and preparation of the land. If we judge from the topics selected in Genesis 1:1–2:4a, we can say that the author has only three specific subjects in his account of Creation: God, human beings, and the land. Having said that there is little mention of the creation of the rest of the universe, we should note that the creation of the sun and moon is given considerable attention. But we should be quick to note, as well, that neither of these celestial bodies is mentioned in its own right. Rather, their creation is recounted in terms of the role they play in human affairs on the land: "to divide the day and night and to be signs for the seasons and for days and years" (1:14–15).

At this point we need to show how the two principles of structure and selectivity work together to give a narrative passage its meaning. First, we have already noted that an internal structural element has defined the scope of the Genesis 1:1–2:4a Creation account. That is, the author employs the disjuncture at 1:2 to focus his Creation account on the land. This point is consistent with our analysis of the selection: one of the author's three specific topics is the land.

Second, we can turn to the external structural relationship of Genesis 1:1–2:4a to the Pentateuch and ask: What does the land as a subject have to do with the Sinai covenant? Or, more precisely stated: How does the material about the land in Genesis 1:1–2:4a serve as an introduction to the author's view of the covenant at Sinai? When Genesis 1:1–2:4a speaks of God's creation and preparation of the land, we are, in fact, introduced to one of the central elements of the Sinai covenant: the promise of God to give the land to Israel: "If you obey me fully and keep my covenant, then out of all nations you will be my treasured possession. Although the whole earth is mine, you will be for me a kingdom of priests and a holy nation" (Ex 19:5–6). What, then, does Genesis 1:1–2:4a tell us about the land? It tells us that God is its owner. He created and prepared the land, and he can give it to whomever he chooses (Jer 27:5). In the ancient world, as in the modern world, the right to own land and grant it to others formed the basis of an ordered society. The author of the Pentateuch, then, is quick to point out that the promise of the land to Israel, made effective in the Sinai covenant, was in every way a right justly belonging to God.

A third example of the interrelationship between structure and selection can be seen in the view of God in Genesis 1:1–2:4a. When viewed as an introduction (structural relationship) to the covenant at Sinai, we can see that Genesis 1 presents a very important view of the covenant God: He is the Creator of the universe (Ge 1:1). Because Israel had come to know God in a close and personal way through the covenant, a certain theological pressure existed that, if left unchecked, could—and at times did—erode a proper view of God. This pressure was the tendency to localize and nationalize God as the God of Israel alone (Mic 3:11), a God who exists solely for Israel and for their blessing. Over against this lesser view of God stands the message of Genesis 1 with its clear introduction to the God who created the universe and who has blessed all humanity. From the point of view of the author of the Pentateuch, the God of the covenant is the Creator of the universe, and he has a plan of blessing for all people. Here lies the theological foundation of all subsequent missionary statements in the Bible.

We can conclude this section with a summary of Genesis 1:1–2:4a. The author intends his Creation account to relate to his readers that God, the Creator of the universe, has prepared the land as a home for his special creature, the human being, and he has a plan of blessing for all his creatures.

4. The Discourse Principles of *Thema* and *Rhema*

A historical narrative is a form of discourse between the author and the audience. The author must always write with an audience in view and must assume some common knowledge and shared experiences with this audience. On its most basic level this means that the author has to use a language that the audience will understand. The OT was written in Hebrew not simply because that was the language of the writers but more importantly because that was the language of those to whom the authors were writing.

At the level of interpretation, however, the idea of an audience means that an author can and must assume that he or she can use certain terms which are already known on the basis of his or her common experience with the audience. It also means, in the case of literature, that an author can use terms which will take on a specific sense in the course of the literary work itself.

We should expect, then, to find two different kinds of terms in any given narrative: those which an author assumes that the reader will already know or will subsequently come to understand better in the work itself (*thema*), and those which an author must elaborate in the passage at hand (*rhema*). Since an author will develop the meaning of *rhema* terms in the passage at hand, one has little difficulty with them in narrative. All that is really necessary is a sensitivity to an author's help in developing the meaning of these terms for the reader. When an author assumes that readers already have an understanding of terms which he or she uses (*thema*), the question at once faces the modern reader: Where does one look for the meaning of a term that the ancient writer does not explain? We may have to go outside the text altogether for a general understanding of the term and then attempt to fit this understanding into the specific text at hand. Usually, however, a safer approach is to follow the external structural relationship back to a passage where the term in question is in fact developed (if such a passage exists).

An example from Genesis 1:1–2:4a may help to clarify this point. The author uses several terms with the full expectation that his audience will comprehend them without explanation: "the deep," "the expanse," "formless and void," "signs," "seasons," "the great sea monsters," and so on. How do we find the meaning that the author intends for these terms? If we follow the structural ties already delineated above, being careful to remain within the boundaries of the Pentateuch (structure), the meaning of these terms, as used by the author, is close at hand. For example, the term *signs*, calls to mind various things for a modern reader; most recently, for many, the term may recall the signs of the zodiac. Could the author have intended this meaning when he recounts that the sun and moon are put in the heavens as "signs"? If we look at the use of this term in the broader structural context (Pentateuch), we can readily see that such a meaning would have been completely inappropriate to the author and his original audience, for elsewhere in the Pentateuch the author gives special attention to "signs." For example, the so-called plagues of Egypt are called "signs" (e.g., Dt 29:2–3). In the Exodus account (here the term is *rhema*, not *thema*) the acts of God in bringing disorder upon the Egyptians were "signs" that God was more powerful and majestic than the Egyptians' gods. This sense of the term "signs" fits well in Genesis 1:14. The author says that not only are the sun and moon to give light upon the land but they are to be visual reminders of the power and majesty of God. They are "signs" of who the God of the covenant is. They are "telling of the glory of God," as the psalmist puts it (Ps 19:1). For the author of the Pentateuch the term "signs" serves as a reminder not only of God's greatness and glory but also of God's grace and mercy (e.g., Ge 4; 9; 17).

Another example of a *thema* term in Genesis 1:1–2:4a is *seasons*. The English word "season" suggests a time of the year (e.g., "winter, fall") but again, the broader context of the Pentateuch gives a more precise meaning. Leviticus 23 is entirely devoted to the term "seasons." This is not easy to see because some English versions render the term "feasts." The term literally means "appointments." These appointments were the annual days when all Israel was to come together and worship the God of the covenant and celebrate the covenant relationship (Lev 23). If this is the meaning of the term in Genesis 1, we see that the author has something very specific in mind when he writes of the creation of the sun and moon. They were not mere lights or reminders of God's glory—they were also calendars for the celebration of the covenant. The world was made for the covenant. Already at creation, the land was being prepared for the covenant. Israel's covenant is at home in God's world.

Genesis 1:1–2:4a also develops new senses of terms (*rhema*) in the narrative. In fact, the concept of humanity's creation in the "image" of God finds its only explanation in this narrative. The explanation of the term comes from the way in which the author selects two features of humanity's creation: the deliberation of God before creating human beings and God's blessing of human beings after their creation. Both features have an important bearing on the author's view of the Sinai covenant. First, God's deliberation shows that he has decided to create human beings differently from any other creatures—that is, in his image and likeness. God and human beings share a likeness that other creatures do not share. Thus a relationship of close fellowship can exist between God and human beings that is unlike the relationship of God with the rest of his creation. What more important fact about God and humanity would be necessary if the covenant at Sinai were to be a real divine-human relationship? Remove this and the covenant is unthinkable. Second, in Genesis 1, humanity, the image bearer, is the object of God's blessing. According to the account of creation in Genesis 1, the chief purpose of God in creating human beings was to bless them. The impact of this point on the remainder of the Pentateuch and the author's view of Sinai is clear: through Abraham, Israel, and the covenant this blessing is to be restored to all humankind.

5. The Principle of Contemporization

In the writing of historical narrative, events of the past often find new meaning and significance in relation to certain issues and ideas present in the author's own day. Thus the author views past events with an eye to the present, and often assumes that the narrative would be read in that way. From this fact a principle emerges: look for thematic development of ideas and issues current during the author's own time. This principle presupposes that we have some indication of when the narrative was written and that we know something of the historical-cultural setting of the narrative's composition. If we cannot discern when or to whom a book was written, it may also mean that the book has been intentionally generalized and contemporized in order to speak to many succeeding audiences in many different contexts.

This principle can be detected in Genesis 1 by the way in which the author uses terms in unusual contexts. For example, he calls the global ocean (the "deep") in 1:2 a "desert."[49] If we again use the notion of *thema* terms and search for the meaning of this word within the Pentateuch itself, we can see its typological significance. The author uses this term (in Dt 32:10) to describe the desert wasteland where Israel wandered for forty years. Why call an ocean a desert? What better way to teach the people that the God who will lead them out of the wilderness and give them the Promised Land is the same God who once prepared the land for them by dividing the waters and producing the "dry land"? The God of the Pentateuch is the one who leads his people from the wasteland to the Promised Land.

---

[49]This is not apparent in the English translation "formless." The NASB margin has "wasteland."

6. Summary

We close this section with one further example of the role of structure and selection in determining the meaning of a unit of historical narrative like Genesis 1:1–2:4a. This example should serve also as a summary of the approach taken in this study of the Pentateuch. We have already suggested that the overall purpose of the author is to show that the Sinai covenant failed for lack of an obedient heart on the part of God's people Israel. We have also suggested that his intention in writing the Pentateuch is not to look back in despair at human failure but to point in hope to the faithfulness of God. The hope of the writer is clearly focused on what God would do to fulfill his covenant promises.

Nowhere is he more clear on this than at the (structural) conclusion to his work: Deuteronomy 30:1–10. Here Moses tells the people of Israel that they will one day fail and that they will be cursed, but he also tells them that God's work with them will not end there. The Lord will again bring them into the Promised Land, gathering them from all the lands where they have been exiled. But this time things will be different. Israel is going to obey God, for God is going to give them a heart that will obey, a heart that will love the Lord and keep his commandments. It is on this high note of expectation that the Pentateuch draws to a close.

If we go beyond the Pentateuch to the later historical books, the Prophets, and finally to the NT, the fulfillment of Moses' hope is made certain. It is also clear in these later books how God is going to give his people a new heart: "I will give you a new heart, a new Spirit I will put within you; I will turn away the heart of stone from your flesh and I will give you a heart of flesh. My Spirit I will put within you and I will make you walk in my statutes, and my judgments you will keep" (Eze 36:26–27). It is by means of God's Spirit that his people will be able to do his will. No one is clearer on this point than Paul (Ro 8:4).

What is often overlooked, however, is that we need not go beyond the Pentateuch itself for the same conclusion. The author has as one of his central purposes to show that God's work must always be done in God's way: by means of the Spirit of God. To show the centrality of this idea in the Pentateuch we need only compare the author's description of God's own work in doing his will (Ge 1:2b) with that of human obedience to God's will (Ex 31:1–5). Viewed on its own, the description of the Spirit of God in Genesis 1:2 has often been only remotely related to the rest of the chapter. Some interpreters have argued that this reference to God's Spirit be eliminated altogether and that the passage be rendered simply as "a mighty wind was blowing over the surface of the waters." When viewed as structurally related to Exodus 31, however, this brief notice regarding the Spirit of God takes on new importance for the meaning of the Pentateuch. In Exodus 31:1–5, God chose Bezalel to do the work of building the tabernacle. What God commanded Moses, Bezalel was to perform. In order to insure Bezalel's accomplishment of the work, the Lord filled Bezalel with the Spirit of God "to do all of the work . . . which I have commanded you." For the author, to do the work of God successfully (with wisdom) one must be filled with the Spirit of God. We may recall what Moses said to Joshua when he complained that someone "unofficial" may have received the Spirit of the

Lord: "Would that the LORD would put his Spirit upon all of them [his people]" (Nu 11:29). If this point is important to the author, then his comment at the beginning (Ge 1:2b) makes perfectly good sense. Even God the Creator, when he did his work of Creation, did so by means of the Spirit of God. How much more then should his people do his will by means of his Spirit?

G. The Structure of the Pentateuch

What is particularly noticeable about the way in which the Pentateuch is put together as a book is the presence of so many collections of laws within the narratives. When the book reaches the giving of the covenant at Sinai (Ex 20), the narrative virtually disappears amid the wealth of legal material. From that point on, the narrative survives as only a trace of a sequence of events leading from Sinai to the plains of Moab. The center of the Pentateuch is dominated by the collections of laws, and the writer does not return to the series of narrated events for the rest of the book. It is only with the books of Joshua, Judges, Samuel, and Kings that we again return to the flow of narrated events like those of Genesis and Exodus.

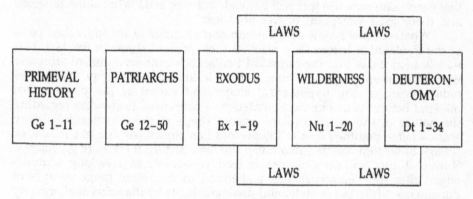

		LAWS	LAWS	
PRIMEVAL HISTORY	PATRIARCHS	EXODUS	WILDERNESS	DEUTERON-OMY
Ge 1–11	Ge 12–50	Ex 1–19	Nu 1–20	Dt 1–34
		LAWS	LAWS	

Having made this observation, we should ask, What is the purpose of the collections of laws? Why has the author abandoned his concern for narratives and stories and left us, the readers, alone with these laws? The answer to these questions is bound up with the answer to the larger question of the purpose of the Pentateuch as a whole. We will thus address the question of the purpose of the laws in the Pentateuch in the course of our discussion of the purpose of the entire Pentateuch (see especially section H.4., below).

H. The Purpose of the Pentateuch

Why was the Pentateuch written? What was its purpose? It is, of course, the aim of the present work to discuss that purpose and the Pentateuch's theological message in detail. The following discussion is intended to give an overview of the Pentateuch's purpose and the ways in which it is developed within and throughout the book.

We will argue that the Pentateuch's purpose is reflected in its composition. What the author intend to say determines the shape of the book. Our procedure here will be to give an account of the various ways one can explain the structure and shape of the Pentateuch. This approach, called compositional analysis, attempts to describe how the various pieces fit into the whole. Throughout the remainder of the book we will attempt to show that the pieces of the Pentateuch do fit together and do reveal a conscious attempt by the author to render the various stories and laws in one coherent picture.

1. A Compositional Analysis of the Pentateuch

In recent years the attention of biblical scholarship has focused as much on textual strategies in the Pentateuch as on textual strata. While source criticism has long been practiced in pentateuchal studies, only recently has equal attention been given to compositional criticism, the attempt to describe the semantics of the arrangement of source material in the biblical texts.[50] What methods and techniques does an author employ in producing a final text? What large units of text has the author employed to build the final text? What functions do the individual units within the final text play in the light of the completed whole? Does the author give any final touches to the text that determine how the text will be read and received? What is the religious and theological viewpoint of the final text?

Whatever one's view of the origin and diversity of the individual parts of the Pentateuch before they reached their present shape in the text, it is widely held today that the canonical Pentateuch exhibits a unified structure with a common purpose. Though there is little agreement in OT studies today regarding the hypothetical shape and extent of the pentateuchal material before its use in the Pentateuch, a consensus is growing regarding the nature of the material in its present shape in the Pentateuch.[51] Many acknowledge that the fabric of the present Pentateuch consists of a mosaic or collage of written sources, much like the later historical books (e.g., Judges, Samuel, Kings, and the Gospels). Indeed, conservatives have long acknowledged that the Pentateuch has embedded in it a wide range of ancient documents "differing in style, and distinguishable by the primitive formality of their introductions."[52]

---

[50]See Georg Fohrer, *Exegese des Alten Testaments* (Heidelberg: Quelle & Meyer, 1983), 139ff.

[51]See Erhard Blum, *Studien zur Komposition des Pentateuch* (Berlin: de Gruyter, 1990), 1ff., for a helpful survey of the recent literature.

[52]Robert Jamieson, A. R. Fausset, and David Brown, *A Commentary Critical, Experimental and Practical on the Old and New Testaments*, 3 vols. (Eerdmans, 1945), 1:xxxv. Jamieson, of course, stood firmly against the critical positions of his day by holding to a single authorship of the Pentateuch. Though he held that "fragments of other compositions" (p. xliv) were evident in the Pentateuch, he strongly rejected the then current "Fragmentary Hypothesis" because it posed a problem for the unity of the Pentateuch as well as for the early date of its composition. "Independently of any hypothesis, it may be conceded that, in the composition of those parts of the Pentateuch relating to matters which were not within the sphere of his personal knowledge, Moses would and did avail himself of existing records which were of reliable authority; and while this admission can neither diminish the value nor affect the credibility of his history as an inspired composition, it is evident that, in making use of such literary materials as were generally known in his time, or had been preserved in the repositories of Hebrew families, he interwove them into his narrative

The Pentateuch as a whole has three major types of literary sources: legal corpora, narrative, and poetry. Each of these plays an important role in the strategy of the final shape of the Pentateuch.[53] We will discuss each type of text and attempt to demonstrate in an introductory way the contribution they make to the literary strategy, and hence purpose, of the Pentateuch as a whole.

2. Poetic Seams in the Pentateuch

Several major poetic texts are found interspersed throughout the narratives of the Pentateuch; most notable are those in Genesis 49:1–27; Exodus 15:1–17; Numbers 23:7–10, 18–24; 24:3–9, 15–24; and Deuteronomy 32–33. A close study of the author's use of narrative and poetry sheds considerable light on the final shape of the work. The technique of using a poetic speech and a short epilogue to conclude a narrative is well known in biblical literature and occurs frequently within recognizable segments of the Pentateuch itself.

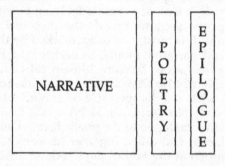

The Creation account in Genesis 1–2 concludes with the short poetic discourse of Adam (2:23) and an epilogue (2:24). The account of the Fall in chapter 3 concludes with the poetic discourse (3:14–19) and an epilogue (3:20–24). The account of Cain in chapter 4 concludes with a poetic discourse (4:23) and an epilogue (4:24–26). That this same pattern can be found throughout the Pentateuch suggests that it is an important part of the compositional technique of the author. Most notable is the occurrence of this pattern in the Joseph story (Ge 37–48), which concludes with the poetic discourse of Jacob's blessing of Ephraim and Manasseh (48:15–16, 20).

More importantly, however, the pattern recurs at a much higher level within the Pentateuch, and this suggests that the technique was extended as part of the structure embracing the whole of the book. First, the pattern is found in the inclusion of the large poetic text (Ge 49:1–27) at the close of the patriarchal narratives, along with the epilogue of Genesis 50. Second, the two major narrative units which follow that of Genesis, the Exodus

conformably with that unity of design which so manifestly pervades the entire Pentateuch" (p. xxxii). See also Harrison, *Introduction to the Old Testament*, 543–53.

[53]There are also many other types of literary texts in the Pentateuch. For example, the genealogical texts play an important role in the early sections of the Pentateuch, especially in Genesis, but do not lead to fruitful conclusions about the shape or structure of the Pentateuch as a whole.

narratives and the wilderness narratives, both conclude with a poetic section, Exodus 15 and Numbers 23–24, respectively. Finally, the pattern embraces the whole pentateuchal narrative, which concludes with the poetic "Song of Moses" and "Blessing of Moses" (Dt 32–33) and the epilogue of Deuteronomy 34.

Since such a compositional scheme seems to lie behind the final shaping of the Pentateuch, it would be wise to begin with the question of the compositional purpose of the book. Do any clues along the seams of these large units point to the author's ultimate purpose? If so, they should guide us in any further probings into the author's purpose at a lower level in the text. We will begin our investigation of the compositional purpose of the Pentateuch with a closer look along the seams of these large units of narrative and poetry. Here we will attempt to uncover the basic hermeneutic of the author, and then demonstrate the use of that hermeneutic at lower levels in the text.

At three macrostructural junctures in the Pentateuch, the author has spliced a major poetic discourse onto the end of a large unit of narrative (Ge 49; Nu 24; Dt 31). A close look at the material lying between and connecting the narrative and poetic sections reveals the presence of a homogeneous compositional stratum. It is most noticeably marked by the recurrence of the same terminology and narrative motifs. In each of the three segments, the central narrative figure (Jacob, Balaam, Moses) calls an audience together (imperative: Ge 49:1; Nu 24:14; Dt 31:28) and proclaims (cohortative: Ge 49:1; Nu 24:14; Dt 31:28) what will happen (Ge 49:1; Nu 24:14; Dt 31:29) in "the end of days" (Ge 49:1; Nu 24:14; Dt 31:29).

The brief narrative prologue to the poetic text in Genesis 49 tells us that the central figure, Jacob, had called together his sons to announce to them "that which will happen at the end of days" (Ge 49:1b). Thus, however we may want to translate the terminology he has employed, in this seam introducing the poetic discourse of Jacob the author has provided the reader with an indispensable clue to its meaning. Jacob's poetic discourse was about "what will happen" at "the end of days."

In an identical macrostructural position within the seam connecting the poetic text of Deuteronomy 32 with the whole preceding narrative of the Pentateuch, we find another narrative prologue with the same terminology and motif. The central figure, Moses, had called together (Dt 31:28) the elders of the tribes to announce to them the trouble that "will happen in the end of days" (Dt 31:29b). Again the reader is afforded an all-important clue to the meaning of the poetic text. It was about "what will happen" in "the end of days." Using the same terminology, the author has inserted an identical message in the seams connecting both poetic texts (Ge 49 and Dt 32) to the preceding narrative segments as a clue for the reader that the poetic discourses are "eschatological," that is, they concern "the end of days."

At one other crucial juncture connecting the large units of poetic and narrative texts in the Pentateuch the same terminology occurs—Numbers 24:14. Here, in the narrative prologue to the last words of Balaam, the author again provides the reader with the necessary hermeneutical clue to the meaning of the poetic texts, and again it has to do with "the last days." As in the other two passages, the events that lie ahead in the future days are revealed in the last words of the central narrative figure, Balaam.

Such convergence of macrostructure, narrative motifs, and terminology among these three strategically important poems of the Pentateuch can hardly be accidental. That the only other occurrence of the terms in the Pentateuch is also within a macrostructural seam (Dt 4) argues strongly for our taking these connecting segments to be part of the final work on the Pentateuch. To state it clearly, they reveal the work of the final composer or author of the Pentateuch. As such, they are also a clear indication of the author's hermeneutic. The author shows throughout his work an intense interest in past events. His repeated and strategic return to the notion of "the last days" in giving his work its final shape reveals that his interest is in the future as well.

In sum, the apparent overall strategy of the author in these three segments suggests that one of the central concerns lying behind the final shape of the Pentateuch is an attempt to uncover an inherent relationship between the past and the future. That which happened to God's people in the past portends of future events. To say it another way, the past is seen as a lesson for the future.

For our purposes these observations lead to the following conclusion. A consideration of the macrostructural strategy lying behind the final shape of the Pentateuch suggests that the author works within a clearly defined hermeneutic. Because of the terminology he uses (viz., "the end of days"), we could call it an eschatological reading of his historical narratives. The narrative texts of past events are presented as pointers to future events. Past events foreshadow the future. It is not hard to see that such a hermeneutic leads to a form of narrative typology. We should, then, look for signs of such a typology in the composition of the smaller units of narrative in the Pentateuch as well as in the arrangement of the legal material.

3. Narrative Typology

The Pentateuch is put together in such a way that one can discern relationships among its parts. Earlier events foreshadow and anticipate later events. Later events are written to remind the reader of past narratives. We have called this feature "narrative typology." By means of this technique the author develops central themes and continually draws them to the reader's attention. In the following sections we will briefly discuss some examples of this kind of typology. An awareness of such features will greatly enhance one's reading of the Pentateuch.

a. Genesis 12:10–20 Foreshadows Genesis 41–Exodus 12

A small narrative segment that has attracted an extraordinary amount of attention over the years is the account of Abraham's visit to Egypt in Genesis 12:10–20. The similarities between this narrative and that of Genesis 20 and 26 are well known. Such similarities are most often taken to be a sign of historical or literary dependency. But one can also view the similarities as part of a larger typological scheme intending to show that future events are often foreshadowed in past events.[54] In fact, many of the similarities and parallels with the patriarchal narratives may have originated from such a scheme of narrative typology. Further evidence of such a scheme comes from

---

[54]See quote by Cassuto in comments on Ge 12:1–10 below.

a comparison of Genesis 12:10–20 with the large narrative unit which deals with the Israelites' sojourn in Egypt (Ge 41–Ex 12). The chart on Ge 12:10–20 (see the commentary below) suggests that the composition of Ge 12:10–20 has been intentionally structured to prefigure or foreshadow the events of Israel's sojourn in Egypt.

If the similarities between these two narratives are not merely accidental, then some sort of narrative typology clearly lies behind their composition. The author wants to show that the events of the past are pointers to those of the future. An interesting confirmation that this particular text was intended to be read this way is the role played by Lot within the narrative. It can hardly be accidental that Genesis 12:10–20, which forms the frontispiece to the Lot narratives, is virtually duplicated, as a kind of *inclusio*, in Genesis 20, which comes after the last narrative dealing with Lot. This is especially noticeable in light of the fact that chapter 20 is both chronologically and geographically out of place in its present narrative context. The positioning of the Lot narratives between these two remarkably similar narratives about Abraham is apparently a reflection of a narrative strategy. Of special interest is that in Genesis 12:10–13:4 Lot occupies the same position as that of the "mixed multitude" (Ex 12:38) in the narrative of Genesis 41–Exodus 12. In other words the author apparently wants to draw the reader's attention to the identification of Lot with the "mixed multitude." It is as if Lot is seen in these narratives as a prefiguration of the "mixed multitude" that comes out of Egypt with the Israelites.

Along this same line it is significant that the last narrative dealing with Lot shows us that Lot is the father of the Moabites and the Ammonites (Ge 19:36–38), the very group that is prohibited from taking part in the congregational worship (Dt 23:4-5). Thus, as Lot is finally excluded from the assembly of Abraham, the reader is reminded that there is to be no "mixed multitude" in the Israelite assembly.

The question that naturally arises is whether the original or early readers of the book appreciated such a typological reading of these narratives. Fortunately, in this case we have a clear witness to the fact that they did. In Nehemiah 13:1–3 the problem of marriage to foreign wives was handled by an appeal to Deuteronomy 23:4–5, where the Ammonites and Moabites were restricted from the worship assembly. The author of the book of Nehemiah then remarks that when the people heard this, they separated out from them "all of the mixed multitude" (Ne 13:3). Since this is the only other occurrence of the term *mixed multitude* in the Hebrew Bible and since the use of this term in Exodus 12:38 has no association with the Moabites and Ammonites, the association between the "mixed multitude" and the Moabites and Ammonites could only have come from an association of the "mixed multitude" with Lot and his two daughters. In other words, Nehemiah apparently read the pentateuchal narratives typologically, identifying Lot, the father of the Moabites and the Ammonites, with the "mixed multitude." Such evidence offers a very early assessment of how the original readers of the Pentateuch understood and read it.

To sum up: The final shape of the Pentateuch reflects an interest in reading the historical narratives both typologically and eschatologically. The events of the past are read as pointers to the future. The future is portrayed as like the past. The internal composition of smaller narrative units also reflects this interest in typology. For example, Abraham was presented as a picture or type of the future Israel and Lot was presented as a type of the future "mixed multitude."

b. The Spread of Sin in Genesis 1–11 and the Defilement of the Camp in Leviticus 11–16

One can see another example of narrative typology in the parallels between Genesis 1–11 and the arrangement of the cultic purity laws in Leviticus 11–16. The importance of Genesis 1–11 for the rest of the Pentateuch can be seen in the fact that its narrative structure provides a pattern by which the author often shapes subsequent pentateuchal narratives. Thus the order and arrangement of the Creation accounts in Genesis 1–2 exhibit the same pattern as the description of the building of the tabernacle (Ex 25–31); the tabernacle is portrayed as a return to the Garden of Eden. The instructions given to Noah for building the ark foreshadow those given to Moses for building the tabernacle. Furthermore, one can demonstrate that whole sections of laws in the Pentateuch have been grouped and arranged in patterns that parallel the narrative structure of Genesis 1–11.

It has long been recognized, for example, that the order of the purity laws in Leviticus 11 follows that of the creation of animal life in Genesis 1 (Rashi). Moreover, just as in Genesis 1 God distinguished "good" and "evil" in his new creation, so also in Leviticus 11 God distinguished the "clean" from the "unclean." In addition, Leviticus 11–16 has numerous parallels to the pattern of Genesis 1–11.

For instance, at first sight no reason or rationale is apparent for the material selected in Leviticus 12. The subject matter of this chapter deals solely with the question of the impurity of childbirth. What was the "logic" of focusing on this particular topic at this point in the collection of laws? Many consider its placement here completely arbitrary. However, the details of the text as well as the larger structural patterns provide helpful clues about its purpose. For example, the terminology of Leviticus 12 alludes to the curse involving childbirth in Genesis 3. This suggests that beyond the parallels in Leviticus 11, the further arrangement of topics in Leviticus may also fit within the pattern of Genesis 1–11.[55] If this be the case, then the purpose behind the narrative's present structure may be to portray the spread of ritual defilement in Israel's camp as a reversal of God's original plan of blessing. Or, to view the matter from another perspective, the early narratives of Genesis, by paralleling the later rituals dealing with contamination, may be attempting to show that the first sin in the Garden was a form of ritual contamination of God's good creation. Thus the larger parallel between God's work in Creation and his work in establishing a covenant with Israel finds further development along the lines of the spread of sin in both the created world and the covenant community.

Adding to the likelihood that this arrangement of the laws in Leviticus is intentional, the next set of laws in Leviticus 13 deals with the problem of the impurities of the "skin" (עוֹר). Disease of the "skin of the flesh" (עוֹר בשׂר) was a sign of impurity in Israel's camp in a way similar to Genesis 3, where human guilt after the Fall was signified by "nakedness" (עירם). The man and

---

[55] See comments below on Leviticus 12–15.

woman were originally one "flesh" (בשר) and "naked [ערום] but not ashamed" (Ge 2:25). Just as the effects of the first sin were immediately displayed in their skin ("And their eyes were opened and they knew that they were naked [עירם]," Ge 3:7; cf. 9:20–23), so the writer uses the graphic horror of skin (עור) diseases to depict humanity's state of uncleanness before a holy God.

Moreover, it is significant that in Genesis the first man and woman, once they realized their own nakedness, suffered the same consequences for their contamination as the unclean person in Leviticus 13. According to the regulations in Leviticus, if one were found to be unclean, "as long as he has the infection he remains unclean. He must live alone; he must live *outside the camp*" (Lev 13:46). In the same way, when Adam and Eve sinned, "the LORD God banished him from the Garden of Eden to work the ground from which he had been taken. And he drove Adam out" (Ge 3:23–24). They had to live "outside the camp," as it were, until their uncleanness could be removed.

Additional features of the narratives in Genesis 1–11 have interesting parallels to the sequence of laws in the structure of Leviticus. These parallels leave the impression that a conscious attempt has been made in the composition of the Pentateuch to link the two sets of narrative. The following chart lists the laws in Leviticus which are related to the Flood story (Ge 6–9) and the story of Babylon (Ge 11).

Flood Story (Genesis)

1. The waters of the Flood were the means whereby God cleansed the land of "all flesh" that had "corrupted his way" (Ge 6:12).

2. The ark (תבה) was plastered (כפר) with pitch (כפר), inside (מבית) and out (מחוץ) (Ge 6:14).

3. Noah waited at the door of the ark for seven days (Ge 7:4, 10).

4. Noah waited for the bird in the ark for two series of sevens (Ge 8:10, 12).

5. Two birds were sent out of the ark. One, the raven, flew out over the water and the other, a dove, flew over the dry land (Ge 8:7–12). The raven was an unclean bird (Lev 11:15) and the dove was clean.

6. A sacrifice was offered at the conclusion (Ge 8:20).

7. Noah offered a "clean animal" and a "clean bird" on the altar (Ge 8:20).

Purification (Leviticus)

The primary means of cleansing diseased flesh in these Levitical laws was water. Reference to the use of water occurs seven times in this passage (14:5, 6, 8, 9, 50, 51, 52).

The house (הבית) was plastered (טח), with clay (עפר) after the soiled material was removed inside (מבית) and taken out (מחוץ) of the city (Lev 14:41–42). The house was atoned (כפר) for (Lev 14:53b).

The priest was to wait at the door of the house for seven days (Lev 14:38).

The one to be cleansed waited for two series of sevens (14:7, 8).

Two "clean birds" were taken: one was slain "over water," and the other was released "over the face of the field." The slain bird, a sin offering (Lev 14:52), took away the uncleanness; the other bird went free.

A sacrifice was offered at the conclusion (Lev 14:10, 21).

The one to be cleansed offered a male lamb and two doves on the altar (Lev 14:21–22).

8. Noah was given dietary regulations (Ge 9:3) and warned about consuming the blood (Ge 9:4).

Dietary regulations have been given (Lev 11), along with a strict warning about consuming the blood (Lev 17; cf. 7:26).

9. God established a covenant with Noah (Ge 9:9).

God established a covenant with Israel (Lev 26:44).

10. The sign of the covenant was the rainbow in the clouds (Ge 9:14–15).

The sign of God's presence in the covenant was the cloud over the atonement cover (Lev 16:2).

11. Noah drank wine (יין) and became drunk (שכר) and lay naked in his tent (Ge 9:21).

Aaron and his sons were warned not to drink wine (יין) or fermented drink (שכר) when they went into the Tent of Meeting (Lev 10:9).

12. Noah's two sons, Ham and Canaan, were cursed (Ge 9:24–27).

Aaron's two sons, Nadab and Abihu, were cursed (Lev 10:1).

13. Noah's son "Ham, the father of Canaan, saw his father's nakedness" (Ge 9:22).

Lev 18:7, "Do not uncover the nakedness of your father." The whole of this chapter deals with problems of uncovering nakedness, which is called the defilement of the Canaanites (Lev 18:24–30).

14. Story of Babel. At Babylon (בבל from בלל), God's concern was that "nothing they plan [זמם] to do will be impossible for them" (Ge 11:6). The verb זמם is used here and in Dt 19:19.

The holiness laws in Lev 18–20 were intended to insure that there would be no "wickedness" (זמה) from זמם, Lev 18:17; 19:29; 20:14) or "confusion" (תבל from בלל, Lev 18:23; 20:12) in the land. The nouns זמה (from זמם) and תבל (from בלל) are used only here in the Pentateuch.

15. Abram married Sarai, his half-sister (Ge 11:29; 20:12).

The holiness laws prohibited marriage to one's half-sister (Lev 18:11; 20:17).

If the parallels between Genesis 1–11 and Leviticus enumerated above are not fortuitous (which does not appear likely), then the author of the Pentateuch appears to have a larger purpose in mind in the structure of his work. These parallels suggest that he sees Adam's sin as a contamination of God's good creation. It was marked by the effect of the curse on childbirth, by the nakedness of the man and the woman, and by their being cast out of the Garden. The author apparently saw that the Flood and Noah's sacrifice played an important part in the cleansing of humankind after the Fall and in the preparation for God's renewed covenant, first with Noah and then with Abraham. All in all this strategy places the covenant with Abraham within a much broader context and shows that God's purposes in Creation were continued in the call of Abraham and the covenant at Sinai.

c. The Balaam Narratives

The Balaam narratives have long puzzled readers of the Bible. Balaam himself is an enigma, but more important here is the question of the role these narratives play in the overall purpose of the Pentateuch. When viewed in the light of their parallels with other parts of the Pentateuch, these narratives play a strategic role in the overall message of the Pentateuch. Their placement in the book is part of the writer's plan to develop a central theological thesis.

In Genesis 1 the writer shows that at the center of God's purpose in creating human beings was his desire to bless them. Immediately after creating them, God blessed them and said, "Be fruitful and multiply and fill the land" (Ge 1:28). Even after they were cast away from God's protective care in the Garden, God let it be known that this act of disobedience would not thwart his plan for humanity's blessing. God promised that he would provide a means for restoring the blessing: a future "seed" would one day come and crush the head of the serpent (Ge 3:15). Genesis 3:15 shows plainly that God's original intention for the human race was blessing and that his continual concern for humanity remains the same. When God chose Abraham as the channel of the promised "seed" (Ge 12:1–3), his express purpose was to bless Abraham and all the nations of the earth through his "seed." Like his original intent for Adam in the beginning, God's intent for Abraham was that he become a great nation and enjoy God's good land.

When Abraham's seed was on the verge of entering into Egyptian bondage, God furthered his promise by giving a prophecy to the patriarch Jacob. The prophecy was about one of his sons, Judah (Ge 49:8–12). Through the family of Judah, one would come who would be a king and restore God's blessing to Israel and all the nations. As God had forewarned Abraham (Ge 15:13–16), his people would first undergo a time of bondage and oppression. But God also promised that after four generations Abraham's "seed" would return to the land and again enjoy his blessing. God would return Israel to the land when the sin of the Amorites had reached its full measure (Ge 15:16).

With this background in mind, we can now appreciate the plan of the writer of the Pentateuch and his concentration on the prophecies of Balaam. Underlying the narratives which tell the story of Balaam is the author's interest in the promise to Abraham: those who bless his seed will be blessed and those who curse his seed will be cursed. The story opens with Balak's dread of the great numbers of Israel (Nu 22:3). Balak, the king of Moab, hired Balaam to curse the seed of Abraham (22:5–41), but as the story unfolds, God would permit them only to be blessed (24:10).

Thus the Balaam narratives play an important role in the message of the Pentateuch, particularly in the development of the themes of the Abrahamic covenant (Ge 12:1–3). They show that God has already begun to fulfill his promise to Abraham and that his seed had become "a great nation" (Nu 22:6). They also show that God was about to fulfill his promise to give Abraham's seed the land. When Balak sent for Balaam to curse this people, Israel was poised on the plains of Moab ready to go into the land. Finally, the Balaam narratives show that the curses of the nations could not thwart God's promise to bless the seed of Abraham. In spite of all his efforts, Balak (or even Balaam) could not curse God's people.

In the light of this focus on "the nations" we can see the importance of Balaam's not being an Israelite prophet but "one from among the nations." This helps, in large measure, to explain many of the enigmas of the gentile Balaam and his important role within the Pentateuch. In this sense there are significant analogies between Balaam and other important Gentiles in Scripture (e.g., Cyrus, Isa 45; 2Ch 36:23). Not only do the Balaam narratives play an important role in developing the themes of the Abrahamic covenant, but they also serve as an *inclusio* to the Exodus-wilderness narratives. That is, the Balaam narratives restate the central themes of these narratives at their conclusion in a way that parallels the statement of these themes at their beginning.

The Balaam story, which lies at the close of Israel's sojourn in the wilderness, parallels many of the events and ideas of the story of Pharaoh at the beginning of the book of Exodus. Both Pharaoh and Balak were kings of large and powerful nations which represented a major obstacle to Israel's entering the Promised Land. Israel was a threat to these nations only because God kept his promise to Abraham and had greatly increased their numbers. Pharaoh instigated plans to afflict Israel because he saw that they had become "much too numerous" (Ex 1:9). Within the narrative, Pharaoh's words merely reiterate the description of the narrator given two verses earlier: "the Israelites were fruitful and multiplied greatly and became exceedingly numerous" (Ex 1:7).

Moreover, according to the narrator, Pharaoh's plans were an attempt to stop Israel from returning to their land (Ex 1:10); that is, his plan was to block the very blessing which God had promised to Abraham (Ge 15:16)— enjoyment of the Promised Land. Thus, what the writer attempts to show is that the promise to Abraham ("I will make you into a great nation," Ge 12:2) and the blessing of humankind ("Be fruitful and multiply and fill the land," Ge 1:28; 15:16) were beginning to be fulfilled in Israel's sojourn in Egypt, and the nations were set on thwarting that promise. Like Pharaoh's plans, Balak's plans in the book of Numbers were also motivated by the fact that Israel had become "too numerous" (Nu 22:6). Also like Pharaoh, Balak was intent on keeping the Israelites out of the land (Nu 22:6).

In the early narratives of Exodus, Pharaoh made three attempts to counteract the blessing and hence decrease the number of God's people. He put slave masters over the Israelites to oppress them (Ex 1:11–14); he commanded the Hebrew midwives to kill the male children (1:15–21); and he commanded that every male child be thrown into the Nile (1:22). Yet as the narrative unfolds, on each occasion God intervened and Pharaoh's plan was turned into a blessing. Whatever the particular scheme of the Egyptians, the Israelites increased all the more. Moreover, within the structure of the story unfolding in the narrative, by means of Pharaoh's third plan (casting the male children into the Nile) the writer introduces the announcement of the birth of God's chosen deliverer, Moses.

Like Pharaoh before him, Balak also made three attempts to thwart God's blessing for Israel (23:1–12; 23:13–26; 23:27–24:9), but each attempt was turned into a blessing (23:11–12; 23:25–26; 24:10–11). It should be noted that though Balaam gave more than three oracles, the writer has arranged the oracles into three attempts to curse Israel. Balak himself verbalized the writer's own interest when he said, "I summoned you to curse my enemies, but you have blessed them these three times" (Nu 24:10). As was the case with Pharaoh's three attempts, after Balak's third attempt the author turns to the question of the birth of God's chosen deliverer, the prophecy of the star that was to arise out of Jacob (Nu 24:12–25).

In the light of the author's attempt to parallel the events at the beginning of Israel's sojourn in the wilderness with the events at the end, it is not surprising also to find that the content of Balaam's first three oracles is thematically parallel to the content of Pharaoh's three attempts to suppress God's blessing of Israel in Egypt, and that Balaam's last oracle focuses on the coming of a deliverer (see comments below on Nu 22–24).

Other features in the verbal texture of the two narratives also suggest that the above parallels are part of the author's conscious intention. For example, the story line of both passages is guided by the use of the Hebrew term for "heavy" (כבד). Hebrew narratives are often guided by a thematic verbal pattern.[56] The narrative of Pharaoh's opposition to releasing the Israelites is guided by the recurring reference to the "hardening" (כבד) of his heart (Ex 7:14; 8:11, 28; 9:7, 34; 10:1). At the climax of the story, by means of a wordplay on the notion of hardening Pharaoh's heart, the Lord says, "I will gain glory [כבד] for myself through Pharaoh" (Ex 14:4). In Hebrew the word for "glory" (כבד) is from the same root as the word for "harden" (כבד). Furthermore, the story of Balaam is guided by Balak's promise to "reward" (כבד) him richly if he would curse Israel (22:17, 37; 24:11). Again, we have the same root (כבד).

The placement of these similar narratives at either end of the Exodus-wilderness material can thus be diagramed:

1) Israel a mighty nation (רב עצום, Ex 1:9)	Exodus-Wilderness (Ex 16–Nu 21)	1) Israel a mighty nation (רב עוצם, Nu 22:3, 6)
2) Pharaoh "hardened" (כבד)		2) Balaam "honored" (כבד)

Such an arrangement within the larger structure of the Pentateuch can hardly be accidental. It reveals, rather, a conscious attempt by the writer to develop a theme—one centering on God's promise to Abraham and its future fulfillment.

4. Collections of Laws (Legal Corpora)

The legal corpora make up the largest portion of the center section of the Pentateuch. Clearly recognizable corpora in the Pentateuch are the Covenant Code (*Bundesbuch*), Exodus 20:22–23:33, the Holiness Code (*Heiligkeitsgesetz*), Leviticus 17–26, and the Code of the Priests (*Priesterkodex*), Exodus 25–Leviticus 16.[57] Belonging to this last corpus are the instructions

---

[56]For example, the narratives of Genesis 9–12 are linked by the use of the key word "Shem/name" and Genesis 12–26 by the key word "Isaac/laughed."

[57]The Code of the Priests is not to be confused with the so-called Priestly Document, denoted in the documentary hypothesis by the siglum P.

concerning the pattern of the tabernacle, Exodus 25–31, and its construction, Exodus 35–40. Although questions regarding the setting and date of such strata predominate in classical source criticism, from the point of view of compositional strategy, one is confronted with a different set of problems. We are not concerned here with reconstructing the "sources" from which these laws may have derived but rather the role that these various collections of laws play in the overall strategy of the final form of the book. How and why has the author put them where they are within the text? We are concerned here with the question of composition and literary strategy.

It has long been recognized that certain basic differences exist between these collections of laws. For example, the requirements for the building of an altar (Ex 20:24–25) in the Covenant Code are quite different from those in the Code of the Priests (Ex 27:1–8). According to the Covenant Code the Lord told Israel that an altar was to be made of earth or stones "in every place where I cause my name to be remembered" (Ex 20:24–25). This was a very simple form of altar. According to the Code of the Priests, however, the altar was to be made of acacia wood overlaid with bronze (Ex 27:1–8) and was to be placed in the tabernacle, where only the priests would have access to it. This appears to be a different sort of altar. There have been numerous attempts to harmonize these two laws. According to a traditional harmonization, the bronze altar of Exodus 27 was to be hollow (Ex 27:8) and was therefore to be filled with dirt or stones to make the earthen altar of Exodus 20.[58] Thus what appears to be a description of two distinct altars may really only reflect two aspects of the description of one altar. Such an attempt, however, serves better to demonstrate the nature of the problem than to solve it. This has generally been acknowledged even by modern conservative biblical scholars, and nowadays the two passages are simply allowed to coexist without excessive harmonization, the earthen altar often being taken merely as a temporary measure.[59] Though this explanation may provide a solution to the historical problem of the purpose of the two altars, it completely misses the literary question of why two types of altars are prescribed in the Pentateuch without an attempt to harmonize or explain their differences.

Critical scholarship has been unanimous in seeing the two laws as arising out of different historical settings.[60] It is commonly argued, for example, that along with the other laws in the Covenant Code, the instructions for building an earthen altar come from a more primitive period in Israel's religion, a time when their forms of worship were much like that of the patriarchs in the Genesis narratives. Individuals and groups could provide local centers of worship by building an altar and giving gifts to God.[61] In the early stages of their religion, Israel, like Abraham in the Genesis

---

[58]"Under the brass-overlaid wooden frame of this chest-like altar there must have been a centre of earth or stone sufficiently large enough to support the body of the sacrificial victim. . . .The enclosing copper case served merely to keep the earth together" (Jamieson, Fausset, and Brown, Commentary, 1:391).

[59]Walter Kaiser, Jr., "Exodus," EBC, ed. Frank E. Gaebelein, 12 vols. (Grand Rapids: Zondervan, 1990), 2:428.

[60]Otto Eissfeldt, Introduction, 218.

[61]F. Horst, RGG, 3d ed., 1:1523ff.

narratives, built a new altar at each place they settled. By contrast, the laws dealing with the bronze altar are taken to represent the final stages of Israel's religion, when a single, official worship site was recognized.

However, the lack of a convincing explanation of how such an obvious dissonance could have been tolerated in the final text has always imperiled the critical view. Clearly sensing the need for an explanation, Eissfeldt argued that after the Covenant Code had been replaced by the laws of Deuteronomy, it could not be removed from the text because it was "already so rooted in the popular mind that such a transformation of it would not be possible." This "neutralising . . . of the Book of the Covenant . . . seems to us not merely remarkable, but also impracticable. But we must bear in mind that the attempt has been successful not only in this case but also in many others. . . . Older precepts which are allowed to remain, are now quite naturally understood in the light of the newer, or, where that is not possible or necessary, they simply remain unheeded."[62]

Eissfeldt's words betray his own dissatisfaction with this explanation. While it is possible that the biblical writer intends his readers to ignore the Covenant Code in their reading of the Pentateuch, it is by no means likely. On the contrary, its position alongside the Decalogue and within the Sinai narrative itself suggests that the author intends to give it some prominence in the overall structure of his work. Rather than attempt to discount its importance within the Pentateuch as a whole, we should seek a way to explain its placement in the final shape of the Pentateuch.

a. Narrative Strategy in Exodus–Numbers

Numerous narrative texts of varying lengths are found throughout the central portion of the Pentateuch. Not only do these narratives provide the general framework for the legal corpora, but they are also embedded in the midst of the various collections of laws. The general framework of this section of the Pentateuch is formed by three complex narratives: the Exodus narrative (Ex 1–18), the Sinai narrative (Ex 19–34), and the wilderness narrative (Nu 10:11ff.). In addition, several smaller but strategically important narratives within this section are related to the larger framework; for example, the oppression narrative (Ex 1); the call of Moses (Ex 3) and the call of Joshua (Nu 27:12–23); the accounts of the faith of Moses, Aaron, and the people (Ex 4 and 19) and the accounts of their lack of faith (Nu 13–14; 20); the narrative of Aaron's calf idol (Ex 32) and the narrative of Israel's goat[63] idols (Lev 17:1–9); the narrative of Moses and Pharaoh (Ex 7–12) and the narrative of Balaam and Balak (Nu 22–24). Though each of these units of narrative has a discernible internal structure, our interest in them here relates to their relationship with each other and with the legal corpora.[64]

---

[62]Eissfeldt, Introduction, 222–23.

[63]The Hebrew word שְׂעִירִם usually means "goats," but it can also mean "goat idols." According to 2Ch 11:15, these שְׂעִירִם are said to have been "made" by Jereboam along with his "calf idols" (cf. Ludwig Koehler and Walter Baumgartner, Hebräisches und Aramäisches Lexikon [Leiden: Brill, 1990]: 4:1250).

[64]"It is one of the tasks of pentateuchal criticism to explain how this interruption of the narrative by large blocks of law took place" (Eissfeldt, Introduction, 157).

b. Textual Strategy: The Collection of Laws (Legal Corpora) and the Sinai Narratives

The following chart shows the general relationship between the narrative sections[65] of the central part of the Pentateuch and the collections of laws.

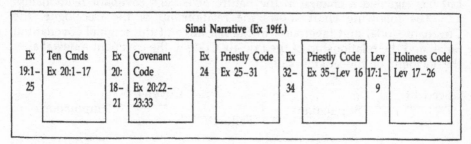

			Sinai Narrative (Ex 19ff.)						
Ex 19:1– 25	Ten Cmds Ex 20:1–17	Ex 20: 18– 21	Covenant Code Ex 20:22– 23:33	Ex 24	Priestly Code Ex 25–31	Ex 32– 34	Priestly Code Ex 35–Lev 16	Lev 17:1– 9	Holiness Code Lev 17–26

A curious feature of the Sinai narratives is the way in which they envelop and thus serve to link the Decalogue, the Covenant Code, and the Code of the Priests, precisely those collections of laws that, at least according to critical theory, differ most markedly from each other.[66] The Decalogue follows the account of the Covenant ceremony in Exodus 19:1–25. This narrative is complex and includes two major segments: an account of the establishment of an initial covenant on Mount Sinai (19:1–16a) and an account of Israel's fearful retreat from God (19:16b–25). The Decalogue (20:1–17), in turn, is followed by a short narrative, again recounting the fear of people at Sinai (20:18–21). The Covenant Code is then embedded in the Sinai narrative between Exodus 20:21 and 24:1ff.; it is followed by the Code of the Priests (Ex 25–Lev 16). Furthermore, the account of the making of the golden calf (Ex 32) and the reestablishment of the Sinai covenant (Ex 33–34), both parts of the Sinai narratives, break into the Code of the Priests just after the instructions for making the tabernacle (Ex 25–31) and before the account of its completion (Ex 35–40). Consequently, the instructions for building the tabernacle are separated from the remainder of the Code of the Priests by the account of the failure of the house of Aaron in the incident of the golden calf (Ex 32) as well as by the account of the renewal of the Sinai covenant (Ex 33–34). These observations raise important literary questions: What is the effect of the arrangement of the laws and the narrative in the present shape of the text? What message is to be gained from the pattern of events and laws reflected in the text as we now have it? Is the shape of the text semantically relevant? We will address these questions by attempting to unravel and retrace the literary strategy lying behind the present shape of the Sinai narrative.

By means of the arrangement of the narrative, the Sinai covenant *before the incident of the golden calf* is characterized by the laws of the Decalogue, the Covenant Code, and the instructions for building the tabernacle. However,

---

[65]"This section, more precisely its actual narrative kernel . . . is exceptionally difficult to analyze" (Eissfeldt, *Introduction*, 193).

[66]In most critical assessments of these two corpora, the Covenant Code is taken as the earlier of the legal codes and the Code of the Priests is assigned the later date.

the Sinai covenant *after the golden calf* is characterized by the fundamentally different and more extensive Code of the Priests (Ex 35–Lev 16). In other words, the bulk of the priestly laws (Ex 35–Lev 16) takes the place occupied earlier in the original Sinai narratives by the Decalogue, the Covenant Code, and the tabernacle (Ex 19–31). It thus appears that the incident of the golden calf has signaled a change in the nature of Israel's covenant relationship.

The following chart shows the relationship of the Decalogue, the Covenant Code, and tabernacle to the narrative of the original covenant at Sinai, and the relationship of the Priestly Code to the covenant renewal after the incident of the golden calf.

Covenant			Covenant	
	Stipulations	Failure		Stipulations
Covenant Established Ex 19:1–25; 20:18–21	Decalogue, Covenant Code, and Tabernacle Ex 20:1-17 20:22– 31:18	Golden Calf Ex 32	Covenant Renewed Ex 32–34	Priestly Code Ex 35–Lev 16

When viewed within the context of the differences between the laws of the Covenant Code and those of the Code of the Priests, alluded to above, the arrangement of this material appears to reflect a definite strategy.

On the face of it, the association of the original Sinai covenant with the Covenant Code and the renewal of that covenant with the Code of the Priests suggests a differing assessment of the two codes. It is also clear that the incident of the golden calf, which has been strategically positioned between these two codes of law, is the underlying cause of the changes in the law codes. In positioning the texts this way, the changes perceived between the laws in the two codes are now narratively presented as part of a larger change in the nature of the Sinai covenant itself—a change resulting from the episode of the golden calf. Rather than seeking to render the differences between the two law codes invisible, as modern critical studies suggest, the author apparently uses these very differences as part of his larger strategy. In their present textual position, these very differences show that a change has come over Israel's covenant with God. Israel's initial relationship with God at Sinai, characterized by the patriarchal simplicity of the Covenant Code, is now represented by the complex and restrictive laws of the Code of the Priests.

What begins to emerge in this assessment of the narrative strategy is the notion that the author does not intend to portray Israel's relationship with God in the Sinai covenant as static. He apparently wants to show that Israel's relationship with God, established at Sinai, underwent important changes because of Israel's repeated failure to obey God's will.[67] What began as a covenant between God and Israel, fashioned after that of the patriarchs (the Covenant Code), became increasingly more complex (the Code of the Priests) as Israel failed to obey God. Israel's propensity to follow "other gods," demonstrated in these narratives by the transgression of the golden calf, necessitated God's giving them the additional laws found in the Code of the Priests.[68]

The placement of the other law codes throughout the narrative shows further signs of the same strategy on the part of the author of the Pentateuch. The Code of the Priests (Ex 25–Lev 16), for example, is followed by the Holiness Code (Lev 17–26). The unique feature of the Holiness Code is the fact that in its introduction and throughout its laws, the audience it addresses is not the priests as such but the whole of the congregation. It calls the entire people of God to holiness. As has long been observed, the Holiness Code is not attached directly to the Priestly Code. Between these two legal codes lies a striking account of Israel's offering sacrifices to "goat idols" (Lev 17:1–9). Though brief and somewhat enigmatic, this short fragment of narrative, usually taken to be the work of the final composer,[69] portrays the Israelites forsaking the tabernacle and sacrificing "outside the camp."[70] The content of the narrative is similar to the incident of the golden

---

[67]Not only is there an *ordo temporum* between the covenants, but there is an *ordo temporum* within the covenants as well.

[68]Eissfeldt's argument that the Covenant Code was shaped as a polemic against a more complex form of worship suits the role that the code has assumed within the strategy of the Pentateuch. It is, in fact, a polemic of sorts against the more complex requirements of the Priestly Code. In this light, the view of Adam Welch (*Deuteronomy, The Framework of the Code*, [London: J. Clarke, 1932]), Wilhelm Caspari ("Heimat und Soziale Wirkung des alttestamentlichen Bundesbuches," *ZDMG* 83 [1929] 97–120), and Henri Cazelles ("L'auteur du code de l'alliance," *RB* 52 [1945] 173–91) that the Covenant Code was compiled in Kadesh or the east Jordan by Moses, or during the time of Moses, is of considerable importance.

[69]Literary critics of the old Wellhausen school took this composer to be a late redactor, usually associated with the priestly circles; see Alfred Bertholet, *Leviticus* (Tübingen: J. C. B. Mohr [Paul Siebeck], 1901), 58. Composition criticism, however, should remain neutral on the question of the historical time period of the final composition of the Pentateuch.

[70]Wenham, along with Keil, suggests that these verses are a prohibition not just of sacrifices but of any kind of animal slaughter and that the prohibition was limited only to the time Israel was in the wilderness. However, the fact that what is prohibited is not every kind of slaughter but specifically slaugher for sacrifice, is shown in the relationship of Lev 17:3–4 to 17:5. According to 17:5, the slaughter of 17:3–4 was specifically and only for sacrifice—that is, it was not a general slaughter for food. It should be noted as well that later in this same chapter (17:13ff.), provision is made for animals slain in hunting. This would also suggest that slaying animals for food was permissible; hence only slaughtering for sacrifice was expressly prohibited. Moreover, in 17:7 the prohibition is called an "eternal ordinance," ruling out its limitation to the time of the wilderness sojourn. Finally, Dt 12:15 appears to clarify this law by restating the provision that mere slaughtering of animals could be done anywhere. What was specifically prohibited in Dt 12:13–14 was the offering of *sacrifices* at any place other than the central altar.

calf:[71] the people forsook the Lord and his provisions for worship and followed after other gods—in this case, the "goat idols." Unlike the narrative of the golden calf, however, which places the blame on the priesthood, this narrative of the goat idols makes the people, not the priests, responsible for the idolatry. Thus within the logic of the text, the incident of the *people's* sacrificing to the goat idols plays a similar role to that of the *priests'* involvement in the golden calf. Just as the narrative of the golden calf marked a transition in the nature of the covenant and its laws, so here also the incident of the goat idols marks the transition from the Code of the Priests to the additional laws of the Holiness Code. The chart below shows this relationship.

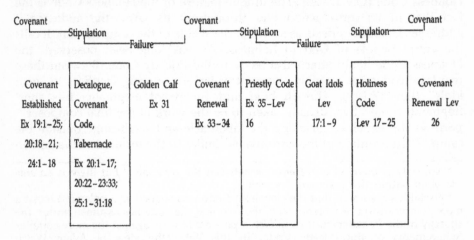

Thus the three major law collections—the Covenant Code, the Code of the Priests, and the Holiness Code—are not only embedded in the whole of the Sinai narratives, but are also arranged around two similar narratives. Both of these narratives focus on the Lord's displeasure with Israel's fall into idolatry, the first involving idolatry in the form of calf worship and the second that of goats.[72] Such a structure betrays a high level of strategy in the structure of the Pentateuch. In this arrangement, the laws of the Covenant Code are intentionally linked to the original covenant at Sinai (Ex 19–24); the laws of the Code of the Priests are associated with the covenant renewal after the sin of the golden calf (Ex 32–34); and the laws of the Holiness Code are placed in the context of the incident of the people's offering sacrifices to the goat idols outside the camp (Lev 17) and the covenant renewal in Leviticus 26.

It will not be possible at this point to trace the strategy apparent in the

---

[71]There are also literary parallels between this text and the opening sections of the other law codes, e.g., the establishment of the proper place of worship in Ex 20:24–26; 25ff.; Dt 12; and Eze 40ff. (see Bertholet, *Leviticus*, 58).

[72]There appear to be intentional compositional links between the golden calf erected by the priests (עֵגֶל,Ex 32:4) and the young bull (עֵגֶל,Lev 9:1ff.) required as a sin offering for the priests, and the goat idols worshiped by the people (שְׂעִיר, Lev 17:7) and the goats (שְׂעִיר, Lev 4:23) required as a sin offering for the people.

detailed arrangement of the laws and the narrative texts of the Pentateuch (see commentary below). We will limit ourselves here to a brief discussion of two central questions raised by our observations. The first is the internal shape of Exodus 19–24: How does the structure of the initial Sinai narrative (Ex 19–24) fit into the larger scheme of the Pentateuch and its view of the law outlined above? The second question concerns the location of the instructions for the tabernacle (Ex 25–31): Why are they placed before the incident of the golden calf (Ex 32) rather than after it? If the addition of the Code of the Priests is the result of the sin of the golden calf, why is a significant portion of this instruction placed before the incident itself?

(1) The Sinai Narrative (Ex 19–24)

It has long been noted that within Exodus 19 there are two different conceptualizations of Israel's covenant with God at Mount Sinai. In one version of the account (Ex 19:1–16a), it is argued, God made a covenant with Israel in which they were to be a "kingdom of priests and a holy nation" (19:5). The only requirement of the covenant was that Israel was to "have faith" (19:9) and "obey God" (19:5). There appear to be no "laws" in this covenant. To ratify the covenant, Moses and the people were to wait three days and then "go up" into the mountain and meet God there (19:10-13). Though this is not always reflected in English translations, there is little doubt that this is the view of the Hebrew text.[73] This same view of the Sinai covenant can also be found both earlier in Exodus (3:12)[74] and in later biblical texts that refer back to this chapter. In Jeremiah 7:22-23, for example, the Lord says, "For in the day that I brought them out of the land of Egypt I did not speak to your fathers or command them concerning burnt offerings and sacrifices. But this command I have them, 'Obey my voice, and I will be your God and you will be my people and you will walk in the way I will command you so that it would be well to you.'"[75]

In the other version of the Sinai covenant in Exodus 19 (vv. 16b–25), however, a much different view is presented. Instead of the notion of Israel being a "kingdom of priests," a distinction is now made between the people and the priests—it is not a kingdom *of* priest but a kingdom *with* priests (19:22-24). Moreover, instead of the people being called to go up before God in the mountain, they were to be kept from going up; only Moses and Aaron were allowed up the mountain to be with God (19:12-13a, 21-23). Finally, instead of simple faith and obedience, the Decalogue and the Covenant Code became the basis of Israel's keeping their covenant with God. Curiously, this is the view of the Sinai covenant found in Ezekiel 20:18-26: " 'I am the LORD your God, walk in my statues and keep my judgments and do them; keep my sabbaths holy and it will be a sign between you and me to know that I am

---

[73]The NJPS has correctly rendered 19:13b, "they may go up on the mountain (בָּהָר)." See the discussion of this verse below.

[74]"When you [sing.] bring the people out of Egypt, you [plur.] shall worship God *on* this mountain (עַל הָהָר הַזֶּה)." This verse clearly anticipates that Moses *and the people* were to worship God on the mountain (cf. Ex 4:27b; 5:3).

[75]The translation above follows the RSV, NRSV, NASB, NJPS, and KJV. The NIV translation, "I did not just give them commands about burnt offerings and sacrifices," appears to be a harmonistic attempt of the translators to remove an obvious problem.

the LORD your God.' But they rebelled against me. . . . And I gave them statutes which did not result in good [for them] and judgments in which they could not have life.''[76]

According to literary critical theory, these two versions of the Sinai covenant reflect the composite nature of the present text. It was the "Elohist" who presented the view that both Moses and the people were to "go up" to the mountain to meet with God (Ex 19:13b). The nature of the covenant was that which we find in 19:2b–8, namely, a simple renewal of the patriarchal covenant of faith and obedience. Owing to their fear of God's presence (Ex 19:16b), however, the people appointed Moses to speak with God on their behalf while they remained behind at the foot of the mountain (19:17,19b).[77] In the "Jahwist" account, however, the people were forbidden to go up the mountain from the very start (19:12-13a). They were to watch the entire display of God's presence at a safe distance (19:18, 20–25).[78]

Long before the rise of literary criticism of the Pentateuch, the tensions within this narrative were already apparent, and various harmonizations were offered. As to the question of the relationship of the covenant made in Exodus 19:3–8 with that of Exodus 24, Rashi argued that we should not read the narrative in chronological order. Thus, the covenant made in chapter 19 is the same as the one later established in chapter 24. Rashi's explanation of this difficulty has had little influence among Christian interpretation.[79] The most common explanation among Christians was that in Exodus 19:3–8, God had only begun to expound to Israel the nature of the Sinai covenant. Before

---

[76]The NIV and New Scofield Reference Bible's translation of נתתי להם חקים in Eze 20:25 as "I also gave them *over to* statutes" is an unfortunate harmonization of this difficult passage (cf. RSV, NRSV, NASB, NJPS, and KJV, which render it as above). The same is to be said of the addition of "in fire" to Eze 20:26 in some English versions, making it appear that the "statutes" in 20:25 relate to offering their firstborn "in the fire." The words "in fire" do not occur in the Hebrew text, nor are they implied. Eze 20:26 is rendered correctly by NJPS: "When they set aside every first issue of the womb" (בהעביר כל־פטר רחם). This phrase relates to identical phraseology concerning God's claim of the firstborn in Ex 13:12: "You are to give over to the LORD the first offspring of every womb" (העברת כל פטר רחם), not to child sacrifice (cf. Ex 34:19; Num 3:12–13). Moreover, "causing one's children to pass through the fire" (העברת בנו ובתו באש) is expressly forbidden in Dt 18:10. The collocation העביר פטר רחם does not occur in the OT with באש, but, as in Ex 13:12, with reference to the firstborn. When העביר occurs with באש, the object is not פטר רחם but rather בן (Dt 18:10; 2Ki 17:17; 21:6; 23:10; 2Ch 33:6; Eze 20:31 [omitted in LXX]).

[77]Otto Eissfeldt, *Hexateuch-Synopse. Die Erzählung der fünf Bücher Mose und des Buches Josua mit dem Anfange des Richterbuches* (Darmstadt: Wisenschaftliche Buchgesellschaft, 1973), 146–47.

[78]Eissfeldt, *Hexateuch-Synopse*, 146–48.

[79]Keil may depend on Rashi when he suggests that Ex 19:3–8 is associated with the proclamation of the "fundamental law of the covenant in the presence of the whole nation (chap. xix.16–xx.18)" (C. F. Keil and F. Delitzsch, *Biblical Commentary on the Old Testament* [Grand Rapids: Eerdmans, 1971], 2.101). Recently, Rashi's view has apparently been adopted by G. C. Chirichigno in "The Narrative Structure of Exod 19–24" (*Biblica* 68 [1968], 479): "We have argued that the awkward surface structure of the narrative, which results in the non-linear temporal ordering of events, can be explained when one takes into account the sequence structure of the narrative, particularly the use of the literary device called resumptive repetition."

he had fully explained it, Israel quickly agreed to the terms. According to Calvin, for example, the people "were carried away by a kind of headlong zeal, and [they] deceived themselves."[80]

The question of who was to go up into the mountain has been the most difficult to solve. According to Rashi, the key to the solution is the mention of the "blast" (במשך) of the horn that signaled Israel's move up the mountain (Ex 19:31b). Rashi reasoned that a long blast (קול ארוך) of the ram's horn signified that God was departing from the mountain and hence, when God had departed, the people were permitted to go up the mountain.[81] Thus, though the people were warned not to go up into the mountain in verse 12, they were allowed to go up into the mountain when the horn was sounded. Rashi's interpretation has found its way into several early scholarly versions,[82] and it is as old as the Septuagint.[83]

Nicolas von Lyra, however, departed from Rashi's explanation by suggesting that "to go up the mountain" meant the people could go only as far as the limits that had been established by Moses (Ex 19:12).[84] This appears to be the sense taken by many modern English versions: "When the horn blasts, they shall come up to the mountain."[85] The obvious problem with this

---

[80]John Calvin, *Commentary on the Four Last Books of Moses Arranged in the Form of a Harmony*, trans. Charles William (Grand Rapids: Baker, 1979), 320. Cf. H. Ainsworth: "The people not yet knowing the unpossibility of the Law, which is weak through the flesh, Rom. 8:3, make promise of more than they were able to performe. After, when the Law was pronounced, they feare and flee away, Exod. 20.18,19" (*Annotations upon the Five Bookes of Moses* [London: M. Parsons, 1639], 68).

[81]Rashi's interpretation is represented in several Christian commentaries; for example, Münster: "*Cum prolixius buccina sonuerit; prolixior enim sonus signum erat Dominum majestatis montem deseruisse*"; Fagius: "*Sensus est, Dum satis protractus adeoque finitus est sonitus tubarum, tum ascendere potest populus; at praesente Domino nequaquam. Neque enim veto ut in perpetuum non ascendatis. Dum ergo sonitus cornu cessaverit, potestis ascendere. Prolixior sonus signum erat, Dominum majestatis montem deseruisse.*" According to Eben Ezra, Rashi's explanation was inadequate because the Lord's glory was always on the mountain until the completion of the tabernacle.

[82]Calvin, *Commentary* (1563): "quum protaxerit buccina, ipsi ascendent in montem"; Münster, *Biblia sacra* (1534): "cum prolixius buccina insonuerit, tunc poterunt ascendere montem"; Tyndale, *The Seconde Boke of Moses* (1530): "when the horne bloweth: than let them come up in to the mounten"; Geneva Bible (1599): "When the horne bloweth long, they shall come up into the mountaine"; Junius and Tremellius, *Biblia sacra* (1575): "cum tractim sonabit cornu, ea ascendere poterunt in ipsum montem"; NJPS: "When the ram's horn sounds a long blast, they may go up on the mountain."

[83]The LXX translated the sense of the phrase, not the words: "Whenever the sounds and the trumpets and the cloud departs from the mountain, they may go up the mountain" (ἐπὶ τὸ ὄρος). Cf. the Vulgate: "cum coeperit clangere bucina tunc ascendant in montem"; and Targum Onkelos: "When the horn blast is protracted, they may go up into the mountain" (במיגד שופרא אנון מרשן למסק בטורא).

[84]"*In montem* hic est versus montem, usque ad terminos a Mose Dei jussu praefixos" (*Synopsis Criticorum*, 1.398). Lyra apparently followed Eben Ezra on Ex 19:17: "[under the mountain] means outside the borders set by Moses" (מחוץ לגבול שהגבילם משה). A similar interpretation may already be present in the Samaritan Pentateuch's reading of ההר in Ex 19:12a rather than העם, as in the MT.

[85]This translation is represented in the NIV, NASB, and KJV. That it is a harmonistic

view is that the text does not say "up *to* the mountain" but "up *in* the mountain," just as in Exodus 19:12.[86]

Still another problem within the narrative is the statement in 19:12, "Beware of going up the mountain" (JPS). This statement is often taken by literary critics as an absolute prohibition of the people's going up the mountain, but it does not necessarily have this sense. The warning could just as well be, "Watch yourselves going up" (עֲלוֹת), as, "Beware not to go up" (מֵעֲלוֹת).[87] In either case, however, if read in the context of Israel's waiting three days (19:11) until "the horn is blown" (19:13b), the warning in 19:12 (according to critical theory, a Yahwist verse) is merely a warning not to enter the mountain *until* the appropriate time. According to the narrative, then, God expects the people to go up the mountain with Moses to meet with Him.

In other words, God's intention to meet the people on the mountain itself is not merely the viewpoint of a hypothetical document, such as the Elohist, but is, in fact, the consistent view of the entire narrative. And it is also clear from the narrative that the people are subsequently barred from going up the mountain (Ex 19:21, 23). However, as 19:23–24 makes clear, the people are first barred from the mountain in 19:21, not in 19:12.[88] In 19:12 the people cannot go up the mountain until the horn blast; in 19:21 the people cannot go up the mountain at all.

The above consideration of the strategy of the composition of this passage raises several important questions. Why does the viewpoint of the narrative change so radically with respect to the people's going up into the mountain? Is it merely that two conflicting accounts have been preserved intact in this chapter, as critical theory suggests? Or are there clues of a changing situation within the narrative that account for such a shift in God's purpose? Furthermore, does the change in the people's right to go up the mountain reflect the intention of the author of the Pentateuch? In other words, are the tensions that are so transparent in the Hebrew narrative

---

attempt to avoid the problem of the Hebrew text is suggested by the fact that these same versions render the identical expression (עֲלָה בָהָר) in the preceding verse not by "go *up to* the mountain," but rather "go *up (or into)* the mountain" (Ex 19:12). Only the NJPS renders עֲלָה בָהָר in 19:12 and 13b as to "go up (on) the mountain."

[86]A third explanation was offered by Drusius. Following Eben Ezra, he identified the pronoun "they" (Ex 19:13b) with Moses, Aaron, Abihu, and the elders, thus avoiding the suggestion that the people were allowed to go up the mountain (*Critici Sacri*). This is also the position of Targum Neofiti 1: "When the trumpet is sounded, Moses and Aaron are authorised to come up into the mountain." That it was the people rather than Moses and the elders, however, is seen from 19:17 and 19:12, where "the people" are expressly in view.

[87]The variant suggested in the *Biblia Hebraica* (Stuttgart edition) apparatus (מֵעֲלוֹת) shows precisely what would be expected of an unequivocal negative sense.

[88]The similarity of the terms, e.g., הָעֵד in 19:21 and 19:23, as well as identical meaning, shows that 19:23 is explanatory of 19:21 and not 19:12. The use of הַגְבֵּל in 19:12 and 19:23 is sometimes taken as grounds for seeing 19:23 as a harmonization of 19:12 and 19:13b. However, the phrase "set limits *for the people*" (19:12) is not the same as "set limits *for the mountain*" (19:23). The reading of the Samaritan Pentateuch in 19:12 (ההר rather than העם) points precisely back to the difficulty of making 19:23–24 refer to 19:12.

merely the result of conflicting sources or are they semantically and theologically relevant? Are they part of the author's intent?

Fortunately, the narrative does not leave us without an answer to these questions. According to Exodus 19:16, on the third day, when the people were to be ready to "go up the mountain," the horn was blown. Curiously enough, however, the text says that when the people saw the great display of God's power on the mountain, they "were afraid in the camp." Moreover, the text goes on to recount that "Moses brought the people out from the camp to meet with God and they stood at the base of (בְּתַחְתִּית) the mountain" (Ex 19:17). When they saw the Lord's appearance on the mountain, "they were afraid in the camp" and remained standing at the foot of the mountain (19:17b); Moses thus ascended to meet with God alone. Important from the standpoint of narrative strategy is the fact that at precisely this point in the narrative the people were warned not to "break through to look upon the LORD" (19:21). This is not, as we have seen, a repeat of the warning in 19:12 but a new warning. According to Moses' own words in 19:23, God had "testified against the people" (19:21) that they were not to go up the mountain. What the whole of Exodus 19 then shows is that God's original intention to meet with the people on the mountain (19:13b) was fundamentally altered because of the people's fear of God (19:16b). At this point it is also important to note that in 20:18–21, a later reflection on this same incident,[89] we find exactly the same point of view about the failure of the people to draw near to God. We will thus turn to a brief discussion of that narrative.

There are marked similarities as well as differences between the two narratives on either side of the Decalogue (Ex 19;16–24 and 20:18–20). Both narratives explain why Moses went up to the mountain alone and not with

---

[89]This similarity of viewpoint raises the question of the relationship of the narrative in chapter 19 with that of chapter 20. It is frequently argued that the narrative about Israel's retreat from the mountain and their fear of God in Ex 20:18–21 most naturally follow 19:25 rather than the Decalogue (20:1–17; cf. Eissfeldt, *Synopse*, 45–46). Moreover, the Decalogue begins with God speaking ("And God spoke all the words, saying. . . ." [20:1]) rather than with Moses, as is suggested by its current position after 19:25, "And Moses said to them. . . ." Therefore, according to literary critical theory, the narrative in its present state has been rearranged, with the Decalogue now coming before 20:18–21 rather than after it, where it more naturally belongs (cf. Dt 5:5–6). The purpose of this rearrangement, it is held, was redactional. It was to include the Covenant Code along with the Decalogue as part of the "word" which God spoke to Israel in the Sinai covenant. Whereas originally the Decalogue was the only "word" which God spoke at Sinai, in its present shape the "word" which God spoke at Sinai also includes the Covenant Code. Hence Ex 24:3a, "and all the judgments" is taken as a harmonistic gloss. Though there is little grounds for this hypothetical reconstruction, the basic structural observation on which it rests is sound. As the narrative now stands, the Decalogue (Ex 20:1–17) is presented not as the word which God spoke to the people but rather the word which Moses spoke to the people in 19:25. To be sure, Moses' words to the people in 19:25 recounted what God had spoken to him earlier on the mountain (19:19). However, these words are in fact presented here as first given to Moses by God (19:19) and then given to the people by Moses (19:25ff.). In other words, the narratives show that there is now a growing distance between God and the people—one that was not intended at the outset of the Sinai narrative (19:12–13).

the people (190:16b; 20:19–20). Regarding differences, in 19:21, the Lord instructed Moses to keep the people from the mountain, "lest they break through to see the LORD and many of them fall [dead]." In 20:18–19, however, the people flee "a great distance" from the presence of the Lord on the mountain, telling Moses, "You speak to us and we will hearken so that the LORD not speak to us, lest we die." Furthermore, according to 19:19, the Lord spoke only to Moses, whereas in 20:19 the narrative infers that God intended to speak with the people as well as Moses.

Without raising the question of whether such variations can be related to hypothetical literary documents,[90] we will turn directly to the question of the role these variations play in the composition of the Pentateuch. Do the above-mentioned similarities and differences in the two narratives advance the author's purpose or intention?

It can be argued that in the present shape of the Pentateuch, the Decalogue (Ex 20:1–17) is intended to be read as the content of what Moses spoke to the people *upon his return* from the mountain in 19:25.[91] After the Decalogue, the narrative in 20:18–21 looks back once again to the people's fear in 19:16–24.[92] In retelling this incident, the second narrative fills the important "gaps" in our understanding of the first. Whereas 19:16–24 looks at the people's fear from a divine perspective, 20:18–21 approaches it from the viewpoint of the people themselves.[93] What we learn from both

---

[90]Eissfeldt identified Ex 19:19a, 20–25 with the Jahwist and 20:18–21 with the Elohist (*Synopse*, 147–50).

[91]By the time Moses speaks the words of the Decalogue to the people in Ex 19:25–20:17, however, the narrative suggests he had already received both the Decalogue and the Covenant Code. It thus makes sense that when Moses spoke the Decalogue (20:1–17) to the people in 19:25, it is introduced with, "And God said. . . ." (20:1). Rather than betraying the presence of a mislocated text, the clause structure of 20:1 follows precisely that sense of the whole. Moreover, as can be seen from the syntax of 20:22 and 24:1, the narrative of the events at Sinai, which began in Ex 19, continues further (24:1) on the other side of the Covenant Code. The narrative link is established syntactically in 24:1 by means of a chiastic coordination from 20:22: ויאמר יהוה אל משה (20:22) is continued by ואל משה אמר (see Francis I. Anderson, *The Sentence in Biblical Hebrew* [The Hague: Mouton Publishers, 1980], 122–26). Thus, in Ex 24, we find Moses still on the mountain receiving God's "word." In 24:3, when God had finished speaking, Moses went down the mountain to bring God's words to the people. The expression "all the words of the LORD *and all of the judgments*" (24:3) shows an intentional linking of the Decalogue *and the Covenant Code* to the final ceremony of 24:3–8. The mention of Moses, Aaron, and the priests in 24:1, then, anticipates the role of Moses, Aaron, and the priests in 24:9 and is a carryover from 20:21, where the people's "fear" necessitated a mediator and priesthood.

[92]The syntax of 20:18, which begins with a circumstantial clause (W + NC), suggests that the narrative in Ex 20:18–21 is not to be read sequentially as a new narrative event but rather as a return to the previous events of Ex 19, or more specifically, 19:16ff.

[93]The position taken here, though arrived at independently, is in some respects similar to that of Chirichigno, that the two passages reflect two different perspectives on the covenant: 19:16ff represents the Lord's perpsective and 20:18–21 the people's perspective. Also for Chirichigno, 20:18–21 "elaborates in detail the fear of the people" ("The Narrative Structure of Exod 19–24," 479). I also agree with Chirichigno

narratives, therefore, is that there was a growing need for a mediator and a priesthood in the Sinai covenant. Because of the people's fear of God's presence, they are now standing "afar off" (20:21). Already, then, we can see the basis being laid within the narrative for the need of the tabernacle (Ex 25–31). The people who are "afar off" must be brought near to God. This is the purpose of the instructions for the tabernacle which follow this narrative.

The following chart depicts the dynamic state of the Sinai covenant throughout Exodus 19–25.

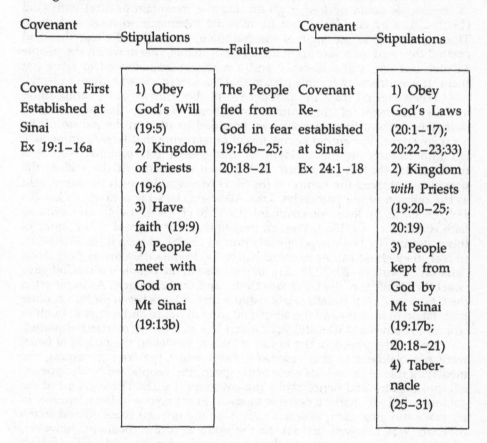

Covenant └──Stipulations──┘ Failure		Covenant └──Stipulations──┘	
Covenant First Established at Sinai Ex 19:1–16a	1) Obey God's Will (19:5) 2) Kingdom of Priests (19:6) 3) Have faith (19:9) 4) People meet with God on Mt Sinai (19:13b)	The People fled from God in fear 19:16b–25; 20:18–21 Covenant Re-established at Sinai Ex 24:1–18	1) Obey God's Laws (20:1–17); 20:22–23;33) 2) Kingdom *with* Priests (19:20–25; 20:19) 3) People kept from God by Mt Sinai (19:17b; 20:18–21) 4) Tabernacle (25–31)

(2) The Place of the Tabernacle Instructions (Ex 25–31)

We can now turn briefly to our second question: Why are the instructions for the tabernacle given before the sin of the golden calf? If it was the golden calf that led to the priestly laws, why do the tabernacle instructions precede the golden calf? Rashi maintained that the sequential arrangement in the Pentateuch does not reflect the chronological order of the events. In actual fact, says Rashi, "the incident of the golden calf happened

---

that 20:18–21 "acts as a causal link between the fear of the people and their sinful acts below the mountain in Exod 32" (ibid.).

much earlier than the instructions for the building of the tabernacle."[94] For Rashi, then, the giving of all the priestly laws, including those for the tabernacle, came after the sin of the golden calf.

However, the sense of the narrative strategy in Exodus 19–24, as outlined above, suggests another reason for the position of the tabernacle instructions in the present narrative. We have seen above in the depiction of the Sinai covenant that an emphasis was placed on the need for a mediator as well as a priesthood. The people, in their fear of God, stood "afar off." Just as the people could no longer go up into the mountain to meet with God (19:21–22), they could also not go into the tabernacle to meet with him. Thus, according to the logic of the narrative, it was Israel's fear that had created the need for a safe approach to God, that is, one in which the people as such were kept at a distance and a mediator was allowed to represent them. It was precisely for this reason that the tabernacle was given to Israel.

When viewed from the perspective of the strategy of its composition and its treatment of the various collections of laws, the pentateuchal narratives present themselves as an extended treatise on the nature of the Sinai covenant. The author seems intent on showing that Israel's immediate fall into idolatry in the incident of the golden calf brought with it a fundamental shift in the nature of the Sinai covenant. At the outset, the narrative portrayed the nature of the Sinai covenant in much the same light as the religion of the patriarchs. Like Abraham, Israel was to obey God (Ex 19:5; cf. Ge 26:5), keep his covenant (Ex 19:5; cf. Ge 17:1–14), and exercise faith (Ex 19:9; cf. Ge 15:6). Though they immediately agreed to the terms of this covenant (Ex 19:8), Israel quickly proved unable to keep it (Ex 19;16–17). In fear, they chose Moses to stand before God while they themselves stood "afar off" (Ex 19:18–20; 20:18–21). In response to the people's fear, God gave Israel the Decalogue, the Covenant Code, and the tabernacle. As depicted in the Covenant Code, Israel's relationship with God was based on the absolute prohibition of idolatry and the simple offering of praise and sacrifice. In other words, the covenant was still very much like that of the patriarchal period.

Led by the priests of the house of Aaron, however, the people of Israel were not obedient to this covenant. Even while the laws governing the mediating role of the priests were being given, the people, led by the priests, fell into idolatry and hence broke the covenant (Ex 32). The incident of the golden calf, then, marks a decisive moment in the course of the narrative. In his grace and great compassion (Ex 33), God did not cast Israel off and so the covenant was renewed (Ex 34). In the renewal of the covenant, however, additional laws were given and these are contained in the Code of the Priests (Ex 35–Lev 16). As the title of this code suggests, these laws were aimed almost entirely at the priesthood. Although these laws had the same purposes as the Covenant Code—to keep Israel from idolatry and to maintain purity in worship—they were not stated in the simple, straightforward ideals of the Covenant Code. On the contrary, the Code of the Priests sought to ensure Israel's obedience through an elaborate system of priestly requirements. As the Sinai narrative unfolds, then, the simple "everyman's" altar of the Covenant Code (Ex 20:24–25) gives way to the singular and more

---

[94]*Rashi's Commentary on the Torah* (Hebrew), ed. Chaim Dov Shual (Jerusalem: Mosad Harav Kook, 1988), 303.

elaborate bronze altar of the tabernacle (Ex 27:1–8; 38:1–7), one that was to be used solely by the priests (Lev 1ff.).

After listing a rather large portion of the priestly requirements (Ex 35– Lev 16), the author proceeds to show, by means of the narrative, that God's purpose in giving these laws was accomplished. The author's primary means of demonstrating that the Code of the Priests had had a positive effect on the priesthood is his use of the narrative of Israel's sacrificing to goat idols (Lev 17:1–9). As the narrative shows, after the consecration of the priests, they remained free of idolatry and false worship. Leviticus 16, dealing with the Day of Atonement, thus represents the final act of the consecration of the priests and of their role in ensuring the well-being of the nation.

In the course of the narrative, however, it becomes clear that the situation with the people was quite different from that of the priests. Since the early Sinai narratives (e.g., Ex 24ff.), the focus had been on the priests and the means of ensuring their holiness. If one looks back over that period it becomes clear that the narrative had given little or no attention to the question of the people as a whole and whether they had been given laws to keep them from idolatry and to ensure their holy living. Thus, in turning to the question of the life of the ordinary citizen, the author uses the narrative of Leviticus 17:1–9 to show that they had "played the harlot after their idols" (Lev 17:7). The placement of the Holiness Code (Lev 17–26) at this point in the narrative, then, plays an important role in the author's strategy. It aptly shows that God gave further laws designed specifically for the ordinary people. These laws are represented in the Holiness Code. Thus, as is characteristic of the Holiness Code, its laws pertain to specific situations in the everyday life of the people. Once again one can explain the differences among the various law codes in the Pentateuch not on the basis of conflicting documents but in terms of the author's intention in the final composition of the work.

The differences and primary characteristics of the legal corpora in the Pentateuch, then, follow closely the line of thought reflected in its larger compositional strategy. The Decalogue and the Covenant Code, which reflect a kind of patriarchal worship, are used to portray the religious ideals of the Sinai covenant. The Code of the Priests, which focuses on the regulations of the priesthood, is used to show God's concern to keep the nation from falling further into idolatry after the incident of the golden calf. The Holiness Code, which is largely made up of laws dealing with the everyday life of the people, shows what further efforts were necessary to ensure that the whole of the nation, not merely the priests, be kept from idolatry and apostasy.

I. The Mosaic Law and the Theology of the Pentateuch

We can now raise the question of the role of the Mosaic Law in the purpose of the Pentateuch.[95] We should ask specifically what our understanding of the composition of the Pentateuch tells us about the author's view of the Law.

---

[95]The material presented in this section can be found in an expanded form in the author's article "The Mosaic Law and the Theology of the Pentateuch," *WTJ* 53 (Fall 1991), 241–61.

1. The Final Composition of the Pentateuch

Much has been written in recent years about the final composition of the Pentateuch.[96] In the previous sections, I have attempted to demonstrate the influence of prophetic hope and eschatology on its composition. The Pentateuch, I have suggested, represents an attempt to point to the same hope as the later prophets, namely, the new covenant.[97] The narrative texts of past events are presented as pointers to future events. Past events foreshadow the future.

Along similar lines, though working from quite different assumptions, Hans-Christoph Schmitt has argued that the Pentateuch is the product of a unified compositional strategy that lays great emphasis on faith.[98] According to Schmitt, the same theme is found within the composition of the Prophetic Books, like Isaiah, and ultimately can be traced into the NT (e.g., the book of Hebrews).

Schmitt's approach differs from many critical approaches in that he treats the Pentateuch as one would the later historical books, that is, as the product of an intentional theological redaction or composition. One must start from the final form of the book and ask what each part of the whole contributes to its theological intention. Schmitt argues that each major unit[99] of narrative in the Pentateuch shows signs of a homogeneous theological redaction. A characteristic feature of this redaction is the recurrence of the terminology of "faith" (e.g., ב האמין).[100] At crucial compositional seams throughout the Pentateuch, Schmitt finds convincing evidence of a "faith theme"—that is, a consistent assessment of the narrative events in the light of the rule of "faith" (ב האמין).[101] For Schmitt, this redaction represents the

---

[96]Erhard Blum, *Studien zur Komposition des Pentateuch* (Berlin: de Gruyter, 1990); Rolf P. Knierim, "The Composition of the Pentateuch," *SBL 1985 Seminar Papers* (Atlanta: Scholars Press, 1987) 393–415; Erhard Blum, *Die Komposition der Vätergeschichte* (Neukirchen-Vluyn: Neukirchener, 1984); Rolf Rendtorff, *Das überlieferungsgeschichtliche Problem des Pentateuch*, BZAW 147 (Berlin: de Gruyter, 1977).

[97]This does not necessarily imply that the final composition of the Pentateuch is later than that of the Prophetic Books. On the contrary, if the composition of the Pentateuch were dated before that of the Prophetic Books, it would help explain the origin of the message of the those books. In the discussion which follows, the date of the final composition of the Pentateuch as such is taken to be Mosaic.

[98]Hans-Christoph Schmitt, "Redaktion des Pentateuch im Geiste der Prophetie," *VT* 32/2 (1982): 170–89.

[99]The largest literary units ("grösseren Einheiten") which are linked in the final redaction of the Pentateuch, according to Schmitt, are the Primeval History, the Patriarchal Narratives, the Exodus Narratives, the Sinai Narratives, and the Wilderness Narratives. See Rendtorff, *Das überlieferungsgeschichtliche Problem*, 19ff.

[100]It is important to note that, according to Schmitt, the terminology of "faith" (ב האמין) occurs only at the redactional seams. See next note.

[101]The key texts of that redaction are Ge 15:6, "And Abraham believed in [ב האמין] the LORD and he reckoned it to him for righteousness"; Ex 4:5, "In order that they might believe [יאמינו] that the LORD, the God of their fathers . . . has appeared to you"; Ex 14:31, "And they [the people] believed in [ב האמין] the LORD and in Moses his servant"; Nu 14:11, "How long will they [the people] not believe in [ב האמין] me"; Nu 20:12, "And the LORD said to Moses and Aaron, 'Because you did not believe in [ב האמין] me. . . .'" See also Dt 1:32 and 9:23. Schmitt has not discussed Ge 45:26, the

final stages in the composition of the Pentateuch—later even than the so-called priestly redaction. According to Schmitt, it does not reflect an emphasis on keeping the priestly law codes (viz., the Mosaic Law) but rather on preserving a sense of trust in God and an expectation of his work in the future. In the light of this eschatological expectation of God's future work the redaction lays great stress on "faith."[102]

Schmitt's study goes a long way in demonstrating an important part of the theological intention and orientation of the Pentateuch as a narrative text. Put simply, Schmitt shows that the Pentateuch is intended to teach "faith" in God.[103]

An important question raised by Schmitt's study is whether the concept of "faith" in the Pentateuch is intended to stand in opposition to the Mosaic Law or whether this faith is to be understood simply as "keeping the law."[104] In other words, can we find evidence in the composition of the Pentateuch that the author is concerned with the question of "faith versus works of the law"?

It is well known that this issue surfaces a number of times in other OT texts. In Psalm 51:16–17 (MT 18–19), for example, David says, "For thou hast no delight in sacrifice. . . . The sacrifice acceptable to God is a broken spirit"; and Micah 6:6–8 says, "With what shall I come before the LORD. . . ? Shall I come before him with burnt offerings? He has showed you, O man, what is good . . . to do justice, and to love kindness, and to walk humbly with your God." Since such texts do in fact exist within the OT, we may with some justification look for similar ideas within the theological macrostructure of the Pentateuch.

Here we will attempt to show that the issue of "faith versus works of law" was, indeed, central to the theological purpose of the Pentateuch. We will argue specifically that, among other things, the Pentateuch is an attempt to contrast the lives of two individuals, Abraham and Moses. Abraham, who lived before the Law (*ante legem*), is portrayed as one who kept the law,

---

only occurrence of the term for "faith" (הַאֲמִין) outside Schmitt's redactional seams, because it does not show other signs of belonging to the *Glaubens-Thematik*.

[102]"So steht am Ende der Pentateuchentstehung nicht die Abschliessung in ein Ordnungsdenken theokratischen Charakters. Vielmehr geht es hier darum, in prophetischem Geiste die Offenheit für ein neues Handeln Gottes zu wahren und in diesem Zusammenhang mit dem aus der prophetischen Tradition entnommenen Begriff des "Glaubens" eine Haltung herauszustellen, die später auch das Neue Testament als für das Gottesverhältnis zentral ansieht" (Hans-Christoph Schmitt, "Redaktion des Pentateuch," 188–89).

[103]It is important to note that such a reading of the Pentateuch, as a lesson on faith, can be found throughout the subsequent canonical literature. Both Pss 78 and 106, which look at the meaning of the whole of the Pentateuch, read the events of the Pentateuch as evidence of the Israelites' faith or faithlessness (cf. Ps 78:22, 32, 37; 106:12, 24). A similar reading is found in Ne 9, which is a rehearsal of the pentateuchal narrative in its present form (cf. Ne 9:8). The example of Heb 11 has already been pointed out.

[104]There are indications in Schmitt's study that the notion of faith in the Pentateuch is put in opposition to that of "obedience to the law." Schmitt has argued, for example, that the "faith" seams overlay and reinterpret the narratives which have stressed obedience to the Law (cf. comments below on Nu 20:12).

whereas Moses, who lived under the Law (*sub lege*), is portrayed as one who died in the wilderness because he did not believe. If such a contrast between faith and works is a part of the compositional strategy of the book, then we may rightfully conclude that part of the Pentateuch's purpose was to show not merely the way of faith, but also the weakness of the Law.

2. The Genre of the Pentateuch

In a recent article, Rolf Knierim has focused attention on the question of the *genre* of the Pentateuch as a whole.[105] In it he argues that the Pentateuch consists of two major generic sections: (a) Genesis and (b) Exodus–Deuteronomy. According to Knierim, Genesis is to be taken as an introduction to the whole of the Pentateuch. The genre of the central section of the Pentateuch, Exodus–Deuteronomy, is not so much narrative history (of Israel), as is commonly supposed in biblical scholarship, but rather *biography*, specifically, a biography of Moses.

This is not the place to enter into a full discussion of Knierim's description of the genre of the Pentateuch. It is enough to say that his general observations about the Pentateuch are convincing. The Pentateuch devotes its attention more to the individual Moses than to the nation of Israel. Hence its overall purpose in all likelihood should be understood in relationship more to the life of Moses per se than to the history of the nation. As such it is reasonable to conclude that the Pentateuch reads much like, and apparently aims to be, a biography.

Since the purpose of a biography is the presentation or conceptualization of the work or life of an individual person, the Pentateuch can well be viewed generically as a presentation (conceptualization) of the work of Moses. The events of the life of Moses (*Vita Mosis*) are not told entirely for their own sake but are intended as a narrative explication of the nature of a life lived within the context of the call of God and the covenant at Sinai. The Pentateuch seeks to answer the question of how well Moses carried out his calling, that is, his work under the Sinai covenant.

One may doubt, however, whether Knierim's description of the *whole* of the Pentateuch as a biography of Moses is entirely adequate. First, collections of laws, which make up a major part of the final composition of the Pentateuch, do not fit within the narrow limits of a biography. According to Knierim's reckoning, these laws (i.e., the Sinai pericope and Deuteronomy) make up 68.5 percent of the total text of the Pentateuch. Although Knierim treats these legal sections as part of the Moses texts, they clearly are not part of the Moses narratives per se. The course of the narratives is distinctively broken into and suspended until these large collections of laws are exhausted. It appears that in the final stage of the composition, the focus on Moses, the individual lawgiver, was intentionally expanded to include a substantial portion of the Law itself. This state of affairs raises the question of why, in the light of the genre of the Pentateuch, these laws were placed in the midst of the biography.

The traditional answer to this question has been that they were put there simply as legislation, that is, as laws which were to be kept—thus the Pentateuch's reputation as a "book of the Law." In this view the Pentateuch

---

[105]Knierim, "The Composition of the Pentateuch," 393–415.

is read as if it were a collection of laws intended to guide the daily living of its readers. This view of the purpose of the laws is so pervasive that it is often merely assumed in works dealing with the problem of the Law.

It is also possible, however, that the Pentateuch intentionally included this selection of laws for another purpose: to give the reader an understanding of the nature of the Mosaic Law and God's purpose in giving it to Israel. Thus it is possible to argue that the laws in the Pentateuch are not there to tell the reader how to live but rather to tell the reader how Moses was to live under the law. To use an example from the Pentateuch itself, it is clear to all that the detailed instructions on the building of the ark in Genesis 6 were not given to the reader so he or she could build an ark and load it with animals; rather, those detailed instructions were given to show what Noah was to do in response to God's command. These instructions are included as narrative information *for* the reader.

The same may be true for the instructions found in the Mosaic Law. Though the nature of the instructions to Noah and those to Moses (e.g., the building of the tabernacle in Ex 25–31) are similar in form and narrative function, we often read them entirely differently. We read the instructions to Noah as given *for* the reader and the instruction to Moses as given *to* the reader.[106] It is possible, however, that the two sets of instructions within the Pentateuch are intended to be read in the same way. In other words, to use terms introduced into OT studies by Mendenhall, the inclusion of the selection of laws (viz., the Mosaic Law) in the Pentateuch was intended less as a source for legal action (technique) than as a statement of legal policy.[107]

This understanding of the purpose of the pentateuchal laws is supported by the observation that the collections of laws in the Pentateuch appear to be incomplete and selective. The Pentateuch as such is not designed as a source of legal action. That the laws in the Pentateuch are incomplete is obvious; many aspects of ordinary community life are not

---

[106]"From the earliest days of the church Christians have asked about the commands of the Old Testament: do they apply to us? The question, however, is ambiguous. It may be a question about authority, or it may be a question about prescriptive claim. A prescription, we said, instructs somebody to do, or not to do, something. We may ask in each case who is instructed and who instructs. If, as I walk down the street, somebody in a blue coat says, 'Stop!', I shall have to ask, first, 'Is he speaking to me?'—the question of claim—and, then, 'Is he a policeman?'—the question of authority. And so it is with the commands of the Old Testament: we must ask, 'Do they purport to include people like us in their scope?'—the question of claim—and, 'If so, ought we to heed them?'—the question of authority. In the patristic church, after the rejection of the Gnostic temptation, especially in its Marcionite form, the question of authority was not really open for discussion; Old Testament commands were evaluated entirely in terms of their claim. Our own age, conversely, has been so dominated by the question of authority that the question of claim has been obscured and forgotten" (O. M. T. O'Donovan, "Towards an Interpretation of Biblical Ethics," *Tyndale Bulletin* 27 [1976]: 58–59).

[107]"That common body of what might be called the sense of justice in a community we shall call 'policy'. What happens in a law court, however, is usually much more directly related to the technical corpus of specialized legal acts and tradition. These are 'techniques'" (George E. Mendenhall, "Ancient Oriental and Biblical Law," *The Biblical Archaeologist Reader*, ed. E. F. Campbell and David Noel Freedman [New York: Anchor Books, 1970], 3:3.

covered in these laws. Moreover, at least one text in the Pen..ateuch mentions a "statute given to Moses by the LORD" but does not actually record it.[108] The selective nature of the laws included in the Pentateuch is further suggested by two "structural observation related to the author's use of numbers": the number of laws, 611, is the same as the numerical equivalent of the Hebrew title of the Pentateuch, "Torah" (תורה),[109] and within the structure of the collections of laws the number seven and multiples of seven predominate. For example, the listing of 42 (7 x 6) laws in the Covenant Code (Ex 21:1–23:12) equals the numerical value of the title of that section (ואלה, "And these [are the judgments]"). This is not to suggest that secret numerical codes were intended to conceal mysteries within these texts. The use of the numerical values of titles and catchphrases was a common literary device at the time of the composition of Scripture. The same principle of numerical selectivity may also be seen within the book of Proverbs: the total number of proverbs in 10:1–22:16, 375, equals the numerical value of the name "Solomon."[110] This suggests that, as in the publication of law generally in the ancient Near Eastern world,[111] the laws in the Pentateuch were not intended to administrate justice; they were not a collection of laws to be enforced.

In his study of law codes in the ancient world, F. R. Kraus has provided a helpful analogy to the nature and purpose of the laws included in the final composition of the Pentateuch.[112] According to Kraus, literary works such as the Code of Hammurapi were not intended for the actual administration of law; they were not associated with the systems of justice in the ancient world. Rather, they were intended to tell us something about the lawgiver (viz., important people like Hammurapi himself).[113] For example, when one considers the whole of the present shape of Hammurapi's Code, including the important but often overlooked prologue, it becomes clear that a text such as Hammurapi's was not intended to administer justice but rather to promote the image of Hammurapi as a wise and just king.[114]

What Kraus has argued for the Code of Hammurapi suits the phenomenon of law in the Pentateuch remarkably well. It explains the

---

[108]The "statute of the law that the Lord gave Moses," referred to by Eleazar in Nu 31:21, is not found elsewhere in the Pentateuch, though a part of what Eleazar commands (the water of cleansing) was given in Nu 19. This shows either that the laws included in the Pentateuch are selective, i.e., not every law given to Moses was included, or that any law given by a priest could have been called a "statute of the law that the Lord gave Moses" (cf. Dt 33:10). The former alternative appears more likely because the text expressly says "the Lord gave [it] to Moses." The omission of "to Moses" in the Samaritan Pentateuch is evidence that at an early period there was already a tendency to read the laws of the Pentateuch as complete.

[109]The traditional number of laws in the Pentateuch, 613, is obtained by treating both the Shema (Dt 6:4) and Ex 20:2, "I am the LORD your God," as laws.

[110]Barry J. Beitzel, "Exodus 3:14 and the Divine Name: A Case of Biblical Paronomasia," *TrinJ*, n.s., 1 (1980): 6. See also J. M. Sasson, "Wordplay in the OT," *IDBS*, ed. Keith Crim (Nashville: Abingdon, 1976), 968–70.

[111]See F. R. Kraus, "Ein Zentrales Problem des Altmesopotamischen Rechtes: Was Ist der Codex Hammu-rabi?" *Genava* 8 (1960): 283–96.

[112]Ibid.

[113]See ibid., 290–91.

[114]Ibid., 291.

existence of the relatively large collections of laws strategically placed throughout the pentateuchal narratives dealing with the life of Moses. Applying the analogy of the Code of Hammurapi helps confirm the judgment that the selection of laws in the Pentateuch is not there as a corpus of laws as such (*qua lex*), but was intended as a description of the nature of divine wisdom and justice revealed through Moses (*qua institutio*).

An interbiblical example of a similar collection of "sayings" is found in the book of Proverbs, with its prologue and selection of wise sayings. The book of Proverbs was not intended to be read as an exhaustive book of right actions but as a selective example of godly wisdom.

In the narratives of the Pentateuch, then, in Exodus–Deuteronomy, we are to see not only a picture of Moses but also a glimpse of the nature of the Law under which he lived and of God's purpose for giving it. If we return to Knierim's thesis of the genre of the Pentateuch, what emerges from a genre analysis of the Pentateuch in its present shape is that it is a biography of Moses, albeit a modified one. It portrays him as a man who lived under the Law given at Sinai. It is a biography of Moses *sub lege*.

A second difficulty in Knierim's assessment of the genre of the Pentateuch is his treating Genesis as an introduction to the life of Moses; there are significant problems in accounting for this section of the Pentateuch within the genre of biography (of Moses). According to Knierim, Genesis adds the dimension of "all of human history" to the biography of Moses. But clearly not all of Genesis is about "all of human history"; only the first eleven chapters have all of humanity specifically in view. Though the rest of Genesis is drawn into the scope of "all humanity" by means of the reiterated promise that in the seed of Abraham "all the families of the land will be blessed," the narratives in chapters 12–50 focus specifically on the family of Abraham. Indeed, the three major sections of Genesis 12–50 appear to consist of genres nearly identical to that of Knierim's view of the whole Pentateuch, namely, biographies of Abraham (chaps. 12–26), Jacob (chaps. 27–36), and Joseph (chaps. 37–50).

Knierim rightly makes much of the fact that the whole of Genesis, covering some two thousand years, takes up only about 25 percent of the total text of the Pentateuch, whereas Exodus–Deuteronomy, which covers only the span of Moses' life, takes up the other 75 percent. "The extent of material allotted to each of the two time spans is extremely disproportionate, a factor that must be considered programmatic."[115] However, when the Moses narratives (Ex 1–18 and Nu 10:11–36:13) are counted alone, without the laws (Deuteronomy and the Sinai pericope), they make up only about 20 percent of the whole Pentateuch. The material in Genesis devoted to the patriarchs (chaps. 12–50) is also about 20 percent; hence the narratives about Moses and those about the patriarchs appear equally important within the final text.

It is thus not satisfactory to group the patriarchal narratives together with Genesis 1–11 and consider them both as the introduction to Moses' biography. It appears more probable within the framework of the entire Pentateuch that the patriarchal material in Genesis is intended on its own to

---

[115]Knierim, "Composition of the Pentateuch," 395.

balance the material in the Moses narratives. The biographies of the patriarchs are set over against the biography of Moses.

The early chapters of Genesis (1–11) play their own part in providing an introduction to the whole Pentateuch; they stress the context of "all humanity" for both the patriarchal narratives and those of Moses. The Moses material, for its part, has been expanded with voluminous selections from the Sinai laws in order to show the reader the nature of the Law under which Moses lived.

If this is an adequate description of the Pentateuch, then its genre is not simply biography (of Moses) but rather a series of biographies, similar perhaps to those in Kings or Samuel (where the life of Saul, for example, is counterbalanced with that of David). Within this series of biographies in the Pentateuch a further textual strategy appears evident.

The chronological framework of Genesis (periodization) and the virtual freezing of time in Exodus–Deuteronomy (a single period of time only, viz., the life span of Moses) suggests a conscious effort to contrast the time before (and leading up to) the giving of the Law (*ante legem*) with the time of Moses under the Law (*sub lege*).[116] Abraham lived *before* the Law and Moses lived *after* it was given.

With this background to the compositional strategy of the final shape of the Pentateuch, we can now turn to its treatment of Abraham and Moses. We wish to raise the specific question of what the Pentateuch intends to say about the lives of these two great men that contributes to our understanding of faith and keeping the Mosaic Law.

A complete answer to this question cannot be given here. We will limit ourselves to two strategically important pentateuchal texts from the standpoint of its final composition, Genesis 26:5 and Numbers 20:12. These texts are similar in that they offer a reflective look at the lives of Abraham and Moses respectively and give an evaluation that stems from the final stages of the book's composition.

Furthermore, both texts evaluate the lives of these two great men from the perspective of the theology of Deuteronomy. We will see that Genesis 26:5 portrays Abraham as one who "kept the Law," whereas Numbers 20:12 portrays Moses as one who "did not believe."

3. Abraham and the Mosaic Law (Ge 26:5)

In Genesis 26:5, God says, "Abraham obeyed my voice [שמע . . . בקלי] and kept my charge [וישמר משמרתי], my commandments [מצותי], my statutes [חקותי], and my laws [תורתי]." Though the meaning of this verse seems clear, questions arise when one views it within the larger context of the book. How was it possible for Abraham to obey the commandments (מצותי), statutes (חקותי), and laws (תורתי) before they were given? Why is Abraham here credited with keeping the Law when the previous narratives took great pains to show him as one who lived by faith (e.g., Ge 15:6)? There has been no

---

[116]Though it is not part of our immediate concern, one could also note indications within the final shape of the Pentateuch of a time "after the law" (*post legem*). For example, Deuteronomy 30 looks to a future time quite distinct from that of Moses' own day. There are close affinities between this chapter and passages in the prophetic literature which look to the time of the new covenant, e.g., Jer 31:31ff.; Eze 36:22ff.

mention of Abraham's having the Law or keeping the Law previous to this passage. Why, at this point, does the text say that Abraham had kept the Law?

The verse is recognized as "deuteronomic" by most biblical scholars, both critical and conservative.[117] Earlier biblical scholars went to great lengths to explain the verse in view of its inherent historical and theological difficulties. For those who saw the verse as a description of Abraham's legal adherence to the Law, the major problem was how Abraham could have had access to the Mosaic Law. For example, early rabbinical approaches attempted by word associations to identify each of the terms used here with a specific act of obedience by Abraham within the patriarchal narratives. In that way it could be demonstrated that Abraham knew the Mosaic Law and thus kept it.[118] This approach did not gain wide acceptance, however, because, apart from a remote link to circumcision, none of the terms in 26:5 could be associated with events or actions from the life of Abraham within the biblical narratives.[119]

Another more common, rabbinical explanation of 26:5 made use of the talmudic teaching of the "Noahic laws."[120] The early Protestant scholars also

---

[117]See Blum, *Komposition der Vätergeschichte*, 363, for a discussion of the critical views. See also F. Delitzsch: "Undoubtedly verse 5 in this passage is from the hand of the Deuteronomist" (*A New Commentary on Genesis* [Edinburgh: T. & T. Clark, 1888], 137ff.). C. F. Keil also recognized that these same terms were later used to describe the Mosaic Law. "The piety of Abraham is described in words that indicate a perfect obedience to all the commands of God, and therefore frequently recur among the legal expressions of a later date [in der späteren Gesetzessprache]" (*Commentary on the Old Testament*, I: *The Pentateuch*, 3 vols. [Grand Rapids: Eerdmans, repr. 1971]), 1:270). Cf. Benno Jacob, "Aber diese Ausdrücke besagen, dass er auf den verschiedensten Gebieten sein Leben ähnlich den späteren Ordnungen des Gesetzes nach den speziellen Weisungen Gottes, wie sie ihm erteilt wurden oder er sie sich selbst erschliessen mochte, eingerichtet hat" (*Das erste Buch der Tora, Genesis* [Berlin: Schocken, 1934], 548). Since, throughout the Pentateuch and especially in Deuteronomy, this same expression denotes the Mosaic Law (e.g., Dt 11:1; 26:17), this passage says, in no uncertain terms, that Abraham kept the Mosaic Law.

[118]E.g., the terms משמרתי and מצותי were related to Abraham's obedience in circumcision since, according to Ge 17:9, Abraham was to "keep" (תשמר) God's covenant in circumcision, and in 21:4, Abraham circumcised Isaac "as God had commanded [צוה] him."

[119]The terms חקותי and תורתי could not otherwise be associated with Abraham's piety in the patriarchal narratives, and no amount of midrashic attempts to do so proved successful. A similar attempt to demonstrate that Abraham had the Law of Moses is that of Walter Kaiser: "In spite of its marvelous succinctness, economy of words, and comprehensive vision, it must not be thought that the Decalogue was inaugurated and promulgated at Sinai for the first time. All Ten Commandments had been part of the law of God previously written on hearts instead of stone, for all ten appear, in one way or another, in Genesis. They are: The first, Genesis 35:2: 'Get rid of the foreign gods.' The second, Genesis 31:39: Laban to Jacob: 'But why did you steal my gods?' The third, Genesis 24:3: 'I want you to swear by the Lord.'" (*Toward Old Testament Ethics* [Grand Rapids: Zondervan, 1983], 81–82).

[120]The Talmud teaches that all descendants of Noah who did not follow the practices of idolatry were given seven divine laws. See L. Goldschmidt, *Der Babylonische Talmud*, 12 vols. (Berlin: Jüdischer Verlag, 1930), 2:373.

accepted this approach.[121] Thus some identified the deuteronomic terms for the Law in 26:5 as those general laws given to all humankind since the time of Noah.[122] Because these specific terms are used later in the Pentateuch to represent the whole of the Mosaic Law, however, it proved difficult to limit them only to the concept of the Noahic laws. Thus for this particular passage (26:5) the Talmud itself rejected the notion of Noahic laws and took the position that, in his own lifetime, Abraham was given the whole of the Mosaic Law.[123]

As to how Abraham would have known the Law, the assumption was that God had revealed it to him.[124] Many also held that Abraham derived the laws of Moses from his own observations, or even from written tradition, which could be traced back to Enoch.[125] In Jubilees 21:10, for example, when explaining the various laws for sacrifice, Abraham says, "For thus I have found it written in the books of my forefathers, and in the words of Enoch, and in the words of Noah."[126] The tractate *Nedarim* 32a states that Abraham was three years old when he first began to obey the Law. By means of *gematria*, the rule that permits deriving significance from the numerical value of the consonants of a word, the first word, עקב, is read as the number 172 (years).[127] Thus 26:5 was read as if it said, "For 172 [עקב] years Abraham

---

[121]"Observantia Sabbati et Circumcisionis, esus Sanguinis, cultus unius Dei, et multa hujusmodi" (Sebastian Münster [1489–1552], *Critici Sacri: Annotata Doctissimorum Virorum in Vetus ac Novum Testamentum*, ed. J. Pearson, A. Scattergood, F. Gouldman, and R. Pearson [Amsterdam, 1698], 1:616). Münster explicitly cites Ibn Ezra's commentary on this passage.

[122]E.g., Seforno, שנצטוו בני נח. *Torat Chaim Chumash* (Jerusalem: Mossad Harav Kook, 1987), 13.

[123]*Yoma* 28b, *Die Babylonische Talmud*, ed. Lazarus Goldschmidt (Berlin: Jüdischer Verlag, 1930), 3:75. See H. L. Strack and Paul Billerbeck, *Kommentar zum Neuen Testament aus Talmud und Midrasch*, 6 vols. (Munich: C. H. Beck, 1926), 3:204–5, for further examples. Benno Jacob suggested that this talmudic interpretation was an attempt to counter the argument of Paul in Gal 3:17ff ("polemisch gegen Paulus") (*Das erste Buch*, 549). Andreas Rivetus specifically rejected this view as "false," *Opera Theologica* (Rotterdam, 1651), 1:457. According to the Kabbalah, the laws mentioned in this verse are those of the Decalogue. The explanation is based both on the fact that this verse contains ten words and that the Decalogue has 172 words, the same number as the Hebrew word עקב in Ge 26:5. See Baal Hatturim, *Chumash* (New York: Philipp Feldheim, 1967), 81.

[124]"God disclosed to him the new teachings which He expounded daily in the heavenly academy" (Louis Ginzberg, *The Legends of the Jews*, 7 vols. [Philadelphia: Jewish Publication Society, 1968], 1:292). Rivetus held that "praeter naturae legem, habuisse patres multas observationes, praesertim circa divinum cultum ex speciali Dei revelatione, et majorum qui ea acceperant imitatione, ut de mundis animalibus offerendis et talia, praeter circumcisionem, et alios mandatos ritus" (*Opera Theologica*, 1:457). According to rabbinic teaching God himself was guided by the Torah in creating the world, but he hid the Torah from humankind until the time of Abraham עד שלא נברא העולם צפן הקבה את התורה עד שעמד אברהם שנאמר עקב אשר שמע אברהם בקולי) *Yalkut Shemoni* [Jerusalem, 1960], 972).

[125]Strack and Billerbeck, *Kommentar zum Neuen Testament*, 3:205–6.

[126]R. H. Charles, *The Apocrypha and Pseudepigrapha of the Old Testament in English*, 2 vols. (Oxford: Clarendon, 1913), 2:44.

[127]The number 172 is derived from ע = 70; ק = 100; and ב = 2. See Wilhelm Bacher,

obeyed me." Since Abraham lived for 175 years, he would have been three years old when he first began to obey God's law.[128]

It is difficult to see in these early rabbinical attempts a convincing explanation of the Genesis passage. They are rather attempts at harmonization. If to keep the "commandments, statutes, and laws" meant to keep the Mosaic Law as the rabbis had understood these terms in Deuteronomy, then no other explanation remained. Abraham must have known the Mosaic Law.

As with all readers of a text, the rabbis' understanding of the sense of the whole determined their interpretation of this part. What was clearly not open to these commentators was the possibility that this verse was intended as an interpretation of the life of Abraham from another perspective than that of the Law.[129]

In contrast, the view of the later medieval Jewish commentaries was that these "laws" were merely a form of general revelation of moral and ethical precepts.[130] Many Christian commentaries have a similar interpretation.[131] The difficulty of such an interpretation is not merely that elsewhere in

---

Die Exegetische Terminologie der Jüdischen Traditionsliteratur (Hildesheim: Georg Olms, 1965), 127.

[128]*Midrash Rabbah* (New York: KTAV, n.d.), 135. The purpose of this explanation was apparently to deal with the problem of idolatry in Terah's household (Jos 24:2). If Abraham had received the Mosaic Law already at age three, he could not have been influenced by his father's idolatry.

[129]Although Calvin is not clear in his comments on this passage, he appears to follow the same line of interpretation as that reflected in the rabbis. "And although laws, statutes, rites, precepts and ceremonies, had not yet been written, Moses used these terms, that he might the more clearly show how sedulously Abraham regulated his life according to the will of God alone—how carefully he abstained from all the impurities of the heathen" (John Calvin, *Commentaries on the First Book of Moses Called Genesis*, trans. John King [Grand Rapids: Baker, repr. 1979], 2:60).

[130]See Benno Jacob, *Das erste buch der Tora, Genesis*, 549. Rashi says, "'my commandments' are those things which even if they had not been written [in the Law] it is evident [ראויין] that they are commanded [להצטוות], such as stealing and murder" (*Torat Chaim Chumash* [Jerusalem: Mossad Harav Kook, 1987], 2.13). Regarding the last two terms, "my statutes" and "my laws," however, Rashi held that they were unobtainable by reason alone; they were given as a command from God.

[131]The Belgic Confession (1561) takes the מצות here to be the moral law (*praecepta*), the תורות as doctrine (*leges*) necessary to be believed, and the משפטים as political law (*judicia*). Thomas Cartwright (1535–1603) followed Nicholas of Lyra (1270–1340), who followed Rashi, "Lyra ait, *ea esse, quae sunt de dictamine rationis rectae, et servanda etiamsi nulla lex esset posita*" (*Critici Sacri*, 1:632). Lyra, however, did not follow Rashi on the last two terms, much to Cartwright's surprise, "a quo mirum est Lyram dissentire." Lyra understood these terms as follows: "חקות cerimonias, seu statuta, ea esse, quae pertinent ad modum colendi Dei; תורות leges esse ista, quae non obligant, nisi quia sunt a Deo, vel homine instituta, vel praecepta." See Matthius Pol, *Synopsis Criticorum Aliorumque Sacrae Scripturae Interpretum*, 5 vols. (Utrecht: Leusden, 1684), 1:206. Ultimately the dependency on Rashi and innovations (see previous note) go back to Lyra, "cerimonias meas, seu statuta mea, et leges meas," and to the Vulgate, "praecepta et mandata mea et caerimonias legesque" Johannes Drusius (1550–1616) defined these terms as "[משמרתי] quaecunque mandavi ut custodiret . . . [מצותי] praecepta moralia quae post decalogo comprehensa sunt . . . [תורתי] forenses, sive quae ad judicia pertinent" (*Critici Sacri*, 1:622). Johannes Mercerus distinguished

the Pentateuch each of these terms is used specifically to describe an aspect of the Mosaic Law, but, more importantly, elsewhere in the Pentateuch the same list of terms denotes the *whole* of the Mosaic Law (e.g., Dt 11:1). Thus there seems little room for doubt that this passage is referring to the Mosaic Law.

Literary critics are virtually unanimous in assigning the verse to a "deuteronomic redactor."[132] Gunkel assigned it to a later (more legalistic) period, though he agreed that the terms are "Deuteronomistic."[133] Westermann associated the verse with the "post-Deuteronomic" interpretation of Israel's relationship to God in terms of obedience to the law (*Gesetzesgehorsam*).[134]

Though such responses are predictable of critical methodology, they serve better as illustrations of the nature of the problem than they do as its solution. Critical scholarship is unanimous in affirming that at some point in the composition of the Pentateuch this statement about Abraham's piety was inserted to show that he kept the Mosaic Law. Critical scholarship has also affirmed that the verse stems from the same process of composition that resulted in the addition of Deuteronomy to the Pentateuch.[135]

We should ultimately attempt to find the meaning of this verse in the Pentateuch's larger strategy and purpose.[136] Does the author of the Penta-

---

sharply among each of the five terms: the first term refers generally to Abraham's obedience in such cases as the command to leave Ur of the Chaldeans and the binding of Isaac; the second term refers to general religious practice which Abraham carried out diligently as God had prescribed; the third term refers to general moral principles, such as the Decalogue, that are posited in the natural mind; the fourth term refers to rituals by which God is worshiped as well as statutes whose rationale is not immediately obvious, such as the red heifer; and the fifth term refers to documents by which one is instructed in doctrine. "Sic Dei voluntatem partitur Moses hoc loco, ut postea in Lege tradenda divisa est [but the Jewish view that Abraham had the whole of the Mosaic Law is to be rejected]. . . . Non est quidem dubium quin ante Legem multa seruarint, quae postea in Legem sunt redacta, ut de mundis animalibus immolandis, aut edendis, et alia. Sed non sunt minutiis astringendi. . . . Sed nondum haec in legem certam abierant, ut postea sub Mose, ubi sacerdotium certa familia, et certis ritibus est institutum, etc. . . . Cum ergo hic Moses in Abrahamo, hac legis in suas partes distributione utitur, significat eum absolutissime Dei voluntati paruisse, et per omnia morigerum fuisse, ut nihil omiserit eorum quae tunc praescripserat Dominus agenda aut seruanda" (*In Genesin Primum Mosis Librum, sic a Graecis Appellatum, Commentarius* [Genevae, 1598], 458).

[132]H. Holzinger, *Einleitung in den Hexateuch* (Freiburg: Mohr [Siebeck], 1893), 3; Otto Procksch, *Die Genesis übersetzt und erklärt*, KAT, 1st ed. (Leipzig: A. Deichert, 1913), 151.

[133]"The thought that Abraham had fulfilled so many commandments does not suit the spirit of the ancient narratives [*Sage*], but betrays that of a later (legalistic) piety" (Hermann Gunkel, *Genesis* [Göttingen: Vandenhoeck & Ruprecht, 1977], 300).

[134]Claus Westermann, *Genesis*, 3 vols., trans. John J. Scullion (Minneapolis: Augsburg, 1984–86), 2:425.

[135]On the "deuteronomic redaction of the Pentateuch" see Rendtorff, *Das überlieferungsgeschichtliche Problem*, 164; Blum, *Komposition der Vätergeschichte*, 362ff.; C. Brekelmans, "Die sogenannten deuteronomischen Elemente in Genesis bei Numeri. Ein Beitrag zur Vorgeschichte des Deuteronomiums," *VTSup* 15 (Leiden: Brill, 1966), 90–96.

[136]Such an approach follows from the observation that, on most reckonings, the verse belongs to the work of the author in shaping the final form of the Pentateuch.

teuch intend to depict Abraham as a model of faith or as a model of obedience to the Law? Curiously enough, the overwhelming majority of biblical scholars have read this passage as if the verse intended to show Abraham's life as an example of obedience to the Law (*Gesetzesgehorsam*).

However, several considerations make this assumption unlikely. First, the final shape of the Abrahamic narratives is closely aligned with the faith theme that forms the larger structure of the Pentateuch. This same faith theme is also part and parcel with the "Deuteronomic composition" of Genesis 26:5. Thus it is unlikely that the same author would want to stress faith at the expense of law at one point in the composition of the Pentateuch and law at the expense of faith at another.

The chronological setting of the patriarchal narratives offers further evidence that this text (Ge 26:5) intends to teach Abraham's faith and not obedience to the Law as such. It is well known that the early chapters of the Pentateuch are governed by an all-embracing chronological scheme. This scheme runs throughout the patriarchal narratives up to the time of the giving of the Law at Sinai. At that point, the linear chronology broadens out into a literary present. Thus the events of the Pentateuch are divided between those before and those during the giving of the Law. Within this scheme, then, the patriarchs are necessarily portrayed as those who lived before the Law (*ante legem*). They are chronologically separated from those who lived under the Law (*sub lege*).[137] Thus any statement about Abraham would likely be intended as a contrast to life under the Law.

Furthermore, the very existence of such a wide range of explanations of Abraham's "living under the Law" (*sub lege*), so common in rabbinical and Christian exegesis, testifies to the difficulties of reading Genesis 26:5 as a statement about Abraham's obedience to the Mosaic Law.[138]

It appears reasonable to conclude, therefore, that the importance of Genesis 26:5 lies in what it tells us about the meaning of the Deuteronomic terms it uses. It is as if the author of the Pentateuch has seized on the Abrahamic narratives as a way to explain his concept of "keeping the Law."

The author uses the life of Abraham, not Moses, to illustrate that one *can* fulfill the righteous requirements of the Law. In choosing Abraham and not Moses, the author shows that "keeping the Law" means "believing in God," just as Abraham believed God and was counted righteous (Ge 15:6). In effect the author says, "Be like Abraham. Live a life of faith, and it can be said that you are keeping the Law."

We turn now to a consideration of the Pentateuch's portrayal of Moses. We will not attempt a survey of the whole of Moses' life; rather, we will look only at the assessment of Moses that lies within the compositional seams.

---

[137]For change of time as a segmentation marker in narrative see Elisabeth Gulich and Wolfgang Raible, "Überlegungen zu einer makrostrukturellen Textanalyse: J. Thurber, The Lover and His Lass," in *Untersuchungen in Texttheorie* (Göttingen: Vandenhoeck & Ruprecht, 1977), 132–75.

[138]Moreover, the *Glaubens-Thematik*, which is central to the Abrahamic narratives, is also related to the assessment of the life of Moses. The Pentateuch tells us that Moses died in the wilderness, not entering into the good land, because he "did not believe" God (Nu 20:12). At that point the author labeled the action of Moses as "faithlessness." Within such a scheme it would follow that the Pentateuch would also view Abraham's faith as obedience to the Law.

4. Moses and the Faith of Abraham (Nu 20:1–13)

According to Schmitt, Numbers 20 contains an original account of the rebellion of Moses and Aaron that has been secondarily reworked into the faith theme. He argues that the narrative of Numbers 20:1–13 was originally a self-contained unit which, apart from verse 12, formed a coherent whole. Verse 12, however, intrudes into this original narrative and gives it a specific theological interpretation (*Glaubens-Thematic*). The original theme of the passage was the rebellion of the people. This theme, however, was replaced in verse 12 by a focus on faith—an idea that had not hitherto played a part in the narrative.[139]

As chapter 20 opens, the Israelites were encamped at Kadesh (20:1) but had begun to contend (וירב) with Moses on account of the lack of food and water. When the Lord told Moses to take a rod and speak to the rock to bring forth water, he did "as [the Lord] commanded him" (20:9). This statement gives an initial impression that Moses and Aaron were obediently following the Lord's commands. Then Moses, saying to Israel, "You rebellious ones" (המרים, 20:10), struck the rock twice and water came out for both the people and their animals (20:11).

Though popular exposition emphasizes the nature of Moses' sin, it is not immediately clear from the text why the Lord said Moses (and Aaron) "did not believe" (20:12). Only the bare outline of the events is retained in the narrative.[140] Nevertheless, attempts to find the error of Moses and Aaron and relate it to their lack of faith are numerous.[141] Moses' sin has generally been related to three aspects of the narrative; (1) his striking the rock with the rod (20:11), (2) his (harsh) words to the people (20:10), and (3) the lacunae within the narrative itself.

(1) Some argue that Moses exhibits a lack of faith in striking the rock rather than merely speaking to it. According to the narrative, however, the Lord certainly intended Moses to use the rod in some way since it was the Lord who told Moses to get the rod, and Moses is commended for doing "as he had commanded" (20:9). But the narrative does not recount the Lord's instructions concerning how or why Moses was to use the rod. Thus Keil, like many, supposed that the Lord's instructions to "speak to the rock" meant that Moses was merely to hold the rod in his hand while he spoke to

---

[139]In Dt 1:37; 3:26; and 4:21, Moses says he could not enter the land because of the rebellion of the people—an idea consistent with Nu 20:10–11, 13. The presence of the theme of rebellion underlying the present text is betrayed by several wordplays throughout the narrative between the people's rebellion (e.g., המרים, וירב, ורבו) and the place name Meribah (מריבה). The fact that later allusions to the Meribah incident speak of the people's rebellion there and not the "unfaithfulness of Moses and Aaron" further supports Schmitt's argument that originally that was the theme of the story. See Nu 20:24; 27:14; Dt 32:51.

[140]The difficulty of determining the nature of Moses' sin because of the brevity of the narrative was already acknowledged by early biblical scholars. Regarding this problem Münster said, "Et quidem verba Mose sunt tam succincta ut nemo facile ex illis advertere possit in quo peccaverit" (*Critici Sacri*, 2:323).

[141]Drusius, "De peccato Mosis variae sunt interpretum opiniones, quas omnes recensere longum esset" (*Critici Sacri*, 2:328).

the rock.[142] In this way one infers from the narrative that Moses erred in striking the rock.[143]

That such a meaning is not likely a part of the author's intention is clear from other narratives where Moses was explicitly commanded to strike (הכה) an object with his rod to work a sign demonstrating God's power. In Exodus 17:5–6, for example, the Lord told Moses: "I will stand before you there on the rock at Horeb; and you shall strike [והכית] the rock, and water shall come out of it, that the people may drink." Moreover, if God told him to take the rod, what else would have been expected but to use it to strike the stone?[144] In response, some have argued that the rod was the budding rod of Aaron and hence should not have been used for striking.[145] Hence Jamieson argued that the error of Moses consisted of his striking the rock "*twice* in his impetuosity, thus endangering the blossoms of the rod."[146] Some have stressed merely that Moses struck the rock twice.[147]

(2) Another line of explanation of Moses' faithlessness in Numbers 20:7–13 focuses on what he said when he struck the rock. The Septuagint translators apparently attempted to resolve the problem by translating Moses' words to the people by "Hear me, you faithless ones [οἱ ἀπειθεῖς]."[148] This was a convenient solution to the passage in Greek because it took advantage of the semantic range of the Greek word ἀπειθεῖν, used elsewhere in the Pentateuch to render the Hebrew word "to rebel" (מרה, Dt 1:26; 9:7, 23–24). The Greek ἀπειθής can mean either "disobedient" or "unbelieving."[149]

---

[142]Keil, *Pentateuch*, 3:130.

[143]E.g., Rashi interprets the passage this way: "God did not command him to strike the rock but to speak to it."

[144]"Quorsum virga sumenda erat, nisi ut percuterent," Thomas Malvenda, *Commentaria in sacram Scripturam una cum nova de verbo ad verbum ex hebraeo translatione, variisque lectionibus* (1650), quoted in Pol, *Synopsis*, 689.

[145]Franziscus Junius, 1587, quoted in Pol, *Synopsis*, 689, "At florida illa virga Aaronis non erat ad percutiendum vel imperata, vel commoda." Also Johannes Drusius (1550–1616), "Sed si verbo educenda erat aqua, cur jussus est accipere virgam? Nam ea nihil opus, si sermone res transigi debebat" (*Critici Sacri*, 2:328).

[146]Jamieson, Fausset, and Brown, *Commentary*, 1:564.

[147]Also Ainsworth, "the doubling of his stroke shewed also the heat of his anger" (*Annotations*, 127). Jamieson wrote, "Hence some writers consider that his hasty smiting of the rock twice was an act of distrust—that such a rebellious rabble would be relieved by a miracle; and that as the water did not gush out immediately, his distrust rose into unbelief, a confirmed persuasion that they would get none" (*Commentary*, 564). Keil turned Moses' striking the rock into an evidence of lack of faith by suggesting that striking the rock was an exercise of human works rather than trust in God: "He then struck the rock twice with the rod, 'as if it depended upon human exertion, and not upon the power of God alone,' or as if the promise of God 'would not have been fulfilled without all the smiting on his part' " (*Pentateuch*, 3:131). Rashi suggested that the first time Moses struck the rock only a few drops (טפין) came out because God had told him to speak to it.

[148]The Vulgate follows the LXX with the conflated *rebelles et increduli*.

[149]LSJ, 9th ed., 182. It is also possible that an attempt has been made to associate the word מרה with סרה or סרר, which was translated with ἀπειθής in Dt 21:18. It may also be an unintended variant in the *Vorlage* of the LXX, but that is less likely in this case.

For some the sin of Moses consisted simply of his speaking to the people rather than to the rock.[150] Others have argued that the source of Moses' error lay rather in the harsh words he spoke to the people. Rather than speaking to the rock, as the Lord had commanded, Moses spoke harshly to the people.[151] Some have read the Hebrew מורה (Nu 20:10) as the Greek word μωρός, "fool," and thus said Moses sinned in calling God's people fools.[152] According to Jamieson, "his speech conveyed the impression that it was by some power or virtue inherent in him or in the rod that the miracle was wrought."[153] Jamieson was apparently dependent on Sebastian Castellio (1515–1563), who understood the sin of Moses and Aaron to consist of their saying "shall we draw water?" which showed that they were taking credit for doing that which only God could do.[154] Others have argued that when Moses struck the rock the first time no water came out, and at that point the people began to murmur and doubt that God would give them water. Thus Moses called the people "you rebellious ones" and struck the rock a second time.[155] Several early biblical scholars have read the interrogative in המן הסלע in the sense of "whether" (num)[156] and hence rendered Moses' words: "Are we really able to bring water out for you?" In so doing, they are able to show Moses' words to be an expression of doubt. Drusius noted an equally ingenious, though hardly possible solution: the verb דברתם (דבר) in verse 8, "you shall speak [to the rock]," was to be derived from the noun דבר, "pestilence, plague," and hence should be translated "you shall destroy [the rock]."[157]

(3) Finally, the sparsity of the narrative itself (i.e., the lacunae) has provided the occasion for various explanations of Moses' error. Jamieson suggested that there were perhaps circumstances "unrecorded which led to so severe a chastisement as exclusion from the promised land."[158] Münster thought that the people wanted to receive water from one particular rock and Moses wanted to give them water from a different rock, saying, "We are not able to give water from that rock, are we?" Thus, Münster argued, Moses

---

The history of the difficulty in interpreting this passage argues against an unintended variant.

[150]Paul Fagius, Critici Sacri, 2:324. According to Fagius, this was a view known as inter Hebraeos.

[151]"Instead of speaking to the rock with the rod of God in his hand, as God directed him, he spoke to the congregation, and in these inconsiderate words, . . . which, if they did not express any doubt in the help of the Lord, were certainly fitted to strengthen the people in their unbelief, and are therefore described in Ps cvi. 33 as prating (speaking unadvisedly) with the lips" (Keil, Pentateuch, 3:130–31).

[152]Matching the Hebrew consonants מורה to their Greek equivalents, מ = μ, ו = ω, and ר = ρ, with the nominative ending ος. See Münster, Critici Sacri, 2:323.

[153]Jamieson, Commentary, 1:564.

[154]"In eo peccatum est quod dixerunt, Eliciamus, quod Dei erat, sibi tribuentes" (Critici Sacri, 2:326).

[155]See Drusius, Critici Sacri , 2:328. Drusius was probably referring to Rashi when he attributed this view to the "antiquissimi Ebraei."

[156]Following the Vulgate; see Fagius, Vatablus, Drusius, Grotius (Critici Sacri , 324ff.), and Cornelius à Lapide (1567–1637). See Pol, Synopsis, 1:689.

[157]Critici Sacri, 2:328. Drusius rejected the view because the verb did not have a direct object with את but rather an object with אל.

[158]Jamieson, Commentary, 1:565.

caused the people to think that God could give them water from some rocks but not others.[159] Lightfoot contended that the miracle of the water from the rock, having been given already at the beginning of the wilderness wanderings, implied to Moses that a still longer time of waiting in the desert was to follow. The sin of Moses, then, lay in "discrediting God's promise to lead the people into Canaan."[160]

Another major element of uncertainty in the story is the nature of the sin of Aaron. Because the story itself is silent about the actions of Aaron, the common, but implausible, explanation is that he sinned in remaining silent and not correcting Moses.[161]

These many and varied attempts to explain verse 12 illustrate that which is already obvious from the text itself: the passage does not explicitly tell us the nature of Moses' (or Aaron's) lack of faith.[162]

On the basis of the passage alone, the faithlessness of Moses does not appear to have consisted in his striking the rock or in his harsh words but rather lies just out of reach somewhere in the numerous "gaps" of the story.[163] We should stress that this is not a result of a deficiency in the story.[164] Rather, it appears to be part of the story's design. It is just at the point of recounting the nature of their sin that the author abbreviates the narrative and moves on to the divine speech (Nu 20:12). Moreover, it is just this divine speech that "fills the gap" with the word about faith and gives the story a sense far larger than that of its own immediate concerns. Thus, Schmitt concludes, the reason the exact nature of the error of Moses is not immediately clear from the passage is because the author has deliberately

[159]*Critici Sacri*, 2:323.
[160]See Jamieson, *Commentary*, 1:565.
[161]Pol, *Synopsis*, 1:689.
[162]Gray's comment has merit: "The sin which excluded Moses and Aaron from Canaan is described in v. 12 as unbelief, in v. 24 [and] 27:14 as rebellion. But in vv. 8–11, as they now stand, neither unbelief nor rebellion on the part of Moses and Aaron is recorded; either the one or the other has often been read into the verses, but neither is there" (George Buchanan Gray, *A Critical and Exegetical Commentary on Numbers*, ICC [Edinburgh: T. & T. Clark, 1903], 261).
[163]"From the viewpoint of what is directly given in the language, the literary work consists of bits and fragments to be linked and pieced together in the process of reading: it establishes a system of gaps that must be filled in. This gap-filling ranges from simple linkages of elements, which the reader performs automatically, to intricate networks that are figured out consciously, laboriously, hesitantly, and with constant modifications in the light of additional information disclosed in later stages of the reading" (Meir Sternberg, *Poetics*, 186).
[164]Critical scholarship shows little patience with the story as it now stands. "The truth is, the story is mutilated" (Gray, *Numbers*, 262). The classic critical study of Nu 20:1–13 is that of Hugo Gressmann in *Mose und seine Zeit, ein Kommentar zu den Mose-Sagen* (Göttingen: Vandenhoeck & Ruprecht, 1913), 150–54. Gressmann divided the account into two separate stories. One, the Elohist, is an *Ortssage* explaining the abundant oasis at Kadesh. The other, the later *Priesterkodex*, is only partially preserved and attempts to explain why Moses and Aaron did not go into the land. Cornill treated Nu 20:1–13 as an original unity but saw it largely "mutilated" (*verstummelt*) by a later redactor. See H. Holzinger, *Einleitung in den Hexateuch* (Freiburg: Mohr, 1893), Appendix I, 9.

suppressed it in order to stress the divine pronouncement of Moses' lack of faith.[165]

Though we may not want to follow Schmitt's line of argument fully,[166] we believe that his analysis points the way to the central message of the narrative. The rebellion of Moses and Aaron (מריתם, 20:24), which appears at some point to have been an important feature of the narrative, has been replaced with the focus on their faithlessness (לא האמנתם, 20:12). Such an interpretation has raised the actions of Moses and Aaron in the narrative to a higher level of theological reflection—the issue of faith versus obedience to the Law.[167] Their actions epitomize the negative side of the message of faith.

---

[165]The importance of the divine word about Moses' lack of faith in Nu 20:12 can be seen all the more in that it abruptly breaks into a narrative that appears to be primarily concerned with Israel's rebellion. The centrality of the idea of rebellion in the narrative can be seen in the fact that at the close of the chapter (20:24), when the death of Aaron is recounted, there is a reference back to the earlier failure of Moses and Aaron. Surprisingly, according to the narrative of 20:24, it was not their lack of faith that disqualified them from entering into the land, as in 20:12, but rather their rebellion (מריתם). Furthermore, the reference to their rebellion (מריתם) in 20:24 provides the basis for a wordplay on the name of the waters, "Waters of Meribah" (מריבה). Then again, later in the book, as the death of Moses approached and he was reminded that he could not enter the land with the people (27:14), there is another reference back to 20:1–13. It is recalled that Moses could not enter the land because, the Lord said, "You rebelled [מריתם] to sanctify me (להקדישני) . . . at the waters of Meribah [מריבת]." Similarly, in Dt 32:51 the Lord states that Moses (and Aaron) "acted treacherously [מעלתם] with me not sanctifying me [לא קדשתם] in the midst of the Israelites at the waters of Meribah [מריבת]." In each case the Nu 20 passage is read without reference to the lack of faith of Moses and Aaron (20:12). Mention should also be made here of the reading in Ps 95, which also does not make reference to their "lack of faith" at Meribah. The failure of this psalm to mention their lack of faith, however, is probably due to the fact that the primary text for Ps 95 was the similar passage in Ex 17 rather than Nu 20. When the allusions to the Meribah passage in Nu 20 are compared with the text in its present state, one can see quite easily, Schmitt argues, that the terms for rebellion (e.g., מריתם, 27:14; מעלתם, Dt 32:51) have been interpreted by the term "faith" (לא האמנתם) in Nu 20:12. Since, according to Schmitt, the theme of faith forms the motif of the completed version of the Pentateuch, the account of the rebellion of Moses and Aaron at the waters of Meribah has become an example of the theme of faith found throughout the Pentateuch. A similar type of interpretation can be seen in the reading of Ps 95 in Heb 3:7–18. After an extensive quotation of the psalm, which does not make reference to the faithlessness of Moses, the writer of Hebrews proceeds to interpret the psalm in the light of the theme of faith. The crucial statement in Ps 95 is verse 10: "They always go astray in their hearts" (תעי לבב הם). It is just this statement that the writer of Hebrews then interprets as: "Take care, brethren, lest there be in any of you an evil, unbelieving [ἀπιστίας] heart, leading you to fall away from the living God."

[166]E.g., we need not work from Schmitt's premise regarding the priestly material or draw the same conclusion regarding the time of this redaction. V. 12, in fact, is linked to the rest of the narrative by means of the repetition of the notion of "sanctifying God," להדיישני (20:12) and ויקדש (20:13). Cf. D. A. Carson, "Redaction Criticism: On the Legitimacy and Illegitimacy of a Literary Tool," in Scripture and Truth, ed. D. A. Carson and John Woodbridge (Grand Rapids: Zondervan, 1983), 119–42.

[167]Schmitt has argued that this Glaubens-Thematik can be traced to the influence of Deuteronomy. This is not without significance for those who hold to a Mosaic authorship of the Pentateuch. Given the fact that in Deuteronomy Moses is the

Moses and Aaron, who held high positions under the Law, did not enjoy God's gift of the land. They died in the wilderness because they did not believe.[168]

5. Conclusion

The narrative strategy of the Pentateuch contrasts Abraham, who kept the Law, and Moses, whose faith was weakened under the law. This strategy suggests a conscious effort on the part of the author to distinguish between a life of faith before the Law (*ante legem*) and a lack of faith under the Law (*sub lege*). This distinction is accomplished by showing that faith and trust in God characterized the life of God's people before the giving of the Law, but after the giving of the Law faithlessness and failure characterized their lives. Abraham lived by faith (Ge 15:6), in Egypt the Israelites lived by faith (Ex 4), they came out of Egypt by faith (Ex 14:31), and they approached Mount Sinai by faith (Ex 19:9). After the giving of the law, however, the life of God's people was no longer marked by faith.[169] Even their leaders, Moses and Aaron, failed to believe in God after the coming of the Law.

If we have accurately described this aspect of the compositional strategy of the Pentateuch, then we have uncovered an initial and clear indication of the Pentateuch's view of the Mosaic Law. The view is remarkably similar to that of Jeremiah 31:31ff. Just as Jeremiah looked back at the failure of the Sinai covenant and at the Mosaic Law, which the Israelites had failed to keep, so the author of the Pentateuch already held little hope for blessing *sub lege*. Jeremiah looked forward to a time when the Torah would be internalized, not written on tablets of stone (cf. Eze 36:26) but written on their heart (Jer 31:33). In the same way the Pentateuch holds up the example of Abraham, a model of faith, one who did not have the tablets of stone but who nevertheless kept the Law by living a life of faith. At the same time it offers the warning of Moses, who died in the wilderness because of his lack of faith. In this respect it seems fair to conclude that the view of the Mosaic

---

speaker, Schmitt's *Glaubens-Thematik* is, narratively at least, Mosaic in origin. In Dt 9:23, e.g., Moses tells the Israelites, "And when the LORD sent you from Kadesh Barnea, . . . you rebelled [וַתַּמְרוּ] against the commandment of the LORD your God and did not believe [וְלֹא הֶאֱמַנְתֶּם] him or obey [וְלֹא שְׁמַעְתֶּם] his voice." The view which Moses expresses here in Deuteronomy is precisely that of the *Glaubens-Thematik*.

[168]An identical interpretation can be found in Nu 14:11, where the Lord says of the rebellion (מָרַד, v. 9) of the people: "How long will this people despise me? And how long will they not believe [לֹא יַאֲמִינוּ] me?"

[169]This strategy of the author can be seen clearly in the vocabulary of faith (הֶאֱמִין) which he employs in the Pentateuch. For example, throughout the Pentateuch, each use of the word "faith" (הֶאֱמִין) as part of the *Glaubens-Thematik* before the giving of the Law at Sinai is positive. Abraham believed, Israel believed, and so on. After the giving of the Law, however, the positive statements of faith disappear. The statements about Israel's faith are all negative, that is, after Sinai, Israel (Nu 14:11) and Moses and Aaron (Nu 10:12) "did not believe." Thus, standing between the narratives that stress the faith of God's people and those that stress their faithlessness is the account of the giving of the law at Sinai. The last positive statement of faith in the Pentateuch is Ex 19:9a, the prelude to the giving of the law. It is significant that in Heb 11:29, the writer ends his examples from the Pentateuch with the crossing of the Red Sea and moves immediately to the book of Joshua. He is clearly following here the line of argument of the *Glaubens-Thematik* in the Pentateuch.

Law found in the Pentateuch is essentially that of the new covenant passages in the Prophets.[170]

J. Basic Principles Taught in the Torah

The way in which the various laws are collected and inserted into the narratives throughout the Pentateuch has given rise to the question of the total number of laws contained in the Pentateuch. There also appear to be numerous duplications of laws at several points within the Pentateuch, particularly in the parallel passages in Deuteronomy. It is thus no surprise that discussions about the number of laws in the Pentateuch are found early in Jewish literature. We may suppose that already in Jesus' day such a list existed, since he was once asked, "Which is the greatest commandment in the Law?" (Mt 22:36). Interestingly enough, when he gave his answer, the first and second commandments in his list were not the same as those in the traditional list of later Judaism. The first (and great) commandment which Jesus gave is traditionally counted as the third commandment, "You shall love the LORD your God" (Dt 6:5). Jesus' second commandment, "Love your neighbor as yourself" (Lev 19:18), is later reckoned by tradition as the 206th commandment. Once, in the Gospel of Luke (10:26–27), Jesus asked an "expert in the Law" to tell him the chief commandment, or at least, the central commandment of the Law. To this question the expert replied, "Love the Lord your God with all your heart . . . and your neighbor as yourself." Thus Jesus appears to have agreed with the Jews of his day regarding the order of at least the first two commandments.

One might think it would be simple to arrive at a number by merely counting all the distinct laws in the Pentateuch, but in reality it is quite difficult. For example, a major problem is what to do with laws that appear to be similar but not identical. Should these be counted as one law or two?

The earliest tradition appears to have settled on the number 611 as the total number of distinct laws found in the Pentateuch, though this was usually put alongside the more official number of 613. This tradition is based not only on carefully counting the laws and treating similar laws as distinct but also, in some cases, counting identical laws as distinct. For example, the prohibition "Do not boil a kid in its mother's milk" is treated as two distinct laws. When the prohibition occurs in Exodus 23:19, it is taken to mean one should not *cook* meat with milk; when the same prohibition occurs again in Exodus 34:26, it is taken to mean that one should not *eat* meat with milk. Moreover, groups of similar laws, such as the eight types of unclean "creeping things" in Leviticus 11:29–31, are treated as a single law.

While it is true that the number 611 closely approximates the actual number of laws found in the Pentateuch, this number also equals the *gematria*[171] value of the Hebrew word for "law" (תורה), that is, 611. It is

---

[170]This view of the nature of the Pentateuch and its view of the Law is similar to that of Walther Eichrodt, who argued that in the Pentateuch the Law is presented in such a way that it is "impressed on the heart and conscience. Application to individual concrete instances is then left in many cases to a healthy feeling for justice" (Eichrodt, *Theology of the Old Testament*, trans. J. A. Baker, OTL, 2 vols. [Philadelphia: Westminster, 1961], 1:77).

[171]An example of its use in the Bible is the familiar passage in Rev 13:18: "If anyone

difficult to determine which came first, the count of 611 laws or the recognition of the numerical value of the word "law." In any case the proof text came to be Deuteronomy 33:4, "the law [תורה] that Moses gave to us," which was read by *gematria*, "the 611 [laws] that Moses gave to us." The number 613 was also based on this text. It was maintained that Moses gave Israel 611 laws (Dt 33:4), but God gave them two extra laws directly when he spoke to them "face to face out of the fire on the mountain" (Dt 5:4).

In the twelfth century A.D. the Jewish philosopher and exegete Maimonides published a definitive list of the laws in the Pentateuch. Maimonides' list of laws has particularly lasting value in that it represents an attempt to state comprehensively the principles represented in the collection of pentateuchal laws. One sees quite clearly in Maimonides' list an attempt to comprehend the whole of the will of God expressed in these various laws in the Pentateuch. It is for this reason that we have thought it helpful to include Maimonides' list in an appendix to this book. In cases where Maimonides has focused more on justifying later traditional law than on formulating the precise principle found in the biblical text, we have cast the law in the terms in which it is stated in the biblical text rather than the later law. In those cases we have included Maimonides' interpretation in brackets and marked it with "M."

Throughout the commentary itself, we have also listed each of Maimonides' 613 laws in the contexts in which they occur in the scriptural text. The purpose of this listing is to enable the reader to see each of the 613 laws in its particular biblical context. Though this expression of the meaning of the laws in the Pentateuch is an important part of the tradition surrounding the biblical text, no special theological or exegetical value is attached to it here. It does, however, represent a careful and sensitive reading of the text. As a part of this commentary, its value lies in the example it gives of the way in which the pentateuchal laws can and have shaped the moral conscience of Judaism and Christianity. Christians through the ages have been fundamentally influenced in their understanding of biblical law by the particular statement of it found in Maimonides' list.[172]

---

has insight, let him calculate the number of the beast, for it is a man's number. His number is 666."

[172]For an excellent discussion of the influence that Maimonides' interpretation of the pentateuchal laws in his *Mishneh Torah* has had on Christian theology and exegesis, see Aaron L. Katchen, *Christian Hebraists and Dutch Rabbis: Seventeenth Century Apologetics and the Study of Maimonides' Mishneh Torah*, Harvard University Center for Jewish Studies (Cambridge: Harvard Univ. Press, 1984).

Chapter 1

GENESIS

I. INTRODUCTION TO THE PATRIARCHS AND THE SINAI COVENANT (1:1–11:26)

Chapters 1–11 form an introduction to both the book of Genesis and the Pentateuch as a whole. One should read these chapters with this dual purpose in mind. They set the stage for the narratives of the patriarchs (Ge 12–50) as well as provide the appropriate background for understanding the central topic of the Pentateuch: the Sinai covenant (Exodus–Deuteronomy).

The author of the Pentateuch has carefully selected and arranged Genesis 1–11 to serve its function as an introduction. Behind the present shape of the narrative lies a clear theological program. Nearly every section of the work displays the author's theological interest, which can be summarized in two points. First, he intends to draw a line connecting the God of the fathers and the God of the Sinai covenant with the God who created the world. Second, he intends to show that the call of the patriarchs and the Sinai covenant have as their ultimate goal the reestablishment of God's original purpose in Creation. In a word, the biblical covenants are marked off as the way to a new Creation.

A. The Land and the Blessing (1:1–2:24)

A close look at the narrative style of the opening chapters of Genesis suggests that the first two chapters form a single unit. This unit has three primary sections. The first section is 1:1, which stands apart from the rest of chapter 1. The remaining two sections are 1:2–2:3 and 2:4b–25. The heading entitled "generations" in 2:4a serves to connect these last two sections.

Two primary themes dominate the Creation account: the land and the blessing. In recounting the events of Creation, the author has selected and arranged his narrative to allow these themes full development. The preparation of the land and the divine blessing are important to the author of Genesis (and the Pentateuch) because these two themes form the basis of his treatment of the patriarchal narratives and the Sinai covenant. In translating the Hebrew word אֶרֶץ ("earth") in 1:1–2, the English versions have blurred the connection of these early verses of Genesis to the central theme of the land in the Pentateuch. Although אֶרֶץ can be translated by either "earth" or "land," the general term *land* in English more closely approximates its use in chapter 1. Thus from the start the author betrays his interest in the covenant by concentrating on the land in the account of creation. "Nothing is here by chance; everything must be considered carefully, deliberately, and precisely."[1]

1. The Beginning (1:1)

The account opens with a clear, concise statement[2] about the Creator and the Creation. Its simplicity belies the depth of its content. These seven words (in Hebrew) are the foundation of all that is to follow in the Bible. The purpose of the statement is threefold: to identify the Creator, to explain the origin of the world, and to tie the work of God in the past to the work of God in the future.

The Creator is identified in 1:1 as God, that is, Elohim. Although God is not further identified here (cf., e.g., Ge 15:7; Ex 20:2), the author appears confident that his readers will identify this God with the God of the fathers and the God of the covenant at Sinai. In other words, the proper context for understanding 1:1 is the whole of the book of Genesis and the Pentateuch. Already in Genesis 2:4b God (Elohim) is identified with the Lord (Yahweh), the God who called Abraham (Ge 12:1) and delivered Israel from Egypt (Ex 3:15). The God of Genesis 1:1, then, is far from a faceless deity. From the perspective of the Pentateuch as a whole he is the God who has called the fathers into his good land, redeemed his people from Egypt, and led them again to the borders of the land, a land which he provided and now calls on them to enter and possess. He is the "Redeemer–Shepherd" of Jacob's blessing in 48:15. The purpose of 1:1 is not to identify this God in a general way but to identify him as the Creator of the universe.

---

[1] Gerhard von Rad, *Genesis*, trans. John H. Marks, OTL (Philadelphia: Westminster, 1961), 45.

[2] The first verse, a verbal clause, should be taken as an independent statement rather than a summary of the rest of chapter 1. Thus 1:1 describes God's first work of creation *ex nihilo*, and the rest of the chapter describes God's further activity. The author's usual style in Genesis is to use nominal clauses as summary statements at the beginning of a narrative (e.g., 2:4a; 5:1; 6:9; 11:10), and verbal clauses as summaries at the end of the narrative (e.g., 2:1; 25:34b; 49:28b). Moreover, the conjunction at the beginning of 1:2 shows that 1:2–2:3 is coordinated with 1:1 rather than appositional. If the first verse were intended as a summary of the rest of the chapter, it would not be followed by a conjunction (e.g., 2:4a; 5:1). The conjunction in 2:5a further demonstrates the role of the conjunction in coordinating clauses, e.g., "When the Lord God made earth and heaven, *now* there was not yet any shrub of the field. . . . The LORD God made man" (2:4b–7). Furthermore, the fact that 2:1 is already a well-formed summary of 1:2–31 suggests that 1:1 has another purpose.

It is not difficult to detect a polemic against idolatry behind the words of this verse. By identifying God as the Creator, the author introduces a crucial distinction between the God of the fathers and the gods of the nations, gods that the biblical authors considered mere idols. God alone created the heavens and the earth. The sense of 1:1 is similar to the message in the book of Jeremiah that Israel was to carry to all the nations: "Tell them this," Jeremiah said, " 'These gods, who did not make the heavens and the earth, will perish from the earth and from under the heavens' " (Jer 10:11). Psalm 96:5 shows that later biblical writers appreciated the full impact of Genesis 1:1 as well: "For all the gods of the nations are idols, but the LORD [Yahweh] made the heavens."

The statement in Genesis 1:1 not only identifies the Creator but also explains the origin of the world. According to the sense of 1:1, God created all that exists in the universe. As it stands, the statement is an affirmation that God alone is eternal and that all else owes its origin and existence to him. The influence of this verse is reflected throughout the work of later biblical writers (e.g., Ps 33:6; Jn 1:3; Heb 11:3).

Equally important in 1:1 is the meaning of the phrase "in the beginning" within the framework of the Creation account and the book of Genesis.[3] The term *beginning* in biblical Hebrew marks a starting point of a specific duration, as in "the beginning of the year" (Dt 11:12). The end of a specific period is marked by its antonym, "the end," as in "the end of the year" (Dt 11:12).[4] In opening the account of Creation with the phrase "in the beginning," the author has marked Creation as the starting point of a period of time. "Hence will here be the beginning of the history which follows. . . . The history to be related from this point onwards was heaven and earth for its object, its scenes, its factors. At the head of this history stands the creation of the world as its commencement, or at all events its foundation."[5] By commencing this history with a "beginning," a word often paired with its antonym "end," the author has not only commenced a history of God and his people but also prepared the way for the consummation of that history at "the end of time."[6]

The growing focus within the biblical canon on the times of the "end" is an appropriate extension of the "end" already anticipated in the "beginning" of Genesis 1:1. The fundamental principle reflected in 1:1 and the prophetic vision of the end times in the rest of Scripture is that the "last things will be like the first things":[7] "Behold, I will create new heavens and a new earth" (Isa 65:17); "Then I saw a new heaven and a new earth" (Rev 21:1). The allusions to Genesis 1 and 2 in Revelation 22 illustrate the role that these

---

[3]For a discussion of the syntax of the first word, בראשית, "In the beginning," see my "Genesis," *EBC* (Grand Rapids: Zondervan, 1990), 2:21.

[4]H. P. Müller, *THAT*, 709.

[5]Franz Delitzsch, *A New Commentary on Genesis*, trans. Sophia Taylor (Edinburgh: T. & T. Clark, 1888), 76.

[6]See Otto Procksch, *Die Genesis übersetzt und erklärt*, KAT, 1st ed. (Leipzig: Deichert, 1913), 425: "Already in Genesis 1:1 the concept of 'the last days' fills the mind of the reader."

[7]Ernst Böklen, *Die Verwandtschaft der jüdisch-christlichen mit der Parsischen Eschatologie* (Göttingen: Vandenhoeck K. Ruprecht, 1902), 136.

early chapters of Genesis played in shaping the form and content of the scriptural vision of the future.

The phrase "the heavens and the earth," or more precisely, "sky and land," is a figure of speech for the expression of totality. Its use in the Bible appears to be restricted to the totality of the present world order. It is equivalent to the "all things" in Isaiah 44:24 (cf. Ps 103:19; Jer 10:16). Of particular importance is that its use elsewhere in Scripture suggests that the phrase includes the sun and moon as well as the stars (e.g., Joel 3:15–16 [MT 4:15–16]). Since Genesis 1:1 describes God's creating the universe, we should read the rest of the chapter from that perspective. For example, the "light" of verse 3 is the light of the sun created already "in the beginning." It has long been apparent that the notion of God's creating the universe in the beginning raises the question of what God did on the fourth day; it appears that on that day, rather than "in the beginning," God created the "sun, moon, and stars." We will attempt to answer that question in the discussion of the fourth day.

2. Preparation of the Land (1:2–2:3)

As a praise of God's grace, the theme of the remainder of the Creation account (1:2–2:25) is God's gift of the land. God first prepared the land for men and women by dividing the waters and furnishing its resources (1:2–27). Then he gave the land and its resources as a blessing to be safeguarded by obedience (2:16–17). Since a similar pattern is reflected in the psalm of Moses (Ex 15:1–18), where God leads his people to the promised land through the divided waters of the Red Sea, the creation account appears to be the narrative equivalent to such a hymn. The purpose is the same in both texts: "This is my God, I will praise him, my father's God, I will exalt him" (Ex 15:2). At another point in the Pentateuch—the poem in Deuteronomy 32—the author draws a similar connection between God's gracious work of Creation and his gracious covenant with Israel. There, in terminology clearly reminiscent of Genesis 1, Moses portrayed God's loving care for Israel over against Israel's chronic disobedience. In that poem the loss of the land, which was to come in the future exile, was portrayed as the height of folly over against God's gracious and loving provision for his people. We will see throughout these early chapters that the viewpoint reflected in Moses' final song plays a major role in the theological shaping of these narratives.

a. Day One (1:2–5)

Verse 2 describes the condition of the land before God prepared it for human beings. The sense of the phrase "formless and empty"[8] must be

---

[8]The English translation of tōhû wābōhû as "formless and empty" (NIV) or "without form and void" (RSV) often leads to an understanding of the description of the earth as a chaotic, amorphous mass, rather than calling to mind an uninhabitable stretch of wasteland, a wilderness not yet inhabitable by human beings, as is suggested in the first chapter. The translation often stirs up images of the earth and the universe in a primeval stage of existence, much like the view of the origin of the universe in the physical sciences: a mass of cooling gases, whirling aimlessly through space not yet in its present spherical shape (e.g., "an original formless matter in the first stage of the creation of the universe," New Scofield Bible [New York: Oxford Univ. Press, 1967],

gained from the context alone. The immediate context (1:2a, 9) suggests that the land was described as "formless and empty" because "darkness" was upon the land and because the land was "covered with water." The general context of chapter 1 suggests that the author means "formless and empty" to describe the condition of the land before God made it "good." Before God began his work the land was "formless" (*tōhû*), and God then made it "good" (*tôb*). Thus the expression "formless and empty" refers ultimately to the condition of the land in its "not-yet" state—in its state before God made it "good." In this sense the description of the land in 1:2 is similar to the description of the land in 2:5–6. Both texts describe the land as "not yet" what it shall be.[9]

In the light of the fact that the remainder of the chapter pictures God preparing the land as a place for human beings to dwell, we should understand verse 2 to focus our attention on the land as a place not yet humanly inhabitable.[10]

Having described the land as uninhabitable, the author uses the remainder of the account to portray God's preparing the land as the place of human dwelling.[11] The description of the land as "formless and empty" in

---

1). Though such a picture could find support in the English expression "without form and void," it is not an image likely to arise out of the Hebrew.

The origin of the English translation is apparently the Greek version (LXX), which translates with "unseen" and "unformed." Since both terms play an important role in the Hellenistic cosmologies at the time of the Greek translation, it is likely that the choice of these terms, and others within the LXX of Genesis, was motivated by an attempt to harmonize the biblical account with accepted views in the translators' own day rather than a strict adherence to the sense of the Hebrew text (Armin Schmitt, "Interpretation der Genesis aus hellenistischem Geist," *ZAW* 86 [1974]: 150–51). The later Greek versions, e.g., Aquila ("empty and nothing") and Symmachus ("fallow and undistinct"), decidedly moved away from the LXX. It is also important to note that the early Semitic versions have no trace of the concepts found in the LXX; e.g., Neophyti I appropriately paraphrases with "desolate without human beings or beast and void of all cultivation of plants and of trees." The Vulgate (*inanis et vacua*) also shows little relationship to the Greek.

Within the English versions the influence of the LXX is at least as old as the Geneva Bible ("without form and void," 1599), reflecting Calvin's own translation, *informis et inanis* (p. 67). Calvin's commentary on these words, however, shows that his understanding of the translation *informis et inanis* is quite different from the image suggested to the modern reader in the English equivalent "formless and void": "Were we now to take away, I say, from the earth all that God added after the time here alluded to, then we should have this rude and unpolished, or rather shapeless chaos" (p. 73). In the days of the early English versions, the terms *formless* and *void* would not have suggested the same cosmological images as they do in a scientific age such as our own.

[9]Hans Westermann, *Genesis*, trans. John J. Scullion, 3 vols. (Minneapolis: Augsburg, 1984–1986), 1:94–95, 102.

[10]Ibn Ezra, *Torat Chaim Chumash* (Hebrew), ed. M. L. Gesinlinburg (Jerusalem: Mossad Harav Kook, 1986), 7.

[11]The meaning of the word *tōhû* (formless) here is identical to its meaning in Isa 45:18 "[God] did not create it [the land] to be empty [*tōhû*], but formed it to be inhabited." The term *empty* (*tōhû*) in the Isaiah passage stands in opposition to the phrase "to be inhabited." This is the same meaning of the word (*tōhû*) in Dt 32:10. There "formless" (*tōhû*) parallels "desert" (*midbār*), an uninhabitable wasteland.

verse 2a, then, plays a central role in the Creation account because it shows the condition of the land before God's gracious work has prepared it for humanity's well-being (ṭôḇ). Deuteronomy 32 draws on the same imagery (v. 10) to depict Israel's time of waiting in the wilderness before their entry into the good land. The prophets also drew from the same source to depict God's judgment of exile. When Israel disobeyed God, the land became again "uninhabitable" (tōhû) and the people were sent into exile: "I looked at the land and it was formless and empty [tōhû wāḇōhû] and at the heavens and their light was gone. . . . The fruitful land was a desert" (Jer 4:23–26). The land after the Exile was depicted in the same state as the land before God's gracious preparation of it in Creation. The description of the land in Genesis 1:2, then, fits well into the prophet's vision of the future. The land lies empty, dark, and barren, awaiting God's call to light and life. Just as the light of the sun broke in upon the primeval darkness heralding the dawn of God's first blessing (1:3), so also the prophets and the apostles mark the beginning of the new age of salvation with the light that shatters the darkness (Isa 8:22–9:2 [MT 3]; Mt 4:13–17; Jn 1:5, 8–9).

Similar ideas are already at work in the composition of Genesis 1. Just as the future messianic salvation would be marked by a flowering of the desert (Isa 35:1–2), so also God's final acts of salvation are foreshadowed in Creation. The wilderness waits for its restoration. Henceforth the call to prepare for the coming day of salvation while yet waiting in the wilderness would become the hallmark of the prophets' vision of the future (Isa 40:3; Mk 1:4–5; Rev 12:6, 14–15).

The way in which later biblical writers reuse the terminology and themes of Genesis 1 suggests that the notion of "land" in this chapter is more circumspect than it is usually taken to be. The common understanding of the term *land* (אֶרֶץ) in Genesis 1:2 is "earth," or the "inhabited earth." Jeremiah 27:5, however, shows that later biblical writers read Genesis 1 as referring primarily to the "land" promised to the patriarchs and to Israel. This raises the question of whether the "Promised Land" is the land described here in Genesis 1:2 and hence whether the whole of Genesis 1:2–31 and 2:1–14 are primarily about God's preparation of the Promised Land as the "good land" for humanity's dwelling. So, then, 1:1 describes God's creation of the universe and 1:2–2:3 narrows the reader's focus to just one small but, from the perspective of the writer, all-important place, the land to be promised to Abraham and his descendants (15:18–19).[12]

---

[12]The following points suggest reading "land" in Ge 1:2 as specifically referring to the land promised to the patriarchs in Ge 15:18–19. (1) The sense of the term *land* (אֶרֶץ) throughout Ge 1 is that of "the dry land" as opposed to a body of water (1:10). The notion of the "earth," as opposed to the other heavenly bodies, is not a feature of the term אֶרֶץ in Ge 1. (2) The compositional links between Ge 1 and 2 suggest that the location of the events of Ge 2 are the same as those of Ge 1. The boundaries of the location of Ge 2 are the Tigris, Euphrates, and the river that goes through Kush (Egypt). These are the same boundaries which are given for the Promised Land in Ge 15:18–19. (3) Though the text is clear that the flood was widespread over all the earth, the "land" (אֶרֶץ) that is the focus of the Flood account is the same as the "land" (אֶרֶץ) in the narrative in Ge 11. The "land" in Ge 11 is clearly the Promised Land in that it is from this "land" that humankind travels "eastward" (12:2) and settles in the "land of Babylon."

The second part of verse 2 has received remarkably diverse interpretations. The central question is whether the last clause in verse 2 ("The Spirit of God was hovering over the waters") belongs with the first two clauses and hence further describes the state of the uninhabitable land, or whether it belongs to the following verse (3) and describes the work of God, or the Spirit of God, in the initial stages of Creation. In the first instance it would be translated "a mighty wind," while in the second instance it would be translated "the Spirit of God," as in most English versions.

Although many modern interpreters have read the clause as "a mighty wind," the traditional reading "Spirit of God" seems the only reading compatible with the verb "hovering," a verb not suited to describing the blowing of a wind. Moreover the image of the Spirit of God hovering over the waters is similar to the depiction of God in Deuteronomy 32:11 as an eagle "hovering" over the nest of its young, protecting and preparing their nest. The use of a similar image of God at both the beginning and end of the Pentateuch suggests that the picture of the Spirit of God is intended here.

Another observation in support of the meaning "Spirit of God" in verse 2 comes from the parallels between the Creation account (Ge 1) and the account of the construction of the tabernacle in Exodus. Although many lines of comparison can be drawn between the two accounts, showing that the writer intends a thematic identity between the two narratives, it will suffice here to note that in both accounts the work of God (Ge 2:2; Ex 31:5) is to be accomplished by the "Spirit of God." As God did his "work" of creation by means of the "Spirit of God," so Israel was to do their "work" by means of the "Spirit of God."

In verse 3, God said, "Let there be light." Not until verse 16, however, does the text speak of God making the sun. Consequently, verse 3 has often been taken to mean that God created light before he created the sun. It should be noted, however, that the sun, moon, and stars are all included in the usual meaning of the phrase "the heavens and the earth," and thus according to the present account these celestial bodies were all created in verse 1. Verse 3 then does not describe the creation of the sun but the sun's breaking through the morning darkness, much the way the sunrise is described in Genesis 44:3; Exodus 10:23; and Nehemiah 8:3. The narrative does not explain the cause of the darkness in verse 2, just as it does not explain the cause of the similar darkness in the land of Egypt in Exodus 10:22. The absence of an explanation in either case is, however, insufficient grounds for assuming that the sun had not yet been created. The expression "the heavens and the earth" does not easily permit that assumption. (See further on 1:14–16.) The division between "the day" and "the night" in verse 4 also leaves little room for an interpretation of the "light" in verse 3 as other than that of the light from the sun.

Given the frequent repetitions of the phrase "And God saw that it was good" (1:4, 10, 12, 18, 21, 25, 31), we may assume that the narrative intends to emphasize this element. In the light of such an emphasis at the beginning of the book, it is hardly accidental that throughout Genesis and the Pentateuch the activity of "seeing" is continually at the center of the author's conception of God. The first name given to God within the book is that of Hagar: "El Roi," the "God who sees" (16:13). Moreover, in 22:1–19, a central chapter dealing with the nature of God in Genesis, the narrative concludes on the theme that God is the one who "sees." Thus the place where the Lord appeared to Abraham is called "The LORD will see" (22:14). Though the English versions often translate the verb *rā'â* ("see") in this passage as "provide," as it should be, the Hebrew word *rā'â* comes to mean "provide" only secondarily. The translation is dependent on the particular context, but the sense is the same in either case. This is similar to the expression "to see to it" in English, which is the same sense as "to provide."

The close connection between the notion of "seeing" and "providing," which is brought out so clearly in chapter 22, likely plays an important role in the sense of the verb "see" in chapter 1. In a tragic reversal of his portrayal of God's "seeing" the "good" in Creation, the author subsequently returns to the notion of God's "seeing" at the opening of the account of the Flood. Here too the biblical God is the God who "sees," but at that point in the narrative, after the Fall, God no longer "saw" the "good," but rather he "saw that human evil was great upon the land" (6:5). The verbal parallels suggest that the author intends the two narratives to contrast the state of humanity before and after the Fall.

The "good" which the author has in view has a very specific range of meaning in chapter 1—the "good" is that which is beneficial for humankind. Note, for example, how in the description of the work of the second day (1:6–8) the narrative does not say that "God saw that it was good." The reason is that on that day nothing was created or made that was, in fact, "good" or beneficial for humanity. The heavens were made and the waters divided, but the land, where human beings were to dwell, still remained hidden under the "deep." The land was still "formless" (*tōhû*); it was not yet a place where a human being could dwell. Only on the third day, when the sea was parted and the dry land appeared, could the text say, "God saw that it was good."

Throughout this opening chapter the author depicts God as the one who both knows what is "good" for humankind and is intent on providing the good for them. In this way the author has prepared the reader for the tragedy that awaits in chapter 3. It is in the light of an understanding of God as the one who know "good" from "evil" and who is intent on providing humanity with the good that the human beings' rebellious attempt to gain the knowledge of "good and evil" for themselves can be seen clearly for the folly that it was. The author seems bent on portraying the fall of humanity not merely as a sin but also as the work of fools. When we read the portrayal of God in chapter 1 as the provider of all that is good and beneficial, we cannot help but see an anticipation of the author's depiction of the hollowness of that first rebellious thought: "And the woman saw that the tree was good . . . and able to make one wise" (3:6). Here again the verbal parallels between God's "seeing the good" in chapter 1 and the woman's "seeing the good" in chapter 3 cannot be without purpose in the text. In drawing a parallel between the woman's "seeing" and God's "seeing," the author has given a graphic picture of the limits of human wisdom and has highlighted the tragic irony of the Fall.

The fact that many English translations render 1:5b as "the first day" gives the impression that the author views this chapter as describing the first day of creation. The Hebrew text, however, appears deliberately to avoid this impression by stating, "It was evening and morning; one day."[13]

b. The Second Day (1:6–8)

The sense of the account of the second day of Creation is largely determined by one's understanding of the author's perspective. The central question is how the author understands and uses the term *expanse*. Is it used from a cosmological perspective, that is, is it intended to describe a major component of the structured universe?[14] Or does the term describe something immediate in the everyday experience of the author (e.g., the "clouds" that hold the rain)? We must be careful to let neither our own view of the structure of the universe nor what we might think to have been the view of ancient people control our understanding of the biblical author's description of the "expanse."[15] We must seek clues from the text itself. One such clue is the purpose which the author assigns to the "expanse" in verse 6: "to separate water from water." The "expanse" holds water above the land; that much is certain. A second clue is the name given to the "expanse." In verse 8 it is called the "sky." Finally, we should look at the uses of the term *expanse* within chapter 1. The "expanse" refers not only to the place where God put the sun, moon, and stars (v.14) but also to that place where the birds fly (v. 20, "upon the surface of the expanse of the sky").

Is there a single word or idea that would accommodate such uses of the term *expanse*? Cosmological terms such as "ceiling," vault," or "global ocean," which are often used for "expanse" in this first chapter, do not suit the use of the term in v. 20. Such explanations, though drawn from analogies of ancient Near Eastern cosmologies, appear far too specific for the present context. Thus it would be unlikely that the narrative would have in view here a "solid partition or vault that separates the earth from the waters above."[16] It appears more likely that the narrative has in view something within the everyday experience of the natural world: In a general way, that place where the birds fly and where God placed the lights of heaven (cf. v. 14). In English the word *sky* appears to cover this sense well. The "waters above" the sky is likely a reference to the clouds. That is at least the view that appears to come from the reflections on this passage in later biblical texts. For example, in the account of the Flood in chapter 7, the author refers to the "windows of the sky" which, when opened, pour forth rain (7:11–12; cf. 2Ki 7:2; Pss 104:3; 147:8; 148:4). Furthermore, the writer of Proverbs 8:28 has clearly read the term *expanse* in Genesis 1 as a reference to the "clouds."

In recent years it has become customary to point to a subtle but significant tension between the accounts of verse 6 and verse 7. Whereas verse 6 recounts the creation of the "expanse" by God's "word" alone ("And

---

[13]See my "Genesis," *EBC*, 2:28, for a further discussion of the meaning of this expression.

[14]See, e.g., Delitzsch, *Genesis*, 86: "the higher ethereal region, the so-called atmosphere, the sky, is here meant; it is represented as the semi-spherical vault of heaven stretched over the earth and its water."

[15]See Hermann Gunkel, *Genesis übersetz und erklärt*, 9th ed. (Göttingen: Vandenhoeck & Ruprecht, repr. 1977), 107.

[16]Westermann, *Genesis*, 1:116.

God said"), it is maintained that verse 7 presents an alternative account of the creation of the "expanse" by God's "act" ("So God made"). It is apparent that throughout chapter 1 there is a consistent alternation between accounts of God's speaking and acting, often giving the impression of duplication (compare v. 11 with v. 12; v. 14 with v. 16; v. 24 with v. 25). This impression is heightened by the presence of the recurring expression "and it was so," which suggests that what God had commanded had been accomplished. A close reading of chapter 1 could make it appear that the author at first recounts God's creative work as the result of God's speaking ("And God said . . . and it was so"), and then recounts God's work as an act or deed that he carried out to completion ("And God made"). If such observations are correct, we are left with the impression that the Creation account of chapter 1 has very little internal consistency and coherence. Though such a view cannot be ruled out, it is worth asking whether there might be another explanation for the apparent duplicity which runs throughout the whole chapter.

A possible explanation lies in a consideration of the nature of narrative texts like the present account of Creation. A twofold task lies before the authors of such narrative texts. Their responsibility is not only to recount and report events of the past, that is, to maintain a consistent and continuous flow of narrated events within the world of the narrative text. Often they must also supply the reader with more than the bare facts about those events; they must supply a measure of commentary on the events recorded, that is, monitor the reader's understanding and then manage his or her appreciation of those events. Such is the case for the author of Genesis, for example, in 2:4. There he momentarily set aside the flow of narrative to address the reader directly with a word of advice and application: "For this reason a man will leave his father and mother and be united to his wife, and they will become one flesh." At that point in the narrative, the author is directly managing the reader's response to the events of the narrative.

Although in the past, little attention was paid to such features of narrative texts, it has become increasingly apparent that narratives have such features to one degree or another.[17] It may be possible to explain some of the difficulties and irregularities in Genesis by looking for such reader-conscious techniques in the narrative. For example, in 1:24, the author recounts that God spoke and the animals came into being ("And God said . . . and it was so"). But then he follows that description of God's work by a reader-oriented comment: God made the animals according to their own kind, and he saw that it was good (v. 25). The purpose of such a comment was presumably to assure the reader that God—no one else—made the animals and, in addition, to underscore that God made the animals according to their kind, a key theme in this chapter that has its ultimate focal point in the one major exception, the creation of human beings according to the image of God.

In other words, behind the Creation account of Genesis 1 there appears to lie the same concern as in Psalm 104, especially verses 27–30: "These all look to you . . . when you take away their breath, they die and return to the dust. When you send your Spirit, they are created, and you renew the face of

---

[17]Robert de Beaugrade and Wolfgang Dressler, *Introduction to Text Linguistics* (London: Longman, 1981), 163ff.

the earth." God is the Creator of all life, both animal and human. Such a reading of Genesis 1 not only accounts for the duplications within the whole of the chapter but more importantly, allows for a more explicit reckoning of the author's overall intention. By monitoring his own text, the author reveals his chief interest in the events he is recounting and can be seen at each point along the way preparing the reader for a proper understanding of the narrative.

c. The Third Day (1:9–13)

There are two distinct acts of God on the third day: the preparation of the dry land and the seas, and the furnishing of the dry land with bushes and fruit trees. Unlike the work of the second day, both acts are called "good." They are "good" because they are created for human benefit. Both acts relate to the preparation of the land, a central concern of the author (cf. Ge 12:7; 13:15; 15:18; 26:4). The separation of the waters and the preparation of the dry land is to be read in light of the subsequent accounts of the Flood (Ge 6–9) and the parting of the Red Sea (Ex 14–15). In all three accounts, the waters are an obstacle to humanity's inhabiting the dry land. The water must be removed for human beings to enjoy God's gift of the land.

But as we learn in the accounts of the Flood and the Red Sea, the waters are also God's instrument of judgment on those who do not follow his way. The author of Genesis 1 is not merely recounting past events—he is building a case for the importance of obedience to the will of God. In the Creation account of chapter 1, the author begins with the simple picture of God's awesome power at work harnessing the great sea. It is a picture of God's work on behalf of humanity's "good." But in the Flood account, when the narrative returns to the picture of God's power over the waters of the great sea, the water is a bitter reminder of the other side of God's power. The sea has become an instrument of God's judgment.

In his second act on the third day God furnished the land with bushes and fruit trees. In the present shape of the narrative it is likely that the author intends the reader to connect God's furnishing the land with fruit trees in chapter 1 and his furnishing the "garden" with trees "good for food" in chapter 2. Whatever our opinion may be about whether the two accounts of Creation in chapters 1 and 2 originally belonged together, there is little doubt that as they are put together in the narrative before us, they are meant to be read as one account.

The implications of reading the two chapters together are greater than has been acknowledged. For example, if the two accounts are about the same act of Creation, then the narrative has identified the "land" of chapter 1 with the "garden" of chapter 2. The focus of the Creation account in chapter 1, then, is on the part of God's creation that ultimately becomes the location of the Garden of Eden. We will say more about the location of Eden in our discussion of chapter 2, but for now it is enough to point to the connection between "the land" and its "fruit trees" in chapter 1 and the trees of the Garden in chapter 2. One can see the selectivity of the Creation account in its focus on only the "seed bearing bushes" and "fruit trees." Those are the plants which are food for human beings. No other forms of vegetation are mentioned. Even the origin of the food for the animals, mentioned at the close of this first chapter (1:30), is not recounted here.

d. The Fourth Day (1:14–19)

The narration of events on the fourth day raises several questions. Does the text state that the sun, moon, and stars were created on the fourth day? If so, how could the universe, "the heavens and the earth," which would have surely included the sun, moon, and stars, have been created "in the beginning" (1:1)? Could the author speak of a "day and night" during the first three days of Creation if the sun had not yet been created? Were there plants and vegetation on the land (created on the third day) before the creation of the sun?

Keil represents a common evangelical viewpoint; he suggested that though "the heavens and the earth" were created "in the beginning" (1:1), it was not until the fourth day that they were "completed."[18] Keil's explanation can be seen already in Calvin, who stated that "the world was not perfected at its very commencement, in the manner in which it is now seen, but that it was created an empty chaos of heaven and earth." According to Calvin, this "empty chaos" was then filled on the fourth day with the sun, moon, and stars. Calvin's view is similar to that of Rashi: "[The sun, moon, and stars] were created on the first day, but on the fourth day [God] commanded that they be placed in the sky."

The Scofield Bible represents another common line of interpretation (the "Restitution Theory" or "Gap Theory"), which can be found much earlier in the history of interpretation: "The sun and moon were created 'in the beginning.' The 'light' of course came from the sun, but the vapor diffused the light. Later the sun appeared in an unclouded sky."[19] According to this view the sun, moon, and stars were all created in 1:1 but could not be seen from the earth until the fourth day.

Both of these approaches seek to avoid the seemingly obvious sense of the text, that is, that the sun, moon, and stars were created on the fourth day. Both views modify the sense of the verb "created" so that it harmonizes with the statement of the first verse: God created the universe in the beginning.

There is, however, another way to look at this text that provides a satisfactory and coherent reading of 1:1 and 1:14–18. First, we must decide on the meaning of the phrase "the heavens and the earth" in 1:1 (see comments above on 1:1). If the phrase means "universe" or "cosmos," as is most probable,[20] then it must be taken with the same sense it has throughout its uses in the Bible (e.g., Joel 3:15–16 [4:15–16]); thus it would include the sun, moon, and stars. So the starting point of an understanding of Genesis 1:14–18 is the view that the whole of the universe, including the sun, moon, and stars, was created "in the beginning" (1:1) and thus not on the fourth day.

Second, we must consider the syntax of verse 14. When one compares it to that of the creation of the "expanse" in verse 6, one can see that the two verses have a quite different sense. The syntax of verse 6 suggests that when God said, "Let there be an expanse," he was creating an expanse where

---

[18]Keil, Pentateuch, 1:59.

[19]Cf. O. Zöckler, "Schöpfung," RE, 3d ed. (Gotha: Verlag von Rudolf Besser, 1866), 20:735–36.

[20]H. H. Schmid, THAT, 1:229.

none existed previously (creation out of nothing). Thus there seems little doubt that the author intends to say that God created the expanse on the first day. In verse 14, however, the syntax is different, though the English translations do not always reflect this difference. We should be careful to note that in verse 14 God does not say, "Let there be lights . . . to separate. . . ," as if there were no lights before this command and afterward the lights were created. Rather, the Hebrew text reads, "God said, 'Let the lights in the expanse be for separating. . . .'" In other words, unlike the syntax of verse 6, the syntax in verse 14 assumes that the lights were already in the expanse, and in response to his command they were given a purpose, "to separate the day and night" and "to serve as signs to mark seasons and days and years." If the difference between the syntax of verse 6 (the use of היה alone) and verse 14 (היה with an infinitive) is significant,[21] then it suggests that the author does not understand his account of the fourth day as an account of the creation of the lights but, on the contrary, he assumes that the heavenly lights have already been created "in the beginning."

A third observation comes from the structure of verses 15 and 16. At the end of verse 15, the author states, "and it was so." This expression marks the end of the author's report and the beginning of his comment in verse 16 (see comments above on 1:6–7). Thus, verse 16 is not an account of the creation of the sun, moon, and stars on the fourth day, but rather a remark directed to the reader to draw out the significance of that which had previously been recounted: "So God [and not anyone else] made the lights and put them into the sky." In other words, behind this narrative is the author's concern to emphasize that God alone created the lights of the heavens and thus no one else is to be given the glory and honor due only to him. The passage also states that God created the light in the heavens for a purpose: to divide day and night and to mark the "seasons, days, and years." Both of these concerns form the heart of the whole of chapter 1, namely, the lesson that God alone is the Creator of all things and worthy of the worship of his people.

e. The Fifth Day (1:20–23)

The creation of living creatures is divided into two days. On the fifth day, as the account reads, God created the creatures of the sea and the sky. On the sixth day (1:24–28) God created the land creatures, which included men and women. In verse 20 God spoke ("And God said"), and in verse 21 God acted ("So God created"). The word for "created" (Heb. *bārā'*) is used six times in the Creation account (1:1, 21, 27 [3 times]; 2:3). Elsewhere the verb *'āśâ*, "make," is used to describe God's actions.

Why is "create" used with reference to the "great sea creatures"? Are the "great sea creatures" (1:21) singled out by the use of a special term? One suggestion is that the use of the word *bārā'* (create) just at this point in the narrative is intended to mark the beginning of a new stage in the Creation, namely, the creation of the "living beings," a group distinct from the vegetation and physical world of the previous six days. Each new stage in the account is marked by the use of the verb "create": the universe (1:1), the living creatures (1:2), and human beings (1:26).

---

[21]Cf. *GKC*, par. 114h.

The orderliness of the account is evident, as is its lack of specificity. The author's primary interest is to show the creation of all living creatures in three distinct groups: on the fifth day, sea creatures and sky creatures, and on the sixth day, land creatures.

For the first time in the Creation account, the notion of "blessing" appears (v. 22). The blessing of the creatures of the sea and sky is identical with the blessing of humanity, with the exception of the notion of "dominion," which is given only to human beings. As soon as "living beings" are created, the notion of "blessing" is appropriate because the blessing relates to the giving of life.[22]

f. The Sixth Day (1:24–31)

The account of the creation of the land creatures on the sixth day distinguishes two types: the "living creatures" that dwell upon the land and humankind. In turn, the "living creatures" of the land are divided into three groups: "livestock," "creatures that move along the ground," and "wild animals." Humankind is distinguished as "male" and "female."

Once again the author begins with the divine command ("And God said") in verse 24, and then follows with the comment to the reader in verse 25 ("So God made"). At first reading, the comment in verse 25 does not appear to add significantly to the command of verse 24. However, a comparison of these verses with similar verses (vv. 11–12) shows that verse 25 does add an important clarification to the report of verse 24. In verse 11 God said, "Let the land produce vegetation," and in verse 12 the author adds, "So the land produced the vegetation." The point of the comment is apparently that the land, not God, produced the vegetation. In verses 24 and 25, however, the emphasis shifts. Verse 24 reports a command similar to verse 11: "Let the land produce living creatures"; but the comment which follows in verse 25 stresses that God made the living creatures: "God made the wild animals." Apparently the author wants to show that though the command was the same for the creation of both the vegetation and the living creatures on land, the origin of the two forms of life was distinct. Vegetation was produced from the land, but the living creatures were made by God himself. Life stems from God and is to be distinguished from the rest of the physical world (cf. the creation of humankind and the animals in chap. 2).

The creation of humanity is set apart from the previous acts of creation by a series of subtle contrasts with the earlier accounts of God's acts. First, in verse 26, the beginning of the creation of humanity is marked by the usual "And God said." However, God's command which follows is not an impersonal (third person) "Let there be," but rather the more personal (first person) "Let us make." Second, whereas throughout the previous account the making of each creature is described as "according to its own kind," the account of humankind's creation specifies that the man and the woman were made according to the likeness of God ("in our [God's] image"), not merely "according to his own kind." The human likeness is not simply of himself and herself; they also share a likeness to their Creator. Third, the creation of humanity is specifically noted to be a creation of "male and female." The

---

[22]See my "Genesis," EBC, 2:35, for a discussion of the use of the term ברא in the Creation account.

author has not considered gender to be an important feature to stress in his account of the creation of the other forms of life, but for humankind it is of some importance. Thus the narrative stresses that God created humankind as "male and female." Fourth, only human beings have been given dominion in God's creation. This dominion is expressly stated to be over all other living creatures: sky, sea, and land creatures.

If we ask why the author has singled out the creation of humanity in this way, one obvious answer is that he intends to portray human beings as special creatures, marked off from the rest of God's works. But the author's purpose seems to be not merely to mark human beings as different from the rest of the creatures but also to show that they are like God. It is important not to lose sight of the fact that behind the portrayal of the creation of humanity in this narrative lies the purpose of the author of Genesis and the Pentateuch. The author gives the reader certain facts to serve as the starting point for his larger purposes within the Pentateuch. Human beings are creatures, but they are special creatures, made in the image and likeness of God.

There have been many attempts to explain the plural forms: "Let us make man in our image, according to our likeness."[23] Westermann summarizes the explanations given to the plurals under four headings: (1) a reference to the Trinity; (2) a reference to God and his heavenly court of angels; (3) an attempt to avoid the idea of an immediate resemblance of human beings to God; (4) an expression of deliberation on God's part as he sets out to create humanity.[24] The singulars in verse 27 (cf. 5:1) rule out the second explanation (that the plural refers to a heavenly court of angels), since in the immediate context humanity's creation is said to be "in his image" with no mention of the image of the angels.[25] Both the third and fourth explanations are possible within the context, but neither is specifically supported by the context. Where we do find unequivocal deliberation, as in Genesis 18:17, it is not the plural that is used but the singular ("Shall I hide from Abraham what I am about to do?"). As Westermann has stated, the first explanation is "a dogmatic judgment," though we could add that it is not a judgment that runs counter to the passage itself. If we seek an answer from the immediate context, however, we should turn to the next verse for our clues.

Verse 27 stated twice that humankind was created in God's image and a third time that humankind was created "male and female." The same pattern is found in Genesis 5:1-2a: "When God created humankind . . . male and female he created them." The singular, "human being," is created as a plurality, "male and female." In a similar way, the one God created humanity through an expression of his plurality. Following this clue, one may see the divine plurality expressed in verse 26 as an anticipation of the

---

[23]See Westermann, *Genesis*, 1:144–45; Eduard König, *Die Genesis: Eingeleitet, übersetzt, und erklärt,* (Gutersloh: Bertelsmann, 1919), 153.

[24]See Westermann, *Genesis*, 1:144–45.

[25]Ne 9:6 may also be an attempt to insure that the plurals of Ge 1:26 are not read as referring to angels. In the liturgical rehearsal of the events of Ge 1, Ne 9:6 states, "You alone, O Lord, made the heavens," thus ruling out the participation of angels in Creation.

human plurality of the man and woman, thus casting the human relationship between man and woman in the role of reflecting God's own personal relationship with himself. "Could anything be more obvious than to conclude from this clear indication that the image and likeness of the being created by God signifies existence in confrontation, i.e., in this confrontation, in the juxtaposition and conjunction of man and man which is that of male and female, and then to go on to ask against this background in what the original and prototype of the divine existence of the Creator consists?"[26]

The importance of the blessing in verse 28 cannot be overlooked. Throughout Genesis and the Pentateuch the "blessing" remains a central theme.[27] The living creatures have already been blessed on the fifth day (1:22); thus the author's view of the blessing extends beyond humanity to all of God's living creatures. In verse 28 human beings are also included in God's blessing. The blessing itself in these verses is primarily one of posterity: "Be fruitful and multiply and fill the land." Thus already the fulfillment of the blessing is tied to human "seed" and the notion of "life"— two themes that will later dominate the narratives of Genesis. Since the introductory statement identifies them as a "blessing," the imperatives are not to be understood as commands in this verse. Moreover, the imperative, along with the jussive, is the common mood of the blessing (cf. 27:19).

Command #212, Ge 1:28, You must be fruitful and multiply: "Be fruitful and multiply."[28]

g. The Seventh Day (2:1–3)

The author has set the seventh day apart from the first six not only by stating specifically that God "sanctified" it but also by changing the style of the account markedly. On this day God neither "spoke" nor "worked" as he had on the previous days. On this day he "blessed" and "sanctified" but he did not "work." The reader is left with a somber and repetitive reminder of only one fact: God did not work on the seventh day. While the author recounts little else, he repeats three times that God did not work. The author surely intends to emphasize God's "rest."

It is also likely that the author intends the reader to understand the account the seventh day in the light of the "image of God" theme of the sixth day. If the purpose of pointing to the "likeness" between human beings and their Creator is to call on the reader to be more like God (cf., e.g., Lev 11:45), then it is significant that the account of the seventh day stresses that very thing which the writer elsewhere so ardently calls on the reader to do: "rest" on the seventh day (cf. Ex 20:8–11). If, as we have earlier suggested, the author's intention is to point to the past as a picture of the future, then the

---

[26]Karl Barth, *Church Dogmatics* (New York: Scribner, 1956), 3/1:195.

[27]See Claus Westermann, *Theologie des Alten Testaments in Grundzügen* (Göttingen: Vandenhoeck & Ruprecht, 1978), 75.

[28]According to ancient Jewish tradition, the command listed here is the first commandment found in the Pentateuch. These commandments were arranged and enumerated by the medieval Jewish scholar Maimonides. Throughout this commentary we will list each of the 613 commandments and prohibitions at the point in the text where they find their primary support. For more on this, see the last two paragraphs of the introduction as well as the Appendix.

emphasis on God's "rest" forms an important part of the author's understanding of what lies in the future. At important points along the way, the
author will return to the theme of God's "rest" as a reminder of what lies
ahead (2:15; 5:29; 8:4; 19:16; Ex 20:11; Dt 5:14; 12:10; 25:19). Later biblical
writers continued to see a parallel between God's "rest" in Creation and the
future "rest" that awaits the faithful (Ps 95:11; Heb 3:11).

3. Gift of the Land (2:4–24)

It is important to read chapter 2 as an integral part of the first chapter.
(The chapter divisions are not original and are sometimes very arbitrary.
They are referred to here only for the sake of convenience.) It seems
apparent that the author intends the second chapter to be read closely with
the first and that each chapter be identified as part of the same event. Thus
the author explicitly returns to the place and time of chapter 1 at the point
where he links it to chapter 2: "When the LORD God made the land and the
sky" (2:4b). It is likely that the author's central theological interests in chapter
1 would be continued in chapter 2 as well—the theme of humanity's creation
in the "image of God." Thus we may expect to find in chapter 2 a
continuation of the theme of the "likeness" between humankind and the
Creator.

a. Creation of Humanity (2:4–7)

Chapter 2 begins with a description of the condition of the land before
the creation of humanity. In this respect it resembles the description of the
land in 1:2. The focus of the description is on those parts of the land that
were to be directly affected by the Fall (3:8–24). The narrative points to the
fact that before the man was created (in 2:7), the effects of human rebellion
and of the Fall had not yet been felt on the land. In the subsequent
narratives, each of the parts of the description of the land in verses 4b–6 is
specifically identified as a result of the Fall. The "shrub of the field" and
"plant of the field" are not a reference to the "vegetation" of chapter 1, but
rather anticipate the "thorns and thistles" and "plants of the field" which are
to come (in 3:18) as a result of the curse.[29] In the same way, when the
narrative states that the Lord God had not yet "caused it to rain upon the
land," we can sense the allusion to the Flood narratives at which time the
Lord explicitly stated: "I will cause it to rain upon the earth." The reference
to "no man to work the ground" (2:4b–5) points us to the time when the
man and the woman were to be cast from the garden "to work the ground"
(3:23). Thus, as an introduction to the account of the man's creation, we are
told that a "good" land had been prepared for him: "streams came up from
the earth and watered the whole surface of the ground" (2:6). In the
description of that land, however, we can already see the coming of the time
when human beings would become aliens and strangers in a foreign land.

At first glance the description of the creation of the man in verse 7 is
quite different from that of chapter 1. Man was made "from the dust of the
ground" rather than "in the image of God." However, we should not
overlook the fact that the topic of the creation of humankind in chapter 2 is

---

[29]U. Cassuto, *A Commentary on the Book of Genesis*, Part 1, *From Adam to Noah*, trans.
Israel Abrahams (Jerusalem: Magnes, 1972), 102.

not limited to verse 7. In fact, the topic of the creation of the man and the woman is the focus of the whole chapter. What the author had stated as a simple fact in chapter 1 (humankind, male and female, were created in God's likeness) is explained and developed throughout the narrative of chapter 2. We cannot contrast the depiction of the creation of humanity in chapter 1 with only one verse in chapter 2; we must compare it to the whole chapter.

The first point that the author is intent on making is that the human being, though a special creature made in God's image, was nevertheless a creature like the other creatures which God had made. The man did not begin as a "heavenly creature"; he was made of the "dust of the ground." In the light of the special treatment given to humanity's creation in chapter 1, the emphasis on human creatureliness in chapter 2 is not without importance. This narrative deliberately excludes the notion that humanity's origin might somehow be connected with the divine. Man's origin was from the dust of the ground. One can also see an anticipation of human destiny in the Fall, when human beings would again return to the "dust of the ground" (3:19)—in Creation a human being arose out of the dust, but as a result of the Fall human beings returned to the dust. This is a graphic picture of the author's lesson on the contrast between the work of God and the work of humankind.

Still another contribution to the picture of humanity's creation in God's image can be seen in the author's depiction of the land which was prepared for human dwelling. The description of the Garden of Eden appears to be deliberately cast to foreshadow the description of the tabernacle found later in the Pentateuch (see commentary on Ex 25:1–31:18). The Garden, like the tabernacle, was the place where human beings could enjoy the fellowship and presence of God.

b. Preparation of the Garden (2:8–14)

The inordinate amount of attention given in chapter 2 to the description of the "garden" signifies that we must pay attention to these details. First, we are told that the Lord God planted the garden and "put" the man there. Later in the same narrative this is repeated, though, as we shall see, with significant differences. We should also note that the garden was planted "in Eden to the east." The word *Eden* appears to be a specific place, and since, in the Hebrew Bible, the word means "delight," we may assume that the name was intended to evoke a picture of idyllic delight and rest.

The fact that the garden was "to the east" in Eden is somewhat striking. Elsewhere in Genesis the notion of "eastward" is associated with judgment and separation from God (e.g., 3:24; 11:2; 13:11). Also, when the man and woman were expelled from the garden, the cherubim were placed "on the east" (3:24) of the Garden of Eden, giving the impression that the garden itself was not in the east. Such an apparent difficulty in the coherence of the passage may account for the fact that in 2:8 the garden is not actually called the "garden of Eden," as it is elsewhere, but rather the "garden in Eden," a designation found only in this verse. Thus, according to 2:8, the garden was planted in Eden, which was apparently to be taken as a location larger than the garden itself; and if "on the east" is taken with reference to Eden itself, the garden was on its eastern side.

It is still unclear how the reference to "east" in 2:8, which seems positive, is to be associated with the references to "eastward" in the subsequent narratives, which are all to be taken negatively. One solution may be that of the early versions. For example, Targum Onkelos translated מקדם as "long ago" rather than as "eastward" (cf. the Vulgate's *a principio*). Both meanings are possible for the Hebrew expression. In any event, if a geographical direction is meant here, the author is apparently establishing an important distinction between "east" and "west" which will be of great thematic importance throughout the remainder of the book (see below). For now we are given only a hint that the location of the garden may be important.

In the garden are beautiful, lush trees, including the elusive "Tree of Life" and "Tree of Knowledge of Good and Evil," as well as a river that divided into four "headstreams." The author takes special care to locate the rivers and to describe the character of the lands through which they flowed. The lands were rich in gold and precious jewelry, and their location was closely aligned with the land later promised to Abraham and his descendants[30]—another example of the author's continual interest in drawing comparisons between the events in primeval history and specific events and places in the life of Israel. Later biblical prophets also made an associative link between the Garden of Eden and the land promised to the fathers.[31]

The location of the Garden of/in Eden has long been debated. Two of the rivers mentioned in association with the garden can be identified with certainty, the Euphrates and the Tigris. It is difficult to identify the other two, the Pishon and the Gihon. Since the "land of Cush" is identified in the Bible as Ethiopia, the Gihon is most likely the river which passes through the land of Ethiopia. If so, the author apparently has in mind the "river of Egypt." The land of "Havilah," however, cannot be identified.

It should be noted that the amount of description given to each of the four rivers is in inverse proportion to the certainty of the identification of each of the rivers. The narrative gives most attention to the river Pishon, but there is least certainty regarding that river's identification and location. By contrast, the narrative merely states that the well-known Euphrates is the fourth river. The author's attention to detail with the two lesser-known rivers (e.g., the gold and jewels) can be tied to the parallels between the role of the Garden and that of the tabernacle later in the Pentateuch (see below). Moreover, the mention of the Euphrates and Tigris rivers can be linked to the identification of the Garden of Eden and the Promised Land. It can hardly be a coincidence that these rivers, along with the "River of Egypt," again play a role in marking boundaries of the land promised to Abraham (Ge 15:18).

Another important detail in the description of the Garden of Eden in

---

[30]See Ibn Ezra and Rashi, in *Torat Chaim Chumash*, 46.
[31]Cf. Eze 36:35: "This land that was laid waste has become like the garden of Eden"; Joel 2:3: "Before them the land is like the garden of Eden, behind them, a desert waste"; Isa 51:3: "The Lord will surely comfort Zion and will look with compassion on all her ruins; he will make her deserts like Eden, her wastelands like the garden of the Lord"; Zec 14:8: "On that day living water will flow out from Jerusalem"; Rev 22:1–2: "Then the angel showed me the river of the water of life, as clear as crystal, flowing from the throne of God and of the Lamb down the middle of the great street of the city. On each side of the river stood the tree of life, bearing twelve crops of fruit, yielding its fruit every month."

chapter 2 is the close similarity between the appearance and role of the Garden and that of the tabernacle in Exodus 25–27.[32] We have already called attention to the similarities between the account of Creation in chapter 1 and the account of the building of the tabernacle in Exodus 25–27. Thus it is no surprise to find that the description of the "garden" erected by God in chapter 2 should also suggest similarities to the tabernacle. In describing the Garden the author's primary interest is to stress the beauty of the gold and precious stones throughout the lands encompassed by the Garden. If we take the purpose of such descriptions in the later literature as a guide, the point of the description of the Garden is to show the glory of God's presence through the beauty of the physical surroundings. The prophet Haggai later proclaimed the glory of God's presence in the new temple with a description of the gold and precious metals of that temple: " 'I will fill this house with glory,' says the LORD Almighty. 'The silver is mine and the gold is mine,' declares the LORD Almighty" (Hag 2:7–8); so also John's description of the New Jerusalem stressed the gold and precious stones which pictured the glorious presence of God among his people: "The wall [of New Jerusalem] was made of jasper, and the city of pure gold, as pure as glass. The foundations of the city walls were decorated with every kind of precious stone" (Rev 21:18). In the light of such an attempt to depict the Garden as foreshadowing the tabernacle of God, it is especially interesting to find that the description of God's placing the man in the Garden also bears a strong resemblance to the later establishment of the priesthood for the tabernacle and temple.

c. Man's Place in the Garden (2:15–24)

The author has already noted that God "put" the man into the Garden (2:8). In verse 15, however, he returns to this point by stating the purpose for God's putting the man there. Two important points from verse 15 are in danger of being obscured by the traditional English translations. The first is the change in vocabulary for the Hebrew word for "put." Unlike verse 8, where the author uses a common term for "put," in verse 15 he uses a term that he elsewhere has reserved for two special uses: God's "rest" or "safety" which he gives to human beings in the land (e.g., Ge 19:16; Dt 3:20; 12:10; 25:19), and the "dedication" of something before the presence of the Lord (Ex 16:33–34; Lev 16:23; Nu 17:4; Dt 26:4, 10). Both senses of the term appear to lie behind the author's use of the word in verse 15. The man was "put" into the Garden where he could "rest" and be "safe," and the man was "put" into the Garden "in God's presence" where he could have fellowship with God (3:8).

A second observation from verse 15 concerns the specific purpose for God's putting the man in the Garden. In most English translations of the verse the man is "put" in the Garden "to work it and take care of it." Although this interpretation is found in translations as early as the LXX (2d century B.C.), there are serious objections to it. For one, the suffixed pronoun in the Hebrew text rendered "it" in English is feminine, whereas the noun

---

[32]This relationship has also been discussed by Gordon J. Wenham, "Sanctuary Symbolism in the Garden of Eden Story," *Proceedings of the World Congress of Jewish Studies* 9 (1986): 19–25.

"garden," which the pronoun refers to in English, is masculine. Only by changing the pronoun to a masculine singular, as the LXX has done, can it have the sense of the English translations, namely, "to work" and "to keep." Moreover, later in this same narrative (3:23), "working the ground" is said to be a result of the Fall, and the narrative suggests that the author has intended such a punishment to be seen as an ironic reversal of humanity's original purpose (see comments below on 3:22–24). If such is the case, then "working" and "keeping" the Garden would not provide a contrast to "working the ground." In view of these objections, which cannot easily be overlooked, a more suitable translation of the Hebrew text would be "to worship and obey."[33] The man is put in the Garden to worship God and obey him. The man's life in the Garden was to be characterized by worship and obedience; he was to be a priest, not merely a worker and keeper of the Garden. Such a reading not only answers the objections raised against the traditional English translation but also suits the ideas of the narrative. Throughout chapter 2, the author has consistently and consciously developed the idea of the human "likeness" to God along the same lines as the major themes of the Pentateuch as a whole—worship and sabbath rest.

A further confirmation of our translation "to worship and obey" is that in the following verse we read for the first time that "God commanded" (2:16) the man whom he had created. As in the remainder of the Torah, here enjoyment of God's good land is made contingent on keeping God's commandments (cf. Dt 30:16). The similarity between this condition for enjoyment of God's blessing and that laid down for Israel at Sinai and in Deuteronomy is clear. Indeed, one can hardly fail to hear in these words of God to the first man the words of Moses to Israel: "See, I set before you today life and blessing [the good], death and calamity [the evil]. For I am commanding you today to love the LORD your God, to walk in his ways, and to keep his commandments, decrees, and laws; then you will live and increase, and the LORD your God will bless you in the land you are entering to possess. . . . But if your heart turns away and you are not obedient . . . you will not live long in the land you are crossing the Jordan to enter and possess" (Dt 30:15–18).

The inference of God's commands in Genesis 2:16–17 is that God alone knows what is good for human beings and God alone knows what is not good for them. To enjoy the "good" we must trust God and obey him. If we disobey, we will have to decide for ourselves what is good and what is not good. While to modern men and women such a prospect may seem desirable, to the author of Genesis it is the worst fate that could have befallen humanity.

Having put this in general terms in verses 16–17, the author turns in the remainder of the chapter to give a specific example of God's knowledge of the "good": the creation of the woman. Not only has the first chapter stressed that God knows the good (e.g., "and God saw that it was good"), but now in the present narrative the creation of the woman has become an archetypal example of God's knowledge of the good. When he sees the man alone, God says, "It is not good that the man should be alone." At the close of chapter 2 the author puts the final touches on his account of what it means

---

[33]See further my "Genesis," EBC, 2:45, 47–48.

for humankind to be "in God's image and likeness." In the first chapter, the author has intimidated that humanity's creation in the "image of God" somehow entailed their creation as male and female: "In the image of God he created him; male and female he created them" (1:27). In the narrative of the creation of the woman in chapter 2, the author has returned to develop this theme by showing that humankind's creation "in God's image" also entails a "partnership" between the man and his wife. The "likeness" which the man and the woman share with God in chapter 1 finds an analogy in the "likeness" between the man and his wife in chapter 2. Here also, as in the first chapter, the human likeness to God is shown against the background of their distinction from the other creatures. That the author intends the account of the naming of the animals to be read as part of the story of the creation of the woman is made certain in verse 20, where at the conclusion of the man's naming the animals the author remarks: "but for Adam, he did not find a partner like himself." The clear implication is that the author sees in the man's naming the animals also his search for a suitable partner. In recounting that no suitable partner had been found, the author has assured the reader that the man was not like the other creatures. The author then records in graphic detail the words of the man when he discovered the woman who was one like himself: "This is now bone of my bone and flesh of my flesh" (2:23). Thus the man recognized his own likeness in the woman.

B. The Land and the Exile (2:25–4:26)

If chapter 2 portrayed humanity's earliest state as a prototype of God's gift of the good land to Israel, then it should come as no surprise that the account of the Fall should also be recounted in terms that bring to mind Israel's future exile from the land.

1. Disobedience (2:25–3:7)

A more studied attempt to treat the problem of evil and temptation cannot be found in all the Scriptures. As a part of his deliberate strategy, the author of the Pentateuch has left the reader virtually alone with the events of the story. He does not reflect or comment on the events that transpired. We, the readers, are left to ourselves and our sense of the story for an answer to the questions it raises. We must seek our clues to the story's meaning from the few signs of the author's own shaping of the story.

a. Transition (2:25)

Verse 25 is clearly intended to link the account of the land and the blessing (1:1–2:24) with that of the Fall (2:25–3:24). The reference to the "two of them" looks back to the previous narrative, while their description as "naked and unashamed" anticipates the central problem of the narrative which is to follow. It is important to note that two different but related words are used to describe the "nakedness" of the man and his wife in this narrative. Apart from the obvious meaning of עָרֹם ("naked"), its nuanced sense can be gained from the immediate context: "they were not ashamed."

The choice of this term at the beginning of the narrative is likely motivated by two considerations. First, there is an alliteration between עָרוֹם ("nakedness") and עָרוּם ("crafty"). There is an obvious play on the two words. The effect of such a pun is both to draw the reader into the story by providing an immediate connecting link with the previous narrative and to provide a presage to the events and outcome of the subsequent story. The link provides an immediate clue to the potential relationship between the serpent's "cunning" and the innocence implied in the "nakedness" of the couple. The story unfolds the nature of that relationship.

Second, there is a difference in meaning between עֲרוֹם ("naked") in 2:25 and עֵירֹם ("naked") in 3:7. Although both terms are infrequent in the Pentateuch, the latter is distinguished by its used in Deuteronomy 28:48, where it depicts the state of Israel's exiles who have been punished for their failure to trust and obey God's word: "Because you did not serve the LORD your God joyfully and gladly in the time of prosperity, therefore in hunger and thirst, in nakedness and dire poverty, you will serve the enemies that the LORD sends against you." In distinguishing the first state of human nakedness from the second, the author has introduced a subtle yet perceptible clue to the story's meaning. The effect of the Fall was not simply that the man and the woman came to know that they were עֲרוֹם ("naked"). Specifically, they came to know that they were עֵירֹם ("naked") in the sense of being "under God's judgment," as in Deuteronomy 28:48 (cf. Eze 16:39; 23:29).

b. The Tempter (3:1)

The author has chosen to disclose a small but important clue to the story by revealing a detail about the snake: he was more "crafty" than any of the creatures. The word *crafty* is not primarily a negative term in the Bible but suggests wisdom and adroitness (besides its use here it occurs eight times in Proverbs and two times in Job). The description of the serpent as "crafty" is in keeping with several features of this story which suggest that the author wants to draw a relationship between the Fall and the human quest for wisdom. The disobedience of the man and the woman is depicted not so much as an act of great wickedness or a great transgression as an act of great folly. They had all the "good" they would have needed, but they wanted more—they wanted to be like God. The forbidden tree is the Tree of Knowledge of "Good and Evil." When they take of the tree and eat, it is because the woman "saw that the tree was able to make one wise" (3:6). Thus, even the serpent is represented as a paragon of wisdom, an archetypical wiseman. However, the serpent and his wisdom lead ultimately to the curse (3:14). It should not be overlooked that the serpent is said to be one of the "beasts of the field" which the Lord God had made (cf. 1:25; 2:19). The purpose of this statement is to exclude the notion that the serpent was a supernatural being. "The serpent is none other than a serpent."[34]

c. Temptation (3:2–7)

The story of the temptation is told with subtle simplicity. The snake speaks only twice, but that is enough to offset the balance of trust and obedience between the man and the woman and their Creator. The centerpiece of the story is the question of the knowledge of the "good." The snake implied by his questions that God was keeping this knowledge *from* the man and the woman (3:5), while the sense of the narratives in the first

---

[34]Benno Jacob, *Das erste Buch der Tora, Genesis,* 102.

two chapters has been that God was keeping this knowledge *for* the man and the woman (e.g., 1:4, 10, 12, 18, 21, 25, 31; 2:18). In other words, the snake's statements were a direct challenge to the central theme of the narrative of chapters 1 and 2: God will provide the "good" for human beings if they will only trust him and obey him.

However, a narrative clue already points to the woman's assuming God's role of "knowing the good" even before she ate of the fruit—that is, the description of the woman's thoughts in the last moments before the Fall. The narrative states that the woman "saw that the tree was good" (3:6). Up until now in the narrative, the expression "and he saw that it was good" has been used only of God. Now, instead of God, it is the woman who "saw that it was good." Precisely at this point the author raises the issue of becoming "wise": "And the woman saw that the tree was . . . also desirable for gaining wisdom" (3:6). Thus, the temptation is not presented as a general rebellion from God's authority. Rather, it is portrayed as a quest for wisdom and "the good" apart from God's provision.

Having thus shown the temptation to be a quest for "wisdom" apart from God, the story comes to an abrupt conclusion in the act of the transgression itself: "and she took some and ate it and also gave some to her husband, who was with her, and he ate it" (3:6b). How quickly the transgression comes once the decision has been made. The thrust of the story, with all its simplicity, lies in its tragic and ironic depiction of the search for wisdom. That which the snake promised did, in fact, come about: the man and the woman became "like God" as soon as they ate of the fruit. The irony lies in the fact that they were already "like God" because they had been created in his image (1:26). In the temptation the serpent promised that they would know "good and evil," just as God knew "good and evil." It is clear in the story that the man and the woman had believed that when they obtained the knowledge of "good and evil" they would, on their own, enjoy the "good." Prior to their eating the fruit, the narrative did not raise the possibility that they would know only the "evil" and not the "good." Yet when they ate of the fruit and their eyes were opened, it was not the "good" that they saw and enjoyed. Their new knowledge was that of their own nakedness. Their knowledge of "good and evil" which was to make them "like God" resulted in the knowledge that they were no longer even like each other—they were ashamed of their nakedness, and they sewed leaves together to hide their differences from each other. Like Qohelet (Ecclesiastes), they sought wisdom but found only vanity and toil. As the next segment of the narrative shows, not only did the man and his wife attempt to cover their shame from each other by making clothing from the trees of the garden, but they also tried to hide themselves from God at the first sound of his coming.

Why was the man held responsible for the actions of both he and his wife? There are some clues in the text and its context. For example, the author stresses in 3:13 that the woman was "deceived." Since the text does not explicitly state that the man was also "deceived," the author apparently means to suggest that the man was, in fact, not deceived and hence was to be held responsible for his own action. The woman, being deceived, was not responsible. There is a further indication within the text why the man was being held responsible for the woman's actions. That is, in the larger context of the Pentateuch (e.g., Nu 30:1–16), the Mosaic Law teaches that the husband is responsible for those vows which his wife has made (see comments below on Nu 30:1–6). The author of the Pentateuch allows the reader's knowledge of the Mosaic Law to guide the reading of this passage. In Numbers 30, if the husband hears his wife make a vow and does not speak out, he is responsible for it. It may be important, then, that the author states specifically in Genesis 3 that the man was with his wife when she ate of the tree, and that he said nothing in reply to the serpent or the woman. His silence may be a clue as to why the man must bear the responsibility for the actions of his wife.

2. Judgment (3:8–20)

a. The Scene (3:8)

The judgment scene opens with the "sound" of the Lord's coming (3:8). Again the author's depiction of the scene is ironic. The expression "the sound of the LORD God" is common in the Pentateuch, especially in Deuteronomy (5:25; 8:20; 13:19; 15:5; 18:16; 26:14; 27:10; 28:1, 2, 15, 45, 62; 30:8, 10), where along with the verb שָׁמַע (hear/obey) and the preposition בְּ, it is the common form of expression for the Lord's call to obedience. It can hardly be without purpose that the author opens the scene of the curse with a subtle but painful reminder of the single requirement for obtaining God's blessing: "to hear/obey the voice of the LORD God."

The coming of the Lord at the mountain of Sinai is also foreshadowed in this scene of the Lord God's coming to the first disobedient couple. When the Lord came to Sinai (Dt 5:25; 18:16; cf. Ex 20:18–21), the people "heard the sound of the LORD God." The response of Adam in the Garden was much the same as that of Israel at the foot of Sinai. When the people heard the sound of the Lord at Sinai they were afraid "and fled and stood at a great distance and said . . . 'let not God speak with us lest we die'" (Ex 20:18–19). So also Adam and his wife fled at the first sound of the Lord in the Garden. Not only is the Fall a prototype of all sins, but also the failure of Israel at Sinai is cast as a replica of this first sin.

The time of the Lord's visit is often translated as "the cool of the day" or "the time of the evening," but the text reads only "at the wind of the day." Indeed, nothing in the context suggests that this refers to a time of day. In the light of the general context of the picture of God's coming in judgment and power, the "wind" which the author envisions is more likely intended to resemble that "great and powerful wind" which blew on the "mountain of the LORD" in 1 Kings 19:11. Thus the viewpoint of the narrative would be much the same as that in Job 38:1, where the Lord answered Job "from the whirlwind."[35] It is significant that the author calls attention to the hiding place: they fled to the trees. Throughout this chapter and the previous ones, the trees play a central role in depicting humanity's changing relationship with God. First, in chapters 1 and 2, the fruit trees were the sign of God's bountiful provision. Then, at the beginning of chapter 3, the trees became the ground for inciting the man and the woman to rebellion and the place where the rebellious man and woman sought to hide

---

[35]So Rambam, *The Commentary of Rambam on the Torah* (Hebrew), ed. H. D. Shual (Jerusalem: Mossad Harav Kook, 1984), 40.

from God. Finally, when the man and the woman are cast out of the Garden, their way is barred from the Tree of Life (3:24). The full sense of this focus on the trees should perhaps be understood in the light of the role of the tree as the place of the punishment of death (Dt 21:22–23) and also in the light of the later role of the tree as the place of the gift of life (Gal 3:13).

b. Trial (3:9–13)

Before meting out the judgment, God's only words to the rebellious man and woman come in the form of questions: "Where are you?" (3:9); "Who told you that you were naked? Have you eaten from the tree?" (v. 11); "What is this you have done?" (v. 13). The picture of God's questioning before his act of judgment suggests the proceedings of a court session much like that of 4:9–10: "Where is your brother Abel? . . . What have you done? Your brother's blood cries out to me from the ground"; and 18:21: "I will go down and see whether what they have done is as bad as the outcry that has reached me." Skillfully, by the repetition of the word *naked* (3:7, 10, 11), the author allows the man to be convicted with his own words: "I was afraid because I was naked." Then, as though to show that alienation between the man and the woman went far beyond the shame that each now felt in the presence of the other, the author recounts the petty attempt on the man's part to cast blame on the woman ("she gave to me") and, obliquely, on God ("whom you gave to me"). The man's words are an ironic reminder of God's original intention: "It is not good that man should be alone. I will make a helper, fit for him" (2:18). As an index of the extent of humanity's fall, the author shows that the man saw God's good gift as the source of his trouble.

c. Verdict (3:14–20)

Although much can be said about the curse on the snake, the woman, and the man, it is important to note that the text says very little. In this passage we can see most clearly the artful composition that produced the Pentateuch. There are no long discourses on the appearance of the snake before and after the curse. Did he have feet? Did he have wings? The thoughts of the snake, if there were such, or the thoughts of the man and woman are left completely out of view. The narrative gives nothing to help us understand their plight as individuals. The snake, the woman, and the man are not depicted as individuals involved in a personal crisis; rather, they are representatives. We are left with the impression that this is not their story so much as it is our story, the story of humankind. With great skill the author has presented these three participants as the heads of their race. The snake on the one hand and the man and the woman on the other are as two great nations embarking on a great struggle, a struggle that will find its conclusion only by an act of some distant and as yet unidentified "seed."

Whereas once the snake was "crafty," now he was "cursed." His "curse" distinguished him "from all the livestock and wild animals," that is, he must "walk upon his belly and eat dust all the days of his life." This curse does not necessarily suggest that the snake had previously walked with feet and legs as the other land animals. The point is rather that now and for the rest of his life, as a result of the curse, when the snake walks on his belly, as snakes do, he will "eat the dust." This expression elsewhere carries the meaning of "total defeat" (cf. Isa 65:25 and Mic 7:17). The curse of the snake, then, as a result of his part in the Fall, is to be the perennial reminder of the ultimate defeat of the rebellious "seed." So strongly was this imagery of the snake's defeat felt by later biblical writers that in their description of the ultimate victory and reign of the righteous "seed," when peace and harmony are restored to creation, the serpent remains under the curse: "dust will [still] be the serpent's food" (Isa 65:25).

As representatives, the snake and the woman embody the fate of their seed, and the fate of their seed is their fate as well. The author has brought about this headship of the snake and the woman by means of a careful but consistent identification of the snake and his "seed." At first in verse 15 the "enmity" is said to have been put between the snake and the woman and between the "seed" of the snake and the "seed" of the woman. But the second half of verse 15 states that the "seed" of the woman ("he") will crush the head of the snake ("your head"). The woman's "seed" is certainly intended to be understood as a group (or individual) which lies the same temporal distance from the woman as the "seed" of the snake does from the snake itself. Yet in this verse, it is the "seed" of the woman who crushes the head of the snake. Though the "enmity" may lie between the two "seeds," the goal of the final crushing blow is not the "seed" of the snake but rather the snake itself—his head will be crushed. In other words, it appears that the author is intent on treating the snake and his "seed" together, as one. What happens to his "seed" in the distant future can be said to happen to the snake as well. This identification suggests that the author views the snake in terms that extend beyond this particular snake of the Garden. The snake, for the author, is representative of someone or something else, and is represented by his "seed." When that "seed" is crushed, the head of the snake is crushed.

Consequently, more is at stake in this brief passage than the reader is at first aware. A program is set forth. A plot is established that will take the author far beyond this or that snake and his "seed." It is what the snake and his "seed" represent that lies at the center of the author's focus. With that "one" lies the "enmity" that must be crushed.

No attempt is made to answer the ancillary question of the snake's role in the temptation over against the role of a higher being (e.g., Satan). This was, however, the drama which later biblical writers saw behind the deed of the snake (cf. Ro 16:20; Rev 12:9, "That ancient serpent called the devil, or Satan, who leads the whole world astray"). From what has been said, such a reading of this passage does not lie outside the narrative implications of the verse. We must mark the fact that in the last analysis the reader is left with only the words of the Lord to the snake. It is unlikely that at such a pivotal point in the narrative the author would intend no more than a mere reference to snakes and their offspring and the fear of them among humankind.

If one looks at the passage within the larger scope of the purpose of the Pentateuch and the pains taken by the author to construct a whole narrative out of just these small segments of discourse, much more appears to lie in these words (the Lord's first spoken words after the Fall). In the light of the fact that such programmatic discourses are strategically important throughout the remainder of the book, it seems likely that the author intends these words to be read as programmatic and foundational for the establishment of the plot and characterization of the remainder of the book. In the narrative to follow, there is to be war ("enmity"). The two sides are represented by two seeds, the "seed" of the snake and the "seed" of the woman. In the ensuing battle, the "seed" of the woman will crush the head of the snake. Though wounded in the struggle, the woman's "seed" will be victorious.

There remains in this verse a puzzling yet important ambiguity: Who is the "seed" of the woman? It seems obvious that the purpose of verse 15 has not been to answer that question, but rather to raise it. The remainder of the book is, in fact, the author's answer.

The judgment against the woman (3:16) relates first to her children and then to her husband. She would now bear children in increased pain or toil. Her "desire" will be for her husband and he will "rule over" her. The sense of this judgment within the larger context of the book lies in the role of the woman which is portrayed in chapters 1 and 2. The woman and her husband were to have enjoyed the blessing of children (1:28) and the harmonious partnership of marriage (2:18, 21–25). The judgment relates precisely to these two aspects of the blessing. What the woman once was to do as a blessing—that is, have children and be a marriage partner, had now become tainted by the curse. In those moments of life's greatest blessing, children and marriage, the woman would now sense most clearly the painful consequences of her rebellion from God.

We should not overlook the relationship between the promise of verse 15 and these words to the woman. In that promise, the final victory was to be through the "seed" of the woman. In the beginning, when the man and the woman were created, childbirth was at the center of the blessing which their Creator had bestowed upon them ("Be fruitful, multiply, and fill the land," 1:28). Now, after the Fall, childbirth is again to be the means through which the snake would be defeated and the blessing restored. The pain of the birth of every child was to be a reminder of the hope that lay in God's promise. Birth pangs are not merely a reminder of the futility of the Fall; they are as well a sign of an impending joy: "We know that the whole creation has been groaning as in the pains of childbirth right up to the present time. Not only so, but we ourselves, who have the firstfruits of the Spirit, groan inwardly as we wait eagerly for our adoption as children, the redemption of our bodies. For in this hope we were saved" (Ro 8:22–24); cf. Mt 24:8).

As the man's judgment, the "good land" provided by the Creator in the narrative of chapters 1 and 2 was cursed (3:17–20). He could no longer "freely eat" of the produce of the land. Throughout chapters 2 and 3, the author has carefully monitored the man's ongoing relationship with his Creator by means of the theme of eating. At first, God's blessing and provision for the man are noted in the words: "from all the trees of the garden you may freely eat" (2:16), recalling the good gifts in chapter 1 and the pronouncement that all was then "very good" (1:31). Then, in chapter 3, it was precisely over the issue of "eating" that the tempter raised doubts about God's ultimate goodness and care for the man and his wife (3:1–3). Finally, the man and the woman's act of disobedience in chapter 3 is simply though thoughtfully described as "she ate it . . . and he ate it." It is not surprising, then, that the author calls attention to precisely the aspect of eating in his description of the judgment on the man: "Cursed is the ground because of you; in pain you will eat all the days of your life" (3:17). Such a focus on eating, which seems to dominate the author's depiction of the Fall, is connected with the author's interest elsewhere in the importance of eating and its association with humankind's relationship to God, that is, in the Torah's teaching regarding the clean and the unclean food (Lev 11; Dt 14) and the regulations for annual feasts to celebrate God's gift of the good land in the covenant (Lev 23). To this material one could also add the larger context of the role of feasts and eating in the biblical eschaton (Rev 19:9).

The description of the "land" in verse 18 ("you shall eat of the shrub of the field") is a reversal of the state of the land as it was described in chapter 2: "no shrub of the field had yet appeared on the land, and no plant of the field had yet sprung up" (2:5). In drawing a contrast between the condition of the land before and after the Fall, the author shows that the present condition of the land was not the way it was intended to be. Rather, the state of the land was the result of human rebellion. In so doing, the author has paved the way for a central motif in the structure of biblical eschatology, the hope of a "new heaven and a new earth" (cf. Isa 65:17; Ro 8:22–24; Rev 21:1).

Just as verse 18 was intended to show the reversal of the state of the land before and after the Fall, so verse 19 intends to show the same for the condition of human beings themselves. Before the Fall, the man was taken from the ground and given the "breath of life" (2:7). As a result of the Fall, however, the man must return to the ground and to the dust from which he was taken (3:19). The author's point in showing such a reversal is to stress that the verdict of death, of which the man was warned before the Fall (2:17), had now come upon him. As a perennial reminder of the effect of the Fall, the author draws a connection between the man's name (אָדָם) and the ground (אֲדָמָה) from which he was taken. The man, Adam, curiously enough named his wife Eve (חַוָּה), "because she was the mother of all living [חַי]" (3:20). This was the second time Adam had named his wife (cf. 2:23). The first name given to her pointed to her origin ("out of man"), whereas her second name pointed to her destiny ("the mother of all living").

3. God's Protection (3:21)

In striking contrast to God's rest from work in chapter 2, immediately after the statement of God's judgment the author returns to the description of God at work: "And the LORD God made for the man and his wife a tunic of skin and he clothed them." After, and because of, the Fall, there is more work to be done. The author characterize that work as "covering the nakedness" of the man and the woman. The mention of the type of clothing which God made—a "skin [עוֹר] tunic"—is perhaps intended to recall the state of the man and the woman before the Fall: "they were naked [עֲרוּמִּים] and not ashamed" (2:25). The author may also be anticipating the notion of sacrifice in the slaying of the animals for the making of the skin tunics, though he has given no clues of this meaning in the narrative itself.

Later in the Pentateuch the Lord instructed the people to make tunics for the priests who were to enter into the presence of God at the tabernacle. The purpose of the tunics was to cover the priests' nakedness (עֶרְוָה), lest they incur guilt and die (Ex 28:42). The author may be anticipating this "lasting ordinance" (Ex 28:43) in drawing our attention to God's covering the nakedness of the man and the woman. In this way the role of the priests, developed later in the Pentateuch, is foreshadowed by God's work in ages past—his work of restoring to humanity the blessing of his presence and fellowship.

In addition to the above points, there are other important links between this text and the later purity laws in the Pentateuch (see comments below on Lev 13:1–14:57 for a discussion).

4. The Exile (3:22–24)

The verdict of death now brought against the man and the woman consisted of their being cast out of the Garden and barred from access to the Tree of Life. The penalty is identical to that established by the Mosaic Law: to be put to death ("he shall surely die") is to be "cast off from the midst of one's people" (Ex 31:14). In this sense, the transgression of Adam and Eve means that they must be cast off from the protective presence of the community in the Garden (cf. Ge 4:14).

The depiction of the man and woman being cast out of the Garden has an interesting parallel with the casting out of the one plagued with skin disease in Leviticus 13:46. This parallel is part of a larger strategy within the Pentateuch of depicting the Fall as a form of contamination that must be dealt with along lines similar to the cultic regulations described in Leviticus (see comments below on Lev 13:1–14:57).

The author uses irony to show the folly of humanity's fall. He shows that even though the human quest to "be like God" (3:5–7) was obtained, the goal itself proved to be undesirable. The man and the woman, who had been created "like God" in the beginning (1:26), found themselves, after the Fall, curiously "like God"—but no longer "with God" in the Garden. In this subtle verbal interchange the author has shown that human happiness does not consist in being "like God" but rather being "with God," enjoying the blessings of his presence: "You have made known to me the path of life; you will fill me with joy in your presence, with eternal pleasures at your right hand" (Ps 16:11 [MT 12]).

In order to underscore the reversals which the man and the woman suffered in their rebellion, the author uses a wordplay on two key terms from his earlier depiction of humankind's blessing in the Garden. In 2:15 the man was put into the Garden for "worship" (עבד) and "obedience" (שמר), but here in 3:23, after the Fall, the man was cast out of the Garden "to work [עבד] the ground" and he is "kept [שמר] from the way of the Tree of Life."

In his depiction of the Garden and the Tree of Life after the Fall, the author has again anticipated God's plan to restore human blessing and life in the covenant at Sinai and the Torah. The Tree of Life stands guarded by the "cherubim" (3:24), just as in the Sinai covenant the Torah lies in the ark of the covenant guarded by the "cherubim" (Ex 25:10–22; Dt 31:24–26). Only through the covenant can human fellowship with God be restored: "There, above the cover between the two cherubim that are over the ark of the testimony, I will meet with you and give you all my commands for the Israelites" (Ex 25:22). In the covenant, human beings returned to the state they enjoyed in Genesis 2:15—serving God, obeying his will, and enjoying his blessing.

The author's mention of the direction "eastward" is not a mere geographical detail. Throughout Genesis, the author carefully apprises the reader of the direction of the characters' movement. In doing so, he plants a narrative clue to the meaning of the events he is recounting. At this point in the narrative, "eastward" has only the significance of "outside the garden." Later in the book, however, the author will carry this significance further by showing "eastward" to be the direction of the "city of Babylon" (11:2) and the "cities of Sodom and Gomorrah" (13:11). Moreover, he will show that to return from the east is to return to the Promised Land and to return to the "city of Salem" (14:17–20).

5. Life in Exile (4:1–26)

In chapter 4 the author has given a brief glimpse of life outside the Garden of Eden. The woman bore sons (cf. 3:16), and the sons became both workers of the ground (cf. 3:23) and tenders of sheep. Thus the narrative assumes the effects of the Fall recorded in chapter 3 ("by the sweat of your face you shall eat food"). The chapter is framed by the accounts of the births of Adam's sons at the beginning (4:1–2), in the center (4:17–22), and at the conclusion (4:25–26). The many diverse events included within the small space of the chapter give it an appearance of being a transition and staging narrative connecting the preceding events to those that are to follow. On the basis of Jude 11 ("Woe to them. They have taken the way of Cain") and Hebrews 11:4 ("By faith Abel offered God a better sacrifice than Cain"), Cain has often been taken as a type of a godless humanity and Abel as a type of the spiritual humanity.[36] Though there is no doubt truth in seeing both Cain and Abel as narrative examples of godlessness and godliness, there are hints in the text that the author also sees in Cain an example of repentance and forgiveness. The central question in the narrative is the meaning of Cain's words in 4:13 (see discussion below). If his words are to be understood as an expression of remorse and repentance, then Cain's city (4:17) and the line of Cain's descendants (4:17–24) are cast in a new light.

a. The First Worship (4:1–8)

Eve's first words after the Fall raise many questions. The translation "With the help of the LORD I have brought forth [or acquired] a man" leaves the impression that her words are positive. Her acknowledging God's help makes it look as though she were hopeful that the promise of a "seed" to crush the head of the serpent (3:15) might find its fulfillment in this son. But her words can also be read in a less positive light: "I have created a man equally with the Lord." In this sense, Eve's words are a boast that just as the Lord had created a man, so now she also had created a man.[37]

The immediate context offers little help to decide between two such diverse readings of the passage. Two considerations, however, suggest that the latter interpretation is more likely. First, throughout the narratives of Genesis, a recurring theme is that of the attempt and failure of human effort in obtaining a blessing that only God can give. God continually promised a

---

[36]Cf. the Scofield Bible, p. 8, nn. 3–4: "Cain is a type of the mere man of the earth . . . Abel is a type of the spiritual man"; and Augustine: "Cain then was the first-born . . . who belonged to the city of men; Abel . . . belonged to the city of God" (*The City of God Against the Pagans*, Loeb Classical Library, ed. Philip Levine [Cambridge: Harvard Univ. Press, 1966], 4:413).

[37]See Cassuto, *Genesis*, 1:201.

person a blessing, and that person pushed it aside in favor of his or her own attempts at the blessing. The story of the building of Babylon (chap. 11) is the most familiar of such narratives. In particular, Eve's situation brings to mind that of Sarah's attempt to achieve the blessing through her handmaiden Hagar. Just as Sarah had tried to bring about the fulfillment of God's promised "seed" (16:1–4) on her own, so also Eve's words expressed her confidence in her own ability to fulfill the promise of 3:15.

The second consideration is Eve's later words about the birth of Seth ("God has granted me another seed in place of Abel," 4:25), which shed a great deal of light on her words in 4:1. The contrast between her words at the beginning of the narrative and those at the close is striking and revealing. At the beginning Eve said, "I have begotten a man," whereas at the close of the narrative she acknowledged, "God has given me another seed." Moreover, Eve did not say that Seth was given to replace Cain—he was to replace Abel. This suggests that within the story Eve had not placed her hope in Cain but in Abel. True to the plot of the remaining narratives in Genesis, Cain, the older son, did not stand to inherit the blessing; rather, the younger son was to inherit the blessing. Also true to the plot of the remaining narratives, God himself provided the other "seed" through yet another younger son.

In view of the parallels between the previous scene (3:21–24) and the worship of God in the Sinai covenant (see above), it is appropriate that the author has turned immediately to the question of God's acceptance of the offering and worship of Cain and his brother. The author's purpose is apparently to use the narrative of Cain and Abel to teach a lesson on the kind of worship that is pleasing to God. Worship that pleases God is that which springs from a pure heart. How does the narrative teach a lesson about a pure heart? It does so by allowing the reader to see, behind the scenes, the *response* of Cain to God's rejection. In that response, we see the heart that lay behind the unaccepted offering; Cain's worship was not acceptable, whereas Abel's worship was. The author does not explicitly draw out the difference between the two offerings. Contrary to the popular opinion that Cain's offering was not accepted because it was not a blood sacrifice, it seems clear from the narrative that both offerings, in themselves, were appropriate— both were described as "offerings" and not "sacrifices"; hence, Cain, a farmer, had no need to shed blood in his gift to God. The narrative suggests, as well, that they were both "firstfruits" offerings (4:4); thus, as a farmer, Cain's offering of "fruits of the soil" was as appropriate for his occupation as Abel's "firstborn of his flocks" was for his occupation as a shepherd. Rather than attempting to discover what was wrong with Cain's offering, we would be better advised simply to note that the author omitted any explanation. He is apparently less concerned about Cain's offering than he is about Cain's response to the Lord's rejection of his offering. At least, that is what the author focuses on. Whatever the cause of God's rejection of Cain's offering, the narrative itself focuses our attention on Cain's response. It is there that the narrative seeks to make its point.

Cain's response was twofold: (1) anger against God (4:4b), and (2) anger against his brother (4:8). By stating the problem in this way, the author surrounds his lesson on pleasing offerings with a subtle narrative warning: "by their fruits you shall know them" (Mt 7:20). In portraying the importance of a pure heart in worship, the author is close to the ideas expressed by Jeremiah against the hypocritical worshipers in his day. Just as Jeremiah pleaded with his people "to do well [אִם־הֵיטֵיב תֵּיטִיבוּ] and not shed innocent blood" lest they be exiled from their land (Jer 7:5–7), so God pleaded with Cain to "do well" (אִם־תֵּיטִיב) or face the consequences of shedding innocent blood and exile from the land (Ge 4:7–12).

It is possible that the author intends the present narrative to be read in the light of the Deuteronomic legislation of the "cities of refuge." The terse description of Cain's offense against Abel is similar to the description of an intentional homicide in Deuteronomy 19:11. The similarity appears to play into the author's purpose. The purpose of the cities of refuge was to insure that "innocent blood not be shed in the land" (Dt 19:10). That, of course, is the central point of the Cain and Abel narrative: "The voice of your brother's blood is crying out to me from the ground" (4:10). In setting out the types of offenses for which the "cities of refuge" were to be used, Deuteronomy 19:11 specified that a guilty murderer was one who "lies in wait for his neighbor and rises up [וְקָם] against him and slays him." The narrative of Genesis 4 states that "while they were in the field, Cain rose up [וַיָּקָם] against Abel and slew him" (4:8). According to the law in Deuteronomy, Cain's offense was punishable by death, though, of course, he would still have had recourse to the cities of refuge. In any event, the fact that God showed mercy on Cain and the fact that later in the story God's mercy was connected with Cain's building a city suggest that a more than coincidental relationship exists between the story of Cain and the later Deuteronomic legislation dealing with the cities of refuge. The narrative may be suggesting not only that Cain's offense was punishable by death but also that the city which Cain built (4:17) was a prototype of the cities of refuge.

b. Repentance (4:9–14)

Again, as in chapter 3, when the Lord came in judgment, he first asked questions ("Where is Abel you brother?" "What have your done?"), then meted out the punishment ("Cursed are you from the ground. . . . When you work the ground it will no longer give its strength to you; you will wander to and fro over the land"). The picture of Cain's judgment is remarkably similar to the Exile that Israel was warned of in Deuteronomy: "Cursed are you in the city and cursed are you in the field. Your basket and your kneading trough will be cursed. The fruit of your womb will be cursed, and the crops of your land, and the calves of your herds and the lambs of your flocks" (Dt 28:16–19).

The imagery of God's judgment against Cain appears to have become a metaphor to the prophets (Isa 26:21) in picturing the judgment of God against Israel in the Exile: "See, the LORD is coming out of his dwelling to punish the people of the land for their sins. The land will disclose the blood shed upon her; she will conceal her slain no longer." It should be noted that Isaiah 27:1–5 continues with images drawn from the early chapters of Genesis: of God's final victory over the "snake" and God's watchful care over his "fruitful vineyard" where no "briers and thorns" are allowed to grow.

The meaning of this passage turns on how we understand Cain's reply in verse 13. Did Cain complain that his "punishment" was too great to bear? Or should we understand his reply to be that his "iniquity" was too great to forgive? Although most English versions read "my punishment is too great to bear," the sense of the Hebrew word עוֹן and the Lord's response to Cain's words in verse 15 suggest that Cain's words are not to be understood as a complaint about his punishment but rather an expression of remorse over the extent of his "iniquity."[38] Cain acknowledged that God's punishment (v. 12) would result in his own death, since he would not have the protection of an established community (v. 14). Like his parents, Adam and Eve, who were driven out (3:24) of their home, the penalty of death was to be carried out against Cain by banishment (4:14) from a protective community: "Today you have driven me from the land, and I will be hidden from your presence; I will be a restless wanderer on the earth and whoever [or whatever] finds me will kill me." By themselves Cain's words do not necessarily suggest repentance, but the Lord's response of mercy and protection ("Very well, anyone who kills Cain will be avenged seven times," v. 15) implies that Cain's words in verse 13 are indeed words of repentance.

c. Divine Protection (4:15–24)

The major issues at stake in this narrative seem identical to those that lie behind the narrative of the cities of refuge (Nu 35:9–34). In both narratives God provides a protection against the "avenger of blood." The question was not first whether one was actually guilty of the crime of murder—that could be settled by due process (Nu 35:12). The more basic question lying behind Cain's statement and the provision of the cities of refuge was the protection of the accused against the threat of a blood avenger. In both narratives God's provision was intended to put an end to the further bloodshed that even an unintentional killing engenders: "Bloodshed pollutes the land" (Nu 35:33).

The background of the cities of refuge may provide a clue to the sense of the "sign" given to Cain in this passage. It is clear that the purpose of the sign was to provide Cain with protection from vengeance. It is often said that the "sign" was put "on" Cain (cf. English versions), though the passage states that the sign was given "to" or "for" Cain (cf. Ge 21:13, 18; 27:37; 45:7, 9; 46:3 with 21:14; 44:21).

What was the "sign" given to Cain for his protection? Though the narrative does not explicitly identify the sign,[39] we should note that after the mention of the sign, the narrative continues with an account of Cain's departure to the land of Nod, "east of Eden," where he built a city. In view of the parallels with those texts relating to the cities of refuge, it may be significant that in this text the "sign narrative" is followed by the "city narrative." In the present shape of the text, Cain's city may have been intended as the "sign" which gave divine protection to Cain. One element of the narrative that seems to be in favor of such a reading is that, within the narrative itself, the purpose of the "sign" was to provide protection for Cain from anyone who might attempt to avenge Abel's death. Such was the express goal of the cities of refuge ("They will be places of refuge from the avenger, so that a person accused of murder may not die before he stands

---

[38]See Cassuto, Genesis, 1:222.

[39]Many attempts have been made to identify the sign, e.g., a dog, a bright colored coat, a horn on his forehead; see L. Diestel, Geschichte des Alten Testaments in der christliche Kirche (Jena: Mauke's Verlag, 1869), 497.

trial before the assembly," Nu 35:12). The subsequent narrative testifies to the association of Cain's sign and the cities of refuge in that even in Lamech's day (vv. 23–24) Cain's city was a place of refuge for the "manslayer" (see comments below). Thus within the narrative as a whole, Cain's city may be viewed as a city of refuge given him by God to protect him and his descendants from blood revenge (see Dt 19:11–13).

The importance which the author attaches to the city which Cain built can be seen in the fact that the remainder of the chapter is devoted to the culture which developed in the context of that city. In verses 20–24 the author names the originators of the primary components of city life: agriculture (Jabal, v. 20), arts (Jubal, v. 21), craftsmanship (Tubal-Cain, v. 22), and, it appears, law (Lamech, vv. 23–24).

Lamech's words to his two wives have been interpreted many ways, frequently as an example of boasting arrogance and rebellion. When read in the context of the Mosaic Law and of the teaching regarding the cities of refuge, however, Lamech's words appear to be an appeal to a system of legal justice.[40] The Mosaic Law provided for the safe refuge of any "manslayer" until a just trial could be held (Nu 35:12). By referring to the "avenging of Cain," Lamech made it known that in his city he too had been "avenged." To show that he had not shed innocent blood Lamech appealed to the fact that he killed a man "for wounding" him. He did not "hate his neighbor and lie in wait for him and rise up against him and kill him" (Dt 19:11) as Cain had done; rather, he based his appeal on a plea of self-defense.

Lamech's appeal to the law of lex talionis bears striking resemblances to the Mosaic Law, which provided for a just penalty on the basis of lex talionis: "an eye for an eye and a tooth for a tooth" (Ex 21:23–25; Lev 24:18–20; Dt 19:21). The classic statement of this principle was given in Exodus 21:23–25, which concludes with the same words used by Lamech: "a wound for a wound and a bruise for a bruise." The purpose of the principle was not to allow for revenge but to prevent it. The force of the principle was to ensure that a given crime was punished only by a just penalty. Like the laws establishing the cities of refuge, the principle of lex talionis was to prevent the escalation of an offense in blood revenge. Thus, Lamech killed a man for wounding him, that is, in self-defense, not because he "hated him" (Dt 19:6). If Cain, who killed his brother with malice, could be avenged, then Lamech would surely be avenged for a killing in self-defense. The point of the narrative is not to show that Lamech's sense of justice was correct or even exemplary. Rather it is to show that Cain's city and descendants had a system of law and justice representative of an ordered society. Not only did his city have agriculture, music, and crafts, it also had an ordered base from which human beings could run their affairs by law. The picture of Lamech is reminiscent of that of many ancient monarchs whose contribution to the peace and order of their realms was epitomized in their legal decisions (e.g., Hammurapi's "Laws").

d. God's Blessing (4:25–26)

The scene at the conclusion of the chapter returns to that of the beginning. A new son is born. Though Cain's sons have prospered and have

---

[40]See my "Genesis," EBC, 2:68.

become the founders of the new world after the Fall, the focus of the narrative turns from the line of Cain to that of the new son born "in the place of Abel." The woman called him Seth (שֵׁת) because, she said, "God has given [שֵׁת] me another seed." In such narratives as these the author clearly betrays his interest in the "seed" (Ge 3:15) of the woman. Chapter 5 shows just how seriously the author takes the promise in 3:15. The focus is on the "seed" and the one who will crush the head of the snake. A pattern is established in chapter 4 that will remain the thematic center of the book. The one through whom the promised seed will come is not the heir apparent, that is, the eldest son, but the one whom God chooses. Abel, the younger of the two sons, received God's favor (4:4); Seth, still the younger son, replaced Abel. Cain takes his place in the narrative as one who was not to become part of the line of the "seed." With him throughout the remainder of the book of Genesis are Japheth (10:2–5), Ham (10:6–20), Nahor (11:29; 22:20–24), Ishmael (17:20), Lot (19:19–38), and Esau (chap. 36).

To underscore the importance of the line of Seth, the author notes that in his days humankind already practiced true worship of the God of the covenant ("At that time people began to call on the name of the LORD," 4:26). Such a note is a sign that, for the author, the worship of the Lord established at the time of Moses was not something new, but rather a restoration of the worship of the only and true God. In the light of such statements in the Pentateuch as Deuteronomy 31:27–29, which focus on the failure of the people to worship properly the God of the covenant, it is remarkable that the author not take a similar view of the patriarchs before the Flood. At least as far as the line of Seth was concerned, these men, like Abraham after them, are described as true worshipers of the covenant God.

C. Story of Noah (5:1–9:29)

At the beginning of chapter 5 a new heading signals a major break in the narrative: "This is the book of the generations of Adam." This section of narrative, which concludes in 9:29, is built around a list of the descendants of Adam. The list focuses on ten men. The first man is Adam, the last is Noah. The list continues until the death of Noah is recorded (9:29), at which time a new list of the sons of Noah begins (10:1–11:26). The second list ends with the birth of Abraham (11:26). Several narrative passages, varying greatly in size, are interspersed within these lists of names. The largest narrative is the account of the Flood in the days of Noah (6:5–9:19), but there are other important narratives as well: Enoch's translation (5:24), Lamech's naming of Noah (5:29), the sons of God (6:1–4), Noah's drunkenness (9:20–27), Nimrod the mighty hunter (10:8–10), the Philistines (10:14), the division of the land (10:25), and the city of Babylon (11:1–9). The interweaving of bits of narrative and genealogical lists is one of the most characteristic features of the author's narrative technique. Scholars often take the genealogical lists to be mere interludes in the course of events being described in the narratives. A close reading of the text, however, suggests that the author has something more specific in mind in including these lists of names and that they play an important role in shaping the context within which the narratives of the book are to be read.

1. Ten Men of Name (5:1–6:4)

The first question that one must ask is the relationship of chapter 5 to the first four verses of chapter 6. We have taken 6:1–4 to be the epilogue to the list of names in chapter 5. When read with chapter 5 rather than the remainder of chapter 6, these four verses (6:1–4) take on a specific meaning within the narrative. They form a conclusion to the author's list of the sons of Adam, summarizing the main points of the passage before moving on to the story of the Flood. (See discussion on these verses below.)

a. Prologue (5:1–3)

The effect of this prologue on the genealogical list which follows in chapter 5 is striking. The prologue first redirects the reader's attention back to the course of events in the first chapter: the creation of the man and the woman. In so doing, the prologue reiterates the central point of that earlier account: the creation of the man and the woman in the image and likeness of God. Second, the prologue ties chapter 5 together with the preceding verses in chapter 4 (4:25–26) by continuing the pattern of birth and naming. Just as the first parents named their sons (4:25–26), so also in the prologue to chapter 5 God named Adam, and he, in turn, named his son (Seth).

The picture of the first parents and their sons is similar to that of God and Adam. This connection is most readily seen in the fact that God's naming of Adam appears here for the first time in Genesis. It was not a feature of the earlier account of the creation of humankind in chapters 1 and 2. It appears that the author brings it in here specifically to heighten the comparison between 4:25–26 and the role of God in the prologue. In other words, the effect of the prologue is to cast God in the role of a father, who has named Adam as his son.

Third, the role of God as a father is heightened even further by the parallels between his creating Adam "in the image of God" and Adam's begetting "[one] in his likeness according to his image" (5:3). The author has gone to great lengths to depict God's creation of humankind in terms of a patriarch establishing and overseeing his family. The motive behind drawing such a parallel lies in the purpose of the list of patriarchs in chapter 5. Not only is Adam the father of Seth and Seth the father of Enosh and so on, but God is the father of them all. If we follow the lines of these genealogical lists throughout the subsequent chapters of Genesis, two important points emerge: (1) God is shown to be the father of all humankind (chap. 10), and (2) God is specifically shown to be the father of Abraham and his seed.

The point of the prologue in 5:1–3 is much the same as that of the Song of Moses in Deuteronomy 32:6. In that song, Moses had addressed a disobedient people with the rebuke, "Is not the one who created you your father?" In view of such a purpose behind the prologue to Genesis 5, it is not surprising that the author should return to the theme of the "sons of God" at the conclusion of this section in 6:1–4.

The author's return to the theme of God's blessing humanity (in Ge 5:2) is also part of his overall scheme to cast God's purposes for humanity in terms that will recall a father's care for his children. Throughout the remainder of the book of Genesis, a recurring theme is that of the father blessing his children (9:26–27; 27:27; 48:15; 49:29). In keeping with such a theme the author shows at each turning point in the narrative that God himself renewed his blessing to the next generation of sons (1:28; 5:1; 9:1; 12:3; 24:11). Seen as a whole, the picture that emerges is that of a loving father insuring the future well-being of his children through the provision of an inherited blessing. In this way the author has laid a theological foundation for the rest of Scripture. God's original plan of blessing for all humankind, though thwarted by human folly, will nevertheless be restored through the seed of the woman (3:15), the seed of Abraham (12:3), and the "Lion of the tribe of Judah" (49:8–12; cf. Rev 5:5–13). It is on this same foundation that Paul built his view of Jesus as the one through whom God has "blessed us" (Eph 1:3) and "adopted us as his sons" (1:5) so that "we also have obtained an inheritance" (1:11) from the one we may call "Abba, Father" (Ro 8:15).

b. Sons of Adam (5:4–32)

The genealogical list in chapter 5 is nearly identical in form to the one in 11:1–26, the genealogy of Shem. A comparison of the formal elements of the two genealogies shows that the only difference between them is the inclusion of the clause "and he died" at the end of each of the names in chapter 5. Why would the author have felt it important to remind the reader specifically of the death of each of these patriarchs, whereas in the other genealogical lists he allows the matter of the individual's death to remain implicit in the statement of the total number of the years of his life? The answer is not hard to find in chapter 5 because in this chapter alone one of the patriarchs, Enoch, did not die. The total number of the years of his life is given, as with the other genealogies, but only here is there an exception. Enoch "was no more, because God took him away" (v. 24). In other words, the author purposefully underscores the death of each patriarch in chapter 5 in order to highlight and focus the reader's attention on the exceptional case of Enoch.

Why does the author want to point to Enoch so specifically as an exception? It is not merely because he did not die. That in itself is reason enough to merit special attention, but it does not sufficiently explain the author's purpose in this case. The author's purpose can better be seen in the way he has emphasized, through repetition, that Enoch "walked with God" vv. 22, 24). The phrase "walked with God" clearly has a special meaning to the author since he uses the same expression to describe Noah as "a righteous man, blameless among the people of his time" (6:9), and Abraham and Isaac as faithful servants of God (17:1; 24:40; 48:15). Its use here shows that the author views it as the reason why Enoch did not die. Enoch is pictured as one who did not suffer the fate of Adam ("you shall surely die") because, unlike the others, he "walked with God."

The sense of the author is clear. Enoch is an example of one who found life amid the curse of death. In Enoch the author is able to show that the pronouncement of death is not the last word that need be said about a person's life. One can find life if one "walks with God." For the author, then, a door is left open for a return to the Tree of Life in the Garden. Enoch found that door in his "walking with God" and in so doing has become a paradigm for all who seek to find life. It is significant that the author returns to this theme at the opening of chapter 17, where God establishes his covenant promise with Abraham. Here the meaning is clear: "walk before me and be perfect, and I will establish my covenant with you" (17:1–2). To "walk with God" is to fulfill one's covenant obligations.

For the author, "walking with God" is the way to life. As Moses tells the people in the wilderness, "See, I set before you today life and blessing, death and destruction. For I command you today to love the LORD your God, to walk in his ways, and to keep his commands . . . and the LORD your God will bless you in the land you are entering to possess" (Dt 30:15–16). It is important to see that for the author of the Pentateuch "walking with God" could not have meant a mere keeping of a set of laws. Rather, it is just with those who could not have had a set of "laws" that the author associates the theme of "walking with God." By choosing such individuals to exemplify "walking with God," the author shows his desire to teach another way to life than merely a legalistic adherence to the Law. We must not lose sight of the fact that from the author's perspective the way of the Law at Sinai has not proved successful (e.g., Dt 31:27). A better way lay still in the future (Dt 30:5–16). For him the way to life is exemplified best in people like Enoch ("he walked with God," 5:22), Noah ("he walked with God," 6:9), and Abraham ("he believed God and he reckoned it to him for righteousness," 15:6). It is to these patriarchs who lived long before the giving of the Law at Sinai that the author turns for a model of faith and trust in God.

The second of the ten patriarchs that the author singles out for special attention is Noah. The genealogical list in chapter 5 has been purposefully restructured at its conclusion in order to accommodate the Flood narrative. The Flood narrative has been inserted into the genealogy between the notation of Noah's age at the time he engendered his three sons and the notation of the total length of his life (9:28) and his death (9:29). As a result the material relating to Noah varies greatly from that of the rest of these early patriarchs.

Two points in particular call for attention. First, in a section that breaks into the formal pattern of the list of names and shows clear affinities with the structure and content of the prologue (5:1–3), we are told that Noah will bring comfort from the labor and painful toil of the curse (5:29). In the light of Genesis 8:21, it is likely that the comfort which Noah brings is the salvation of humankind in the ark as well as the reinstitution of the sacrifice after the Flood. In so doing, Noah averted any future destruction of humankind.

Second, it is then significant that the narrative of the Flood, in which Noah and his family were the sole survivors, is inserted into the genealogical list just before the final word about Noah's death. Thus that final word does not appear until 9:28–29, where it in effect has become a part of the following Table of Nations (10:1–32). The reason for this adjustment of the genealogy of Noah and the insertion of the account of the Flood is clear from the way in which the author has reintroduced part of the genealogy of Noah into the Flood account (6:9–10). The same explanation for Enoch's rescue from death ("he walked with God") is made the basis for Noah's rescue from death in the Flood: "he walked with God" (6:9). Thus in the story of Noah and the Flood, the author is able to repeat the lesson of Enoch: life comes through "walking with God."

At the close of the Flood account, by means of a brief genealogical note, the author appends the story of Noah's drunkenness (9:18–27). It is a strikingly different picture of Noah than that of the Flood account, but it well serves the author's purpose because it provides a basis for the final word he has to give concerning Noah: "and he died" (9:29). In other words, while Noah, along with Enoch, provided a lesson in the way of life that pleases God ("he walked with God"), Noah also provided the opposite lesson. Whatever the actual nature of his conduct might have been (see comments below on 9:18–27), the author presents his deed as one of disgrace and shame ("nakedness," as in Ge 3), and he seems intent on depicting the scene in such a way as to establish parallels between Noah's disgrace (he took of the fruit of his orchard and became naked) and that of Adam and Eve (who took of the fruit of the Garden and saw that they were naked). Having thus depicted Noah, the narrative concludes with the remaining sections of Noah's genealogy and the account of his death (9:28–29).

c. Epilogue (6:1–4)

At the conclusion of the list of patriarchs and before the account of the Flood, the author summarizes the state of affairs of Adam's descendants. (For similar summaries at the close of a genealogical list see Ge 10:31–32; 11:27–32; Ex 1:7.) This short passage has had many diverse interpretations, most of which have arisen out of the viewpoint that these verses introduce the story of the Flood. If the events of these verses are an introduction to the Flood account, then they must be about the wickedness of humankind and the horrendous deeds that caused the Flood (e.g., Calvin: "For, in order to make a transition to the history of the deluge, he prefaces it by declaring the whole world to have been so corrupt, that scarcely anything was left to God, out of the widely spread defection").[41] Such a starting point for reading these verses, then, has led to a number of interpretations of the supposed wickedness depicted in them.

Historically, there have been three primary interpretations. The "sons of God" are (1) angels (the oldest view, e.g., Codex Alexandrinus, an early manuscript of the LXX); (2) royalty (also very old, e.g., Targum Onkelos, though Levy suggests that these may be "angels" in Onkelos;[42] see also Targum Neophyti I: בני דייני, "sons of judges";[43] and (3) pious men from the "line of Seth."[44] The first view has not been widely held since it appears to contradict the statement in Matthew 22:30: "At the resurrection people will neither marry nor be given in marriage; they will be like the angels in heaven." The commonly accepted view is that the "sons of God" refer to the godly, pious line of Seth.[45] All such interpretations, however, originate from the assumption that 6:1–4 is an introduction to the account of the Flood and

---

[41]John Calvin, *Commentaries on the First Book of Moses Called Genesis*, trans. John King (Grand Rapids: Baker, repr. 1979), 237.

[42]*Chaldäisches Wörterbuch über die Targumim*, 2 vols. (Leipzig: Baumgärtner's Buchhandlung, 1881), 2:403.

[43]A marginal reading has "kings," or possibly "angels"; see Alejandro Diez Macho, *Neophyti I Targum Palestinense MS de la Biblioteca Vaticana* (Madrid: Consejo Superior de Investigaciones Cientificas, 1968), 1:33.

[44]L. Diestel, *Geschichte des Alten Testaments in der Kirche* 499.

[45]Calvin: "It was therefore, base ingratitude in the posterity of Seth, to mingle themselves with the children of Cain," *Genesis*, 237; Scofield Bible: "verse 2 marks the breaking down of the separation between the godly line of Seth and the godless line of Cain."

is therefore to be understood as the cause of the Flood. If we read 6:1–4 as a summary of chapter 5, however, there is little to arouse our suspicion that the events recounted are anything out of the ordinary. As a summary of the preceding chapter, this little patch of narrative is a reminder that the sons and daughters of Adam had greatly increased in number, had married, and had continued to have children. The impression it gives is that of an interlude, a calm before the storm. For a brief moment we see a picture of human beings in the midst of their everyday affairs "marrying and giving in marriage, up to the day Noah entered the ark; and they knew nothing about what would happen until the flood came and took them all away" (Mt 24:38–39).

As in 2:24, where the author turned briefly to the theme of marriage before moving on to the account of the Fall, so also in 6:1–4, on the eve of the Flood, the narrative turns briefly again to the theme of marriage. It is interesting to note that the description of the marriages hinges on several key terms already well developed by the author. For example, in the statement that "human beings began to increase [רב] on the face of the earth" (6:1), the author recalls the blessing of God in Genesis 1:28: "be fruitful and multiply [רב]" (cf. Ex 1:7).

What is the meaning of the Lord's statement in verse 3: "My Spirit will not remain in man forever, for he is only flesh, his days will be a hundred and twenty years"? Though the statement is terse and open to several interpretations, its sense is clear if read within the context of what precedes and follows. It is interesting to note that this is the first time the Lord has spoken since 5:2, where, after creating the male and female, "he named them man [Heb. 'ādām]." In that context the term man (Heb. 'ādām) clearly had a wider scope ("humankind") than the personal individual ("Adam") of chapter 4. In the remainder of chapter 5 the focus of the author has been on the lives of individuals again; thus in 5:3 he turned immediately to the genealogy of Adam, the individual. So it is only in 6:3, as God speaks a second time, that the focus of the term man (Heb. 'ādām) is again on humankind as a whole. The point is that between these two statements of God about humankind, the author has put the list of ten great individuals whose length of life stands in stark contrast to the "one hundred and twenty years" of the life of "humankind."

The inference of such an arrangement of the narrative is that it was God's Spirit dwelling with these individuals that gave them their long lives and not their own "flesh" (6:3). The sad reality of the narrative is that such long lives do not belong to humanity as a whole; rather, they belonged to another age. The long lives of the ten great men in chapter 5 are thus shown to be exceptions rather than the rule. Henceforth a person's life would be "one hundred and twenty years" only. Such a short life, in comparison with the long lives of the previous chapter, marks the fall and separation of human beings from their Creator.

In keeping with this point the author continues to show the ages of the descendants of Noah throughout the remainder of the Pentateuch and notes that their ages grow increasingly shorter (cf. 11:10–26). Only at the close of the Pentateuch do we finally reach an individual who died at the age of 120 years, Moses, who was in the wilderness and who died as a result of unbelief and divine punishment (Nu 20)—he died though he was still in good strength (Dt 34:7).

Luther (also Calvin and the Scofield Bible) understood the 120 years to refer to a time of reprieve granted by God to humankind before the sending of the Flood ("I want to give to them yet a reprieve of 120 years," Luther Bible). Such an interpretation is apparently an attempt to resolve the discrepancy between the limit of 120 years put on human life and the record of the length of the human lives in Genesis 11:10–26 that exceeded 120 years (cf. Augustine: "They cannot be taken as foretelling that thereafter men would not live beyond a hundred and twenty years, since we find that after the flood, as before, men lived even beyond five hundred years"),[46] a discrepancy that does not exist in the above interpretation. It may also reflect the influence of 1 Peter 3:20 ("when God waited patiently in the days of Noah while the ark was being built"), which has been taken by many to refer to the period of 120 years in Genesis 6:3.[47] Such an understanding of the 120 years can already be found in Targum Onkelos ("A reprieve will be given to them") and Targum Neophyti I ("Behold, I have given you the space of a hundred and twenty years [hoping that] perhaps they might do repentance and they did not do [it]"), but it is not in the LXX or the Vulgate.

The mention of the "Nephilim," sometimes rendered "giants," ties these verses to the preceding chapter. The author uses the term *Nephilim* elsewhere in the Pentateuch to refer to the great men who were in the land of Canaan at the time of the exodus (Nu 13:32–33). Here in Genesis 6:4 the term *Nephilim* also appears to refer to the great men of antiquity. In the light of the fact that the author has just completed a list of the names of ten great men from antiquity (chap. 5), it is possible that he has these ten men in mind in referring to the "men of name" (6:4). The mention of the Nephilim in Numbers 13:33, however, suggests that they still survived in the days of the Exodus, which would appear to conflict with our taking them as the ten great men of chapter 5.[48]

2. The Flood (6:5–9:19)

The account of the Flood gives every indication of being a carefully wrought and intricately complex narrative. There are seven principal stages in the narrative: (1) the decision to send the Flood and to rescue Noah (6:5–12), (2) the command to build the ark (6:13–22), (3) the command to enter the ark (7:1–5), (4) the floods come (7:6–24), (5) the floods abate (8:1–14), (6) the command to exit the ark (8:15–19), and (7) the building of the altar and the covenant (8:20–9:19). Within each stage the author has arranged a whirling array of activities which catch the reader up in the fury of the Flood and the sense of the impending wrath of God.

It is significant to note how the author guides the readers' participation in the narrative by tightly controlling the point of view from which the story is told. At the beginning of the story, the reader follows the course of events from a divine perspective. We, the readers, are allowed to look down from

---

[46]Augustine, *City of God*, 15.24.

[47]See Gustav Wohlenberg, *Der erste und zeite Petrusbrief und der Judasbrief* (Leipzig: A. Deichert, 1915), 114.

[48]See *EBC*, 2:78–79.

heaven over all the earth and see what the Lord himself sees; we are allowed to listen in on his conversations and to follow his judgments (6:5–7:5). With the onset of the Flood, however, we lose our privileged position. We no longer see what God sees. We see only what the characters of the story themselves see as the heavens pour forth rain and the fountains of the deep break apart. Our perspective as readers is horizontal. The floods rise up around us; we cannot stand alongside God and look down on those in the narrative who are experiencing God's judgment.

As the Flood progresses God becomes strangely absent. Only the waters and those fleeing the waters are kept in narrative view. The author refuses to allow the reader to stand in a neutral corner and watch while God judges the world. We are forced to take sides like those in the narrative itself. Like Lot's wife (19:26), we cannot look on while others experience God's judgment. We are left either to enter the ark with Noah or to remain outside in the Flood. The only glimpse of God we are allowed as the waters of the Flood close in around "all flesh" is his closing the door behind those who have entered the ark (7:16). After 150 days of flood waters (8:1–4), the reader catches a brief glimpse of God's actions (God remembered Noah and sent a wind to dry up the waters); but, here again, we are not allowed to continue to view the rest of the story from such a lofty perspective. Immediately the narrative returns us to the ark where, with Noah, we must wait for the waters to recede and rely only on the return of the raven and the dove sent out through the little window of the ark (8:5–14). Once the dry land has appeared (8:13–22), the reader's perspective returns to that of the Lord in heaven, and we hear and see his point of view again as at the beginning of the story.

a. Introduction (6:5–8)

These verses form the introduction proper to the Flood story. As such they tie the story together with previous narratives and provide the central themes of the narrative to follow. Here and throughout the Flood story the author establishes numerous ties with the Creation account in chapter 1. The effect is to show that the Flood was a reversal of God's good work of Creation. In chapter 1 God is the one who prepared the good land for human beings. In the account of the Flood, God is the one who takes this good land from human beings when they act corruptly and do not walk in his way. The central themes introduced in these opening verses are God's judgment of human wickedness and his gracious salvation of the righteous.

The cause for the Flood is tied directly to the earlier account of the Fall in chapter 3. As a result of the Fall, humankind had obtained the "knowledge of good and evil" (3:22). The previous narratives make clear that the author does not consider humankind's having obtained this knowledge to be beneficial. From the author's perspective, human beings were far better off when they had to trust God for "the good."

One of the ways the author is able to teach this lesson in chapter 1 is through the recurring expression "and God saw that it was good." The central theme of "God's good provisions for humanity" is embodied in the recurring picture of God's "seeing" what is good. After the Fall, when human beings had to find the "good" on their own, what God "sees" (6:5) is not that his creation is good; rather, "the LORD saw that the evil of man was great upon the earth and that all the intentions of his heart are only evil" (6:5).

In verse 6, "The LORD was grieved [נחם] that he had made man on the land and his heart was filled with pain," the author describes the Lord's response to human wickedness by making a curious wordplay on Lamech's naming Noah: "This one will comfort [נחם] us . . . from the painful toil of our hands" (5:29). Thus both passages introduce Noah with wordplays associating his name, Noah (נח), with the "comfort" (נחם) from the grief and pain caused by human rebellion. By making God the subject of the verbs in 6:6, the author has shown that the grief and pain of human sin was not something that only human beings felt. God himself was grieved over human sin. In returning in this way to the role of "comforter" invested in the significance of Noah's name, the author has suggested that Noah brought comfort not only to humankind in their grief but also to God.

Noah alone among all the others "found grace in the eyes of the Lord" (6:8). Here again the narrative makes a play on Noah's name in that the word *grace* (חן) is a reversal of the consonants of the name Noah (נח). The purpose of verse 8 is to say no more than that Noah found favor with God. In the following section (6:9–12) the author explains why God found Noah to be an exception. In that explanation lies the central purpose of the Flood account in the book of Genesis.

b. Noah's Righteousness (6:9–12)

The Flood account begins in verse 9 with the description of Noah's righteousness. It seems clear from the way the author begins the account that the main purpose of the story of the Flood is not to show why God sent a flood but rather to show why God saved Noah. This opening section contrasts Noah's "righteousness" with the "violence" of "all flesh." The message of the narrative is quite straightforward. The reason why God saved Noah is that he "walked with God" and did not "corrupt" God's way. In describing Noah in this way, the author intentionally draws a parallel between the deliverance of Noah from the Flood and Enoch's deliverance from death (5:22–24). The point is clear enough: God delivers those who "walk with" him and who do not "corrupt his way."

As in the account of Enoch's deliverance, here in verses 9 and 10 the author is not specific about the nature of Noah's "righteousness" or what it means to "walk with God." In the following section, however, the author allows the reader to peer more closely into the nature of Noah's righteousness. We are allowed to see him at work. The picture of Noah that emerges from the Flood story thus becomes a model of the kind of life that finds grace in the sight of God. It is a picture of simple obedience to God's commands and trust in his provision. In view of the predominance of the concept of "faith" elsewhere in the Pentateuch[49] it is appropriate to say that the author pictures Noah very much as the writer of Hebrews does: one who "by his faith condemned the world and became heir of the righteousness that comes by faith" (Heb 11:7).

---

[49]See Hans-Christoph Schmidt, "Redaktion des Pentateuch im Geiste der Prophetie, Beobachtungen zur Bedeutung der 'Glaubens'-Thematik innerhalb der Theologie des Pentateuch," *VT* 32/2 (1983): 170–89.

c. Command to Build the Ark (6:13–22)

There are important similarities between the account of the building of the ark and two other narratives in the Pentateuch, viz., the account of Creation in Genesis 1 and the building of the tabernacle in Exodus 25–39. Each account has a discernible pattern: God speaks, an action is commanded (imperative/jussive), and the command is carried out according to God's will. The key to these similarities lies in the observation that each narrative concludes with a divine blessing (Ge 1:28; 9:1; Ex. 39:43) and, in the case of the tabernacle and Noah's ark, a divinely ordained covenant (Ge 6:8; Ex 34:27). In this regard it is of some importance that later biblical tradition also associated the events of Genesis 1–3 with the making of a divine covenant (e.g., Hos 6:7). Like Moses, Noah followed closely the commands of God and in so doing found salvation and blessing in his covenant.

It is not hard to see in these examples the lesson that the author of the Pentateuch intends. He states it directly to the readers in Deuteronomy 30:2–3: "When you and your children return to the LORD your God and obey him with all your heart and with all your soul according to all I command you today, then the LORD your God will restore your captivity and have compassion on you and gather you again from all the nations where he scattered you." The author's purpose in drawing out the list of specifications for the ark in chapter 6, as with the details of the building of the tabernacle, is not that readers might be able to see what the ark or the tabernacle looked like, but rather that readers might appreciate the meticulous care with which these godly and exemplary individuals went about their tasks of obedience to God's will. They obeyed God with "all their hearts."

d. Command to Enter the Ark (7:1–5)

The command to make the ark has been given and followed to its completion (6:22). The next scene opens with the command to enter the ark before the coming rains. This section, which emphasizes the special provisions for the "clean animals" to be taken into the ark, follows the same pattern as the previous one, in which we saw important parallels with the provisions for the building of the tabernacle. It is noteworthy that this narrative of Noah's entering the ark has parallels to the narrative of the provisions for making ready the tabernacle in the wilderness. For example, the narratives emphasize that entry into the ark or the tabernacle is to be accompanied by an animal offering. At the close of the description of the building of the tabernacle (Ex 35–39), when the completion of the tabernacle has been recorded (Ex 39:43), the command is given for it to be set up and readied for use (Ex 40:1–33). When it is readied and the glory of the Lord has filled the tabernacle (Ex 40:34–38), provisions are made for "drawing near" to the tabernacle (Lev 1ff.). One may "draw near" only by bringing an animal offering that is "unblemished" (1:3). Thus just as the completed tabernacle can be entered only with the "unblemished animals" as an offering, so Noah's entry into the ark is tied to his taking with him "seven pairs" of every clean animal.

The specific mention of the "clean animals" which Noah took with him into the ark is perhaps intended to suggest that while in the ark, he ate only "clean meat," as is the requirement in the tabernacle (Lev 7:19–21). Such parallels suggest that the author has intentionally drawn a comparison between the salvation that lies in the ark of Noah during the impending "forty days and forty nights" of rain (7:4) and the salvation in the presence of the tabernacle during the impending "forty years" in the wilderness. Again it is the centrality of the idea of a covenant relationship that lies behind the author's work.

In the light of such parallels it is significant that the author refers directly to the sacrificial importance of these "clean animals" taken into the ark when, at the close of the Flood account, he shows that these animals were in fact to be used for an offering to the Lord (8:20–21). In describing the Lord's acceptance of these offerings (8:21), the author employs the specific terminology used in Leviticus 1:17, and again it is tied to the notion of a covenant (9:8, 11). Such typological shaping of the Flood narrative by the author is remarkably similar to the later reading of this passage in 1 Peter 3:21. In that passage the ark is understood to prefigure the saving work of Christ as it is pictured in NT baptism.

e. The Floods (7:6–24)

Most apparent in the description of the onset of the Flood is the author's focus on the occupants of the ark. With great detail the procession of those entering the ark passes by the impatient eyes of the modern reader. Noah's age, the month and the day of the beginning of the rain, the source of the waters, the kinds of animals and their number—no bit of information is too insignificant if it can contribute to the author's purpose of holding this picture before the reader as long as literarily possible. It is first and foremost this picture of Noah's salvation that the author wants his readers to take a long look at. It is only at the conclusion of chapter 7, when the ark is resting safely over the highest mountains in the surging flood, that the author cast his glance in the direction of those who did not seek refuge in the ark (7:21–23). But even then, the author's attention on those who did not survive the Flood is motivated less by an interest in what happened to them specifically ("they died," 7:22) than by the reason why they perished: "Only Noah and those with him in the ark remained" (7:23).

In the repetitions the author's message comes through most clearly. Thus when the author repeats four times that those who survived the Flood were those who had done "as the LORD had commanded" (6:22; 7:5, 9, 16), his point is clear. Obedience to the will of the Lord is the way to salvation. In the way that Noah is here an example of obedience and salvation, later narrative figures, such as Abraham (Ge 21:4) and the Israelites (Ex 12:28), will be called upon to exhibit the same lesson.

f. The Floods Abate (8:1–14)

While those in the ark may have been safe, they had not yet been saved. The author has not finished his story until Noah and his family are back on dry ground (8:14). But those in the ark must wait ("a hundred and fifty days," 7:24) before God sends his deliverance. Just as the author later passes over the four hundred years that Israel waited in Egypt (Ex 1:7) and then the forty years of waiting in the wilderness (Nu 14:33ff.) in order to focus on God's deliverance, so now the story passes over the time of waiting in the ark and proceeds immediately to the decisive moment when "God remembered Noah and those with him in the ark" (8:1). The description of God's rescue of Noah foreshadows God's deliverance of Israel in the Exodus. Just as God "remembered his covenant" (Ex 2:24) and sent "a strong east wind to dry up the waters before his people" (Ex 14:21) so that they "went through on dry ground" Ex 14:21–22), so also in the story of the Flood we read that God "remembered" those in the ark (8:1) and sent a "wind" (8:1) over the waters so that his people might come out on "dry ground" (8:13–14).

It hardly seems likely that so many verbal and thematic parallels within the Pentateuch could be a mere coincidence. The author of Genesis, who frequently seizes on wordplays (e.g., 11:9) and recounts wordplays within narratives (e.g., 21:6), would not have been unaware of the parallels suggested by his narratives. We must reckon with the fact that the author is deliberately recounting these various events in such a way to highlight their similarity. God's dealings in the past prefigure his work in the present and the future.

Again it is noticeable how the author has prolonged the picture of God's deliverance. God is depicted at work stopping the flow of the waters and removing the sources of the floods (8:2). But it still takes time before Noah can be back on dry land (v. 3). He still has to wait. With this picture of God at work as background, the author turns his attention to Noah inside the ark. The narrative now focuses on the patience of Noah as he waits on God's deliverance. At the end of forty days, Noah began to look for signs of his impending deliverance. He sent out a raven (v. 7) and a dove (vv. 8–12) but no signs of dry land appeared. Noah continued to wait (vv. 10, 12). When the sign of the return of the dry lands finally appeared and the dove did not come back (v. 12), the author reminds us that Noah had waited exactly one year (cf. 7:6, 11 and 8:13–14). But even then Noah could only open the window to look out of the ark. He still had to wait for God's command to go out before leaving the ark (8:15–17).

The image that emerges from this portrait of Noah in the narrative is that of a righteous and faithful remnant (7:23) patiently waiting for God's deliverance. It is a common image in later biblical literature (e.g., Isa 8:17–18; 40:31; James 5:7–11), and its development here in the Flood narrative has contributed greatly to its later use. Henceforth, within the biblical text, "the Flood" is synonymous with eschatological judgment (e.g., Isa 8:7–8), and Noah's deliverance is an image of the salvation of the faithful (e.g., Mt 24:37–39).

g. *Command to Exit the Ark (8:15–19)*

In the same epic style of the description of the entry of the ark (cf. the sentence structure of 7:7–9 with 8:18–19; both are examples of "epic repetition"),[50] the author depicts the exit. He is careful to show that even here Noah left the ark only at God's command (8:15–16). The description, though condensed, follows closely the pattern of Creation in Genesis 1 (e.g., "let them swarm upon the earth and let them be fruitful and multiply upon the earth," 8:17). The picture given is that of a return to the work of Creation "in the beginning." It is significant that right at this point in the narrative the

---

[50]See F. I. Andersen, *The Sentence in Biblical Hebrew*, 39.

author takes up a lengthy account of the covenant (8:20–9:17). The restoration of God's creation was founded on the establishment of a covenant.

There is a striking thematic parallel between the picture of God's calling Noah out of the ark (8:15–20) and the call of Abraham (12:1–7).

Genesis 8:15–20	**Genesis 12:1–7**
a. And God said to Noah (8:15)	a. And God said to Abram (12:1)
b. Go out from the ark (8:16)	b. Go out from your land (12:1)
c. And Noah went out (8:18)	c. And Abram went out (12:4)
d. And Noah built an altar for the LORD (8:20)	d. And Abram built an altar for the LORD (12:7)
e. And God blessed Noah (9:1)	e. "And I [God] will bless you" (12:2)
f. "Be fruitful and multiply" (9:1)	f. "I will make you a great nation" (12:2)
g. "I will establish my covenant with you and your seed" (9:9)	g. "I will give your seed this land" (12:7)

Both Noah and Abraham represent new beginnings in the course of events recorded in Genesis. Both are marked by God's promise of blessing and his gift of the covenant.

h. The Altar and the Covenant (8:20–9:19)

In the account of Noah's altar and the covenant, the author continues his close associations with Genesis 1. As a result of Noah's altar and offering, the state of humankind before the Flood is restored. Human beings are still fallen (9:21), but through an offering on the altar they may yet find God's blessing (8:21–9:3). It is significant that just as in Genesis 1, the focus of the author's interest in human beings after the Flood is their creation in God's image (9:6).

Just as significant as the associations of this passage with the Creation account, however, are the several close associations between Noah's altar and Moses' altar at Mount Sinai following the Exodus (Ex 24:4–18). A brief list of some key parallels gives a sense of the verbal and thematic similarities: (1) The building of the altar in both accounts follows a major act of God's salvation—God's rescue of Noah from the Flood and God's deliverance of the Israelites from bondage in Egypt; (2) the altar and the offering in both accounts mark the establishment of a "covenant" with God (Ge 9:9; Ex 24:7); (3) the outcome of both covenants is God's "blessing" (Ge 9:1; Ex 23:25); (4) the central provisions in both covenants are protection from "wild animals" (Ge 9:2; Ex 23:29) and human enemies (Ge 9:5–6; Ex 23:22); (5) both accounts mention specifically that the "land" will be preserved from destruction (Ge 9:11; Ex 23:29); (6) in Genesis the visible "sign" of the establishment of the covenant is the rainbow in the "clouds" (9:13–17), and in Exodus the conclusion of the covenant making is marked by the appearance of the glory of God in the "clouds" (Ex 24:15) that cover the mountain; (7) both covenants give stipulations which the people must obey (Ge 9:4; Ex 24:3).

These observations suggest that the author intentionally draws out the similarities between God's covenant with Noah and the covenant at Sinai. Why? The answer that best fits with the author's purposes is that he wants to show that God's covenant at Sinai is not a new act of God. The covenant is rather a return to God's original promises. Once again at Sinai, as he had done in the past, God is at work restoring his fellowship with humanity and bringing humanity back to himself. The covenant with Noah plays an important role in the author's development of God's restoration of blessing. It lies midway between God's original blessing of all humankind (1:28) and God's promise to bless "all the families of the earth" through Abraham (12:1–3).

Verses 18 and 19 are the conclusion of the Flood story, but at the same time they form an introduction to the short episode of Noah's drunkenness. These verses are a good example of the author's style of composition throughout Genesis. By means of these short transitional units the author ties together individual, self-contained narratives into a larger line of stories. In this particular transitional unit one should not overlook the identification of Canaan as one of the sons of Ham (9:18). That bit of information is crucial to the meaning of the narrative to follow (cf. 9:22, 25).

3. Noah's Drunkenness (9:20–29)

In placing the story of Noah's drunkenness at this point in the story line, the author continues to follow the plan of casting the Flood narrative as a recursion of the Creation account. Just as in the account of creation in the early chapters of Genesis God planted (וַיִּטַּע, 2:8) a garden for the man and woman to enjoy, so now, as the narrative has returned the reader's attention to the point of God's "blessing" (9:1) and covenant relationship (9:17), the story of Noah picks up again with the planting (וַיִּטַּע, 9:20) of an orchard. The outcome is remarkably similar to the outcome of the story of the Garden of Eden. Noah ate of the fruit of his orchard and became naked. The author's intent is to point to the similarities of Noah and Adam. He wants to show even here, too, after the salvation from the Flood, that human enjoyment of God's good gifts could not be sustained. Like Adam, Noah sinned, and the effects of that sin were to be felt in the generations of sons and daughters to follow. As in chapter 3, the effect of Noah's sin is seen in his "nakedness" (cf. 2:25; 3:7). When read in the context of the events of the Garden of Eden (chap. 3), the allusive details of Noah's drunkenness become quite transparent. In a subtle parody of humanity's original state ("They were both naked and not ashamed," 2:25), Noah in his drunkenness "uncovered himself in his tent."

Ham looked on his father's nakedness but Shem and Japheth did not. Instead, they covered their father's nakedness without looking at him. Many have regarded the actions of the three sons, as this narrative describes them, to be the mere outline of a much more sinister deed. Whatever the details of the actual act might have been, taken at face value the sons' actions suit the author's purpose quite well. He apparently wants to show simply the contrast between the deeds of Ham and those of Shem and Japheth. That contrast becomes the basis for the curse and blessing which follow (9:25–26).

The significance of the contrast between the actions of the sons is seen from the author's account of the fall in chapter 3. In covering their father's nakedness, Shem and Japheth (cf. 2:25; 3:7; 9:23) were like Adam and Eve (3:7) and like God (3:21), who did not look upon human nakedness but covered the nakedness with coats of skin (cf. 2:25). By contrast, Ham did not follow that lead. His actions were more like those of whom God warned later in the Torah, who "expose their own nakedness" before God and human-kind (Ex 20:26; cf. the commentary below on Lev 17:18ff.). So important is this matter to the author of the Torah that he includes among the rules for the priests that they should wear "linen undergarments" as a covering for their "naked flesh" when they go near the presence of God at the altar (Ex 28:42–43). The sons of Noah are here shown to belong to two groups of humankind, those who like Adam and Eve hide the shame of their nakedness and those who like Ham, or rather the Canaanites, have no sense of their shame before God. The one group, the line of Shem, will be blessed (9:26); but the other, the Canaanites (not the Hamites), can only be cursed (9:25).

It is important to see how the author uses these narratives to teach the importance of acknowledging the guilt of one's sin. His point is not simply that all Canaanites were cursed. That would certainly not fit what he later writes about Abraham as the one through whom "all the families of the earth [including the Canaanites] will be blessed" (12:3). Rather, his point is simply that these three sons, as later the "seed of Abraham" and the "nations," represent two responses to human guilt and disobedience. Ultimately, the author will show that simply because one is born into a certain family line does not render one blessed or cursed. In the figure of Abraham, the author will set forth his final case for the way of blessing: "he believed God and righteousness was accounted to him" (15:6).

There are also narrative similarities between the incident in this section of Genesis and the narrative about the punishment of the two sons of Aaron, Nadab and Abihu (see comments below on Lev 10; 13–14).

D. Sons of Noah (10:1–32)

The author's purpose in giving a list of names at this point in the narrative can be seen in the statement at the end of chapter 10: "from them the nations spread out in the land after the flood" (v. 32). These names give the reader a panoramic view of the nations as a backdrop for the remainder of the events in Genesis and the Torah. The list is complex and shows many signs of selection and shaping to fit a pattern. The pattern that emerges is determined by the number seventy. There are exactly seventy nations represented in the list. Thus, like other biblical genealogies,[51] the present list of names owes its shape to a kind of numerical symbolism in which the concept of a totality of nations is expressed in the number seventy. In other words, "all nations" find their ultimate origins in the three sons of Noah. Humanity in its totality is closely circumscribed. The author does not want the reader to lose sight of the unity among human beings.

It is out of this one humanity that Abraham will be called. Though he is

---

[51]E.g., Mt 1: see D. A. Carson, "Matthew," *EBC* (Grand Rapids: Zondervan, 1984), 8:68–69.

on the verge of narrowing his focus to the "seed of Abraham" and the "Israelites," the author first lays a solid foundation for his ultimate purpose in God's choosing Abraham: through his "seed" God's blessing will be restored to "all the families of the earth" (12:3). It is not without purpose that the author reminds his readers that the total number of Abraham's "seed" at the close of Genesis is also "seventy" (46:27; cf. Ex 1:5). Before Abraham, the nations numbered "seventy." After Abraham, at the close of the book, the seed of Abraham numbered "seventy." He who was taken from the nations has reached the number of the nations. Such careful attention to detail suggests that the author of the book has in mind a specific understanding of the role of the "seed" of Abraham. By correlating the number of nations with the number of the seed of Abraham, he holds Abraham's "seed" before the reader as a new humanity and Abraham himself as a kind of second Adam, the "father of many nations" (Ge 17:5). In this chosen "seed" God's original blessing will be restored.

There is, then, much theological reflection behind the shaping of these early sections of Genesis. In Deuteronomy 32:8, Moses alludes to this chapter by saying, "When the Most High gave the nations their inheritance, when he divided all humankind, he set up boundaries for the peoples according to the number of the Israelites" (cf. Paul's view of Abraham in Ro 4:16: "he is the father of us all").

Chapter 10 is not simply a list of seventy names. Throughout the list the author has inserted several historical notes (vv. 8–12, 14, 19, 25) as well. Each of these notes is of special relevance to a particular event yet to be recorded in Genesis. For example, the note about Nimrod and his kingdom in Babylon provides a wider context for the narrative of the "tower of Babel" in the next chapter. By and large the notes focus on those nations which are the subject of God's judgment in the remainder of the book (e.g., Babylon, vv. 8–12; the Philistines, v. 14; the Canaanites, including Sodom and Gomorrah, v. 19).

1. Shem, Ham, and Japheth (10:1)

Chapter 10 is bracketed (vv. 1, 32) with an identification of the list of names as "sons of Noah" and the temporal marker "after the flood." The author is clearly concerned that the list in chapter 10 not be read outside its context within the line of narrative coming out of the Flood. Such conspicuous attention to context is another indication that the author has a plan to unfold in this narrative and that he did not want the reader to lose sight of it.

2. Sons of Japheth (10:2–5)

The list begins with those nations that are considered the "islands of the nations" (v. 5). They are the nations that make up the geographical horizon of the author, the outer fringe of the known world, a kind of third world over against the nations of Ham (Canaan) and Shem. In later biblical literature, when the focus is on the establishment of God's universal kingdom, these nations again come into view to show that the scope of God's plan includes all humankind: "He will rule from sea to sea. . . . The kings of Tarshish and of distant shores will bring tribute to him" (Ps 72:8–10). Already in the Pentateuch, the writer turns his attention to these nations in his view of the future. At the coming of the future king, foretold by Balaam (Nu 24:7ff., 17ff.), these nations will again be included in God's rule (Nu 24:23–24; see commentary below on Nu 24).

A pattern in the author's selection is clearly discernible in the list of the sons of Japheth. Fourteen names are listed in all: seven sons of Japheth (Ge 10:2), then seven grandsons (vv. 3–4). The author has omitted the sons of five of Japheth's seven sons (Magog, Madai, Tubal, Meshech, and Tiras) and lists only the sons of Gomer and Javan (vv. 3–4). Thus his intention is not to give an exhaustive list but rather a representative list, one which, for him, is obtained in the number seven.

3. Sons of Ham (10:6–20)

The author has thoroughly worked over the list of the sons of Ham. It begins in the same way as the list of the sons of Japheth, with the simple naming of Ham's four sons: Cush, Mizraim, Put, and Canaan (v. 6). Then, as also in the Japheth list, he named the grandsons of the first listed (Cush, v. 7a). But before going on to the next son (Mizraim, v. 13), he lists the great-grandsons (sons of Raamah, v. 7b). The result is a list of names that again numbers "seven sons"—thus a complete list. Immediately following these seven names, the author inserts a narrative on the exploits of Nimrod and his cities (vv. 8–12) that breaks into the pattern of sevens that has characterized the lists thus far. The importance of this small narrative lies in its introduction of the city of Babylon, which is the subject of the following chapter (11:1–9). The deliberate association of Assyria with Babylon (10:11–12) is also significant; otherwise, in the lists of names which follow, Assyria is associated with the sons of Shem (10:22). By means of this narrative insertion, then, the author has not only introduced a key city, Babylon, but also has taken Assyria out of its natural associations with Shem and given it a new identification with Babylon (cf. Nu 24:24, where Assyria is again associated with Babylon [Eber]).[52] Thus the author has opened the way for an association and identification of any city with Babylon. These appear to be the initial stirrings of a larger-than-life symbolic value for Babylon, one known in a fully developed sense in the book of Isaiah (cf. chaps. 13–14, where Assyria is identified with Babylon) and fully developed in the image of "Mystery Babylon the Great" in Revelation 17. The prophet Micah could also speak of Assyria as the "land of Nimrod" (Mic 5:6).

The author returns to the genealogy of the sons of Ham with a list of the sons of Mizraim, once again containing seven names (Ge 10:13–14). This is the last list to be shaped by the numerical pattern of seven. The remainder of the lists of names appears to be influenced by no particular numerical pattern except that of the total number of "seventy nations," which dominates the list of names as a whole. Since it is clear that the author of the "list of the sons of Noah" has intentionally worked out a final pattern of seventy names, it is likely that, where it is found, the pattern of the smaller

---

[52]Eber in Nu 24:24 is not the Eber mentioned in Ge 10:24, the descendant of Shem, but rather the Hebrew term meaning "beyond (the river)," hence a reference to Babylon. Cf. Targum Onkelos, "beyond the river." See Franciscus Zorelli, *Lexicon Hebraicum et Aramaicum Veteris Testament* (Rome: Pontificium Institutum Biblicum, 1968), 569.

lists of seven names is also intentional. As with the number seventy, the idea of completeness likely lies behind the number seven. Thus, for those lists which contain seven names, we may conclude that the author intends to give a complete accounting of the sons of that group, without actually listing all the sons. He is, as it were, passing them by without further comment.

With the lists which now occupy the attention of the author (those that do not number in the "sevens," vv. 15–29), however, the focus is more comprehensive because these sons, the Canaanites and the Shemites, play more prominently in the narratives of Genesis and the Pentateuch. The author is especially interested in the exact boundaries of the area of Canaan (v. 19; cf. Nu 34:1–12) since that area of land lay at the heart of his purpose in writing the book. This was the land promised to Abraham, though "the Canaanites were still living in the land" (12:6).

4. Sons of Shem (10:21–31)

The author begins the list of the sons of Shem with a prosaic introduction (10:21). The purpose of the introduction is to draw out the major lines of continuity running through chapter 10. The author calls attention to the relationship of Shem and Japheth ("Shem, the brother of Japheth, the elder"), and the relationship of Shem to the following generations ("he is the father of the sons of Eber"). The reference to Shem and Japheth together without Ham may be significant, possibly intended to recall Noah's blessing of Shem and Japheth in 9:26–27, where Canaan is also excluded. If so, it is another reminder of the ways in which the author uses allusions to past narratives to retain the reader's focus on the major points of the narrative— in this case, the line of the blessing. The mention of the "sons of Eber" anticipates the genealogy that lies ahead, that one which results in the birth of Abraham (11:10–26; cf. Nu 24:24). So, before moving on to complete the list of the sons of Noah, the author inserts this short summary to tie the list to the preceding and following narrative contexts.

The list of descendants of Shem is also highly selective, though it does not follow any particular numerical scheme, as the earlier lists do. Rather, the line of Shem is traced up to the two sons of Eber, and there continues to follow the line of the second son, Joktan (10:26–29). It is significant that another genealogy of Shem is repeated after the account of the building of Babylon (11:1–9), and there the line is continued to Abraham through the first son of Eber, Peleg (11:10–26). In arranging the genealogy of Shem in this way, the author draws a dividing line through the descendants of Shem on either side of the city of Babylon. The dividing line falls between the two sons of Eber, that is, Peleg and Joktan. One line leads to the building of Babylon and the other to the family of Abraham. The author supplies a hint to this division of the line of Shem with the comment that in Peleg's day "the land was divided" (10:25). As throughout the biblical text, the "land" is often a reference to the "inhabitants of the land." Thus, not only is the land divided in the confusion of languages (11:1), but more fundamentally, two great lines of humanity diverge from the midst of the sons of Shem. Those who seek to make a name (שֵׁם, 11:4) for themselves in the building of Babylon and those for whom God will make a name (שֵׁם, 12:2) in the call of Abraham.

5. Families of Noah (10:32)

In the subscription to chapter 10, the author again takes up the theme of the division of the nations: "From these the nations spread out over the earth." His purpose is to provide a context for the narrative of Babylon which follows. What he has described geographically and linguistically in chapter 10, he will describe theologically in chapter 11, namely, God's judgment of Babylon and the dispersion of the nations.

E. Babylon (11:1–9)

As was stated above, it is important to note the position of the account of the building of Babylon within the lists of names that form the subject matter of chapters 10 and 11. It is located between the two lines that are traced from Shem: first, the line that extends from Shem (10:22) through Eber (10:24) through Joktan (10:26–29); second, the line extending from Shem (11:10) through Eber (11:14) through Terah (11:25). As it is presently situated in the text, the account of the founding of Babylon falls at the end of the list of fourteen names from the line of Joktan (10:26–29). At the end of the list of the ten names of Peleg's line, however, is the account of the call of Abraham (11:27–12:10). So two great lines of the descendants of Shem divide in the two sons of Eber (10:25). One ends in Babylon, the other in the Promised Land. It is hard not to see this positioning of the account of Babylon as deliberate on the part of the author, especially in view of the continuous interplay between the name Shem שֵׁם and the quest for "making a name" (שֵׁם) in both the account of the building of Babylon (11:4) and the account of God's election of Abraham (12:2).

We should begin by setting out the main points of the account of the building of Babylon. The first scene of the story opens outside the "plain in Shinar." The narrative specifically notes that the builders "moved eastward" to the plain where they founded the city (11:2). It is important to the author that we picture the starting point of the events of the story as a "land" west of Babylon. Thus in the movement of the story the builders moved eastward to build Babylon. As early as Genesis 3 the author has shown his interest in marking the directions of travel that human beings take in their search for a home. When the man and his wife were driven from the Garden because they had chosen the knowledge of good and evil for themselves, they were made to settle in a land "eastward" from the Garden (3:24). When Cain was cast out from the presence of God after he refused God's instruction (4:7), he went to dwell in a land "east of Eden." When Lot divided from Abraham and sought for himself a land "like the garden of the Lord," he moved "eastward" while Abraham remained in the land.

In the light of such intentional uses of the notion of "eastward" within the Genesis narratives, we can see that here too the author intentionally draws the story of the founding of Babylon into the larger scheme at work throughout the book. It is a scheme that contrasts God's way of blessing (e.g., Eden and the Promised Land) with humanity's own attempt to find the "good." In the Genesis narratives, when people go "east," they leave the land of blessing (Eden and the Promised Land) and go to a land where their greatest hopes will turn to ruin (Babylon and Sodom). It is not without importance, then, that when the Israelites set out from Mount Sinai to travel into the wilderness, the text specifically returns to the notion that the direction of their travel is "eastward" (Nu 10:5). Only a few chapters later (Nu 13–14) we learn that this whole generation will die in the wilderness and not enjoy God's good blessing because they "did not believe" in the Lord (Nu 14:11). Thus, even in the Lord's directive to the tribes camping "eastward" (Nu 10:5), there is a narrative clue to the unfortunate turn of events that lay ahead in the text.

The central question surrounding this story is why God judged the builders of the city. Though the story is quite brief, the author gives the reader definite, if subtle, indications of the story's meaning. The clues lie in the repetition of key words within the story, key words that also tie the story to the larger narrative context.[53] We have already noted the importance of the word *name* within the larger context of chapters 10–12. Within the story itself, the word *name* also plays a central role. First, according to the builders of the city, the reason for building a city was "to make a name" for themselves (11:4). Second, the conclusion of the story returns to the "name" of the city and ironically associates it (בבל, Babylon/Babel) with the "confusion" (בלל) of their language (11:9). Thus the builders' attempt to make a name for themselves is a central feature of the story in terms of both its internal structure and its linking with the surrounding narratives.

Another key word tying the story together internally and externally with the surrounding narratives is *scattered*. The purpose of the city was to keep its inhabitants from "being scattered [פוץ] over the face of all the land" (11:4). Ironically, at the conclusion of the story it is the Lord who "scattered [פוץ] the builders from the city over the face of all the land" (11:8), a fact repeated twice at the conclusion (11:8–9).

A third key expression in the story is *all the land*. They had left "all the land" (11:1–2) to build a city in the east. The purpose of the city was to keep them from being scattered throughout "all the land" (11:4). But in response the Lord reversed their plan and scattered them over "all the land" (11:8–9).

Thus the story of the founding of the city of Babylon has been carefully constructed around key terms and ideas. The people of the land were at first united as one people sharing one language and living in the "land." They moved "eastward" and built a city to make a name for themselves in order not to be scattered over the land. When God saw their plan, he initiated a counterplan, one that resulted in the very thing that the city builders were attempting to prevent: "the LORD scattered them over all the land" (11:8).

Although, by itself, the story of the building of Babylon makes good sense as the story of human plans thwarted in God's judgment, the real significance of the story lies in its ties to the themes developed in the surrounding narratives. The focus of the author since the beginning chapters of Genesis has been both on God's plan to bless humankind by providing them with that which is "good" and on the human failure to trust God and enjoy the "good" that God had provided. The characteristic mark of human failure up to this point in the book has been the attempt to grasp the "good" on their own rather than to trust God to provide it for them. The author has centered his description of God's blessing on the gift of the land: "Be fruitful and multiply and fill the land" (1:28). The good land is the place of blessing.

---

[53]Cf. *EBC*, 2:106.

To leave this land and to seek another is to forfeit the blessing of God's good provisions. It is to live "east of Eden."

Within this context, the events of the story of the building of Babylon take on a greater significance. As Cain left the land and went eastward (4:16) and there built a city (4:17), the people, who were once united in the land (the last-mentioned location of the sons of Noah was the garden planted by Noah, 9:20), left the land, moved "eastward," and founded their own city, there to make a name for themselves (11:4). God, who saw that their plans would succeed, moved to rescue them from those very plans and return them to the land and the blessing that awaited there.

The story of the building of Babylon ends with only a hint of a return to the land of blessing, but in the continuation of the Genesis narratives (chap. 12ff.), the next series of events brings God's plans into sharp focus: "The LORD said to Abram, 'Leave your country, your people and your father's household and go to the land I will show you. . . . I will bless you and I will make your name great'" (12:1–2).

F. Genealogy of Shem (11:10–26)

This list of ten descendants of Shem functions similarly to that of the list of ten descendants of Adam in chapter 5. It draws the line of the "faithful" from Noah to Abraham and bypasses the line of the "unfaithful" (10:26–30). Moreover, the list of the ten descendants of Shem (11:10–26) closely resembles the list of the ten descendants of Adam (5:1–32). A comparison of the use of the two lists within the larger narrative complex suggests that both are a result of the author's careful attention to the final shape of the text. In chapter 5, the list of ten patriarchs from Adam to Noah provided the necessary linkage between the "seed" promised to the woman (3:15) and the seed of Noah, the survivor of the Flood (7:23). Not only does the list mark the "line of the promise," but it also is the means for bypassing the other line that occupies the attention of the author, the line of Cain (4:17–22), which also consists of a list of ten names. It is Cain's line that represents those who were builders of the city (4:17) and the civilization (4:20–24) that was destroyed in the Flood. The list in chapter 5, then, reveals a highly developed theological reflection on the promise which had been made concerning the seed of the woman in 3:15. It shows that the author is conscious of the impending failure of the line of Cain and the city they had built. The judgment and destruction that awaited that city, however, would not mean the end of God's promise. Noah would survive and his seed would carry the hope of the promise. Such theological reflection achieves full expression in the words of the woman at the birth of Seth: "God has given me another seed in the place of Abel because Cain has slain him" (4:25). There are two seeds, that of Cain and that of the woman. The line of Cain may rise up against the seed of the woman, but God had provided another seed in place of the one who was slain. The line of Cain may lead to judgment and destruction, but God would preserve the line of Seth, through whom the promise would be fulfilled.

The same theological reflection on God's promise lies behind the list of ten names in 11:10–26. Here the author's aim is to show that God's promise concerning the seed of the woman cannot be thwarted by the confusion and scattering of the nations at Babylon. Though the seed of Noah were scattered at Babylon, God had preserved a line of ten great men from Noah to the chosen seed of Abraham. Out of the ruins of two great cities, the city of Cain and the city of Babylon, God has preserved his promised seed. By beginning the list of names over again with Shem, the author shows his intention to bypass the other line that had been traced to Shem in the previous chapter (10:26–30).

II. ACCOUNT OF ABRAHAM (11:27–25:10)

A. Line of Abraham (11:27–32)

Still another genealogy precedes the narrative of Abraham. The function of this genealogy is not so much to connect Abraham with the preceding events, as the previous genealogies have done, but to provide the reader with the necessary background for understanding the events in the life of Abraham which follow. The list includes eight names. All the individuals named are relevant for understanding the events of the narrative to follow except "Iscah" (11:29). The inclusion of this otherwise insignificant name in the list suggests that the author is seeking to achieve a specific number of names. Thus far in Genesis, the author has followed a pattern of listing ten names between important individuals in the narrative. This short list gives only eight names; hence, if we are expecting ten names, the number of individuals in this list appears to be short by two names. By listing only eight names, the author leaves the reader uncertain who the ninth and, more importantly, the tenth name will be. It is only as the narrative unfolds that the ninth and tenth names are shown to be the two sons of Abraham, Ishmael (16:15) and Isaac (21:3).

In his genealogical introduction, then, the author anticipates the central event in the forthcoming narrative: the birth of Isaac, who will mark the tenth name. This is one of many ways in which the author carefully guides the reader toward the focus of his narrative—yet also holds the reader back in anticipation. The same concern can be seen in the initial reminder that "Sarah was barren; she had no child" (11:30), and in the prominence given in the following narrative to the wordplay on Isaac's name ("he laughs," 17:17; 18:12–13, 15; 19:14; 21:3, 6). The unusual spelling of the word *child* (וְלָד) in verse 30 may be an attempt to call attention to this important element of the introduction. Later in the narrative, in Abraham's response to the announcement of the birth of this child, there appears to be a deliberate allusion to this unusual spelling, as well as to the name (יִצְחָק, "Isaac") of the child: "Abraham fell facedown; he laughed [וַיִּצְחָק] and said to himself, 'Will a son be born [יִוָּלֵד] to a man a hundred years old?' " (17:17).

Interspersed in the list of names is the brief notice that Terah and his family, including Abraham and Lot, had left Ur of the Chaldeans and traveled as far as Haran, en route to the land of Canaan. There is no mention of the call of God until 12:1, and that appears to be after the death of Terah (11:32). The initial impression is that, while in Haran, Abraham was called to leave his homeland—after the death of his father Terah and not while he was in Ur of the Chaldeans. That impression is further sustained by the narrative in 12:4–5, which recounts Abraham's obedient response to the call of God and explicitly states that he left Haran, not mentioning Ur of the Chaldeans.

A closer look, however, suggests that the author intends us to understand the narrative differently. In 11:27–32, we are explicitly shown that Ur of the Chaldeans, not Haran, was the place of Abraham's birth (vv. 28, 31). Thus, when the command is given Abraham to leave "the place of [his] birth" (12:1), only Ur of the Chaldeans can be meant, despite the fact that the narrative of chapter 12 does not mention it. The role of 11:27–32 in providing the geographical context of chapter 12, then, should not be overlooked, especially in view of the author's close attention to geography in working out his key themes (e.g., his emphasis on traveling "eastward"; see comments above on 11:2). Even though the narrative of chapter 12 might suggest otherwise, the author seems clearly intent on having the reader understand Abraham's call as a call to leave "Ur of the Chaldeans." That this is the view of the author is confirmed by the later reference to Abraham's call in 15:7. There the author looks back to the call of Abraham and sees it as a call from "Ur of the Chaldeans" rather than from Haran. This is also the view of the author of the book of Nehemiah (9:7) and the author of Acts (7:2–3) in the NT.

The importance of this detail goes far beyond the question of harmonizing the biblical accounts. By putting the call of Abraham within the setting of Ur of the Chaldeans, the author aligns his narrative with themes that will prove central in the later prophetic literature. For Isaiah the "glory of the Chaldeans" is the city of Babylon, which God will overturn "like Sodom and Gomorrah" (Isa 13:19; cf. 48:14). In Jeremiah (24:5; 25:12; 50:1, 8, 35, 45; 51:24, 54) and Ezekiel (1:3; 12:13; 23:15, 23), the "Chaldeans" are those who live in Babylon and who have taken God's people into captivity. So it is in harmony with the view of these prophets that the author of Genesis already puts Abraham's call in the context of "Ur of the Chaldeans," drawing a line connecting the call of Abraham (12:1–3) with the dispersion of Babylon (11:1–9) and thus making Abraham prefigure all those future exiles who, in faith, wait for the return to the Promised Land. In much the same way the prophet Micah pictures the remnant who await the return from exile as descendants of Abraham faithfully trusting in God's promise (Mic 7:18–20).

Marked similarities between this introduction to the narrative of Abraham and the introduction to the narrative of Isaac (25:19–26) indicate that the author sees the two narratives as related. Abraham's brother, Haran, died "before" his father (11:28), just as Isaac's brother, Ishmael, died "before his brothers" (25:17–18). At the beginning of the Abraham narratives is a brief introduction of Nahor (11:29), who is to become a key character in the subsequent narratives concerning the quest for a bride for Abraham's son (24:24). So also at the beginning of the Isaac narratives Laban (25:20), the father of the bride of Isaac's son, Jacob, is briefly introduced (28:2). In both the Abraham and the Isaac narratives, the introductions turn quickly to the key characters: Abraham and Lot in the Abraham narratives, and Isaac-Jacob and Esau in the Isaac narratives.

As an introduction to the Abrahamic narrative the author recounts that Abraham took a wife, Sarah, and that she was barren (11:29,30). So also in the Isaac narratives we read that Isaac took a wife, Rebekah, and that she was barren (25:20–21). Unlike the Abraham narratives, where the motive of barrenness occupies center stage throughout, the barrenness of Isaac's wife is treated in a single verse (25:21), and the narrative moves on to the theme of the struggle between the brothers, Jacob and Esau. Both narratives, however, contain an element of struggle between "brothers," and the introductions to both narratives are centrally concerned with setting forth the necessary background of that struggle. Abraham was accompanied by Lot from birth (11:27), and Jacob was accompanied by Esau from birth (25:22–24). In the struggle that ensued from Abraham's companionship with Lot (13:7) and Jacob's companionship with Esau (chaps. 25–28), Abraham must be "separated" from Lot (13:9, 11, 14) and Jacob must be "separated" from Esau (25:23).

There are striking verbal parallels between the accounts of the struggle that arose between Abraham and Lot and the struggle between Jacob and Esau. In 13:6 the narrative reads, "The land was not able to support them both because their possessions were great; they were not able to live together." In the same manner, in 36:7 the narrative reads, "Because their possessions were great, the land of their sojourning was not able to support them because of their cattle." Such parallels have the effect of drawing the themes of the two narratives together so that they reinforce a central theme. The theme in this case is the fulfillment of the blessing: "Be fruitful and multiply and fill the land" (1:28).

Along with the theme of "blessing," the theme of "separation," so prominent in chapter 10 (vv. 5, 32), continues to play a central role in the author's purpose. The ideas that lie behind such a theme can be seen clearly in the final words of the Pentateuch: "When the Most High gave the nations their inheritance, when he divided all humankind, he set up boundaries for the peoples . . . because the LORD's portion is his people, Jacob his allotted inheritance" (Dt 32:24).

B. Call of Abraham (12:1–9)

We have already suggested that by placing the call of Abraham after the dispersion of the nations at Babylon (11:1–9), the author intends to picture Abraham's call as God's gift of salvation in the midst of judgment. As a way of sustaining this theme even further, the author has patterned the account of Abraham's call and blessing after an earlier account of a similar gift of salvation in the midst of judgment, the conclusion of the Flood narrative (see comments above on 8:15–19). The similarities between the two narratives are striking and show that Abraham, like Noah, marks a new beginning as well as a return to God's original plan of blessing "all humankind" (1:28).

The theme of Abraham and his descendants marking a new beginning in God's plan of blessing is developed in a number of other ways as well in Genesis. Most notable is the frequent reiteration of God's "blessing" in 1:28 (and 9:1) throughout the narratives of Abraham and his descendants (e.g., 12:1–3; 13:15–16; 15:5, 18; 17:6–8; 22:17–18; 25:11; 26:2–4; 27:27–29; 49:28). The "promise to the fathers" is none other than a reiteration of God's original blessing of humankind (1:28). To make this clear the author has given a representative list of "all humankind" in chapter 10 according to their "families" (10:32) and has shown how their dispersion was the result of Babylon's rebellion (11:1–9). These same "families of the earth" are to be blessed in Abraham and his seed (12:3). Abraham is represented here as a new Adam and the "seed of Abraham" as a second Adam, a new humanity. Those that "bless" him, God will bless; those that "curse" him, God will curse. The way of life and blessing, which was once marked by the "tree of the knowledge of good and evil" (2:17), and then by the ark (7:23), is now marked by identification with Abraham and his seed. The identity of the "seed" of Abraham will be one of the chief themes of the following narratives.

At the close of the book, a curtain on the future is drawn back and a glimpse of the future seed of Abraham is briefly allowed (49:8–12). This one "seed" who is to come, to whom the right of kingship belongs, will be the "lion of the tribe of Judah" and "to him will be the obedience of the nations" (49:10). The importance which the author attaches to the connection of the fulfillment of the "blessing" and coming of this one from the tribe of Judah can be seen in the narrative framework given to the prophetic poem of Jacob in chapter 49. At the conclusion of Jacob's words, the author has repeated three times that his words are to be understood as a renewal of the theme of the blessing: "and he blessed them each according to his blessing he blessed them" (49:28). The interest of the author in this king who is to come does not stop here. The future reign of this king and the blessing that is to ensue is the focus of other poetic texts in the Pentateuch (see comments below on Nu 24).

The account of Abraham's entry into the land of Canaan is selective. Only three sites in the land are mentioned: Shechem (12:6), the area between Bethel and Ai (v. 8), and the Negev (v. 9). As Cassuto has pointed out, it can hardly be accidental that these are the same three locations visited by Jacob when he returns to Canaan from Haran (Ge 34–35) as well as the same sites occupied in the account of the conquest of the land under Joshua:

> The Torah does not recount its narrative simply to instruct about ancient history. Rather, its aim is that of teaching religion and heritage and it uses ancient tradition for this purpose. By carefully choosing its words, the Torah signals to the reader key relationships within the ancient tradition that show its meaning. Already in the first section of Genesis 12 it is possible to recognize this method. Abram comes up out of the north and passes through all the land of Canaan in three journeys. In the first journey he goes to the place of Shechem and there he builds an altar to the Lord, marking the "ideal conquest" of the land and its sanctification to the Lord (vv. 6–7). In the second journey he arrives on the east of Bethel, with Bethel on the west and Ai on the east. Again he builds an altar at this place and calls on the name of the Lord (v. 8). In the third journey he travels to the Negev (v. 9), and there, in Hebron, he purchased later the field of Machpelah (Ge 23).
>
> Jacob's return from the east and his journeys in the land are like those of Abraham. First, he goes to Shechem and purchases a section of a field where he puts his tent and erects an altar to the God of Israel (33:18–20). Before he leaves this site, he commands his household to put away the foreign gods which are in their midst (35:2) and hides all the idols he has received from Shechem beneath the oak tree which is there (35:4). Then he journeys to Bethel and sets up there a pillar to the glory of his God (35:14–15). Finally, he travels on to the south, which is the Negev, and comes to Hebron (35:27).
>
> The key points in the journeys of Abraham, then, parallel those of Jacob, and both of these, in turn, parallel the key points in the conquest of

the land as it is recounted in the book of Joshua. There it is noted that the first city which they themselves conquered was Ai, and it uses the same expression as Genesis 12:8—" east of Bethel, between Bethel and Ai, west of Ai" (Jos 7:2; 8:9; cf. also v. 12). Immediately after this the book of Joshua recounts that Joshua built an altar at Mount Ebal, that is, next to Shechem (Jos 8:30). From there, the Israelites spread out into two further regions: south of Bethel and Ai (Jos 10) and north of Shechem (Jos 11). This is precisely the same three regions which we see with Abraham and Jacob. In Shechem Joshua commanded the Israelites to put away the foreign gods which were in their midst (Jos 24:23), using almost the same words as those of Jacob in his day. There Joshua erected a large stone under the oak which was in the sanctuary of the Lord (Jos 24:26)—under the oak as in Genesis 35:4.

These parallels show clearly the method of demonstrating that the deeds of the fathers in former times prefigure those of their descendants in the present. Its intention is to show that what happened to Abraham also happened to Jacob and then also to their descendants. This is to show that the conquest of the land had already been accomplished in a symbolic way in the times of the fathers, demonstrated by means of their building their altars and purchasing property. Thus it shows that in the deeds of the fathers there is a source of trust that the Lord has cared for them from the very start and that he will still remain trustworthy in the days of the descendants of the fathers later on.[54]

C. Abraham in Egypt (12:10–13:4)

Verse 10 opens a new episode with a notice that a famine has forced Abraham to seek refuge in Egypt. Almost as if to justify Abraham's somewhat incongruous journey to Egypt, the author emphasizes at the end of the verse that the "famine was severe." The narrative continues to 13:4, where we are returned to our point of departure, with Abraham worshiping God at the altar he had built between Bethel and Ai.

A recurring theme can be traced throughout the subsequent narratives in Genesis, one that is first noted in the present story. That theme is the threat to God's promise in 12:1–3. In nearly every episode which follows, the promise of a "numerous seed," "blessing to all families of the earth," or the "gift of the land" is placed in jeopardy by the actions of the characters of the narrative. The promise looks as if it will fail. In the face of such a threat, however, the narratives show that God always remains faithful to his word and he himself enters the arena and safeguards the promise. The purpose of such a recurring narrative theme is to show that only God can bring about his promise. Human failure cannot stand in the way of God's promise.

The account of Abraham's sojourn in Egypt bears the stamp of having been intentionally shaped to parallel the later account of God's deliverance of Israel from Egypt (Ge 41–Ex 12). Both passages have a similar message as well. Thus, here, at the beginning of the narratives dealing with Abraham and his seed, we find an anticipation of the events that will occur at the end. As with other sections of the book, the parallels are striking:

---

[54]*Encyclopaedia Biblica*, 8 vols. (Jerusalem: Bialik Institute, 1955–1956), 1:65–66.

Abraham		Joseph	
12:10	— There was a famine in the land	41:54b	— There was a famine in all the lands
12:11	— When he drew near to go into Egypt . . .	46:28	— When they came toward the land of Goshen . . .
12:11	— He said to Sarai his wife	46:31	— Joseph said to his brothers . . .
12:11	— I know that . . .	46:31	— I will go up and say to Pharaoh . . .
12:12	— And it shall come to pass when the Egyptians see you, they will say . . .	46:33	— And it shall come to pass when Pharaoh calls you, he will say . . .
12:13	— Say . . .	46:34	— Say . . .
12:13	— That it might be well with me on account of you	46:34b	— That you might dwell in the land of Goshen
12:13	— And the officers of Pharaoh saw her and declared it to Pharaoh	47:1	— And Joseph came and declared to Pharaoh. . .
12:15	— And the wife was taken into the house of Pharaoh	47:5	— And Pharaoh said '.". . .settle your father and brothers in the best part of the land."
12:15	— And Abraham acquired sheep and cattle . . .	47:6	— Put them in charge of my livestock.
		47:27	— They acquired property and were fruitful and increased greatly
12:17	— And the Lord struck Pharaoh with great plagues	Ex 11:1	— One more plague I will bring against Pharaoh
12:18	— And Pharaoh called to Abram and said	12:31	— And Pharaoh called to Moses and Aaron and said
12:19	— Take and go	12:32	— Take and go
12:20	— and sent them away	12:33	— to send them away
13:1	— And Abram went up from Egypt toward the Negev	12:37	— And the sons of Israel traveled from Rameses toward Succoth.
13:1	— And Lot went with him	12:38	— And also a great mixed multitude went with him
13:2	— And Abram was very rich with livestock, silver, and gold	12:38	— And they had very much livestock,
		12:35	— silver, and gold
13:4	— Returned to altar and worshiped God	12:42	— Passover

By shaping the account of Abraham's sojourn in Egypt to parallel the events of the Exodus, the author permits the reader to see the implications of God's past deeds with his chosen people. The past is not allowed to remain in the past. Its lessons are drawn for the future. Behind the pattern stands a faithful, loving God. What he has done with Abraham, he will do for his people today and tomorrow.

The whole of God's plan, from beginning to end, is thus contained within the scope of this simple story. It is in the light of such parallels that we should also understand the close similarity of the account of Abraham's sojourn in Egypt in chapter 12, the account of his sojourn in Gerar in chapter 20, and the account of Isaac's sojourn in Gerar in chapter 26. The similarities among these texts have long been recognized, though not always appreciated. We must avoid two extremes. We cannot be content to reduce the importance of the similarities to evidence of a "common tradition." Nor is it enough to attribute the similarities to mere coincidence. It is more likely that the similarities are intentional and part of the larger scheme of parallels found throughout the Pentateuch. For example, within the Joseph narratives sets of parallel dreams with marked similarities are recounted. Though different in their details, each set of dreams is about the same thing (37:5–7, 9; 40:5–19; 41:17–21, 22–24). In his interpretation of Pharaoh's dreams, Joseph voices the meaning lying behind not only the repetition of the dreams but also, apparently, to all the repetitions and parallels within the Pentateuch: "The reason the dream was repeated in two forms is that the matter has been firmly decided by God, and God will do it soon" (41:32). The reason for repetitions and recursions of similar narratives throughout the Pentateuch is to show that the matter has been firmly decided by God and that God will act quickly to bring about his promise.

D. Abraham and Lot (13:5–19:38)

1. Struggle and Separation (13:5–18)

A new section begins at 13:5, though its connections with the preceding section are clear. The narrative is governed by the theme of struggle and shaped around the separation (13:9, 11, 14), which results from the struggle. At its conclusion stands the second statement of the promise (13:14–17). Just as the first statement of the promise was preceded by Abraham's separation from among the nations (10:32) and from his father's house (12:1), so the second statement of the promise is put in the context of Abraham's separation from his closest kin, Lot (13:14). It is not without purpose that the final statement of the promise to Abraham comes immediately after he has demonstrated his willingness to be separated from his only son and heir, Isaac (22:15–18).

Abraham's separation from Lot also carries on the theme of "the promise in jeopardy." As the story reads, Abraham is on the verge of giving the Promised Land to Lot ("If you go to the left, I'll go to the right; if you go to the right, I'll go to the left," 13:9). What is particularly striking about Abraham's offer is that, in a subsequent narrative (19:37–38), Lot is shown to be the father of the Ammonites and the Moabites. Abraham is about to hand the Promised Land over to the same people who, in the author's own day (e.g., Nu 22–25) and throughout Israel's subsequent history (Dt 23:3–6; Ezr 9:1), were the primary obstacle to the fulfillment of the promise. Because of Abraham, the promise now teeters on the whim of the father of the Moabites. But, as the narrative shows, Lot chose to go "east" (13:11), so Abraham remained in the land (13:12). God's promise is secure, in spite of Abraham.

Thus even the plans of the nations are shown to fit into the will of God for his people. Nothing can stand in the way of God's promise to Abraham. The same viewpoint that is reflected in this narrative is found in the later prophetic literature. In Isaiah 45 the prophet describes the rise of the Persian king Cyrus as the work of God's own hand. All of Cyrus's plans and military campaigns had only one purpose, according to Isaiah—that God's people Israel might return and dwell safely in the Promised Land: "He will rebuild my city and set my exiles free" (Isa 45:13).

The author provides the reader with a subtle foreshadowing of the fatal results of Lot's choice. The land he chose was "like the garden of the Lord" and "like the land of Egypt," a positive description within the context of Genesis. But the author then adds that the land chosen by Lot is found in the area "as you go toward Zoar." As the subsequent narrative will show, Zoar was the city where Lot had to flee for safety from the destruction of Sodom and Gomorrah (19:22). Already in Lot's choice of a land "to the east" that was "like the garden of the Lord," we can see anticipated in the reference to "Zoar" the final outcome of that choice.

Within this narrative one can see definite ties between Lot's "separation" and the "separation" (10:32) of the nations at Babylon (11:1–9) and the judgment of the nations at Sodom (19:1–29). The ties between chapter 13 and the destruction of Sodom (chap. 19) can be seen in 13:10: "before the LORD destroyed Sodom and Gomorrah," and 13:12–13: "And Lot lived among the cities of the plain and pitched his tents in Sodom. Now the men of Sodom were wicked and were sinning greatly against the LORD." This is the same information restated at the beginning of chapter 19. One of the interesting implications of the author's mention of the destruction of Sodom at this point in the text is that it shows that he assumes that his readers have already read Genesis 19. The Torah was written to be read more than once. In fact, much of its message comes into focus only after one has read through the whole Pentateuch several times.

The ties between chapter 13 and the account of the destruction of Babylon stem from the fact that Lot's separation from Abraham and his journey eastward appear to have been consciously shaped by the account of the fall of Babylon in Genesis 11. In 10:32, the author closes the account of the dispersion of the nations with the statement: "From these the nations separated throughout the land after the flood." Then the narrative of the dispersion of Babylon opens with the account of the people of the land "traveling eastward" (מִקֶּדֶם) into "the plain of Shinar," where they set out to build the city of Babylon (11:1–2). In the same way Lot is said to have "traveled eastward" (מִקֶּדֶם) from the land into "the cities of the plain of the Jordan" when he "separated" from Abraham (13:11).

Following the "separation" of the nations at Babylon, the narrative resumes with Abraham traveling throughout the land of Canaan, receiving it as a promise and then building an altar in response to God's promise (12:1–9). So also, after Lot "separated" to Sodom, Abraham traveled throughout the land of Canaan, received it a second time as a promise, and built an altar in response (13:14–18). Lot, then, is the link connecting the author's treatment of the two cities, Babylon and Sodom. The close parallels between the two which are created in the narrative of chapter 13 suggest that the author intends both cities to tell the same story. As in the case of parallels and repetitions throughout the book, the double account of God's destruction of the "city in the east" is intended to drive home the point that God's judgment of the wicked is certain and imminent (cf. 41:32).

2. Abraham and the Nations (14:1-24)

At first glance the ties between chapters 13 and 14 seem meager. With respect to both the time and the place, the two narratives seem only distantly related. Somewhat abruptly the narrative begins in the time frame marked as "In the days of Amraphel," with no point of reference to the time of the preceding chapter. Just as abruptly the location of the narrative moves from Abraham's tent in Hebron (13:18) to that of an event of international importance, the wars of the four kings (14:1-11). Several indications within the narrative, however, suggest that the author intends chapter 14 to be read closely with that which has preceded. In 14:12, the focus of the account of the war between nations is quickly reduced to the scope of chapter 13 by recounting that Lot had been captured and Sodom had been sacked. Immediately following the report of Lot's capture, the narrative returns to the scene of 13:18, with Abraham dwelling at the "oaks of Mamre" in Hebron (14:13). At that point Abraham is brought into the center of the account of the battle with the four kings and, somewhat surprisingly, is capable of marshaling his forces to defeat the kings (14:14-17). The mention of "Mamre" at the end of the account (14:24) returns the reader to the scene at the close of chapter 13.

In putting these two narratives together in this way the author has allowed an event of international importance to sweep past Abraham's tent in Hebron and thus to involve Abraham in an event that will show on an enormous scale the implications of Abraham's faith—yet without losing its simple and everyday character. "Yahweh," the God Abraham worships at his altar in Hebron (13:18), is "the creator of heaven and earth" (14:22), who delivers the four kings of the east into his hands. Abraham, who asks nothing and wants nothing from the kings of this world (14:22-23), is the only one who proves able to dwell peacefully in the land. As 12:3 has forecast, those who join with Abraham (14:13) will enjoy his blessing (14:24), but those who separate from him, as Lot had done (13:12), will suffer the same fate as Sodom and Gomorrah (14:11-12).

Another feature of the composition of chapter 14 shows clearly the author's intent to link this chapter with the themes of the preceding narratives. At the outset of the account of the war of the four kings, the reader is alerted to the fact that the events of chapter 14 "happened in the days of Amraphel, king of Shinar." The author has already clearly and consciously identified Shinar as Babylon (10:10; 11:2, 9). He appears to have deliberately arranged the opening of this narrative so that the king of Shinar's name would come first in the list, thus aligning the narrative with the theme of "Babylon" introduced in chapters 10 (10:10) and 11 (11:2). This point is suggested by the fact that the list of kings in verse 1 differs from the lists of the names of these four kings throughout the remainder of the chapter. Whereas in 14:1 it is Amraphel king of Shinar who comes first in the list, throughout the chapter it is not Amraphel who is first among the four kings but Kedorlaomer king of Elam (vv. 4, 5, 9, 17). In verse 9, which lists the kings, Kedorlaomer is first and Amraphel is third, but in verse 1 Amraphel is first and Kedorlaomer is third. When one compares the sequence of the names in both lists, one can see that Kedorlaomer is followed by Tidal in the lists and Amraphel is followed by Aroch; thus the break in the sequence of the names comes only at Amraphel's name.

14:9	Kedorlaomer, Tidal,	Amraphel, Arioch	
14:1	Amraphel, Arioch,	Kedorlaomer, Tidal	

If the sequence in verse 9 is the original one, as is suggested by the fact that elsewhere in the lists Kedorlaomer is always first (as simply "Kedorlaomer," v. 4, or as "Kedorlaomer and the kings with him," vv. 5, 17), then at the beginning of the narrative the author has apparently broken the list into two sections, putting the section beginning with Amraphel first and the other section second.

a. Four Kings Conquer Canaan (14:1–11)

What immediately strikes the reader in this account of the conquest of Canaan by the four kings is that very little information is given about the actual battles while the account is overladen with geographical and political details. The author is apparently more interested in the geographical extent of the warfare than in the actual course of the battles. From this feature of the narrative it is certain that the events recounted were global in scope and that they ended in the disgraceful defeat of the kings of Sodom and Gomorrah. The kings were completely routed (14:10–11).

b. Lot Captured (14:12)

At this point in the account, the perspective of the narrative changes markedly. The reader's field of vision is directed away from the global scope of the war with the four eastern kings to the sudden change in the fate of Lot. Lot, who departed from Abraham to pitch his tent in Sodom, has been taken captive along with the possessions of Sodom and Gomorrah (v. 12). In the midst of the harried description of the deteriorating course of events, the reader is reminded of the ultimate cause of Lot's unfortunate fate: "He was dwelling in Sodom" (14:12b). Thus, again, the narrative is brought into the larger context of the blessing in the land (12:1–3; 13:14–17) and the fate of all those who separate themselves from Abraham.

Lot's fate is a lesson, or rather, the first stage in a lesson that will bring him still further in need of the intercession of Abraham (18:23–32). Twice, by means of Abraham, Lot's welfare is restored: first here in the war with Babylon, and then later in chapters 18 and 19 in the destruction of Sodom. Here Abraham with his band of 318 men rescued Lot. In chapters 18 and 19 Abraham's intercession (18:23–32; 19:29) effected Lot's rescue. The picture of Abraham that emerges from these narratives is the same as that given voice in 20:7: "He is a prophet, he will pray for you, and you will live." God's blessing of humankind is tied to Abraham and his seed.

c. Abraham Rescues Lot (14:13–16)

The focus of the narrative returns to the scene at the close of chapter 13. Abraham was dwelling with his three friends at Hebron (14:13), strangely unaffected by the events recorded in the previous narrative. In this brief scene, strikingly similar to Job 1:17, Abraham was able to muster a select army, defeat the four kings, and return Lot with the rest of the captives.

d. Abraham Meets Two Kings (14:17–24)

After his return from battle, Abraham was met by two kings in the "Valley of the King." It has been suggested that the present shape of this narrative is disheveled and in disarray owing to the insertion of the section on Melchizedek (14:18–20). It appears to have been inserted into the section dealing only with the king of Sodom. It is true that Melchizedek appears in the narrative as if out of nowhere and just as quickly is gone, not to be encountered again or subsequently explained. But the structure of the narrative is not unusual,[55] and the insertion of the encounter with Melchizedek (vv. 18–20) into the section dealing with the king of Sodom is done in such a way as to suggest that it is to be read as the background to the encounter with the king of Sodom.[56] Thus a contrast is established between Abraham's positive response to the king of Salem and his negative response to the king of Sodom.

Lying behind Abraham's response to both kings is the contrast between the offer of the king of Salem and that of the king of Sodom. The king of Salem brings "bread and wine" as a priestly act (v. 18) and acknowledges that it was the "Most High God, creator of heaven and earth," who delivered the adversaries into Abraham's hand (v. 19). In other words, the perspective of the king of Salem is precisely that of the author himself, who has also acknowledged at the start of his work that the God who delivered Israel from the hand of the Egyptians (see Ex 20:2) is the Creator of heaven and earth (Ge 1:1). Abraham's response to the king of Salem, then, is an appropriate recognition of the validity of Melchizedek's offer as well as of his priesthood: Abraham paid a tithe (see Nu 18:21).

The offer of the king of Sodom was quite different: he would give to Abraham all the "possessions" recovered in the battle (Ge 14:21). Abraham's response not only speaks for himself but also shows how the author views this gesture. It was an offer of reward from the king of Sodom, and Abraham would have nothing to do with it. As his solemn speech at the close of the narrative showed, Abraham's reward would not come from the kings of this world but from "Yahweh, the creator of heaven and earth." Any "possessions" he was to have would come from the Lord, as the following chapter sets out to show (e.g., 15:1, 14).

In a number of points, the events of chapter 14 reflect the same concerns as those of Deuteronomy 20:1–15, the instructions concerning carrying out wars with foreign nations. Abraham's actions are described in ways reminiscent of the conduct of warfare against "cities that are afar off and do not belong to the nations nearby" (cf. Dt 20:15). He does not hesitate to go into battle against an army greater than his (cf. Dt 20:1). Thus the author informs us that he took with him only 318 men, a number that

---

[55]The Hebrew construction is a chiastic coordination with the *wayyiqtol* of (v. 17) followed by the *qatal* of (v. 18), and the word order of predicate-subject (v. 17) followed by subject-predicate (v. 18); cf. F. I. Andersen, *The Sentence in Biblical Hebrew*, 123ff.

[56]The pattern *w + x + qatal*, when *in* precedes the main clause, e.g., *wayyiqtol*, depicts background; see W. Gross, "Syntaktische Erscheinungen am Anfang althebräischer Erzählungen: Hintergrund und Vordergrund," *VTSup* 32 (Leiden: Brill, 1981), 131–45.

corresponds to Gideon's 300 men in Judges 7:6 ("The LORD said to Gideon, 'With the three hundred men that lapped I will save you and give the Midianites into your hands.'"). Abraham went into battle specifically with only the "dedicated young men in his house" (Ge 14:14). The Hebrew expression used here for "dedicated" is not found elsewhere in the Bible, nor is its meaning clear within the context of ancient history and customs. The use of the word here, however, provides another link with Deuteronomy 20:5, which states that one who goes into battle should only be one who has already "dedicated" his house. Since within the Pentateuch the verb occurs only in this passage of Deuteronomy, a link between the two texts by means of the terminology seems likely.

Though he rejected the offer of a reward from the king of Sodom, Abraham laid claim to own rightfully that which his young men have eaten (Ge 14:24). Deuteronomy 20:14 says explicitly that those who go into war with nations afar off may "eat" of the spoils taken in battle (the NIV has translated "eat" in Dt 20:14 as "use"). Abraham also recognized that his three friends had their own rightful share in the spoil (Ge 14:24), which corresponds to the provisions of Deuteronomy 20:14. Nevertheless, Abraham flatly rejected the offer to take from the possessions of the king of Sodom (Ge 14:23), as was prescribed in Deuteronomy 20:17 for the spoils of those nations who live within the boundaries of the land of inheritance. Along these same lines it is to be noted that Deuteronomy 20:2 assigned to the "priest" the role of reminding the people that "the LORD your God is the one who goes with you to fight for you against your enemies to give you victory" (cf. Dt 20:13, "When the LORD your God delivers it into you hand"). In much the same way, Abraham was met by Melchizedek, "a priest" of the Most High God, who proclaimed to him that it was "the Most High God who delivered your enemies into your hand" (Ge 14:20).

In the light of such similarities it appears that the author has intended to show that Abraham lived a life in harmony with God's will even though he lived long before the revelation at Sinai. Abraham was one who pictured God's Law written on his heart. He obeyed the Law, though the Law had not yet been given. Such an understanding of the life of Abraham is not foreign to the author of Genesis. Indeed, one of the last statements made about Abraham in Genesis is that he kept God's "commandments, statutes and laws" (Ge 26:5). These terms are well-known from the pages of Deuteronomy (e.g., Dt 11:1; 26:17), where they are the stock vocabulary for describing the keeping of the Torah revealed at Sinai. The author's point appears to have been to show that Abraham, as a man of faith, "kept the law." He did not have the Law written out before him; nevertheless he kept it. In this respect, the picture of Abraham that emerges from chapters 14 and 26 is much like that of the new covenant promise in Jeremiah 31:33, in which God has promised to write the Torah on the heart of his covenant people so that they will obey it "from the heart." This is the same picture of Abraham that later emerges as the central figure in the NT writers' portrayal of life under the new covenant (e.g., Ro 4, Gal 3).

3. Abraham and the Covenant (15:1–21)

a. Introduction (15:1–4)

In a later chapter (20:7) Abraham is explicitly called a "prophet." Here in chapter 15, the author goes to great lengths to cast him in that role. The central subject of the chapter deals with the announcement of events that lie far in the future (vv. 13–16), and thus it is of utmost importance to the author that Abraham's credentials as a prophet be clearly set forth and defended. God's address to Abraham is introduced in an elevated style that is typical of the later prophetic literature: "The word of the Lᴏʀᴅ came to Abram saying. . ." (15:1, 4; cf. Jer 34:12). To this is added the fact that, like the seer Balaam (Num 24:6, 16), Abraham saw the word of the Lᴏʀᴅ in a "vision" (בַּמַּחֲזֶה, Ge 15:1). This word occurs only here and in Numbers 24 (the prophecies of Balaam in Pentateuch.

Such an introduction to the events of chapter 15 is intended to show that these events were, in fact, that which Abraham saw in the vision. Thus, like prophetic visions elsewhere in Scripture, there may be more than a little symbolic value to the events. This is especially likely to be true of the visual display which Abraham saw in verse 17.

It may also be significant to note that here, for the first time, it is recorded that Abraham spoke to God. Up to this point in the narrative of Genesis, when God spoke to him, Abraham obeyed but did not speak to God in return. Indeed, Abraham will speak to God only on rare occasions in the remainder of the narratives (15:2–3, 8; 17:18; 18:23–33; 22:11). In the vision of chapter 15, however, Abraham not only replied to God's promise but raised a question of how the promise would be fulfilled. In fact, Abraham raised so many questions in this chapter that the author seems compelled to remind the reader of his unwavering faith (15:6).

Abraham's questions provide the necessary backdrop for the central issue of the chapter, that is, God's apparent delay in fulfilling his promises. The prophet Jeremiah faced the same issue in his own day. God's people, who should have been enjoying the promised blessing, instead found themselves about to enter captivity in Babylon. The promise appears to have come to naught: "This whole country will become a desolate wasteland, and these nations will serve the king of Babylon seventy years" (Jer 25:11). But in Jeremiah's warning of impending judgment there is as well the promise of ultimate blessing. The time of exile in a foreign land has a limit: "When the seventy years are fulfilled," the Lord told Jeremiah, "I will punish the king of Babylon and his nations, the land of the Chaldeans, for their guilt" (Jer 25:12). Thus the faithful in exile can, like Daniel (9:2), wait in hope that in spite of the present affliction in Babylon, God would remain faithful to his promise: "I, Daniel, understood from the Scriptures, according to the word of the Lᴏʀᴅ to Jeremiah the prophet, that the desolation of Jerusalem would last seventy years. So I turned to the Lord God and pleaded with him in prayer and petition, in fasting, and in sackcloth and ashes" (Dan 9:2–3). The limit to God's judgment is set at seventy years.

In much the same way, the present chapter of Genesis addresses an audience awaiting the fulfillment of the promises to the fathers but who could see no present evidence of the fulfillment. They are like those whom Isaiah calls upon to "wait on the Lord" (Isa 40:31) and who Habakkuk says will ultimately live through the present affliction only because they have been made "righteous by their faith" (Hab 2:4). As the author of Genesis 15 has shown, Abraham's predicament is not too far from that of later generations of God's people. Abraham too must wait in faith for the fulfillment of the promise, as one counted righteous in his faith (15:6) but realizing that the promise was afar off to another generation (vv. 15–16). "All these people were still living by faith when they died. They did not receive the things promised; they only saw them and welcomed them from a distance" (Heb 11:13). So the message to the reader is to stand fast. When they say, "Where is the promise of his coming?" remember that "the Lord is not slack in keeping his promise, as some understand slackness. He is waiting for you to come to repentance" (2Pe 3:4, 9).

The statement "Do not fear—I am a shield to you; your reward will be great" (Ge 15:1) raises a number of questions. What is Abraham afraid of? What "reward" does God have in mind? Are the military events in chapter 14 still posing a threat to Abraham? Since the chapter opens by making a major break with the preceding chapter (that is the sense that the phrase "after these things" has elsewhere in Genesis [22:1; 39:7; 40:1]), God's first words to Abraham are probably not to be understood within the immediate context of chapter 14. We are left, then, with the subject matter of chapter 15 itself to determine the sense of these first words to Abraham. From that perspective, it becomes apparent that Abraham had begun to fear for the final outcome of God's promise to make his "seed like the dust of the earth" in number (13:16). The questions Abraham raised within the narrative betray the fact that such a fear did lie behind God's first words of comfort. Abraham asked, "What can you give me since I remain childless?" (15:2); then he objected, "You have not given me a seed" (v. 3); finally, as he was again reminded that his "seed" (v. 5) would be greater than one could number and would inherit the land of promise, he asked, "How can I know I will inherit it?" (v. 8). Not only do his questions betray the fear that lies within him, but also the Lord's continued assurances point in the same direction: "A son coming from your own body will be your heir" (v. 4). In the present shape of the narrative, then, Abraham is portrayed as one who has reason to fear that God's promises will not be fulfilled. From all appearances around him, Abraham has little to give him hope that God will remain faithful to his word. He is still childless and all his possessions will one day again be in the hands of one from "Damascus" (v. 2).

The mention of "Damascus" in chapter 15 is apparently intended to draw a connection to Abraham's victory near "Damascus" in chapter 14 and to tie the themes behind the events of chapter 15 to those of chapter 14. The latter chapter showed that the fulfillment of God's promises lay not in the strength of "Damascus," where Abraham defeated the four kings, but in the "faith" of his chosen "seed." In much the same way, the prophet Isaiah warned the weakhearted of his day: "Do not fear. . . . It will not take place, it will not happen, for the head of Aram is Damascus, and the head of Damascus is only Rezin. . . . If you do not stand firm in your faith, you will not stand at all" (Isa 7:4–9).

At the close of the narrative Abraham was given a vision of the distant future as a source of comfort in the face of the apparently unfulfilled promises of God. The events in the vision fit precisely those which actually occurred to Abraham's seed—events which are recorded in Exodus 1–12. The importance of the vision lies not so much in the assurances it may have given Abraham in his own day, but rather in the assurances it was to give the reader. The reader knows, from reading the rest of the Pentateuch, that the vision was to be fulfilled in the days of Moses. Thus, within the narrative of Genesis and the Pentateuch, the vision and its fulfillment are a confirmation of the prophetic words of Abraham. He was given a true vision. What he saw in the vision did, in fact, come to pass and has been recorded within the Pentateuch itself. Thus for the readers who know that the vision is true, Abraham is shown to be a true prophet according to the test in Deuteronomy 18:22: "If what a prophet proclaims in the name of the LORD does not take place or come true, that is a message that the LORD has not spoken." Like Jeremiah after him (Jer 27–29), Abraham was a true prophet even though he spoke of exile and not blessing. But also like Jeremiah (30:3ff.), Abraham's vision looked beyond the coming exile to the time when God would restore his people and judge their oppressors: "But I will punish the nation they served and afterward they will come out with great possessions" (Ge 15:14).

It is in the light of this vision, then, that God's first words to Abraham in chapter 15 are to be understood. With these same words Jeremiah comforted those awaiting exile in his day: "Fear not, O Jacob my servant, do not be dismayed, O Israel. I will surely save you out of a distant place, your seed from the land of their captivity" (Jer 30:10). It is significant that the next words which Abraham spoke to the Lord were those in Genesis 17:18: "Would that Ishmael would live before you," spoken after he had said to himself in laughter: "Will a son be born to a man a hundred years old?" Throughout the Genesis narratives, when Abraham speaks he gives expression to questions that appear to reveal doubt. By contrast, when he is silent in the narratives, his actions exhibit faith.

b. Seed Like Stars (15:5)

The appeal to the number of the stars of "the heavens" looks back to Abraham's own words in 14:22, where his hope for reward was based solely on the "Creator of heaven and earth." If Yahweh was the creator of the great multitude of the stars in heaven, it follows that he was able to give Abraham an equal number of descendants ("seed"). Thus God's faithfulness in the past was made the basis for Abraham's trust in the future.

The comparison of the number of Abraham's seed to that of the stars of the heavens occurs several times in the Pentateuch: twice the promise was reiterated to Isaac (22:17; 26:4), and then again by Moses at a crucial moment when God was on the verge of destroying the whole nation (Ex 32:13). Deuteronomy 1:10 alludes to this promise in reference to the great multitude that came out of Egypt, but as Deuteronomy 28:62 makes clear, the promise remained to be fulfilled in a future generation. It is possible that the image of the "star" which is to arise out of the house of Jacob in Numbers 24:17 owes part of its sense to this particular feature of the promise to the fathers.

c. Abraham Counted Righteous (15:6)

The syntax of 15:6 suggests that it is to be read as background information for the scene that unfolds in verse 7. God was about to enter a covenant with Abraham that would provide the foundation for all God's future dealings with him and his seed (15:7–21). Verse 6 opens the scene by setting the record straight: Abraham had believed in Yahweh and had been accounted righteous. The covenant did not make him righteous; rather it was by his "faith" that he was reckoned righteous. Only after he had been counted righteous by his faith could Abraham enter into God's covenant. The precise position and use of the concept of "faith" here in chapter 15 is no more accidental than its use throughout the remainder of the Pentateuch. At key moments throughout the course of the book, the author returns to the notion of "faith" and points to it as the decisive factor in God's dealings with Abraham's seed.[57]

d. Account of the Covenant (15:7–17)

As 15:18 shows, these verses recount the establishment of a covenant between the Lord and Abraham. Thus it is fitting that in many respects the account should foreshadow the making of the covenant at Sinai. The opening statement in 15:7: "I am the LORD, who brought you up out of Ur of the Chaldeans," is virtually identical to the opening statement of the Sinai covenant in Exodus 20:2: "I am the LORD your God, who brought you up out of the land of Egypt." The expression "Ur of the Chaldeans" refers back to Genesis 11:28, 31 and grounds the present covenant in a past act of divine salvation from "Babylon," just as Exodus 20:2 grounds the Sinai covenant in an act of divine salvation from Egypt. The coming of God's presence in the awesome fire and darkness of Mount Sinai (Ex 19:18; 20:18; Dt 4:11) appears to be intentionally reflected in Abraham's pyrotechnic vision (Ge 15:12, 17). In the Lord's words to Abraham (15:13–16) the connection between Abraham's covenant and the Sinai covenant is explicitly made by means of the reference to the four hundred years of bondage of Abraham's seed and their subsequent "exodus" ("and after this they will go out," v. 14). Such considerations lead to the conclusion that the author intends to draw the reader's attention to the events at Sinai in his depiction of the covenant with Abraham.

If we ask why the author has sought to bring in the picture of Sinai here, the answer lies in the purpose of the book. It is part of the overall strategy of the book to show that what God did at Sinai was part of a larger plan which had already been put into action with the patriarchs. Thus, the exodus and the Sinai covenant serve as reminders not only of God's power and grace but also of God's faithfulness. What he sets out to accomplish with his people, he will carry through to the end.

e. Boundaries of the Land (15:18–21)

The author again draws the promise of the land back into the narrative by concluding with a description of the geographical boundaries of the covenant land. It has been pointed out (see above on 2:4b–27) that the borders of the Promised Land coincide with those of the Garden of Eden (cf. 2:10–14).

---

[57]E.g., Ex 4:5, 31; 14:31; 19:9. See H.-C. Schmitt, "Redaktion des Pentateuch."

4. Hagar (16:1–16)

Chapter 16 alludes to three other important passages in the Pentateuch: Genesis 3:6; 12:3; and Deuteronomy 7:1–6. By bringing the events of Hagar and Abraham into the larger context of these other passages, the author enlarges the reference of the story beyond Abraham and Hagar as individuals and ties their actions to the themes of the Pentateuch as a whole. The first sign of an intentional interdependence of the Hagar story on surrounding texts is the notice at the beginning of the narrative that Hagar was an "Egyptian" maid of Sarah (Ge 16:1, 3). Only at the beginning of the story is Hagar identified as an Egyptian, however. Throughout the remainder of the story she is identified only by name or as "the maid."

The second reference to Hagar as "the Egyptian" is strikingly different from the first. The adjective does not modify "the maiden" as in verse 1 ("Egyptian maid"), but stands alone as a substantive along with "maid" in apposition to the personal name Hagar ("Hagar, the Egyptian, her maid"). In verse 3, then, "the Egyptian" serves as a conspicuous reminder of Hagar's identity in verse 1, "an Egyptian maid." The mention of Hagar's geographical origin appears to function as a connecting link with the geographical list immediately preceding the story (15:18–21), since in that list, the first geographical name is Egypt (15:18). If such a connection is intentional, then it appears that the author is attempting to position the account of Hagar (Ge 16) so that her story is representative of those nations in the preceding list. A way was thus opened for the events in the life of Hagar and Abraham to be interpreted within the larger theological context of Genesis and the Pentateuch where these lists of names occur. Particularly important in this regard are the similarities between Genesis 16 and Deuteronomy 7:1–6, the prohibition of taking foreign wives, a text which had enormous importance to later generations of Israelites.[58]

The account of Sarah's plan to have a son has not only been connected with the list of nations in chapter 15, but also appears to have been intentionally shaped with reference to the account of the Fall in Genesis 3. Each of the main verbs (*wayyiqtol* forms) and key expressions in 16:2–3 finds a parallel in Genesis 3.

Ge 16:2a "so she [Sarai] said to"	Ge 3:2 "The woman said to"
Ge 16:2b "Abram listened to Sarai"	Ge 3:17 "you listened to your"
Ge 16:3a "Sarai . . . took"	Ge 3:6a "she took some"
Ge 16:3b "and [she] gave her to her husband [Abram]"	Ge 3:6b "she also gave some to her husband"

---

[58]Cf. Ezr 9:1ff. See Michael Fishbane, *Biblical Interpretation in Ancient Israel* (Oxford: Clarendon, 1985), 114ff.

At the same time that these parallels establish an association between the Hagar narrative and the Fall (Ge 3), the repeated use of the verb "curse" in 16:4–5 appears also to mark an intentional association of the passage with the patriarchal blessing in 12:3. This word ("to curse") occurs with a similar meaning only in these two passages in Genesis. It is mentioned twice within 16:4–5 that Hagar the Egyptian "despised" Sarah, the very thing which 12:3 warned would end in God's curse: "Those who despise you I will curse." (It is noteworthy that one of the few other occurrences of the verb is Dt 23:5, a passage with longstanding association with Dt 7:1–6 and the theme of "foreign wives" within the OT canon.)

As a consequence of her despising Sarah, Hagar is forced into the "wilderness" where she must stay until she submitted herself again to Sarah. It is only in association with her return to Sarah and her submission to her that the Lord offered her a blessing: "I will greatly increase your seed so that they cannot be counted" (Ge 16:10). This was the same "blessing" which Abraham himself was to receive (17:2) and which Ishmael was to receive in 17:20 ("I will make him fruitful and will greatly increase his numbers"). The association of this blessing with the primeval blessing in 1:26 is unmistakable. In other words, just as the author has positioned the Hagar narrative as representative of the list of nations in 15:18–21, so also within the narrative Hagar's actions are exemplary of the nations who will find either blessing or curse in their relationship with the family of Abraham.

a. Sarah's Plan (16:1–6)

The first section of the Hagar narrative is concerned with Sarah's plan to deal with her own barrenness. Offering her maid to Abram to bear him a child was apparently acceptable within the social custom of the day. There is reason to doubt, however, that the biblical author approves of the scheme. From his vantage point, Sarah's plan was one more example of the futility of human efforts to achieve God's blessing—not to mention the difficulties his approval of Sarah's plan would pose in the light of the fact that he had already extolled the virtues of monogamy in previous sections of his narrative (2:24). His overall disapproval is further suggested by the observation made above that he recounts the story in a way that associates Sarah's action with that of Eve in Genesis 3, and thus shows her plan, like Eve's scheme to be like God, to be an attempt to circumvent God's plan of blessing in favor of gaining a blessing on her own. Another indication that the author does not approve of the plan is that in the subsequent narrative (Ge 17), Sarah's plan does not meet with God's approval (vv. 15–19).

Finally, there is the matter of the position of this narrative immediately following the establishment of a covenant to affirm the promise of a child (15:4). By placing the Hagar story here the author suggests that Sarah's scheme was intended to head off that divine promise by supplying it with a human solution. Thus the story falls in line with the theme of the stories which preceded it in demonstrating the unacceptability of human effort in fulfilling the divine promise. Sarah's plan, though successful, does not meet with divine approval (17:15–19), just as the plans and schemes of those in the previous narratives had ended in failure (3:6–8; 4:3–7; 11:1–9; 12:10–20; 13:1–12; 14:21–24).

b. Hagar in the Wilderness (16:7–12)

The location of the narrative shifts in this second section from the household of Abraham to the wilderness. The author's identification of the well as the "well on the way to Shur" (16:7) assures the reader of what might otherwise only be suspected: Hagar was returning to Egypt (see 25:18).

The associations between chapter 16 and chapter 3 continue in this section of the narrative as well. Just as the Lord sought Adam and Eve after the Fall (3:9), so the angel of the LORD found Hagar in the wilderness and greeted her with the similar question (16:8): "Where have you come from and where are you going?" Furthermore, as in 3:15, where a renewed hope of blessing was sounded amid the chords of despair, so also in 16:10–12 the angel of the Lord offered a blessing to a distraught Hagar wandering through the wilderness. The child to be born will be named "Ishmael" because "the LORD has heard her affliction." The key term throughout the chapter is *affliction*, which occurs as a noun in 16:11 and as a verb in verses 6 and 9. Hagar was afflicted by Sarah (v. 6); she was told to put herself back under that affliction (v. 9); and the Lord heard her affliction (v. 11).

The second half of Hagar's "blessing" did not portend well for her son. The text says that he would be a "wild donkey of a man" (there is a wordplay between "donkey" and "Paran," the location of the tribes of Ishmael in later history), that is, "his hand will be against everyone and everyone's hand against him" (v. 12). The sense of the last statement in the blessing is uncertain, but its meaning can perhaps be gained from the author's final statement regarding Ishmael in 21:21, which says that he "dwelt in the wilderness." Thus, the sense of "he shall dwell upon the face of all his brothers" is taken by the author to mean "he shall dwell over against all his kinsmen" (RSV). He was to dwell on the outskirts of civilization, that is, in the wilderness.

c. Birth of Ishmael (16:13–16)

The final section of the narrative consists of Hagar's naming God and the actual birth of Ishmael. The two events go together in that the birth of the child was the confirmation of the name given to God in this section: "the God of seeing" (16:13).

5. Abraham, Sarah, and Ishmael (17:1–27)

a. Abraham's Age (17:1a)

The report of Abraham's age serves as a link to the preceding narrative of Ishmael's birth. At the close of chapter 16 Abraham was eighty-six years old when Ishmael was born. At the beginning of chapter 17 Abraham's age is put at ninety-nine years. The close attention to his age comes up again at the conclusion of the chapter, where the reader is reminded that Abraham was ninety-nine years old when he was circumcised (v. 24) and Ishmael was thirteen (v. 27). Thus the age of Abraham functions as a framework for the events of the chapter as well as a link to the preceding context. The next reckoning of the age of Abraham after chapter 17 comes in the account of the birth of Isaac (21:5). At that point it is reported that Abraham was one hundred years old. Between these two notices, the text contains a diverse collection of narratives with little close attention to their chronological coherence. The age of Abraham, however, provides the outside chronological boundaries for the events of the narratives, showing that they all are to be understood as taking place within the year before the birth of Isaac.

b. God's First Speech (17:1b–2)

Chapter 17 is one of a small group of narratives in which the author explicitly states that the Lord appeared to someone (12:7; 18:1; 26:2, 24; 35:9). Unlike the similar statement in chapter 18, where the author devotes special attention to the actual nature of the Lord's appearance, here the interest of the author seems solely in what the Lord said, not in the nature of the appearance itself. The Lord's first speech to Abraham is brief and serves mainly as a summary introduction to the second speech, which by comparison is long. As a summary, however, the first speech establishes the interpretive boundaries for the rest of the chapter. Most importantly, it establishes the fact that the events of the chapter represent the making of a covenant between the Lord and Abraham. The substance of the covenant is the promise of abundant descendants.

The author has immediately identified God as the Lord (17:1b), the God of the covenant at Sinai (Ex 3:15). Within the narrative, however, God identified himself to Abraham as "God Almighty." In so doing, the author has removed all doubt regarding the faith of Abraham at this stage in the narrative. Abraham worshiped the covenant God, Yahweh, but he knew him as "God Almighty." (This is also the viewpoint of Ex 6:3: "I appeared to Abraham, to Isaac, and to Jacob as God Almighty, but by my name Yahweh I did not make myself known to them.") After identifying himself, the Lord gives a brief synopsis of the covenant, stressing Abraham's obligation: "Walk before me and you will be blameless."[59]

The choice of words in 17:2 ("I will make my covenant," RSV) poses a question of the coherence of chapter 17 with the preceding narrative. Had not God already made a covenant with Abraham in 15:18? Why does he establish a covenant with Abraham a second time? Several solutions to this problem have been proposed. The simplest answer lies in seeing the two covenants as distinct covenants—a covenant made in regard to the promise of the land (15:18–21) and a covenant made in regard to the promise of a great abundance of descendants (17:2). It should also be noted that between these two covenants was the incident with Hagar. There may thus have been a need to reestablish the earlier covenant after that unsuccessful attempt to take the promise into their own hands. A similar line of argument can be seen in the narratives of the covenant at Sinai. The covenant is first established in Exodus 24 and then, again, in Exodus 34. Between these two accounts, however, is the narrative of the incident of the golden calf (Ex 19:16; 32:1–35), which implied a failure on Israel's part in keeping the covenant.

---

[59]See GKC, par. 110f. The imperative, since it is dependent on a preceding imperative, should not be read as an English imperative (as NIV), but as a consequence which follows from an initial condition and the divine promise, "I will greatly increase your numbers."

c. Abraham's Response (17:3a)

The report of Abraham's response to the Lord's words is also brief. The author simply recounts that he "fell on his face," a sign of deep respect. The significance of this brief description of Abraham's response can be seen in the similarities between it and the account of Abraham's response to the Lord's second speech. At that point he not only "fell upon his face" but also "he laughed." In other words, when Abraham heard that God would greatly increase his descendants, he responded with respect and submission. But when he heard how God would carry out his plan, his respect contained a hint laughter. The notion of "laughter" (יִצְחָק) and the announcement of the birth of "Isaac" (יִצְחָק), an obvious wordplay, plays an important role in the composition of the next several chapters (see commentary below).

d. God's Second Speech (17:3b–16)

The second divine speech is divided into three sections (vv. 3b–8, 9–14, 15–16), each marked by the reintroduction of the clause "and God said": (vv. 3b, 9, 15. Each section deals respectively with one of the parties of the covenant (the Lord, Abraham, and Sarai), each of whom is specifically named or identified at the beginning of each section: the Lord ("as for me," v. 4a), Abraham ("as for you," v. 9a), and Sarai ("as for Sarai, your wife," v. 15a). The specific content of each section of the covenant is memorialized by a specific sign within that section: the change of Abraham's name in the first section (v. 5), the circumcision of all males of the family in the second section (vv. 10–14), and the change of Sarai's name in the third section (v. 15).

God's part of the covenant (vv. 3b–8) consists of two promises: abundant descendants (vv. 4–6) and eternal faithfulness (vv. 7–8). As the narratives have already stressed, the descendants of Abraham who belong to this covenant will owe their existence to God alone: "I will make you a father of many nations." They will be "children born not of natural descent, nor of human decision or a husband's will, but born of God" (Jn 1:13). The promise of abundant descendants is memorialized in the change of Abram's name to Abraham, which is interpreted to mean "father of many nations" (17:4b, 5). The choice of the word *be fruitful* in verse 6 and *multiply* in verse 2 seems intended to recall the blessing of all humankind in 1:29: "Be fruitful and multiply and fill the land," and its reiteration in 9:1: "Be fruitful and multiply and fill the land." Thus the covenant with Abraham was the means through which God's original blessing would again be channeled to all humankind.

A new element is added in verse 6b: "Kings will come forth from you," which seems not only to anticipate the subsequent history of Abraham's seed as it is recorded in the later historical books (e.g., Samuel and Kings), but also, more importantly, to provide a link between the general promise of blessing through the seed of Abraham and the author's subsequent focus of that blessing in the royal house of Judah (Ge 49:8–12; Nu 24:7–9). The notion that the blessing would come from a king is not new to the author's argument (cf. Ge 14:18–19), but what he here develops for the first time is the idea that this king would come from the seed of Abraham. At work here is the same theological planning that lies behind the structure of the genealogy of Matthew 1: "A record of the genealogy of Jesus Christ the son of David, the son of Abraham." Keeping in mind the close association of the term *messiah* ("anointed one," as in Greek *christos*) with the kingship elsewhere in biblical literature (e.g., 1Sa 24:7, 11), one could speak of a "Christology" of Genesis in such passages.

The focus of verses 7 and 8 lies in the repetition of the term *everlasting*. The covenant promised is an "everlasting covenant" (v. 7a) and the possession of the land an "everlasting possession" (v. 8). The promises contained in these verses are not given here for the first time (cf. 13:14–15; 15:18–21), but the everlasting nature of the covenant—that which is to assure the fulfillment of the promises—is new. The eternality of the land covenant was certainly implied in the "forever" of the promise (13:15), but when the covenant was granted in chapter 15, there was no mention of its being "eternal." Thus as God reiterated his role in the covenant, the focus was on his everlasting faithfulness: "I will establish my covenant as an everlasting covenant. . . . and the whole land of Canaan. . . . I will give as an everlasting possession" (vv. 7–8).

Abraham's part in the covenant consisted in his obedience to the covenant: "You must keep my covenant" (v. 9). What this meant was immediately explained: "This is my covenant which you must keep . . . every male among you shall be circumcised" (v. 10). To keep the covenant was to practice circumcision faithfully; to break (v. 14b) the covenant was to be uncircumcised (v. 14a). Lest the reader conclude that the whole of the covenant was simply the rite of circumcision, the author included the words "and it will be the sign of the covenant" (v. 11).

Command #215, Ge 17:10, Circumcision: "You must circumcise every male."

Sarah's part in the covenant was to be the one through whom the seed of Abraham was born. She was to be the mother of nations and "the kings of nations will come from her" (v. 16). In her old age, she was to be the one through whom it would be demonstrated that God alone could fulfill his covenanted promise. As with Abraham, Sarai's new name was to be a sign of her part in the covenant. She would no longer be called Sarai, but would be called Sarah (v. 15). The author does not explain the meaning of Sarah's new name as he had with the renaming of Abraham (v. 5). He apparently takes it for granted that the reader will understand verse 16 as an explanation of her name. Since in Hebrew Sarah self-evidently means "princess," the reader could easily recognize that she was to be called "princess" because "kings will come forth from her" (v. 16b).

e. Abraham's Response (17:17–18)

Abraham's response to God's promise is not what the reader would expect: "Abraham fell on his face and laughed" (v. 17a). In the light of the author's portrayal of Abraham thus far in Genesis (e.g., 15:6), it seems unlikely that his laughter is intended to point to a lack of faith—although one must admit that the text leaves that impression. Without commenting directly on Abraham's surprising reaction to God's promise, however, the author allows Abraham's own words in verse 17b to uncover the real motivation behind his laughter ("Will a son be born to a man a hundred years old? Will Sarah bear a child at the age of ninety?"), and thus leave a final verdict on the nature of his laughter somewhat in the lurch.

In the following chapter, when Sarah also responded to God's promise with laughter, the author shows that her laughter met with divine disapproval ("Then the LORD said, 'Why did Sarah laugh?'" 18:12–13). The absence of such a rebuke of Abraham's laughter here in chapter 17 may suggest that his laughter did not reflect so much a lack of faith as a limitation of his faith in what God must do to fulfill his promise. Abraham is depicted here not as one whose faith in God has reached full maturity; rather, he is one whose faith must still be pushed beyond its present limits. In Abraham's laughter we are allowed to see the outer limits of his faith. His faith must grow if he is to continue to put his trust in God's promise. In any event, one clear purpose of the author in including the note about Abraham's laughter can be seen in the fact that the Hebrew expression "he laughed" (יִצְחָק) foreshadows the name Isaac (יִצְחָק).

The irony of Abraham's response is evident. Even in his surprising response of laughter in the face of God's promise, Abraham's laughter became a verbal sign marking the ultimate fulfillment of the promise in Isaac. Throughout the remainder of the narratives surrounding the birth of Isaac, a key word within each major section is *laughter*. Sarah laughed (18:12); Lot's sons-in-law laughed (19:14); all who heard of Sarah's birth to Isaac laughed (21:6); the son of Hagar laughed (21:9) at Isaac; finally, Isaac's own failure to trust in God (26:7) is uncovered when the Philistine king sees him "laughing" (26:8; NIV has "caressing") with Rebekah. Thus, for the author, both the power of God and the limitations of human faith are embodied in that most ambiguous of human acts, laughter.

For the first time the name *Abraham*, rather than *Abram*, is used as the subject of a verb: "Abraham fell on his face and laughed" (v. 17; cf. v. 3: "Abram fell on his face"). The author's irony is apparent in that Abraham was laughing at the very thing which his new name was intended to mark: "You will become a father of many nations" (v. 4).

f. God's Third Speech (17:19–22)

The content of the third divine speech extends the covenant to include Isaac, who is to be born of Sarah, and consequently to exclude Ishmael, the son of Hagar. Thus Isaac was not to be one of the anonymous "seed" who was to receive the benefits of the covenant. He is here brought to the level of a participant in the original covenant: "I will establish my covenant with him as an everlasting covenant for his descendants after him" (v. 19). Thus the identification of the covenant "seed" of Abraham is made more specific. The descendants of Abraham who are heirs of the covenant are those through Sarah, that is, the "seed" of Isaac. In this respect God's words to Abraham concerning Isaac in 17:19 already anticipate the reiteration of these words in the covenant with Isaac (26:3—"I will establish the oath which I swore to Abraham you father"). In this final speech, however, the author is careful to show that although Ishmael had been excluded from the covenant with Abraham, he and his descendants were still to live under the blessing of God (v. 20). In fact, in God's blessing of Ishmael (v. 20), he reiterated both his original blessing of all humankind in 1:28 ("I will surely bless him; I will make him fruitful and will greatly increase his numbers," 17:20) and his blessing of Abraham in 12:2 ("I will make him into a great nation," 17:20b). Just as the "seed" of Isaac would form a great nation of twelve tribes (49:1–

27), so the "seed" of Ishmael, under God's blessing, would form a great nation of twelve princes (17:20b). The list of these twelve princes is given in 25:12–16.

g. Abraham's Final Response (17:23)

Abraham's final response shows that he obeyed the covenant as commanded in 17:9—he circumcised all male members of his household, "as God had spoken to him" (v. 23). This final remark about Abraham's obedience carries the reader back to the beginning of the narrative where the injunction was given: "walk before me [הִתְהַלֵּךְ] and be blameless [תָמִים, v. 1]." This portrait of an obedient Abraham is reminiscent of the picture of Noah, who also "walked with God" (הִתְהַלֶּךְ) and was "blameless" (תָמִים, 6:9). In the light of the sparsity of these terms in Genesis it seems likely that the author expects the reader to make an association between these two great men based on the close recurrence of both terms. "Blameless" occurs in Genesis only in these two texts; "walk before God" occurs more frequently, but in carefully chosen contexts (Enoch, 5:22, 24; Noah, 6:9; Abraham, 17:1; 24:40; 48:15 [with Isaac]). Thus Abraham and Noah are presented as examples of those who have lived in obedience to the covenant and are thus "blameless" before God, because both obeyed God "as he commanded them" (17:23; cf. 6:22; 7:5, 9, 16).

h. Conclusion (17:24–27)

The ages of Abraham and Ishmael mark an inclusio to the narrative, which opened with the age of Abraham (17:1) and, by implication, the age of Ishmael. The final word at the close restates Abraham's obedient response to the covenant. The chiastic structure of verses 26 and 27 adds a certain formality to the conclusion as well as stresses the major topic of the chapter: Abraham obeyed God's will in carrying out his covenant obligations.

6. Three Visitors (18:1–33)

a. The Lord Appears to Abraham (18:1a)

Chapter 18 is an extensively developed narrative showing clear signs of theological reflection at several key points. The issues that appear to be central to the chapter (the announcement of the birth of Isaac and the question of the fate of the righteous amid divine judgment) are dealt with not only in this chapter but also in chapters 17 (announcement of Isaac's birth) and 19 (fate of the righteous amid divine judgment). The author's treatment of these two themes in chapter 18, however, shows his concern to push beyond a mere reporting of the events to develop them into a lesson in theology. The narrative begins, in the same way as chapter 17, with the author's report that "the LORD appeared to Abraham." The importance of this comment at the beginning of the narrative should not be overlooked. Its effect is to help clarify one of the most puzzling features of the narrative, namely, who were the three men who visited Abraham and what was their mission?

In opening the narrative with the statement that the Lord "appeared" to Abraham, the author leaves no doubt that in some (albeit unexplained) way, these men represented the Lord's appearance to Abraham. Not all questions are answered by beginning the narrative in this way, however. In fact, such an opening gives rise to several new questions. But opening the narrative with a reference to the Lord's "appearing" to Abraham provides an important context that serves as a guide throughout the reading of the remainder of the chapter. However one sorts out the details of the story, the fact remains that, in sum, the events of the chapter constitute an account of the Lord's appearance to Abraham.

The mention of the "oaks of Mamre" reestablishes the location of Abraham during these events. When last noted he had moved his tents near the "oaks of Mamre" (13:18). It appears that the author wants us to see that Abraham had not moved since he settled near the "oaks of Mamre at Hebron," and thus, at the beginning of chapter 18, he updates the reader on Abraham's whereabouts. Perhaps the purpose is to reestablish the scene at the close of chapter 13, where Abraham was dwelling in the land God had promised to him and Lot had turned away to "pitch his tents near Sodom" (13:12). At that time the reader had already been apprised of the condition of the people of Sodom: "Now the men of Sodom were wicked and were sinning greatly against the LORD" (13:13).

In verse 1 the Hebrew text does not have "to Abraham," as the NIV does, but rather "to him." The antecedent of "him" is "Abraham" (cf. 17:26). The identification of Abraham within chapter 18 does not occur until verse 6. Thus the opening section of chapter 18 is closely bound with the end of chapter 17 and the account of the circumcision of Abraham and his household.

That the whole chapter is to be understood within the context of the Lord's appearance to Abraham can be seen in the final verse (v. 33), which recounts that after he had finished speaking, "the LORD went away." Elsewhere the conclusion of the expression "the LORD/God appeared" is marked by a brief notice of the Lord's departure (cf. 17:1b and 22a; 35:9 and 35:13). Consequently, we are to understand the whole of chapter 18 to fit within the account of the Lord's appearance to Abraham.

b. Three Men Arrive (18:1b–8)

The narrative of the arrival of three men at Abraham's tent is complicated by several uncertainties within the text. First, the relationship between the three men and the appearance of the Lord (17:1a) is not explicitly explained. Second, there appears to be a conscious shift in the verbal forms between verse 3 and verses 4–9. In verse 3 the verbs and pronouns are all masculine singular, whereas in verses 4–9 the forms are masculine plural (e.g., v. 4).[60]

Finally, there is the question of the nature of the relationship between the uncertainties just raised in chapter 18 and their apparent counterparts in chapter 19, where, for example, the relationship between the "two angels" (or "messengers," 19:1) and the Lord remains unexplained (e.g., the two "men" [19:12] tell Lot that they will destroy Sodom [v. 13], but the text states

---

[60]Also, there is uncertainty about the ultimate value of the vowel points in the MT, which in v. 3 have rendered Abraham's greeting ("my lord," NIV) as an address to God, "O Lord" (by lengthening the final vowel to a *qāmeṣ*, rather than *patah*, as in 19:2).

that "the LORD rained down burning sulfur on Sodom and Gomorrah" [v. 24]). The verbs and pronouns in Lot's greeting are all masculine plural (e.g., 19:2) and continue to be so until the end of the story, where the same sort of unevenness found in chapter 18 reappears (e.g., 19:17: "As soon as they [masculine plural] brought them out, he said [masculine singular]"; or 19:18: "Lot said to them [masculine plural] . . . 'Your servant ['your' is masculine singular] . . .'"). Also, unlike 18:3, the Masoretes' vocalization of "my lords" (NIV) in 19:2 reflects an address to persons other than God (אֲדֹנַי rather than אֲדֹנָי), whereas when the same persons are addressed in 19:18, the Masoretic form of "my lords" (NIV) is again the form used only to address God (אֲדֹנָי).

Such features have left the impression that the text of these chapters has come down to us in a highly irregular and uneven form, leading many to suppose that more than one version of the story lies behind the present narrative. For example, Hermann Gunkel concluded that the "interchange of the singular and plural forms does not follow a recognizable principle but is rather completely unmotivated."[61] Over against such an evaluation, however, one can confidently say that the text as it presently stands does evoke a singular and coherent interpretation, if one reads it with an eye to the importance of every detail and apparent irregularity. As the following comments will attempt to demonstrate, throughout the narrative the apparent irregularities in the text can be seen not as the result of a haphazard weaving together of divergent stories, but as the result of the author's careful balancing of two central theological positions with respect to the divine presence and power. Such irregularities as exist in the narrative are best understood as the result of a conscious attempt to stress at one and the same time the theological relevance of the promise of God's presence along with his transcendent, sovereign power. Thus the final unevenness of the narrative should not be traced to its diverse origin (however much that may have played a part in its present shape) or to a careless disregard for cohesion, but rather to the author's struggle to remain faithful to the central theological constraints of his task, namely, the need to reconcile two equally important views of God.

The close similarities between this account of Abraham's visit by "three men" (18:1–3) and that of Lot's visit by the "two angels/men" (19:1–2) suggest that the narratives should be explored further for clues regarding their interrelationship. First, the scene in chapter 18 opens with Abraham sitting "at the entrance to his tent" (18:1), just as in the opening of chapter 19 Lot is found "sitting in the gateway of the city" (19:1). Second, just as when Abraham "saw" the men he ran "to meet them," "bowed low to the ground," and said, "O LORD, if now. . . ," so also in the account of Lot in chapter 19, when he "saw" the angels/men, he got up "to meet them," "bowed down with his face to the ground," and said, "Behold now, O lords. . . ." The effect of these unmistakable similarities between the two accounts is to highlight the one primary difference between them: the way the visitors are greeted. Abraham addressed the visitors as "Lord" and appropriately used the singular to address all three men in verse 3 (see

---

[61]Hermann Gunkel, *Genesis übersetzt und erklärt*, 9th ed. (Göttingen: Vandenhoeck & Ruprecht, 1977), 194.

above). Lot addressed the visitors as "lords" and thus used the plural to address the two angels/men. What is the reader to make of this difference? The most apparent explanation is that the author wants us to see that Abraham, who had just entered the covenant (chap. 17), recognized the Lord when he appeared to him, whereas Lot, who now lived in Sodom, did not recognize the Lord. The lives of the two men continue to offer a contrast. Abraham knew God, but Lot did not.

We should note that the statement in 18:1, "the LORD appeared to him," has prepared the reader for Abraham's greeting the three men as "the Lord." In the case of Lot's greeting the two men as simply "my lords," the reader is also in a position to judge Lot's response. In 18:21, the reader had been informed that the Lord was on his way to Sodom; thus when the two angels/men arrived, the most likely inference is that they represented the Lord's visit. That such is the case is later confirmed within the narrative. As the narrative progresses, Lot comes to the point of recognizing his visitors as emissaries of the Lord. Thus the last time he addressed these same two angels/men (19:18), he called "them" (note the plural, 19:18) "Lord," and appropriately, like Abraham, he addressed them both with the singular. In keeping with Lot's recognition of the identity of the two angels/men, in 19:19 Lot stated his requests to them in the same words that Abraham (in 18:3) had addressed his three visitors (compare also Lot's words in 19:19a—"If your servant has found favor in your eyes"—with those of Abraham in 18:3—"If now I have found favor in your eyes").

The interchange between the singular and plural verbs and pronouns in 18:3 (where the singular is used) and 18:4ff. (where the plural is used) appears to be one of the ways in which the author attempts to clarify a crucial point in the narrative, namely, the nature of the divine-human relationship. The biblical God is one who makes himself known intimately and concretely to his covenant people. He can make himself known through "speaking" (1:3), "in a vision" (15:1), or through his "angel" (16:7) who speaks for him. He can even "appear" to individuals, as in 12:7; 17:1; and 18:1. Those narratives which speak of God's making himself known through words, visions, and angels would not be expected to pose a difficulty to the reader of the Pentateuch who was familiar with the strict prohibition against the presentation of God in any physical form in passages such as Deuteronomy 4:15 ("You saw no form of any kind the day the LORD spoke to you at Horeb"). But passages that expressly state that God "appeared" to someone (12:7; 17:1; 18:1) would naturally raise difficult questions. How is it that God can "appear" and yet his form not be seen ("You did not see his form," Dt 4:15)? How can God "appear" and yet say, "My face must not be seen" (Ex 33:23)? Such questions appear to lie behind the apparent unevenness of the narrative in chapter 18.

By carefully identifying and distinguishing the characters in the narrative by means of the singular and plural verbal forms, the author is able to show that the Lord's appearing to Abraham and the visit of the three men are one and the same event. God appeared to Abraham, but not "face to face" in his own physical form. Rather, the author has so arranged the singular and plural forms that the three men always represent God's presence and can be identified with God's presence while remaining clearly distinct from him.

A reading of the narrative with an eye for the alternations between singular and plural reveals the remarkable skill and timing of the author and makes clear his theological program. First, we should not overlook the fact that the author has identified the scene as a visit from the Lord ("And the LORD appeared to him," 18:1). Second, Abraham saw the three men, greeted them, and then addressed them as the Lord, using the singular throughout verse 3. Once it is established that this is a visit from the Lord, Abraham addressed the three men in the plural, and the author himself follows Abraham's lead by using the plural in the description of the three men in verses 4–9 ("and they said," 18:5, 9).

At verse 10, without reidentifying the speaker, the author picks up the narrative again with the singular, "And he said."[62] By not identifying the speaker in verse 10, the author has minimized the break which naturally would arise from the alternation between the plural "and they said" (18:5, 9) and the singular "and he said" (v. 10), but the break remains intact. First the men spoke, then an unidentified "he" (later identified as the Lord) spoke; thus one has the impression within the narrative as a whole that this "he" has spoken in behalf of the men and, consequently, the men spoke for "him."

The reader is left the task of filling the gaps with the most contextually appropriate explanation. That explanation seems to be that the three men, as such, are to be understood as the physical "appearance" of the Lord to Abraham. In other words, though God himself did not appear to Abraham in physical form, the three men represent his presence. Similarly, the burning bush of Exodus 3:2–3 was a physical representation of God's presence but was not actually the physical presence of God. In such a way the actual presence of God among his covenant people was assured without leaving the impression that God may have a physical form.

The identity of the "he" is explicitly recovered in verses 13–14, where the author supplies "the LORD" as the verbal subject whose words are a continuation of those in verse 10: "I will return to you at the appointed time next year and Sarah will have a son" (v. 14). Thus the "he" of verse 10 can be none other than the Lord, though he was not at that point in the narrative identified as such in order to maintain the close connection between his words and those of the three men.

This same interweaving of the three men and the Lord continues throughout the narrative. In verse 16 the men made their way toward Sodom and Abraham accompanied them; but in verse 17, it is the Lord who spoke (first to himself, vv. 17–19, and then to Abraham, vv. 20–21). But as the Lord finished speaking, the men departed from Abraham to go toward Sodom (v. 22); the Lord remained with Abraham (v. 22) and did not depart until verse 33. Thus the narrative teaches that the Lord can speak to Abraham with or without the men, but he has appeared to Abraham in the form of the three men (v. 2a).

In a similar way, the "two angels" of 19:1 (later called simply "the men," e.g., v. 10) were addressed with the plural at the beginning of the narrative because Lot did not recognize them for who they are, emissaries of

---

[62]The NIV has correctly added "the LORD" in its translation, but one should keep in mind that the Hebrew text does not have this reidentification of the subject.

the Lord. But after he learned who they were and who had sent them, Lot addressed them both in the plural ("them," v. 18a, and the plural form "the Lord," v. 18b) and in the singular (e.g., "your servant," v. 19). Moreover, in this narrative, the author even follows Lot in this usage (viz., "and he said"; the MT already has the singular in v. 17).

The plural pronoun in verse 18, along with the plural verbal forms in verse 16, make the singular form of the MT very difficult and thus, according to the rules of textual criticism, to be preferred. The plural of the LXX, Peshitta, and Vulgate are likely the translators' attempt to smooth out the difficulty of the singular in the light of the plurals in verse 16 as well as the plural pronoun "to them" in verse 18a, though it is not impossible that they represent an early Hebrew text with the same intention. In verse 21 the author also conceals the identity of the "he" to smooth over (but not to eliminate) the break caused by the change from plural to singular. As was the case in 18:13, in 19:24 the "he" is finally identified as "the LORD." This identification was done at considerable distance in the narrative from the switch to the singular so as not to disturb further the already difficult break caused by the shift to the singular. The reader, however, has already been given advance notice that the "two angels/men" in chapter 19 are the Lord in that the Lord had said (18:20), "I will go down and I will see this outcry that has come to me"(v. 21). By means of this statement, the reader is able to draw the obvious conclusion at the beginning of chapter 19 that the visit by the "two angels/men" represents the Lord's visit to the city spoken of in 18:21—a conclusion Lot himself failed to draw. By thus depicting Lot's failure to recognize the Lord, the author gives the reader advance insight into Lot's own state of awareness of the Lord's presence.

c. Promise of a Son (18:9–15)

Although the announcement of the birth of a son is made to Abraham, the focus of the narrative is clearly on Sarah's response. In her laughter (צָחַק, 18:12), the name of the son Isaac (יִצְחָק) is foreshadowed. But the significance of Sarah's laughter goes beyond that. Her laughter becomes the occasion to draw an important theological point from the narrative, namely, that what the Lord was about to do to fulfill his promise to Abraham was a matter "too wonderful" (v. 14) even for his own people to imagine.

(1) Where Is Sarah? (18:9–10)

These verses set the stage for the brief but intricate narrative which follows. The three men inquired about Sarah, but they spoke only to Abraham. Sarah remained "off camera" through most of the narrative, though the author apprises the reader of her thoughts and motives as she listened to the conversation. Only in verse 15 was she finally addressed directly, but even then she was given no opportunity to respond.

(2) Sarah's Age (18:11)

As background to Sarah's response, the author inserts an explanation. Abraham and Sarah were too old to have children. As all women her age, Sarah was no longer physically capable of even conceiving a child. The structure of the Hebrew sentence suggests that the last statement ("Sarah was past the age of childbearing") is a restatement of the sense of the first.[63] In such a statement it is possible to detect an attempt to ensure a harmony between this passage and Genesis 25:1–4. There it was stated that Abraham took another wife, apparently after the death of Sarah, and that she bore him sons. Thus, although Abraham's age was a factor, the primary obstacle to the fulfillment of the promise was Sarah's old age. The central importance of Sarah's age, over against that of Abraham, can be further seen in her own restatement of the problem in verse 12. Here she looks at her own old age first and then that of Abraham: "After I am worn out, will I now have pleasure, and my husband is old." Finally, within the narrative itself, the Lord rephrases Sarah's thoughts (v. 13) as, "Will I really have a child, now that I am old?" with no mention of Abraham's old age.

The point is that these verses bring the promise to the brink of failure, pushing the unlikelihood of its fulfillment far beyond the previous levels. It was not only that Sarah was barren (11:30; 16:1) or that Abraham was old (since he will later again have children without any apparent divine intervention, 25:1–4). These obstacles are in themselves great enough to demonstrate that the promise, when fulfilled, came from God alone. But the author takes the reader a step further. Sarah was even past the physical age of bearing children. A child was not simply unlikely—it was now impossible (v. 14) that Sarah should have a child.

(3) Sarah Laughs (18:12–15)

The key to the sense of this short passage lies in the Lord's question to Abraham about Sarah's laughter. The subtle changes in the wording of Sarah's thoughts reveal that the Lord was not simply restating her thoughts but was interpreting them as well. In this way the writer is able to give the reader a deep insight into the meaning of the passage. First, the Lord restated Sarah's somewhat ambiguous statement ("After I am worn out, will I now have pleasure?") as simply, "Will I really have a child?" Then he took Sarah's statement about her husband ("My husband is old," 18:12) and reshaped it into a statement about herself ("I am old," v. 13). Finally, he went beyond her actual words to the intent of those words: "Is anything impossible with the LORD?" (v. 14). By means of these questions to Abraham, the underlying issue in the narrative is put before the reader, that is, the physical impossibility of the fulfillment of the promise through Sarah.

Once the obstacle of the physical impossibility of Sarah's giving birth to a son was firmly established, the Lord then repeated his promise to Abraham: "I will return to you at the appointed time next year, and Sarah will have a son" (v. 14b). At this point in the narrative, Sarah, who had only been "listening at the door of the tent" (v. 10), entered the conversation with the terse reply, "I did not laugh" (v. 15). The author quickly dismisses this reply as a lie (v. 15) and goes on to explain that "she was afraid" (v. 15b). (The NIV reverses the order of the clauses here, but the sense remains the same.) The narrative then concludes with the Lord's reiteration of what the reader by now certainly knows to be the truth, namely, that Sarah did laugh (v. 15b).

In the course of this brief but strategically important narrative, the

---

[63]See F. I. Andersen, *The Sentence in Biblical Hebrew*, 46ff.

reader has come to a new level of understanding regarding the promise of a son and its potential fulfillment. The promise was beyond all physical possibility. No one could know this more than Sarah herself, and through the course of the narrative the author has artfully and delicately revealed her most intimate knowledge about the promise to the reader. Having made that point, the author immediately brings the narrative to a close and moves on to a new section of the story.

d. Departure of the Three Men (18:16)

As the three men rose and looked out toward Sodom, Abraham accompanied them to send them off. The men had been strangely out of the picture for most of the immediately preceding narrative, but the author brings them back into view just before the Lord speaks in verse 17. In so doing, the author once again establishes an association between the Lord's presence and the appearance of the three men. In the middle of verse 16, the author begins skillfully to turn the narrative toward chapter 19 by directing the reader's attention to a seemingly insignificant gesture on the part of the three men as they rose to leave: "They looked down toward Sodom." As the men's heads turned to look down over the doomed city, the author directs the reader's attention also toward that city in anticipation of the events of the next chapter. The intense preoccupation with the events surrounding the announcement of the birth of Isaac, which has played such a dominate role in the narrative thus far, suddenly vanishes and is not again seen until the time of its fulfillment two chapters later (21:1). The narrative now proceeds to follow the glance of the three men as they look out toward Sodom.

e. The Lord Reflects on What Is About to Happen (18:17–19)

The syntax of verse 17 suggests that the author intends the Lord's words to be read as the background to what follows. Without these verses, the narrative would read directly from verse 16 into verse 20. The intervening verses, however, provide an important context for the discourse between the Lord and Abraham, because, like the direct discourse throughout Genesis, the words of the Lord here reveal the inner motivation for his actions ("what I am about to do"). The Lord's words are concise but they have far-reaching consequences. Verse 18 looks back to the original promise that Abraham would become a "great nation" (cf. 12:2) and that "in him all the nations of the land will be blessed" (cf. 12:3).

Verse 19 appears to be an expansion on the ideas of 17:1 ("Walk before me and be blameless"). Nowhere else in the book, however, do we have such a reflective perspective on the events of the whole of the Abrahamic narratives. First, the Lord puts into words that which has been a central part of the narrative but has not yet been expressly verbalized, namely, Abraham's election: "I have chosen him." Second, the Lord goes on to express his purpose in choosing Abraham; as it turns out, this purpose goes beyond that revealed in the preceding narratives. Here the attention is directed internally ("to keep the way of the LORD") with the end in view that Abraham and his descendants should "do that which is righteous and just." Only then will the Lord fulfill what he had promised to Abraham ("so that the LORD may bring about that which he had promised"). The notion of an internalized obedience found in this verse is remarkably close to the terms of the new covenant found in the prophetic literature: "I will put my law in their minds and write it in their hearts" (Jer 31:33) and is deeply rooted in the theology of Deuteronomy ("The LORD your God will circumcise your hearts and the hearts of your descendants, so that you may love him with all your heart . . . in order that you might live," Dt 30:6).

f. Outcry of Sodom and Gomorrah (18:20–21)

Although verse 20 is a continuation of the Lord's speaking, the syntax of the verse suggests that his words are in a different setting than those preceding. In verses 17–19, it appears that the Lord was speaking to himself or that the author was simply recalling what the Lord had said on another occasion, not within the immediate sequence of events. In any case, Abraham was not addressed directly in those verses. In verses 20–21, however, Abraham was most certainly the one addressed. The Lord's words to Abraham in verses 20–21 were the answer to the question posed by the Lord in verse 17 ("Shall I hide from Abraham what I am about to do?"). In verses 20–21, the Lord revealed to Abraham what he was about to do: go down to investigate the wickedness of the cities of Sodom and Gomorrah.

g. The Men Leave; Abraham Remains Before the Lord (18:22)

It should be noted that the narrative first states that the Lord said, "I will go down and see" (v. 21), and then recounts that "the men turned away and went toward Sodom" (v. 22). Thus once again the Lord and the men are brought into such close association that the actions of the one are identified with the actions of the other. It is important to note the inherent logic of the narrative at this point since this same logic applies in the next chapter. If "the men" are the emissaries of the Lord and represent his presence amid everyday affairs, then when they journey to Sodom and Gomorrah, as in verse 22, it can rightly be said that the Lord himself was visiting these cities, as in verse 21 ("I will go down and see"). As has been the case throughout this narrative, "the men" represent the Lord's appearance but are not actually identified as the Lord. Thus that the Lord remained behind (v. 22b) after "the men" had left (v. 22a) is no more a surprise than that the Lord was again present with Lot in Sodom along with "the men" (19:12, 16; see discussion above). So when the Lord said, "I will go down and see," the reader is led to conclude that, as in chapter 18, "the men" in chapter 19 represented the Lord's presence with Lot.

One question remains, however. If the three men left Abraham, why did only "two messengers" (19:1) arrive in Sodom? It seems reasonably clear that the two messengers who visited Lot are two of the "three men" who visited Abraham, especially in view of the fact that in chapter 19 the "messengers" are subsequently referred to simply as "the men." But what happened to the other "man"? This question has given rise to several speculations about the identity of the one man who did not visit Sodom. The most common explanation is that the "man" is a christophany, that is, an appearance of the second person of the Trinity in human form, before the Incarnation. Thus, when the text says that "the men turned away and went toward Sodom" (18:22a), and that the Lord remained with Abraham (18:22b), and then further that only "two messengers" (19:1) came to Sodom, it seems to follow that one of the men must have stayed behind with Abraham. Since we know that the Lord stayed behind, that man must have been the Lord. Abraham was thus visited by the preincarnate Christ, who was accompanied by two "angels" (19:1).

Although this interpretation has many features of the narrative in its favor, the primary difficulty with such an explanation is that it overlooks the fairly clear indication that although Lot failed to appreciate it, the author sees the "two messengers" as representing the presence of the Lord (e.g., "And Lot said to them, 'Lord,'" 19:18), like the three men in chapter 18. Thus the fact that the men in chapter 18 are referred to as "the Lord" does not mean that one of them is actually the Lord; rather, it means that all three represent the Lord's presence. If the two men in chapter 19 can be addressed as "the Lord" even though they merely represent the Lord, so also the three men in chapter 18 (e.g., 18:3). Hence, after calling attention to the fact that Lot is visited by only two messengers, the author subsequently refers to them simply as "the men" (19:12, 16), as in chapter 18.

The question still remains, however, that if all three men left Abraham and traveled toward Sodom, why then is Lot visited by only two men rather than the three men of chapter 18? Where did the third man go, if not to Sodom? The answer to that question is readily at hand in chapter 18. It seems quite clear that the two men in Sodom represent the fulfillment of the Lord's intention to "go down and see if what they have done is as bad as the outcry." But how did the Lord investigate the "outcry of Gomorrah"? Did he not say he was going down to Gomorrah to see their deeds as well? Since the narrative records only the events of the men's visit to Sodom, because that is where Lot lived (13:12), and since the conclusion of chapter 19 mentions the Lord's destruction not only of Sodom but also of Gomorrah (19:24), the question is left open in the narrative whether the Lord also investigated the "outcry of Gomorrah" as he said he would. Thus, according to the logic (the "outcry" that had reached the Lord was the "outcry of Sodom and Gomorrah" [18:21], and the Lord destroyed both Sodom and Gomorrah [19:24]) of the narrative of chapters 18 and 19, the author apparently intends to imply that the third man went to Gomorrah and investigated that city. In other words, by specifying the number of men who visited Lot, the author leaves the narrative of chapter 19 open to a reading that harmonizes at all points. By specifying the number of men who visited Sodom, the author has left the reader with an answer to the question of the Lord's righteous and just treatment of Gomorrah—the third man visited Gomorrah, and thus "the judge of all the land" has "dealt justly" (18:25). It is precisely this theme which is dealt with in the intervening narrative.

h. Abraham Intercedes (18:23–33)

The central issue of the discourse between Abraham and the Lord is expressed in Abraham's question: "Will not the judge of all the earth do right?" (18:25). The Lord's answer, which is echoed throughout the narrative, is a resounding yes. Abraham persisted with the question until that answer became absolutely clear.

The sequence which Abraham followed has been variously interpreted. He started with a question about fifty righteous persons in a city and concluded with the question of ten righteous persons. Why did he stop at ten persons? Why not ask if there are nine, eight, and so on? Did he not care about Lot and his family who only numbered four? The narrative of 19:29 shows that the author considers Lot to have been the central "righteous" one under discussion. Why then did Abraham not continue his line of questions down to four righteous ones in the city?

One possible solution is that the sequence fifty down to ten, in units of ten, would naturally end with ten—the next question would have been "if there were no righteous left in the city?" The answer to that question was not the concern of Abraham since he was interested only in the salvation of the righteous amid the unrighteous, not the broader question of the destruction of the wicked. Abraham had his answer in general terms and did not need to pursue the question to the exact number. Thus the author of the narrative cuts off the questioning at ten persons in order to allow the issue to remain at a more general level.

In Abraham's concern for Lot, the narrative addresses the larger issue of God's treatment of any righteous one (not merely Lot) in his judgment of the wicked. It is also important to note that in the narrative which follows (chapter 19), the city of Sodom was not spared on Lot's behalf. The city was destroyed and Lot was taken out of the city—a scenario not anticipated in Abraham's line of questions in Genesis 18. It may then be that within the narrative at the close of chapter 18, Abraham's abrupt conclusion to his questions is intended to suit the events of the narrative in chapter 19. By ending the questions at ten righteous in the city, the narrative leaves open the question of what God would do if less than ten righteous were found in the city. Thus Abraham's questions and God's reply are shown to harmonize with the actual course of events in chapter 19, where the city was not spared on Lot's behalf. It should be pointed out, however, that as the narrative continues in chapter 19, though Sodom was not spared for Lot's sake, the "little city" of Zoar was spared on Lot's behalf (see commentary below on 19:17–22).

7. Lot and Sodom (19:1–38)

a. *Two Angels Meet Lot (19:1a)*

According to 19:10, 12, 16, the two "messengers" of verse 1 were "men." The definite article on the word *messengers* suggests that the two men have already been identified and thus must have been the men who visited Abraham in the previous chapter (18:3). The mention of the fact that only two of the three men (18:2) were sent to investigate the "outcry" of Sodom (18:20) allows the inference that the third man was sent to investigate the "outcry" of the city of Gomorrah (18:20; see previous discussion on chap. 18). We hear nothing more about the third man. After 19:1, the narrative refers to the "messengers" both as "the men" (vv. 10, 12, 16) and as "the messengers" (v. 15). More important is that toward the end of the narrative, the men, as in chapter 18, are represented as a visitation of the LORD (19:18, "And Lot said to them, 'No please, O Lord' "; see previous discussion on chap. 18). The men have come to carry out the Lord's retribution against the wickedness of the city (19:13); but in response to Abraham's prayer for the righteous (18:23–32), they have also come to rescue Lot (19:29).

b. At Lot's House (19:1b–11)

The depiction of the events at Lot's house on the eve of the destruction of Sodom and Gomorrah is intended to give justification for the divine judgment on the two cities. Even Lot, the righteous one who was ultimately rescued, is shown to have been tainted by his association with Sodom. Unlike Abraham, who immediately recognized God's presence in the visit of the men (18:2), Lot appears quite insensitive to God's presence with the messengers—he addresses them only as "sirs" (19:2). Though he was just as hospitable as Abraham and can certainly not be put in the same class as the men of Sodom, Lot's suggestion that the men of the city take his own daughters and do with them as they please can hardly be taken, within the present narrative at least, to be a sign of his good character. In fact, at the close of the narrative, in an ironic turn of events, Lot himself inadvertently carried out his own horrible proposal by lying with his own daughters (19:30–38).

The contrasting picture of Abraham and Lot, then, appears to show the consequences of Lot's earlier decision to "pitch his tent toward Sodom" (13:12). At the close of the narrative, Lot is pictured as the father of the Moabites and Ammonites. Thus the fate of Lot was the fate of Moab (19:37) and of Ammon (19:38). Though they lived on the border of the promised land, they would not enjoy its blessings (Nu 24:17).

c. Warning (19:12–14)

The messengers stated clearly their twofold purpose: They had been sent to destroy the city and to rescue Lot and his family. The response of the two sons-in-law (v. 14) shows that they are at one with the rest of the men of the city. This provides a further vindication of the divine punishment that was to follow. A curious wordplay in the response of the two sons-in-law serves as a link with the previous chapter. When they heard of the impending divine their city, the sons saw Lot's words as an occasion for "laughter" (כִּמְצַחֵק, v. 14; NIV "thought they were joking"). The wordplay of their "laughter" (צחק), the "laughter" (צחק) of Sarah (18:12–13, 15), and the "laughter" (צחק) of Abraham (17:17) is obvious and provides a link across these narratives to the ultimate fulfillment of God's promise in the birth of Isaac, whose name means "laughter" (צחק).

d. Lot's Deliverance (19:15–16)

In contrast to the account of the wickedness of the city of Sodom, which was placed in the darkness of night (19:2, 4–5), the rescue of Lot occurs at the break of day. In turning the reader's attention to such details the writer uses a common biblical image that pictures salvation as a sunrise dispelling the evil darkness (see comments above on Ge 1:2) and consequently provides a larger context for viewing the events of this chapter. In contrast to the men of Sodom who blindly groped for the door of Lot's house, Lot and his family were taken by the hand (19:16) and led out of the city to safety. In order to show that the rescue of Lot was in response to the prayer of Abraham, the narrative reads so that the words of the messengers recall explicitly the words of Abraham's prayer in behalf of the righteous in the previous chapter. Abraham had prayed, "Will the righteous be swept away along with the wicked?" (18:23); similarly, the messengers warn Lot and his family to leave the city, "lest you be swept away on account of the iniquity of the city" (19:15, and again in v. 17). In fact, the narrator explicitly reminds the readers that Lot's rescue was an answer to Abraham's prayer in the previous chapter: "And God remembered Abraham and sent Lot from the midst of the destruction of the cities where Lot lived" (v. 29). The picture of Lot then is that of a righteous man living amid the unrighteous—a righteous man who has been rescued from the fate of the wicked through the intercession of God's chosen one.

One further important detail is added to the narrative picture of Lot's rescue. Surprisingly, the basis of God's saving Lot was not Lot's righteousness but the Lord's compassion. When the men took hold of Lot and led him and his family out of the doomed city, the writer is careful to note that this was "on account of the compassion of the LORD" (v. 16). Lot's righteousness is not apparent from the narrative of chapter 19. It comes only from the connection that the writer establishes between Abraham's prayer "for the righteous" in chapter 18 and the events of Lot's rescue in chapter 19. When 19:29 states that God remembered Abraham and rescued Lot from the destruction of the cities, the natural inference is that Lot was the "righteous one" whom Abraham had in mind in his prayer in chapter 18. In the account of the rescue itself, however, the emphasis is not on Lot's righteousness but on God's compassion. Lot's words to the messengers (19:19) reinforce the importance of God's grace. Lot freely acknowledged that he had found "grace" and "mercy" before God.

e. Lot's Flight to Zoar (19:17–22)

A brief episode recounted at the conclusion of Lot's rescue prolongs the reader's attention. Lot requested shelter in the nearby city of Zoar, and granting the request, the Lord saved the city of Zoar from destruction (19:21). The effect of this short episode is to strengthen further the author's point that Lot's rescue was the result of prayer, both Abraham's and his own (v. 19). One can see a reminder of the importance of Abraham's prayer (chap. 18) in the fact that with Lot's request the actual circumstances envisioned in Abraham's prayer are realized: God saved the city on account of the few righteous ones in it. God had promised not to destroy the city "on behalf of" the righteous in it (18:26, 28–29, 30–32). So now, though Sodom was destroyed, Zoar was saved from the destruction on account of Lot (19:21). Thus, by including this episode in the narrative, the writer has resolved a potential interpretive problem between chapters 18 and 19. If Lot was the "righteous one" whom Abraham had in mind in his prayer in chapter 18, why did the Lord not save the city of Sodom on his behalf? Whatever the specific answer given to that question (see discussion above on chap. 18), the point of 19:17–22 is that in spite of the destruction of Sodom, Abraham's prayer was answered at Zoar—God saved the city of Zoar on account of the righteous one living in it.

f. Sodom and Gomorrah Destroyed (19:23–28)

The perspective of the narrative widens considerably as it begins to recount the destruction of the cities. The scope returns to that of 18:20–21, where both Sodom and Gomorrah and the surrounding cities are in view.

We are reminded of two things before the onset of the description of God's judgment. First, according to the sequence in the MT, "the sun had arisen over the land" (19:23a), and second, "Lot had gone [safely] to Zoar" (v. 23b). The mention of the sun ties this section together with Lot's early morning rescue (v. 15) as well as with the larger biblical picture of the "sunrise" as an image of divine salvation for the righteous and divine judgment on the wicked (Isa 9:2–4 [MT 3–5]: "The people who walked in darkness have seen a great light . . . on them has light shined . . . for the yoke of his burden . . . the rod of his oppressor, you have broken as on the day of Midian"; Mal 4:1– 2 [MT 3:19–20]: "For behold, the day comes, burning like a furnace. All the arrogant and every evildoer will be stubble. . . . But for you who revere my name, the sun of righteousness will rise with healing in its wings"). With that as introduction, the author depicts the scene that would become the classic image of the fate of every wicked one: "The LORD rained down upon Sodom and Gomorrah brimstone and fire" (19:24–25).

As in the story of the destruction of the Flood (Ge 6–8), the narrative does not dwell on the destruction of the cities. It rather centers our attention on the response of two individuals, Lot's wife and Abraham, both of whom "looked" at the destruction of the cities but with very different consequences. Few details are given about either.

Lot's wife became a "pillar of salt" because she looked back (19:26). Apparently she suffered the same fate as the wicked upon whom rained brimstone and fire because she disobeyed the words of the men ("Do not look behind you; do not tarry in all the valley, escape to the mountain," v. 17). The double warning, "do not look, do not tarry," which the men gave to Lot and his family, may provide a narrative clue to the exact nature of the misdeed of Lot's wife. In view of the warning, we are perhaps to infer that she did not simply look behind her, but rather "tarried to look in the valley" and hence was swept away with the wicked.

By contrast, Abraham looked from a vantage point consistent with the men's words in 19:17: "Do not stand in all the valley." Thus the writer reminds us that Abraham "was standing" (v. 27) where he had earlier stood before the Lord (18:22) and that he "looked down upon Sodom and Gomorrah and upon all the land of the valley" (19:28). In any event, Abraham, though obviously unaware of the words of the men to Lot and his family, still obeyed the words and escaped the destruction.

This picture of Abraham is consistent with the overall picture of Abraham as one who obeys and pleases God, though with little external instruction. In contrast, Lot's wife knew what to do but failed to do it. It is important to note that the narrative allows us to view the smoldering ruins from Abraham's perspective rather than Lot's. The central figure in the narrative is clearly Abraham. It was his intercession that resulted in Lot's rescue; so we return to the perspective of Abraham, to the place where he was at the time of the intercession, to see a final glimpse of the effect of that prayer. (The picture of Abraham here at the close of the story is similar to that of Moses when he interceded for Israel in the battle with the Amalekites [Ex 17:11–12].)

The reader is not told what Abraham might have been thinking as he watched the smoke billow up from the ruined cities. Abraham was silent, his thoughts were his own. But in view of the fact that the writer has deliberately turned our attention back to the scene of Abraham's prayer in chapter 18, it is hard not to see in this final scene a reminder of the central question of that prayer: "Will the judge of all the earth judge righteously?" At this point in the narrative the answer to Abraham's question is made graphically clear. Sodom, in its wickedness, has been shown to be truly deserving of divine wrath. Lot has been rescued and Abraham himself spared from the destruction. Only the disobedient—among them, Lot's sons-in-law and wife—have perished along with the wicked. The whole of the narrative seems carefully planned to focus the reader's attention on just these points. The lesson of this chapter is turned against the Israelites themselves in Deuteronomy 29:23 (MT 22) (see commentary on Dt 29:2–28 [MT 1–27]).

g. Lot's Incest (19:29–38)

The writer returns to Lot in the concluding narrative of chapter 19. Verse 29 is a clear reminder of the role of Abraham in Lot's rescue: "God remembered Abraham and sent Lot out from the destruction." Any merit on Lot's part that may have resulted in his rescue has obviously been subordinated to the central importance of Abraham's intercession on his behalf. Thus the writer is carrying through with the theme of God's promise—in Abraham and his seed, "all the nations of the earth will be blessed" (12:3). With that reminder, the writer is free to recount the events of the final days of Lot, events which cast Lot in a very different light. In tragic irony, a drunk Lot carried out the very act which he himself had suggested to the men of Sodom (19:8)—he lay with his own daughters.

The account is remarkably similar to the story of the last days of Noah after his rescue from the Flood (9:20–27). There, as here, the patriarch became drunk with wine and uncovered himself in the presence of his children. In both narratives, the act had grave consequences. Thus at the close of the two great narratives of divine judgment, the Flood and the destruction of Sodom, those who were saved from God's wrath subsequently fell into a form of sin reminiscent of those who died in the judgment. This is a common theme in the prophetic literature (e.g., Isa 56–66; Mal 1).

E. Abraham and Abimelech (20:1–18)

The focus of the narratives of chapters 20 and 21 is on the relationship between Abraham and the nations. Abraham's role is that of a prophetic intercessor, as in the promise "in you all the families of the earth will be blessed" (12:3). He prayed for the Philistines (20:7), and God healed them (v. 17). In this narrative, Abimelech plays the role of a "righteous Gentile" with whom Abraham could live in peace and blessing. There is, then, an implied contrast between the narratives in chapters 19 (Lot, the mixed multitude) and 20 (Abimelech, the righteous sojourner).

1. Abraham Moves to Gerar (20:1)

Abraham left the "oaks of Mamre" (18:1, 34) and traveled "southward" (20:1) to sojourn in Gerar. The author's reminder in chapter 21 (vv. 23, 34) that Abraham was still sojourning in Gerar suggests that the events of these two chapters took place in the "land of the Philistines" (v. 34).

2. Abimelech Takes Sarah (20:2)

Sarah was taken into Abimelech's house. Note how truncated this part of the narrative is compared to the story of a similar event in chapter 12. What was there developed into a full story is here condensed into a single verse. The author's interest is clearly not so much the fate of Sarah as the fate of the Philistines. Many of the details of the event recorded here (e.g., Abraham's motive and intention in the deception, as well as a partial rationalization of the deception itself) are withheld until Abraham is given an opportunity to speak on his own behalf (vv. 11–13). At that point, however, his actions cast more light on the Philistines' inner motives than on his own. Abraham's words (vv. 11–13) serve to show that he had mistakenly judged the Philistines to be a wicked people, something which the actions of the Philistines proved false.

3. God, Abimelech, and Abraham (20:3–16)

The narrative goes to great lengths to demonstrate the innocence of the Philistine Abimelech. Before Abimelech pled his own innocence (20:4b), the author makes certain that we have the facts straight by informing us that "Abimelech had not drawn near to her" (20:4a). Thus when Abimelech claimed to be "righteous" and appealed to his own innocence in the face of Abraham's deception, the reader can do no other than acknowledge his innocence and side with him. All the information in the narrative itself points in his favor. Indeed, the matter is finally settled when God himself concurred with Abimelech's plea of innocence. God said, "I know you did this with a clear conscience" (v. 6).

Having shown Abimelech to be innocent, the narrative then points to a feature of Abimelech's relationship with Abraham that threatens disaster. Though he was innocent, he was in need of a warning lest he lose his innocence by his mistreatment of Abraham's household. Abraham's wife was to be returned, and Abraham the prophet must pray in behalf of the life of Abimelech. The surprising outcome of God's visit to Abimelech is that he responded immediately by rising early in the morning (v. 8) and declaring his dream to his servants and then to Abraham. The last statement in verse 8 shows the mood of the Philistines: "The men feared greatly." Like the sailors and the king of Nineveh in the book of Jonah (1:16; 3:6–9), the Philistines responded quickly and decisively to God's warning. Like Jonah, however, Abraham in this narrative was a reluctant prophet.

Abraham's reply seems intended not only to justify his action with Sarah but also to provide a larger picture for understanding his similar actions while in Egypt in chapter 12. At the same time, by tracing the plan back to the very beginnings of his departure from his father's house, he showed that his plan in this instance was not based on an actual assessment of the Philistine's religious life but was simply part of a longstanding scheme. Thus the narrative explains why Abraham misjudged the Philistines. The reader, however, is at a loss to evaluate Abraham's explanation. Though we have followed the life of Abraham closely since he left his father's house in chapter 11, this is the first we have heard of such an overarching strategy on Abraham's part or of this aspect of his relationship with Sarah. In the last analysis we are left only with the opinion of Abimelech himself, who, within the narrative, accepted Abraham's explanation and faulted only himself in this unfortunate situation. Just how sincerely Abimelech accepted Abraham's story can be seen in the fact that in speaking to Sarah he called Abraham "your brother," showing that he accepted the explanation and in turn was attempting to restore the broken relationship with expensive gifts.

4. Abraham Prays for Abimelech (20:17–18)

Abraham, on his part, accepted the gifts from the Philistines and offered a prayer on their behalf in return. Only at this point do we discover the meaning of the words which God had spoken to Abimelech in 20:7: "You are about to die, you and all your household." The death the Lord apparently had in mind was his closing "up every womb in Abimelech's household" (v. 18). Thus God's words "you are about to die" are interpreted by the context to mean that Abimelech's household would not continue.

F. Abraham, Isaac, Ishmael, and Abimelech (21:1–34)

1. Birth of Isaac (21:1–7)

Verse 1 takes up the central line of narrative from 18:10: "I will surely return to you according to the time of life, and Sarah your wife will have a son." The story of Lot and and the story of Abraham's sojourn with the Philistines have occupied most of the narrator's attention for the last three chapters; only now does he return to the promise of a son. One can hardly fail to ask why the writer has delayed and treated so anticlimactically the news of Isaac's birth. Certainly more attention was paid to the announcement of the birth of the son in chapter 18 than here in the report of the birth itself. If we look for an answer to this question in the clues that come out of the text, we may find it in the emphasis given in the narrative to the Lord's faithfulness to his word. The birth of Isaac came about "as the LORD had said," a fact stressed three times within the first two verses. The plan not only came about, but more importantly, it happened as it was announced. Thus the narrative focuses our attention on God's faithfulness to his word and to his careful attention to the details of his plan.

2. Hagar and Ishmael (21:8–21)

The celebration of Isaac's coming of age was the occasion for the account of the expulsion of Ishmael. The similarities between this chapter and the events in chapter 16 can hardly escape the attention of even the casual reader. The writer's close attention to the similarities in the details of the two chapters is perhaps best explained by the frequent use of foreshadowing in these narratives to draw connections between important narratives. In this case, the Lord's promise to Hagar (16:11–12) was recounted in a strikingly similar fashion to the actual fulfillment of the promise (21:18–21). Thus the promise foreshadows the fulfillment.

3. Abraham and Abimelech (21:22–34)

The reappearance of Abimelech in 21:22, though something of a surprise in the narrative, shows that the setting of these narratives had not changed and that Abraham was still living with the Philistines. This situation is confirmed at the conclusion of the narrative, which states explicitly that

Abraham continued to sojourn with the Philistines "many days" (v. 34). The reader is forced to ask why the author constantly draws attention to the fact that Abraham was dwelling with the Philistines during this time. The purpose of such reminders may be to portray Abraham as one who had yet to experience the complete fulfillment of God's promises. Without these recurring accounts of Abraham's dealings with Abimelech, the other events in these narratives might otherwise be read within the context of the Promised Land. We are forced to see a picture of Abraham spending many of his days in exile, out of the land, and thus not living out his days in the Land of Promise. As these narratives show, even Isaac, the son of the promise, was not born in the Promised Land. He was born in exile and had to sojourn there with his father, "wandering from nation to nation, from one kingdom to another" (Ps 105:13). The intention of the narrative is much like that which the writer of the book of Hebrews saw in these texts: Abraham lived "like a stranger in a foreign country. . . . They were aliens and strangers on earth" (Heb 11:8–13).

The picture of Abraham in exile is exemplary of God's caring for the righteous who must suffer while waiting to enter the land. The servants of Abimelech have stolen Abraham's wells, but because God was with him in all that he did (21:22), he entered a covenant with their king (v. 27) and all was restored to him (v. 32).

G. The Seed of Abraham (22:1–24)

1. Binding of Isaac (22:1–14)

Verse 1 of this narrative provides a necessary preliminary understanding of the events of the chapter. Without it, God's request that Abraham offer up Isaac as a "burnt offering" would be inexplicable. By stating clearly at the start that "God tested Abraham," the writer quickly allays any doubt about God's real purpose. There is, then, no thought of an actual sacrifice of Isaac in the narrative, though within the narrative that, of course, was the only thought Abraham entertained. The whole structure of the narrative focuses so strongly on the Lord's request that the writer has apparently sensed the need to dispel any suspense or suspicion about the Lord's real intention.

Several features of the narrative serve to keep the reader's attention focused directly on the inward struggle of Abraham as he carried out the Lord's request—all, we might add, without any mention of Abraham's actual thoughts and with very little talk on Abraham's part. First, there is the abruptness of the Lord's request within the narrative. Apart from the remark in verse 1 that the narrative represented a test, the reader has no warning of the nature of the request or of its severity. Nothing in the preceding narratives would have hinted at this sort of request. In other words, the reader is as surprised and shocked by the Lord's request as Abraham himself would have been. Second, the reader is given no further explanation of the request. The whole request is made up of three simple imperatives: "take Isaac," "go," and "offer him" (v. 2). Moreover, the reader is given no reason to believe that Abraham himself had any further explanation.

Like many biblical narratives, the reader often knows information that the characters in the narrative do not. In this case, the reader knows that this was a test. But, apart from this, we know no more about God's plans and ways than the characters within the narrative itself. We are as much in the dark about God's intention as Abraham is. Thus we, the readers, are forced to rely on the assessment of Abraham himself within the narrative, and to view the events of the narrative through his eyes and by means of his response. At the same time, in the absence of any explanation from the narrator, we are forced to read our own thoughts and feelings into those of Abraham. In the case of this narrative, the reader has ample opportunity to do that as the ensuing events are narrated. What is particularly noticeable is how the writer prolongs the narrative with excessive and deliberate details of Abraham's preparation for the journey and the journey itself. By narrating one incidental and perfunctory act after the other (e.g., "he saddled his donkey," "he cut the wood," "he took two young men with him"—none of these acts proves relevant to the narrative), the writer allows or, indeed, forces the reader to look beyond these narratively meaningless external events to ponder the thoughts of Abraham himself as he so matter-of-factly carried them out.

The writer gives no hints as to the nature of Abraham's inner thoughts, but this is certainly only because no hints were necessary. What reader cannot imagine what Abraham felt? When, at last, someone in the narrative speaks, it is Isaac, not God, who breaks the silence, and the question he raises ("Where is the lamb for the burnt offering?") serves only to heighten the anguish which the Lord's request has brought to Abraham and by now to the reader. When Abraham finally ends his narrative silence and speaks in his reply to Isaac, for the first time a hint at an answer is given: "God will provide the lamb for the burnt offering, my son" (v. 8). Such a reply has not been anticipated within the narrative thus far, but the reply itself anticipates precisely the final outcome of the story ("The Lord will provide," v. 14). Thus midway through the narrative the writer allows the final words of the story to appear and to foreshadow the end. The reader is assured thereby both of the outcome of the narrative and of the quality of Abraham's faith.

Abraham's words cast a new light on his silence. Amid the anguish which the reader has read into Abraham's silence, there is now also a silent confidence in the Lord who will provide. Abraham's words should not be understood as merely an attempt to calm the curious Isaac; but in the light of the fact that they anticipate the actual outcome of the narrative, they are to be read as a confident expression of his trust in God.

Few narratives in Genesis can equal this story in dramatic tension. The writer seems deliberately to prolong the tension of both Abraham and the reader in his depiction of the last moments before God interrupted the action and called the test to a halt. Abraham's every action is described in exaggerated detail. At the last dramatic moment ("Abraham stretched out his hand and grasped the knife to slay his son"), the Lord intervened and, as Abraham had already anticipated, provided a fitting substitute for the burnt offering. Abraham therefore named the altar he had built "The Lord Provides" (v. 14), and the writer adds: "So today it is said, 'On the mountain of the Lord it will be provided.'"

2. Abraham and the Angel of the Lord (22:15–19)

Attached to the end of the narrative is an account of a "second" (22:15) encounter between Abraham and the angel of the Lord. Since in verse 19 Abraham returned to the two young men who had accompanied him, it appears that this second encounter with the angel is to be understood as having occurred on the same occasion as the first. Why then does the writer call attention to it as a "second" meeting? Perhaps the purpose is to emphasize that this second discourse came at a separate time and thus after Abraham had finished the burnt offering. By drawing attention to this fact, the writer has subtly but intentionally separated the account of the renewed promise (vv. 16–18) from the narrative of Abraham's test (vv. 1–15). Perhaps this feature of the narrative is intended to show that the renewal of God's original promises to Abraham was not based on Abraham's specific actions in carrying out the test, but rather on the faith and obedience of Abraham which showed themselves through this test. That interpretation would account for the general expression "this thing" in verse 16. However, as B. Jacob has suggested, the general statement in verse 16, "because you have done this thing," is explained by the more specific reference to the deed of Abraham in fulfilling the test: "and did not withhold your only son."[64] Against Jacob one could point out that the second of the two clauses, "and did not withhold your only son," is connected with a *waw* and thus is more likely a further reason for the promise[65] rather than a more specific explanation of "this thing" which he did.

The promise reiterated here is similar to that of chapters 12, 13, 15, 17, and 18. The promise of "blessing" (22:17) is similar to 12:2. The increase of Abraham's "seed" (22:17) is similar to 13:16; 15:5; and 17:2 . The view of the "nations'" enjoyment of and participation in Abraham's blessing (22:18) is similar to 12:3 and 18:18. The reference to Abraham's act of obedience as the basis of the promise (22:18) is similar to 18:19. Perhaps, also, the reference to Abraham's seed possessing the "gates of the enemy" (22:17) is a reference to the gift of the "land" which is found throughout the earlier narratives (e.g., 12:7; 13:15; 15:18; and 17:8).

3. Abraham's Relatives (22:20–24)

Immediately after the reiteration of the promise of a great multitude of descendants, the writer attaches a notice regarding the increase of the family which Abraham and Sarah had left behind in their homeland. The fact that the number of names in the list is twelve suggests that the writer intends to draw a comparison with the twelve sons of Jacob (Ge 49:28) or the twelve sons of Ishmael in 25:12–15. In any event, the central purpose of listing the names is to introduce into the flow of the narrative the source of the future bride of Isaac, Rebekah (22:23a), and to show that she was of the lineage of Milcah (v. 23b) and not of her concubine (v. 24).

H. Machpelah and Sarah's Death (23:1–20)

Sarah died in Hebron, and Abraham came there to mourn her death. Although the text is not clear, it appears that he came from Beersheba, where

---

[64]Benno Jacob, *Das erste Buch der Tora, Genesis,* 502.
[65]Cf. F. I. Andersen, *The Sentence in Biblical Hebrew,* 99–101.

he had been dwelling at the close of chapter 22 (v. 19). The point of the narrative of chapter 23 is to show how Abraham first came into legal possession of a parcel of land in Canaan. Through what appears to be a hard bargain, Abraham bought not only a cave in which to bury his wife but also a large field with many trees. The chapter shows that Abraham came by this property fairly and legally. The field and particularly the cave in it became an important burial site for the patriarchs and their wives. According to Genesis 49:30–32, this is not only where Sarah and Abraham were buried but also Isaac, Rebekah, Leah, and Jacob (50:13).

The sense of this chapter within the larger context of Genesis can be seen in the similarity between Abraham's response to the offer of the Hethites and to that of the king of Sodom in chapter 14. In both cases, the writer wants to show that Abraham would not accept a gift from the Canaanites. When the king of Sodom offered to reward Abraham, he replied that it should never be said that the king of Sodom made Abraham wealthy (14:23). In the same way, Abraham adamantly refused to accept the parcel of land as a gift. Apparently against the wishes of the Hethites, he paid the full price for the land.

If viewed from the perspective of God's covenant promises to Abraham, both these narratives fit well within the overall themes of the book. God, not any human being, was the source of Abraham's hope of blessing. He would not seek to become wealthy or to own land apart from the promises of God. The same purpose also lies behind the note in 33:19 that when Jacob returned to the land after his sojourn in the east, he purchased a portion of a field to pitch his tent. Wherever possible, the writer seizes the opportunity to show that the patriarchs came by their possession of the land fairly and that it was a gift from God, not from those who were dwelling in the land at the time.

Still another idea in this narrative can be seen in the book of Jeremiah. In Jeremiah 32:6–15, on the eve of the Babylonian captivity, Jeremiah's trust in God's promise of the land was expressed in his purchase of a parcel of land. Though the people would soon be removed from the land in captivity, Jeremiah purchased a plot of ground because he was confident that they would one day return and enjoy the good land God had given them. The writer of Genesis appears to have a similar idea in mind in the picture of Abraham in chapter 23. He purchased only a portion of the land which would some day belong to his seed. In this small purchase was embodied the hope in God's promise that one day in the future it would all belong to him and his seed. In the same way, Joseph's last request was that his bones be returned to the land promised to Abraham, Isaac, and Jacob (Ge 50:24). His request was carried out when the Israelites buried his bones in the parcel of land purchased by Jacob from the sons of Hamor (Jos 24:32).

I. Bride for Isaac (24:1–67)

1. Servant's Oath (24:1–9)

The story begins with an account of the oath which Abraham made his servant swear. The point of the section is to show Abraham's concern for God's promise which was to come to the seed of Isaac. In this sense the story picks up and continues the theme of the promised seed (Isaac) from 21:1.

Though Isaac is a central figure in Genesis 22, he is not portrayed there as the promised seed but as the beloved son of Abraham. Abraham's faith was tested and Isaac's role within that narrative was directed toward that end. The focus on Isaac as the chosen seed, which is at the center of chapter 24, however, takes the reader back to the account of his birth in chapter 21 and to the announcement of his birth in chapter 18. At the end of the Abrahamic narratives, then, the writer returns to the themes that loomed large at the beginning—the promised seed and the blessing.

Two important points are made regarding the future of Abraham's seed in this opening section. First, the seed was not to be mixed with the seed of the Canaanites (24:3). Though no explanation is given, Abraham's desire that Isaac not take a wife from the Canaanites appears to be a further expression of the notion of the two lines of blessing and curse seen in 9:25–27—"cursed be Canaan" but "blessed be the Lord the God of Shem." As has been the case throughout the narratives thus far, the inhabitants of Canaan are considered to be under divine curse for their iniquity (e.g., 15:16). Thus, the seed of Abraham is to be kept separate from the seed of Canaan.

Second, this section makes the point that the seed of Abraham is not to return to the land of their fathers. The Promised Land is their home, and Abraham is careful to ensure that Isaac not be taken back to the place of his father. There is to be no reversal of Abraham's original act of faith and trust in God in leaving the land of his fathers.

Finally, the writer uses this section to portray once more the faith of Abraham. The questions raised by the servant provide the occasion. What if the young woman does not want to return (24:5)? As so many times before, Abraham's reply proves to be both prophetic, in that it anticipates the final outcome of the story, and thematic, in that it announces the central motive of the narrative: "The LORD God will send his angel and you will take a wife for my son from there" (v. 7). In the light of this focus on God's action, the key word in the narrative is "divine providence" (הַקְרֵה, "give [me] success," v. 12), and the key idea is that of God's going before the servant to prepare his way. The primary means of conveying this message in the narrative itself is the speeches of the loquacious servant.

2. Servant Meets Rebekah (24:10–27)

At the beginning of the narrative, the servant states quite specifically the nature of the sign that he sought from the Lord (vv. 12–14). To add force to the picture of God's preparing the way, the writer states that even before the servant had finished speaking, the young girl in question arrived on the scene. We immediately see God's hand at work. The reader is given all the details of the young girl's background as soon as she enters the picture. There is no doubt that this is the right girl. While the servant himself must wait, within the narrative, to find out the identity of the girl, the reader already knows that this is Rebekah, the daughter of Bethuel, the son of Milcah. The point is to show from the start that the Lord has answered the servant's prayer. Thus the writer has sacrificed a certain amount of narrative suspense for the sake of his main idea. Indeed, from the type of information given about the girl in verse 16 (e.g., she was beautiful, she was a virgin, no man had known her), the writer leaves no doubt that this was the girl the servant had asked for and that God had indeed sent his messenger out ahead

of him to prepare the way. The rest of the story only confirms what the
writer has given away here at the beginning—this is the girl. Thus when the
writer continues to recount all the details to show that this was in fact the
girl, it only serves to underscore the extent to which the Lord had prepared
this wife for Isaac.

What is unusual about this particular narrative, and also what makes it
unusually long, is that even though we, the readers, by now already know
the young girl, who she is, and what family she was from, we must still wait
for the servant to inquire of the girl and to find out for himself. Rather than
finding out such information at the same time as the character in the
narrative, the reader's part in the story is to look on as the servant himself
learns about the girl and how the Lord had prepared his way. Thus the point
of the narrative is not the reader's discovery of what God has done but the
servant's response to it. The narrative purpose behind this point, apparently,
is to give due attention to the Lord's role in the events. The writer is not
content to leave the reader alone with such an amazing picture of God's
work. Rather, in the character of the servant and in his response, the reader
is shown the proper response to such events. Such divine preparation for the
seed of Abraham and the line of the blessing must be accompanied by the
kind of appreciation seen in the servant: "Then the man bowed down and
worshiped the LORD, saying, 'Praise be to the LORD, the God of my master
Abraham, who has not abandoned his kindness and faithfulness to my
master'" (vv. 26–27). The servant is a model for all godly readers and their
proper response to the work of God.

3. Servant and Laban (24:28–49)

Another striking feature of this story is that after introducing the new
characters of Laban and his household, the writer allows the servant to retell
the narrative (24:34–49). But as with most repetitions in biblical narrative, the
retelling is not a mere repeating. It is rather a reassertion of the central points
of the first narrative. The point of the retelling can be seen in the fact that the
servant adds to what was originally reported by Abraham. Originally, we
heard Abraham say, only generally, that God would send a messenger and
that the servant would find a wife for Isaac (24:7). When the servant retold
the story to Laban, he included the idea that God would send the angel, but
he added that the angel would make his journey a success by gaining a wife
for Isaac from his own family (v. 40). As we overhear the servant recount
more details, we see that the miracle of God's provision was even more
grand than that originally suggested by the narrative itself.

4. Laban's Response (24:50–61)

Again, at the conclusion of the servant's account of the events, Laban
and Bethuel express their view of the events. They too acknowledge that it
was the Lord who prepared the way for the servant to meet Rebekah. Thus,
the reader has been given several witnesses that these events have been the
work of God: the narrator (vv. 15–16), the servant (vv. 26–27), and Laban
(v. 50). The final witness is Rebekah herself, who, against the wishes of her
brother and mother, returned with the servant to Isaac. The simplicity of her
response ("I will go," v. 58) reveals the nature of her trust in the God of
Abraham. The similarity between Rebekah's response and that of Ruth (Ruth

1:16) suggests that there may be more than a mere coincidental relationship between the narratives of the two women.

5. Rebekah Meets Isaac (24:62–67)

The importance of the blessing of Rebekah by her family lies in the similarity of this blessing to that which the Lord gave to Abraham in 22:17: "May your seed possess the gates of their enemy." The purpose is once again to show the Lord's careful attention to detail in choosing this wife for Isaac. In God's plan, the same blessing has been given to both Isaac and his bride.

Just as the servant was returning with the young woman, Isaac enters the narrative for the first time. They both lift up their eyes and see each other in the distance. The narrator, along with the readers, knows who it is that Isaac and Rebekah see, but within the narrative neither Isaac nor Rebekah recognizes the other. Note how the narrator writes, "she saw Isaac," though it is not until the next verse that Rebekah herself learns that it was Isaac. Here again is an example of the curious perspective of the reader throughout the narratives. The reader learns nothing new as the narratives progress. Only the characters continue to discover the providential ordering of the events. We, the readers, are allowed merely to watch as the characters discover the greatness of God's leading.

Verse 66 shows that the writer knows just how long to tell the story and stops short of going beyond that point. He says merely that the servant "recounted all the things that he did." A less talented writer might have allowed the servant to retell the story once more, but by this time the events of the story are so clear that even the casual reader could have supplied Isaac with most of the details. The final remarks again show that God's ways are good for those who put their trust in him. When Isaac took Rebekah as his wife, he loved her and was comforted with her after the death of his mother. This is the way the writer shows that Rebekah had taken the place of Sarah in the line of the seed of Abraham.

J. Abraham's Final Days (25:1–10)

Chapter 25 is a transition chapter. Abraham dies, and the blessing is renewed with Isaac. Ishmael passes from the scene, and the new generation is born: Jacob and Esau.

1. Abraham's Other Sons (25:1–6)

According to the narrative, after the death of Sarah, Abraham took another wife, Keturah. There is little basis in the Hebrew text for the translation, "Abraham had taken a wife" (as in the NIV note), as though Keturah had been a wife or "concubine" of Abraham in his younger days at the same time he was married to Sarah. Some have suggested that Keturah was one of the concubines mentioned in 25:6, and hence these sons were born to Abraham and Keturah while Sarah was alive. Support for that interpretation appears to come from the fact that the Chronicler calls Keturah a "concubine" (1Ch 1:32). Though Keturah is called a "concubine" in Chronicles, she is called a "wife" here in Genesis 25:1, which would seem to preclude her being a mere concubine during the time Sarah was alive.

The picture that emerges of Abraham's life after the death of Sarah is that of a complete rejuvenation of the old man of the previous narratives. He continued to be rewarded with the blessing of many offspring. The writer is careful to point out, however, that none of these sons had any share in the promised blessing: Abraham gave gifts to the other sons and sent them away, but "to Isaac he gave all that he possessed" (v. 5). The focus on Isaac is reasserted clearly in verse 11, where the writer shows that God himself blessed Isaac after the death of Abraham.

2. Abraham's Death (25:7–10)

The author gives surprisingly little attention to the details of Abraham's death. The length of his life is given (v. 7), which serves to connect him to the patriarchs listed at length in the previous chapters (cf. 11:32). The narrative adds the epitaph that Abraham died "in a good old age," which recalls the word of the Lord to Abraham in 15:15: "You will go to your fathers in peace and you will be buried in a good old age." The mention of Abraham's "good old age" also serves as a contrast to the life of Jacob, which is later characterized as "few [years] and evil" (47:9). Thus within the context of Genesis, Abraham and Jacob provide a narrative example of the contrast of "good" and "evil," a theme begun in the first chapters of the book and carried through to the end (cf. 50:20). The emphasis of the narrative in this section is on the fact that Abraham was buried in the field which he purchased from Ephron the Hittite (25:9–10). The final resting place of Abraham was in a portion of the Promised Land that he rightfully owned.

III. THE ISAAC NARRATIVES (25:11–35:29)

A. Introduction (25:11)

Verse 11 opens the portion of Genesis that deals specifically with Isaac, and it gives this important but simple introduction: "After Abraham died, God blessed Isaac his son." Relatively few narratives are devoted to the theme of blessing in the life of Isaac. Most of them are woven into the busy tapestry of chapter 26. All the more important, then, is this brief statement that God blessed Isaac. Such a reminder shows again the writer's overarching purpose to draw out the line through which the divine blessing would come and to show it as a part of God's plan announced long before (cf. 17:21).

B. Line of Ishmael (25:12–18)

At the opening of the Isaac stories is a final statement regarding the line of Ishmael. It consists of a genealogy of the twelve leaders of Ishmael's clan, a report of the length of Ishmael's life, and, finally, a report of his death. As with other lists of names throughout the book, the number twelve seems to be a deliberate attempt to set these individuals off as founders of a new and separate people (cf. 22:20). The mention of "twelve princes" recalls the word of the Lord regarding the future of the line of Ishmael (17:20), which promised that he too would be blessed and that "twelve princes" would be born to him and become a great nation. It is apparently sufficient for the writer to recall Ishmael's blessing only by way of this allusion to the earlier promise. Perhaps explicit mention of a blessing promised to Ishmael at this point in the narrative would have been too easily confused with the larger theme of the blessings of the Abrahamic covenant. In any case, no further mention is made of the blessing of Ishmael which was recounted in 17:20, and henceforth, though there is mention later of the "Ishmaelites" (e.g., 37:27), we hear nothing more about Ishmael in Genesis (cf. comments below on 28:9). The writer's interest turns quickly to Isaac.

C. Descendants of Isaac (25:19)

The narratives which have the life of Isaac for their backdrop are introduced as "the account of Abraham's son Isaac." Almost immediately, however, the narratives themselves turn out to be about the sons of Isaac rather than about Isaac himself. Isaac is an important link in the line of Abraham, but as an individual character within the narratives he is given little attention. Only in chapter 26 does the narrative turn specifically to him. In most other narratives he plays a secondary role.

D. Birth of Jacob and Esau (25:20–28)

The Isaac narratives and other patriarchal narratives have several similarities. Like Esau, Isaac (26:34) was forty years old when he took a wife. Like Sarah (11:30), Rebekah was barren. Like Abraham (20:17), Isaac prayed for his wife, and the Lord answered and she bore two sons. The concentration on the barrenness of both Sarah and Rebekah, as well as Rachel (29:31) and Leah (29:35), enables the writer to reiterate the point that the promised blessing through the chosen seed of Abraham is not to be accomplished merely by human effort. The fulfillment of the promise is possible at each crucial juncture only because of a specific act of God. The struggle that ensues between Jacob and Esau was already anticipated in the womb of their mother (25:22).

A central theme of the remainder of the book—the struggle between brothers—is introduced in the brief account of the wrestling of the two twins in the womb. The conflict between brothers or within families is not a new motif in Genesis. Already in chapter 4 the struggle between Cain and Abel foreshadowed a whole series of such conflicts within the book: the sons of Noah (9:20–27), Abraham and Lot (13:7–12), Isaac and Ishmael (21:9), Jacob and Laban (chaps. 29–31), and Joseph and his brothers (chaps. 37–50). This emphasis on enmity and struggle appears to stem from the first words of judgment in the book, namely, God's statement: "I will put enmity between your seed and her seed" (3:15). The writer waits patiently until the end of Genesis to express the lesson behind these struggles in the words of Joseph to his brothers: "You meant it for evil but God meant it for good" (50:20). Out of each of the struggles, God's will was accomplished. The point is not that the struggles were necessary for the accomplishment of the will of God, but rather that God's will was accomplished in spite of the conflict.

Another important motif is present in this account: "The older shall serve the younger" (25:23). As far back as chapter 4 the narrative has portrayed God as choosing and approving the younger and the weaker through whom to accomplish his purpose and to bring about his blessing. The offering of the older brother Cain was rejected, whereas the offering of the younger brother Abel was accepted. The line of Seth, the younger brother, was the chosen line (4:26–5:8); Isaac was chosen over his older brother Ishmael (17:18–19); Rachel was chosen over her older sister Leah (29:18); Joseph the younger brother was chosen over all the rest (37:3); and Judah was chosen over his older brothers (49:8). Behind each of these "reversals" was the recurring theme of God's sovereign plan of grace. The blessing was not a natural right, as a right of the firstborn son would be. Rather, God's blessing was extended to those who had no other claim to it. They all received what they did not deserve.

E. Esau Rejects His Birthright (25:29–34)

The story of Esau's rejection of his birthright is purposefully attached to the end of the narrative that introduces the motif of the older serving the younger. It is a narrative example that God's choice of Jacob over Esau did not run contrary to the wishes of either of the two brothers. It is clear from the narrative that Esau was one who "despised" his birthright, while Jacob is portrayed as one who would go to great lengths to gain it. The importance of the contrast between the two brothers can best be seen in that the writer himself explicitly states the point of the narrative in the story's conclusion: "So Esau despised his birthright" (25:34). In few cases in Genesis do we find such a clear and forthright statement of the writer's own understanding of the sense of the individual stories. We are left with no doubt that the writer sees in this story of Jacob's trickery a larger lesson—that Esau, though he had the right of the firstborn, did not value it over a small bowl of soup. Thus, when in God's plan Esau lost his birthright and consequently his blessing, no injustice was dealt to him. The narrative has shown that he did not want the birthright. He despised it.

F. Isaac and Abimelech (26:1–35)

There are several similarities between the events of this chapter and those in the life of Abraham (12:10–20; 20:1–18). The writer is not only fully conscious of the similarities but also appears to use them to advance the theme of God's faithfulness to his promises. While the stories and narratives of this chapter seem at first glance to be only loosely related, without a clear guiding theme, when seen from the perspective of the life of Abraham, the chapter shows a remarkable unity of structure and purpose. Each of the brief narratives that make up chapter 26 portrays Isaac in a situation or circumstance that has a parallel in the life of Abraham. In the short span of one chapter, the writer shows how Isaac's entire life was a repetition of that which happened to Abraham. Thus the lesson is that God's faithfulness in the past can be counted on in the present and the future. What he has done for the fathers, he will also do for the sons.

1. Isaac Goes to Gerar (26:1)

The account opens with a reminder that the present famine was new, not the same famine that forced Abraham to go to Egypt (12:10). By including this reminder, the writer calls attention to the connection between the two passages. God's dealings with Abraham had foreshadowed his dealings with Isaac, just as his dealings with the patriarchs in general would foreshadow his ongoing ways with Israel.

At first we are told only that Isaac went down to Gerar to Abimelech, but the warning he received in the vision of verse 2 informs the reader that

Isaac was on his way to Egypt and thus further associates this sojourn of Isaac with that of Abraham in 12:10–20. No explanation is given why Isaac should not go to Egypt, except that he is to "dwell in the land" (26:2). We are apparently to read this verse in the light of the promise that "the land" is to be given to the seed of Abraham. Thus immediately following this word from the Lord is the first major reiteration of the Abrahamic covenant and of the promise that "the land" is to be given to Isaac and his seed.

It is initially surprising that Isaac remained with Abimelech (26:6). Was not Gerar also outside "the land" promised to Abraham? Apparently in anticipation of this problem, the writer notes that the gift of the land included also the land of the Philistines. He does this by showing that the Lord's promise was to give "all these lands" to the seed of Abraham, not just "the land" where there was famine. The use of the plural expands the notion of the land to include all those places where the patriarchs sojourned. The picture of the Promised Land in this narrative is consistent with that of 15:18–19, where the border of "the land" is the "river of Egypt" and the Euphrates.

2. The Lord's Promise to Isaac (26:2–5)

The Lord's warning to Isaac that he should remain in the land became the occasion for a formal restatement of the blessing. In the face of the impending famine, the Lord promised to be with Isaac, to bless him, and to bring about all that was promised to his father Abraham. Essentially the same promise given to Abraham was given to Isaac. His seed would be great in number (cf. 12:2), the land would be his (12:7), and all the nations of the land would be blessed in him (12:3).

The Lord then added a remarkable note: Abraham "kept my requirements, my commands, my decrees, and my laws" (26:5). What is remarkable is that this is precisely the way in which obedience to the Sinai covenant is expressed in Deuteronomy (e.g., "And you shall love the LORD your God and keep his requirements, his decrees, his laws, and his commands," Dt 11:1). Did Abraham know the Law? If so, how? If not, what was the meaning of the Lord's words? These narratives give no indication that Abraham had an actual copy of the laws of the Pentateuch or of any oral tradition. Thus it would seem unlikely that the writer would expect the reader to understand the Lord's words in such a way.

The key, rather, lies in the writer's portrayal of Abraham throughout the book. We have already seen that at several points in the narrative, Abraham acted in accordance with the Law, particularly Deuteronomy, yet the writer has never assumed that Abraham actually had a knowledge of the Law itself. In Genesis 14, when Abraham fought with the kings from a far country, his actions followed quite closely the stipulations of Deuteronomy 20. The same can be said regarding his treatment of the nations who were nearby (e.g., the king of Sodom). He obeyed the Law from the heart, much as the ideal picture given in Deuteronomy 30:6 would have it. Thus Abraham is an example of one who shows the Law written on his heart (cf. Jer 31:33). He is the writer's ultimate example of true obedience to the Law, the one about whom the Lord could say, "He obeyed me" (Ge 26:5).

Thus, by showing Abraham to be an example of "keeping the law," the writer has demonstrated the nature of the relationship between the Law and faith. Abraham, a man who lived in faith, could be described as one who kept the Law. The view of faith and the Law reflected in this narrative is the same as that in Deuteronomy 30:11–14, where Moses said "this commandment is not too difficult for you or beyond your reach. . . . It is in your heart to do it." It is also in keeping with Paul's understanding of Deuteronomy 30 in Romans 10, where he writes that the "word" which Moses said was "in your heart" is "the word of faith which we are proclaiming" (Ro 10:8).

3. Isaac, Rebekah, and Abimelech (26:6–11)

Several similarities between Isaac and Abraham are apparent in this section. Abraham "dwelt in Gerar" (20:1); so did Isaac (26:6). Abraham once devised a scheme with his wife Sarah and called her his sister (20:2); Isaac did the same with Rebekah. Just as Abraham was rebuked by the Philistine king Abimelech for the great shame he might have brought on his people (20:9), so was Isaac (26:10). Such similarities can hardly be merely coincidental. The writer intends to portray to the reader that the lives of the two patriarchs did in fact run a similar course. Unlike the same incident in the life of Abraham, however, here God did not warn Abimelech not to touch the wife (cf. 20:6), but rather Abimelech himself forbade anyone to touch the wife (26:11). It was not God who protected the wife with the threat of capital punishment (cf. 20:7) but Abimelech (26:11).

In view of the similarities between the two narratives, we would do well to ask why there is a change in perspective on these two similar events. The writer's intention is perhaps best seen by the effect that these differences have on the reader's understanding of the characters themselves. Though Abimelech was said to have been "pure of heart" in 20:6, in chapter 26 his actions alone showed that his heart was right. Abimelech did not need to be warned in the dream. All that was necessary was to discover that Rebekah was not Isaac's sister (26:8)—that was enough for him to fear that a great shame (26:10) might come upon his people. The picture of the Philistine king that emerges at this point in chapter 26 is clearly that of a righteous, even pious, Gentile: one who did that which was right and, by contrast, showed Isaac to be less righteous than he. Such a view of the surrounding nations is a far cry from the picture given of Sodom and Gomorrah and of Lot and his daughters. Apparently at this point in the book the writer wants to portray a broader picture of the nations: he sees them as both wicked, thus deserving judgment, and righteous, hence capable of entering into covenant with the chosen seed (21:27, 32; 26:28). This, however, is not the full picture of the Philistines to be gained from chapter 26. The Philistines also caused great hardship for Isaac in the controversies over the wells (26:14–22).

4. Isaac Prospers (26:12–13)

Just as Abraham prospered while sojourning among the Gentiles (12:16; 20:14), so now Isaac prospered while sojourning with Abimelech. Lest we fail to see the significance of Isaac's prosperity, the writer adds, by way of explanation: "The Lord blessed [Isaac]." This is the second time the writer has spoken of Isaac's blessing. Its repetition is apparently to underscore the connection between Isaac's prosperity and God's promise to Abraham in chapter 12: "I will make you a great [גדל] nation and I will bless you" (v. 2).

What God promised to Abraham has been fulfilled with Isaac; hence the text emphasizes that Isaac "became great" (גדל).

5. Contention Over Wells (26:14–23)

Just as Abraham's prosperity became the occasion for the conflict between Abraham's shepherds and those of Lot (13:2–7), so also Isaac's wealth angered the Philistines. They became jealous and contention arose. Again the writer is intent on drawing a line of comparison between Abraham and Lot (chap. 13) on the one hand, and Isaac and Abimelech on the other. Thus this section relates that "the shepherds of Gerar contended with the shepherds of Isaac" (26:20), virtually using identical terms as in the narrative of contention which broke out between the shepherds of Abraham and the shepherds of Lot (13:7). As the names given to the wells show, there is a progressive resolution of the conflict as Isaac continued to move away from the Philistines and dug new wells. After finding no conflict at Rehoboth, they said, "We have become fruitful in the land" (26:22), which recalls in identical terms the original blessing of 1:28: "be fruitful . . . and fill the land."

The whole depiction of Isaac in this narrative, then, shows that Isaac, like Abraham, enjoyed the firstfruits of God's blessing—even though it resulted in and took place amid bitter contention with those among whom they lived. Clearly the narrative intends to point to the patriarchs as those whose lives best pictured the kind of blessing God intended his people to enjoy. At the same time, these narratives point to the stark reality that even the fathers did not enjoy the full blessing. They too had to face adversity, but they trusted God, and God blessed them amid the conflict.

6. The Lord Appears to Isaac (26:24–25)

Just as the Lord had spoken to Abraham after he had separated from Lot (13:14–17) and renewed his promise of land and great prosperity, so now with Isaac, after he had returned to Beersheba, the Lord appeared and renewed the promise. For a third time it is said that the Lord blessed Isaac. Like his father Abraham (12:7; 13:3), Isaac responded by building an altar and worshiping God (26:25).

7. Abimelech Comes to Isaac (26:26–31)

Just as Abimelech and his people came to Abraham and acknowledged, "God is with you" (21:22), and sought to enter into a covenant with him, so now Abimelech came to Isaac and acknowledged, "The LORD is with you," and sought to enter into a covenant with him (26:28). Like Abraham before him, Isaac was the source of blessing to those nations who sought him out. Isaac, like Abraham, trusted God and lived in peace with his neighbors.

8. A New Well (26:32–33)

As a final picture of Isaac in this brief collage of images, the writer concludes with the account of the news that Isaac's servants had discovered a new well. The point of the brief notice can be seen in the writer's emphasis that the announcement was made "on the same day" (that Isaac had made peace with his neighbors). Consequently, the writer associates the name of the city, Beersheba ("well of the oath," שבע), with this "oath" (שבעה).

9. Esau's Marriage (26:34–35)

At first glance the short notice of Esau's marriage to two Hittite women does not seem to play a significant role within the larger narrative context. When read as an introduction to chapter 27, however, it casts quite a different light on the events of that chapter. Just before the account of the mischievous blessing of Jacob, we are told that Esau, from whom the blessing was stolen, had married Hittite women and that they were a source of grief to both Isaac and Rebekah. These verses, then, take their place along with 25:29-34 as background to the central event of chapter 27, the blessing of Jacob. These preliminary notices put into perspective the cunning deed of Jacob and Rebekah. They demonstrate that Esau was not fit to inherit the blessing.

G. The Stolen Blessing (27:1–40)

We can hardly overlook the fact that in this narrative the writer wants not only to convey an important lesson but also to tell an interesting and suspenseful story. One can see that he has gone to great lengths to make the story what it is. Particularly noticeable is the way in which he develops the characters of the story. As we shall see, at several points along the way he provides helpful characterizations to enable the reader to see behind the mere events of the narrative to the underlying story that develops. In telling a good story, however, the writer does not lose sight of his primary purpose, which is to maintain and to develop further the themes of the Pentateuch. At the climactic end of the central portion of the story, as the disheartened father, Isaac, and the rejected son, Esau, reflect upon Jacob's successful plan to steal the blessing, the writer allows their words of dismay and anger to express the central theme of the story: Isaac: "I have blessed him; indeed, he shall be blessed" (v. 33); Esau: "He has deceived me twice; he has taken my firstborn rights and now he has taken my blessing" (v. 36). Jacob had obtained that which belonged to Esau, and Isaac, his father, had given him the blessing. In the course of it all the will of God, expressed before the two sons were born, was brought to full realization: "The older son [Esau] shall serve the younger [Jacob]" (25:23).

1. Jacob the Deceiver (27:1–26)

In recounting the story the writer pays close attention to all those elements that heighten the suspense and highlight the deception of Jacob. In this regard the writer demonstrates that Jacob's name (יעקב), which means "the deceiver" (cf. וַיַּעְקְבֵנִי, v. 36), has been appropriately chosen. This is one of several stories that bring out this aspect of Jacob's character. Isaac is depicted as one too old and too blind to distinguish between his two sons. In some respects, the writer's drawing out these details may be an attempt to ameliorate Isaac's culpability in the story. However, Isaac's insistence on a "good meal" before the blessing recalls all too clearly Esau's own trading of the birthright for a pot of stew (25:29–34), and thus casts Isaac in a role similar to that of Esau. The purpose of telling the reader about Isaac's blindness was perhaps to make the story more believable and consequently more suspenseful. If Isaac were old and blind, the events of the story make sense and the suspense in the story itself is real. The point of telling the reader such information at the beginning of the story is to ensure that the question of the success of the plan would not be settled beforehand. The writer's interest in a truly suspenseful story is carried right to the end, where Jacob is shown leaving "at the same moment as" his brother Esau returned from the hunt. The plan is in danger of not succeeding right up to the end.

2. Isaac Blesses Jacob (27:27–29)

As the story has stressed throughout, the goal of Jacob's strategy had been to wrestle the blessing from Isaac. Although Isaac did not appear completely convinced, in the end he blessed Jacob. The theme of "blessing" within this story points out the relationship of this narrative to both the preceding and the following narratives. The final words of the blessing allude to the promise to Abraham (12:2–3): "Those who curse you, I will curse, and those who bless you will be blessed" (27:29). In a similar fashion Isaac's blessing foreshadows Jacob's later prophecy concerning the kingship of the house of Judah: "May you be lord over your brothers and may the sons of your mother bow down to you" (cf. 49:8). Thus the words of Isaac are a crucial link in the development of the theme of the blessing of Abraham's seed. In what may appear only as a selfish attempt to rob his brother's blessing, Jacob's daring scheme turns out to be a link in the chain connecting the blessing of Abraham's seed with the rise of the kingship in the house of Judah.

3. Isaac and Esau (27:30–40)

The reverse side of the blessing of Jacob is the disappointment and anger of Esau. There is no attempt in this narrative to revel in Esau's misfortune. He is presented merely as a tragic figure, a victim of a brother who was more resourceful and daring than he. Upon hearing of his misfortune, "he burst out with a loud and bitter cry" (27:34), and immediately his words turn the reader's attention back to the events of chapter 25 and his loss of the birthright: "He has deceived me these two times: My birthright [בְּכֹרָתִי] he took [לָקַח], and now he has taken [לָקַח] my blessing [בִּרְכָתִי]" (27:36). The chiastic structure of this last remark (object + לָקַח . . . לָקַח + object) as well as the wordplay (בְּרָכָתִי . . . בְּכֹרָתִי) suggests that the writer intends Esau's remarks as a concise summary of the sense of the narrative thus far: Esau had lost everything and Jacob had gained it all.

Within the narrative itself, Isaac recounted the main points of the blessing a second time: "I have made him lord over you, I have made his brothers into servants, I have provided him with grain and wine" (v. 37). The writer thus underscores the fact that Isaac had blessed Jacob rather than Esau. Finally, Isaac answered Esau's tearful pleas for a blessing with a third reiteration of the central point of Jacob's blessing: "You will serve your brother" (v. 40). The point of these repetitions of the various aspects of the blessing is primarily to underscore the irretrievability of the lost blessing and hence the certainty of the fulfillment of the blessing itself. By showing that the blessing was irrevocable, even by the father who gave the blessing, the writer underscores an important feature of the blessing—its fulfillment is out of human hands. It cannot even be revoked. It will come to pass, just as it was given.

H. Jacob Flees to Laban (27:41-28:5)

Jacob's scheme not only resulted in his obtaining the blessing which Isaac had intended for Esau but also became the occasion for Jacob's journey to the house of Laban in search of a wife. The picture of Esau at the conclusion of this story is that of a bitter, spiteful brother and son. He made plans to slay Jacob and to regain by force his birthright and blessing. Again, Rebekah thwarted the plans by having Isaac send Jacob back to her own homeland to find a wife.

As has been the case in many of the narratives of Genesis, Jacob's parents' final words of blessing to their departing son anticipate precisely the eventual outcome of the ensuing story: Jacob would visit Laban "for a while," Esau's anger would subside, and Jacob would find a wife and return as a great assembly of people (27:41-28:3). Within Isaac's farewell blessing is a final reiteration of the central theme of the preceding narrative: the blessing of Abraham was to rest on the family of Jacob; the promises of Abraham and the promises of Isaac are now the promises of Jacob.

I. Esau Marries (28:6-9)

The final picture of Esau in this narrative is that of a bitter son seeking to spite his parents through deliberate disobedience. The writer's purpose, however, is not merely to dwell on Esau's bitterness but to prepare the reader for the events that lay ahead in the narrative and to tie the present narrative to the preceding one. Esau was a bitter man when Jacob left; but, just as Rebekah had said (27:45), when Jacob returned, Esau had changed. The point of the narrative is to highlight the changing relationship between the two brothers. Though at first Esau was angry, in the end, when Jacob returned, Esau "ran to meet Jacob and embraced him; he threw his arms around his neck and kissed him. And they wept" (33:4). The brothers were reconciled, and Esau partook of the blessing (בִּרְכָתִי) which Jacob had received (v. 11).

This view of the reconciliation between Jacob and Esau, Israel and Edom, is an important element in the future hope of the later Prophetic Books (Am 9:12; cf. Ac 15:17). It is a picture of the ultimate fulfillment of God's promise to Abraham: "In your seed all the families of the earth will be blessed" (12:3). Such a view seems firmly rooted in the theological structure of the present narrative. The marriage of Esau to the daughter of Ishmael is a reminder that the promised seed of Abraham was determined not by the will of human beings but ultimately by the will of God. The families of the two "older" sons (Ishmael and Esau) were united in the marriage, but by now neither had received the blessing promised to Abraham. The families of the "younger" sons (Isaac and Jacob), however, had already received the promise of the blessing.

J. Jacob at Bethel (28:12-22)

Like Abraham in chapter 15, Jacob received a confirmation of the promised blessing while asleep in the night (cf. 15:12; 18:11). Abraham received a "vision" (15:1), and Jacob saw the Lord in a "dream" (28:12). In both narratives, however, a divine confirmation was given regarding the establishment of the same covenant of promise: (1) the gift of the land;

(2) the promise of great posterity; and (3) blessing to all the nations. In a remarkably similar fashion, the viewpoint of both chapters turns to the future "exile" of Abraham's seed and the promise of a "return." Abraham's vision looked forward to the sojourn of God's people in Egypt and also to the Lord's deliverance in the Exodus. Jacob's dream looked forward to his own sojourn to Haran and to the Lord's eventual return of Jacob to the land promised to Abraham. In both cases, the promise was that God would not forsake them and would return them to their land. As Abraham's vision anticipated narratives from the latter part of the Pentateuch, so Jacob's vision anticipated the events which were to come in the next several chapters.

The purpose, then, of the account of Jacob's dream in this chapter is to show that in all the events of the narratives which follow, we are to see a fulfillment of the promise made here to Jacob. The Lord said, "Behold, I will be with you and I will keep you wherever you go and I will return you to this land" (28:15). Within this carefully constructed narrative, those words become the guiding motif and principle that governs the course of the story. So, when Jacob returned from Laban's house after many years, he returned to the same place, Bethel, where God again blessed him, promised to give him the land he had already promised to Abraham (35:12), and reaffirmed his promise to make Jacob's seed into a great nation (35:11). Just as Jacob erected a "pillar" at the outset of his journey and then named the place "Bethel" (28:18–19), so also when he returned he erected another "pillar" and named the place "Bethel" (35:14–15). At either end of the Jacob narratives, then, the writer has placed the reminder that God was with Jacob in all that he did and that God was faithful to his promises.

K. Jacob's Marriages (29:1–30)

1. Jacob Meets Rachel (29:1–14)

In keeping with the picture of Jacob's sojourn as an exile from the Promised Land, the writer opens the account with the words, "and he traveled toward the land of the sons of the east" (29:1). Jacob's journey to find a wife was similar to that of Abraham's servant who sought a wife for Isaac. In chapter 24 the writer uses the words of the servant to guide the narrative and to show that it was God alone who directed the servant to the right young woman for Isaac. In this chapter, Jacob is relatively silent. He does not reflect on God's guidance or on the Lord's promise to be with him wherever he goes (28:15). Jacob's actions, not his words, tell the story of God's help and guidance.

As with the servant in chapter 24, God directed Jacob to the well where Rachel watered her flocks. One gets the impression early in the story that Jacob was going to do a mighty deed because of the special care with which the writer describes the size of the rock covering the well and the number of shepherds already on hand. Only when all the shepherds were present were they able to lift the rock from the well and water the flocks (29:8), because the rock was big (v. 2). When Jacob saw Rachel, however, and the shepherds identified her as the daughter of Laban, he single-handedly removed the stone and watered her sheep. Then, in a great show of emotion, Jacob kissed Rachel and cried with a loud voice (v. 11). Clearly the writer wants us to see in this emotional response that, though he did not say it specifically, as

Abraham's servant had done (24:27), Jacob saw in these circumstances the guiding hand of God.

We are apparently also expected to see Jacob's physical strength as further evidence that God was with Jacob and that he had not forsaken his promises (28:15; cf. 24:27). Throughout the Jacob narratives, God's guidance is shown in Jacob's strength and cunning. No attempt is made to glory in that strength as such; rather, the author uses it as a sign of God's protective presence. It was the fulfillment of God's promise to be with Jacob in all that he did (28:15). The account is very similar to that of Exodus 2:17, where Moses meets his wife by fighting off the shepherds who have driven away the seven daughters of the priest of Midian and by then watering their sheep.

2. Laban Deceives Jacob (29:15–30)

For the first time in the narrative, Jacob is the object of deception. Laban had turned the tables on him. The similarity between what Laban did to Jacob and what Jacob had done to Isaac (chap. 27) is patent. Jacob was able to exchange the younger for the older, whereas Laban reversed the trick and exchanged the older for the younger. The narrative shows that Jacob got what he deserved. In this light, then, the seven extra years that Jacob had to serve Laban appear as a repayment for his treatment of Esau. By calling such situations to the attention of the reader, the writer begins to draw an important lesson from these narratives. Jacob's deceptive schemes for obtaining the blessing did not meet with divine approval. Through Jacob's plans God's will had been accomplished, but the writer is intent on pointing out, as well, that the schemes and tricks were not of God's design.

Jacob was indignant: "Why have you deceived me?" (29:25). But Laban's reply left him speechless: "In our place one does not give the younger before the older [הַבְּכִירָה]." After this the narrative says only that Jacob conceded the point ("and Jacob did so," v. 28). Unbeknown to him, Laban's words had deftly expressed the very circumstances that had led Jacob on his present journey. The irony of such a circumstance speaks for itself. The reader was certainly expected to interpret such irony as the work of a divine plan. Jacob's past had caught up with him, and he could do no more than accept the results and serve Laban seven more years. At first it had looked as if Jacob's journey was following the course which Rebekah had anticipated: "You shall live with him [Laban] only a few days" (27:44). Thus we are not surprised to read that Jacob's first seven years working for Laban seemed as if it were "only a few days" (29:20). But with Laban's trick, seven more years are added to Rebekah's "few days," and Jacob's plans, as well as Rebekah's, begin to unravel.

L. Birth of Jacob's Sons (29:31–30:24)

In a way that calls to mind the beginning of the Abrahamic narratives (11:30), the writer now introduces the central problem of the narrative: "And God opened Leah's womb, but Rachel was barren" (29:31). It is at first surprising to read that the Lord was behind Rachel's barrenness. In the preceding chapter (28:14), God had promised that the seed of Jacob would be more numerous than the "dust of the ground." Now Rachel, Jacob's intended wife (29:30), was barren, and it appeared to be the Lord's doing

(v. 31). By means of such a twist in the narrative, the writer shows again that Jacob's plans have come to naught. Jacob had planned to take Rachel as his wife, but God intended him to have Leah.

Thus in two major reversals in Jacob's life, we can begin to see the writer's theme taking shape. Jacob sought to marry Rachel, but Laban tricked him. Then Jacob sought to build a family through Rachel, but she was barren and God opened Leah's womb. Jacob's schemes, which had brought him fortune thus far, were now beginning to crumble. Such schemes would not be sufficient to carry out the further plans of God. Jacob, too, would have to depend upon God to bring about the divine blessing. In the conflict that ensued between Jacob and his two wives, a conflict over the birth of their sons, the pattern is set for the remainder of the narratives in Genesis. Leah was the mother of Judah (29:35), among others, while Rachel was the mother of Joseph (30:24). Though all twelve sons are important, these two sons (Joseph and Judah) stand out markedly in the narratives that follow. God used both in important ways, but each had a different role to play in the accomplishment of God's blessing. Here, at the beginning, it appeared that ultimately Judah, the son of Leah, was given the place of preeminence. Counter to Jacob's plans, God had opened the womb of Leah and not Rachel. In the end, however, the Lord hearkened to Rachel and the son Joseph was born (30:22). But as Jacob's words to Rachel underscore, God had withheld sons from Rachel so that the seed of Abraham would be built from Leah. Even after Leah had ceased bearing children (29:35), by means of a clever plan she managed to have two more sons and a daughter by Jacob (30:14–21). Just as Jacob had purchased the birthright for a pot of stew (25:29–34), so also Leah purchased the right to more children by Jacob with the mandrakes of her son Reuben (30:14–16). All the conflict and tension that existed between Joseph and his brothers, particularly between Joseph and Judah, in the narratives that follow are anticipated and foreshadowed here at the beginning in this narrative of their births.

M. Jacob and Laban's Sheep (30:25–43)

After the account of the birth of the sons, the writer turns immediately to the first mention of Jacob's departure from Haran. Seeking the Lord's blessing by means of Jacob, Laban attempted to settle his account for the work Jacob had done for him over the years of his sojourn. So Laban asked Jacob to name his wages (30:28). Laban's offer apparently contained a request that he stay on with him and continue to watch over his herds. In any event, Jacob struck a bargain with Laban that resulted in great blessing and wealth for Jacob. The point of the narrative is to show that such blessing did not come from Laban; rather, it was a gift from God. As Abraham had rejected the offer of wealth from the king of Sodom (14:21), so now Jacob refused to take anything from Laban. What he took instead was the right to stay on and to shepherd Laban's flocks and to keep a part of the herd which he raised (30:31). After the deal was struck, Jacob was allowed to keep all the speckled or spotted goats and all the black sheep in Laban's herds. From this stock he would build his own herds. Although the writer does not specifically state it within the narrative, the passage is surely to be read as an example of the Lord's promise in chapter 28 to be with Jacob during his sojourn in the east.

Jacob's strange use of the peeled poplar branches was not so much intended to demonstrate his resourcefulness as to further the theme of God's continued faithfulness to his word. The clue to the meaning of the passage is the last verse of the chapter, which summarizes the whole narrative (v. 43). The summary recalls quite clearly God's blessing of both Abraham (12:16) and Isaac (26:14) and thus puts the events of this chapter within the larger context of the themes developed throughout the book, namely, God's promise of blessing and his faithfulness to that promise. Jacob's wise dealings with Laban, then, are an example of the way God caused him to prosper during this sojourn. Further confirmation that such is the sense of the narrative comes from the words of Jacob himself in the next chapter. Looking back, he told his wives that it was God who had taken Laban's herds and given them to him (31:7). As with many of the tricks which Jacob attempts in these narratives, God blessed Jacob in spite of them, not because of or through them.

N. Jacob and Laban (31:1–54)

1. Conflict and Promise (31:1–3)

Just as Isaac's wealth had made the Philistines jealous (26:14), so now Jacob learned that Laban was angry and jealous of his wealth. At this time the Lord also directed Jacob to return to the land of his fathers. We are again reminded of the Lord's promise to be "with" Jacob on his journey, and thus the direction of Jacob's life points toward Bethel, the place of the original promise. We seem to have reached the middle point, the turning point, of the narrative and of Jacob's life. He was on his way back to Bethel.

It is interesting that later on, in 32:9 (MT 10), when Jacob looked back at this point in the narrative, he repeated the Lord's words of comfort and promise. Instead of the promise "I will be with you" (31:3), however, Jacob recalled God's words as "I will make you prosper" (32:9 [MT 10]). Thus Jacob's own words offer an expansion and commentary on the sense of God's earlier promise to be "with" him. Such an understanding of the divine presence illustrates the writer's own expansion of the notion of God's promise of his presence to include the continual care and blessing of Abraham's seed.

2. Jacob Tells His Wives (31:4–13)

Jacob's words of explanation to his wives repeat the primary events of the preceding chapter. It is as if the writer lets Jacob retell the confusing events of that chapter from his own perspective. Jacob's explanation not only helps his wives understand the course of events which have transpired, but also provides a helpful guide to the reader in understanding the narratives which precede and follow. Though the events of chapter 30 may look to the reader as though Jacob was getting the best of Laban, from another perspective Jacob's actions may be understood as the Lord's enabling Jacob to be repaid for Laban's mistreatment of him. As Jacob explained the events of the preceding narratives to his wives, the reader could begin to see the same events in a clearer light. The events were all a part of the outworking of God's plan—the plan which began with Jacob's vow at Bethel and the Lord's promise to be with him. Now, even Laban's change of attitude toward Jacob and the jealousy of his sons are seen as part of the plan of God.

3. Flight (31:14–35)

Like Rebekah (24:58) before them and Ruth (1:16) after them, Jacob's wives were willing to leave their own family and go back with him to the land of Canaan. More importantly, they were ready also to put their trust in God and to seek his blessing (31:16). With such an apparent approval of the wives' response to Jacob, it is curious that the writer mentions Rachel's theft of Laban's "household gods" (v. 19). What point does this make within the narrative? Are we to view Rachel's actions favorably or do they reveal a weakness of character in her?

One element in the narrative that may point to an answer is the similarity and contrast between Rachel's stealing her father's "household gods" when fleeing home with her husband and Jacob's stealing his father's blessing when fleeing home to find a wife (chap. 27). In both cases the younger stole what rightfully belonged to the elder. Jacob's stealing the blessing seems to be consciously recast here in the form of Rachel's stealing her father's wealth. Yet in this case, the writer is careful to absolve Jacob of any part in the deed. We are reminded that Jacob did not know that Rachel had taken the gods (31:32). It is through Rachel's resourcefulness alone that Laban's prized possessions are successfully taken.

4. Jacob Argues with Laban (31:36–42)

The dispute over the stolen household gods gives the writer an occasion to restate his central theme, expressed in Jacob's words to Laban: "If the God of my father, the God of Abraham and the Fear of Isaac, had not been with me, you would surely have sent me away empty-handed. But God has seen my hardship and the toil of my hands, and last night he rebuked you" (31:42). Jacob's wealth had not come through his association with Laban. On the contrary, it had come only through God's gracious care during his difficult sojourn.

5. Covenant Between Jacob and Laban (31:43–54)

The narrative concludes with an account of a covenant between Jacob and Laban. As Isaac parted ways with Abimelech by entering into a covenant (26:28–31), so also Jacob and Laban parted ways with a covenant.

O. Jacob, Angels, and Esau (31:55–32:32 [MT 32:1–33])

1. First Encounter with Angels (31:55–32:2 [MT 32:1–3])

The events of this chapter are placed between two accounts of Jacob's encounter with angels ("And the angels of God met him," 32:1 [MT 2]; "And a man wrestled with him until dawn," 32:24 [MT 25]). The effect of these two brief pictures of Jacob's meeting with angels on his return to the land is to align the present narrative with the similar picture of the Promised Land in the early chapters of Genesis. The land appears to be guarded at its borders by angels. The same picture was suggested early in Genesis when Adam and Eve were cast out of the Garden of Eden and "cherubim" (apparently angelic beings) were positioned on the east of the garden to guard the way to the Tree of Life. It can hardly be accidental that as Jacob returned from the east he was met by angels at the border of the Promised Land. This brief notice may also be intended to alert the reader to the meaning of Jacob's later wrestling with the "man" at Peniel (32:24–29 [MT 25–30]). That Jacob met with angels here suggests that the "man" at the end of the chapter may also be an angel.

2. Jacob Fears Esau (32:3–21 [MT 4–22])

The emphasis of this chapter is on the wealth of Jacob and the restoration of Jacob and Esau. Much suspense surrounds Jacob's reunion with his brother Esau. Like Jacob, we the readers are not sure of Esau's intentions in gathering four hundred (32:6) men to meet Jacob on his return. The last words we heard from Esau were that he was intent on slaying Jacob in revenge for the stolen blessing (27:41). Jacob's fear that Esau had now come to do just that seems well founded within the narrative.

In the light of this possibility, Jacob's prayer (32:10–13) plays a crucial narrative role in explaining the reversal of the state of affairs. Jacob prayed: "Save me, please, from the hand of my brother" (v. 11), and then, appealing to the promises God had made throughout the preceding chapters, he said, "You [O Lord] said, 'I will surely make you prosper and will make your descendants like the sand of the sea'" (v. 12 [MT 13]).

True to form, Jacob then made elaborate plans to save himself and his family in the face of Esau's potential threat. He provided his servants with abundant gifts for Esau and instructed them carefully on how to approach Esau when they met. In it all, his thought was that he would pacify Esau and deliver his family from his hand. A very familiar picture of Jacob emerges in this narrative: Jacob the planner and schemer. As he had taken Esau's birthright and blessing, as he had taken the best of Laban's herds, so now he had a plan to gain Esau's favor. As the narrative unfolds, however, it is not his plan that proves successful but his prayer. When he meets Esau, he finds that Esau has had a change of heart. Running to meet Jacob, Esau embraced and kissed him and wept (33:4). All of Jacob's plans and schemes have come to naught. In spite of them all, God had prepared Jacob's way.

3. Jacob Wrestles with Angel (32:22–32 [MT 23–33])

There are many unanswered questions in this brief narrative of Jacob's wrestling with an angel. It is clear, however, that the picture of Jacob's struggle with God is meant to epitomize the whole of the Jacob narratives. Throughout them, Jacob's life has been characterized by struggle, particularly by a struggle to obtain a blessing from God—just as in this narrative. He had struggled with his brother (chaps. 25, 27), his father (chap. 27), and his father-in-law (chaps. 29–31), and now with God (chap. 32). Jacob's own words express the substance of these narratives about him: "I will not let you go unless you bless me" (v. 26 [MT 27]). Here we see a graphic picture of Jacob struggling for the blessing, struggling with God and with men (v. 28 [MT 29]). Most significant is that according to this narrative, Jacob had emerged victorious in his struggle: "You have struggled with God and men and have overcome" (v. 28 [MT 29]). Jacob's victory, even in his struggle with God, comes when, as the text says, the angel "blessed him" (v. 29 [MT 30]). The importance of Jacob's naming the location "Peniel" (v. 30 [MT 31]) is that it identified the one with whom Jacob was wrestling as God. Jacob said, "I saw God face to face" (v. 31 [MT 32]). Jacob's remark does not necessarily mean that the "man" with whom he wrestled was in fact God. Rather, as with similar statements (e.g., Jdg 13:22), when one saw the "angel of the LORD," it was appropriate to say that one had seen the face of God.

Prohibition #183, Gen 32:33 (EVV 32), One must not eat the sinew of the thigh: "The Israelites do not eat the tendon attached to the socket of the hip."

P. Jacob Meets Esau on the Way to Shechem (33:1–20)

1. Jacob Meets Esau (33:1–17)

When he saw Esau and the four hundred men approaching, Jacob divided his entourage again (cf. 32:7 [MT 8]). Jacob showed his preference for Rachel and Joseph by putting them last, after his wives' maidservants and Leah and her sons. Neither Jacob nor the reader had expected Esau's greeting. Right up to the present point in the narrative, Jacob had expected revenge from Esau, or, if not revenge, then heavy bargaining and appeasement. The reader has had no clue that Jacob's fears were not well founded. But, seemingly in response to Jacob's prayer (cf. 32:11 [MT 12]), Esau had had a change of heart. The change in Esau is depicted graphically in the contrast between Jacob's fearful approach ("he bowed seven times as he approached his brother," 33:3) and the eager excitement of Esau to see his brother ("And Esau ran to meet him and embraced him and kissed him," v. 4). All Jacob's plans and preparations pale in the light of Esau's joy at his arrival. Ironically, the four hundred men accompanying Esau turn out not to be for battle with Jacob's household or for taking his spoils but rather for safeguarding the final stage of Jacob's journey (v. 15). Once again Jacob is portrayed as one who has gone to great lengths to secure his own well-being but one whose efforts have proved pointless in view of the final outcome. Jacob continued to scheme and plan, yet God's own plans ultimately make Jacob's plans worthless.

The picture of Jacob and Esau in these narratives curiously foreshadows the relationship between the historical Israel of the Davidic monarchy and Esau's own descendants, Edom, as the later Prophetic Books depict that relationship. Though there was often bitter resentment between the two nations, which God frequently used to chastise his disobedient people (e.g., 1Ki 11:14; Ob 1–18), in the end God's kingdom was to be extended even to include the land of Edom (Ob 21).

2. Jacob in Shechem (33:18–20)

These last verses form a transition in the narrative between Jacob's sojourn in the east and events of the later years of his life in the land of Canaan. As he left Canaan in chapter 28, Jacob vowed that if God would be with him and watch over him so that he returned to the land "in peace" (בְּשָׁלוֹם), he would give to God a tenth of all he had (28:20–22). The narrative has been careful to follow the events in Jacob's life that have shown the Lord's faithfulness to this vow. Thus here we are told that Jacob returned "in peace" (שָׁלֵם) to the land of Canaan. Though he was not yet back to Bethel, he was "in the land of Canaan," and thus God had been faithful. Jacob returned to Bethel in chapter 35 and built an altar there (v. 7). None of these texts mentioned Jacob's giving a "tenth" of all he had to the Lord. Most scholars assume that the erection of an altar here and in chapter 35, along with the offerings, represented his "tenth."[66] It may be also that the "hundred pieces of silver" (NIV) which he paid for the portion of land where an altar was built was intended to represent part of that "tenth."

The portion of land purchased by Jacob at Shechem plays an important role in the later biblical narratives. This was the portion of land where the Israelites buried the bones of Joseph (Jos 24:32); thus it represented their hope in God's ultimate fulfillment of his promise of the land.

Q. Dinah and Shechem (34:1–31)

The birth of Dinah was recorded without much comment in 30:21. Now she becomes the center of the conflict between Jacob and the inhabitants of Canaan. The point of the narrative is to reiterate the portrait of Jacob that has been central throughout these stories. That portrait is of a man who planned and schemed for what appeared to be his own gain, but who in the end actually accomplished God's purposes.

In the present narrative, God's purpose in setting apart the seed of Abraham comes into jeopardy with the proposal of marriage between Dinah and Shechem. Throughout the narrative we are reminded that the purpose of the marriage was that the family of Jacob should become "one people" (34:16, 22) with the inhabitants of Canaan. The last time such a proposal ("one people") was made was in the building of the city of Babylon (11:6). The wording of the proposal runs counter to Abraham's admonition to the servant who sought a wife for his son Isaac: "Swear by the LORD, the God of heaven and the God of earth, that you will not get a wife for my son from the daughters of the Canaanites, among whom I am living" (24:3); and to Rebekah's fear in the case of Jacob: "If Jacob takes a wife from among the women of this land, from Hittite women like these, my life will not be worth living" (27:46); and finally to Isaac's command: "Do not marry a Canaanite woman" (28:1).

While the story in this chapter operates at a level of family honor and the brothers' concern for their ravaged sister, the story nevertheless also carries along the theme that runs so clearly through the Jacob narratives, namely, that God works through and often in spite of the limited self-serving plans of human beings. The writer's purpose is not to approve these human plans and schemes but to show how God, in his sovereign grace, could still achieve his purpose through them.

1. Shechem Defiles Dinah (34:1–4)

Though the narrative is clear that the Hivite son genuinely loved Dinah (34:3), the point of the story is that he had taken her and laid with her (v. 2), apparently against her will, and had thus humiliated her. Simeon and Levi's final words about the incident express clearly how they viewed the situation: "Should he have treated our sister like a prostitute?" (v. 31).

2. Jacob's Sons' Plot (34:5–24)

Jacob was curiously silent about the incident. When he heard what had happened to Dinah, he waited for the return of his sons. The reason behind Jacob's silence is not clear at the beginning of the story. Did he have a plan

---

[66]See, e.g., Keil, *Pentateuch*, 1:283.

and now was he merely waiting for the right occasion? Or was he afraid to act in the absence of his sons? Was he afraid to act at all? Such questions remain unanswered in the narrative.

It is significant, however, that throughout the story it was the sons of Jacob, not Jacob himself, who carried out the deception, and at the end of the story Jacob admonished his sons for their actions. The plans and schemes were no longer Jacob's—they were now the plans and schemes of his sons. The sons of Jacob have taken the place of their father in the thematic structure of the narratives.

In his last words to the two sons, Simeon and Levi, Jacob was very harsh on them concerning the events of this chapter: "Let me not enter their council, let me not join their assembly, for they have killed men in their anger. . . . Cursed be their anger, so fierce, and their fury, so cruel" (49:6–7). The present narrative does not linger to explain Jacob's passive role but goes on quickly to describe the cunning vengeance of Simeon and Levi, who had taken up where their father left off.

That Simeon and Levi had a plan of deception to repay the offense is already suggested in the report of their anger at hearing the news of Dinah (34:7). The reader knows from the bitterness of their anger that they would not let such an act go unpunished. The course of action they chose played remarkably well into the hands of the writer in the development of his themes.

In chapter 17 the rite of circumcision was a sign (v. 11) of the unity of the covenant people and their separation from the rest of the nations. Circumcision was not limited to the seed of Abraham but was rather given as a sign of one's participation in the hope of God's promises to Abraham. It was, in fact, a sign of the covenant promise that Abraham would become the father of "a multitude of nations" (v. 5).

But the way the sons of Jacob carried out the request that these Canaanites be circumcised was a curious reversal of God's intention. They offered circumcision as a means for the two families to become "one people" (34:16). The Canaanites were not joining the seed of Abraham; rather, the seed of Abraham were joining with the Canaanites. The importance of this point is stressed when Shechem repeated it to his countrymen: "Won't their livestock, their property, and all their other animals become ours?" (v. 23).

A thematic interplay between chapters 17 and 34, then, lies behind the writer's including this narrative in the book. A further indication of this narrative interrelationship is the wordplay in the two chapters between the word *sign* (אוֹת, 17:11) and the *consent* (אוֹת, 34:15, 22–23) of the two families to live as "one people."

What is the overall purpose of the association between the two chapters? What point is the writer making? Again, the solution lies in the way in which the present narrative fits into the larger thematic development within the Jacob narratives. Jacob and his family have continuously been characterized as those who attempted to carry out God's intentions by means of their own plans and schemes. On the surface, their plans worked reasonably well, though they always involved cunning and deceit to succeed. The writer does not wish to suggest that such plans represented God's own plans. On the contrary, Jacob's plans and those of his family are always depicted as the plans of those who were far ahead of God and his plans. Nevertheless, the ultimate purpose of these narratives is to show that in spite of the fact that such plans ran counter to God's own, they could not thwart the eventual success of his intentions.

3. Jacob, Simeon, and Levi (34:25–31)

When the sons of Jacob carried out their deception to the end, the writer is careful not to let their actions go unrebuked. Jacob's words apparently express the writer's own final judgment on the actions of the sons: "You have brought trouble on me by making me a stench to the Canaanites and Perizzites, the people living in this land" (34:30). The writer then lets the sons' reply stand as the last words of the narrative, apparently to show that their motive had not been mere plunder but had been the honor of their sister (v. 31).

R. Jacob Returns to Bethel; Rachel and Isaac Die (35:1–29)

1. Jacob's Flight to Bethel (35:1–5)

As Jacob had once fled to Bethel to escape the anger of his brother Esau, so now the Lord told him to return to Bethel and dwell there in the face of the trouble that his two sons, Simeon and Levi, had stirred up. When Jacob obeyed and went to Bethel, the Lord delivered him from the anger of the Canaanites who lived nearby (35:5).

It is significant that Jacob called God "the one who answered me in the day of my distress and who has been with me wherever I have gone" (v. 3). That epitaph serves as a fitting summary of the picture of God that has emerged from the Jacob narratives. Jacob was in constant distress, yet in each instance God remained faithful to his promise and delivered him.

What were the "gods" which Jacob put away? The only previous mention of the "gods" (v. 4) which Jacob's household might have had is that of the "household gods" (31:19) which Rachel stole from her father. These may be included in the expression "foreign gods" (35:4). In view of the fact that the writer mentions that they buried their "earrings" (v. 4) along with these "foreign gods," however, it is likely that Jacob's household had picked up other religious objects while they were living in Shechem. In any case, the point of the narrative is that Jacob and his family were leaving such things behind and purifying themselves in preparation for their journey to Bethel.

2. Jacob in Bethel (35:6–15)

The arrival at Bethel marked the end of Jacob's journey and the final demonstration of God's faithfulness. He had been with Jacob throughout his journey, and now Jacob had returned to Bethel in safety. As Abraham and Isaac had done on numerous occasions, Jacob built an altar and named it in commemoration of the Lord's appearing to him there when he left for Haran (28:10–22). In response, the Lord appeared again to Jacob and "blessed him" (35:9).

For a second time, Jacob's name was changed to "Israel" (cf. 32:28 [MT 29]). Why twice? It is significant that there is no explanation of the name Israel in this second naming, as there was in 32:28 (MT 29). Thus it appears that the negative connotation of the name Israel ("struggled with God") has been deliberately omitted. At this point, Jacob was not the same Jacob who "struggled with God and men." The purpose of the second renaming then is to erase the original negative connotation and to give the name Israel a more neutral or even positive connotation—the connotation it is to have for the remainder of the Torah. It does so by removing the notion of struggle associated with the wordplay in 32:28 (MT 29) and letting it stand in a positive light, contrasting it with the name Jacob, which has been frequently associated throughout these narratives with Jacob's deceptions (e.g., "Isn't he rightly named Jacob? He has deceived me," 27:36). In Jacob's successive names, then, we can see the writer's assessment of his standing before God.

The importance of God's words to Jacob in 35:11–12 cannot be overemphasized. First, God's words "be fruitful and increase in number" recalled clearly the primeval blessing of Creation (1:28) and hence showed God to be still at work in bringing about the blessing to all humankind through Jacob. Second, for the first time since 17:16 ("kings of peoples will come from her"), the mention was made of royalty ("kings," 35:11) in the promised seed. Third, the promise of the land, first given to Abraham and then to Isaac, was renewed here with Jacob (v. 12). Thus within these brief words, several major themes of the book have come together. The primeval blessing of humankind was renewed through the promise of a royal seed and the gift of the land.

In the course of the narrative, this section represents a major turning point and thematic focus. Two lines which have thus far run parallel are about to converge, and out of them both will emerge a single theme. Jacob has two wives, each representing a possible line through which the promise would be carried on: the line of Rachel, namely, the house of Joseph, and the line of Leah, the house of Judah. Just as Abraham had two sons and only one was the son of promise, and just as Isaac had two sons and only one was the son of the blessing, so now Jacob, though he has twelve sons, has two wives (Leah and Rachel), and each has a son (Judah and Joseph) who could rightfully contend for the blessing. In the narratives that follow, the writer holds both sons, Joseph and Judah, before the readers as rightful heirs of the promise. As the Jacob narratives have already anticipated, in the end it is Judah the son of Leah, not Joseph the son of Rachel, who gains the blessing (49:8–12).

3. Rachel Dies (35:16–20)

Rachel, Joseph's mother and Jacob's favorite wife, died giving birth to her second son, Benjamin. The account of the birth of this youngest son is separated from that of the rest of the sons (29:32–30:24), but it follows closely on that passage. The last son to be born was Rachel's first son, Joseph.

It was important to the author that the site of Rachel's burial, Ephrath, be clearly identified with Bethlehem, an important city in later biblical history (cf. 1Sa 17:12; Mic 5:2). This site is further identified by the pillar that Jacob set up to mark Rachel's grave (Ge 35:20). Some such identification of Rachel's burial place was still known at the time of Samuel (1Sa 10:2). Although in Genesis only one other passage even briefly alludes to this site (48:7), this passage continued to play an important role in later biblical text. Thus Jeremiah alluded to it in his description of the destruction of Jerusalem (Jer 31:15), and Micah perhaps alluded to it in his vision of the future Davidic King (Mic 5:2 [MT 1]). It appears that Rachel's agony in the birth of Benjamin later became a picture of Israel's painful waiting for the promised Messiah (cf. Mt 2:18).

4. Jacob's Sons (35:21–26)

The narrative is concerned to show that the oldest sons of Jacob fell from favor because of their horrendous conduct. The writer has already recounted the violence of Simeon and Levi (chap. 34), and now he briefly notes the misconduct of Reuben. As the list which follows shows, the next brother in line was Judah, the son of Leah. With the older sons out of the way, the stage is set for the development of the line of Judah and the line of Joseph. The narratives which follow are devoted primarily to Joseph, but that by no means is an indication of the final outcome. The last word regarding the future of these two lines of the seed of Abraham is not heard until chapters 48 and 49.

5. Isaac Dies (35:27–29)

The end of the Jacob narratives is marked by the death of his father Isaac. After this point the narrative turns to Esau (chap. 36) and Joseph (chaps. 37–50). The purpose of this notice is not simply to record Isaac's death but to show the complete fulfillment of God's promise to Jacob (cf. 28:21). According to Jacob's vow, he had asked that God watch over him during his sojourn and return him safely to the house of his father. Thus, the conclusion of the narrative marks the final fulfillment of these words as Jacob returned to the house of his father Isaac- before he died.

IV. ACCOUNT OF ESAU (36:1–43)

A. Esau's Journey (36:1–8)

The separation of Jacob and Esau is cast in the same form as the separation of Abraham and Lot in chapter 13. The possessions of the two brothers were too great and the land was not able to sustain both of them (36:7; cf. 13:6); so, just as Lot parted from Abraham and went eastward, Esau parted from Jacob and went to Seir. The heirs of the promise remained in the land and the rest moved eastward. The writer is careful to note that their parting of ways was beneficial to both. It was because of their great wealth that they had to part company.

In the remainder of this chapter, the writer goes to great lengths to show the progress and well-being of the line of Esau. He is particularly careful to note that Esau is Edom. The name Esau is identified by "that is, Edom" throughout this chapter. Why such a concern? The answer lies in the importance of Edom during the later periods of Israel's history. For example, in the book of Obadiah, Edom became a small picture of Israel's relationship to the other nations at large. In the future reign of the messianic King, Edom will once again, as in the days of David, be part of his kingdom: "Deliverers will go up on Mount Zion to govern the mountains of Esau. And the kingdom will be the LORD's" (Ob 21). So also within the Pentateuch, the possession of Edom is a mark of the strength and victorious reign of the "Star" that would arise "from Jacob" (Nu 24:17). It is no wonder, then, that the NT writers could look to such passages and see in "Edom" a promise that relates to "all humankind." For example, in Acts 15:17, James, quoting a reference to "the remnant of Edom" (Am 9:12), applies it to "the remnant of humankind."

B. Esau's Sons (36:9–14)

In the remainder of the chapter, the writer includes an unusually long list of the "genealogy" of Esau. The list is made up of several smaller lists. Together these smaller lists make apparent a meaningful structure and reveal the author's conscious effort to present the family of Esau as a coherent and distinct whole.[67] There is first a list of the names of Esau's sons, largely dependent on the brief narratives regarding Esau's wives (26:34; 28:9; 36:3). Verse 10 divides the sons of Esau into two groups: the sons of Adah and the sons of Basemath. Adah's sons (and grandsons) are listed in verses 11–12, then Basemath's in verse 13, and finally Oholibamah's in verse 14.

C. Chiefs of Esau's Sons (36:15–19)

Verses 15–19 list the tribal "chiefs" of the sons of Esau, beginning with the eldest, Eliphaz, and again grouped according to their mothers: Adah (vv. 15b–16), Basemath (v. 17), and Oholibamah (v. 18). The term chief is used in the Bible only for the tribal leaders of Edom, with the exception of Zechariah 12:5-6, where it is also used of the leaders of Judah. The title denotes primarily a political or military function. The names are virtually the same in both lists, with the exception of Korah in verse 16, who is not in the first list (v. 11); the order of Kenaz and Gatam is also reversed.

D. Seir's Sons (36:20–30)

To the two above lists is added a list of "the sons of Seir the Horite, who were living in the region" (vv. 20–28), and then a list of their tribal "chiefs" (vv. 29–30). Seir is ordinarily the name of the geographical territory occupied by the Edomites, but here it refers to an individual. He and his descendants are listed here because they occupied the territory of Edom. In 2 Chronicles 25:11, 14, the "sons of Seir" are called "Edomites."

E. Edomite Kings (36:31–39)

The list of Edomite kings in verses 31–39 is introduced by the heading, "These were the kings who reigned in Edom before any Israelite king reigned." This expression presupposes a knowledge of the kingship in Israel, or at least an anticipation of the kingship. Thus it is part of those texts (e.g., 17:6, 16; 35:11) that look forward to the promises of 49:10; Nu 24:7, 17–18; and Dt 17:14; 33:5. It also presupposes the promise to Abraham in Genesis 17:6.

F. Trial Chiefs of Esau's Clan (36:40–43)

The chapter closes with a final list of the tribal "chiefs" of Esau's clan. Several names in this list overlap with those in vv. 10–14.

---

[67]See Westermann, Genesis, 2:563.

V. ACCOUNT OF JACOB AND JOSEPH (37:1–49:33)

A. Joseph's Dreams and His Brothers' Plot (37:1–36)

1. Transition (37:1)

Verse 1 belongs structurally to the preceding narrative as a conclusion to the Jacob story. It shows Jacob back in the land of promise but still dwelling there as a sojourner like his father before him. The writer's point is to show that the promise of God had not yet been completely fulfilled and that Jacob, like his fathers before him, was still awaiting its fulfillment. From verses like this, the NT writers read the lives of the patriarchs as "aliens and strangers on earth" (Heb 11:13).

The verse also provides a fitting transition to the next section, the Joseph narratives. That section traces the course of events by which the sons of Jacob left the Land of Promise and went into the land of Egypt. Verse 1 sets the stage for that narrative. According to 25:11, Jacob's father, Isaac, lived in Beer Lahai Roi, which was evidently where Jacob now lived.

2. Joseph's Dreams (37:2–11)

The formal title of the section is "This is the account of Jacob," but as the rest of verse 2 suggests, the remaining narrative is not about Jacob but about Joseph, and as we shall see, it is also about Judah. The writer begins immediately to tell the story of Joseph by giving a number of pertinent details about him. He is seventeen years old; along with his brothers he is a shepherd of his father's sheep; and he is only a young lad compared with his other brothers. Most importantly, however, the writer introduces the fact that Joseph brought a "bad report" about his brothers to his father and also that his father Jacob loved him more than the other brothers because he was the son born to him in his old age. In the context of the preceding narratives about Jacob and his wives, we can see that Jacob's special love for Rachel (29:30) has carried over to that of her son Joseph (37:3). Since the story of Joseph is filled with wordplays and reversals, it seems likely that the reference to the "bad [רָעָה] report" in 37:2 foreshadows the brothers' intended "evil" (רָעָה) mentioned in 50:20. The "richly ornamented robe" which Jacob made for Joseph visually illustrates the father's preferential love for Joseph. The writer continually returns to the coat throughout the story as a way of reminding the reader of this central issue (37:23, 31–33).

Jacob's preferential treatment of Joseph was the central problem that initiated the action of the story. The special treatment of Joseph angered the brothers and turned them against him. Eventually their anger resulted in a plan to do away with Joseph altogether (v. 18). But first, adding to their hatred, Joseph recounted to his brothers two dreams, both of which end with the picture of his brothers "bowing down" (vv. 7, 10) to him. This picture of the brothers bowing down to Joseph foreshadows the conclusion of the story where, because he is ruler of the land of Egypt, his brothers "bowed down" (42:6) to him. Thus on that occasion, the narrative informs us that Joseph "remembered the dream which he had dreamed about them" (42:9). Ironically, however, the manner in which Genesis was composed suggests that the picture of Joseph and his brothers foreshadows even further the relationship between Judah and his brothers pictured in Jacob's words in

49:8: "Judah . . . your father's sons will bow down to you." The picture of Joseph is transcended by that of Judah, just as the blessing which the sons of Joseph received in chapter 48 is transcended by that of Judah in chapter 49.

The fact that Joseph has two dreams that foreshadow his future ascendancy over his brothers is to be understood in the light of Joseph's own words in chapter 41. There he explained to Pharaoh, "The reason the dream was given to Pharaoh twice is that the matter has been firmly decided by God, and God will do it soon" (41:32). So here the matter is already settled at the beginning of the story. God would surely bring to pass the fulfillment of Joseph's dream. The writer is careful to show throughout this narrative that Joseph's dreams do come to pass. The significance of the dreams is stated in the words of Joseph's brothers: "Will you reign over us?" (37:8)—words showing that the sense of the "bowing down" (v. 10) is an acknowledgment of royalty and kingship. The irony of the narrative composition is that in the end such royal honor would not reside in the house of Joseph but in the house of Judah ("The scepter shall not depart from Judah," 49:10).

3. Joseph Searches for His Brothers (37:12–18)

After a minor difficulty in which Joseph temporarily lost his way and had to seek help from a stranger, he found his brothers in Dothan. The purpose of this small account of Joseph's seeking his brothers can be seen by comparing it with the brief and similar prelude to the second part of the story, where he met his brothers in Egypt (chaps. 42–44). The symmetry of the two passages and the verbal and thematic parallels serve to reinforce the sense in the narrative that every event is providentially ordered. Here at the beginning of the Joseph story, when Joseph's brothers saw (ראה) him approaching, they "made plans" (נכל) to kill (מות) him (37:18). In the same way, midway through the narrative, when Joseph first saw (ראה) his brothers in Egypt, he eluded them by disguising himself (נכר, 42:7) so that they did not recognize him (נכר, v. 8), and then planned a scheme that, at least on the surface, looked as if he intended to kill them (מות, v. 20).

4. The Brothers Plot (37:19–36)

The writer gives the details of the brother's plans as well as their motivation. Their plans were motivated by Joseph's two dreams. Little did they suspect that the very plans which they were then scheming were to lead to the fulfillment of those dreams. In every detail of the narrative the writer's purpose shows through, that is, to demonstrate the truthfulness of Joseph's final words to his brothers: "You meant it for evil, but God meant it for good" (50:20). The first plan was simply to slay Joseph, to throw his body in a pit, and then to tell their father that an "evil" (37:20) animal had eaten him. Again, the brothers punctuated their plan with a reference to Joseph's dreams in an obviously ironic statement: "We will see what will become of his dreams" (37:20; cf. 42:9). This initial plan, however, is interrupted by Reuben, who, the writer tells us, saved Joseph from their hands. The reference to Reuben is countered later in the narrative by a similar reference to Judah (37:26). The writer apparently wants to show that it was not merely Reuben who saved Joseph from the plan of his brothers, but that Judah also played an important role. Again we can see the central importance of Jacob's last words regarding Judah in 49:8–12. In the end Judah is placed at the center of the narrative's focus on the fulfillment of the divine blessing. It is the seed of Judah who will ultimately figure in the coming of the promised seed.

Reuben's ostensive plan is to persuade the brothers merely to throw Joseph into a pit and, apparently, leave him to die. We learn from the narrative, however, that his actual plan was to return later and rescue Joseph. Reuben's plan succeeded, and the brothers threw Joseph into the pit alive and left him there. The reference to Joseph's coat, by turning our attention briefly back to the earlier events of the narrative, highlights the central point of the story, namely, that the present plan is all part of a larger divine plan foreshadowed in Joseph's dreams.

The story takes an important turn with the arrival of the "Ishmaelites," who were bearing spices down to Egypt (37:25). The "Ishmaelites" become the occasion for Judah to enter the story with the suggestion that rather than letting Joseph die (v. 26) in the pit, they could sell him to the "Ishmaelites." It should be noted here that Judah's plan is in direct violation of the law in Deuteronomy 24:7: "If a man is caught kidnapping one of his brothers from the sons of Israel and treats him as a slave or sells him, the kidnapper must die" (see below). Only a cursory account of Joseph's fate follows in the text. The Ishmaelites, who are also called "Midianites" in this narrative,[68] arrive, and Joseph is sold to them for twenty shekels of silver (about 300 grams or 10 ounces). They then take him to Egypt with them. When the focus of the narrative returns to Reuben and to the outcome of his plan to deal with Joseph, ironically it serves only to underscore the role of Judah in the actual rescue of Joseph.

The Hebrew text of 37:28 is ambiguous. It is unclear who actually sold Joseph to the Ishmaelites. Several English translations add the words "his brothers" to this verse and thus suggest to the reader that it was "his brothers" who sold Joseph. Though such an interpretation and translation may ultimately be correct (cf. 45:4), it nevertheless detracts from the fact that the original Hebrew text appears to say that the Midianites sold Joseph to the Ishmaelites (cf. 37:36). This ambiguity in the text may be an attempt to absolve Judah and his brothers from the appearance of breaking the law of Deuteronomy 24:7. It may have been Judah's idea, but it was the Midianites who actually carried out the deed.

Verse 29 suggests that Reuben had no part in the plan to sell Joseph to the Ishmaelites. He returned to the pit expecting to find Joseph there and thus to rescue him, but Joseph was not there. Reuben's surprise is shown in his rage upon seeing that Joseph is gone. Thus in no uncertain terms we learn that it was Judah, not Reuben, who saved the life of Joseph.

Ultimately, the brothers had to fall back on their original plan of telling their father that an "evil" (v. 33) animal had killed Joseph. Once again, the coat which Jacob had given to Joseph provides the narrative link in the story. The symbol of the brothers' original hatred for Joseph now becomes the means by which the father recognizes his loss. In the end, the bloodstained coat is all that remains of Joseph, and upon seeing it, Jacob tears off his own coat and exchanges it for sackcloth (v. 34).

Thus Jacob's own fate and that of his sons is briefly sketched out in this

---

[68]See my "Genesis," *EBC,* 2:230.

opening narrative. What happens to Joseph foreshadows all that will happen
to the sons of Jacob. They will be carried down into Egypt and there put into
slavery. In this sense, then, Jacob's final words set the goal of the narratives
to follow: "I will go down to my son in death in mourning" (v. 35).
Ironically, the Joseph narratives conclude with Jacob's going down (46:3–4)
to Egypt to see his son and then with his own death (chap. 50).

B. Judah and Tamar (38:1–30)

1. Judah and His Sons (38:1–11)

The narrative of chapter 38 has only a loose connection with the Joseph
story. The first verse notes only that these events occurred "at the same
time." The importance of that remark can be seen in that without it we
would have little basis for relating these events to the story of Joseph. In the
overall strategy of the book, however, this chapter plays a crucial role. The
fact that the narrative seems to lie outside the course of events of the Joseph
story shows that the writer has put it here for a special purpose. It plays an
important part in the development of the central themes of the book.

As so often before in Genesis, the narrative begins with the mention of
three sons (cf. the three sons of Adam, Noah, and Terah). Two of the sons
died because of the evil they did, and now the seed of Judah was put in
jeopardy. Who would prolong the seed? The point of this introductory
information is to show that the continuation of the house of Judah lay in
Judah's hands. The narrative which follows will show that Judah does
nothing to further the seed of his own household. It would take the
"righteousness" of the woman Tamar (38:26) to preserve the seed of Judah.
A nearly identical theme is found in the book of Ruth, which itself alludes to
this chapter of Genesis (Ru 4:18). The story of chapter 38, then, is much like
the other patriarchal narratives outside the story of Joseph that show the
promised seed in jeopardy and the patriarch demonstrating little concern for
its preservation. As in chapter 20, where the seed of Abraham was protected
by the "righteous" (20:4) Abimelech (as also in 26:9–11), here it is the woman
Tamar, not Judah the patriarch, who is ultimately responsible for the survival
of the seed of the house of Judah.

The text is not clear from whose house Jacob originally took Tamar for
his son's wife. Since we are told that Judah's own wife was a Canaanite
(38:2), we should probably assume that had Tamar also been a Canaanite, the
author would have mentioned it in the narrative. If Tamar was not a
Canaanite, as appears likely, then this introduction shows another point at
which the promise to Abraham would have stood in jeopardy. Judah had
married the daughter of a Canaanite (38:2). By so doing, he had realized the
worst fears of Abraham (24:3) and Isaac (28:1), and so, according to the logic
of the narrative, the promise regarding the seed of Abraham and Isaac was in
danger of being unfulfilled. Through Tamar's plan, however, the seed of
Abraham was preserved by not being allowed to continue through the sons
of the Canaanite, the daughter of Shua. The line was rather continued
through Judah and Tamar. The genealogy at the close of the narrative serves
to underscore this point. It was, of course, also the case that a line of the
house of Judah was continued through the seed of Shelah (Nu 26:20). What
is important to note is that this line is not mentioned here, and thus the focus

of the narrative is on the line of Judah that would ultimately lead to the house of David.

2. Tamar's Plan (38:12–26)

Tamar's plan resembles that of Jacob and Rebekah (chap. 27). Through a disguise she obtained a part in the blessing of the firstborn. In so doing, just as with Jacob and Rebekah, she obtained that which the patriarch should have rightfully given. Shelah, the son of Judah, was of age (38:14), and Tamar should have been given to him for a wife (v. 11). The law of levirate marriage (Dt 25:5–10) is assumed here by the author. The brother was to take his brother's widow as a wife in order to prolong the family line. Thus, in the end, the continuation of the line of Judah was not due to the righteous actions of the patriarch Judah; rather, it lay in the hands of the "righteous" Tamar. This has been a recurring theme throughout the patriarchal narratives: God alone will bring about the fulfillment of his promises.

3. Tamar's Sons (38:27–30)

The whole of the Jacob narratives has reached a fitting summary in this brief account of the birth of the two sons, Perez and Zerah. As the Jacob narratives began with an account of the struggle of the two twins, Jacob and Esau (25:22), so now the conclusion of the Jacob narratives is marked by a similar struggle of two twins. In both cases, the struggle resulted in a reversal of the right of the firstborn and of the right of the blessing. The result of both struggles was that the younger gained the upper hand over the elder. As Jacob struggled with Esau and overcame him, so Perez overcame Zerah, the elder, and gained the right of the firstborn (cf. Nu 26:20, where Perez is regarded as the firstborn). The brevity and austerity with which the narrative is recounted leaves the impression that the meaning of the passage would be self-evident to the reader. Indeed, coming as it does on the heels of a long series of reversals in which the younger gains the upper hand on the elder, its sense is readily apparent from the larger context.

C. Joseph in Potiphar's House (39:1–23)

1. Potiphar Buys Joseph (39:1)

Fully conscious of the intervening Judah narrative, the text resumes the account of Joseph by taking up where chapter 37 left off. As in 37:26, those who brought Joseph into Egypt are called "Ishmaelites," while in 37:28, 36, they are known as "Midianites."[69]

2. Joseph Prospers (39:2–6)

Verse 2 establishes the overall theme of the narrative: "The LORD was with Joseph and he prospered." Verses 3–6 relate the theme to the specific series of events to follow: Joseph's blessing from the Lord is recognized by his Egyptian master and Joseph is put in charge of his household. Joseph's sojourn in Egypt, like that of his father Jacob's (30:27), has resulted in an initial fulfillment of the Abrahamic promise that "in you all the families of the earth will be blessed" (12:3). Thus we are told that "the LORD blessed the

---

[69]See my "Genesis," EBC, 2:230.

house of the Egyptian on account of Joseph" (39:5). Such a thematic introduction alerts the reader to the underlying lessons intended throughout the narrative. This is not a story of the success of Joseph, but rather of God's faithfulness to his promises. The last note about Joseph in this introductory section ("Joseph was well built and handsome") sets the stage for what follows.

3. Potiphar's Wife (39:7–20)

This story about Joseph reverses a well-known plot in the patriarchal narratives. Whereas in previous narratives the beautiful wife (12:11; 26:7) of the patriarch was sought by the foreign ruler, now the handsome patriarch himself, Joseph (39:6), is sought by the wife of the foreign official. Whereas in the earlier narratives either the Lord (12:17; 20:3) or the moral purity of the foreign ruler (26:10) rescued the wife, and thus not the patriarch himself, here Joseph's own moral courage saves the day.

Joseph's reply explicitly expresses his motives: "How could I do this great evil and sin against God?" (39:9). The purpose of this reversal perhaps lies in the writer's change of emphasis in the Joseph narratives. In the preceding narratives, the focus of the writer had been on God's faithfulness in fulfilling his covenant promises; in the story of Joseph, however, the writer's attention has turned to the human response. We have seen in the preceding narratives that Abraham, Isaac, and Jacob repeatedly fell short of God's expectations, though of course they continued to have faith in God. In the Joseph narratives, however, we do not see him fall short. On the contrary, Joseph is a striking example of one who always responds in total trust and obedience to the will of God. Behind the Joseph narratives, then, lies an emphasis that has been little felt in the earlier stories, where the stress has been on God's overriding commitment and faithfulness to his promises. The Joseph narratives express that part of the promise found in 18:19: "that they may do righteousness and justice in order that the LORD may fulfill what he has promised to Abraham." There was a human part to be played in the fulfillment of God's plan. When God's people respond as Joseph responded, then their way and God's blessing will prosper.

The Joseph narratives are intended then to give balance to the narratives of Abraham, Isaac, and Jacob. Together the patriarchal narratives and the Joseph narratives show both God's faithfulness in spite of human failure and the necessity of an obedient and faithful response on the part of human beings. The theological emphasis of these narratives is remarkably similar to that of the new covenant theology of Jeremiah (Jer 31:31–34) and Ezekiel (Eze 36:22–32), where the two themes of divine sovereignty and human responsibility are woven together by means of the concept of God's Spirit and the "new heart"—a heart given to human beings by God that responds with obedience and faith. It can hardly be accidental then that in all the book of Genesis, only Joseph is described as one who was filled with the Spirit of God (41:38). This theological emphasis on the "new heart" is not found only in the later prophetic literature; it is also found already in Deuteronomy 30:6–10, where Moses grounds his hope in the future of God's covenant promises regarding the divine work of giving human beings a new heart.

We should note that Joseph was imprisoned through no fault of his own. In fact, the narrative emphasizes explicitly the total uprightness of Joseph throughout the attempted seduction by the Egyptian's wife. He was in jail because of false witness laid against him.

4. God with Joseph (39:21–23)

The epilogue to the story is clear in its emphasis. God has turned an intended evil against Joseph into a good. God was with Joseph (39:21) and prospered his way. Lying behind the course of events, then, is the lesson which the whole of the Joseph narratives intends to teach: "You intended it for evil but God intended it for good" (50:20). Like Daniel during the Exile, Joseph suffered for doing what was right, but God turned the evil done to him into a blessing.

D. Joseph in Jail (40:1–23)

Chapter 40 represents an intermediary stage in the development of the plot of the Joseph story. Joseph has been cast into jail and has risen to a position of prominence there. We are apparently to assume that Joseph's position was responsible for his being assigned to wait on the two incarcerated royal officials. They each had a dream, which Joseph correctly interpreted. This matter was initially to no avail, since the surviving official soon forgot it.

What could have been the writer's purpose in including at such great length the events of this part of the narrative? Later in the story, when Pharaoh himself has a dream, the butler then remembers the events of this chapter and tells Pharaoh of Joseph. From that perspective the events recorded here prove decisive. But is there more to it than that? Why so much detail regarding each dream? Why such an elevated style in the telling of the story? The writer clearly wants to impress upon the reader the picture of Joseph that comes through these events. It is a Joseph who, like Daniel, is an interpreter of dreams and mysteries. He discerns the course of future events which to others are in total darkness. Even when we, the readers, hear the dreams recounted, we are at a loss to find their meaning. The sense of the cupbearer's dream may seem self-evident, but as the sense of the baker's dream shows, such apparently self-evident meanings are by no means certain. Who could, on the face of it, discern between the meanings of the two dreams? One is favorable and the other not so. There is clearly more to the dreams than a plain reading of each would suggest.

The picture of Joseph that emerges from this narrative is precisely that which Pharaoh himself would later express. Joseph is "a man in whom is the Spirit of God" (41:38). He knows the interpretation of dreams, which, in his own words, "belongs only to God" (40:8). The narrative serves, then, to set Joseph apart from all those who have preceded him in the book. He is "wise" and "understanding" (41:39) and "things turned out exactly as he interpreted them" (v. 13). This is a picture quite different from that of the other patriarchs. Abraham was a "prophet" (20:7), but Joseph is a "wiseman" (41:39). Whereas Abraham passively saw the course of future events "in a vision" (15:1), Joseph wisely discerns (41:39) the course of the future in the mysterious dreams of others. What lies behind the writer's portrayal of Joseph in these terms, so distinct from the earlier narratives? Why the contrast with Abraham?

The answer may lie in the perspective of the Pentateuch in general. As the last chapters of Deuteronomy show, the Pentateuch addresses itself to an audience that has seen the passing of Moses, the great prophet (Dt 34:10), and yet has not seen the fulfillment of all his great prophecies. Much lies ahead to be fulfilled. It is to this audience that the leadership of Joshua is presented, not as a prophet but as one "filled with the spirit of wisdom" (Dt 34:9)—a "wiseman," much like Joseph. Unlike the other patriarchs, Joseph, then, represents the kind of leadership that the readers of the Pentateuch would themselves be called upon to follow—a leader like Daniel, needing to "discern" (Da 9:2) the visions of the prophets to find the course of God's future dealings with his people rather than wait upon new prophecies to come. Like Solomon, Joseph is a picture of a truly wise leader, who understands and sees the will of God in the affairs of those around him. In this sense, Joseph stands as a prototype of all the later wisemen in Israel. All future leaders must be measured against him. It is hardly surprising, then, that one sees foreshadowed in the picture of Joseph elements that later resemble David, Solomon, and ultimately the Messiah himself.

E. Joseph and Pharaoh (41:1–57)

The central theme of chapter 41 is expressed clearly and forthrightly within the narrative itself by Joseph in verse 32: "The matter has been firmly decided by God, and God will do it soon." As the narratives of this chapter show, the assurance that God would surely bring future events to pass comes from the fact that the dreams relating those events are repeated twice. "Two" dreams with the same meaning show that God would certainly bring about that which was foreseen in the dreams. Throughout the narrative this theme is kept alive by a continuous return to the pattern of twos. In the previous chapter, the "two" (40:2) officials of the king each had a dream. One dream was good and the other was bad. The dreams and their interpretations are repeated twice, once by the writer in the narrative of chapter 40 and then again by the cupbearer before Pharaoh in 41:9–13. After "two years" (שְׁנָתַיִם, v. 1), the king himself had "two" (שְׁנִית, v. 5) dreams; one part of each dream was good ("years of plenty") and the other was bad ("years of famine"). Within the narrative, each of the two dreams is repeated twice, once by the writer (vv. 1–7) and once by Pharaoh (vv. 17–24). When the dream is "repeated," it is to show that the matter is certain and swift (v. 32). The point of the narrative is that such symmetry in human events is evidence of a divine work. The writer, along with Joseph, is able to see the handiwork of God in the events which he recounts, and he passes them along to the readers in these subtle interplays within the text itself.

1. Pharaoh's Dreams (41:1–8)

The two dreams of Pharaoh are more transparent than those of the two officials. The sense of the two dreams can be seen in the elements of the dream. Seven good cows and seven good heads of grain are the seven good years. The seven ugly cows and seven blighted heads of grain are the seven bad years to follow. But to show that their simplicity conceals rather than reveals their meaning, the writer tells us that all the king's magicians and wisemen were unable to give their meaning (v. 8). The inability of the court officials to interpret the dreams is similar to the powerlessness of Nebuchadnezzar's court officials in the face of the king's mysterious dreams (Da 2:4–12). In the latter case, however, they had not only to interpret the dream but, to insure against fraud, they had to recount the dream as well. Joseph's interpretation of Pharaoh's dreams then was different from that of Daniel. It lay not only in forecasting from the dreams what was to happen, but also, and it appears more importantly, in the advice he gave on how to prepare for what was to come. Thus Joseph's wisdom in dealing with the situation forecast in the dreams is portrayed as equally important to the interpretation of the dreams itself. His wisdom consists more in planning and administration than in a knowledge of secret mysteries. There is also a similarity between the Egyptian king's magicians here and those in Exodus 8:14. Like Joseph, Moses was able to do that which the Egyptian magicians were not.

2. Cupbearer Remembers Joseph (41:9–13)

The words of the cupbearer redirect the reader's attention to the first occasion of Joseph's interpretation of the dreams. Though he had forgotten, the cupbearer now recalled that Joseph's interpretation had stood the test of time: "Things turned out exactly as he interpreted them to us" (v. 13). As it turns out, even the cupbearer's forgetfulness works in Joseph's favor, since just at the opportune moment he remembered Joseph and recounted his wisdom before the king. This short reflection on the events of the previous passage, by drawing the reader's attention to them, serves to highlight the wisdom of Joseph as well as the sovereign workings of God. Joseph's wisdom is highlighted by the fact that, in contrast to the wisemen of Egypt, the interpretation of Joseph, "a Hebrew lad" (v. 12), proved true. God's sovereign power is highlighted in the fact that, though the cupbearer did forget Joseph at the time, he remembered just at the right moment and thus served as the means for Joseph's ultimate rise to power.

3. Joseph Interprets Pharaoh's Dreams (41:14–36)

Pharaoh repeated his two dreams to Joseph in virtually the same terms as the writer originally recounted them. Why then does the writer allow the dreams to be told twice? It is not unusual for the writer to include such repetitions, but in each case the reader should look for the reason behind it. As was suggested above, the writer has gone out of his way to present the whole narrative in a series of pairs, all fitting within the notion of the emphasis given by means of the repetition: "The matter is certain and swift" (v. 32). The repetition of the dreams, then, fits this pattern.

But there may be still more to it. When Pharaoh repeats the dreams, he adds only two major parts: the comment in verse 19b ("I had never see such terrible [רע] cows in all the land of Egypt") and the whole of verse 21, which states that these cows looked just as terrible (רע) as before they ate the good cows (טוב). In both cases, the repetition seems to stress the "evil" (רע) appearance of the cows in contrast with the good of the first group. The writer's emphasis on the "good" and "evil" represents Joseph's wisdom and discernment as an ability to distinguish between the "good" (טוב) and the "evil" (רע). Such a picture suggests that in the story of Joseph the writer is returning to one of the central themes of the beginning of the book, the knowledge of "good" (טוב) and "evil" (רע). While Joseph is able to discern between "good and evil," it is clear from this story that such knowledge comes only from God (41:39). It is ultimately God who gives such knowledge to him. Joseph is the embodiment of the ideal that true wisdom, the ability to discern between "good and evil," comes only from God. Thus the lesson of the early chapters of Genesis is artfully repeated in these last chapters.

Consistent with such an intention is the fact that at the end of Genesis (50:20), the writer returns to the picture of God so clearly portrayed at the beginning (1:1–31), namely, that of the covenant God who alone brings about all things for the "good" of his own. Moreover, at the close of the Pentateuch itself (Dt 30:15), Moses returns to the notion of God's provision of the "good" (טוב) and his warning against the "evil" (רע). In that context, it is God's gift of the Torah that again reveals to humanity the "knowledge of good and evil" which was lost in the Garden. In view of such considerations, it can hardly be accidental that the following narrative picks up just on this point by recounting that Joseph's plan seemed "good" (41:37) to Pharaoh and all his servants.

4. Joseph Rules over Egypt (41:37–57)

The account of the king's appointment of Joseph over all his kingdom continues to present a picture of him that recalls the portrait of Adam in Genesis 1. Just as Adam is seen in the Creation account as dependent on God for his knowledge of "good and evil," so Joseph is portrayed here in the same terms (see above comments). Just as Adam is made God's "vice-regent" to rule over all the land, so Joseph is portrayed here as Pharaoh's "vice-regent" over all his land (41:40). As Adam is made in God's image to rule over all the land, so the king here gives Joseph his "signet ring" and dresses him in royal garments (41:42). The picture of Joseph resembles the psalmist's understanding of Genesis 1: "You have . . . crowned him with glory and honor. . . . and have made all things subject under his feet" (Ps 8:5–6 [MT 6–7]). Just as God provided a wife for Adam in the Garden and gave human beings all the land for their enjoyment, so the king gave a wife to Joseph and put him over all the land (41:45).

What is one to make of such correspondences between Adam and Joseph? Are they intentional or coincidental? While they may be merely accidental similarities, such patterns in the description of key characters are often found in biblical texts and would not be thematically out of place here. At many points in the story, Joseph seems to be represented as an ideal of what a truly wise and faithful man is like. He is a model of the ideal man or the ideal king. He accomplishes that which Adam failed to do. It seems likely, then, that a conscious purpose lies behind these similarities with Genesis 1. The story of Joseph is a reflection of what might have been, had Adam remained obedient to God and trusted him for the "good." At the same time, the picture of Joseph is an anticipation of what might yet still be, if only God's people would, like Joseph, live in complete obedience and trust in God. The picture of Joseph, then, looks back to Adam; but more, it looks forward to one who is yet to come, the one from the house of Judah "to whom the kingdom belongs" (Ge 49:10). Thus, in the final shape of the narrative, the tension between the house of Joseph and the house of Judah, which lies within many of these texts, is resolved by portraying the life of Joseph as a picture of the one who is to reign from the house of Judah.

F. Joseph and His Brothers (42:1–38)

The preceding chapter has recorded Joseph's rise to power. The present chapter turns to the divine purpose behind his miraculous rise. At the conclusion of this long and complicated section, Joseph recounts to his brothers the ultimate purpose behind the narratives: "God sent me ahead of you to preserve for you a remnant on earth and to save your lives by a great deliverance" (45:7). Joseph is cast in the role of a savior of his people. Though that is the primary meaning of the narratives, there are still many subplots along the way. Indeed, this section of Genesis becomes extremely complex in both plot and motive, and, like chapter 24, it is complicated even further by numerous repetitions in the reporting of the events. Nearly every major event is told twice—once by means of the narration of the event itself and then by one of the chief characters in the narrative.

1. Jacob Sends His Sons to Egypt (42:1–2)

As is frequently the case in biblical narratives, the words of Jacob at the beginning of this story foreshadow the final outcome of the events of the story. Sending his sons to Egypt, Jacob said, "Go down there . . . that we may live and not die" (cf. 45:2). Jacob's words also serve to align the deeds of Joseph with the larger themes of the Torah, namely, "life" (חַיִּים) and "death" (מָוֶת) (Ge 2:7, 9; 3:22; Dt 30:15). In so doing, the events that follow are cast as a narrative picture showing the way to return to the gift of life which was lost in the Garden.

2. Joseph Meets His Brothers (42:3–13)

The twelve (שְׁנֵים עָשָׂר, 42:13, 32) sons of Jacob are divided into two groups throughout the narrative. There are the "ten brothers of Joseph" (42:3) and then the "two" (שְׁנַיִם,44:27) sons of Jacob by Rachel, Joseph, and Benjamin. These two sons of Rachel are contrasted with the two sons of Leah, Reuben, and Judah. Both Reuben and Judah play an important and similar role in the narrative (cf. Reuben, 42:22, 37; Judah, 43:3, 8). They speak on behalf of the other brothers and are the catalysts in the resolution of the plots instigated by Joseph. It was Judah, however, who saved the day by offering himself as a pledge (43:9) for the young Benjamin, and it was Judah who repeated Jacob's own thematic words "that we may live and not die" (43:8; cf. 42:2). Finally, it was Judah who spoke before Joseph and offered himself as a substitute for Benjamin, lest he cause any evil (רַע) to come upon his father Jacob (44:33–34). Throughout the narrative, then, the plot is woven around the interplay between Joseph and Judah, and in the end it is Judah who resolves the conflict. By contrast, it is Joseph who creates the conflict and tension throughout the narrative. When his brothers approached to buy grain, he "pretended to be a stranger" (42:7) and spoke harshly, accusing them of being spies. What motivated Joseph? Was it revenge? Was he trying to get even with his brothers for what they did to him? The writer immediately pushes aside such a possibility with the comment that Joseph "remembered the dreams which he dreamed about them" (v. 9). Thus the reader is advised that Joseph's schemes and plans against his brothers were motivated by the dreams of the earlier narratives and not by revenge for what his brothers had done to him.

Little more is said specifically regarding the purpose that Joseph saw in his continuous schemes to perplex his brothers. But several subtle reminders throughout the narrative reveal further his intention. For example, in response to Joseph's accusation that the brothers were spies, the brothers defended their integrity by saying, "Your servants are twelve brothers" (v. 13). Lest their integrity be gainsaid, however, they were forced to add "and one is no more." Joseph's schemes have provoked the first hint that their evil deed, accomplished long past, may yet rise up against them. As proof that this point was not lost on the brothers, the writer allows us to listen in on the brothers' own version of this event when they recount it to their father (v. 32). On that occasion, they reported their own words in a different order than that of the narrative in verse 13. In the narrative account the brothers mentioned last the "one who is no more"; but when they tell their father about Joseph's accusations and their response, they mention first the "one who is no more" and then tell of Benjamin, who was home with their father. Though subtle, such a reversal appears to be a narrative hint that the memory of what they did to Joseph was beginning to grate on their conscience.

Another reminder in the narrative that serves to reveal Joseph's motives is the conclusion that the brothers draw from Joseph's trick of having their money returned to them in their grain sacks. When each saw his own money returned, they asked, "What is this that God has done to us?" (v. 28). Whatever they might have meant by it, in the logic of the narrative itself their words have an ironic ring of truth about them. Though we, the readers, know it was Joseph who had the money put back into their sacks, their words point us to the work of God and serve to confirm the direction the narrative as a whole appears to be taking. God is at work in the schemes of Joseph, and we are allowed to see in this narrative a preliminary reminder of the ultimate theme: "God meant it for good" (50:20).

3. Joseph Tests His Brothers (42:14–24)

Joseph devised two plans to test his brothers. The first was that "one" (v. 16) of the brothers should return for the youngest and the rest remain in prison. After three days, the second plan was announced: "one" (v. 19) of the brothers was to remain behind and the others were to return to get the youngest. The double plan fits into the overall narrative scheme of repetition in that for both plans it is the "one" brother who rescues the others that is central. Within the narrative this "one" brother appears to be an echo of the "one who is no more." It is no wonder then that the brothers' own conclusion from within the narrative is that their present distress had been caused by the distress which they had brought upon Joseph (vv. 21–22).

Joseph's explanation of the change in plans also ties the narrative to the larger themes of the book. He said about his plan, "Do this and you will live. . . . and you will not die" (vv. 18–20), which again aligns the narrative with the themes of "life" and "death" that run throughout the Pentateuch (cf. 2:16–17; 50:20; Dt 30:15). Joseph also said, "for I fear God" (42:18), which again identifies his plans with the will of God (50:20, "God meant it for good").

When the brothers begin to talk among themselves about the distress they had brought upon Joseph, the reader can again catch a glimpse of where Joseph's plans were leading. Reuben's words focus our attention on the central point of the narrative: "Now we must give an accounting for his blood" (42:22). At this point we can see that Joseph's plans were not in revenge for how his brothers once treated him; rather, they were to show how, in God's world, the guilt (v. 21) of the brothers came back upon them and called for justice. The remarkable message of the narrative, however, is that Joseph had already forgiven his brothers of the evil they had done to him. As verse 24 shows, Joseph had to turn away from them to hide his sorrow for the distress his plan now caused. What awaited the brothers was not the "evil" (רַע) they intended for Joseph but the "good" God intended for them through Joseph (50:20).

4. Money in the Sacks (42:25–28)

Joseph's next plan was to fill the brothers' sacks with the money they had brought to buy grain. Though nothing was said about Joseph's intention, the words of the brothers as they discovered their money tell the whole story: "What is this that God has done to us?" (v. 28). We, the readers, know that it was Joseph who put the money in their sacks, but the brothers give expression to the underlying lesson of the narrative. God was behind it all, and through it all was working out his purposes (cf. 50:20).

5. The Brothers Tell Jacob (42:29–38)

The events of this chapter are now retold in the words of the brothers themselves, but in an abbreviated form. Their focus is on the plan of Joseph for the return of the youngest son. We must again ask why the writer has allowed this portion of the narrative to be retold. It certainly is part of his overall strategy in telling the story, but what specifically does he intend here? The answer lies in Jacob's response: "You have deprived me of my children—Joseph is no more and Simeon is no more" (v. 36). As if he knew all that had happened between his sons and Joseph, Jacob's words ring truer than he would ever have suspected. To the sons, and to the reader, his words were curiously true. The brothers had deprived him of Joseph, and it was because of them that Simeon was not now with them and that Benjamin was to be taken away. Thus now, in the words of their father, there was a reminder of the guilt that lingered over their treatment of Joseph.

In the light of Jacob's words, Reuben's response was very unusual: "You may put both of my sons to death if I do not bring him back to you" (v. 36). Reuben certainly meant his words to insure confidence in his own resolve to return Benjamin, but within the context of the narrative they appear only to add insult to injury. Jacob's reply to Reuben not only summarily dismissed Reuben's pledge but also raised one more time the matter of the loss of Joseph: "His [Benjamin's] brother [Joseph] is dead and he alone survives" (v. 38).

G. The Brothers Return to Egypt (43:1–34)

1. Judah and Jacob (43:1–14)

In keeping with the general motif of pairs of events throughout the Joseph narratives, the story now begins the second journey of the sons into Egypt. The famine was still in the land and the grain purchased earlier was gone, so the father sent his sons back for more. This time it was Judah who insisted on taking Benjamin back with them in accordance with Joseph's demands. In the previous chapter it had been Reuben (42:37). In persuading his father, Judah gave expression once more to the central themes of "life" and "death" that have been carefully interwoven throughout these narratives: "that we may live [חיה] and not die [מות, 43:8; cf. 50:20]." In a way similar to Reuben (42:37), Judah offered to take full responsibility for Benjamin if he was allowed to accompany the brothers to Egypt: "I myself will guarantee his safety" (43:9).

That both Reuben and Judah had suggested ways in which Benjamin could be safely taken to Egypt provides another reminder that the events depicted here have already been foreshadowed in the events of chapter 37, the brother's maltreatment of Joseph. In that narrative, both Reuben and Judah attempted to save Joseph's life in the face of the brothers' evil plan (37:21, 26). Now both Reuben and Judah have attempted to save Benjamin from the plan which Joseph had initiated against the brothers. Such reversals are commonplace by now throughout these narratives and serve to show that the whole series of events recorded here was part of a larger plan, a divine plan (cf. 50:20). As a further reminder to the reader of the repetition throughout the narrative, Judah is allowed to express his impatience with Jacob by referring explicitly to the fact that this was the "second" time a journey to Egypt has been made: "If we had not delayed we could now have return a second time" (43:10; cf. 41:32).

Jacob (or Israel, as he is known throughout this chapter) gave in to Judah's plan. Just as it was Judah's plan in chapter 37 which ultimately saved the life of Joseph (37:26), so now it was Judah's plan that saved the life of Benjamin. Jacob's farewell words provide the narrative key to what follows: "May God Almighty grant you mercy [רחם] before the man" (43:14). As so often in the patriarchal narratives, the events that follow seem to be guided by just these words. At the conclusion of the narrative, when the sons reached Joseph and he saw Benjamin, we are told that "his mercy [רחם] was kindled toward his brother" (v. 30). It is important that in these words of Jacob the compassion which Joseph was to find toward his brothers was given by "God Almighty." Again, in these subtle and indirect ways the writer informs the reader of the power of God in directing the lives of his people and in carrying his plans to completion.

2. The Brothers and Joseph's Steward (43:15–25)

Curiously, the whole problem of the brothers being "spies" is not raised again. The readers, of course, know the brothers were not spies, so the writer simply allows the whole issue to drop without further comment. We are left instead with the apprehensions of the brothers themselves as they were ushered into the royal house of Joseph. Their fears and misgivings reveal to the reader their conviction that nothing good was going to come of this. The reader, however, is told at the start that the brothers were being taken into the house for a great feast. We know that the brothers' fears were misguided. They need not have feared becoming Joseph's slaves. But the writer wishes to draw our attention to their misguided fear.

To show the underlying cause of their misgivings and to show just how misguided the brothers actually were, the writer allows them to repeat to the steward the account of their finding the money in their grain sacks. The purpose of this repetition is to present before the readers the response of the steward. The picture that emerges is that of the brothers vainly trying to explain themselves to anyone who will listen and vainly trying to return the money which they had found in their sacks. But no one seemed to take their explanation seriously nor would anyone take their money. Joseph's steward brushed off their explanation with the penetrating reply, "It's all right. Your God and the God of your father has given you treasure in your sacks. I received your silver" (v. 23). The reader surely knows that the steward's words cannot be taken seriously. There has been no mention of money given to the steward. From the narrative itself we are apparently to understand that the steward has been in on Joseph's secret plan all along. But, as is often the case in these narratives, the steward expresses unwittingly one of the central themes of the book: "The God of your father has given you treasure."

3. Banquet (43:26–34)

The writer goes to great lengths in depicting the scene of the banquet. Joseph was conspicuously careful to ask about the well-being of their father and the lad, Benjamin, whom the brothers had brought back with them. The readers almost have to remind themselves that the brothers still did not know it was Joseph who was entertaining them. It is only when we see Joseph hurry to another room to hide his tears that we are sure his identity was still unknown.

The question that naturally arises out of this passage is what the brothers themselves thought about Joseph's questions and their treatment in his house. They came expecting to be made into servants and now it was they who were being served. Did they not suspect something? Did they not have questions about Joseph's curiosity about their father and his special treatment of Benjamin? The writer answers all such questions by simply stating that the brothers were "dismayed" (v. 33). They asked no questions and seemed to accept the words of Joseph's steward ("The God of your father has given you treasure," v. 23) and Joseph's words to Benjamin ("God be gracious to you, my son," v. 29) as the most plausible solution. For the writer, of course, Joseph's steward had unwittingly given the correct explanation and Joseph's words have provided a cryptic confirmation.

H. The Silver Cup (44:1–34)

1. Joseph's Trick (44:1–6)

Once again Joseph tricked his brothers by having his cup and Benjamin's money returned in his sack of grain. The purpose of the act is clear from Joseph's instruction to his men. When they overtook the brothers they were to say, "Why have you repaid evil for good?" (v. 4), and "You have done evil in what you have done" (v. 5). If we are to judge by the brothers' response when the servants reached them with Joseph's message, the word which the servants spoke was more detailed than what we are given in the narrative. The brothers immediately made reference to the silver and gold that was supposedly in their sacks. But why are Joseph's words reported only in such general terms? The answer lies in the fact that as spoken by Joseph, his words have expressed the central question of the

Joseph narratives: the contrast between the "evil" (רָעָה) done by the brothers and the "good" (טוֹב) intended and accomplished by God (cf. 50:20). When stated in such a general way, Joseph's question looks as if it included the question of the brothers' treatment of him in chapter 37. The question raises again the matter of the brothers' guilt in their treatment of Joseph. Whether the brothers realized this point, the function of Joseph's question within the narrative is to indicate to the reader that a residue of guilt still lingered over the brothers' heads. It seemed as if everywhere they turned they heard the echo of their mistreatment of Joseph. The effect of such narrative strategies is to present a picture of a world in which justice does ultimately prevail and where an "evil" once done will not go unnoticed or unattended. This is, indeed, one of the most important elements of this narrative.

2. The Brothers Return (44:7-13)

Joseph's plan worked as if every detail had been carefully orchestrated in advance. Not knowing that the cup and money were in Benjamin's sack, the brothers made a rash vow and put the life of Benjamin and their own freedom in jeopardy. When the cup was discovered, their response was one of complete hopelessness. They tore their clothing and returned to the city. There was nothing else to do. Curiously, their response was a mirror image of their father's response upon hearing their own report of the loss of Joseph (37:34). The grief they had caused their father had now returned upon their own heads. In a word, they were trapped.

3. The Brothers Before Joseph Again (44:14-17)

When Joseph's plans turn out as if perfectly orchestrated, we begin to see what his purpose has been all along. While it had looked as if he was working a slow revenge upon his brothers, we can now see that his purpose was not revenge but repentance. Through his schemes, his brothers were coming to an awareness of their guilt and were now ready to acknowledge it. Their utter frustration was expressed in their repetition of the question, "What can we say?" (44:16). Finally comes their expression of guilt: "How can we show ourselves to be right?" The rhetorical answer to these questions is an implied negative: "We have nothing to say, we cannot show ourselves to be right." Thus the conclusion they are forced to draw is: "God has found the iniquity of your servants" (v. 16).

Though we can clearly see that the brothers have only the immediate issue of the lost cup in mind, within the compass of the whole Joseph narrative their words take on the scope of a confession of their former guilt as well. We, the readers, know that the brothers have not taken the cup. Joseph had it put into Benjamin's sack. We also know that the brothers know that they did not take the cup. So, when they speak of God "finding out their guilt" (v. 16), we are forced to generalize their sense of guilt within the context of the narrative as a whole. We, along with the author of the narrative, read their words with a broader significance than they might have intended on that occasion. We see the narrative interconnections that were, obviously, not a part of their own understanding within the situation itself. In Joseph's response, he steers the matter in a direction that even more closely resembles his brothers' treatment of him. The young lad is to be sold into slavery in Egypt and the brothers are to return to their father.

4. Judah's Speech (44:18–34)

Judah's final speech, in which he retold the whole Joseph story, reveals the brothers' perception of the events as well as the hopelessness of their situation. The overall sense of Judah's version of the story is that the brothers have been mistreated. The implication was that if anyone was to blame it was Joseph. According to Judah's version, Joseph was the one who initiated the series of mishaps that had ended in the present predicament. All that the brothers had done was to follow his instructions and the instructions of their father.

Judah's words, however, reveal more to the reader than even he intended. They show that the fault did not lie with Joseph but with the "evil" intention of the brothers toward Joseph. Once again, his words raised the issue of the brothers' mistreatment of Joseph.

Curiously, at this point Judah said of Joseph, "He is dead" (v. 20). This is quite different from what was said of Joseph on other occasions, namely, "He is no more" (42:13). The meaning of the expression "he is no more" within Genesis does not imply death (cf. 42:36, "Simeon is no more"; Ge 5:24, "Enoch walked with God; then he was no more, because God took him away"). We can see, then, that in retelling the story, Judah has added a dimension to the brothers' recounting of the events that was not previously there. The net effect is that the story now resembles the original intention of the brothers, which was "to kill" Joseph (37:18). Furthermore, it corresponds to the story which the brothers themselves gave to Jacob. What in real life would have perhaps been a slip of the tongue is now, within the strategy of the narrative, a clue to the brothers' state of mind as well as to their guilt.

But Judah's account of Jacob's own response to the issue with Benjamin raises even further the issue of the brothers' guilt regarding Joseph. In this narrative Judah also recalled that Jacob had said to them, "You know that my wife bore me two sons, and one went out from me, and I said, 'He has surely been torn to pieces' " (44:28). When he recounted the story this way, Judah, along with the readers, surely knew that Jacob's words were mistaken. It was not a wild animal that killed Joseph—it was the brothers themselves who had sold him into slavery. But could Judah have told the story any other way? Clearly not. To tell the story the way it happened would be to admit to a guilt even greater than that of which they were presently accused. Thus even when retelling the story to demonstrate his own innocence, Judah gives testimony, to the reader at least, of his own guilt and the guilt of his brothers. Though it is through Judah's speech that the reader is again reminded of the brothers' guilt, we should not lose sight of the fact that once again it was Judah who intervened on behalf of Benjamin and ultimately, within the narrative, it was his words which saved the day. After this speech, Joseph could contain himself no longer. He now had to unveil his identity to his brothers.

I. Joseph's Revelation (45:1–28)

1. Joseph's Speech (45:1–8)

The narrative is clear that Joseph had taken no personal enjoyment in the deception of his brothers. When he could hold back no longer, he revealed his true identity. We are never told why he chose not to reveal his identity to his brothers immediately, but we can see from the narrative itself that the effect of his scheme has been to further the primary themes of the Pentateuch. In his words of explanation and comfort to his brothers, Joseph returns once again to the central theme of the narrative: though the brothers were responsible for Joseph's being sold into Egypt and though they intended "evil," God was ultimately behind it all and had worked it out for the "good." As he told his brothers, "God sent me before you to save life" (v. 5), and, "God sent me before you to preserve for you a remnant in the land and to save your lives" (v. 7).

In the narrative thus far, this theme has been expressed by Jacob (42:2) and Judah (43:8), and Joseph himself has also indirectly alluded to it (42:18). Here, however, and in 50:20, Joseph's words give the theme its full expression. Joseph's words pull back the narrative veil and allow the reader to see what has been going on behind the scenes. It was not the brothers who sent Joseph to Egypt—it was God. And God had a purpose for it all. We have seen numerous clues throughout the narrative that this has been the case, but now the central character, the one ultimately responsible for initiating the plots and subplots of the narratives, reveals the divine plans and purpose behind it all. Joseph, who can discern the divine plan in the dreams of Pharaoh, also knew the divine plan in the affairs of his brothers. Through it all he saw God's plan to accomplish a "great salvation" (v. 7). In describing God's care over him, Joseph alluded to the brothers' initial question regarding his dreams as a young lad. They had said, "Do you intend to reign over us?" (37:8). Now he reminded them that he had been made "ruler over all the land of Egypt" (45:8).

2. Joseph Sends His Brothers Back to Jacob (45:9–20)

In the second part of his speech to the brothers, Joseph made plans to bring his father to Egypt. He repeated twice that the brothers were to go to Jacob and with all haste bring him down to Egypt. He had set aside the "land of Goshen" (אֶרֶץ־גֹּשֶׁן, v. 10), where they could continue to raise their families and livestock during the five remaining years of famine. In the midst of the famine the family of Israel was to be well provided for in the land of Goshen. It can hardly be without purpose that this picture of God's chosen people dwelling safely and prosperously in the land which God has provided for them comes at the close of the book of Genesis and that it is a near replica both of the way things were in the beginning and of the way things were to be in the future. The writer appears intentionally to draw our attention to the connection between the "end" and the "beginning." Thus when Pharaoh restates Joseph's offer and "twice" gives the brothers the "good" (vv. 18, 20) of the land of Egypt, it is hard not to see in the purpose of this narrative a conscious allusion to the "good" (1:31) land given to Adam in Genesis 1. The picture of Joseph is a picture of restoration—not just the restoration of the good fortune of Jacob, but, as a picture, the restoration of the blessing that was promised through the seed of Jacob. This picture is also a blueprint for the hope that lies for the people of Israel at the end of the Pentateuch. They are to go into the land and enjoy it as God's good gift (e.g., Dt 30:5).

3. Jacob's Response (45:21-28)

Jacob's response to the news of Joseph plays a key role in connecting these narratives to the message of the Pentateuch as a whole. Throughout the Pentateuch there is a focus on the response of God's people to the work of God. At important moments in the narrative the people's response to the work of God is interpreted as either one of "faith" (Ge 15:6; Ex 4:31; 14:31; 19:9) or "no faith" (Nu 14:11; 20:12).[70] Jacob's response appears to play a part along with these other examples. Here, however, the writer gives a deeper insight into the nature of his faith. At first, when Jacob hears the news that Joseph is alive, "his heart grew numb" and "he did not believe" (45:26). But when he heard the words of Joseph and saw all that he had sent to take him back to Egypt, "the spirit of Jacob came alive" (v. 27) and he set out to go to him (v. 28). The faith of Jacob bore the same marks as that of the other occurrences of faith throughout the Pentateuch, but this text alone stresses a different dimension in the contrast between his "numbed heart" and his "renewed spirit." Jacob's lack of faith is identified with his "numbed heart." When his spirit was renewed, however, he believed. The viewpoint expressed here is very similar to that of the later prophetic literature where faith and the "new heart" are synonymous (cf. Jer 31:33-34; Eze 36:26) and where lack of faith (Hab 1:5) is synonymous with "numbness" (Hab 1:4). All these texts seem to be summed up in the words of David in Psalm 51: "Create a pure heart in me, O God, renew a steadfast spirit within me" (v. 10 [MT 12]).

J. Jacob Goes to Egypt (46:1-34)

1. Jacob at Beersheba (46:1-4)

Before Jacob went to Egypt, he traveled to Beersheba, where he built an altar and offered sacrifices to the God of his father, Isaac. The writer is careful to remind the reader in this way that the patriarchs all worshiped the same God. Jacob worshiped the God of his father, Isaac. In the light of this fact there appears to be a remarkable contrast between God's words to Jacob in this chapter and his words to Isaac earlier in chapter 26. The Lord had said to Isaac, "Do not go down to Egypt" (26:2), but he now said to Jacob, "Do not be afraid to go down to Egypt" (46:3). Such a change in attitude toward the patriarchs' traveling to Egypt indicates that the Lord was following a specific plan with regard to his people. His instructions to Isaac in chapter 26 might have left the impression that he was opposed, in principle, to the seed of Abraham going into Egypt. That, in turn, might have left the impression that the whole Joseph story, which resulted in Jacob's going to Egypt, was running counter to God's purposes. Thus when the Lord now speaks to Jacob, it becomes clear that this sojourn to Egypt plays a part in God's plan. Such a perspective is consistent with the overall theme of the Joseph narrative, which is that God was working all things for the good of Jacob and his house (50:20).

God's words to Jacob in the night vision also reiterate the promise to Abraham that from his seed would come a "great nation" (46:3; cf. 12:2), but these words add that God would do this in Egypt. Egypt was to be the place

---

[70]See Hans-Christoph Schmitt, "Redaktion des Pentateuch," 170-189.

where the house of Jacob would become the nation of Israel. In these words then is anticipated the whole of the great work of God that was yet to be recounted in the Torah. God would bring his people into Egypt and be with them there. After they had become a great nation, he would bring them back to the Promised Land. This is the second great "vision" in which God revealed his future plans for the seed of Abraham. In 15:1, God revealed in a vision to Abraham that his seed would be taken into bondage and serve for four hundred years (15:13) and that afterward they would come out with "great wealth" (v. 14).

2. Journey to Egypt (46:5–7)

Special attention is given to the journey of Jacob and his household into Egypt. Just as Abraham had left Ur of the Chaldeans and journeyed to Canaan (12:4–5), so now Jacob leaves the land of Canaan and journeys to Egypt. Both men were leaving the land of their birth in obedience to the will of God. Just at this point in the narrative, the obedience of both men plays a pivotal role in God's election of Abraham's seed. Thus, by means of their repetition, verses 6 and 7 emphasize that "all his seed" went with Jacob into the land of Egypt. To demonstrate graphically the importance of this point, the writer now lists the names of "all his seed" and numbers them at "seventy" (v. 27).

3. Jacob's Descendants (46:8–27)

The list of names in these verses appears to have been selected to total "seventy" (46:27). It can hardly go without notice that the number of nations in Genesis 10 is also "seventy." Just as the "seventy nations" represent all the descendants of Adam, so now the "seventy sons" represent all the descendants of Abraham, Isaac, and Jacob—the children of Israel. Here in narrative form is a demonstration of the theme in Deuteronomy 32:8 that God apportioned the boundaries of the nations (Ge 10) according to the number of the children of Israel. Thus the writer has gone to great lengths to portray the new nation of Israel as a new humanity and Abraham as a second Adam. The blessing that is to come through Abraham and his seed is a restoration of the original blessing of Adam, a blessing which was lost in the Fall. The picture of God that emerges from these pages is not merely a God who works with his own chosen people for their good alone, but also a God who works with the nations to bring about his plan of salvation and blessing. The picture is similar to that of Isaiah 45, which portrays the rise of the kingdom of Persia as the handiwork of God—all for the sake of the universal salvation and blessing which God intended through his chosen seed.

Deuteronomy 10:22 views the number "seventy" as very small in comparison to the fulfillment of God's promise of making Abraham's seed outnumber the stars of the heavens. Thus, in preparation for the idea of God's faithfulness to his promise to the patriarchs, we are reminded of the relatively few descendants of Israel who went into the land of Egypt. Exodus 1:5 returns to this same theme by reminding the reader of the "seventy" descendants of Jacob who went into Egypt and of their great increase during their sojourn there: "The Israelites were fruitful and multiplied greatly and became exceedingly numerous and the land was filled with them" (Ex 1:7)— a clear allusion to the promised blessing (cf. Ge 1:28).

4. Reunion of Jacob and Joseph (46:28–34)

Curiously, in the narrative itself it was Judah, not Joseph, who led the family of Israel into the land of Goshen. Once again it appears as though the writer has singled out Judah for special attention and highlighted his activity even over against Joseph. Though in the Joseph story as a whole Joseph was responsible for the preservation of the family in Egypt, here, within the detail of the passage, it was Judah who "pointed out the way" to the land of Goshen. Such a special focus on Judah is part of the writer's overall strategy to emphasize the crucial role of Judah in God's plan of bringing about Israel's deliverance. The prominence of Judah is seen most clearly in Jacob's words of blessing to his twelve sons (Ge 49:8–12).

The chapter ends with Joseph's plan to secure the land of Goshen as a dwelling place for the family of Israel. The plan was simply to tell Pharaoh that they were shepherds. As the writer informs us, the Egyptians hated shepherds and thus would allow the Israelites to dwell off by themselves in the land of Goshen. In the next chapter, Joseph's plan succeeded and the people were given the land of Goshen. In these two brief narratives, Joseph and Judah are contrasted markedly. Judah led the brothers to the land of Goshen, but it was Joseph's wise plan that resulted in their being able to live there.

K. Jacob Settles in Goshen; Famine (47:1–31)

1. In Goshen (47:1–12)

Throughout the Joseph narratives the writer has been careful to allow the key events to be recounted twice. The events of chapters 46 and 47 are no exception. Joseph has recounted his plan to his brothers in chapter 46, and now, in chapter 47, the writer recounts the outcome of the events of the plan. The point is to show that Joseph's plan was successful and thereby to reinforce a central theme of the narrative: "And the LORD was with Joseph and the man was successful" (39:2). Joseph's wisdom has resulted in the family of Israel dwelling safely in the land of Goshen while there was severe famine in the land of Canaan.

Pharaoh's response was even more generous than the previous narrative would have suggested. Not only did he grant their wish and allow Joseph's brothers to settle in Goshen; he also put the brothers in charge of his own livestock, a result curiously reminiscent of Joseph's own rise to power in the house of Pharaoh (cf. 41:41). Thus the narrative shows that Joseph's fortune was duplicated in the fortune of his brothers. The land of Goshen is called the "best part [מיטב] of the land" (47:6), which perhaps is a wordplay on the "good" (טוב) which God intended in all of these recorded events (50:20).

It is significant that the central concern of the narrative is to show that Jacob "blessed Pharaoh" (47:7, 9) when he was brought before him. Its importance can be seen from the fact that it is mentioned twice. Behind such an emphasis in the narrative is God's promise to Abraham that he would bless those who bless the seed of Abraham. The passage shows that in Joseph and Jacob the promise to Abraham was being fulfilled with the nations around them.

The words of Jacob to Pharaoh in 47:9 ("My years have been few and difficult; they do not equal the years of the sojourning of my father") sound unusual in the way they contrast with the two accounts of his blessing of Pharaoh. What do his words mean? These words appear to be the author's attempt at a deliberate contrast to the later promise that one who honors his father and mother should "live long and do well upon the land" (Dt 5:15). Jacob, who deceived his father and thereby gained the blessing, must not only die outside the Promised Land but also, we learn here, his years were few and difficult. From his own words, then, we can see a final recompense for Jacob's actions earlier in the book. As Abraham obeyed God and lived long in the land (Ge 26:5), so Jacob's years were short and difficult. In spite of this final verdict on the life of Jacob, the narrative goes on to show that he lived out his remaining years "in the good of the land," though not the Promised Land (47:11), and that Joseph, his son, provided for him and his household.

2. Joseph's Rule in Egypt (47:13-27)

The writer goes into great detail to show the final steps by which Joseph extended his authority and the authority of Pharaoh over every region of Egypt. The narrative returns to the story line of 41:57 (Joseph's ruling Egypt) with an account of the affairs of Joseph in Egypt and his work on behalf of Pharaoh. The brothers are no longer the center of attention. The writer sets them aside, at least temporarily, to focus on Joseph and his sons. The narrative returns to the theme of the brothers in chapter 49, though at that point it is not concerned with Joseph and his brothers per se but with Jacob and his sons—with Joseph being simply one of the brothers. It is only in the end (50:15) that we return to the theme of Joseph and his brothers.

We might ask what is the writer's strategy in inserting the account of Joseph and his brothers (chaps. 42-46) in the midst of the narratives dealing with Joseph's rise to power in Egypt (chaps. 39-41, 47). The answer may lie in the way in which this final narrative resembles the story of Joseph and his brothers. Throughout those narratives the theme was repeatedly expressed that Joseph's wisdom and administrative skills saved the life of his brothers and father. Thus at the beginning of the story, Jacob had told his sons to go down to Egypt to buy grain "that we may live and not die" (42:2). Then Judah, "in the second year" (45:6), told his father to let them return to Egypt "that we may live and not die" (43:8). Finally, when he revealed himself to them, Joseph told his brothers that God had sent him to Egypt "to save life" (45:5). In keeping with that emphasis, the present narrative opens with the statement of the Egyptians to Joseph as they seek to buy grain from him: "Why should we die before you?" (47:16); then it continues with the account of their return to Joseph "the second year" (v. 18), when they again say "Why should we die?" and "that we might live and not die" (47:19). Such repetitions in the surface structure of the narrative suggest a thematic strategy at work. First with his brothers and then with the Egyptians, Joseph's wisdom is seen as the source of life for everyone in the land.

A further evidence of a distinct strategy behind the present narrative in chapter 47 can be seen in the ironic twist that the outcome of this chapter gives the earlier narratives. The whole story of Joseph and his brothers began with Joseph being sold (37:28) into slavery (39:17) for twenty pieces of silver (37:28). Now, at the conclusion, Joseph sells (47:20) the whole land of Egypt into slavery (vv. 19, 25) and takes "all the silver in the land" (v. 18). In the end, because of the wisdom of Joseph, the seed of Abraham have become "fruitful" and have "multiplied exceedingly" (v. 27) and are dwelling safely and prosperously in the land of Goshen. Such a picture appears to be an obvious replication of the intended blessing of the early chapters of Genesis: "Be fruitful and multiply and fill the land" (1:28).

3. Jacob's Age (47:28)

The thread of narrative continues from verses 8–12 where, at the last mention of Jacob, his age had been given as 130 years. To return to the subject of Jacob, the writer bridges the narrative gap with a summation of all the years of his life: 17 years in Egypt and the 130 give a total of 147 years. The initial impression from this verse is that the Jacob narratives are coming to a close, but such is not the case. Two crucial chapters remain.

The function of verse 28 is twofold. First, it provides continuity within the Jacob narrative, which had been broken into by the account of Joseph's further rise to power (vv. 13–27); second, it moves the narrative to a new time frame, seventeen years later. Perhaps the underlying assumption is that by now the famine was over and Joseph's position in Egypt had been well established. With such matters now behind, the writer moves to the last days of Jacob.

4. Jacob's Burial Instructions (47:29–31)

As he approached death, Jacob's only request was that he not be buried in the land of Egypt. The manner of the request suggests that it is intended as an allusion to the sending of Abraham's servant for a bride for Isaac: "Put you hand under my thigh and promise" (v. 29; cf. 24:2). The similarities between the two requests are transparent. As he approached death (24:1), Abraham did not want his son to take a wife from among the people in the land where he was then dwelling but rather to take a wife from among his own family (24:3–4). In the same way, as he approached death (47:29), Jacob did not want to be buried among the Egyptians but to be buried with his fathers (v. 30) in his own land. The same theme is taken up in chapter 50, when Joseph makes his sons swear that they will carry his bones back to the Promised Land, a request carried out by the Israelites in Joshua 24:32.

What lies behind such requests? Do they give expression to any central themes in the book? The answer is yes. A central element of the promise to Abraham was the promise of the land. The request of the patriarchs to be buried in the land "with their fathers" brings to the fore their trust in the faithfulness of God to his word. Henceforth a key symbol of Israel's faith in the promises of God is the bones of the faithful seed that are buried in the Promised Land.

One other chapter of the Bible pays specific attention to this symbol— Ezekiel 37, the prophecy of the "dry bones." There the hope embedded in the symbol is given full expression when the Lord says, "O my people, I am going to open your graves and bring you up from them; I will bring you into the land of Israel. . . . and you will live" (Eze 37:12–14). It is no wonder then that in this same chapter Ezekiel returns directly to one of the central underlying issues of the Joseph narratives, namely, the rivalry between Joseph and Judah.

As early as the rivalry between Leah, Judah's mother, and Rachel, Joseph's mother (Ge 30), the question of the preeminence of one of the brothers over the other has occupied a central role in the narratives. In chapters 48 (the blessing of Joseph) and 49 (the blessing of Judah), the issue comes to a final resolution in the choice of one from the tribe of Judah who will reign over the rest of the brothers (49:8–10). So also in Ezekiel 37, the prophet returns to the theme of the Joseph narratives and the rivalry between the brothers. Here, as in Genesis, the brothers are reunited under the king from the tribe of Judah, David: "Son of man, take a stick of wood and write on it, 'Belonging to Judah.'. . . Then take another stick of wood and write on it, 'Belonging to Joseph.'. . . Join them together into one stick so that they will become one in your hand. . . . There will be one king over them and they will never again be two nations or be divided into two kingdoms. . . . My servant David will be king over them. . . . They will live in the land I gave to my servant Jacob" (37:22–24).

We can see then that the writer of Genesis has much the same concern underlying his narratives as the prophecies of Ezekiel: the fulfillment of God's promises to Jacob. Those whose faith is like that of Jacob are those who look for the time when the "dry bones" will again be given life in the reign of the one from the tribe of Judah. Of further interest is the fact that Ezekiel's prophecy leads from this theme directly into his vision of the defeat of Gog and Magog (Eze 38). In the same way, the book of Revelation weaves together the defeat of Gog and Magog (cf. Eze 38–39) with the victory of the "Lion of the tribe of Judah" (cf. Ge 49:8–12; Nu 24:7;[71] Rev 5:5; 19:11–16).

L. Ephraim and Manasseh Blessed (48:1–22)

The phrase "after these things" suggests an important break in the narrative and separates this passage from the preceding events. Chapter 48 forms a fitting conclusion to the Joseph narratives. As in the earlier patriarchal narratives, the blessing of the father is passed along to the next generation. Two features of this passage stand out. First, as with the earlier instances of the patriarchal blessings, the younger son, Ephraim, was blessed as the firstborn rather than the older, Manasseh (v. 19). In this respect the passage continues the well-established theme that the blessing did not follow the lines of natural descent or natural right. The blessing was a gift bestowed upon those who could not claim it as a right. Second, the blessing recorded in this chapter is largely subordinated to and superseded by the blessing of Jacob which follows in chapter 49.

It has been a curious feature of the whole of the Joseph narratives that Judah, rather than Joseph, ultimately gains the position of preeminence among his brothers. As important as Joseph is in the structure of the Genesis narratives, his role is subordinate to that of Judah. Consequently, the blessings of the sons of Joseph recorded in this passage do not play an important role in the later biblical story. Rather, it is the blessing of Judah in

---

[71]In the textual history of Nu 24:7b, there is evidence of an eschatological interpretation of the Balaam oracles similar to that of Eze 38 and 39. The MT reads "his king [מַלְכּוֹ] will be greater than Agag [אֲגַג]," but the original reading may have been "Gog" (גּוֹג), which is represented by most early witnesses apart from the MT and is the *lectio difficilior*.

chapter 49 that plays the dominant role in the continuing story of the promise and the blessing. From Judah comes the house of David and from David comes the Messiah (2 Sam 7)—that is the focus of the biblical story which follows. The two sons of Joseph, Ephraim and Manasseh, play an important role in the texts dealing with the divided northern kingdom, but the biblical writers' attention to that kingdom, which ultimately was exiled and lost in the dispersion, pales quickly in the light of the rising star of David.

1. Jacob Ill (48:1–4)

Once again we are reminded of the frailty of Jacob, and we can see that his life was drawing to a close. As soon as he saw Joseph and his two sons, however, Jacob was revived (48:2), and he prepared to bestow God's blessing on the house of Joseph. Jacob's recollection of God's promise to him at Bethel (35:9–13) is significant. He repeated the Lord's words almost verbatim, but in the minor alterations we can see not only Jacob's assessment of the promise but also the writer's perspective. As he had acknowledged in 35:9, so now Jacob recalled that God had "blessed him." But when he recounts what God said, Jacob brings out a nuance to God's words that helps clarify the reader's own understanding of the Lord's promised blessing.

In 35:11 the Lord had said, using the imperative mood, "Be fruitful and multiply, a nation and an assembly of nations will be from you." The use of the imperative in blessings is not unusual and should be understood not as a command but as a form of "well-wishing." The Lord was saying, "May you be fruitful and multiply," just as in 1:28. But, as Jacob retells the story to Joseph in this chapter, he does not use the imperative but changes the verbal forms to stress that God is the one who would bring about all that had been promised: "I am going to make you fruitful and will increase your numbers. I will make you a community of people, and I will give this land as an everlasting possession to your descendants after you" (48:4). As he reflects back on the blessing and recounts it to his sons, Jacob brings out just that aspect of the blessing that had been the theme of the Joseph narratives: God will ultimately bring about all that he has promised. All that had happened to the house of Jacob had been in God's plan and was intended by him "for the good" (50:20).

A second nuance is noticeable in Jacob's recounting of the promise. When he recounts God's promise of the land he again does so verbatim: "I will give this land to your descendants after you" (cf. 35:11). But there is a significant addition to Jacob's retelling of the blessing. He has added "for an everlasting possession" (48:4), a statement not recorded in chapter 35. Only one other time is the promise of the land called an "everlasting possession" (cf. 13:15), that is, in 17:8. There too, in chapter 17, when the promise was given to Abraham, the form of the blessing was not the imperative ("Be fruitful and multiply") but the indicative, denoting God as the subject of the action: The Lord said, "I will multiply you exceedingly" (17:2) and "I will make you exceedingly fruitful" (17:6).

It may also be significant that Jacob omitted one of the key elements of the promise which the Lord had made to him in chapter 35. The Lord had said, as in 17:6, 16, "Kings will come from you" (35:11), but the present chapter makes no mention of that part of the promise. Why is this part omitted in chapter 48? It is likely that the stress on the role of Judah with regard to the kingship in chapter 49 has precluded any mention of the promise of kings in reference to Joseph.

2. Jacob Adopts Ephraim and Manasseh (48:5-7)

The two sons of Joseph, Ephraim and Manasseh, were taken into the family of Jacob and were to be treated just as one of his own. Along with the other sons of Jacob, they would inherit the promise of Abraham. Henceforth, the families of Ephraim and Manasseh were counted among the sons of Jacob and later became two of the most important tribes of Israel. In later biblical texts (e.g., 1Ki 12), these two names became synonymous with the northern kingdom of Israel, which stood in bitter opposition to the kingdom of Judah.

Verse 7 has long puzzled biblical interpreters. Why the mention of Rachel at this point in the narrative and why the mention of her burial site? If we relate the verse to what precedes it, then the mention of Rachel just at this point could have been prompted by the fact that just as she bore Jacob "two sons" (44:27, Joseph and Benjamin) at a time when he was about to enter (48:7) the land, so also Joseph gave Jacob "two sons" just at the time when he was about to enter Egypt (48:5). Such symmetry suggests that Ephraim and Manasseh are seen as a replacement of Joseph and Benjamin, and thus it serves to further the sense of divine providence behind the events of Jacob's life.

Furthermore, Jacob's recollection of Rachel's death (48:7) is quite close to the actual account of her death in 35:16-19. Both passages stress the site of "Ephrath," which the writer identifies in both passages as Bethlehem. As in the earlier cases of the concern for the burial of the patriarchs in the Promised Land, Jacob's mention of Rachel's burial is tied to the promise that the land would be an "eternal possession" of the seed of Abraham. Rachel's burial place, like that of Abraham and Sarah and that of Jacob's own impending burial site (47:29-30), serves as a reminder of the faithfulness of God to his covenant promise.

3. Jacob Blesses Ephraim and Manasseh (48:8-14)

The blessing of Ephraim and Manasseh is recounted in great detail. In the next chapter—the account of Jacob's blessing his sons—these two sons are not mentioned. The overall function of the present account then is to augment the blessings of chapter 49 with an account of the blessing of the two sons who have taken their place in the house of Jacob along with the other sons (48:5-6). The writer takes great care to emphasize that in the blessing of these two sons, Ephraim, the younger brother, was given the blessing of the firstborn instead of Manasseh (v. 20). As has been the case throughout the patriarchal narratives, it was the younger son who was chosen to carry the line of blessing.

Before Jacob went on to address the two sons specifically in the blessing, Joseph interrupted him in an attempt to get his father to place his right hand on Manasseh rather than Ephraim and thus to give the right of the firstborn to Manasseh, the eldest son. After refusing Joseph's efforts, Jacob went on to bless the two sons specifically (v. 20) and thus give Ephraim preeminence over Manasseh.

4. The Blessing (48:15–16)

The first blessing, verses 15–16, appears to be a blessing of Joseph (v. 15) rather than the two sons. The blessing itself, however, refers to the "young sons" (v. 16), and the blessing of Joseph ultimately focuses on them.

Jacob's blessing is a storehouse of key thematic terms that direct the reader's attention to several major themes at work in the book as a whole. God is identified as the "God before whom my fathers, Abraham and Isaac, walked" (v. 16). Not only does the mention of Abraham and Isaac connect Jacob's faith in God to his immediate forefathers, but it also helps tie together the faith of the earliest patriarchs in Genesis with that of Abraham, Isaac, and Jacob. At two earlier points in the book the primeval patriarchs are described as those who "walked with God" (5:22, 24; 6:9). The early fathers were at one with the later patriarchs—they walked with God.

At the same time, this description of God also serves to link the faith of the fathers with that of the later generations of God's covenant people. As Moses said in Deuteronomy 30:16, the essence of the covenant relationship was that God's people were to love God and "walk in his ways," and as the prophets were later to say, "What does the Lord require of you? To act justly and to love mercy and to walk humbly with your God" (Mic 6:8).

Jacob's short catechism of faith, then, provides a theological link connecting and identifying the faith throughout all the ages. God is also described in Jacob's blessing as the "God who has been my shepherd all my life to this day" and the "angel who has delivered [me] from all harm" (Ge 48:16). It is unusual that God himself should be described as "the angel," since earlier in the book it is said that God sent "his angel" (24:7) or simply that one of the patriarchs was visited by "the angel of the LORD" (22:11). The blessing of the two sons picks up the theme of the promise to Abraham. They are to be called by the "name" of Jacob and the "name" of Abraham and Isaac, just as God had promised Abraham: "I will make your name great" (12:2). They are to increase greatly, just as God had promised Abraham: "I will make you a great nation" (12:2).

5. Ephraim Precedes Manasseh (48:17–20)

The central concern of this section is to underscore the fact that Ephraim, the younger son, was given preeminence over Manasseh, the elder. There is an interesting reversal of the scene in which Jacob received the blessing from his father Isaac in chapter 27. Isaac, who was nearly blind, was deceived into blessing the younger son rather than the older. Though nearly blind himself (48:10), Jacob appeared to be making the same mistake. When Joseph attempted to correct him, however, he stated his intentions clearly: "His younger brother will be greater than he" (v. 19). The writer reinforces his words by stating further that "he put Ephraim ahead of Manasseh" (v. 20).

We may well ask why there is so much concern over whether Ephraim or Manasseh was put first, especially in view of the fact that in the next chapter it was Judah—not Joseph or his two sons—who received the preeminent place. The answer is that the issue of preeminence in these texts is meant to address the larger question of who stands in a position to receive God's blessing. Over and over in these narratives the answer to that question has been the same. Receiving the blessing which God offers does not rest with one's natural status in the world. On the contrary, the blessing of God is based solely on God's grace. The one to whom the blessing did not belong has become heir of the promise.

6. Jacob's Words to Joseph (48:21–22)

These last two verses are difficult to understand not only in the immediate context but also within the context of the entire picture of Jacob that emerges from the Genesis narratives. Throughout these narratives, Jacob has not been pictured as a man of "sword and bow" (48:22), but as "a quiet man, staying among the tents" (25:27). Elsewhere, Jacob had said of the inhabitants of the land of Canaan: "If they join forces against me and attack me, I and my household will be destroyed" (34:30). Now suddenly, on his deathbed, Jacob revealed another picture of himself as he bequeathed to Joseph the portion of land he had taken by force. Though he spoke to Joseph, his use of the plural pronouns ("you") shows that he was addressing a larger audience. In the light of the fact that he spoke of a time when they would again return to the land of their fathers, that larger audience appears to be the house of Joseph, which was to be represented in the tribes of Ephraim and Manasseh.

M. Blessing of Jacob (49:1–33)

1. Jacob Calls His Sons (49:1–2)

The poetic discourse of chapter 49 plays a key role in the overall strategy of the patriarchal narratives as well as the strategy of the book as a whole (see the introduction above). Jacob's last words to his sons have become the occasion for a final statement of the book's major theme: God's plan to restore the lost blessing through the seed of Abraham. The key to the writer's understanding of Jacob's last words lies in the narrative framework that surrounds them. In verse 1 we are explicitly told that Jacob was speaking about those things that will happen "in the last days." The same expression occurs in the Pentateuch as poetic discourses, the oracles of Balaam (Nu 24:14–24) and the last words of Moses (Dt 31:29). On all three occasions the subject matter introduced by the phrase "in the last days" is that of God's future deliverance of his chosen people. At the center of that deliverance stands a king (Ge 49:10; Nu 24:7; Dt 33:5). In Genesis 49 that king is connected with the house of Judah.

At the close of Jacob's discourse (49:28), the writer goes to great lengths to connect Jacob's words in this chapter to the theme of "the blessing" that has been a central concern of the book since chapter 1 (1:28). He does this by repeating the word bless(ing) three times in the short span of this one verse: "And he blessed them, each according to his blessing he blessed them." By framing Jacob's last words between verses 1 and 28, the writer shows where his interests lie. Jacob's words look to the future ("in the last days") and draw on the past (God's blessing of humankind). It is within that context that we are to read and understand Jacob's words in this chapter.

The order of the sons in this chapter follows roughly the order of the record of their birth in chapters 29 and 30. The sons of Leah (Reuben, Simeon, Levi, Judah, Zebulun, Issachar) lead the list, followed by the sons of the handmaidens, Bilhah (Dan), Zilpah (Gad, Asher), and again Bilhah (Naphtali), and then the sons of Rachel (Joseph, Benjamin).

2. Reuben (49:3–4)

The key to the saying regarding Reuben is the statement, "You will not excel" (v. 4). The word *excel* is a play on the two phrases that have preceded it, "excelling in honor" and "excelling in power." Though Reuben has excelled, he will no longer excel. The reason given is brief but to the point: "because you defiled my couch." The reference is to an episode briefly noted in 35:22: "While Israel was living in that region, Reuben went in and slept with his father's concubine Bilhah, and Israel heard of it." Reuben no longer had the right of the firstborn of the household of Jacob because he had violated the honor of his father. The purpose behind these initial sayings is ultimately the elimination of the otherwise rightful heirs to make room for Judah and Joseph at the top. Many years later the author of the Book of Chronicles offered the following explanation: "He [Reuben] was the firstborn, but when he defiled his father's marriage bed, his rights as firstborn were given to the sons of Joseph son of Israel; so he could not be listed in the genealogical record in accordance with his birthright, and though Judah was the strongest of his brothers and a ruler came from him, the rights of the firstborn belonged to Joseph" (1Ch 5:1–2). In his reference to the sons of Joseph taking the birthright, the Chronicler was no doubt thinking of Genesis 48:5 where Jacob said, "Ephraim and Manasseh [the two sons of Joseph] will be mine, just as Reuben and Simeon are mine."

3. Simeon and Levi (49:5–7)

Simeon and Levi are grouped together because they were the instigators of the bloodshed against the city of Shechem (35:25). At that time Jacob protested vehemently against the two sons and their attack on the defenseless city (35:30). Now he has given his final verdict on their action. According to Jacob's words here, the result of their action was that the two tribes of Levi and Simeon would not have their own portion in the inheritance of the land. The fulfillment of Jacob's words can be found in the fact that the tribe of Simeon virtually disappears from the biblical narratives after the time of the conquest and in the fact that the tribe of Levi was given the responsibility of the priesthood and hence was not given its own inheritance in the apportioning of the land.

4. Judah (49:8–12)

Having eliminated the older brothers as rightful heirs of the blessing, Jacob foretold a future for the tribe of Judah that pictured him as the preeminent son. We have seen that the author of the book of Chronicles did not understand Jacob's words to mean that Judah was given the right of the firstborn, which, according to Genesis 48:5, belonged to Joseph (1Ch 5:1–2). Though he did not have the right of the firstborn, Judah had been chosen over all the others as the royal tribe. According to the book of Chronicles, Judah "prevailed" over his brothers and thus became heir to the throne (1Ch 5:2). As the writer of Psalm 78 later put it, The Lord "rejected the tents of Joseph, he did not choose the tribe of Ephraim, but he chose the tribe of Judah, Mount Zion, which he loved" (vv. 67–68). As both these later biblical texts suggest, the words of Jacob regarding Judah in Genesis 49 anticipated in many details the future rise of David to Israel's throne.

Unlike the imagery used of the other sons, the words of Jacob regarding Judah are quite transparent, though they are, of course, made up of poetic images. Judah is described as a victorious warrior who returns home from battle and is greeted by the shouts of praise from his brothers. The parallelism of verse 8 is extended by the statement, "Your father's sons will bow down to you." It is difficult not to see in this statement an intentional allusion to the dream of Joseph (37:10) in which his father's sons would come to bow down before him. In other words, that which was to happen to Joseph, and did happen in the course of the narrative (e.g., 42:6), has been picked up by way of this image and transferred to the future of the house of Judah. That which happened to Joseph is portrayed as a picture of that which would happen to Judah "in the last days" (49:1).

The image of the victorious warrior is extended with the picture of Judah as a "young lion" (v. 9). The young lion is pictured as sleeping in its den after having just devoured its prey. The question at the end of verse 9 speaks for itself: "Who dares to rouse him?" Verse 10 fills out the picture with a description of the young warrior as a king. He is the one who holds the "scepter" and the "ruler's staff." The point of Jacob's words is that Judah will hold such a status among the tribes of Israel until one comes "to whom it truly belongs." Those who reign from the house of Judah will do so in anticipation of the one to whom the kingship truly belongs. The word *Shiloh*, found in some English versions, is simply an untranslated form of the Hebrew expression meaning "one to whom it belongs."[72] It is not a name as such, nor is it to be associated with the site of the tabernacle in the days of Samuel (1Sa 1:3).

The most startling aspect of the description of this one from the tribe of Judah comes next: "and the obedience of the nations is his" (49:10b). The use of the plural word *nations* rather than the singular suggests that Jacob had in view a kingship that extended beyond the boundaries of the Israelites to include other nations as well. There may be an anticipation of this view in the promise of God to Jacob in 28:3 and 48:4: "I will make you a community of peoples." In any case, later biblical writers were apparently guided by texts such as this in formulating their view of the universal reign of the future Davidic king: for example, Psalm 2:8: "Ask of me, and I will make the nations your inheritance"; Daniel 7:13–14: "There before me was one like a son of man. . . . He was given authority, glory and sovereign power; all peoples, nations and men of every language worshiped him"; Revelation 5:5, 9: "See, the Lion of the tribe of Judah, the Root of David, has triumphed. . . . And they sang a new song: 'You are worthy . . . with your blood you purchased men for God from every tribe and language and people and nation.'"

Verses 11 and 12 draw an extended picture of the reign of this one from the tribe of Judah. In his day there will again be abundance for everyone. This idea of plenitude is poetically expressed with the image of a donkey tethered to the choicest of vines and clothing washed in vintage wine. The sense of the imagery is that wine, the symbol of prosperity and blessing, will be so abundant that even the choicest vines will be put to such everyday use

---

[72]See further discussion in my "Genesis," *EBC*, 2:279–80.

as tethering the animals of burden, and vintage wine will be as commonplace as wash water. Verse 12 returns to the picture of the king of Judah. His eyes are darker than wine and his teeth whiter than milk. He is a picture of strength and power.

Later biblical writers drew heavily from the imagery of this short text in their portrayal of the reign of the coming Messiah. Isaiah 63:1-6 envisions the coming of a conquering king whose clothes are like those of one who has treaded the winepresses. His crimson clothing is then likened to the bloodstained garments of a victorious warrior. He is the one who has come to carry out the vengeance of God's wrath upon the ungodly nations (Isa 63:6). The book of Revelation applies this same image to the victorious return of Christ. He is the rider on "the white horse" who is "dressed in a robe dipped in blood" (Rev 19:11, 13). "Out of his mouth comes a sharp sword with which to strike down the nations. . . . He treads the winepress of the fury of the wrath of God Almighty" (Rev 19:15).

5. The Remaining Sons (49:13-27)

Jacob's words regarding the remaining sons, with the exception of Joseph, are noticeable not only for their brevity but also for their cryptic allusions to epic events that at the time lay yet in the future of the particular tribe. True to the poetic qualities of the text, the images of the destiny of the remaining sons are in most cases based on a wordplay of the son's name. The central theme uniting each image is that of prosperity. Just as in the image of the victorious king from the tribe of Judah who will reign over all nations in a time of rich blessing, so also each of the remaining brothers will experience the same sort of prosperity and blessing.

a. Zebulun (49:13)

Zebulun, whose boundaries in Joshua 19:10-16 do not touch the sea, will extend its borders to the sea as far as Sidon. The Hebrew name Zebulun, which means "lofty abode," has become a cipher for the extension of the Promised Land into the "far recesses" of Sidon. There is apparently an intended wordplay between the meaning of Zebulun's name and the sense of the Hebrew word here translated "abide."

b. Issachar (49:14-15)

Issachar, whose name is a play on the word *wages* (cf. Ge 30:18), is pictured as a strong donkey who sees that his land of rest is good and applies his back to the burden. The expression "he saw that his land of rest was good" is perhaps an allusion to chapter 1, where the similar expression "and God saw that it was good" is a constant reminder that God's purpose in Creation was to provide the "good" for humanity. The use of the word *resting place* or *land of rest* aligns the words of Jacob with the theme of the future rest which God will give his people in the Promised Land (cf. Ps 95:11).

c. Dan (49:16-18)

Dan (דן), whose name is a play on the expression "he will judge" (דין), is the one who will judge his people. He is likened to a snake along the path that attacks the heels of the horse and cunningly defeats the horseman.

Though the sense of the image itself is unclear, Jacob's final words regarding Dan show that the image was meant in a positive way: "I wait for your salvation, O LORD" (v. 18). Breaking in as it does on the increasingly terse poetic images, this expression of hope in the Lord's salvation provides the much-needed clue to the meaning of Jacob's words. In the individual and future destiny of the sons is embodied the hope of all Israel. That hope is of a future prosperity for the nation and a future victory over their enemies. At the center of that hope is the king from the tribe of Judah.

d. Gad (49:19)

The brief statement regarding Gad contains a wordplay on nearly every word: "Gad [גד] will be attacked [גד] by a band of raiders [גדד], but he will attack [גד] them at their heels." Again, though it is very brief, the saying falls in line with the others following in the path of the prophecy regarding Judah in that it expresses the hope of the final defeat of the enemy.

e. Asher (49:20)

The statement regarding Asher has no clear wordplays, and its meaning is self-evident. In the future, Asher's sons will enjoy great abundance and rich delicacies.

f. Naphtali (49:21)

The words regarding Naphtali are also brief. The picture they present, which is similar to the others, is of great future prosperity and abundance.

g. Joseph (49:22–26)

As might be expected from the importance of Joseph in the earlier chapters, Jacob has much to say about the future of his tribe. In substance, Jacob's statements regarding Joseph repeat much of what was said about the other brothers after Judah. The difference in the words to Joseph, however, is the repetition of the word *blessing*. Whereas Jacob's words regarding the other brothers paint a picture of the future well-being of the sons and thus speak figuratively of a future blessing, Jacob's words to Joseph refer explicitly to this future well-being as a "blessing." As such, the words to Joseph fall in line with all those earlier passages in the book that speak specifically of the promised "blessing" and prepare the way for the writer's final remarks about Jacob's words in verse 28: "He blessed them, each according to his blessing, he blessed them." The reference to the "Shepherd" in verse 24 appears to be an allusion to Jacob's earlier blessing of Ephraim and Manasseh (48:15).

h. Benjamin (49:27)

The picture of Benjamin is similar to that of Judah. Both depict the patriarchs' future in terms expressing a conquest over the enemy. In both, the conqueror is a vicious predator, the lion and the wolf. The stark simplicity of these words to Benjamin, however, brings out the sense of sudden victory and conquest in much stronger terms than the imagery of Judah.

6. Summary (49:28)

The writer sums up in unequivocal terms the substance of Jacob's words to his sons. They are an expression of the theme of the blessing which was to be passed along through the seed of Abraham, Isaac, and Jacob. Within Jacob's words to each of the sons (after Judah), the theme of blessing has been evident in two primary images. First, the notion of blessing is stressed in the imagery of the victorious warrior. The defeat of the enemy is the prelude to the messianic peace. Second, the positive side of the blessing is stressed in the imagery of great prosperity and abundance. Behind such imagery of peace and prosperity lies the picture of the Garden of Eden—the paradise lost. The focus of Jacob's words has been the promise that when the one comes to whom the kingship truly belongs, there will once again be the peace and prosperity that God intended all to have in the Garden.

7. Death of Jacob (49:29–33)

As he lay dying, Jacob once more made a request that his sons bury him in the Land of Promise with his fathers. The specific place he had in mind was "Machpelah," the burial place purchased by Abraham in chapter 23. He had made a similar request in 47:29–30, but this final request was far more specific. He wanted to be buried in the land with Abraham, Sarah, Isaac, Rebekah, and Leah, the central figures of the preceding narratives. The point of the request within the present narrative is the renewal of the reader's awareness of the promise of the land—the promise that Jacob's seed would live in peace in the land promised to Abraham and Isaac. It is to show that Jacob's faith in God's promises remained firm to the end. With such an expression of faith still on his lips, the narrative concludes with the fitting remark: "He breathed his last and was gathered to his people."

VI. FINAL JOSEPH NARRATIVE (50:1–26)

A. Jacob's Burial (50:1–14)

Over half the final chapter describes the mourning and burial of Jacob. Joseph himself mourned (v. 1) and then the Egyptians (v. 3). Great preparations were made by both Joseph and the Egyptians. Pharaoh granted a special request to bury Jacob in his homeland, and he provided a large entourage as a burial processional to carry Jacob's body back to Canaan. "All the officials of Pharaoh and all the elders of the land of Egypt," along with Pharaoh's chariots and horsemen, accompanied Joseph on his journey back to Canaan. Even the Canaanites recognized this as "a very large ceremony of mourning" (v. 11). The writer himself seems to go out of his way to emphasize in detail the magnitude of the mourning.

The question naturally arises why the text gives such detail on the burial of Jacob when the accounts of the death of the other patriarchs give only the bare facts that they died and were buried. Even the account of Joseph's death, which is also recorded in this chapter, consists only of the brief notice that he died and was embalmed and entombed in Egypt. Was his burial of any less magnitude than Jacob's? Surely it was not, but the narrative devotes virtually no attention to it. Why then the emphasis on Jacob's burial? Perhaps such a description is intended merely as a concluding flourish at the end of this section of the book; or does it play a part in the ongoing strategy of the text? In the light of the writer's careful attention to his overarching themes in these narratives, it is appropriate to seek a motive for his emphasis within the narrative. We can do that by asking what themes may be sustained or highlighted in such a full description of the burial party.

One theme that immediately comes to mind has already been a concern of the writer at a number of points throughout the narrative: the focus on God's faithfulness to his "land" promises and the hope of God's people in the eventual return to the land. In the later prophetic literature, a recurring image of the fulfillment of the promise to return to the land pictures Israel returning to the land accompanied by many from among the nations. The prophets of Israel saw the return as a time when "all the nations" would "stream into" Jerusalem and "many peoples will come and say, 'Come, let us to up to the mountain of the LORD, to the house of the God of Jacob'" (Isa 4:2–3); or as Zechariah saw it, "In those days ten men from all languages and nations will take firm hold of one Jew by the edge of his robe and say, 'Let us go with you'" (Zec 8:23).

It is difficult not to see the same imagery at work in the present narrative. In his final return to the Land of Promise, Jacob was accompanied by a great congregation of the officials and elders of the land of Egypt. With him was also the mighty army of the Egyptians. Thus the story of Jacob's burial in the land foreshadows the time when God "will bring Jacob back from captivity and will have compassion on all the people of Israel" (Eze 39:25).

B. Joseph Forgives (50:15–21)

The narrative turns once more to the scene of Joseph and his brothers and, in so doing, returns to the central theme of the Joseph narratives: "You intended to harm me but God intended it for good . . . to save many lives" (50:20). Behind all the events and human plans recounted in the story of Joseph lies the unchanging plan of God. It is the same plan introduced from the very beginning of the book, where God looks out at what he has just created for humanity and sees that "it is good" (1:4–31). Through his dealings with the patriarchs and Joseph, God had continued to bring about his good plan. He had remained faithful to his purposes, and it is the point of this narrative to show that his people can continue to trust him and to believe that "in all things God works for the good of those who love him, who have been called according to his purpose" (Ro 8:28).

The last description of Joseph's dealings with his brothers is the statement that "he comforted them and spoke kindly to them" (50:21). It is again difficult not to see in this picture of Joseph and his brothers a foreshadowing of the future community of the Israelites in exile awaiting their return to the Promised Land. To that same community the call went out by the prophet Isaiah to "'comfort, comfort my people,' says your God, 'speak kindly to Jerusalem . . . for she has received from the hand of the LORD double for all her sins'" (Isa 40:1–2).

C. Death of Joseph (50:22–26)

Though his words are few, Joseph's final statement to his sons gives the clearest expression of the kind of hope taught in these narratives. Again, like his father Jacob, Joseph wanted his bones returned to the Promised Land. Also like Jacob, he saw to it that his sons swore to return his bones when they returned to the land. Though he knew he would die and not see the time when his sons returned to the land, he expressed clearly the hope and trust that he had in God's promise: "God will surely come to your aid and take you up out of this land to the land he promised on oath to Abraham, Isaac and Jacob" (v. 24). As has been characteristic of the literary technique of the Joseph narratives, Joseph repeated a second time (cf. 41:32) his statement of trust in God's promise: "God will surely come to your aid, and then you must carry my bones up from this place" (v. 25).

Chapter 2

EXODUS

I. THE OPPRESSION OF THE ISRAELITES (1:1–22)

The story of Exodus continues without interruption from the book of Genesis by recounting the genealogical list of Jacob's sons who came down to Egypt (1:1–5; cf. Ge 46:3). The total number of persons given is seventy. This is the same as the number of nations listed in Genesis 10, that is, the descendants of Adam and Noah (see comments above on Ge 46:8–27).

Exodus 1:6 marks an important starting point for the next series of events. It recounts the passing of the old generation. Verse 7, then, is a transitional verse passing over the majority of the four hundred years that Israel was in Egypt (cf. Ex 12:40). The structure of the narrative thus follows the prophetic word about Israel's future given to Abraham in Genesis 15:13: "Then the LORD said to him, 'Know for certain that your descendants will be strangers in a country not their own, and they will be enslaved and mistreated four hundred years.'" During this time, Israel had grown into a nation: "the land was filled with them" (referring to the "land of Goshen," not to the whole land of Egypt; cf. Ge 47:6).

Exodus 1:8 brings us into the time frame of the major events of the book. Many generations had passed, the Israelites had greatly increased in number (cf. Ge 12:2), and "a new king" had arisen over Egypt. The Bible does not identify this "new king." It is likely that what is meant is a new dynasty. Many identify this new dynasty with that of the Hyksos, an Asiatic people who reigned over Egypt during the Second Intermediate Period (1786–1558 B.C.).[1] The identity of the king, however, was obviously not a concern of the writer of the Pentateuch.

---

[1] See Carl G. Rasmussen, NIV Atlas of the Bible (Grand Rapids: Zondervan, 1989), 85.

The writer wishes to show that the new king moved quickly to prevent the Israelites from using their great strength to gain their freedom. The first measures taken by the king proved fruitless. In fact, as the narratives progress we can see that the king's efforts begin to work against him and help only to increase further the number of the people (1:12).

There is an apparent irony behind the narratives of Exodus 1 and 2. The way in which the narrative proceeds, the more the king tries to thwart God's blessing the more that blessing increases. Down to the last measure taken by the Egyptian king there is the theme of a providential irony in these events. The author's point is clear enough: God is at work in these events to bring about his plan, and no one, not even the great power of the gentile nations, can stand in his way (cf. Isa 45).

We can see the irony at work in the king's command that all Hebrew male babies be cast into the Nile (Ex 1:22). Although Moses' mother obeys this command, she does so in a way that recalls the story of God's salvation of Noah in the days of the Flood—the child is put into an "ark" and then cast into the water. Such shaping of the narrative is clearly intended to show that a sovereign God is at work in Israel's history.[2]

It is interesting to note that the author has placed two quite similar narratives on either side of his lengthy treatment of the Exodus and wilderness wanderings. The two narratives are Exodus 1–2, the Egyptian king's attempt to suppress Israel, and Numbers 22–24, the Moabite king's attempt to suppress Israel. Both narratives focus on the futility of the nations' attempts to thwart God's plan to bless the seed of Abraham (see the discussion of these texts in the Introduction above and in the commentary below on Nu 22–24).

II. THE PREPARATION OF A DELIVERER—MOSES (2:1–25)

A. Moses' Birth (2:1–10)

Chapter 2 offers a narrative glimpse of what one family did to protect their newborn son from the decree of Pharaoh. The son was in fact the deliverer, Moses. His mother hid him for three months. When she could no longer hide him, she constructed a reed basket (an "ark"), sealed it, and placed the baby "in the Nile River" (Ex 2:3)—ironically, just as Pharaoh had decreed (1:22). Furthermore, the child was saved not only by the carrying out of Pharaoh's decree but in fact by Pharaoh's own daughter.

The writer has not wasted our time with stories about the hardships of the people in general. He has, rather, focused on the life of a single child. Not only was this one of the Hebrew children which the king was attempting to kill; this was the very child whom the Lord had intended to bring his people up out of the land—the very eventuality that the king of Egypt feared most (1:10). The king's grand scheme was thwarted by what seems to be a mere coincidence. We, the readers, have a privileged view of the whole process.

This use of irony is common in the OT narratives. It shows that God is indeed at work in the affairs of the world and that, despite human efforts to

---

[2]This point has recently been made by Erhard Blum, *Studien zur Komposition des Pentateuch*, BZAW 189 (Berlin: de Gruyter, 1990), 10.

the contrary, he will bring about his purposes. This was no mere coincidence; this was God at work.

B. Moses' Early Life (2:11-22)

Two short narratives dealing with the early life of Moses are placed here between the account of his birth and that of his call. The total number of years of Moses' life was 120 (Dt 34:7). Since the bulk of the Pentateuch has focused on the last forty years of Moses' life (cf. Nu 14:34; 20:12), it is commonly held that these first two periods in his life also consisted of forty years each (cf. Acts 7:23, 30). The text, however, does not specifically mention Moses' age in this context.

These two narratives appear consciously to foreshadow the central role of Moses in the narratives which follow. Just as Moses rescued the Israelite being beaten by the Egyptian (Ex 2:11-15), so in the near future he was to deliver the Israelites from their Egyptian oppressors (3:10). Just as Moses was to provide water for God's people and their flocks throughout their time in the wilderness (17:6; Nu 20:7-11), so also Moses provided water for the daughters of Jethro and their sheep (Ex 2:17-19).

These two narratives also serve to underscore the important role God's power plays in Moses' success. The first narrative (vv. 11-15) shows that without the specific call of God that Moses received in Exodus 3, he could not win the trust of the people. The guilty Israelite's question: "Who appointed you as leader and judge over us?" (2:14), anticipates Moses' own questioning of God in the next chapter: "Who am I, that I should go to Pharaoh and bring the Israelites out of Egypt?" (3:11). Only after God promises to be with him (3:12) can Moses win the trust of the people (3:16-18; 4:31).

Moses' meeting his wife, Zipporah, at the well (2:17) finds a close parallel in the account of Jacob's meeting Rachel (Ge 29:2-14) and that of Abraham's servant meeting Rebekah (Ge 24:10-28). The account of Judah's meeting Tamar at the "springs" (Ge 38:14; the NIV translates "springs" as a place-name, "Enaim") is also similar.

	Isaac	Jacob	Judah	Moses
Outside the land	Ge 24:10	29:1	38:1	Ex 2:15
Father	Ge 24:15	29:5	38:1	Ex 2:16
Daughters	Ge 24:13	29:16	38:2	Ex 2:16
A well	Ge 24:11	29:2	38:14	Ex 2:15
Daughters water father's sheep	Ge 24:13	29:9		Ex 2:16
Shepherds gather		Ge 29:2		Ex 2:17
Test	Ge 24:12	29:8	38:11	Ex 2:17
Saves daughters		Ge 29:10		Ex 2:17
Sheep watered	Ge 24:18	29:11		Ex 2:17
Daughters tell of deed	Ge 24:28	29:12	38:24	Ex 2:18
Patriarch invited to stay	Ge 24:31	29:13-14	(38:26)	Ex 2:20-21
Married daughter	Ge 24:67	29:23, 28	(38:26)	Ex 2:21
Son(s) born	Ge 25:21	29:31-30:23	38:27-30	Ex 2:22

Besides the basic pattern noted above, in each of these narratives one of the leading patriarchs of the Pentateuch takes a wife from a people and a land not already aligned with the chosen people. That this may be an important feature of these narratives is suggested by the fact that in the conclusion of the present passage the name of Moses' son stresses his living outside the Promised Land. The name Gershom, it is explained, means "I have become an alien in a foreign land" (2:22). We should further note that of the central patriarchal characters in the Pentateuch, only Abraham takes a wife from his own immediate household. It may be significant that it is Abraham alone whose wife is not introduced by a "woman at the well" narrative. Joseph also takes a wife from outside the land and the chosen people (Ge 41:45), but in contrast to the other patriarchs after Abraham, he does not meet her at a well. Joseph and his seed, however, are probably not considered part of the central line of promised blessing or leadership of God's people (cf. 1Ch 5:2).

After the statement of the promise in Genesis 12:1–3, those in the central line of blessing (i.e., Isaac, Jacob, Judah, and Moses) take wives from outside the land and the chosen people. In each case the wife is introduced by means of the scene at the well. It seems proper, in the light of the parallels in these narratives, to raise the question of their overall purpose within the Pentateuch as a whole. An important clue is the meaning given to the events in Genesis 24. In that narrative it is repeatedly stressed that the pattern of events demonstrates that it was the Lord who had led the servant to the proper wife (Ge 24:27). It is possible, then, that the pattern established by means of these well narratives is intended to show that behind the apparent anomaly of an important and prominent patriarch taking a wife from another land and people there lies the ever-present will of God. Repeated patterns are often used in these narratives to stress the continuing work of God.

C. God Remembers (2:23–25)

Exodus 2:23 marks another important transitional stage in the events of the book. As in 1:8, a new stage is marked by the rise of a new king. Moses has been in the wilderness, where he had escaped for his life, and now he is free to return to Egypt.

In verse 24 the writer gives us the all-important clues to the meaning of the events that he is about to recount. When the Israelites cried out to the Lord for help, God not only heard their cry, but he also "remembered his covenant" with Abraham, Isaac, and Jacob (cf. Lev 26:42). Just as God had "remembered" Noah in the ark and rescued him (Ge 8:1), so now God turns to bring his people up out of bondage and into the land he had promised to their forefathers. The point of the narrative is to show that the basis of God's dealings with Israel was and is his covenant promises to Abraham.

The emphasis on God's covenant promises to the patriarchs, so clearly stated within these narratives, is also found in the message of the later prophets. For example, Micah saw God's promises to Abraham and Jacob as the basis on which Israel's hope in God's future salvation could rest: "You will again have compassion on us; you will tread our sins underfoot and hurl all our iniquities into the depths of the sea. You will be true to Jacob and show mercy to Abraham, as you pledged on oath to our fathers in days long ago" (Mic 7:19–20). Moreover, the NT viewed God's work of redemption in sending his son, Jesus, as a fulfillment of these same promises to Abraham and the fathers (Lk 1:54–55).

The Exodus from Egypt thus becomes an important biblical image of God's faithfulness in remembering his promises and the sending of his redeemer. In this account of the Exodus itself we can see the same concerns already at work. In this context, the call of Moses already anticipates and foreshadows the future redeemer. It is not by chance that henceforth in the Pentateuch the mediator Moses becomes one of the central narrative vehicles for depicting the messianic hope (cf. Dt 34:10).

III. THE CALL OF MOSES (3:1–4:31)

A. God Calls Moses (3:1–10)

The first result of God's "remembering his covenant" with Abraham is his call of Moses, a deliverer. God begins his discourse with Moses by warning him not to come near to him because he is holy (v. 5). As we will later see, the idea of God's holiness is a central theme in the remainder of the book. Indeed, the whole structure of Israel's worship of God at the tabernacle is based on a view of God as the absolutely Holy One who has come to dwell in their midst. We should not lose sight of the fact, however, that at the same time that God warns Moses to stand at a distance, he also speaks to him "face to face" (cf. Nu 12:8).The fact that God is a holy God should not be understood to mean that he is an impersonal force—God is holy yet intensely personal. This is a central theme in the narratives of the Sinai covenant that follow.

God now identified himself to Moses as "the God of your father, the God of Abraham, the God of Isaac, and the God of Jacob" (v. 6), and proceeded to tell Moses of his plan: Moses was to be the one who would deliver the Israelites from bondage in Egypt and to bring them into the land promised to their forefathers (vv. 7–10). He was to form them into a nation whose central concern would be the worship of God.

B. Moses Responds to God's Call (3:11–4:31)

1. First Objection: Who Am I? (3:11–12)

Moses' response to God's call shows that he immediately realized the responsibility of his task. He replied to God, "Who am I?" We should probably not understand his question as an expression of doubt or fear. Rather, it seems to derive from a genuine humility. Moses was now a shepherd, and we know from the preceding narratives that the Egyptians did not have dealings with shepherds (cf. Ge 46:34). Moses knew well that he would have no official recognition among the Egyptians.

God responded to Moses' question not by building up Moses' confidence in himself but by the reassurance that he would be with him in carrying out his task. Thus God's words here restate and reinforce the lesson of the Joseph narratives, which preceded this account. As with Joseph, God would provide the kind of recognition that Moses would need before Pharaoh by the "signs" and "great wonders" that he would perform through Moses. The signs Moses was to give to the people and to Pharaoh were miraculous signs that demonstrated God's power.

It should be noted, however, that the sign given to Moses in Exodus 3:12 itself called for faith: "When you have brought the people out of Egypt, you will worship God at this mountain." We should further note that within the narratives of the Pentateuch, the reader is well aware that this specific sign would be fulfilled in Exodus 19. Thus, when viewed as an element of the text, God's word of assurance to Moses has more certainty to it than might at first have appeared. It is a sign to the reader as much as to Moses.

2. Second Objection: What Is Your Name? (3:13-22)

Moses' next response has prompted much discussion among biblical scholars and theologians: he said, "Suppose I go to the Israelites and say to them, 'The God of your fathers has sent me to you,' and they ask me, 'What is his name?' Then what shall I tell them?" In other words, Moses realized that what he was being called to do would meet with opposition in Egypt. Moreover, the nature of the opposition would be theological. The people would want to know about the God whom they were to follow into the wilderness.

When Moses asked about the "name" of God, he was inquiring about more than just the identity of God. He was asking a question about the very nature of God. Within the world of the biblical text, the name was the expression of the nature of its bearer (cf. 1Sa 25:25). Adam's naming the animals meant that he was looking at their essential nature—looking, in fact, for a "suitable partner" (Ge 2:20)—the "name" was an expression of the very essence of the one who bears the name. Thus when Moses asked God's name, the answer he received may not seem like the answer we would have expected. In some translations, the Lord's answer looks more like an evasion of the question. God simply replied, "I am who I am."

If Moses was in fact seeking to know God's essential nature in asking for his name, then the answer he received from the Lord was precisely that which he sought. The Lord's reply, "I am who I am," may be paraphrased as, "It is I who am with you."[3] Thus in his reply to Moses, the Lord let it be known to the Israelites that "the one who promises to be with [them]" has sent Moses to them.

The following verse uses the actual name of God, "Yahweh" or "Jehovah."[4] Its association with the expression "I am who I am" suggests that the name of God, "Yahweh," is meant to convey the sense of "he who is present" or "he who has promised to be present with his people." In giving his name to Moses, then, God not only promised to be present with him and his people but also recalled the promise itself: "he who is with us."

---

[3]U. Cassuto, *A Commentary on the Book of Exodus*, trans. Israel Abrahams (Jerusalem: Magnes, 1967), 38.

[4]In English Bibles, the name "Yahweh" is often translated by the word LORD (initial capital followed by small capital letters), not by "Yahweh." Why? It is because translators follow the ancient Jewish custom of not pronouncing the divine name. Rather than read "Yahweh" in the synagogue or in private reading, Jews replaced the name of God by the title "Lord" ("ʾ*dōnāy* in Hebrew). The English translation "LORD" is an attempt to follow this custom and to distinguish the occurrence of the divine name (Yahweh) from the occurrences of the word 'ʾ*dōnāy* (Lord) in the text. The form LORD occurs when the Hebrew text has *Yahweh*, and the word *Lord* occurs when the Hebrew text has 'ʾ*dōnāy*. See my "Genesis," *EBC*, 2:146.

God's words to Moses in Exodus 3:16–22 are an important link in the structure of the pentateuchal narratives. God's words first reflect back to God's promise to the patriarchs in the mention of the "God of your fathers, the God of Abraham, the God of Isaac, and the God of Jacob" (3:16). God then turns his attention to the events that are about to be recorded—Moses' confrontation with Pharaoh. As is the case in many biblical narratives, the description which God gives of these events before they actually happen proves to be a near replica of those events as they are then recorded in the narrative (cf., e.g., Ge 12:10–20). It is important to note this feature of the narrative because it is one of the ways that the Scriptures attempt to show God's sovereign control over all the various events narrated in the Pentateuch. We, the readers, are allowed to view the events from a divine perspective. God describes what is about to happen, and the narrative follows the same pattern in depicting the events.

We should note, however, that even though the events of the Pentateuch turn out as expected from such a vantage point, we often find significant modifications in the narration of the events. That the actual record of the events as they transpire contains such modifications further contributes to the overall effect and sense of the biblical narratives. We should note that within these narratives, when such modifications do occur, they are usually a result of human actions not anticipated in the initial preview. Moses or Israel or the Egyptians do something unexpected. Hence the narratives, as they unfold the events, remain open to human action. The events narrated are not merely determined by God. God knows what will happen, but the narratives have room for the actions of human beings.

For example, in the present narrative, when God first describes to Moses what will happen when he goes before Pharaoh, the role of Aaron as the speaker for Moses is not specifically mentioned. Aaron comes into the picture only because of Moses' reluctance to obey God's call. Moreover, when God recounts the events about to transpire, he anticipates the obedience of the people (Ex 3:18). This obedience is explicitly and verbally realized only in chapter 4, after Moses shows them the signs (4:31). As the narrative now stands, however, the obedience of the people was short-lived. Chapter 6 recounts that the people proved to be disobedient "because of a lack of spirit" (6:9). Thus, though God's words prove determinative for the events of the narrative, they do not preclude the new directions taken by human actions. Such narrative features are subtle, yet they are important guideposts for appreciating the sense and meaning of the biblical narratives.

The importance of this section, then, is not only that it gives the readers an overview of the events that are about to be recounted and a preview of their outcome; but also, even more importantly, these words, spoken before the events themselves, show that God is in control of the outcome. As he sends Moses before Pharaoh, God already knows Pharaoh's choice not to let the people go. God's words show further that ultimately Pharaoh will let his people go, but not without an occasion for demonstrating God's "wonders" in their midst (3:20). Thus the Exodus is already in view at the start. Such structuring of the narratives shows also that even in those areas where events turn out differently than anticipated in the narrative (as in the case of Israel's disobedience), God is still in control of the events as well as the final outcome.

This section ends with a reference to God's promise to Abraham in Genesis 14:14 that his people would go out of Egypt with great wealth (Ex 3:22). This was fulfilled in Exodus 12:35, when "the Israelites did as the Lord had commanded Moses, and they asked from the Egyptians vessels of silver and gold and clothing."

3. Third Objection: What If They Will Not Believe Me? (4:1–9)

In 4:1 Moses asked another question which revealed his understanding of the true gravity of the task God had given him: "What if they will not believe me. . . . For they may say, 'Yahweh has not appeared to you.'" In answer to this question, God gave Moses three "signs": (1) his staff became a snake (vv. 2–5); (2) his hand became leprous (vv. 6–7); (3) the water from the Nile River became blood when poured out (v. 9). Each of these signs bears the unmistakable mark of God's creative power. These signs were not intended for the Egyptians, but rather for the Israelites. They were signs that the Lord was present with Moses and were intended to produce assurance and faith in the Israelites that Moses had been sent by God. To this end the signs achieved their purpose (see v. 31: "so the people believed").

4. Fourth Objection: I Am Not Eloquent (4:10–17)

Moses raised one final objection—he was not an eloquent speaker. Again, the Lord's response was an appeal to his creative power: "Who made man's mouth? Or who makes him dumb or deaf, or seeing or blind? Is it not I, Yahweh?" Then the Lord repeated his promise: "I will be with your mouth," that is, "I will teach you what to say" (v. 12).

At this point Moses appeared to overstep his mark and to resist too much. The Lord was angered by Moses' refusals, but he again provided an answer to Moses' objection: Aaron would go with him and speak for him.

Through the whole of the narrative, Moses is depicted as a reluctant but ultimately willing leader. The writer has shown that the leadership which Moses provided was not motivated by a hunger for power. It was a divine call and God alone would be able to fulfill the task. With such leadership God would do his work, and the people would follow in faith (v. 31).

5. Return to Egypt (4:18–31)

As Moses prepared to return to Egypt to deliver God's people, the Lord warned him of his purposes: "I will harden [Pharaoh's] heart and he will not let the people go" (v. 21). Further on in the narrative (7:3–5) the divine purpose for hardening Pharaoh's heart is given: "so that the Egyptians will know that I am the Lord." God's desire was to make himself known to the Egyptians.

A very odd event occurs in the brief narrative of Moses' return to Egypt (4:24–26). As Moses rested for the night, the Lord sought to kill him. According to the Hebrew text, God sought the life of the child, not that of Moses. Thus, the child's life was spared only because his wife, Zipporah, immediately circumcised her son and laid the foreskin at Moses' feet. When she did this she said, "You are a bridegroom of bloodshed for me" (v. 26). The Lord then withdrew from him and his life was spared.

We are apparently to see this event as a form of judgment or warning regarding the necessity of keeping the commandment of circumcision (Ge

17:10–14). It is impossible to reconstruct the details of the incident recorded here; fortunately, it is not necessary to do so. The point is clear enough. God takes his word seriously, and thus he must be obeyed. Here, at the outset of Israel's covenant with God, the reader is reminded of the importance of obedience and the dire consequences of disobedience. We should note that in the verse immediately preceding this incident (4:23), God said he would slay the firstborn son of Pharaoh when he disobeyed. Here we see the Lord doing the same thing to the firstborn son of Moses when he disobeyed.

At several other points in the narratives of the Pentateuch the writer has included similar incidents. When Jacob returned to the land in fulfillment of God's command (Ge 31:3), for example, he was met at night by God (32:30 [MT 31]) in the form of a man or an angel (32:24 [MT 25]; cf. Hos 12:5), and he wrestled with him until dawn. Just after the sin of the golden calf, God warned Israel: "I will send an angel before you. . . . But I will not go with you, because you are a stiff-necked people and I might destroy you on the way" (Ex 33:2–3). Moreover, when the Israelites were told to leave Mount Sinai and return to the land (Nu 10:5), they "complained" and God sent fire down on their camp (Nu 11:1–3). Thus at each major transition point in the progression of the narrative, the writer uses such opaque and ominous narratives to remind the readers of God's serious intention that Israel obey his commandments and walk in his ways. (See comments below on Nu 11:1–3.)

A confirmation of this reading of the story comes in the immediately following narrative. When Moses and Aaron ask Pharaoh to let their people go into the wilderness to worship and sacrifice to God, the reason they give is "lest he meet [פגע] us with a plague or with the sword" (Ex 5:3). The present narrative (Ex 4:24–26) shows that their reasons were not without merit. The Lord had already "met" (פגע) Moses to strike him down. There was thus good reason to fear lest he meet (פגע) them also with plague or sword. It may also be the case that this short narrative is intended to explain the context within which Moses returned his family to his father-in-law in Midian (see comments below on Ex 18:1–27).

IV. THE DELIVERANCE FROM EGYPT (5:1–15:21)

A. Oppression Worsens, Promises Renewed (5:1–6:30)

1. Pharaoh's Refusal to Free God's People (5:1–3)

After the events of 4:27–31, which recounted that the people believed the signs which Moses performed and were ready to accept his leadership, Moses and Aaron went in to Pharaoh to request permission to leave Egypt for three days. Pharaoh's negative response to their request provides the theological setting for the following narratives: "Who is the LORD that I should obey him? . . . I do not know the LORD" (5:2). These words form the motivation for the events that follow, events designed to demonstrate who the Lord is.

Within the narratives themselves it is Pharaoh and the Egyptians who learn the lesson. The purpose of the narratives, however, is of course to teach the reader this same lesson. Thus as the plague narratives begin, the purpose of the plagues is clearly stated: "so that the Egyptians will know that

I am the LORD" (7:5). Throughout the plague narratives we see the Egyptians learning precisely this lesson (8:19; 9:20, 27; 10:7). As the narratives progress, the larger purpose also emerges. The plagues which God had sent against the Egyptians were "to be recounted to your son and your son's son. . . so that you may know that I am the LORD" (10:2).

2. Israel's Oppression Increased (5:4–18)

The second part of the Pharaoh's response also sets the stage for the events that follow. He increased their labor by cutting the supply of straw for making bricks. Thus, as at the beginning of the book, Pharaoh has made Israel's labor more difficult, and the people now cried out in their distress (cf. 2:23 and 5:15). In 2:23 the cry of the people went up before God. By contrast, here in 5:15 the cry of the people is before Pharaoh. It is as if the author wants to show that Pharaoh was standing in God's way and thus provides another motivation for the plagues which follow.

3. The Lord's Plan Announced (5:19–6:1)

The Israelite leaders were powerless before Pharaoh. By drawing this out, the narrative has begun to stress the importance of the leadership exemplified in Moses. Moses was a leader called by God and empowered to do his work. The key to the effective work of Moses is shown quite clearly here at the beginning: "And the LORD said to Moses, 'Now you will see what I will do to Pharaoh'" (6:1). The work of Moses was the work of God. God used Moses, but it was God who did the work. Thus it is important to note that Moses is not portrayed here as a miracle worker. Rather, he is portrayed as the Lord's servant. As if to stress this aspect of the narrative, the Lord repeated to Moses twice that the work about to be carried out through him was "by the strong arm" of the Lord (6:1).

Moses' own words to God in 5:22–23 further stress God's role in the work that is about to be done. He says to God, "Why have you done this to the people? Why have you sent me? . . . You have not rescued your people." By allowing us to listen to Moses' prayer to God, the author uncovers Moses' own view of his calling. It was God's work, and Moses was sent by God to do it.

4. God, Moses, and the Patriarchs (6:2–8)

Because the previous narratives have greatly stressed that it was God alone who would carry out his work through Moses, the author delays the action of the narrative momentarily in order to identify more clearly the nature of God's relationship to Moses and to specify further his plan. God had already made his name known to Moses in chapter 3. Here in chapter 6 this relationship between God and Moses is contrasted with God's previous relationship to the patriarchs. The patriarchs did not know God "by [his] name Yahweh" as Moses and the Israelites did. The patriarchs—Abraham, Isaac, and Jacob—knew God as "El Shaddai." The key to understanding God's words here lies in the fact that he does not say that the patriarchs did not know the name of God (i.e., Yahweh). He says, rather, that he was known "by [the name] El Shaddai" (Ex 6:3).

We are helped in our understanding of this verse by the fact that in the book of Genesis, the patriarchs use the name "Yahweh" (Ge 15:2, 7), though note that when God "appeared" to the patriarchs (e.g., Ge 17:3), he was known as "El Shaddai." The narrative is also clear, however, that when Abraham saw God "in a vision," he spoke with him as "Yahweh" (Ge 15:1–2). Thus Exodus 6:3—"I appeared to Abraham . . . as El Shaddai" and not as Yahweh—reflects accurately the wording of the Genesis narratives. In Genesis, when God "appeared" to Abraham, he addressed him as *El Shaddai*, but when Abraham saw God "in a vision," he spoke with him as *Yahweh*. Thus, the present text intends to tell us that, unlike the patriarchs, Moses "knew Yahweh," not by means of a vision but "face to face" (Dt 34:10).

This small section of narrative also sketches out the argument of the whole Pentateuch. God made a covenant with the patriarchs to give them the land of Canaan (Ex 6:4). He remembered his covenant when he heard the cry of the Israelites in Egyptian bondage (v. 5). He is now going to deliver Israel from their bondage and take them to himself as a people and be their God (v. 6). He will also bring them into the land which he swore to give to their fathers (v. 8). The die is cast for the remainder of the events narrated in the Pentateuch.

5. Moses Refuses Again, God Commands Again (6:9–13)

In view of the fact that the Israelites had obeyed God and hearkened to Moses in 4:31, it is somewhat surprising to find that they have so soon disobeyed (6:9). The author is quick to remind us, however, that it was their own "shortness of spirit" and the hard work that caused their disobedience. Even Moses questioned God when he was told to go before Pharaoh and to speak. If the people of Israel would not hearken to him, why would Pharaoh?

Moses himself appeared to falter along with the people and to lose sight of what has been a central theme in the narratives thus far—it was God, not Moses, who was to bring the people out of Egypt: "How will Pharaoh listen to me? I am a man of uncircumcised lips" (v. 12). Unlike chapter 4, in this narrative Moses' objections are cut short by God's command: "and God spoke to Moses and Aaron and commanded them to bring the people out of Egypt" (6:13, 26). No mention of signs or call for trust, as in Exodus 4—now God simply commands them to go.

In the last analysis, then, the Exodus was a work of God; even Moses and Aaron had to be commanded to bring the people out. The pattern here is repeated many times throughout the remainder of the pentateuchal narratives. God's initial call for faith and trust is met with doubt and fear. God then responds with a simple call for obedience. This call for obedience, however, does not rule out or replace the necessity of faith and trust, nor does it render "signs" unnecessary (cf. 7:3; 10:1).

6. Family of Moses and Aaron (6:14–27)

As the summary statement at the conclusion of this section suggests, the purpose of this list of names is to identify the leading characters of the following narratives, Moses and Aaron. That the purpose of the list is specifically to introduce Moses and Aaron can be seen in the fact that the list of names is only a fragment of a list of the twelve sons of Jacob (cf. Ge 49:1–27). The beginning of the list of tribal names is abbreviated and ends abruptly after the families of Levi, that is, the family of Moses and Aaron. A brief account of the immediate family of Moses and Aaron is given (cf. Nu 26:59). This concern to give the lineage of the central characters of the narratives has been manifest in the Pentateuch from the beginning (cf. Ge 5; 10; 46).

In 2:1, the name of the mother of Moses was not given. She was called simply "a daughter of Levi." Although the present text appears to suggest that Amram and Jochebed were the parents of Moses and Aaron, they were probably not their immediate parents but rather earlier ancestors. That there were hundreds of "Amramites" in Moses' own day (Nu 3:28) suggests that the description of the birth of Moses and Aaron here in Exodus 6 is abbreviated.

7. Summary (6:28–30)

After the insertion of the list of names (6:14–27), the writer repeats by way of a summary the material of the earlier narrative. We are taken back to Moses objection: "I am of uncircumcised lips, and how will Pharaoh listen to me?" (6:30). What was earlier given as a simple command by God to go before Pharaoh (v. 13) is now expanded into the instructions for carrying out the "signs" or plagues against the Egyptians. Though God's "signs" to the Egyptians are sometimes called "plagues" (e.g., 11:1), they are cast throughout this narrative as signs of God's power over nature.

B. The Plagues (Signs) (7:1–12:36)

1. Purpose of the Plagues (7:1–7)

The purpose of the "plagues" (signs) is suggested in 7:3–5, where God told Moses that he would harden Pharaoh's heart and send signs and wonders upon Egypt. These signs were to be a demonstration of the power of God to the Egyptians (v. 5) as well as to the Israelites (cf. 9:16). The text is clear about this. God was not out to destroy the Egyptians. As Scripture stresses repeatedly, God's plans and ways are aimed at the salvation and blessing of all the nations (Ge 12:3).

Behind such narratives lies the same theological hope of the narrative in Isaiah 19:16–25. Speaking of God's plans and purposes in dealing with Israel and the nations, Isaiah says, "So the LORD will make himself known to the Egyptians, and in that day they will acknowledge the LORD. . . . The LORD will strike Egypt with a plague; he will strike them and heal them. They will turn to the LORD, and he will respond to their pleas and heal them. . . . In that day Israel will be a third, along with Egypt and Assyria, a blessing on the earth. The LORD Almighty will bless them, saying, 'Blessed be Egypt my people, Assyria my handiwork, and Israel my inheritance'" (Isa 19:21–25).

It is possible to argue that the nature of the "signs" themselves appears to be directed against the Egyptians' concept of the universe. Within Egyptian religion, the universe was to exist in a harmonious whole, with each part contributing to the well-balanced system. The Egyptian word for this was *ma'at*. It was the responsibility of the pharaoh, as the incarnate god on earth, to maintain this balance (*ma'at*). The purpose of the "plagues" (signs) was thus to challenge this basic concept by showing that the pharaoh was powerless before the God of the covenant, Yahweh (Ex 12:12).

What we see in the plagues, then, is an unmasking of Pharaoh's claims to deity and his claim to rule the universe. Pharaoh was, in effect, taking credit for something in which he had no part, and the signs that Moses performed demonstrated that unmasking to both the Egyptians and the Israelites. In recording these events, the writer intended to show that only Yahweh is truly God: "Then the LORD said to Moses, 'Go to Pharaoh, for I have hardened his heart and the heart of his servants, that I may perform these signs of mine among them, and that you may tell in the hearing of your son, and of your grandson, how I made a mockery of the Egyptians, and how I performed my signs among them; that you may know that I am the LORD'" (10:1–2). Ultimately, each of the plagues leads up to the final plague—the death of the firstborn. The firstborn of Pharaoh was thought to be a second incarnate god. Hence his death would have meant an even greater threat to Egypt's stability.

There may be some truth to this assessment of the intention of the plagues. One must be careful, however, to note that there is no clear indication that the author intends his readers to see the plagues in this way. There is no mention of the Egyptian concept of *ma'at* in the text itself, nor is there any indication that the author assumes his readers are familiar with the theology of Egyptian religion. It seems more likely that the author is portraying the events of the plagues to a primarily Israelite audience, or at least one who would understand the world in terms of the theology of the Pentateuch itself. Thus this series of plagues need not intend any more than the general but all-important point that the God of the covenant, the Creator of the universe, is superior to the powers of the nations—whether those powers be merely political and military powers or powers that rely on magic and "secret arts."

2. Signs (7:8–13)

As Moses and Aaron approached Pharaoh, they were given a sign to perform before him in order to demonstrate the validity of their mission. Aaron threw down his staff before Pharaoh and it became a snake (or perhaps more accurately, a crocodile, v. 10). The narrative presents this act as wholly a divine sign, not the result of any magic on Aaron's part. In contrast, we are told that Pharaoh's own magicians were able to repeat the sign using their "secret arts" (v. 11). The narrative suggests that magic played an important role in the world of the ancient readers, and the sign of Aaron seems especially directed to this aspect of their life. More importantly, however, the narrative shows clearly to the reader that the work which Moses did was truly different from that of the Egyptians. God worked through Moses to accomplish his own plan. This was not done by the skill or trickery of Moses and the Israelites. Even though the Egyptian magicians were able to reproduce the sign, the Lord demonstrated his power all the more in the fact that their own snakes were swallowed by that of Moses and Aaron (v. 12).[5]

The writer is careful to point out that the events he is recording were

---

[5]According to K. A. Kitchen, the Egyptian magicians' secret arts consisted of a form of hypnosis of the snakes into an immobile state of catalepsy, making them appear as rods until the spell was broken ("Magic and Sorcery," *New Bible Dictionary*, ed. J. D. Douglas [Grand Rapids: Eerdmans, 1962], 769).

already known by God before they came to pass. In 7:3, the Lord had said to Moses, "I will harden the heart of Pharaoh . . . and he will not hearken to you." Thus at the conclusion of this narrative we are told, "and the heart of Pharaoh hardened and he did not hearken to them" (v. 13a). The writer then adds, "just as the LORD had said" (v. 13b). Such an emphasis on the work of God in hardening Pharaoh's heart is intended to explain the condition of Pharaoh at the beginning of the first of the ten plagues. In verse 14, as God sends the first plagues, we are told only that "Pharaoh's heart was heavy [unyielding]."

This introductory narrative thus ensures that the work of God in hardening Pharaoh's heart is not overlooked in the narrative of the ten plagues. Throughout the narrative Pharaoh's refusal to let the people go is traced back to the Lord's hardening his heart. Note the recurring statement: "Just as the LORD had said" (vv. 13a, 22b; 8:15, 19 [MT 11, 15]; 9:12).

3. First Plague: The Nile Became Blood (7:14–25)

The sense of the narrative appears to be that the waters of the Nile did, in fact, become blood. Over against this apparent sense of the text Kitchen suggests that it is more likely that the color of the Nile was simply red like that of blood, just as Joel 2:31 (MT 3:4) said, for example, that the moon would turn to blood. According to Kitchen, that would mean that there was a "red tide" in the Nile—a pollution of the Nile caused by heavy flooding of the Nile valley that would bring large deposits of red dirt from its source in the south and possibly cause an excessive amount of microorganisms (flagellates), which would give off a reddish color in the water.[6] This is not to say that what happened was merely a natural phenomenon, even though such red tides are known to occur in the Nile River. The point of the narrative is that Yahweh, the God of the covenant—not Pharaoh, the king of Egypt—was able to control the balance of nature. That the Nile turned red was perhaps not new to the Egyptians. What was new, however, was that Yahweh, not Pharaoh, was able to turn it red.

The further intensification and explanation of this plague in 7:19, however, suggests that more was involved than a mere red tide in the Nile. For not just the Nile but all the water sources in Egypt, including all the pools of water and water containers, were affected. This would suggest that the narrative intends to teach that the water of the Egyptians did, in fact, become blood. The appeal to Joel 2:31 (MT 3:4) to explain this text as metaphorical overlooks the fact that the Joel passage is poetry and thus should be understood as an image, whereas the passage here in Exodus is narrative and should be read realistically.

Curiously enough, however, the Egyptian magicians were able to duplicate the sign (v. 22), and this suggests that not "all the water" of Egypt had been affected. As is often the case in the everyday language of the biblical narratives, the sense of "all" can be limited by the immediate context. In any event, after the Egyptian magicians carried through their duplication of the signs, there was no "fresh water" available to drink (v. 24). Since the Egyptians had to resort to digging for their water along the banks of the Nile

---

[6]K. A. Kitchen, "Plagues of Egypt," New Bible Dictionary, ed. J. D. Douglas (Grand Rapids: Eerdmans, 1962), 1002.

(v. 24), it is possible that by the same means the Egyptian magicians found fresh water for their duplication of the sign.

4. Second Plague: Frogs (8:1–15 [MT 7:26–8:11])

Along with most creatures in the natural world, the frog was worshiped by the ancient Egyptians. They considered it the giver of the breath of life, and thus it became a symbol of life. At the word of Moses' God, the frogs overwhelmed the Egyptians and Pharaoh had to plead with Moses to have them removed. In answer to the prayer of Moses, on the following day, all the frogs in the land died. Already Pharaoh showed signs of giving in to Moses' request, particularly in the midst of this plague (8:8 [MT 4]). When the plague subsided, however, Pharaoh had a change of heart. We are again reminded that the hardness of his heart was "just as the LORD had said" (v. 15 [MT 11]).

5. Third Plague: Gnats (8:16–19 [MT 12–15])

The importance of this plague lies in the fact that the Egyptians were unable to reproduce it. When they could not succeed, the magicians concluded that "this is the finger of God"—God is truly producing this sign; it is not a trick like their own (8:19 [MT 15]). At this point in the narrative we, the readers, see that the Egyptian magicians were using tricks in their earlier signs. Their confession plays an important role in uncovering the writer's real purpose in recounting these events.

6. Fourth Plague: Swarms of Flies (8:20–32 [MT 16–28])

Still another new element is introduced with this plague—the Israelites were set apart from the swarms of flies, and only the Egyptians were affected (v. 22 [MT 18]). In the Hebrew text this is called a "deliverance" for the people of Israel (note NIV margin), as in Isaiah 50:2: "Was my arm too short to deliver you?"

Again Pharaoh appeared ready to give in to the request to let the people go to worship God. He set a limit, however, by not letting them leave the land (Ex 8:25 [MT 21]). When Moses appealed to him, he gave in further but was vague on what limits he intended for them: "you must not go very far" (v. 28 [MT 24]). Though Moses already anticipated Pharaoh's change of heart (v. 29 [MT 25]), he nevertheless prayed for the removal of the swarms (vv. 30–31 [MT 26–27]). As expected, Pharaoh hardened his heart. There is no reminder here that the Lord already predicted this hardening in 7:3, but that message had already been reinforced throughout the preceding narrative.

7. Fifth Plague: Pestilence upon the Livestock (9:1–7)

The words of Moses to Pharaoh proved true. All the livestock of the Egyptians died of disease, yet not one of the livestock of the Israelites was affected. Moses is not called in this time. Pharaoh's heart hardened, and he did not let the people go.

8. Sixth Plague: Boils upon the Egyptians (9:8–12)

The report of this plague resumes the general pattern of the earlier plagues in referring at the end to God's promise to harden the heart of Pharaoh (cf. 7:3). Moreover, the author states explicitly that "the Lord

hardened the heart of Pharaoh" (9:12). Nevertheless, the nature of Moses'
actions in this plague was unique. He had to throw soot into the air so that
the dust would become boils over all the Egyptians.

In this plague account we learn that the magicians were still hard at
work opposing the signs of Moses. A new twist, however, is put on their
work here. Their problem now is not that they cannot duplicate the sign—
something which they would not likely have wanted to do; rather, they
cannot "stand before Moses because of the boils." This is apparently
intended to show that, like the earlier plagues, this plague did not affect the
Israelites, represented here by Moses and Aaron. It also provides a graphic
picture of the ultimate failure of the magicians to oppose the work of Moses
and Aaron. The magicians lay helpless in their sickbed before the work of
Moses and Aaron.

9. Seventh Plague: Hailstorms (9:13–35)

The result of the hailstorms of this plague was the destruction of the
Egyptians' crops and livestock, that is, "all that was left in the fields" (v. 25).
Again the Israelites were safe in Goshen (v. 26).

The Lord's words to Pharaoh in this plague greatly expand on the
purpose of the plagues developed so far in the narrative. Up to this point,
the purpose of the plagues has been described generally: "so that the
Egyptians will know that I am the LORD" (7:5). That purpose is now
expanded to include "that you [Pharaoh and the Egyptians] may know that
there is none like me in all the earth" (9:14)—an idea that comes close in
meaning to the first commandment (20:2)—and "that my name might be
recounted in all the earth" (9:16)—an idea that resembles the second
commandment, "You shall not take the name of the LORD your God in vain"
(20:7). The narrative thus appears to ground the commandments in the
historical acts of God in the Exodus.

10. Eighth Plague: Locusts (10:1–20)

The eighth plague introduces a new element into the purpose of the
plagues. As before, God has hardened Pharaoh's heart so that he might
perform the signs; but this time the sign is not for Egypt and Pharaoh. It is
rather for Israel and their children, "that you may tell your children and
grandchildren how I dealt harshly with the Egyptians . . . that you may
know that I am the LORD" (10:2).

As the narrative now stands it presents a very fickle Pharaoh. Pharaoh
first appeared to consent to the Israelites' request to leave the land with all
their families and possessions (vv. 8–10). He said literally to Moses, "May
the LORD thus be with you as I send your and your children. See, there is evil
before you" (v. 10). But then, just as quickly, it becomes clear that he
intended to hold back their families and to send only the men (v. 11). At this
point Moses and Aaron were driven out of Pharaoh's presence and the
plague was called down on the Egyptians.

Some translations render Pharaoh's words as if he was speaking
sarcastically: "May the LORD be with you, if I were to send away you and
your children [as you are requesting]." This may be the case. As it stands,
however, there is not much evidence for such a reading within the text, and
the picture of a halting, confused Pharaoh plays well here at the conclusion

of the plague narratives. It shows that Moses and Aaron were beginning to get on his nerves.

11. Ninth Plague: Darkness (10:21–29)

There is a marked finality to the ninth plague. First, Pharaoh was down to his last ruse: the women and children could go but not their livestock. This was unacceptable to Moses because the livestock were needed for offerings. Second, the darkness signaled the end to the plagues. Just as the world began in total darkness (Ge 1:2), so now the land of Egypt had returned to that state. There is thus a narrative finality to the ninth plague. Third, Pharaoh warned Moses and Aaron never to return to him again. All future opportunities for signs were thus removed.

There is still, however, "one more plague" to be unleashed against Egypt. Pharaoh's own words to Moses hint of that plague: "your children may go with you," he said, as his last concession to Moses (Ex 10:24). Little does he know the bitter irony contained in his words. The reader, however, is well aware of the sense his words have. The children of the Israelites will go free, but "every firstborn son in Egypt will die" (11:5). In spite of the fact that they had been warned not to return to Pharaoh, Moses and Aaron must return to warn the Egyptians of the last plague (cf. 11:4–8). When Moses said, "I will not again see your face" (10:29), he may have had in mind that the next time he spoke to Pharaoh it would still be dark (three days later, v. 23). A traditional explanation of Moses' words to Pharaoh is that the announcement of the last plague was spoken "at the same time as the ninth plague."[7]

With the eighth and ninth plagues the narrative shows that Pharaoh was resisting the request of Moses beyond all reasonable limits. Even his own servants appear to scold him with the remark, "Do you not realize that Egypt is destroyed?" (10:7). But Pharaoh continued to hold out because, as the narrative stresses, the Lord had hardened his heart. The more the king resisted, the stronger the message of the narrative comes through. The plagues were "signs" to show the power of God. As long as Pharaoh resisted, the "signs" could continue to make their point.

12. The Last Plague (11:1–12:36)

a. Death of the Firstborn (11:1–10)

Looking at the last plague in terms of what it must have meant for the Egyptians and quite apart from the sense given to the plagues in the biblical account, we can easily see that it was the most severe, both personally and theologically. Not only was it a severe blow to each Egyptian household who lost a firstborn son, but it was also a powerful blow to the Egyptians' idea of royal succession. The ancient Egyptians considered the eldest son of the king to be a god. It is interesting that from what we know of the king who followed the pharaoh of the Exodus, namely, Thutmose IV, he was not the eldest son. In one of his own inscriptions, he recounted how the kingship was promised to him by the gods, which suggests that Thutmose "was not

---

[7]See *Rashi's Commentary on the Torah* (Hebrew) (Jerusalem: Mossad Harav Kook, 1988), 202; Keil, *Pentateuch*, 1:499.

his father's heir apparent, but had obtained the throne through an unforeseen turn of fate, such as the premature death of an elder brother."[8]

Within the context of the biblical narrative, however, we can see that the last plague is central to God's further dealings with Israel. The last plague was memorialized for the Israelites in the celebration of the Passover (Ex 12) and the Feast of Unleavened Bread (Ex 13). Moreover, it was on the basis of the last plague that God was able to claim the "firstborn" for himself and ultimately to substitute the Levitical priesthood for Israel's firstborn (Ex 13:1–2; Nu 3:13, 41).

Thus it is by means of the account of the last plague that the author is able to introduce into the Exodus narrative in a clear and precise way the notion of redemption from sin and death. The idea of salvation from slavery and deliverance from Egypt is manifest throughout the early chapters of Exodus. The idea of redemption and salvation from death, however, is the particular contribution of the last plague, especially as the last plague is worked into the narrative by the author. Hence the commemoration of the Passover was to be more than a remembrance of God's deliverance of Israel from slavery and oppression. It was, as well, a commemoration of salvation from the "angel of death" sent against anyone who did not enter into the Passover.

By means of the last plague, then, the writer is able to bring the Exodus narratives into the larger framework of the whole Pentateuch and particularly that of the early chapters of Genesis. In the midst of the judgment of death, God provided a way of salvation for the promised seed (Ge 3:15). Like Enoch (5:22–24), Noah (6:9), and Lot (19:16–19), those who walk in God's way will be saved from death and destruction.[9]

b. Passover (12:1–36; cf. Nu 9)

The biblical texts describing the Passover require careful reading. They are a mixture of narrative and instruction. At the same time that the writer recounts the events of the Exodus, he also inserts instructions on how later generations were to commemorate the event of the Passover. The Israelites celebrated the first Passover Feast before they left Egypt; hence they needed to know the part of the instructions that related to them. Additional features of the Passover celebration included in this passage, however, are here addressed specifically to later generations.

Command #153, Ex 12:2, Sanctify and calculate the months of the year for the worship of God: "This month shall be to you the beginning of the months."

(1) Chronology of Events

The Exodus occurred in the month of Abib (13:4), which was later called Nisan (Ne 2:1). This month corresponds to March/April. According to Exodus 23:16, the calendar year customarily began in the month of Tishri (September/October), seven months earlier.[10] After the Exodus, the month of

---

[8]William C. Hayes, in *Cambridge Ancient History*, 3d ed. (Cambridge: Cambridge Univ. Press, 1973), 2/1:321.

[9]Each of these narratives is linked within the Pentateuch by the key word חֵן ("grace" or "favor"): Ge 6:8, חֵן and נֹחַ (Noah); 5:22–24, חֲנוֹךְ (Enoch); and 19:19, חֵן.

[10]According to an early tradition, the world was created in the month of Tishri and

the Passover (Abib) was taken to be the first month of the new calendar year (cf. the commentary below on Nu 29:1).

On the tenth day of the month of Abib, each household selected a lamb for a sacrifice. It was to be kept for four days. The text does not give a reason why the animal was to be kept from the tenth to the fourteenth day of the month. Though there are ancient answers to this question, none of them is inherently convincing. It was often suggested that the lamb was chosen several days early to avoid the last-minute rush and final preparations for leaving Egypt; or it was to allow sufficient time for observing the animal to ensure that it was, in fact, "without blemish"; or it was kept during this period of time to allow for reflection on God's salvation and grace shown in the Exodus.[11] Another reason may be tied to the ninth plague, that is, the three days of darkness (Ex 10:22). By choosing the animal on the tenth day, the three days of darkness (the eleventh, twelfth, and thirteenth) would have been avoided. The fourteenth, then, would have been the next day in which there was light. The lamb would not have been chosen during the time of darkness.

On the fourteenth of Abib the animal was slain "at twilight" and eaten. Since twilight marked the end of the day, it would have been the fifteenth of Abib (Nu 33:3)[12] when, at midnight (Ex 12:29), the Lord struck the firstborn of Egypt and the Egyptians swiftly sent the Israelites out of the land. They departed from Rameses, and rather than take the nearest route into the land of Canaan (13:17–18), they turned eastward to Succoth (12:37) and from there to Etham (13:20) on their way to Sinai (14:2).

In the future commemoration of this event, the Feast of Unleavened Bread was to begin on the same day as the Exodus, the fifteenth of Abib (12:17; Lev 23:6; Nu 28:17; 33:3). This was also reckoned as the "evening" of the fourteenth of Abib (Ex 12:18), since it was to follow the Passover, which was celebrated at twilight on the fourteenth day. The Feast of Unleavened Bread, then, lasted from the fifteenth to the twenty-first of Abib (12:18).

(2) Meaning of the Passover Celebration

The Feast of Passover was inaugurated to commemorate the birth of the nation of Israel. That this feast marked a new beginning can be seen in the inauguration of a new calendar shaped around this event as the first event of the year. The feast was also intended to remind Israel of the Lord's salvation when he "passed over" their houses and delivered their firstborn (12:13, 27). The bitter herbs eaten with the meal were to remind Israel of the bitter days of bondage in Egypt,[13] and the unleavened bread was to remind them of God's quick deliverance (vv. 33–34). They left Egypt in such a hurry that their bread dough had not yet been properly prepared (v. 39).

Later biblical writers are careful to remind us that key biblical events

---

hence this was reckoned as the first month of each year. Thus according to the famous chronology of James Ussher, the creation in Genesis 1 is dated at October 23, 4004 B.C. (*Annales Veteris Testamenti* [London, 1650], 1).

[11] See Paul Fagius *Critici Sacri*, 1:202.

[12] See Rashi, ad loc.

[13] See Fagius, *Critici Sacri*, 1:203.

happened during the time of the celebration of the Passover.[14] We are told, for example, that Joshua led Israel through the Jordan and into the Promised Land during the time of the Passover Feast (Jos 4:19). Also, at the time of the preparation for the Passover Feast, Jesus rode into Jerusalem amid a great crowd of people shouting, "Hosanna! Blessed is he who comes in the name of the Lord!" (Jn 12:1, 12). Jewish tradition has it that since the Passover marks the great day of the Lord's salvation, it will also be on that day that the Messiah will come to save God's people.[15] The Gospels show Jesus as the one who fulfilled that expectation. He is the Lamb of God, slain during the days of the Passover Feast (John 18:28). According to Paul, "Christ, our Passover lamb, has been sacrificed. Therefore let us keep the festival, not with the old yeast, the yeast of malice and wickedness, but with bread without yeast, the bread of sincerity and truth" (1Co 5:7–8). For Peter, Christ was "a lamb without blemish or defect, chosen before the creation of the world" (1Pe 1:19–20).

It may be significant that in Peter's reckoning (2Pe 3:8), "a day is like a thousand years." If Peter worked within the traditional chronology of the Bible, which reckons the coming of Christ at four thousand years after Creation, then his concept of Christ, the Passover lamb "chosen before the creation of the world," would fit the requirement of the lamb chosen four days before the Passover. At the end of the Bible, in the book of Revelation, Christ the Passover Lamb stands at the center of John's vision of the future redemption of the heavens and earth, when every creature in heaven and on earth will sing: "Worthy is the Lamb, who was slain" (Rev 5:12).

> Seven famous Passovers are recorded in Scripture to have been kept. The first, this which Israel kept in Egypt. The second, that which they kept in the wilderness, Numbers 9. The third, which Joshua kept with Israel, when he had newly brought them into Canaan, Joshua 5:10. The fourth, in the reformation of Israel by King Hezekiah, 2 Chronicles 30. The fifth under King Josiah, 2 Chronicles 35. The six, by Israel returned out of the captivity of Babylon, Ezr 6:19. The seventh, that which Jesus our Savior desired so earnestly, and did eat with his disciples before he suffered, Luke 22:15 etc. At which time, that legal Passover had an end, and our Lord's Supper came in the place, the memorial of Christ our Passover, sacrificed for us.[16]

(3) Commands Relating to the Passover:

Command #55, Ex 12:6, One must slaughter the Passover lamb on the 14th of Nisan: "Until the 14th day of the month and then all the congregation of Israel shall slaughter it at twilight."

Command #56, Ex 12:8, One must eat the roasted Passover lamb on the night of the 15th of Nisan according to the instructions, e.g., in one house, with matzo upon the bitter herbs: "And they shall eat the meat in that night, roasted with fire, and matzo upon the bitter herbs they shall eat it."

---

[14]Some attempts have been made to link key events in the past to the date of the Passover, e.g., Abraham's arrival in Canaan (Ge 12), Jacob's departure for Egypt (Ge 46), and Isaac's birth (Ge 21).

[15]See Fagius, *Critici Sacri*, 1:203.

[16]Henry Ainsworth, *Annotations upon the Five Books of Moses* (London: M. Parsons, 1639), 40.

Command #156, Ex 12:15, Remove all leaven (on the 14th of Nisan): "On the first day you shall remove the leaven from your houses."

Command #159, Ex 12:16, Rest on the first day of Passover: "On the first day hold a sacred convocation."

Command #160, Ex 12:16, Rest on the seventh day of Passover: "On the seventh day hold a sacred convocation."

Command #158, Ex 12:18, Eating matzo on the night of the 15th of Nisan: "In the evening you shall eat matzo."

Prohibitions relating to the Passover:

Prohibition #125, Ex 12:9, One must not eat the Passover lamb raw or boiled; it must be roasted: "Do not eat the meat raw or cooked in water, but roast it over the fire."

Prohibition #117, Ex 12:10, The meat of the Passover must not be left till morning: "Do not leave any of it till morning."

Prohibition #323, Ex 12:16, One must not work on the first day of Passover: "On the first day. . . do no work at all on these days."

Prohibition #324, Ex 12:16, One must not work on the seventh day of Passover: "On the seventh day . . . do no work at all on these days."

Prohibition #201, Ex 12:19, No yeast must be found in one's house during the celebration of the Passover: "For seven days no yeast is to be found in your houses."

Prohibition #198, Ex 12:20, One must not eat anything mixed with yeast on the day of the Passover: "Eat nothing made with yeast."

Prohibition #128, Ex 12:43, A foreigner must not be allowed to eat the Passover: "No foreigner is to eat of it."

Prohibition #126, Ex 12:45, An alien must not be allowed to eat the Passover: "But a temporary resident and a hired worker may not eat of it."

Prohibition #121, Ex 12:46, One must not break the bone of the Passover lamb: "Do not break any of the bones."

Prohibition #123, Ex 12:46, One must not carry the meat of the Passover lamb outside the house where it is being eaten: "Take none of the meat outside the house."

Prohibition #127, Ex 12:48, An uncircumcised person must not be allowed to eat the Passover: "An alien living among you who wants to celebrate the Lord's Passover must have all the males in his household circumcised; then he may take part."

Prohibition #197, Ex 13:3, One must not eat yeast on the day of the Passover: "Commemorate this day, the day you came out of Egypt. . . . Eat nothing containing yeast."

Prohibition #200, Ex 13:7, No yeast must be seen during the celebration of the Passover: "Nothing with yeast in it is to be seen among you, nor shall any yeast be seen anywhere within your borders."

(4) Instructions on Celebrating the First Passover and Feast of Unleavened Bread (12:1–20)

(a) PASSOVER INSTRUCTIONS (12:1–13)

The instructions to Moses and Israel on the eve of the Exodus are recorded here in such a way that they provide the directions for celebrating the Passover throughout all future generations. Details that would apply only to future generations are recorded later in the chapter (vv. 43–51) after this first Passover Feast had been celebrated (v. 28).

Though later traditions have added much to the celebration of the Passover, the instructions given here are quite simple. A male yearling lamb without blemish was slain and its blood put on the doorposts. After it was properly cooked, it was eaten with unleavened bread and bitter herbs. Anything not eaten was to be destroyed with fire by morning. Those eating the meal were to be dressed for travel and ready at any point to leave. (For instructions relating to the later celebrations of the Passover, see 12:43–49 and the commentary there.)

According to Jewish tradition, some instructions given in these chapters were intended only for the first Passover in Egypt and were not practiced later. These are (1) taking the lamb on the tenth day, (2) applying the blood to the doorposts, and (3) eating the meal in haste. According to Maimonides, "These things were only for those in the land of Egypt and are not required of later generations"[17] This explains why the later description of the celebration of the Passover in the Pentateuch omitted these elements (Lev 23:5; Nu 2–5; 28:16–17; Dt 16:1–8). This also explains why, in the NT, Christ and his disciples did not eat the Passover in haste with staffs in hand, but rather "reclined at the table" (Lk 22:14).[18]

The implication of this passage is that each lamb would be slain at the house where it was to be eaten. Under the Mosaic Law, however, it was forbidden to offer a sacrifice apart from the office of the priests at the tabernacle (Lev 17:1–6). Thus, Deuteronomy 16:5–6 stated clearly that the Passover lamb was not to be slain at each individual house, but rather at the place where all the congregation were gathered. So also in later biblical texts we find that the Passover was celebrated at the temple. Each lamb was brought to the priests to be slain on the altar (2Ch 35:1–11) and then taken home for the celebration. This is the custom followed in NT times as well (Lk 22:1–38).

With the destruction of the second temple in A.D. 70, the biblical instructions for the Passover could no longer be carried out because they necessitated the temple service in Jerusalem. The Feast of Unleavened Bread thus came to be the primary means for remembering the Passover night (see Ex 13:3–7).

(b) THE FEAST OF UNLEAVENED BREAD (12:14–20)

The night of the Passover was to be remembered throughout all generations by means of the Feast of Unleavened Bread. It appears obvious that the instructions regarding the Feast of Unleavened Bread were not given to Israel to be carried out on the night of the first Passover, but are included here in the text because this feast was later to play an important part in the celebration of the Passover. It is unlikely, for example, that the Israelites would have been expected to gather together into a holy assembly on the day of their exodus from Egypt, nor is there any indication in the text that they did this.

Like that of the Passover, the description of the Feast of Unleavened

---

[17]Maimonides, *Qorbenot*, 10.15.
[18]Ainsworth, *Annotations*, 40.

Bread is very simple. Beginning after dark on the fourteenth of Abib (which, since the day began at evening, is in fact the fifteenth of Abib), they were to go without leaven in their food for seven days. The first day (fifteenth of Abib) and the seventh day (twenty-first of Abib) were to be special days in which they were to cease from all unnecessary work and gather together in a holy assembly. A similar set of instructions is given in 13:3–7 (cf. 23:15). Those instructions combine some of the features of the Passover meal with some features of the Feast of Unleavened Bread.

(5) *Carrying Out the Instructions (12:21–28)*

(a) BLOOD ON DOORPOSTS (12:21–23)

The people were instructed that the only way they could avert the "destroyer" was to put the blood of the lamb on their doorposts. Though the text does not explicitly state it, the overall argument of the Pentateuch (see the Introduction above) would suggest that their obedience to the word of the Lord in this instance was an evidence of their faith and trust in him. This is also the way the NT read this text: "By faith he [Moses] kept the Passover and the sprinkling of blood, so that the destroyer of the firstborn would not touch the firstborn of Israel" (Heb 11:28).

(b) STATUTE FOR FUTURE GENERATIONS (12:24–27)

The purpose of the Passover celebration was to remind God's people of his gracious act of deliverance. When the children saw the feas,t they were to ask, "What does this mean?" The parents could then tell them of God's grace and love. Unfortunately, after Israel settled in the land, the Passover was not always celebrated as it should have been (cf. 2Ki 23:22–23; 2Ch 35:18; 30:2–3, 17–20). Thus an important occasion for teaching God's great acts was neglected. Already after the death of Joshua and the elders, for example, "another generation grew up, who knew neither the LORD nor what he had done for Israel" (Jdg 2:10).

(c) THE PASSOVER CELEBRATED (12:28)

The obedience of the people is stressed by the solemn reminder that the people "did all that the LORD commanded them" (12:28).

(6) *Death Angel (12:29–30)*

On the night of the Passover, the Lord went through the land to strike down the firstborn of the Egyptians, that is, he sent his "destroyer" (12:23) to those houses not marked by the blood of the lamb. As elsewhere in Scripture, the Lord's work was carried out by angels. "He unleashed against them his hot anger, his wrath, indignation, and hostility—a band of destroying angels" (Ps 78:49). Note the similar use of angels in 2 Samuel 24:15–16: "So the LORD sent a plague on Israel. . . . When the angel stretched out his hand to destroy Jerusalem, the LORD was grieved because of the calamity and said to the angel who was afflicting the people, 'Enough! Withdraw your hand.'"

It has long been recognized that a certain symmetry exists between Egypt's treatment of Israel in the early chapters of Exodus and God's treatment of Egypt in the present text. As Egypt had killed all the Israelite sons (Ex 1:22) and had oppressed God's firstborn, Israel (4:22–23), so now the Egyptian firstborn were taken and they were repaid for the wrong they had done.

(7) The Departure (12:31–36)

The author is careful to draw a connection between the wealth of the Egyptians given to the Israelites and God's promise of wealth and blessing to the patriarchs. Thus the promise to Abraham was fulfilled—"They shall come out with great wealth" (Ge 15:14).

C. Travel, Mixed Multitude, and Future Observance (12:37–51)

1. Travel from Egypt (12:37)

The Israelites were living in Rameses (1:11), an ancient city in the delta region of Egypt. This was the area of Goshen allotted to them by the Egyptians in the days of Joseph (Ge 47:11). From there they traveled to Succoth en route to Mount Sinai. This route would have taken them southeastward about a day's journey from Rameses. The present location of many of their camps in the wilderness remains uncertain, even that of Mount Sinai itself. It is important to note, however, that the general history and geography of the whole area are quite well known, and hence we have an accurate picture of the conditions of their travel even though we cannot identify most of the sites named here. For the most part it is reasonable to assume that they would have used the established trade routes that ran through the area connecting Egypt with the regions to the east. Because of the small amount of annual rainfall, their travel would have taken them either over dry and dusty flatlands or through precipitous mountain ranges. As the sparse population of the area has attested throughout its history, it was not a region capable of supporting even small numbers of settlers, let alone the number of Israelites in the Exodus (perhaps over two million). As the biblical narrative makes abundantly clear, they could not have survived without the miraculous provisions of water, food, and clothing (Dt 8:2–5).

2. Mixed Multitude (12:38)

Almost as an aside, the author notes that a great many non-Israelites went out with them. The identity of this group and their relationship to Israel is the subject of considerable discussion. A common interpretation is that they were "proselytes" who had abandoned their pagan gods to follow the God of Israel.[19] It may well be, however, that the author intends us to understand them not as true proselytes but as those who had been impressed by the miracles that Moses had performed. Later, in Numbers 11:4, this group is called "the rabble" and is seen as the cause of Israel's incessant complaining against God's good provisions. Just as Abraham had brought Lot with him out of Ur (Ge 12:5), so Israel is accompanied by the "mixed multitude." In the same way, when the Israelites returned from Babylonian captivity they again joined themselves to the "mixed multitude" ("of foreign descent," NIV; cf. Ne 13).

Just as the Lord had brought Abraham out of Egypt with great wealth

---

[19]See, e.g., Rashi, ad loc.; Münster, Critici Sacri, 1:201.

and reward (Ge 13:1–2), so we are again reminded that Israel left Egypt with many possessions.

3. Unleavened Bread in Haste (12:39)

Having left Egypt in haste the night before, the Israelites, in Succoth, now must prepare their food with unleavened bread. The writer reminds us of this point as a way of explaining the Feast of Unleavened Bread. Earlier he had given the instructions for celebrating the feast, but only here does he provide its explanation. The instructions that follow were given to Israel by Moses while they were in Succoth.

4. Chronological Note (12:40–41)

The time of Israel's sojourn in Egypt is calculated "to the very day," that is, 430 years. Genesis 15:13 gave the time in the round number four hundred years.[20] First Kings 6:1 calculates the time from the Exodus to the building of the temple to be 480 years. This figure gives the broad chronological boundaries for the historical books. If the date of the building of the temple was 960 B.C., then the date of the Exodus was 960 B.C. + 480 years, that is, 1440 B.C. If we add the 430 years of Israel's sojourn, then the time of Jacob's entry into Egypt was 1440 B.C. + 430 years, that is, 1870 B.C.[21]

5. Instructions for Future Observance (12:42–51)

These additional instructions for the Passover Feast look to the time when Israel will dwell in their own land and live in their own cities and towns in close contact with the world about them. Thus the basic question is whether "foreigners" could also eat the Passover meal. The answer is no. Only permanent members of the community of God's people could partake.

One of the details of the Passover ritual later became an important element in the identification of Jesus as the Passover lamb: "Do not break

---

[20]The number 430 years, however, appears to be important in the remaining chronologies of the Bible. If the number of years from the judges to the moving of the ark to Jerusalem (1Sa 7:2) are added, without attention to overlapping periods, the total is 430 (410 years of judges plus the 20 years the ark was at Kiriath Jearim, 1Sa 7:2). If the number of years of the kings of Judah are added from the time of the building of the temple, the total is 430.

Time before ark	Time before temple	Time before temple rebuilt	
◄— 430 —►	◄— 430 —►	◄— 430 —►	= 1,290

Curiously enough, this is the same number (of days) given in Daniel for the period before the building of the new temple: "From the time that the daily sacrifice is abolished and the abomination that causes desolation is set up, there will be 1,290 days" (Da 12:11). Daniel was perhaps using this same scheme in the reckoning of time before the building of the future temple.

[21]According to some (Rashi, ad loc.; Ainsworth, *Annotations*, 44), the 430 years includes not only the time Israel lived in Egypt but also the time the patriarchs lived in Canaan. Thus the Samaritan Pentateuch and the LXX read, "And the time the Israelites dwelt in the land of Canaan and the land of Egypt was 430." In Gal 3:17 Paul speaks of the 430 years from the time of the patriarchal covenant of promise to the Mosaic Law.

any of the bones" (Ex 12:46). On the basis of this element of the Passover, the Gospel of John drew a connection between Jesus and the Passover lamb:

> Now it was the day of Preparation, and the next day was to be a special Sabbath. Because the Jews did not want the bodies left on the crosses during the Sabbath, they asked Pilate to have the legs broken and the bodies taken down. The soldiers therefore came and broke the legs of the first man who had been crucified with Jesus, and then those of the other. But when they came to Jesus and found that he was already dead, they did not break his legs. . . . These things happened so that the scripture would be fulfilled: "Not one of his bones will be broken." (Jn 19:31–36, NIV)

John's comment on this verse shows quite clearly that the NT authors often read these OT texts with an eye to their meaning for the events in the life of Jesus.

D. The Firstborn and the Feast of Unleavened Bread (13:1–16)

1. Firstborn of Israel Set Apart (13:1–2)

From the context alone we can conclude that the firstborn were set apart for the Lord because he had "passed over" them in the destruction of the firstborn of Egypt. They thus belonged to him, and as was later seen with the Levites, they were to serve him in worship. This conclusion is confirmed in 13:11–16 (cf. Nu 3:13, 41).

The "consecration to the Lord" was carried out in two ways. On the one hand, the firstborn were to be set apart from ordinary affairs of life and given over to God's service. They were evidently the priests mentioned in Exodus 19:22; 24:5. This consecration was later carried over to the sons of Levi when they became priests (Nu 3:41). On the other hand, the firstborn could be "redeemed" by the payment of a sum of money (Nu 18:15–17).

Command #79, Ex 13:2, Sanctifying the firstborn males: "Sanctify to me all the firstborn males."

2. Instructions for Commemoration of the Feast of Unleavened Bread (13:3–10)

A similar set of instructions had already been given in 12:14–20. The two passages have several differences in emphasis, however. Some of these differences suggest that the present text is an attempt to give a more prominent place to the Feast of Unleavened Bread in the commemoration of the night of the Passover and Exodus from Egypt. In times when there was no possibility of celebrating the Passover Feast (e.g., after the destruction of the second temple in Jerusalem in A.D. 70), the Feast of Unleavened Bread could still function as the time of remembrance of what God had done for Israel. Thus, whereas the Feast of the Passover was previously to have been an occasion of the children's learning the great acts of God in rescuing Israel from Egypt (12:26–27), now, according to 13:8, the Feast of Unleavened Bread was also to serve that purpose.

Other differences serve to focus attention on varying aspects of this feast. For example, earlier in chapter 12, the emphasis fell on the importance of correct celebration of the feast by stressing the stringent penalties for eating leavened bread: "Whoever eats anything with yeast in it must be cut off from the community of Israel" (v. 19). Here, however, the emphasis falls on the continual celebration of the feast, that it is to be observed "at the appointed time year after year."

Whereas during the Passover meal the great deeds of God were to be retold in response to the question of the children (v. 26), the Feast of Unleavened Bread itself was to be the occasion for the retelling of God's acts. There was thus no need to wait for the children to ask. The story was preserved and given as a part of the feast. As Maimonides said, "It is one's duty to inform the children even if they ask no questions."[22]

> Command #157, Ex 13:8, Recounting the story of the Exodus (on the 15th of Nisan): "You shall declare to your son on that day."

3. Redemption of the Firstborn (13:11–16)

Because God had redeemed the firstborn of Israel on the night of the Exodus, it was the duty of the people to devote every firstborn male to the service of worship. The firstborn of the clean animals were to be devoted to the Lord by being offered as a sacrifice. The firstborn of the unclean animals (donkeys, etc.) and of human beings were to be redeemed by substitution (cf. Nu 18:15), a sheep in the case of unclean animals and money in the case of the firstborn male child (five shekels, 18:16). At a later time the tribe of Levi would assume the role of the firstborn and be set apart for service in the tabernacle (3:12–13, 45). Even then, however, a redemption price was still to be paid to the Levites (18:14).

> Command #82, Ex 13:13, One must break the neck of an ass if it is not redeemed: "If you do not redeem it [an ass] you must break its neck."

The dedication of the firstborn was to be a memorial sign of God's redemption of Israel from slavery in Egypt. The same purpose was assigned to the celebration of the Passover Feast and the Feast of Unleavened Bread (Ex 12:14). In the passage of time, Jewish tradition has taken these words to imply more than a mere symbolic function but that actual physical "symbols" were to be worn on the hands and forehead. These are the "phylacteries," small leather boxes containing scriptural quotations (four biblical sections, Ex 13:1–10; 11:16; Dt 6:4–9; 11:13–21), which, according to custom, are strapped to the left arm and forehead. They are also called tefillin. The following is a description of these tefillin in the classical work of Maimonides, Mishneh Torah:

> The head-phylactery is placed on the upper part of the head where the hair next to the forehead ends; it is the place where the child's brain pulsates. The phylactery should be adjusted in the center of the forehead, between the eyes. The knot should be at the top of the neck in the back, which is the end of the skull. . . . The hand-phylactery is attached to the left arm over the biceps, which is the flesh rising above the elbow, between the shoulder-blade and the forearm, so that when the upper arm is held close to the ribs the phylactery will be opposite the heart, in keeping with the precept: "These words . . . shall be on your heart." . . . As long as a man wears the tefillin on his head and arm, he is humble and

---

[22]Maimonides, Chametz and Matzah, 7.2.

God-fearing, is not drawn into frivolity and idle talk, does not engage in evil thoughts but fills his mind with thoughts of truth and justice.[23]

E. Crossing the Red Sea (13:17–15:21)

1. Travel from Egypt (13:17–20)

The shortest route to the land of Canaan was the well-guarded "Way of the Philistines." This route led directly up the coastline and was the main artery of Egypt's defenses against their northern neighbors. The writer gives here an interesting glimpse into God's plans and purposes in dealing with his people. God knew that they were not ready for battle and that at the sight of war they would flee back to bondage in Egypt. He thus led them another way, a way that turned out to be no more successful for this generation of his people and a way that would not be without its own hardships and temptations to return to Egypt (see, e.g., Ex 14:12; Nu 14:1–4). We should also note that the way in which God led them did not exclude war. Only four chapters later they engage in war with the Amalekites and prove victorious with God's help.

The NIV translation of 13:18, "The Israelites went up out of Egypt armed for battle," gives the impression that the people were heavily equipped for war. The Hebrew text, however, suggests only that as they marched out of the land, they formed orderly columns of fifty men abreast, that is, according to the military custom of the day, "in battle array." Since they engaged in war with the Amalekites shortly after this, they obviously were armed and ready for battle, but it was not the intent of the author to say so.

In Genesis 50:24–25 Joseph's faith in God's promise to give the Israelites the land of Canaan had led him to pass on a charge to his brothers and the future generations in Egypt—his bones were not to remain in Egypt but were to be returned to the Promised Land. Unlike Jacob, who was returned to Canaan immediately after his death, Joseph requested that his bones remain with the children of Jacob in Egypt as a reminder of their future return to the land. The writer takes the present occasion to remind us of the fulfillment of that promise and of the people's recognition of it. As in Exodus 2:24 and Joshua 24:32, the writer continues to highlight God's faithfulness to his word of promise. Even in the later prophetic literature (Eze 37:11), the bones of the faithful serve as a sign that the promise of the land still awaits its fulfillment.

This is the second day of their journey out of Egypt. The first day had taken them from Rameses to Succoth.[24] The date would be the sixteenth of Abib. Though the actual location of Etham is not known to us today, the text says, it was at the "edge of the desert," which would put it nearby the present Suez Canal.

2. Pillar of Cloud and Pillar of Fire (13:21–22)

The purpose of the pillar of cloud was to guide the Israelites through the desert. It thus went before the people, and they followed it through the wilderness. The purpose of the pillar of fire was to give them light at night.

---

[23]Maimonides, *Mishneh Torah, Tefillin*, 4.1, 2, 25 (trans. Philip Birnbaum [New York: Hebrew Publishing Co., 1967], 52–53).

[24]See Rashi, ad loc.

The text says that the Lord went with the people in the cloud and the fire. Later, after the building of the tabernacle, the cloud and the fire rested on the tabernacle. If the cloud moved, the people followed. If it did not move, the people remained at their present camp (Ex 40:34–37; Nu 9:15–23).

It is often supposed that the pillar of cloud and the pillar of fire are to be understood as one pillar. In the daylight, the cloud's brightness was subdued in the light of the sun, but in the darkness of night it shone forth to give light.[25] From a straightforward reading of the text, however, it is more likely that two clouds are intended.[26]

The cloud and the fire have other uses in the subsequent narratives. At one point they joined forces against the Egyptians (Ex 14:19–20). The pillar of cloud separated the camp of the Egyptians from the Israelites and shielded the light of the pillar of fire from the camp of the Egyptians.[27]

In the NT, Paul identifies the cloud, along with the Red Sea in the wilderness, as the place of the Israelites' "baptism into Moses" (1Co 10:2).

3. Crossing the Red Sea (14:1–15:21)

a. Narrative of the Red Sea Crossing (14:1–31)

In interpreting the account of the crossing of the Red Sea, we must reckon with the uncertainty of the exact geographical setting of many of the events. Several attempts have been made to identify the various locations mentioned in Exodus 13–14 (e.g., the Red Sea, Etham, Succoth, Pi-Hahiroth, Migdol, and Baal-Zephon), but most identifications remain tentative. The most important location, of course, is the "Red Sea," or, as the Hebrew Bible calls it, the "Reed Sea." We should not let the name "Reed Sea" lead us to think that the sea was merely a marshland and that the biblical account of the dividing of the waters has been exaggerated in any way. The same "Sea of Reeds" served as the port of Solomon's fleet of ships (1Ki 9:26); thus this would have been a sufficiently deep body of water. In any event we know from the account in Exodus that the Israelites passed through this large body of water on dry land and that the Egyptians who tried to follow them were drowned when the waters poured back over them.

It is clear from Exodus 14:2–3 that the Lord had a specific purpose in having Israel cross the sea. That is, it was to be another occasion to reveal his superiority over the power of the Egyptians and to show that he alone was to be honored as Lord (v. 4). To accomplish this purpose, the Lord first instructed Israel to fall back into Egyptian territory (v. 2) and thus lead the Egyptians to believe that Israel was wandering aimlessly in the land, afraid to go out into the wilderness. Second, the narrative tells us that Pharaoh's heart was hardened (vv. 4, 8, 17) and he set out to regain control of the Israelites (vv. 6–7).

The question is often raised here where the Egyptians got horses for their chariots if all their livestock had died (9:6). The answer from the narrative appears to be that, according to 9:20, many Egyptians and their livestock were saved from destruction because they feared God.

The text of 14:3–5 has played an important role in the larger

---

[25]See Keil, *Pentateuch,* 2:41.
[26]See Rashi, ad loc.
[27]See Rashi, ad loc.

chronological discussions. For example, Rashi argued that Pharaoh was prompted to pursue the Israelites because of their failure to return after three days (cf. 5:3). If this is the case, Rashi continued, "on the fifth and sixth day they pursued them . . . and, thus, this was the seventh day of Passover."[28]

The immediate response of the Israelites when they saw the Egyptians was fear and mistrust. Moses, however, stands out as a faithful leader, admonishing the people to be courageous and to "stand by and see the salvation of the LORD which he will accomplish for you today" (v. 13). Moses here demonstrated the necessity of godly leadership and trust. Throughout the rest of the Bible similar examples of godly leadership are men like Joshua, David, Josiah, Ezra, and Nehemiah, and women such as Deborah, Ruth, and Esther.

The result of Moses' example and leadership is the establishment of the faith of the people themselves. When they saw the Lord fight for them and the defeated Egyptians lying along the shore of the sea, "they feared the LORD and put their trust in him and in Moses his servant" (v. 31). In view of the importance of the concept of faith and trust in God for the writer of the Pentateuch, we should take a long look at these verses. Just as Abraham believed God and was counted righteous (Ge 15:6), so the Israelites, under the leadership of Moses, also believed God. It seems reasonable that the writer would have us conclude here in the wilderness the people of God were living a righteous life of faith, like Abraham. As they headed toward Sinai, their trust was in the God of Abraham who had done great deeds for them. It is only natural, and certainly in line with the argument of the book, that they would break out into a song of praise in the next chapter. On the negative side, however, we should not lose sight of the fact that these same people would forget only too quickly the great work of God, make a golden calf (Ps 106:11–13), and thus forsake the God about whom they were now singing.

If the number of adult males was at least 600,000 (Ex 12:37), there would certainly have been over two million persons, plus their livestock, in the whole assembly. For so many people to pass through the sea in one night, the width of the parting of the sea would have to have been at least several miles.

The description of the parting of the sea itself leaves out many details. The expression "the waters were divided" (14:21) has led some to suppose (the Palestinian Targums) that the waters divided at many places so that the people were able to pass through at numerous points (cf. Ps 136:13). Because the text says "waters" rather than "sea," some have supposed that all the waters of the earth parted at this time.[29] Such speculations, though unlikely, show that the text provides us with only a glimpse of the event itself. Much is left unsaid and unexplained. Thus these texts have their own focus on the events that we should not fail to appreciate. We should attempt to understand what is put in the text rather than what is left out.

A caution should be sounded here regarding the description of the crossing of the sea in the narrative portions of Exodus 14 and the poetic portions of Exodus 15. The way events are described in poetry is quite

---

[28]See Rashi on 14:5.
[29]See Rashi, ad loc.

different from the way events are described in historical narrative. Poetry contains a great deal of stock imagery—word pictures used to depict themes and ideas rather than actual events. Thus, if one compares the depiction of the crossing of the sea in chapter 14 with that in chapter 15, one will notice some dissimilarities in the two accounts. In the narrative (Ex 14), for example, the Egyptian armies are drowned when the parted sea folds back over them. In the poem (chap. 15), however, their defeat is expressed by means of the poetical image of the Lord hurling them into the sea (v. 4), where "they sank to the depths like a stone" (v. 5). A possible motive for the use of this image is found in 1:22, where the same expression occurs for Pharaoh's command to throw the Israelite children into the river. Thus we see in these texts that God did to the Egyptians that which they had done to Israel. Though there are differences between the two versions of the event, the depictions of the crossing of the sea in both chapters are close enough to assure us that they are describing the same event.

It is common in the biblical text to describe the work of God in terms of his angels, or, many times, his angel (i.e., the "angel of God" or the "angel of the Lord"). Just as often, however, the biblical writers speak in terms that show God acting directly with his people. Such is the case in Exodus 13 and 14. For example, 13:21 says that the Lord went with them in the cloud and fire, whereas 14:19 says that the "angel of God" accompanied them in the cloud.[30]

b. Song of Moses (15:1–21)

God's defeat of the Egyptians and deliverance of Israel in the crossing of the sea provide the occasion for a hymn of praise sung by Moses and the Israelites. Both the introduction (v. 1) and conclusion (v. 19) of the song make this context clear. The scope of the song itself, however, goes far beyond the event of the crossing of the sea to include the establishment of the city of Jerusalem as the location of the temple (vv. 17–18). There seems to be no doubt that we are to understand Moses' words as prophetic. As in the other major poetic texts in the Pentateuch—i.e., Abraham (Ge 15:13–14) and Jacob (Ge 49:1–27) before him, and Balaam (Nu 23–24) after him, Moses is here cast in the role of a prophet (cf. Dt 18:15) telling of God's continued work for his people. Moreover, as with the other poetic texts, Moses' central concern is with the future King who will reign over God's eternal kingdom. It thus makes sense that Miriam, who led the women in singing this song, is also called here a "prophetess" (Ex 15:20). This is yet another example of the fact that the Pentateuch as a whole is not merely concerned with God's work in the past but is also interested in the work of God that lies in the future.

The poetic imagery that dominates the song is that of the Lord as a mighty warrior (e.g., "The LORD is a warrior; the LORD is his name," (v. 3). The weapon of this warrior is not only his great strength but also the mighty waters of the sea. With the sea he shattered the enemy. Images here are reminiscent of the struggle portrayed in Genesis 3:15. As is the case throughout the poetry of the Bible, God's power is depicted most graphically

---

[30]Later biblical texts have numerous allusions to the crossing of the sea: Jos 3:16; Isa 63:12–14; Pss 18:15 (MT 16); 66:5–6; 77:19–21 (MT 20–21); 78:13; 106:11; 114:5; 136:13–15; 1Co 10:2; Heb 3:8–9; 11:29.

with reference to his control over his creation. Thus the view of God in the first chapter of Genesis can be seen clearly in these poems.

In the poem, God is depicted as one of the judges of Israel: like Samson (Jdg 13–16) delivering the nation from the oppression of the Philistines (Ex 15:14), or like Ehud (Jdg 3:12–31) defeating the leaders of Moab (Ex 15:15). Throughout the poem, however, the picture of God's great deeds foreshadows most closely that of David, who defeated the chiefs of Edom, Philistia, and Canaan and made Mount Zion the eternal home for the Lord's sanctuary (v. 17). Curiously enough, many of the poems in the Pentateuch seem to foreshadow events in the life of David as well as to go far beyond him to even greater days in the future (cf. Ge 49:8–12; Nu 24:17–19). In many respects, this Song of Moses resembles the psalm of Asaph (Ps 78), which, after rehearsing God's great deeds of the past, moves on to describe God's work through David: "He chose the tribe of Judah, Mount Zion, which he loved. He built his sanctuary like the high mountains. . . . He chose David his servant . . . to be the shepherd of his people" (vv. 68–72).

V. WILDERNESS WANDERINGS (15:22–18:27)

A. God's Provision for Israel in the Wilderness (15:22–27)

After the destruction of Pharaoh's army in the sea, the Israelites continued their journey eastward into the wilderness of Shur. Though the text pays little attention to such details as the geography of the region, we know that Shur was a large semidesert region east of the Egyptian border frontier. After three days in the wilderness without finding water, they arrived at Marah. Here the Lord began to provide for the people, and the people learned to depend on his provision.

There is an important narrative lesson in the incident of the bitter waters. When the people were helpless and thirsty, Moses called out to the Lord for help. The Lord answered Moses by giving him an "instruction" on how to make the water sweet. When they followed the "instruction," the water became sweet and their thirst was satisfied (15:25). In the Hebrew text, the word *instruction* is the verbal form of the word *Torah*, that is, (divine) instruction. There is then a lesson about God's instructions to Israel in this incident. The lesson is clear enough—God's people are to "listen carefully to the voice of God" (v. 26). His instruction will be sweet to them and satisfy their thirst.

The mention of "a decree and a law" (v. 25) for Israel before the time of the giving of the Law at Sinai raises several questions and has prompted much discussion. Some say the "decree" or "law" given to Israel was simply the lesson taught to Israel in the testing of the bitter water. The decree was that they must obey God to enjoy his sweet blessings.[31] In the next verse, however, Israel is called upon to pay heed to the Lord's "commands and decrees." Thus, though it is possible to understand verse 25 to refer to the commands of God yet to be given to Israel at Sinai, it seems more probable that already at this stage in their journey we are to understand that God had

---

[31]See Keil, *Pentateuch*, 2:58.

made known his will to them in concrete laws. At least this appears to be the point the author wants to make.

An early Jewish tradition held that God already gave Israel "a few sections of the Torah" at Marah—such commands as the keeping of the Sabbath and those necessary for the administration of justice.[32] Some Christian scholars have followed this interpretation and thus see a distinction between God's initial giving of the Law to Israel, which was not too burdensome to bear, and God's giving of the detailed laws at Sinai after the incident of the golden calf (Ex 32). The law, it is maintained, was originally intended to teach God's people what was "right in his eyes" (15:26). After the failure of the people in the incident of the golden calf, however, more stringent measures were taken to keep the people from falling away into idolatry.[33] The apostle Paul apparently had a similar view of the secondary nature of the Mosaic Law; in Galatians 3:19 he said that the Mosaic Law "was added because of the transgressions."

Having learned the lesson of dependence on God and listening to his voice, the people moved on to Elim, where they found abundant water and nourishment (Ex 15:27).

B. Manna and Quail (16:1–36; cf. Nu 11:4–35)

The chapter opens on the fifteenth day of the second month, the month of Iyar. The Israelites had now been in the wilderness one month. The gathering of the manna and quail, recorded for the first time in this chapter, began then on the sixteenth of Iyar.

After leaving Elim en route to Mount Sinai, the Israelites found themselves in the "Wilderness of Sin" ("Sin" in Hebrew is related to the name "Sinai"; it has nothing to do with the English word *sin*). Here, again, the Lord tested them to see if they would "walk in the Lord's instructions" (16:4; the Hebrew word again is *tôrâ*). The test is brought on by the grumblings of the people over the shortage of food in the desert: "would that we had died by the LORD's hand in the land of Egypt" (v. 3). In other words, they saw themselves as no better off than the Egyptians who died "by the hand of the LORD" when he brought Israel up out of their land. Such a statement appears as a blatant act of unbelief (though we should note that the writer does not call it such) and called for a specific test—the daily supply of manna and quail as well as the keeping of the Sabbath rest. Henceforth, throughout their forty years in the wilderness, the people had to depend daily on the provisions of the Lord. A pattern is thus established here that continues throughout the narratives of Israel's sojourn in the wilderness. As the people's trust in the Lord and in Moses waned in the wilderness, the need grew for stricter lessons.

Though it is true that the Israelites often had other sources of food (e.g., their flocks and herds), through the gathering of the manna and quail the Bible tells us that the people witnessed daily miracles (Dt 8:3). For example, when the people went out to gather the manna, some gathered more than others. Each day, when they measured what they had gathered, the amount

---

[32]See Rashi, ad loc.

[33]J. Coccejus, *Opera Omnia Theologica, Exegetica, Didactica, Polemica, Philologica, Divisa in Decem Volumina* (Amsterdam: P. et J. Blaev, 1701), 7:281–90.

was just what each needed (Ex 16:17–18). The text is clear that this was not the result of their own calculations, but was another sign that God was intimately involved in providing for each of them.

Even amid the blessing of the manna and quail, some of the people did not obey the Lord's instructions for gathering it. They were to take only what they could eat for the day and not to keep it for the next day. There were those, however, who stored some of what they had collected for the next day (v. 20). Their disobedient efforts were to no avail, because "maggots" rose up in the manna and it putrefied by morning. Within the narrative, their disobedient response to God's good provisions provoked Moses to anger (v. 20) and called for a rebuke from the Lord: "How long will you refuse to keep my commands and my instructions?" (v. 28). For the writer, however, this behavior provides yet another lesson of the failure of the people to obey the will of God.

The mention of the forty years that they ate manna (v. 35) anticipates God's judgment of this generation in Numbers 14. It is worthy of note that the account in Numbers 14 follows a second incident with manna and quail (Nu 11:4–35). Moreover, it was because of their lack of faith and trust in God (14:11) that Israel remained in the wilderness forty years and was not allowed to enter the Promised Land (14:21–23). Then, at the end of the forty years, on the day after the Passover when they entered the land of Canaan, "the manna stopped . . . but that year they ate of the produce of Canaan" (Jos 5:12).

manna quail	40 years	manna quail	40 years	manna	end of 40 years
Ex 16:4–34	Ex 16:35	Nu 11:4–34	Nu 14:21–22	Jos 5:12	

Furthermore, it was by means of God's daily provisions for Israel that he also taught them the importance of the Sabbath: setting the seventh day apart for rest and remembrance (Ex 16:23–30). Not only would the double portion of manna keep over the sixth and seventh day, but also on the morning of the seventh day there was no manna. The structure of the Sabbath week was thus already built into the gift of manna.

Prohibition #321, Ex 16:29, One must not travel on the Sabbath: 'Everyone is to stay where he is on the seventh day; no one is to go out."

So great was the miraculous sign of the manna that provision was made for keeping an "omer of manna" as a witness for future generations (16:32–34). Thus we are told here that when the ark was constructed, a jar of manna was kept in it "for the generations to come." Verse 34 is a comment by the writer which updates this narrative by telling us that Aaron did follow through with the Lord's command to store an omer of manna in the ark.

The various biblical texts (including the NT) which speak of the ark show some ambiguity as to where exactly the manna was placed. This much is clear. The manna (Ex 16:33–34) and "Aaron's rod" (Nu 17:25) were put "before [the ark of] the testimony." Neither of these texts, however, says that the manna and Aaron's rod were put "in the ark" itself. Their most natural reading suggests that the manna and Aaron's rod were placed beside and in front of the ark (Ex 40:20). According to 1 Kings 8:9, in Solomon's day only the two tablets were in the ark. It appears, then, that in Solomon's day the manna and Aaron's rod were not placed "in the ark" but rather were placed "alongside the ark." This is consistent with what is said here in Exodus; that is, the manna was "before" the ark. When the writer of the book of Hebrews refers to this aspect of the tabernacle (Heb 9:4), however, he says that both the manna and Aaron's rod were found "in" the ark. It may be that in his day a different custom was followed, but since he appears to be referring to ancient custom, he was likely reading the same texts we have here. There may, then, have been a different interpretation of these texts in his day.[34]

The problem most likely arises from the sense of the prepositions "in" and "before." For example, according to Exodus 40:20 the tablets were put "in" the ark, but Deuteronomy 31:26 said that they were to be "beside" it. Thus, whether the stone tablets were stored "in" the ark or "beside" it is open to interpretation. On the one hand, 1 Kings 8:9 shows how these texts were interpreted in Solomon's day: the stone tablets were placed "in" the ark and all else was "beside" the ark. On the other hand, Hebrews 9:4 is evidence of an equally possible, though difficult, interpretation: the stone tablets, the manna, and Aaron's rod were all kept "in" the ark. Thus these various texts regarding the position of the manna, Aaron's rod, and the stone tablets appear more like different interpretations of the same passage than contradictory accounts. Unfortunately, there is not enough evidence to decide the case; fortunately, the sense of the passage is not dependent on its resolution.

What is manna? The English word *manna* is borrowed from the NT and the LXX, which rendered the Hebrew word *mān* as μάννα (or μαν), that is, "grain" or "granules." The Greek translators apparently associated "grain" with "bread," as can be seen in their identifying μάννα with ἄρτος in Psalm 77(MT 78):24. The Hebrew word used in this passage, however, does not mean "grain" or "bread." Rather, it is an interrogative particle and means "What?"[35] The Hebrew word *mān*, however, sounds like the Greek word μάννα, and that may have influenced its general use in translation. When the Israelites went out to gather their "food from heaven" (v. 4), they said, "What is it?" (v. 15). Henceforth they called it "the what?-food." Since the Hebrew word for "food" is the generic term "bread," it is customary to think of the manna as bread, or as bread-like food. The description of the manna in this passage, however, suggests that it was not simply a kind of bread. It was

---

[34]See Keil, *Pentateuch*, 2:74. No such tradition is known from early Jewish sources, however. See Hermann L. Strack and Paul Billerbeck, *Kommentar zum Neuen Testament aus Talmud und Midrasch* (Munich: C. H. Beck, 1969), 3:737.

[35]The interrogative *mān* ("manna") is found already in the Amarna Letters (14th century B.C.), where Abdu-Heba, prince of Jerusalem, asks the king of Egypt, *ma-an-na ip ša-ti a-na šarri beli-ia*, "What [ma-an-na] have I done to the king, my lord?" (EA 286:5; see J. A. Knudtzon, *Die El-Amarna-Tafeln* [Aalen: Otto Zeller, 1964], 1:859; Ludwig Koehler and Walter Baumgartner, *HALAT* [Leiden: Brill, 1974], fasc. 2, p. 564).

something more than mere bread, perhaps akin to what we might call pastries. Clearly, the Israelites had never seen or tasted anything like it before or since. They tried to describe its looks and taste by comparing it to "thin flakes like frost" (Ex 16:14) and by saying it was "white like coriander seed and tasted like wafers made with honey" (v. 31). (We should note further that manna is also described in Nu 11:7–9). After eating it for over a year, they developed ways to prepare and cook it. It was ground or crushed and either boiled in a pot or baked. It quickly rotted if left until morning (Ex 16:20), and "when the sun grew hot, it melted away" (v. 21), unless it was the Sabbath, in which case it was miraculously preserved (vv. 23–27). In Psalm 78:24 manna is called "the food of angels," in Nehemiah 9:20 it is associated with God's giving Israel his "good Spirit," and in 1 Corinthians 10:3 it is called "spiritual food." At one point the Israelites grew tired of their manna and complained that it was only "light food" (Nu 21:5; NIV "miserable food").

The quail which God provided receive little attention in this chapter or elsewhere in Scripture (cf. Nu 11:31). Even in later allusions to these chapters, little (Ps 105:40) or no mention (e.g., Ne 9; 1Co 10) is made of them. Israel was not commanded, for example, to preserve a quail in a jar in the ark for later generations, as they were the manna. The manna is clearly the center of the biblical writer's attention.

There have been numerous reports of migrating quail passing through the Sinai region from Africa. It is said that by the time the quail reach the desert they are so tired they can be captured by hand.[36] The miraculous feeding of the people during the forty years may then have followed a pattern already established by nature. There is no indication of this in the text, however.

This chapter contains a curious reference to the people's seeing the "glory of the LORD in the cloud" (v. 10). Since the manna is called the "glory of the LORD" in verse 7, it may be that the people saw the manna in the cloud. This is not likely, however, because the people saw the manna for the first time only the next morning (16:13–15). Another possibility is that the people saw the cloud that accompanied them through the wilderness (e.g., 13:21). Thus their seeing the cloud could simply be a reminder to them of the Lord's continual presence. On the face of it, however, the passage appears to recall a special and specific demonstration of God's glory "in the cloud" that served to underscore the importance of what the Lord was about to say to Moses. Some have suggested that the glory which the people saw in the cloud was a glorious appearance of Christ. Paul may have had this in mind when he wrote of Christ accompanying the Israelites in the wilderness when they were "under the cloud" (1Co 10:1–4).

With almost technical precision, the writer adds a note about the measurement of an *omer*. An omer was 3.64 liters, a little over 6 pints.

---

[36]See Keil, *Pentateuch*, 2:67.

C. Water and War in the Desert (17:1–16)

1. Water from the Rock (17:1–7)

Sometime before the third month (cf. 19:1), the Israelites left the Desert of Sin and traveled to Rephidim. According to Numbers 33:12–14, they also camped at Dophkah and Alush before reaching Rephidim. As with many of the camps of the Israelites en route to Sinai, the location of Rephidim is uncertain. That it is close to Mount Sinai is clear from the fact that the rock from which they obtain water is located "in Horeb" (3:1; 17:6), that is, Sinai. In any event, they found water to be in short supply here, and though they already had a daily supply of food in the manna and the quail, they began to complain of thirst.

The incident recorded in this passage is similar to the incident in Numbers 20:1–13, though there are marked differences as well. In both accounts, for example, the place is named Meribah (*merîbâ*) because of the wordplay on the notion of "rebellion" (*rîb*). Both incidents originated with the problem of a shortage of water and concluded with God's provision of water from a rock. In both narratives Moses got water from the rock by striking it. In the present passage, Moses followed the Lord's instructions, whereas in Numbers 20 his striking the rock may be seen as an evidence of his lack of faith. The chief difference between the two accounts is that in this passage *the people* were judged for an act of rebellion, whereas in Numbers 20 *Moses and Aaron* were judged. Furthermore, Moses and Aaron were judged not for their rebellion but for their lack of faith.

Nevertheless, the two accounts are too similar to ignore the fact that the writer wants them to be compared. Here at the beginning of their time in the wilderness and again at the close of that time, God is shown as the one who provided water from the rock for his rebellious people. Thus, by placing these two narratives about the rock both before the Sinai narrative and after it, the author shows that the rock which gave them the water of life accompanied God's people from the beginning until the end of their time in the wilderness. Wherever they camped in the desert, the rock was with them. Perhaps this is what Paul meant when he identified Christ with the "rock which followed" the people in the desert (1Co 10:4).

The narration pattern formed by the sequence of stories is represented as follows:

manna quail	40 years	water from rock	Time in the Wilderness of Sinai	manna quail	40 years	water from rock
Ex 16:4–34	Ex 16:35	Ex 17:1–7		Nu 11:4–34	Nu 14:21–22	Nu 20:1–12

A similar implication from the narrative shape can be seen in the Jacob narratives. Both at the beginning of Jacob's wanderings away from the land (Ge 28) and at the end (Ge 32), the author has placed a narrative that recounts Jacob's meeting God at Bethel. By showing God's presence with Jacob at the beginning and end of the Jacob narratives, the author suggests that God was with him throughout the intervening narratives. This sense of the narrative is confirmed in Jacob's own words in Genesis 48:15–16. Here,

Figure 1

manna quail	40 years	water from rock	Joshua next leader	Time in the Wilderness of Sinai	manna quail	40 years	water from rock	Eleazar next priest
Ex 16:4-34	Ex 16:35	Ex 17:1-7	Ex 17:8-13	11:4-34	Nu 11:4-34	Nu 14:21-22	Nu 20:1-12	Nu 20:23-29

Figure 2

manna quail	40 years	water from rock	Joshua next leader	battle with Amalek	Sinai	manna quail	40 years	water from rock	Eleazar next priest	battle with Canaanites
Ex 16:4-34	Ex 16:35	Ex 17:1-7	Ex 17:8-13	Ex 17:14-16		Nu 11:4-34	Nu 14:21-22	Nu 20:1-12	Nu 20:23-29	Nu 21:1-3-16

reflecting on the past narratives, Jacob alluded to God's presence and care for him throughout the years of his sojourn.

When the people raised the question, "Is the LORD among us or not?" they put God's promise to Moses in Exodus 3:12 to the test. God had promised, "I will be with you." As further confirmation of that promise, the Lord had said, "And this will be the sign to you that it is I who have sent you: When you have brought the people out of Egypt, you will worship God on this mountain" (3:12). Here then, "at Horeb," the people find that God had kept his promise to Moses and had come to the mountain "at Sinai." God's promise had been fulfilled, but they still questioned his presence.

2. Amalekites Defeated (17:8–16)

This narrative has the first mention of Joshua in the Pentateuch. Though in the remainder of the pentateuchal narratives he plays a relatively minor role, he was to be the next great leader in Israel. After the death of Moses (Dt 34:9), he would take Moses' place and lead God's people, with the help of Aaron's son Eleazar, who would take Aaron's place after he died (Nu 20:23–29). We can see then that the larger structure of the narratives in the Pentateuch continues to prepare the way for the events that lie in the future. Just as Joshua is introduced here after the first account of God's providing "water from the rock," so also Eleazar is introduced in Numbers 20 after the second account. Within the narrative strategy of the Pentateuch, God's chosen leaders, whether "king" (e.g., Dt 33:5) or priest, are thus closely associated with the "rock" which brings life to the people. (See Figure 1.)

The Amalekites were the descendants of Amalek, the grandson of Esau (Edom, Ge 36:16). Their home was in southern Canaan (Nu 13:29). According to Deuteronomy 25:17–18, they attacked Israel when they were "weary and worn out" and cut off their stragglers without mercy. For this attack they were known as the "first among the nations" to wage war against God's people (Nu 24:20); thus, according to God's promise in Genesis 12:3, their memory was to be blotted out from under heaven (cf. Nu 24:20; Dt 25:19). This promise was partially fulfilled during the time of Saul (1Sa 15) and Hezekiah (1Ch 4:43). But it was not until the death of Haman the Agagite (Est 7:10) and his descendants (Est 9:7–10) that the last of the Amalekites was destroyed.

The Exodus account gives no indications of the Amalekites' specific act of treachery. Rather, the narrative focuses on the means of their defeat. As long as Moses held up his hands, the battle favored the Israelites, led by Joshua. Even when Moses's arms were tired and had to be propped up by Aaron and Hur (17:12), the battle continued in Israel's favor. The significance of Moses's raised hands is given at the close of the chapter: "For hands were lifted up to the throne of the LORD" (v. 15). Hence the common interpretation of this picture of Moses is one of intercessory prayer. An early Aramaic translation of this passage says, "And the hands of Moses were raised in prayer, recalling the faith of the just fathers, Abraham, Isaac, and Jacob, and recalling the faith of the just mothers Sarah, Rebekah, Rachel, and Leah"[37]

The present narrative in Exodus 17 appears to have been shaped by its

---

[37]*Neophyti 1*, ed. Alejandro Díez Macho (Madrid: Consejo Superior de Investigaciones Científicas, 1970), 2:113.

relationship to the events recorded in Numbers 21:1–3, the destruction of Arad. The two narratives are conspicuously similar. Here in Exodus 17, the people murmured over lack of water and Moses gave them water from the rock (vv. 1–7). They were attacked by the Amalekites but went on to defeat them miraculously while Moses held up his hands (in prayer?). So also in the narrative in Numbers 21, after an account of Israel's murmuring and of getting water from the rock (20:1–13), Israel was attacked but miraculously went on to defeat the Canaanites because of Israel's vow, which the narrative gives in the form of a prayer (21:1–3).

The mention of the place-name Hormah at the conclusion of the account of the defeat of the Canaanites ("They completely destroyed them, so the place was named Hormah," Nu 20:3), provides a further literary link with the earlier account of Israel's defeat at the hand of the Amalekites and Canaanites ("They beat them down all the way to Hormah," Nu 14:45). Thus at the beginning of Israel's time in the wilderness, they were opposed by the Amalekites living in the land of Canaan (Ex 17), and also at the end of their time there they were opposed by the Canaanites (Nu 21). The parallels between the two narratives suggest an intentional identification of the Amalekites in the Exodus narratives and the Canaanites in Numbers 21:1–3. Thus the structure of the narrative appears to reflect Balaam's vision of the fate of the Amalekites: "Amalek was first among the nations, but he will come to ruin at last" (Nu 24:20). As is often the case in biblical narrative, the poetic sections (e.g., Nu 24:20) provide a thematic expression of the intent of the structure of the narratives. Amalek was the first nation to bring destruction upon Israel, but, as can be seen proleptically in the parallels inherent in the present narrative, in the end they too would be brought to destruction. (See Figure 2.)

D. Jethro, Moses' Father-in-law (18:1–27)

The father-in-law of Moses goes by a number of names in the Bible: Reuel (Ex 2:16–22), Jether (4:18), Jethro (3:1), and Hobab (Nu 10:29; Jdg 4:11). It is not uncommon in the Bible for the same person to have more than one name. Moses had lived with his father-in-law as a shepherd (Ex 3:1). In Exodus 3 he was called by God to return to Egypt. Although Exodus 4:19–20 made it appear that Moses took his wife and two sons with him when he returned to Egypt, we learn from this passage that Moses had returned them to his father-in-law before going back to Egypt. Perhaps the purpose of the mysterious narrative in 4:24–26 is to give some motivation for the return of Moses' wife and family to his father-in-law (cf. the comments above on Ex 4:24–26).

The present narrative has many parallels with the accounts in Genesis 14 and 15. Just as Melchizedek the priest of Salem (šālēm) met Abraham bearing gifts as he returned from the battle with Amraphel (Ge 14:18–20), so Jethro the Midianite priest came out with Moses' wife and sons to offer peace (šālôm, 18:7; NIV "they greeted each other") as he returned from the battle with the Amalekites. In Genesis 15:2 the "son of Abraham's house" was Eliezer, whose name epitomized God's help for Abraham, just as in the present narrative the "son of Moses" was Eliezer, whose name means "God is my help" (Ex 18:4). Melchizedek praised God for his rescue of Abraham from his enemies: "Blessed be Abram by God Most High . . . who delivered your enemies into your hand" (Ge 14:19), just as Jethro praised God: "Blessed be the LORD, who rescued you from the hand of the Egyptians. . . . The LORD is greater than all other gods" (Ex 18:10). Melchizedek brought out bread and wine as a priest of God Most High, and Abraham tithed to him (Ge 14:18–20); Jethro brought out a burnt offering and other sacrifices and ate bread with Moses and Aaron. The Lord showed Abraham in a vision that his seed would be "a sojourner [gēr] in another's land" (Ge 15:13), and Moses' other son is named Gershom because he said, "I have become a sojourner [gēr] in a foreign land" (Ex 18:3). The purpose of these parallels appears to be to cast Jethro as another Melchizedek, the paradigm of the righteous Gentile. It is important that Jethro have such credentials because he plays a major role in this chapter, instructing Moses, the lawgiver himself, how to carry out the administration of God's Law to Israel. Thus, just as Abraham was met by Melchizedek the priest (Ge 14) before God made a covenant with him in Genesis 15, so Moses is met by Jethro the priest (Ex 18) before God makes a covenant with him at Sinai (Ex 19).

The account of Moses' sending his father-in-law back to his own country should not be taken to mean that he did this immediately. In Numbers 10:29 (cf. Jdg 4:11), for example, it appears that his father-in-law was still with Israel when they left Sinai. Some have suggested that the whole of Exodus 18 recounts events that occurred after the time at Sinai,[38] and thus the mention of his father-in-law's departure is not included here chronologically. This would explain the present passage as well as why the Israelites already had "statutes and laws" before the giving of the Law at Sinai (Ex 18:16). It is not necessary, however, to say that the whole of Exodus 18 is out of place. It is only necessary to say that the last verse (27) recounts a period after the time of Numbers 10:29. As far as the mention of other "laws" is concerned, the Lord had already given them "commandments and statutes" at Marah (Ex 15:25–26); hence the mention of the "statutes and laws" is not inappropriate here.

VI. THE COVENANT AT SINAI (19:1–24:18)

A. God Meets with Moses (19:1–25)

1. Arrival and Encampment at Sinai (19:1–2)

The writer takes care to note that the covenant at Sinai was established on the fiftieth day since the Exodus from Egypt. The Israelites arrived at the Wilderness of Sinai "on the very day," that is, the third day of the third month, Sivan (May/June). This would have been the forty-eighth day after Israel left Egypt. They camped in the wilderness (19:2a) on the night of the forty-eighth day. The next day, the forty-ninth day, they arrived and camped[39] at the mountain (v. 2b). The next morning,[40] Moses went up to the mountain and received the covenant, on the fiftieth day, Pentecost (see (Ex 34:22; Dt 16:9–11). They remained here for nearly one year, leaving on the

---

[38]See Rashi, ad loc.

[39]The repetition of the clause "they camped" in the Hebrew text implies that they set up a new camp.

[40]See Rashi, ad loc.

twentieth day of the second month, Iyar (April/May), in the second year (Nu 10:11).

2. The Covenant Announced (19:3–15)

On Mount Sinai, God made a covenant with Israel. The covenant called for obedience (19:5a), and its purpose was to set Israel apart as a special people, a kingdom of priests and a holy nation (vv. 5b–6). In the following chapters (Ex 20–23), the stipulations of the covenant are spelled out in great detail. Much more is added in the subsequent books of Leviticus, Numbers, and Deuteronomy. This covenant was intended as a fulfillment of the promises to Abraham, Isaac, and Jacob (2:24), but later in Exodus (chap. 32) it became clear that Israel could not obey this covenant, even while they were at Mount Sinai. Thus Israel broke this covenant (Dt 31:29–32:6; Jdg 2:10–13), and any hope for the future would have to rest in the establishment of a new covenant (Dt 30; Jer 31:31–34; Eze 36).

Moses was the mediator of this covenant at Mount Sinai. God spoke to him on the mountain and he carried these words back to Israel. When Israel agreed to enter the covenant, he carried their response back to God (Dt 5:5). It is important to note that Israel's acceptance of the covenant is called a mark of their faith (NIV "trust") in God and Moses (Ex 19:9).

3. The Lord Came Down to Sinai (19:16–25)

The cloud that had led the people through the wilderness now appeared to rest on Mount Sinai. It was dark with smoke and foreboding, filled with fire, and accompanied by loud bursts of thunder. Mysteriously, amid the tumult, the blasts of trumpets could also be heard, growing louder every moment (v. 16). The mountain where God had come was an inferno. This display of God's power was not lost on any of the people. There was great fear among them. As Moses explained it, "God has come to test you, so that the fear of God will be with you to keep you from sinning." (20:20). Later he again warned the people, "Be careful not to forget the covenant. . . . For the LORD your God is a consuming fire, a jealous God" (Dt 4:23–24). For the identity of the "priests" in this passage, see the comments above on Exodus 13:1–2.

The description of the setting of the giving of the Ten Commandments in 19:25 is somewhat vague. There are at least two ways to view it. It appears on the one hand that God first spoke the Ten Commandments to Moses (v. 19), and then Moses gave these commandments to the people (v. 25). The people were afraid to go near to hear God speak, so they asked Moses to go for them (20:19). However, 19:25 could also be understood as saying that the Lord first spoke the Ten Commandments to both Moses *and all the people* from the mountain rather than to Moses alone. After hearing God speak, the people requested that God speak only to Moses and that Moses then speak to them (20:18–19). This scenario is suggested by Deuteronomy 4:10–13 ("Remember the day you stood before the LORD your God at Horeb. . . . You came near and stood at the foot of the mountain while it blazed with fire. . . . Then the LORD spoke to you out of the fire. . . . He declared to you his covenant, the ten commandments") and 10:4 ("The ten commandments he [the LORD] had proclaimed to you on the mountain, out of the fire, on the day of the assembly"). The preface to the Ten Commandments in Deuteronomy

5:4–5 clarifies the issue further. Moses said, "The LORD spoke to you face to face out of the fire on the mountain. At that time I stood between the LORD and you to declare to you the word of the LORD, because you were afraid of the fire. . . . And he said. . . ."

B. The Decalogue (20:1–17)

At this point in the narrative, the Bible refers to God's commands simply by the expression "these words." Later they are called the "ten words" (Ex 34:28; Dt 4:13; 10:4). According to Deuteronomy 4:13 these words are called "the covenant which he commanded" Israel. The "ten words," then, are the expression of God's will for his covenant people. The words were etched on both sides of two small stone documents (Ex 24:12). The documents, or tablets, were small enough for Moses to carry "in his hand" (32:15; or "hands," Dt 9:15, 17). It is not clear whether all "ten words" were written on each tablet—as some treaty documents in the ancient world required two copies—or whether some of the words were written on one tablet and some on the other. It is often maintained that the first group of commandments, dealing with humanity's relationship to God (commandments 1–4), were written on the first tablet, and the second group, dealing strictly with human relationships (commandments 5–10), were written on the second tablet. The text offers no clear hint of such a division.

Of particular interest is the question of the division of the "words" into ten commandments. Some have traditionally divided Exodus 20:3–6 into two commandments.[41] The first, verses 2–3, is taken as a call for absolute monotheism: "You shall have no other gods before me." The second, verses 4–6, is a command against idolatry: "You shall not make for yourself an idol." To arrive at a total number of ten commands, then, the last command must consist of the whole of verse 17: "You shall not covet your neighbor's house. . . ." This is the view represented in the NIV translation. Others, however, have read the whole of verse 2–6 as merely one command, a prohibition of idolatry, and count it as the first commandment.[42] In other words, the expression "other gods" is taken to mean "idols," a sense the same terminology has elsewhere in Scripture. To arrive at a total number of ten commands in this case, verse 17 is read as two commandments, the ninth—"You shall not covet your neighbor's house"—and the tenth—"You shall not covet your neighbor's wife, or his manservant. . . ." Finally, Jewish tradition reads verse 2: "I am the LORD your God, who brought you out of Egypt, out of the land of slavery," as the first commandment and understands it as a call for strict monotheism. Consequently, verses 3–6 are taken as the second commandment and are understood as a prohibition against idolatry.

One must admit that no clear line of distinction can be drawn between the statements in verses 2–6, potentially the first two commands, and those in verse 17, potentially the last two commands. What is certain, however, is that the author understands the total number to be ten. The reason for certainty here is that the "words" written on the stone tablets are later called the "ten words" (34:28).

---

[41]Greek and Reformed view; Josephus, Philo, Origen. See Keil, *Pentateuch*, 2:109.
[42]Augustine, Luther, MT. See Keil, *Pentateuch*, 2:109.

The question of where the first two commandments are to be divided has an interesting implication. Later in Exodus, in the chapter dealing with the making of the golden calf (Ex 32), the narrative sets out to show that immediately after the commands were given, Israel broke them. The making of the golden calf is presented by the writer as a direct violation of the first commandment. But what is the "first" commandment? Does the golden calf represent "another god," so that the first commandment is a call for monotheism? Or does it represent the making of an image of the Lord, and thus imply that the first commandment is a prohibition of idolatry?

According to the NIV in the narrative of Exodus 32, when the people set up the calf, they said, "These are your gods, O Israel, who brought you up out of Egypt" (vv. 4, 8). The translation "your gods" implies that the sin of the golden calf is understood to be polytheism, the worship of gods other than the Lord. The problem with translating this passage is that the Hebrew word translated as "gods" (אֱלֹהִים) can be rendered either "gods" (plural) or "god" (singular). Furthermore, the same word is rendered elsewhere in Scripture simply as "God." In each case the context must determine whether the plural "gods" or the singular "god/God" is intended. If in this passage the word is rendered in the singular, then the sin of the golden calf is intended to be understood as idolatry. In our judgment this appears to be the sense of the passage.

Two important considerations from the context of chapter 32 suggest that the singular "god" or "God" is intended. First, the calf is specifically called in the text an "idol cast in the shape of a calf" (vv. 4, 8). Thus the writer understands the golden calf not so much as another god (polytheism) as an idol of the one God (idolatry). Second, it is clear in the text that when Aaron built an altar before the calf, he said, "Tomorrow there will be a festival to the LORD" (v. 5). Moreover, the next day, the day that Aaron had called for a "festival to the LORD," the people celebrated before the calf. It appears, then, that the sin of the golden calf was one of idolatry, not polytheism. They were worshiping God by means of an idol; they were not worshiping other gods as such. This is the way Nehemiah 9:18 has rendered this text: "This is your god, who brought you up out of Egypt." Nehemiah's wording in Hebrew is clearly intended to be read as singular, "god."

The narrative of Exodus 32 and its interpretation in Nehemiah 9, then, suggest that the first commandment is the prohibition of idolatry.[43] Thus, to maintain a final count of ten commandments, Exodus 20:17a, coveting the house of one's neighbor, must be understood as the ninth commandment, and the tenth is 20:17b, coveting in general. In taking the division of the commandments this way, the Exodus passage harmonizes well with the repetition of the ten commandments in Deuteronomy 5, where the question of coveting is clearly taken as two commandments.[44] (See further the comments on Ex 20:17a below.)

---

[43]Also Ex 20:23, the prohibition of worshiping God by means of idols, shows the centrality of the problem of idolatry.

[44]Note the addition of the *waw* between each of the last five commandments and the change in vocabulary ("covet," "desire") in Dt 5:21.

1. Prologue (20:1-2)

The basis of the call to obedience in the covenant was God's act of salvation in the Exodus from Egypt. Thus the Lord identifies himself first not merely as the only God but also as the God who delivered Israel from bondage.

2. First Commandment (20:3-6): You shall have no other gods

In the rest of Scripture, the expression "other gods" refers to the wooden and stone idols of the nations around Israel. It does not refer to actual divine beings, that is, "gods" as such (Dt 28:36). The expression is common in Deuteronomy. The reference to such "gods" does not then assume the actual existence of divine beings, or gods, alongside the one and only God of Israel. It merely acknowledges that the other nations worship wooden and stone idols as their gods.

This commandment teaches that God is a jealous God; that is, he will not tolerate anything short of wholehearted worship. He is a personal God and will not be satisfied with anything less than a personal relationship with men and women whom he created in his image. To worship an image of God (idol) rather than God himself violates God's purpose for the creation of man and woman in his image (Ge 1:26). Thus God's will as expressed in these commandments is consistent with his purposes in Creation.

The extended commentary on this commandment (Ex 20:5-6) acknowledges that parents often pass on to their children the misdirected and ill-advised patterns of life they learned from their own parents. Wrong notions about God and worship can be maintained for many generations and can result in generations of hardships. On the positive side, however, the commentary to this commandment recognizes that, in God's grace, the love and obedience of a single generation can change the course of a family for thousands of future generations.

In the OT historical books we can see this pattern play itself out. In Judges 2:10, for example, we are told that a whole generation was lost because of the spiritual neglect of their parents: "another generation grew up, who knew neither the LORD nor what he had done for Israel. Then the Israelites did evil in the eyes of the LORD. . . . They forsook the LORD, the God of their fathers, who had brought them out of Egypt. They followed and worshiped *other gods.*" For this act of neglect and rebellion the children were punished (Jdg 2:12-15). It is part of the purpose of the OT historical books to show that this act of rebellion was passed from one generation to another until ultimately the nation was sent into exile (2Ki 25). Toward the end of the narrative, the biblical writer explains: "All this took place because the Israelites had sinned against the LORD their God, who had brought them up out of Egypt. . . . They worshiped *other gods.* . . . they would not listen and were *as stiff-necked as their fathers.* . . . So the LORD was very angry with Israel and removed them from his presence" (2Ki 17:7-18).

At this same time in Israel's history, the period of the Exile, the prophet Ezekiel addressed this very question raised by the first commandment (Eze 18). Some in Ezekiel's day apparently felt that this commandment could be interpreted to mean that the accumulated sins of the parents were to be taken out on the innocent children. They had possibly appealed to the wording of the first commandment to support their view. According to Ezekiel a proverb had been coined in Israel: "The fathers eat sour grapes, and the children's teeth are set on edge." Ezekiel argued over against such a proverb that "the soul who sins is the one who will die" (Eze 18:1–4). Ezekiel then raised the question of a righteous father and a wicked son, and a wicked father and a righteous son, and concluded that the reward or punishment of the son was not dependent on the deeds of the fathers: "The righteousness of the righteous one will be credited to him, and the wickedness of the wicked will be charged against him" (Eze 18:20).

3. Second Commandment (20:7): Do not misuse the name of the Lord your God

God had revealed to Israel his name (Yahweh) and had given to them the corresponding privilege of calling on that name in worship and in time of need. Along with this privilege came the responsibility of honor and respect. Israel was not to call on God's name "for no good purpose," that is, they were not to presume upon their relationship with God and think that he was merely at their beck and call. The whole of the instructions regarding the nature of Israel's worship and the building of the tabernacle (Ex 25–31) was intended to teach Israel the proper way to call on God's name.

4. Third Commandment (20:8–11): Remember the Sabbath day

Under the covenant at Sinai, Israel was to set apart each seventh day of the week and to keep it holy. In so doing they were following God's own pattern in Creation (Ge 2:2–4). The purpose of the Sabbath day was to give rest from one's labor (Ex 23:12; Dt 5:14) and to provide an occasion for an assembly of the nation in a "holy convocation" (Lev 23:3).

5. Fourth Commandment (20:12): Honor your father and mother

An important part of this commandment is the promise "that you may live long in the land." The commandment is not addressed to small children; it does not primarily admonish them to obey their parents, though it no doubt includes that. The commandment is spoken to adults who are not dependent on their father and mother, but whose father and mother may even be dependent on them. You are to treat your parents with respect not only as long as *they* live, but also as long as *you* live in the land the Lord God is giving you. Long after parents have departed, they are still to be treated with respect by honoring and obeying their instruction. This is the basis of God's showing love to the thousands of generations of those "who love me and keep my commandments" (20:6).

6. Fifth Commandment (20:13): You shall not murder

The basis of this commandment prohibiting murder and manslaughter was laid down at Creation. Human beings were created in God's image; thus "Whoever sheds the blood of man, by man shall his blood be shed; for in the image of God has God made man" (Ge 9:6). That this commandment does not preclude capital punishment is clear from the fact that the OT law calls for the death penalty on numerous occasions (e.g., Ex 21:12, "Anyone who strikes a man and kills him shall surely be put to death"; cf. Ge 9:5).

7. Sixth Commandment (20:14): You shall not commit adultery

Sexual intercourse outside marriage is prohibited. The commandment is based on God's purpose for marriage: "For this reason a man will leave his father and mother and be united to his wife, and they will become one flesh" (Ge 2:24). David, a man exemplary in most respects, nevertheless violated this commandment, and it marked the beginning of the end of his role as leader of God's people (2Sa 11; 24).

8. Seventh Commandment (20:15): You shall not steal

The word *steal* in Hebrew conveys the sense of an act of taking what does not belong to one. It also includes the sense of deception. Thus, while robbery is prohibited in this commandment, the focus is on thievery.

9. Eighth Commandment (20:16): You shall not give false testimony

Honesty and accuracy in the administration of justice and in everyday affairs is assumed here to be essential.

10. Ninth Commandment (20:17a): You shall not covet your neighbor's house

Deuteronomy 5:21 renders this commandment, "You shall not covet your neighbor's wife" rather than "your neighbor's house." In other words, it exchanges one of the elements of the last part of the verse ("neighbor's wife") with the more general category of a "neighbor's house." The Deuteronomy passage also uses a different word for "covet" in the last command, that is, the word "desire." These changes suggest that the two parts of Exodus 20:17 are understood in Deuteronomy as two separate statements that distinguish one's "coveting a neighbor's spouse" from "coveting" a neighbor's property. Moreover, that the author intends these two statements to be read as distinct already in Exodus 20:17 is suggested by the repetition of the verb "covet." If we allow Deuteronomy's interpretation to govern our understanding of the Exodus text, then the expression "coveting a neighbor's house," prohibited in the ninth commandment, is taken euphemistically in the sense of coveting a neighbor's spouse. The "coveting" prohibited in the tenth commandment, then, must be taken in a more general sense of desire for more property. It follows that in Deuteronomy a different word is used to show just this distinction.

11. Tenth Commandment (20:17b): You shall not covet your neighbor's wife, or his manservant or maidservant

If we follow the interpretation of this commandment given in Deuteronomy, this is the last commandment and is a general prohibition of every kind of coveting. It is distinct from the previous command in so far as the previous commandment focuses only on lustful covetousness, whereas the present commandment includes such covetousness along with all other types.

Command #1, Ex 20:1, One must believe that God is: "I am the Lord your God." (Dt 5:6)

Command #155, Ex 20:8, Sanctify the Sabbath: "Remember the day of Sabbath to sanctify it."

Command #210, Ex 20:12, You must honor you parents: "Honor your father and your mother."

Prohibition #1, Ex 20:3, One must not believe in the existence of another god: "You shall have no other gods before me."

Prohibition #2, Ex 20:4, One must not make images to worship: "You shall not make for yourself an idol."

Prohibition #5, Ex 20:5, One must not bow down to idols: "You shall not bow down to them."

Prohibition #6, Ex 20:5, One must not worship idols: "You shall not bow down to them."

Prohibition #62, Ex 20:7, One must not take God's name in vain: "You shall not misuse the name of the Lord your God."

Prohibition #320, Ex 20:10, One must not work on the Sabbath: "You shall not do any work."

Prohibition #243, Ex 20:13, Stealing (M. kidnapping) is prohibited: "You shall not steal [M. kidnap]."

Prohibition #289, Ex 20:13, One must not murder another: "You shall not murder."

Prohibition #347, Ex 20:14; Dt 5:18, "You shall not commit adultery"; Lev 18:20 One must not have a sexual relationship with the wife of another: "Do not have sexual relations with your neighbor's wife."

Prohibition #285, Ex 20:16, One must not give false testimony: "You shall not give false testimony against your neighbor."

Prohibition #265, Ex 20:17, One must not covet another's possessions: "You shall not covet your neighbor's house."

C. Worship and Idolatry (20:18–26)

1. The People Fear (20:18–21)

The statement of the "ten words" (Ex 20:1–17) and the collection of "judgments" (21:1–23:13) are joined with a short narrative link (20:18–26). Here the report of the fear of the people is repeated, as well as the reason for the display of divine power at Sinai (a much fuller account is given in Dt 5:22–33). In the narrative the people were afraid to approach God at the mountain, so they made Moses the mediator of the covenant. Moses then explained that the proper response to a recognition of God's power is not a fear that causes them to flee from his presence but one which causes them to submit to him in godly living. He told the people: "God has come to test you, so that the fear of God will be with you to keep you from sinning." Moses expressed the same idea in Deuteronomy 8:16 when he explained that God's dealings with Israel in the wilderness were intended to humble and test them "so that in the end it might go well" with them.

2. Prohibition of Idolatry (20:22–23)

This segment of the narrative (vv. 22–26) summarizes virtually the whole nature of the religion of the covenant. It begins with the warning against idolatry. Moses is instructed to remind the Israelites that God had spoken to them directly and thus warned them not to stray from God through the worship of idols.

Prohibition #4, Ex 20:23, One must not make forms of living creatures from wood or stone: "Do not make gods of silver or gold."

3. Proper Forms of Worship (20:24–26)

This simple description of true worship is intended to portray the essence of the Sinai covenant in terms that are virtually identical to that of the religion of the patriarchs—earthen altars, burnt offerings, and simple devotion rather than elaborate rituals. A simple earthen altar is sufficient. If more is desired (e.g., a stone altar), then it should not be defiled with carved stones and elaborate steps. The ultimate purpose of any such ritual is the covering of human nakedness that stems from the Fall (Ex 20:26b; cf. Ge 3:7). The implication is that all ritual is only a reflection of that first gracious act of God in covering human nakedness with garments of skin (Ge 3:21). Later the provision was made for the priests to wear linen undergarments "to cover their naked flesh" when they approach the altar (Ex 28:42).

It is notable that this picture of the nature of the true religion of the covenant should precede the countless details yet to be given for the construction of the tabernacle. The detailed and ornate description of the tabernacle seems a far cry from the simple worship envisioned here. These verses, however, play an important role in the lesson of the immediate narrative and ultimately that of the Pentateuch as a whole. They serve to focus our attention on the essential nature of the worship intended in the covenant. Thus the similarity between the nature of the worship described here and that of the patriarchs earlier in the Genesis narratives plays an important role in the narrative. Israel's worship in the Sinai covenant was to be the same as that of the patriarchs, Abraham, Isaac, and Jacob. In fact, this sort of worship is comparable to the fathers' worship of God since the time of Adam (Ge 4:26). God will certainly be honored with all the gold and silver of the tabernacle that is to be built, but his honor is not to be at the expense of the simple call to obedience exemplified in the lives of the patriarchs.

Themes similar to those stressed in this introduction to the judgments (Ex 21:1–23:12)—the prohibition of idolatry and the nature of proper worship of God—are repeated again at the close of the section (Ex 23:10–13). These sections thus provide a prologue and epilogue to the list of forty-two judgments (cf. 34:11–26).

Prohibition of Idolatry (20:22–23) Proper Forms of Worship (20:24–26)
42 (7 × 6) Judgments (21:1–23:12)
Prohibition of Idolatry (23:13) Proper Forms of Worship (23:14–19)

Prohibition #79, Ex 20:25, One must not make an altar of hewn stone: "Do not build it with hewn stones."

Prohibition #80, Ex 20:26, One must not make an altar with steps: "And do not go up to my altar on steps."

D. Judgments (21:1–23:12)

A selection of "judgments" is provided as a sample of the divine judgments which Moses gave the people. A total of forty-two "judgments" is given. The number forty-two apparently stems from the fact that the Hebrew letters in the first word of the section, "and these" (ואלה), add up precisely to the number forty-two (7 × 6).[45] This suggests that the laws in 21:1–23:12 are to be understood merely as a representative selection of the whole Mosaic Law. It is not an attempt at a complete listing of all the laws. The purpose of the selection was to provide a basis for teaching the nature of divine justice. By studying specific cases of the application of God's will in concrete situations, the reader of the Pentateuch could learn the basic principles undergirding the covenant relationship. Whereas the "ten words" provided a general statement of the basic principles of justice which God demanded of his people, the examples selected here further demonstrated how those principles, or ideals, were to be applied to real life situations.

The following is a list of the laws included in this section:
1. Rights of Hebrew servants (21:2–6)[46]
2. Rights of daughters (21:7–11)
3. Murder and manslaughter (21:12–13)
4. Deliberate murder (21:14)
5. Killing of parents (21:15)
6. Kidnapping (21:16)
7. Cursing parents (21:17)
8. Aggravated assault (21:18–19)
9. Assault on servants (21:20–21)
10. Assault on unborn (21:22–23)
    Principle of *lex talionis* stated (21:24–25)
11. Lex Talionis applied to servant's eye (21:24–25)
12. Lex Talionis applied to servant's teeth (21:27)
13. Bull goring a person (21:28–32)
14. Injury from unguarded pit (21:33–34)
15. Bull goring another bull (21:35–36)
16. Stealing cattle and sheep (22:1–4 [MT 21:37–22:3])
17. Damage in grazing cattle (22:5 [MT 4])
18. Damage caused by burning fields (22:6 [MT 5])
19. Loss of money or articles put in safekeeping (22:7–9 [MT 6–8])
20. Loss of livestock put in safekeeping (22:10–13 [MT 9–12])
21. Loss of borrowed property (22:14–15 [MT 13–14])
22. Extramarital pregnancy (22:16–17 [MT 15–16])
23. Prohibition of sorcery (22:18 [MT 17])
24. Prohibition of sexual relations with animals (22:19 [MT 18])
25. Prohibition of sacrifices to other gods (22:20 [MT 19])
26. Prohibition of oppressing the alien (22:21 [MT 20])

---

[45]There may also be a desire to have seven laws for each of the six days of work (cf. Ex 20:11).

[46]Note the relationship of the purchase of the Hebrew servant here and the prohibition of making one's "brother" a servant in Lev 25:39. Was the servant to go free in seven years? Or in the Year of Jubilee? Does "forever" in Ex 21:6 preclude the Year of Jubilee in Lev 25:39? Cf. the commentary below on Dt 15:12-18.

27. Prohibition of afflicting the widow or orphan (22:22–24 [MT 21–23])
28. Regulations on lending money (22:25–27 [MT 24–26])
29. Prohibition of blaspheming God and the ruler (22:28 [MT 27])
30. Giving to the Lord (22:29–30 [MT 28–29])
31. Prohibition of eating meat slain by an animal (22:31 [MT 30])
32. Prohibition of false witness (23:1)
33. Prohibition of siding with the crowd (23:2–3)
34. Returning an enemy's stray livestock (23:4)
35. Helping an enemy's burdened livestock (23:5)
36. Equal justice for the poor (23:6)
37. Warning against false justice (23:7a)
38. Warning against careless justice (23:7b)
39. Prohibition of bribery (23:8)
40. Prohibition against oppression of the alien (23:9)
41. Sabbatical year (23:10–11)
42. Weekly sabbath (23:12)

Commands:

Command #232, Ex 21:2, Treatment of Hebrew servants: "If you buy a Hebrew servant."

Command #233, Ex 21:8, The master must marry his female Hebrew servant: "Her master who designated her for himself."

Command #234, Ex 21:8, The master must redeem his female Hebrew servants: "He must let her be redeemed."

Command #227, Ex 21:16, Capital punishment: "He must be put to death."

Command #236, Ex 21:18, Injury caused by a person: "If men quarrel and one hits the other."

Command #226, Ex 21:20, Capital punishment: "He must be avenged."

Command #237, Ex 21:28, Injury caused by an animal: "If a bull gores a man or a woman to death."

Command #238, Ex 21:33–34, Injury caused by a pit: "If a man uncovers a pit or digs one and fails to cover it."

Command #239, Ex 21:37–22:3 (EVV 22:1–4), Punishment of robbers: "If a man steals an ox or a sheep."

Command #240, Ex 22:4 (EVV 5), Punishment for trespassing: "If a man grazes his livestock in a field or vineyard and lets them stray."

Command #241, Ex 22:5 (EVV 6), Punishment for arson: "If a fire breaks out."

Command #242, Ex 22:6–8 (EVV 7–8), Punishment for guardian (unpaid) who steals: "If a man gives his neighbor silver or goods for safekeeping."

Command #246, Ex 22:8 (EVV 9), Judgments involving all matters of property: "In all cases of illegal possession."

Command #243, Ex 22:9–12 (EVV 10–13), Punishment for guardian (paid) who steals: "If a man gives a donkey, an ox, a sheep."

Command #244, Ex 22:13 (EVV 14), Punishment for loss of borrowed property: "If a man borrows an animal. . . ."

Command #220, Ex 22:15–23, (EVV 16–24), A seducer must be punished: "If a man seduces a virgin."

Command #197, Ex 22:24 (EVV 25), Lend to the poor without interest: "If you lend money to one of my people among you who is needy. . . ."

Command #80, Ex 22:28 (evv 29), Redemption of firstborn sons: "The firstborn of your sons belongs to me."

Command #175, Ex 23:2, Do not pervert justice by following the many: "Do not pervert justice by siding with the crowd." (M. In judgments follow the many: "Incline after the many.")

Command #202, Ex 23:5, You must help an overburdened donkey: "If you see the donkey of someone who hates you fallen down under its load."

Command #134, Ex 23:11, In the seventh year the land belongs to all: "During the seventh year let the land lie unplowed and unused."

Command #154, Ex 23:12, Rest on the Sabbath: "On the seventh day you shall rest."

Prohibitions:

Prohibition #261, Ex 21:8, One must not sell his Hebrew maidservant: "He must let her be redeemed. He has no right to sell her to foreigners."

Prohibition #262, Ex 21:10, If one marries his Hebrew maidservant, he must not deprive her of food, clothing, or marital rights: "He must not deprive the first one of her food, clothing, and marital rights."

Prohibition #319, Ex 21:15, One must not strike one's parents: "Anyone who strikes his father or mother must be put to death."

Prohibition #318, Ex 21:17 (evv 18), One must not curse one's parents: "Anyone who curses his father or mother must be put to death."

Prohibition #188, Ex 21:28, One must not eat an ox that has been stoned: "And its meat must not be eaten."

Prohibition #310, Ex 22:17, One must not allow a sorceress to live: "Do not allow a sorceress to live."

Prohibition #252, Ex 22:20 (evv 21), One must not take advantage of a foreigner (with words): "Do not mistreat an alien."

Prohibition #253, Ex 22:20 (evv 21), One must not oppress a foreigner (M. in trade): "Do not oppress him."

Prohibition #256, Ex 22:21 (evv 22), One must not oppress the widow and orphan: "Do not take advantage of a widow or an orphan."

Prohibition #234, Ex 22:24 (evv 25), One must not charge credit to the needy: "If you lend money to one of my people among you who is in need, do not be like a moneylender."

Prohibition #237, Ex 22:24 (evv 25), One must not participate in agreements with the needy involving interest: "charge him not interest."

Prohibition #60, Ex 22:27 (evv 28), One must not blaspheme God's name: "Do not blaspheme God."

Prohibition #315, Ex 22:27 (evv 28), One must not curse God (M. a judge): "Do not blaspheme God."

Prohibition #316, Ex 22:27 (evv 28), One must not curse a ruler: "Do not curse the ruler of your people."

Prohibition #154, Ex 22:28 (evv 29), One must not change the order of separating the tithes: "Do not hold back offerings from your granaries or your vats."

Prohibition #181, Ex 22:30 (evv 31), One must not eat an animal that was killed by a predator: "Do not eat the meat of an animal torn by wild beasts."

Prohibition #281, Ex 23:1, One should not spread false reports (M. It is forbidden to hear one litigant without the other being present): "Do not spread false reports."

Prohibition #286, Ex 23:1, One must not give false testimony for the guilty: "Do not help a wicked man by being a malicious witness."

Prohibition #282, Ex 23:2, A judge should not be persuaded by the crowd: "Do not follow the crowd in doing wrong."

Prohibition #283, Ex 23:2, A judge should not pervert justice by siding with the crowd: "Do not pervert justice by siding with the crowd."

Prohibition #277, Ex 23:3, A judge must not favor the poor: "Do not show favoritism to a poor man in his lawsuit."

Prohibition #270, Ex 23:5, One should not refuse to help a man or animal who has collapsed under a heavy burden: "Do not leave it there; be sure you help him with it."

Prohibition #278, Ex 23:6, A judge should not discriminate against the poor: "Do not deny justice to your poor people in their lawsuits."

Prohibition #290, Ex 23:7, One must not punish an innocent or honest person (M. convict on the basis of circumstantial evidence alone): "Do not put to death an innocent or honest person."

Prohibition #274, Ex 23:8, A judge must not accept a bribe in a decision: "Do not accept a bribe."

E. Idolatry and Worship (23:13–19)

1. Prohibition of Idolatry (23:13)

The end of this section takes up again the first commandment, that is, the warning against idolatry, which was also sounded at the beginning of this section (20:22–23). The continual return to the theme of idolatry throughout this section of the book is preparation and background for an appreciation of the incident of the golden calf (Ex 32). When Israel made the golden calf and set it up as an object of worship, they broke the first commandment and graphically demonstrated their inability to keep the covenant.

Prohibition #14, Ex 23:13, One must not swear by idols: "Do not invoke the names of other gods."

Prohibition #15, Ex 23:13, One must not seek to persuade another to follow idols: "Let it not be heard from your mouth."

2. Proper Forms of Worship: Feasts (23:14–19)

The ceremonial year was divided into three feasts. The Feast of Unleavened Bread has been described in Exodus 12:14–20; 13:3–9. The Feasts of Harvest (23:16a) and Ingathering (23:16b) are mentioned here for the first time (see Lev 23:5–44; Nu 28:26; Dt 16:9–12). At these three times of the year all the men of the community were to appear before the Lord (Ex 23:17).

A central regulation is given for each of the three feasts. (1) For the Feast of Unleavened Bread there is to be no leaven in the sacrificial blood, and none of the Passover lamb (cf. 34:25) is to be left over for this feast (23:18); this was important because the Passover Feast was held on the previous day (12:8). (2) For the Feast of Harvest, the "best" of the firstfruits are to be brought to the Lord's house. (3) For the Feast of Ingathering, only weaned animals are to be brought as offerings (cf. 22:29; Lev 22:27); a young goat "in its mother's milk" is one that still suckles from its mother (Ex 34:18–26).

Thus the expression "Do not boil a kid in its mother's milk" is intended to state the principle that only weaned animals are to be used as offerings. As such it is similar in function to the maxim "Is Saul also among the prophets?" which is found later in Scripture. In the case of the maxim about Saul, we have the actual situation out of which the maxim was formed. Saul, an unlikely candidate for the prophetic gift, began to prophesy as a sign of his being chosen as king over Israel (1Sa 10:11–12). Henceforth, any surprising act of God could be referred to by the saying, "Is Saul also among the prophets?" (1Sa 19:24). This would be like saying, "This is another miracle."

The origin of the expression "Do not boil a kid in its mother's milk" is not as clear as that of Saul's prophesying, but the present passage provides a helpful context for understanding it. As other passages show, the same expression can be used in quite dissimilar contexts (e.g., Ex 34:26; Dt 14:21), much like that of Saul's prophesying.

> **Command #52**, Ex 23:14, Pilgrimage to the temple three times a year: "Three pilgrimages you shall make for me in a year."
>
> **Command #125**, Ex 23:19, Bring firstfruits to the temple: "The firstfruits of your ground you must bring to the temple."
>
> **Prohibition #156**, Ex 23:15, One must not go on a pilgrimage without an offering: "No one is to appear before me empty-handed."
>
> **Prohibition #116**, Ex 23:18, One must not let fat portions of an offering remain overnight: "The fat of my festival offerings must not be kept until morning."
>
> **Prohibition #186**, Ex 23:19, One must not boil a young goat in its mother's milk (cook meat with milk): "Do not cook a young goat in its mother's milk."

F. Plans for Taking the Land (23:20–33)

God's care and guidance of the Israelites is here linked to his protection of the patriarchs. By means of explicit allusions to key passages in Genesis, the writer shows that what happened to the Israelites was the fulfillment of the promises God had made with the patriarchs. For example, Jacob called God "the angel who had delivered [him] from all harm" (Ge 48:16), just as God is here pictured as protecting his people with his angel. A remarkable number of parallels between this section of text and Genesis 15 show that God's promises to Abraham and the making of his covenant in that chapter are to be fulfilled in the promises of the Sinai covenant. Abraham had foreseen the time when God would bring "fearful" (Ge 15:12; Ex 23:27) judgment on "the Amorites" (Ge 15:16; Ex 23:23) because of their iniquity. Though Israel was to "serve" (Ge 15:13–14) a foreign nation, they were not to "serve" (Ex 23:24) the gods of that nation. Rather, God would bless them (Ex 23:25) and they would not be barren (Ge 15:2–3; Ex 23:26). Their number would be great (Ge 15:5; Ex 23:26), and they would live in the land promised to their fathers (Ge 15:18–21; Ex 23:31). God had made a "covenant" with their fathers to give them the land (Ge 15:18), and they were not to make a "covenant" with those who dwelt in the land (Ex 23:32–33). Though we must not overlook the fact that the failure of the people at Sinai (see Ex 32) meant a postponement of the possible fulfillment of these promises until the next generation (see Nu 14), the intention of the covenant at Sinai can be clearly seen in the relationships between this passage and the promises to the patriarchs.

After the sin of the golden calf and Moses' return to Mount Sinai, God again spoke of sending his angel before the people to give them the land, but, unlike the present text, at that point the promise of sending the angel contained an intimation of judgment (Ex 33:1–6). The angel was sent because the people were "stiff-necked" and unable to live in God's presence (v. 5). Rather than representing God's presence with them, at that time the angel had become a sign that God could not go with them (vv. 2–3). God could not go with them, but he would send his angel to represent his presence. On the one hand the angel represented God's presence, and on the other hand it represented God's absence. We should note here the frequency of warnings against idolatry within this text dealing with God's promise to send his angel (e.g., 23:21, 24, 32–33).

> **Command #5**, Ex 23:25, One must worship God: "You shall worship the Lord your God." (Dt 6:13, "him you shall serve"; 11:13, "to serve him with all your heart"; 13:5, "and him you shall serve.")
>
> **Prohibition #48**, Ex 23:32, One must not make a covenant with the Canaanites: "You shall not make a covenant with them."
>
> **Prohibition #51**, Ex 23:33, One must not allow idolaters to live in the land: "They shall not dwell in your land."

G. Establishment of the Covenant (24:1–18)

As the chapter opens (vv. 1–2), we are reminded of God's instructions to Moses in 19:24. God had said (19:24a) that Moses was to go down to the people, speak his words (viz., 20:1–17) and judgments (viz., 21:1–23:13), and return with Aaron. The priests and the people, however, were not to come up (19:24b). The writer now repeats in 24:3 that which had already been recounted in 19:25, that is, that Moses went down and spoke God's words and judgments to the people. When the people heard Moses, they consented to the covenant and ratified it by means of a covenant ceremony (24:4–8). After this ceremony, Moses and Aaron "went up" (v. 9) to feast with Nadab and Abihu and the seventy elders (vv. 10–11). The location of this feast is not certain, but it seems reasonable to conclude that it was not on the mountain because in the subsequent narratives God called Moses again to "come up the mountain" (v. 12), and he, with Joshua, "went up" (v. 13) at that time, as God had instructed in 19:24 and 24:2.[47] Moses told the elders, Aaron, and Hur to remain until he and Joshua returned (v. 14). That Aaron went up with Moses follows what we might expect from 19:24. That he then remained with Hur and the elders goes along with 24:2, which states that Moses was to go on alone.

The elders were apparently not the same group as the priests, since the text says that the elders "went up" with Moses and Aaron but the priests were not to go up but rather were to remain with the people (19:24).

It should be noted that again the text states that Moses went up the mountain (without Joshua? 24:15). The mountain was covered by the cloud.

---

[47] In 19:24 Aaron was to go with Moses and the priests were to remain behind. In 24:2 Moses was to go alone and the others were not to "go near." The people were not to "go up" at all.

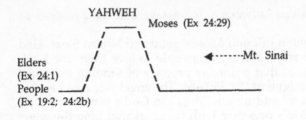

YAHWEH
Moses (Ex 24:29)

Elders
(Ex 24:1)
People
(Ex 19:2; 24:2b)

◄------Mt. Sinai

"Set bounds about the mountain and consecrate it" (Ex 19:23)
"Warn the people, lest they break through to Yahweh to gaze, and many of them perish" (Ex 19:21; cf. 1Sa 6:19)

There Moses waited six days, and on the seventh day God called to him (v. 16). Moses again went up the mountain (v. 18) and remained (alone, v. 2) on the mountain for forty days and nights (v. 18b). According to Deuteronomy 9:9, Moses fasted throughout this period of time (cf. 1Ki 19:8; Mt 4:2). The following chapters (Ex 25–31) recount God's words to Moses during this time on the mountain. At the close of these words of God, the narrative returns to Aaron, who was now standing with the people at the foot of the mountain (32:1). Moses (and Joshua, v. 17) then returned from the mountain to the people at the foot of the mountain (v. 15).

Acting as mediator of the covenant, Moses took "the words" (Ex 20:1–17) and "the judgments" (21:1–23:13) spoken by God on Mount Sinai and carried them down to the people (24:3a). With one accord the people agreed to obey the covenant (v. 3b). The covenant was ratified by the people in the ceremony at the foot of Sinai (vv. 4–8) and by the leaders in the feast upon the mountain (vv. 9–11).

The text says that Moses and the elders "saw the God of Israel" (vv. 10–11). If we are to read this passage as the author apparently understands it (Dt 4:12, 15, "you saw no form")[48] and as it was later interpreted (e.g., Jn 1:18, "No one has ever seen God"), it probably means that they saw his glory, as in verse 16, or they saw God in a vision. That they saw a *vision* of God is supported by the repetition of "they saw God" in the next verse (24:11). In this repetition, a different word for *see* is used (חזה), one that in its other uses in the Pentateuch carries the sense of "to see in a vision" (Nu 24:4, 16).

Excursus: The Tabernacle-(Temple) Complex: The Setting of the Tabernacle (Ex 24; cf. Nu 2–3; 10)

The following discussion is an explanation of the role and importance of the tabernacle, and later the temple, in Israel's worship and in the theology of the OT.

1. The Prototype of the Tabernacle: Mount Sinai (Ex 19)

1. Because of the covenant, Yahweh had come to dwell in the midst of his covenant people.

a. Exodus 19:11—"And let them be ready for the third day, for on the

---

[48]Nu 12:8, "He [Moses] saw the form of the LORD," is apparently a reference to Ex 33:23, "you will see my back; but my face must not be seen"; or 34:5, "And the LORD came down in the cloud and stood there with him." In any event, Moses' words in Dt 4:12 are about the Israelites, not himself.

third day the LORD [Yahweh] will come down on Mount Sinai in the sight of all the people."

b. Exodus 19:20—"And the LORD [Yahweh] came down on Mount Sinai, to the top of the mountain; and the LORD called Moses to the top of the mountain, and Moses went up."

2. Because Yahweh was coming into their midst, the people had to take special measures to set themselves apart in preparation.

a. Exodus 19:10—personal consecration: "Go to the people and consecrate them today and tomorrow, and let them wash their garments; and let them be ready for the third day."

b. Exodus 19:21—special safeguards: Since a holy God was to be in their midst, special safeguards were necessary to protect the people from improperly entering into the presence of this holy God, Yahweh: "And the LORD said to him, 'Go down and warn the people so they do not force their way through to see the LORD and many of them perish.'"

3. Only Moses (with Joshua) came near to God on the mountain (24:2), but even here God was covered from Moses with a cloud (vv. 15–16); and Moses had to wait seven days for God to speak with him (v. 16—not only spatial separation but also temporal separation).

4. Summary: As the people of God gathered around the mountain where God had promised to meet with them (3:12), a special arrangement was provided by the mountain setting—"the people stood at a distance, while Moses approached the thick cloud where God was."

5. The theology of Mount Sinai: Two important theological elements are at work here in the setting of Mount Sinai.

a. The covenant—In the covenant relationship with the chosen descendants of Abraham (24:3–18), the Creator God has come to dwell among his people (25:8). The God of the universe has come to dwell among the people of Israel.

b. The holiness of God—The Lord, who will now dwell among this people, is a holy God. He has not put his holiness aside while he dwells among these people. A holy God is dwelling among sinful human beings. Thus special measures must be taken by the people among whom he will now dwell. These measures are twofold:

(1) Positive measures: Throughout the Pentateuch, positive measures of consecration are provided for the people (e.g., special washings, garments, and anointings of the priests prescribed in Ex 28 and 29, as well as the book of Leviticus, passim).

(2) Negative measures: Under the circumstances discussed above, the possibility existed that an impure person might enter into the presence of the holy God living in Israel's midst. Since such an improper entry into the presence of a holy God had grave results (19:21; 1Sa 6:19), the Israelites must be protected from entering improperly—that is, from entering into God's presence without the blood sacrifice, particularly that effected on the yearly Day of Atonement prescribed in Leviticus 16.

Summary: Thus Mount Sinai was a protection for the people. By means of the physical (and temporal) separation afforded by the mountain, the holy God, Yahweh, could dwell among his covenant people (cf. Nu 8:19).

2. The Structure of the Tabernacle(-Temple) Complex (Nu 2–3)

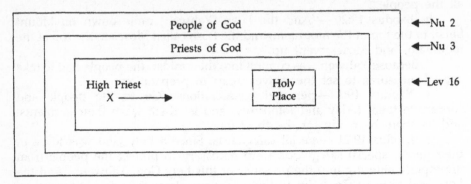

As can be seen in the above sketch of the tabernacle plans, this structure provided the same kind of physical separation between the holy God and his people as did the mountain at Sinai (temporal separation is also provided in the annual feasts and celebrations, e.g., the yearly Day of Atonement, Lev 16). The chief difference lies in the fact that the tabernacle was explicitly made portable. The provisions for the holy God to dwell among his people were not limited to the Sinai desert—they were portable, thus they could be transported into the land promised as a part of the covenant. Once the people were in the land securely, the structure could be made permanent—the temple.

3. Conclusion

In the tabernacle-temple complex, the holy God lived among his chosen people. The special arrangements of the dwelling (e.g., the Holy of Holies, outer court, etc.) were not intended to exclude God from his people but to safeguard the proper approach to this holy God, that is, an approach through the blood of the atonement sacrifice. This theology of the tabernacle-temple complex is the basis of the NT teaching that the individual believer is the temple of the Holy Spirit (1Co 6:19) and that the blood of Christ is the means whereby the believer's heart is made approachable to the holy God (Heb 9:25–26).

VII. THE TABERNACLE (25:1–31:18)

The instructions for the work of building the tabernacle are written in such a way that they provide an interesting parallel to God's own work of creation recorded in Genesis 1. Just as the Creation narrative portrayed the heavens and earth as the arena in which God would have fellowship with humans, so here the tabernacle is pictured as the means of restoring humanity's lost fellowship with God. Thus the account of Creation in Genesis 1–2 and the building of the tabernacle in Exodus 25–30 have several significant similarities.

The first area of similarity is the overall structure of the two accounts. It is well known, for example, that the Creation account in Genesis is structured around a series of seven acts of creation. Each of these acts is marked by the divine speech, "And God said" (Ge 1:3, 6, 9, 14, 20, 24, 26; cf. vv. 11, 28, 29). In the same way, the Torah's instruction for the building of the tabernacle is divided into seven acts, each introduced by the divine speech, "And the LORD said" (Ex 25:1; 30:11, 17, 22, 34; 31:1, 12). Thus the tabernacle is portrayed as a reconstruction of God's good creation. Moreover, the Garden of Eden is described in ways similar to that of the tabernacle. For example, both contained pure gold (Ge 2:12a; Ex 25:3) and precious jewels (Ge 2:12b; Ex 25:7) and were guarded by cherubim (Ge 3:24; Ex 25:18).

At the close of the Creation account in Genesis 2:1–3 was the reminder that God rested on the seventh day, the Sabbath. So also in the account of the building of the tabernacle, the last instruction is the reminder to observe the Lord's Sabbath (Ex 31:12–18). Moreover, in the Genesis narrative, God concluded his last work with an inspection and evaluation of all he had done ("And God saw all he had made, and behold, it was very good," Ge 1:31) and a blessing (1:28), just as in the description of the building of the tabernacle, when the work was completed, Moses inspected and evaluated all that was done ("And Moses saw all the work, and behold, they had done it just as the LORD had commanded," Ex 39:43a), and he blessed them (39:43b). In the Genesis account of Creation, humanity was made according to a specific pattern, that is, according to the "image" of God (Ge 1:26–27). In the building of the tabernacle, the whole as well as the parts were to be made according to the "pattern" God had shown Moses (Ex 25:9).

Furthermore, the Creation account in Genesis 1 and 2 is followed by the account of the Fall (Ge 3). At the center of the Fall account is human disobedience of God's command not to eat of the Tree of the Knowledge of Good and Evil. At the close of the instructions for the building of the tabernacle there is also a "Fall narrative," the account of Israel's sin of the golden calf (Ex 32). Just as in the Genesis account, in the account of the golden calf Israel's disobedience to the divine command resulted in their breaking God's covenant.

That the tabernacle was to be built according to the "plan" or "pattern" that God had shown Moses on the mountain (Ex 25:9, 40; cf. 1Ch 28:11–12, 18–19) gives rise to a number of important points. First, it suggests that the tabernacle was intended as a model or facsimile of God's heavenly abode. It thus was a kind of incarnation of God's presence with humankind. If only in the sense of a "form" or "pattern," God was coming to dwell among his people. Second, that the tabernacle was a "pattern" of something in heaven shows that it had a symbolic value as well as a practical purpose. This symbolism suggests, moreover, that its various physical forms also had a spiritual meaning or sense to them. There was thus already a typology in the various features of the tabernacle.

The problem that faces the readers of the Pentateuch, however, is that the text itself explains very little of the heavenly meaning of the tabernacle and its parts. It appears that we, the readers, are invited to ponder the description of the tabernacle in these chapters with the expectation that they exhibit the pattern of the heavenly temple, but we are not given any help in explaining them. In other words, there appears to be an intentional mystery about the tabernacle and the meaning of its parts, with little desire to resolve it.

There is a lesson to be learned from this mystery, however. That is, the fact that the NT writers explain many of the tabernacle's parts as "shadows" of the reality revealed in Christ (e.g., Heb 9:5) is in keeping with the purpose of these chapters. One could say that these chapters await just the sort of spiritual explanation that the NT gives them. Without such an exposition, their sense would remain uncertain. The NT sees the tabernacle and the service associated with it in these texts as a picture of the work of Christ (Jn 2:19–21; Heb 8:2; 9:11–12), of the individual believer (1Co 6:19), and of the church (1Ti 3:15; Heb 3:6; 10:21).

In the commentary which follows, we will concentrate on two aspects of the description of the tabernacle in these narratives. First, we will attempt to give a simple, straightforward description of each feature of the tabernacle. It will be apparent in almost every case that, in the last analysis, we can understand very little about the exact nature of the tabernacle from these texts. Much of what we know about it is dependent on later tradition, not on the text itself. If anything is certain it is that the Pentateuch itself was not written as a guide or blueprint for constructing the tabernacle. The narratives we encounter here have a different purpose. They are intended to tell us *about* the tabernacle and its *use*, but little more. Much is left up to the imagination of the readers. Second, we will briefly point to the various spiritual meanings usually or traditionally attached to the individual aspects of the tabernacle. We do not mean to imply that the writer had these meanings in mind when he wrote the Pentateuch. As we have said above, he is short on explanation of the spiritual meaning and purpose of the parts of the tabernacle; without his help we can only point to what others after him have said. For the most part, the Christian interpretation of the various parts of the tabernacle has attempted to stay close to the interpretations found in the NT.

A. Offerings for the Tabernacle (25:1–9)

The materials to be used in the construction of the tabernacle are enumerated first: "gold, silver, and bronze; blue, purple, and scarlet yarn and fine linen; goat hair; ram skins dyed red and hides of sea cows; acacia wood; olive oil for the light; spices for the anointing oil and for the fragrant incense; and onyx stones and other gems to be mounted on the ephod and breastpiece." The text does not explain why these metals and materials were to be used and not others, but then, given their obvious value, why would there be a need for further explanation? What is noteworthy, however, is that only a selective list of materials is given here. A more complete list of all the materials needed for building the tabernacle is given later in Exodus 35:4–29. The author, then, has deliberately selected those items of special value to list here at the beginning. He is clearly impressed with these precious materials and he expects the reader to be also.

The common Jewish and Christian tradition by and large identifies these materials with royalty and the kingship. We should not overlook the fact, however, that most of these specific articles have already been mentioned in the description of the Garden of Eden (e.g., "the gold of that land is good; aromatic resin and onyx are also there," Ge 2:9–12.) By depicting the Garden of Eden in conjunction with the tabernacle, the writer apparently wants to show the purpose of the tabernacle as a return to the Garden of Eden. Little is known about the type of tree (שִׁטָּה) used in the construction of the tabernacle and its parts. The common translation is "acacia" trees, but since the term itself is rare in the Bible, we must acknowledge that the exact type of tree is still uncertain. Tradition has associated these "trees of Shittim" with the trees in the Garden of Eden.[49] Indeed, the LXX rendered the term used here as "incorruptible trees," which recalls the notion of the "Tree of Life" from Genesis 3:22.

After the list of building materials, the purpose of the tabernacle is explained: it was to be a sanctuary for God, his dwelling place among the people (Ex 25:8). In constructing the tabernacle, Israel was to follow the plan or pattern which God had shown Moses on the mountain (v. 9). This section, Exodus 25–30, gives the instructions for building the tabernacle.

Following the narratives dealing with the sin of the golden calf, Exodus 32–34, is the account of the actual construction of the tabernacle, Exodus 35–40. From Exodus 37:1, it appears that Bezalel, a highly skilled craftsman, was responsible for all or most of the work on the ark, the table, and the lampstand. He was commissioned by God himself to do the work (31:1–5). For the rest of the tabernacle, however, the narrative is clear that many skilled workers were available and did the work (35:7, 30–35; 36:1–7).

Command #20, Ex 25:8, One must build a temple: "And they shall make for me a temple."

B. The Ark (25:10–22)

The ark was to be made of acacia wood (25:10a). Its size was three and a half feet in length, two and a half feet wide and high (v. 10b). It was overlaid with gold, inside and out (v. 11a) and was to have a gold border (v. 11b). Four gold rings were attached to the sides of the ark for the acacia poles used to carry it (vv. 12–15).

Prohibition #86, Ex 25:15, One must not remove the poles from the ark: "The poles are to remain in the rings of this ark."

The "testimony" was to be put inside the ark (25:16, 21b). According to Deuteronomy 10:2–3, the "testimony" refers to the stone tablets upon which were written the "ten words" (cf. Dt 31:26).

A gold "atonement cover" the same size as the top of the ark (Ex 25:17) was put over the ark. Two gold cherubim were to be placed at either end of the "atonement cover" with outstretched wings covering the cover (vv. 18–20).

The Lord states the purpose of the ark in verse 22: "There, above the cover between the two cherubim that are over the ark of the testimony, I will meet with you and give you all my commands for the Israelites." This promise was fulfilled after the dedication of the altar in Numbers 7:89.

According to a common line of Christian interpretation, the ark is taken to be a type of Christ.[50] That it was to be made of wood denoted Christ's partaking of the physical world in the Incarnation. The gold overlay which covered the wood of the ark denoted his divine nature. The symbolic or typological value of placing the testimony inside the ark has usually been

---

[49]See the Targum to Song of Songs, in *The Bible in Aramaic*, ed. A. Sperber, 4 vols. (Leiden: Brill, 1959–1968), 4:129.
[50]See, e.g., Johann Coccejus, *Opera Omnia*, 1:148; Scofield Reference Bible, 101.

taken to show that Christ, represented by the ark, is the mediator of the covenant and has the Law written within him (cf. Jer 31:33; Ps 40:8 [MT 9]). The NT itself takes the "atonement cover" (mercy seat) as a picture of Christ (Rom 3:25).

C. Table (25:23–30)

The table was to be made of acacia wood (25:23a). Its size was three feet in length, one and a half feet wide, and two and a half feet high (v. 23b). It was overlaid with pure gold (v. 24a) and with golden borders (v. 24b). A golden rim was to be put on the borders (v. 25). There were four gold rings, one by each leg (v. 26). The gold rings and acacia poles for carrying the table were to be overlaid with gold (vv. 27–28). The utensils for the table were also made of gold (v. 29). The purpose of the table was to hold the shewbread, that is, the bread of the Presence (v. 30).

It is common in Christian interpretation to see both the table and the bread of the Presence as a type of Christ.[51] Since there is little support for this in the NT, other explanations are found. For example, the table and the bread of the Presence have been taken as a type of the church which stands in Christ's (the ark) presence.[52]

Command #27, Ex 25:30, Priests must set up the shewbread (bread of the Presence): "And you shall put the shewbread upon the table."

D. Lampstand (25:31–40; cf. Nu 8:1–4)

The lampstand was to be made of hammered gold (Ex 25:31). It had six shafts on either side of a central shaft (v. 32). Each shaft extending from the central shaft was to have three almond-blossom cups, a knob, and a bud (v. 33). On the central shaft were four almond-blossom cups with knobs and buds. A bud was placed at the point where each of the pairs of shafts joined the central shaft (vv. 34–36). Seven lamps were to be put on each shaft (v. 37). There were also gold snuffers and snuffholders (v. 38). The lampstand was not lighted until the dedication of the tabernacle (Nu 8:1–4). The lampstand is commonly taken to be a type of Christ,[53] usually on the basis of Revelation 1:4. It has also been taken as a symbolic image of the Law.[54]

The total amount of gold used was one talent (Ex 25:39; a talent was about 100 pounds or 50 kilograms). The lampstand and the other components of the tabernacle were designed according to the pattern shown Moses on the mountain (v. 40).

E. Tabernacle (26:1–37)

The tabernacle itself, as conceived in this narrative, consisted of curtains attached to wooden boards. There were three distinct structures involved. The tabernacle proper consisted of the boards and a first layer of curtains surrounded by a large courtyard. The second structure was a second layer of curtains made of goat hair. This structure was called "the tent." A

---

[51]See, e.g., Coccejus, *Opera Omnia*, 1:148; Scofield Reference Bible, 102.
[52]See Ainsworth, *Annotations*, 102.
[53]See, e.g., Coccejus, *Opera Omnia*, 1:148; Scofield Reference Bible, 102.
[54]So Ainsworth, *Annotations*, 102.

third structure consisted merely of a layer of skins over the tent. Each of these structures was an integral part of the whole tabernacle, but each was also considered a distinct building, a unit in itself.

As we have shown above, the whole tabernacle is interpreted typologically as referring to Christ (specifically, his earthly incarnation; Coccejus) or to the church (Ainsworth). The same is true for the tent portions of the tabernacle described here. There is ample NT warrant for this interpretation (see above).

1. Curtains (Ex 26:1-6)

The tabernacle consisted of ten curtains joined together into two large sections of five curtains each. Each curtain was to be forty-two feet long and six feet wide. On the edge of each of the two large sections were fifty loops. The two sections were to be joined together with gold clasps by means of these fifty loops. Woven into the fabric of the curtains were images of cherubim, apparently intended to recall the theme of "paradise lost" by alluding to the cherubim which guarded the "Tree of Life" in Genesis 3:24.

2. The Tent (26:7-14)

Covering the tabernacle was a tent made of goat hair. The tent consisted of eleven curtains of goat hair which were made into two large sections, five curtains for one and six curtains for the other. These two sections were joined by fifty loops and bronze clasps. The extra curtain was to be folded over the entrance at the front of the tent. The tent was then covered with ram skins dyed red as well as an additional covering of the hides of "sea cows," an uncertain term indicating a material sometimes rendered "badgers' skins" or "porpoise skins."

3. Frames (26:15-25)

The tabernacle was supported by upright boards of acacia wood. The boards were about fifteen feet in length. Each board was to be set into a pair of silver bases. Along the length of the tabernacle were twenty frames. At the far end, opposite the entrance, there were eight frames, overlaid with gold (v. 29).

4. Crossbars (26:26-29)

Five sets of crossbars of acacia wood provided support for the frame of the tabernacle. These crossbars were overlaid with gold and held in place by gold rings.

5. Curtain (26:31-35)

A curtain was to be set up within the tabernacle to separate the Holy Place from the Most Holy Place. It was hung on four posts of acacia wood standing in silver bases. The ark and its atonement cover were to be placed behind the curtain in the Most Holy Place, and the table and lampstand were to be placed in front of the curtain.

The book of Hebrews takes the inner curtain described here as a symbol of Christ's body (Heb 10:20). It was this curtain, reconstructed for the temple building, that was "torn in two, from top to bottom" when Christ "yielded up his spirit" on the cross (Mt 27:50-51; Mk 15:37-38; Lk 23:45-46). The point of the NT writers was apparently that the death of Christ removed the necessity for the separation between God and his people as well as the system of sacrifices and law denoted in this curtain (cf. Heb 6:19–20; 9:6–10; 10:19–20).[55]

6. Entrance to the Tent (26:36–37)

Five posts of acacia wood were to be set up on bronze bases at the entrance of the tent, and a finely embroidered curtain of blue, purple, and scarlet was hung on them. This was to serve as the entrance to the tent and thus also as the entrance to the tabernacle.

7. Final Plan of the Tabernacle (26:30)

The final plan of the tabernacle was shown to Moses on Mount Sinai.

F. Altar of Burnt Offering (27:1–8)

An altar, seven and a half feet square and four and a half feet high, was to be constructed of acacia wood and overlaid with bronze. It is not specifically said here to be for "burnt offerings," but it is called "the altar of burnt offerings" when constructed in Exodus 38:1. The corners of the altar were made with raised tips. These tips were called its "horns." The utensils used at the altar were also made of bronze. A bronze grating was to go with the altar, apparently placed on the inside of the altar to hold the ashes. The whole of the altar was carried with bronze rings and poles. The altar itself was hollow. It was to be made according to the plan shown to Moses.

The book of Hebrews sees this altar as a picture of the better altar of Christ: "We have an altar from which those who minister at the tabernacle have no right to eat" (Heb 13:10).

G. Courtyard of the Tabernacle (27:9–19)

A courtyard enclosed by curtains was to surround the tabernacle. Its opening faced east. It was about 150 feet in length and 75 feet wide. The height of the curtains, which were attached to posts, was 7.5 feet.

H. Oil for the Lampstands (27:20–21)

The people were to supply oil for burning the lamps. It was to be clear, pressed olive oil. A note explaining the ordinance of maintaining the lamp is attached in verse 21. This note assumes the appointment of Aaron and his sons as priests, which is not recounted until the next chapter.

---

[55]Ernst Lohmeyer, *Das Evangelium des Matthäus*, Kritisch-exegetischer Kommentar über das Neue Testament (Göttingen: Vandenhoeck & Ruprecht, 1962), 395–96. D. A. Carson's comments are helpful here: "It is impossible to grapple with Matthew's fulfillment themes (cf. esp. on 5:17–20; 11:11–13) and see how even the law points prophetically to Messiah and hear Jesus' promise of a new covenant grounded in his death (26:26–29) without seeing that the tearing of the veil signifies the obsolescence of the temple ritual and the law governing it. Jesus himself is the New Temple, the meeting place of God and man. . . ; the old is obsolete" (*EBC* [Grand Rapids: Zondervan, 1984], 8:580–81).

Command #25, Ex 27:21, Priests must light the candles in the temple: "And Aaron and his sons are to arrange it [the lamp] from evening until morning before the Lord."

I. Priestly Garments (28:1–43)

1. Aaron and His Sons (28:1–5)

Aaron and his sons were set apart from the rest of the Israelites as priests. They were to wear special garments to give them "dignity and honor" and "to sanctify" them. The work was to be carried out by those whom God had filled with "the spirit of wisdom." Note that elsewhere in the Pentateuch (Dt 34:9) Joshua is described as one who was filled with "the spirit of wisdom."

The NT sees the priesthood of Aaron as prefiguring that of Christ (Heb 5:5; 7:26; 9:11).

Command #33, Ex 28:2, Priests are to wear special garments: "And they shall make holy garments for Aaron."

2. Ephod (28:6–14)

After a general description of its color and material, the first notable feature of the ephod is the two shoulder pieces studded with onyx stones. The names of the twelve tribes were engraved on these stones, six names on each stone. The purpose of engraving the names on the stones was to show that in his role as high priest, Aaron bore these names as a memorial before the Lord. He represented the name of each tribe of Israel in his duties as priest. Just as Moses had been commanded to write down the events of the battle with the Amalekites (Ex 17:14) as a written memorial to Israel, so these stones would serve as a written memorial to the Lord. Two gold chains were to be attached to the two shoulder pieces.

3. Breastpiece (28:15–30)

The breastpiece, also called the breastplate, was a small (9 inches by 9 inches) pouch worn on the breast of the priest and attached by golden chains to the shoulder pieces. On the outer surface of the breastpiece were twelve different precious stones, arranged in four rows. On each stone the name of one of the twelve tribes of Israel was engraved. As with the shoulder pieces, the purpose of these names was to be a written memorial to the Lord when the priest represented the people in the Holy of Holies. Inside the breastpiece the Urim and Thummim, implements for deciding the will of God, were kept; hence the breastpiece is sometimes called the "breastpiece of decision" (v. 15).

Prohibition #87, Ex 28:28, One must not remove the breastpiece from the ephod: "The rings of the breastpiece are to be tied to the rings of the ephod with blue cord, connecting it to the waistband, so that the breastpiece will not swing out from the ephod."

4. Robe of the Ephod (28:31–35)

A blue tunic was to be worn over the shoulders of the high priest whenever he went into the Holy of Holies. Gold bells were attached to the hem and could be heard while he was in the Holy Place. The purpose of the bells on the high priest's garments was that he might be "heard going in and coming out of the Holy Place, so that he will not die" (28:35). The text does not explain further why it was necessary to hear the high priest going in and out, or why this would prevent his death. It has been suggested that in hearing the high priest, those nearby in worship would be reminded to turn their attention to God.[56] Others have suggested that the bells would distinguish the high priest from the other priests, and thus it would be clear that it was he and no other who entered the Holy Place.[57] Another explanation of the bells is that they were to remind the high priest of his garments, to insure that he was wearing the proper priestly vestments, since entry into the Holy Place without them would have meant certain death (Lev 16:2).[58] Still another explanation is that since it was to be commanded that on the Day of Atonement no one was to be in the sanctuary when the high priest went in and out (Lev 16:17), the bells were to warn anyone hearing them to leave at once.[59]

> **Prohibition #88**, Ex 28:32, One must not make a tear in the coat of the high priest: "There shall be a woven edge like a collar around the opening so that it will not tear."

5. Gold Plate (28:36–38)

A gold plate, or plaque, was to be worn on the priest's turban. Engraved on this plaque were the words, "Holy to the LORD."

6. Tunic, Turban, and Sash (28:39–41)

The basic garment of the priests was the tunic. It was to be woven of fine linen, as were the turban and sash. There were two types of turbans: one for the high priest and another kind, called a "headband," for the other priests. The purpose of such clothing was to "give [the priests] dignity and honor" (28:40). A special act of consecration with anointing oil was necessary for these clothes to be worn and for the duties of the priesthood to be carried out.

7. Undergarments (28:42–43)

The undergarments were made of plain linen. Their purpose was to "cover the naked flesh" (28:42) when they officiated at the Tent of Meeting or approached the altar. The function of the undergarments was similar to the prohibition of steps on the altar: "lest your nakedness be exposed on it" (20:26). This prescription for undergarments alludes to and reminds one of the clothing which God made for Adam and Eve in the Garden of Eden to cover their nakedness (Ge 3:21).

---

[56]J. Drusius, *Critici Sacri*, 1:687. Drusius based his interpretation on the Jewish biblical scholar Hizquni.

[57]See, e.g., Keil, *Pentateuch*, 2:203.

[58]See Rashi, ad loc.

[59]See Rashbam, ad loc. Other explanations: The bells were to tell the people when the high priest arrived in the Holy Place, or to tell the people the high priest was still alive while he was in the Holy Place (Walter Kaiser, *EBC*, [Grand Rapids: Zondervan, 1990], 2:467), or to enable the high priest to "make music with his steps" (Sir [Ecclus] 45:9).

J. The Consecration of the Priests (29:1–46)

1. Aaron and the Priests Clothed (29:1–9)

In the consecration of Aaron and the priests, they were first to be clothed in the garments described in the previous chapter. A "sacred diadem" attached to the turban appears to be mentioned here for the first time. According to Leviticus 8:9, however, the "sacred diadem" was another name for the "gold plate" mentioned in Exodus 28:36.

2. Sacrifices for Aaron and the Priests (29:10–28)

A bull and two rams were required for the consecration of Aaron and the priests. The animals were to be ritually slaughtered "before the Tent of Meeting." Although the nature of the offering is not specified here, the book of Leviticus gives more details. After the description of the sacrificial laws for the priests (Lev 1–7), the slaughter of the bull, mentioned in Exodus 29, is called a "sin offering" (Lev 8:14). Moreover, the slaughter of the first ram is called a "burnt offering" (v. 18) and the second ram an "offering of ordination" (v. 22). The offerings mentioned here in Exodus 29, then, appear to be understood as a "sin offering." This understanding of the nature of the offerings is clearly anticipated at the close of the chapter (vv. 35–43), where the slaughter of the bull is called a "sin offering" (v. 36) and the rams are called "burnt offerings" (v. 42).

That the priest required the sacrifice of a "bull" is probably intended to link the priesthood further with the incident of the golden calf in Exodus 32 (see the commentary below on Lev 17:1–9).

3. Sacred Meal (29:29–34)

The second ram was to be prepared as a sacred meal for Aaron and the priests.

Command #89, Ex 29:33, The priests are to eat the meat of the consecrated offerings (sin and guilt): "They shall eat that by which atonement was made for their ordination."

Prohibition #148, Ex 29:33, A nonpriest may not eat of the holiest sacrifices: "No one else may eat them because they are sacred."

4. Repetition of the Ceremony of Consecration (29:35–37)

The whole ceremony, including the offering of a bull and two rams each day, was to be repeated for seven days.

5. Daily Offering (29:38–46)

Along with the seven-day consecration of Aaron and the priests, instructions are given for the daily sacrifice that was to be carried out perpetually for all generations. Two yearling lambs were to be offered, one at morning and the other at twilight. This instruction is given here because, though it would be a part of the consecration of the priests, it would continue on after that perpetually.

K. Altar of Incense (30:1–10)

An altar for burning incense was to be made of acacia wood, one and a half feet square and three feet high. It was to have raised corners, or "horns," like the sacrificial altar (cf. Ex 27:1–8) and was to be overlaid with gold. Two gold rings were attached to its sides for the acacia wood poles used to carry the altar. The altar of incense was to be put just in front of the curtain that separated the Holy of Holies from the remainder of the Holy Place.

The purpose of the altar was to provide a continual burning of incense before the presence of the Lord at the ark. The high priest (Aaron) was to burn the incense every morning and at twilight every evening. The altar was used only for incense; it could not be used for any other type of offering.

Once a year the high priest (Aaron) made an atonement for this altar with the blood of the atonement.

> **Command #28**, Ex 30:7, Priests must burn the incense on the golden altar: "Aaron must burn fragrant incense on the altar every morning when he tends the lamps."
>
> **Prohibition #82**, Ex 30:9, Only the prescribed incense must be burned on the golden altar in the temple: "Do not offer on this altar any other incense."

L. Atonement Money (30:11–16)

The expense of the tabernacle service was to be shared equally among all Israelites, whether rich or poor. A census was taken and, from that, a donation of silver was required. The requirement was one half-shekel of silver per individual Israelite.

> **Command #171**, Ex 30:12–13, One must give half a shekel every year to the temple: "Each one should pay to the Lord a ransom for his life."

M. Basin for Washing (30:17–21)

A bronze basin was to be constructed for the priests' preparation for service at the altar. Before their work at the altar, they were to wash their hands and feet in the basin. The basin was placed between the altar and the Tent of Meeting.

> **Command #24**, Ex 30:19, Priests must wash before they serve in the temple: "And Aaron and his sons shall wash their hands and feet when they enter the Tent of Meeting."

N. Anointing Oil (30:22–33)

A special oil was to be mixed and used for anointing the various parts of the tabernacle, including the priests. The purpose of the anointing was to set these persons and objects apart, to sanctify them. Thus, it was strictly forbidden to make and use the same oil for profane purposes.

> **Command #35**, Ex 30:31, Holy oil must be prepared: "This is to be my sacred anointing oil for the generations to come."
>
> **Prohibition #83**, Ex 30:32, One must not make oil like that of the anointing oil: "Do not make any oil with the same formula."
>
> **Prohibition #84**, Ex 30:32, The anointing oil is only for the high priest and the king: "Do not pour it on men's bodies."

O. Incense (30:34-38)

A special incense was to be mixed for the incense altar in front of the curtain of the Holy of Holies. Its purpose was to set off the Tent of Meeting as a special holy place. As with the anointing oil, the incense was not to be used for any profane purpose.

Prohibition #85, Ex 30:37, One must not make other incense like that for the altar: "Do not make any incense with this formula for yourselves."

P. Bezalel and Oholiab (31:1-11)

The work of God was to be done by means of the Spirit of God. God chose two skilled craftsmen, Bezalel from the tribe of Judah and Oholiab from the tribe of Dan. Though they were skilled, the narrative emphasizes clearly that they were to do the work of building the tabernacle by means of the skills that the Spirit of God would give them. There is an important parallel here with God's work of Creation in Genesis 1. Just as God did his work of Creation by means of his Spirit (Ge 1:2-2:3), so also Israel was to do their work of building the tabernacle by God's Spirit.

The parallels between God's work in Creation and Israel's work on the tabernacle are part of the Pentateuch's larger emphasis on the importance of the work of God's Spirit among his people. This is the same emphasis found in later biblical books where the new covenant notion of faith and of internal change of heart are put at the center of the human relationship with God. Genuine obedience to the will of God comes only after the renewal of the human heart by the Spirit of God (cf. Eze 36:26-27). It is of interest here to note that the two key characters in the Pentateuch who provide a clear picture of genuine obedience to God's will, Joseph and Joshua, are specifically portrayed in the narrative as those who are filled with the Spirit of God (Ge 41:38; Dt 34:9).

Q. The Sabbath (31:12-17)

The analogy between God's work of Creation and Israel's construction of the tabernacle is made explicit by the reference to the Sabbath at the close of the narrative. We are reminded that God did his work in six days and rested on the seventh day; now Israel is to do likewise. Though it is clear that this pattern is taken up for all future generations (v. 16), in this specific context within the Pentateuch the focus is on the building of the tabernacle. Just as God made the world, so Israel is to make the tabernacle. Like God's work, it is to be a holy work and is to be carried out by observing the holy times. The Israelites' work on the tabernacle was not holy merely because they were working on a holy structure. The work was holy because it was sanctified by the sign of the Sabbath. As such, the building of the tabernacle in the wilderness is a paradigm of all of Israel's work. By setting apart the Sabbath as a sign, the whole of their work was marked as a holy task.

R. Conclusion (31:18)

This last verse returns our attention to the flow of narrative from chapter 24. Throughout this time in the narrative, God had been talking to Moses at the top of Mount Sinai. Now, when he had finished, he gave Moses the two stone tablets on which were written the "ten words." In the next chapter, the narrative returns to the scene of chapter 24 and resumes with the people and Aaron at the foot of Mount Sinai. This is thus an important transitional verse. By means of it, we, the readers, are returned to the scene which Moses had left behind when he went up the mountain.

VIII. THE GOLDEN CALF (32:1–35)

A. Making the Calf (32:1–6)

The narrative returns to the course of events in the Israelite camp during the time in which Moses was receiving the covenant on Mount Sinai. Ironically, while Moses was receiving the Ten Commandments on the stone tablets, Israel was in the process of breaking the first of those commandments. The writer has gone to great lengths in this passage to show that Israel was unable to keep the covenant that God had made with them at Sinai. That covenant found its most concise statement in the Ten Commandments given to Moses and to all the people. Since this covenant was just now being given to them on Mount Sinai, the narrative shows that the covenant was being broken even while Moses was still on the mountain. Throughout the remainder of the Pentateuch, the incident of the worship of the golden calf cast a dark shadow across Israel's relationship with God, much the same way as the account of the Fall in Genesis 3 marked a major turning point in God's dealing with humankind.

The Hebrew text of the narrative is somewhat ambiguous about the intention of the golden calf. Did the calf represent "other gods" that Israel was now seeking to follow, or was it rather an attempt to make an image of the one true God, Yahweh? In other words, did the golden calf represent polytheism (worship of many gods) or idolatry (physical representation of God)? It is possible to translate the passage to reflect either view. Thus we must look to other features of the text and context for a solution.

Two immediate factors in the text affect the interpretation of the expression. First, the Hebrew word *'elōhîm* can be understood and translated either as a plural noun ("gods") or as a singular ("god/God"). Only the context in most cases will determine which sense is intended. In many instances when the plural "gods" is intended, the verb used with the noun will also be plural. Since the verb in this passage is plural, the NIV has rendered the Hebrew noun *'elōhîm* in the plural: "These are your gods, O Israel, who brought you up out of Egypt" (32:4). Often, however, the sense of the noun *'elōhîm* is clearly singular and should be translated "God," even though the verb is plural. In the book of Nehemiah, for example, this very passage is quoted and the singular verb is used, showing that the translation was taken to be, "This is your God who brought you out of Egypt" (Ne 9:8). The book of Nehemiah thus understood the sense to be singular. Appropriately, in that passage, the NIV rendered it with the singular.[60]

Second, the Hebrew expression "other gods" (אֱלֹהִים אֲחֵרִים) or "gods" (אֱלֹהִים) is often, if not always, used specifically as a term for idols and not, as we might have expected, for "other gods" per se. In Deuteronomy 28:36, for example, the expression "other gods" clearly refers not to other deities as

---

[60]Cf. Acts 7:40, "make for us gods to go before us."

such but to "gods of wood and stone," that is, idols. It is widely recognized that the biblical writers had little tolerance for the concept of other deities existing along with the one true God. The expression "other gods" or *'elōhîm* (plural) meant simply physical images or fetishes.

In the present passage the term *gods*, or rather *god*, represented in the golden calf, seems to be understood as an attempt to represent the God of the covenant with a physical image. The apostasy of the golden calf, therefore, was idolatry, not polytheism. Indeed, throughout Scripture Israel was repeatedly warned about the sin of idolatry.

Several points in the narrative suggest this conclusion. First, that the people wanted Aaron to "make" a god(s) for them (v. 1) shows that the term *'elōhîm* was understood as something that could be made—an idol, not a deity as such. For example, the same expression is used in 34:17, where the sense is clearly that of making an idol. In the present chapter, as well, Moses called the calf "a god of gold" (v. 31). Clearly, he saw the calf as an idol. Second, the Hebrew word for "idol" (מַסֵּכָה) is actually used in this passage to describe the "god" that Aaron made: "He took what they handed him and made it into an idol cast in the shape of a calf" (vv. 4, 8). Third, Aaron fashioned only one golden calf. It is not likely that one calf would be called "gods" (in the plural) if actual gods were to be understood. Thus the reference to a single calf suggests that it represented one god/God and not many gods. Fourth, the "god" (*'elōhîm*) which Aaron made is always referred to with the singular pronoun "it." Finally, the celebration of the making of the golden calf is called "a feast for the Lord" (v. 5). Thus the Israelites saw the calf as a representation of the Lord rather than another deity.

It is sometimes held that Aaron had second thoughts about the golden calf and called a "feast for the Lord" at the last minute in an attempt to avert the people's apostasy.[61] Two considerations from the text, however, make such an interpretation unlikely. First, on the next day, the day of the "feast for the Lord," the text says that they "rose early and sacrificed burnt offerings and presented fellowship offerings" (v. 6). It is clear from the text, however, that these offerings on the day of the "feast for the Lord" were presented before the golden calf. We know this because the Lord said to Moses: "They have been quick to turn away from what I commanded them and have made themselves an idol cast in the shape of a calf. They have bowed down to it and sacrificed to it" (v. 8). This shows that the celebration was given in behalf of the calf, not in place of it. Second, the Lord's response to the golden calf shows no recognition of an attempt by Aaron or the people to ameliorate their sinful act of constructing the calf. When the Lord spoke to Moses about the sin of the people (vv. 7–10), he made no mention of the people's turning away from the golden calf to celebrate a separate "feast for the Lord." On the contrary, his attention was directed precisely to the people's refusal to repent: "they are a stiff-necked people. Now leave me alone so that my anger may burn against them and that I may destroy them" (vv. 9–10). When the Lord did act mercifully with them as a result of Moses' intercession (v. 14), the basis of his actions was not any merit of Aaron or the people, but rather his own oath sworn to the patriarchs (vv. 12–13).

---

[61]See Rashi, ad loc.

B. Moses on the Mountain (32:7–14)

The narrative of God's recounting to Moses the news of the golden calf provides the reader with the divine perspective on Israel's sin. God's comments to Moses focus the reader's attention on three central points. First, God said, "They have quickly turned away from what I have commanded them" (v. 8). God had said at the beginning of the Ten Commandments, "Thou shalt have no other gods before me" (20:2), and he had repeatedly warned them not to make or worship an idol (20:23; 23:13, 32, 33); but now Israel had made for themselves just such an idolatrous "god." Second, God said of Israel, "They are a stiff-necked people" (32:9). In their present state, Israel seemed incapable of obedience to the covenant. The narrative shows that God's response was an attempt to destroy the people and start over by making a new nation with Moses (v. 10). Third, however, because of the intercession of Moses and his appeal to the promises to the patriarchs, God had compassion on the people (v. 14). Thus the reference back to the promises God made to the patriarchs (Ge 12:1–3) plays a crucial role in this narrative.

These three points—idolatry of the golden calf, Israel's stiff-necked refusal to obey, and God's compassion—provide the basis of the subsequent narratives and God's further dealings with this people. Though a great act of God's judgment follows immediately (vv. 27–35), the central themes of the subsequent narratives focus on God's compassion and a new start for Israel.

C. God's Judgment on Israel's Sin (32:15–35)

It is important to note that in this narrative, Moses, carrying out his role as mediator, acted and spoke on God's behalf. The divine wrath expressed in 32:9–12 was carried out by Moses and the Levites, "and that day about three thousand of the people died" (v. 28). Moses, who had appealed for clemency on behalf of the people, now led the vanguard of divine judgment. Only in the last verse of the chapter do we see God himself acting in that judgment. The reason for this focus on Moses' role in judgment rather than God's is apparently the writer's desire to stress God's gracious response to Israel's sin. The central theme of the subsequent narrative (Ex 33) is God's great mercy and compassion (33:19). God's dealings with Israel henceforth emphasize his goodness and compassion. What the present narrative shows, however, is that God's gracious dealings with his people are not accomplished in the absence of a clear acknowledgment of his wrath.

Further on in the narrative we are reminded that as a result of the incident of the idolatrous golden calf, the people were "running wild" (32:25). This is a far cry from the picture of the people later in Numbers 10:1–10 as they prepared to leave Sinai. By the time they were ready to leave Mount Sinai, there was a marked order and care by which the people began to move. Why the different pictures of Israel under the single leadership of Moses? It should be noted that between the two narratives—one dealing with Israel's initial stay at Mount Sinai and the other dealing with their departure—there lies in the text an enormous number of laws and regulations. The narrative seems to be saying that Israel's orderly departure from Mount Sinai was not an accident. Rather, it was the result of the countless "laws and regulations" given them by God at Sinai. Moreover, the narrative of Exodus 32 (the incident of the golden calf and the people's "running wild") helps to show clearly that the laws given to Israel at Sinai were not mere arbitrary restrictions but necessary controls on an otherwise desperate and helpless situation (cf. the commentary below on Nu 10:1–10).

It should also be pointed out, in view of the close parallels between the Fall of Israel in the incident of the golden calf (Ex 32) and the Fall of humankind in the Garden (Ge 3), that there is a wordplay in the Hebrew narrative between the "nakedness" (עֵרֹם) of the man and woman after their eating of the fruit and Israel's "running wild" (פָּרֻעַ) after the incident of the golden calf.

When Moses shattered the two stone tablets, it was a clear sign that Israel had broken the covenant. Moses' first act was that of judgment on the people for their "great sin." By means of the Levites, Moses meted out divine wrath on the guilty among them.

On the next day, however, Moses also acted as mediator and atoned for their "great sin" (Ex 32:30–32). It is in the context of Moses' return to the mountain of Sinai that he received the second set of stone tablets and the covenant.

IX. THE RESTORATION OF ISRAEL (33:1–34:35)

Moses had now returned to Mount Sinai and there God spoke with him again. The text has several indications that the author now wants to show that Israel's relationship with God had been fundamentally affected by their "great sin" of worshiping the golden calf. All was not the same. The narrative shows that there was now a growing distance between God and Israel that had not been there before. Each of the following sections of narrative demonstrates specifically the changes that have occurred in God's relationship to Israel. We should also note that the Levites are chosen in this narrative; in Numbers 3 they replace the firstborn Israelites as priests. This represents a further change in Israel's relationship with God in the Sinai covenant.

A. The Angel (33:1–6)

The first intimation that the incident with the golden calf had changed Israel's relationship with God can be seen in the different emphasis the narrative gives to the "angel" which God sent before his people. In most respects, the passage is the same as Exodus 23:20–33, where God had previously promised to send his angel before Israel: "See, I am sending an angel ahead of you to guard you along the way and to bring you to the place I have prepared" (v. 20). At that point in the narrative, the angel clearly represented God's presence among the people of Israel: "My angel will go ahead to you and bring you into the land of the Amorites . . . and I will wipe them out" (v. 23). Moreover, at that point in the narrative Israel was about to finalize their covenant with God at Sinai—Moses was called to go up to the mountain to receive the covenant (24:1). Keep in mind that throughout the earlier narrative dealing with God's sending his angel we find numerous warnings about the danger of idolatry (23:21, 24, 32, 33).

The narrative in chapter 33 now returns to the point in the previous narrative just before the incident of the golden calf. Israel is again waiting at the foot of Mount Sinai, and Moses is waiting to receive God's instruction on the mountain. The first instructions seem the same as before: Israel was to leave Sinai and to enter the land promised to the patriarchs (vv. 1–3a), and God would send his angel before them (v. 2). But in the present narrative, the reason for God's sending his angel to go before them has changed. God now said, "I will send an angel before you. . . . But I will not go with you, because you are a stiff-necked people and I might destroy you on the way" (vv. 2–3). Whereas previously God had sent his angel to destroy Israel's enemies (23:23), now he would send his angel lest he himself would destroy Israel: "If I were to go with you even for a moment, I might destroy you" (33:5). The angel represents not so much God's presence with Israel as his separation from them. A further indication in the narrative of Israel's growing separation from God as a result of the golden calf is the author's stress on the need for the construction of the Tent of Meeting.

B. Tent of Meeting (33:7–11)

The author's conception of a "Tent of Meeting" appears to have fundamentally changed after the narrative of the golden calf. We know from the previous narrative that during the forty days on Mount Sinai, God had given Moses specific instructions for building the tabernacle (Ex 26:1–37). God clearly stated its purpose: "Have them make a sanctuary for me, and I will dwell among them" (25:8). Part of the tabernacle was a goat-hair covering over the inner curtains that was called simply "the tent" (26:7). Moreover, the whole of the tabernacle was sometimes called the "Tent of Meeting" (27:21; 28:43). Its purpose was to be the place where God could meet with his covenant people: "There I will meet you and speak to you; there also I will meet with the Israelites" (29:42–43).

After the incident of the golden calf, however, the narrative tells of another "Tent of Meeting." This "Tent" was not the same as the tabernacle. The "Tent" was a meeting place with God that was "outside the camp some distance away" (33:7). That this was not the tabernacle is clear from the fact that at this point in the narrative the tabernacle was not yet built by Bezalel and his company of skilled workers (36:8–38). Thus the "Tent of Meeting" in this passage was only for Moses and Joshua and was set apart from the people themselves. The people could only stand and watch from the distance of their own tents as Moses went out to enter the tent. The original idea of a "Tent of Meeting" by which God would dwell among his people had now become one of the means whereby God had been set apart from them.

C. Moses and the Glory of the Lord (33:12–23)

Another indication of a change in Israel's relationship with God is the way in which this passage portrays God's glory. A central feature of God's original descent upon Mount Sinai to speak with Moses was the great display of his glory before all the people: "and the glory of the LORD settled on Mount Sinai. For six days the cloud covered the mountain. . . . To the Israelites the glory of the LORD look like a consuming fire on top of the mountain" (24:16–17). In this chapter, however, on the second time that God spoke to Moses on the mountain, the display of his glory was quite different. First, there was no display of God's glory before all the people as there had been earlier. Only Moses could look when God's glory passed by. Second, even as he looked upon God's glory in this passage, Moses's face was covered by God's hand so he could see only the back parts of God's glory. Finally, the next chapter recounts that the Israelite people saw God's glory only as it shone on the face of Moses when he returned from the mountain (34:29). Thus they did not see God's glory; they saw only a reflection of it on Moses' face. Moreover, just as God had covered Moses' face lest he see too much of his glory, so Israel covered Moses' face because "they were afraid to come near to him" (34:30).

Along with this change in the display of God's glory, there was a change in the purpose of revealing God's glory. In the first revelation of God's glory at Sinai, Moses explained to the people that its purpose had been "to test you, so that the fear of God will be with you to keep you from sinning" (20:20). After the incident with the golden calf, however, the revelation of God's glory had a quite different purpose. When Moses asked to see God's glory, the Lord answered, "I will cause all my goodness to pass in front of you. . . . I will have mercy on whom I will have mercy, and I will have compassion on whom I will have compassion" (33:19). Surprisingly, what Moses learned about God's glory after the "great sin" (32:30) of the golden calf was not further fear of God but rather that he was a gracious God, full of compassion. Consequently, in the next chapter, when the Ten Commandments were written on new stone tablets and a covenant was again established, a special emphasis is given to the importance of God's grace: "Then the LORD came down in the cloud and . . . he passed in front of Moses, proclaiming, 'The LORD, the LORD, the compassionate and gracious God, slow to anger, abounding in love and faithfulness, maintaining love to thousands, and forgiving wickedness, rebellion, and sin. Yet he does not leave the guilty unpunished'" (34:6–7).

D. Stone Tablets (34:1–28)

Moses was told to prepare two stone tablets (34:1–10) on which God would write the "Ten Words," just as with the first tablets. Moses carried out God's request (v. 4a) and took the two tablets with him back up the mountain (v. 4b). Once on the mountain, however, God told Moses to write the "words" (v. 27). This is followed by the statement that "he wrote the words of the covenant" on the tablets (v. 28). The text is clear that it was the "Ten Words" which were written (v. 28b). As at the beginning of this narrative (v. 1), the parallel account in Deuteronomy 10:1–4 makes clear that God, not Moses, wrote the "Ten Words" on the two stone tablets. How then are we to understand the present passage, which suggests—in part, at least (Ex 34:28)—that Moses, rather than the Lord, wrote "the words" on the two tablets?

There have been numerous attempts to explain this apparent contradiction. Some have suggested that the biblical writer describes a single act of writing from two different perspectives. It is maintained that God wrote "the words" on the two tablets (Ex 34:1, 28; Dt 10:4) by commanding Moses to write "the words" for him (Ex 34:27).[62] An early and more probable explanation maintains that the Lord, not Moses, is the subject of the verb "he

[62]Cartwrightus, *Critici Sacri*, 1:862; W. Kaiser, *EBC*, 2:485.

wrote" in verse 28.[63] Thus the "words" to be written by Moses in verse 27 were not the same words as those which "[the LORD] wrote" in verse 28. In verse 27, Moses is told to write "the words of the covenant" (i.e., the Covenant Code in 20:23–23:19), but these were not to be written on the two stone tablets.[64] It was God who wrote the "Ten Words" on the stone tablets (34:28).

However the details of the problem are resolved, what seems certain, at least from this passage, is that the covenant was established in this chapter on the basis of the original "Ten Words" which God himself had written on the tablets (v. 1) as well as the additional words which God commanded Moses to write (v. 27). These additional words appear to have included at least those which God spoke to him during his second time on the mountain (vv. 10–26). There are, interestingly enough, "ten words" in this section as well. In some respects, these "ten words" have parallels in the Ten Commandments, but they appear essentially to be merely an expansion of the epilogue of the Covenant Code (23:13–19):

1. Prohibition of idolatry (34:11–17): God's words here open with a strict warning against following "other gods," just as in the Ten Commandments (20:2–6) and in the prologue (20:22–26) and epilogue (23:13–19) of the Covenant Code. Here, as in the Ten Commandments, the expression "other gods" is taken to mean "idols."
2. The Feast of Unleavened Bread (34:18)
3. Dedication and redemption of the firstborn (34:19–20)
4. The Sabbath (34:20)
5. The Feast of Weeks (34:21a)
6. The Feast of Ingathering (34:21b)
7. Prohibition of leaven in the blood of sacrifice (34:25a)
8. Prohibition of preserving the Passover sacrifice (34:25b)
9. The best of the first fruits (34:26a)
10. Prohibition of boiling kid in its mother's milk (34:26b)

It is important to note that the twin themes of warning against idolatry and instructions for proper forms of worship played a significant role in the structure of the Covenant Code in Exodus 20–24. Thus the making of a covenant in this chapter follows the same form as the older one:

1. Warning against idolatry (34:11–17)
2. Instructions on true worship (34:18–26)

For Exodus 34:27–28, see the comments on 34:1 above.

Command #81, Ex 34:20, Redemption of a firstborn ass: "The firstborn of an ass you must redeem with a sheep."

Command #135, Ex 34:21, On the seventh year the ground is left fallow: "Even during the plowing season and harvest you must rest."

Command #53, Ex 34:23, One must appear during each of the three pilgrimages: "Three times in the year all your males must appear." (Cf. Dt 16:16.)

Prohibition #115, Ex 34:25, One must not slaughter the Passover lamb with yeast: "Do not offer the blood of a sacrifice to me along with anything containing yeast."

---

[63]Saadia, Ibn Ezra, Rashbam, Ramban, and Hizquni, ad loc.
[64]Serforno, ad loc.

Prohibition #187, Ex 34:26, One must not eat a young goat in its mother's milk (eat meat with milk): "Do not cook a young goat in its mother's milk."

E. The Glory on the Face of Moses (34:29–35)

Again, as with the preceding narratives, a significant reversal in Israel's relationship with God is noted in the events of this narrative. Near the beginning of the section of narrative in 32:15–35, Moses was depicted as descending from the mountain where he had been with God forty days and nights. In his hand were the two stone tablets. The text says, "When . . . he saw the calf and the dancing, his anger burned and he threw the tablets out of his hands" (v. 19). Now, at the close of the narrative, Moses is shown again returning from the mountain where he had been with God for forty days and nights, and the two tablets are in his hands (34:29). Instead of Moses' amazement at what he saw in the camp, however, those in the camp were now amazed at what they saw in Moses: "When Aaron and all the Israelites saw Moses, his face was radiant, and they were afraid" (v. 30).

What had now happened to Moses was the beginning of the fulfillment of what God had earlier promised him on the mountain: "I am making a covenant with you. Before all your people I will do wonders never before done in any nation in all the world. The people you live among will see how awesome is the work that I, the LORD, will do for you" (34:10). Henceforth, the covenant that God makes with Israel will focus on the role of the mediator. Through him God will display his glory to his people.

X. THE CONSTRUCTION OF THE TABERNACLE (35:1–40:38)

A. The Sabbath (35:1–3)

At the close of the instructions for the building of the tabernacle, Israel had been reminded of the necessity of keeping the Sabbath (31:12–17). All work, presumably that of the tabernacle as well, was to be suspended on the seventh day. After the narrative of Israel's great sin of the golden calf and before the description of the work on the tabernacle, there is again a reminder of the Sabbath rest.

Prohibition #322, Ex 35:3, One must not light a fire (M. inflict punishment) on the Sabbath: "Do not light a fire in any of your dwellings."

B. Materials for the Tabernacle (35:4–29)

A reckoning of the materials needed for building the tabernacle, as well as the generosity of the people in giving and working "from a willing heart," is narrated here. The first part of the list is virtually verbatim that of 25:4–8. Since that list was only a general survey of materials needed, the present chapter completes the list of all items actually gathered for every aspect of the building, and it recounts how the items were made. In the case of the yarn and linens, for example, it says, "Every skilled woman spun with her hands and brought what she had spun—blue, purple, or scarlet yarn or fine linen" (v. 25). The emphasis in this section appears to reflect a focus on the role of women in Israel's worship (cf. 38:8).

C. The Workers: Bezalel and Oholiab (35:30–36:1)

God's preparation and choice of the skilled workers is repeated again in nearly verbatim fashion from 31:2–6. That which the Lord had told Moses in Exodus 31 Moses now repeated to the Israelites. There is one important difference, however. Since the description of the building of the tabernacle will focus not only on Bezalel and Oholiab but also on the many other skilled workers, Moses has given an interesting additional bit of information regarding God's preparation of these workers for his service. At the point in the narrative of Exodus 31 where God gave Oholiab to Bezalel as a helper (v. 6), Moses now has added that God had given both Bezalel and Oholiab "the ability to teach others" (35:34). By adding this information to the narrative, Moses explained how the other workers obtained their skills for the work on the tabernacle: they were taught by the craftsmen whom God had gifted with his Spirit. Even their ability to teach others was a divine gift.

D. Response of the People (36:2–7)

This brief narrative graphically depicts the zeal of the people for the work of the tabernacle. When the workers were brought together to begin the project, the people not only brought what they needed, but they also continued "to bring freewill offerings morning after morning." In fact, the people eventually had to be restrained from bringing any more freewill offerings for the work (v. 7).

E. Construction of the Tabernacle (36:8–38)

The order of recounting the construction of the parts of the tabernacle is not the same as that of the instructions in Exodus 25–30. In those instructions, the individual items in the tabernacle were first described (ark, table, lampstand) and then the tabernacle itself. Here in the description of the construction, however, the writer begins with the tabernacle. The purpose for this change is perhaps to begin with, and thus highlight, the part of the work that involved "all the skilled workers" before moving on to that work which involved only Bezalel. Thus the picture given at the beginning of the narrative is that of the total participation of all the people.

The description of the building of the tabernacle follows closely that which was given earlier in the instructions. The major exception is, of course, that where the details were given as instructions in the first account (Ex 26:1–33), they are recorded here as accomplished. The purpose of such redundancy in the narrative is to show that the workers carried out God's instructions just as he had commanded.

The two accounts differ in two significant ways, however. First, the present account states that the work was done by "all the skilled men among the workmen" (36:8). Second, perhaps because of this additional information, the comment that the tabernacle was to follow the "plan" which Moses saw on the mountain (26:30) is missing in the present account. It appears that the "skill" of the workers was the means by which the "plan" which Moses saw could be followed. If only Moses saw the "plan," it makes sense that the workers would have to be specially gifted if they were to follow it.

F. Ark (37:1–9)

The account given here of the construction of the ark follows closely the instructions given by Moses earlier in 25:10–22. There is, however, no mention of placing the "testimony" in the ark after its completion, as was specified in 25:16, 21, nor is there any mention of placing the "atonement cover" on the ark, as was specified in 25:21. The reason for these omissions is that these two articles were put in place only after the tabernacle had been set up and dedicated with the anointing oil (40:20).

It is specifically mentioned that Bezalel himself made the ark (37:1).

G. Table (37:10–16)

The construction of the table follows closely the instructions in 25:23–30. Though the translation in the NIV suggests otherwise, the Hebrew text is clear that Bezalel himself made the table. The NIV reads: "They made the table," whereas the Hebrew text reads: "And he made the table."

H. Lampstand (37:17–24)

The construction of the lampstand also follows closely the instructions in 25:31–40. As with the ark and the table, the text is clear that Bezalel himself made the lampstand. Of course, it is possible that he had assistants in the work, but the writer is careful to credit Bezalel himself. We should note that in this text there is no mention of the lighting of the lampstand until the dedication of the tabernacle (Nu 8:1–4).

In this account of the construction of the lampstand, the writer has not mentioned the "pattern" which Moses saw on the mountain and which was part of the earlier instructions (25:40). As in the case of the building of the tabernacle, the stress appears to be more on the "skill" of the workers than on the "pattern" given to Moses.

I. Altar of Incense, Anointing Oil, and Incense (37:25–29)

The account of the construction of the altar of incense, which fell near the end in the list of instructions (30:1–10), has been moved up with the other central articles of the tabernacle. Its construction follows the instructions verbatim. There is only a mention of the making of the anointing oil and the incense.

J. Altar of Burnt Offering (38:1–7)

The text suggests that Bezalel himself was responsible for building this altar. In the instructions for building it (27:1–8), the altar was not designated specifically for "burnt offerings," but here it is called "the altar for burnt offerings" (38:1).

In the instructions for making this altar (27:8), Moses was told to make it "just as you were shown on the mountain." As is the case with the construction of the other articles, there is no mention that the workers followed that pattern in this account of its construction. The focus is rather on the "skill" that God had given the workers.

K. Basin for Washing (38:8)

The earlier instructions for building the basin (30:17–21) were brief. The focus there was on the purpose for the basin and its location within the tabernacle. Here, however, an additional factor about the construction of the basin is given. It was made from the mirrors used by the "women who congregated [NIV, 'served'] at the entrance to the Tent of Meeting." As was the case in 35:25, the author appears to go out of his way to show that the women of Israel played an important role in the work of the tabernacle. Behind this concern to highlight the work of the women may lie the overall close association of "wisdom" and women in Scripture (cf. Ge 3:6; Ex 31:3; Prov 8:1–31).

The reference to the "Tent of Meeting" is probably to the tent which Moses had set up (Ex 33:7) outside the camp, since the tabernacle had not yet been erected (cf. 40:2). But this comment may also refer to the tabernacle (also called the Tent of Meeting), which had already been built (36:8) by this time. In either case, the intent of the comment is to show the eagerness of the people to contribute freely to the construction of the tabernacle.

L. Courtyard (38:9–20)

The account of constructing the courtyard follows closely the instructions in 27:9–19. Its inclusion here in the text is to assure the reader that all the divine instructions were fully carried out.

M. Atonement Money (38:21–31)

Exodus 30:11–16 laid out the provision for financing the building of the tabernacle. Each individual adult counted in the census was to pay a half shekel. When the census was carried out (38:26), the money (silver) collected was 301,775 shekels. (A talent was worth 3,000 shekels.) Thus each of the 603,550 men (Nu 1:46) paid a half shekel of silver, as required. The gold collected was 87,730 shekels, and the bronze was 212,400 shekels. The total collection amounted to several tons of precious metals. (A shekel of silver weighed 14.55 grams or .513 ounces, and a shekel of gold [the common shekel] was 16.37 grams or .577 ounces.)

N. The Priestly Garments (39:1–31)

1. The Ephod (39:1–7)

The description of the making of the ephod is somewhat abbreviated here from that of the instructions (28:6–14). It appears that it was not made by one individual but by several. Though the details are not given, it is stressed here that Moses' instructions were followed precisely (39:5).

2. Breastpiece (39:8–21)

The details of the instructions are followed closely from 28:15–28. From the text it appears that several workers were also involved in making the breastpiece. Again it is stressed that they followed Moses' instructions precisely (39:21).

3. The Robe of the Ephod (39:22-26)

A few details are added concerning the way in which the robe was sewn (cf. 28:4). For example, it was made of "cloth which was the work of a weaver." Again, the task involved several workers, and they followed Moses' instruction precisely (v. 26).

4. Tunic, Turban, Sash, and Undergarments (39:27-29)

The text merely adds that these garments were made of "cloth woven by a weaver" and that Moses' instructions were followed precisely (v. 29).

5. The Gold Plate (39:30-31)

The gold plate is identified as a "sacred diadem." Several workers were involved in making it and Moses' instructions were followed carefully.

O. Moses Inspects the Tabernacle (39:32-43)

The description of the tabernacle given here repeats in large measure the instructions of Moses in 35:10-19. As with the earlier descriptions of the work, its purpose is to show that the work was completed "just as the LORD had commanded Moses" (39:42). In a way that recalls God's own inspection of his work in Creation (Ge 1:31, "God saw all that he had made, and behold, it was very good"), the narrative says, "Moses saw all the work, and behold, they had done it just as the LORD had commanded them" (Ex 39:43). As in God's work of Creation a blessing followed the completion of the work (Ge 1:28), so also when the tabernacle was completed Moses "blessed them" (Ex 39:43).

P. Setting up the Tabernacle (40:1-33)

1. Instructions (40:1-16)

The narrative begins with a description of the instructions given Moses for setting up the tabernacle. The Lord told Moses to set it up on the first day of the first month of the second year (v. 17). First the ark was put in place and then covered with the curtains, that is, the tents of the tabernacle and the curtain covering the Holy of Holies. Next came the table, the lampstand, the golden altar of incense, and the curtain covering the doorway to the tabernacle. The altar of burnt offerings was then put before the doorway of the tabernacle, and the basin was put between the altar and the tent. The curtains making the courtyard were then put up all around, with a curtain providing a gateway to the courtyard. When all was in place, the tabernacle with its equipment were anointed with oil and the priests were brought in, dressed, and anointed.

2. Setting up the Tabernacle (40:17-33)

Following the Lord's instruction, Moses now set up the tabernacle. The author is careful to note that the tabernacle was set up on the first day of the first month of the second year. It had been only nine months since Israel arrived at Sinai (19:1); nevertheless, the tabernacle was ready for the celebration of the first Passover, which would have been only fourteen days away (Nu 9:1-5). The writer's careful attention to the chronology of the events is important, for it shows that the restriction of the offering of the

Passover lamb to the central worship center (Dt 16:1–8) could thus have already been carried out during this first celebration of the Passover in the wilderness.

Although the description of the erection of the tabernacle follows closely the instructions of 40:1–16, some extra detail is given regarding the ark. The "testimony"—the stone tablets containing the Ten Commandments and other words spoken by God to Moses—was placed inside the ark and the atonement cover was placed over it. Apparently at this time Aaron put the jar containing the manna "before" the ark, as is described in 16:32–34 (cf. Heb 9:4).

Q. The Glory of the Lord (40:34–38; cf. Ex 13:21–22; Nu 9:15–23)

The Lord's approval of the work of building the tabernacle is shown by the fact that the cloud of God's glory now took its place over the Tent of Meeting (i.e., the tabernacle). This was a visual reminder of the purpose of the tabernacle expressed in 25:8, where the Lord said, "Have them make a sanctuary for me, and I will dwell among them."

This narrative sounds a final note that prepares the way for the instructions which follow in the next section of the Pentateuch, Leviticus. We learn from the narrative that "Moses could not enter the Tent of Meeting because the cloud had settled upon it, and the glory of the LORD filled the tabernacle" (40:35). More provisions were thus necessary before they could enter into the tabernacle. Those provisions are given in Leviticus.

Chapter 3

LEVITICUS

Leviticus is a continuation of Exodus. We should not, in fact, think of it as a new book. The title itself, Leviticus, is the Latin rendering of the Greek translator's Λευιτικόν, meaning "pertaining to the Levitical priests." Its name stems from the fact that in this section of the Pentateuch the author focuses on the requirements of the covenant that relate to the priests, who were from the tribe of Levi.

Exodus 40 concluded with the completion of the tabernacle (v. 17) in the first month of the second year, on the first day of the month. Numbers 1:1 begins on the first day of the second month of the second year after the exodus from Egypt. Leviticus, then, deals with those events which transpired during the intervening month. Its subject matter is the legislation given to Moses at the Tent of Meeting.

The central theme of the book is holiness. The book intends to show how Israel was to fulfill its covenant responsibility to be "a kingdom of priests and a holy nation" (Ex 19:6; Lev 26:5).

I. THE OFFERINGS AND SACRIFICES (1:1–17:16)

These chapters describe briefly the various offerings and sacrifices used in the consecration of the priests and the people. They are not intended as an exhaustive explanation of the sacrificial system. Within the narrative of Leviticus, these regulations provide background for the dedication of the tabernacle and the priesthood in chapters 8–9, as well as for the rest of the Pentateuch.[1] They may be compared to the genealogies in Genesis and those

---

[1]See Gordon J. Wenham, *The Book of Leviticus*, NICOT (Grand Rapids: Eerdmans, 1979), 49–50.

at the beginning of 1 Chronicles, whose purpose is to introduce the main characters of the subsequent narratives. An appreciation for the narrative purpose of these detailed regulations should lead us to focus on what the writer has put in these chapters rather than on what he has left out. That is, we should not attempt to reconstruct from these regulations the whole or even a part of the sacrificial procedures of ancient Israel. Nor should we be concerned to reconstruct and describe what these various regulations meant to the ancient Israelites. Though such things are important in their own right, they do not enhance our appreciation of the writer's intention. The information concerning the regulations given in the narrative before us is sufficient to enable us to understand the events recorded in the subsequent texts. For example, when we read that a woman in Leviticus 12 was instructed to bring "a sin offering" to the Tent of Meeting, one need not be an anthropologist of ancient Israel to understand what that entailed. All that is necessary for an appreciation of the narrative is to have read the first seven chapters of the book.

The book of Leviticus as a whole, being only part of the Pentateuch, has no general introduction. It opens immediately with the instructions for the offerings brought to the tabernacle.

A. Laws of Sacrifice (1:1–7:38)

1. Sacrificial Instructions Pertaining to Laypersons (1:1–6:7 [MT 5:26])

Only a brief introduction to the sacrifices is prefaced to this section (1:1–2). According to this introduction, the instructions that follow for the next six chapters deal with guidelines for bringing "an offering" to the Lord at the tabernacle. The instructions do not introduce the practice of offerings but provide regulations for them in the light of the newly established worship of God at the tabernacle. The narrative assumes that several types of offerings were already well known and practiced by the Israelites (Ex 18:12). Moreover, according to the earlier narratives in the Pentateuch, the earliest patriarchs had already made various kinds of offerings (Ge 4:3–4; 8:20; 46:1). Thus these chapters intend to present regulations which Moses had given for existing practices of sacrifices and offerings among the Israelites. They are not an attempt to inaugurate a new system or to provide a complete description of how each sacrifice was to be carried out. Because there are so many details in these chapters, it is easy to overlook the fact that far more important details have not been given. For example, this section lacks any instructions regarding when and under what circumstances the sacrifices were to be offered. The rest of the Pentateuch will provide many examples of the time and circumstances. The purpose in these early chapters is primarily to describe the offerings themselves.

The narrative framework of Leviticus shows that these instructions were given to Moses by the Lord at the "Tent of Meeting." This was probably the "tent" Moses set up outside the camp where God spoke to him (Ex 33:7–11). According to Exodus 40:35, Moses could not enter the "Tent of Meeting" (i.e., the tabernacle). Thus God continued to speak with Moses from the tent outside the camp. We can already see in the strategy of the writer the importance of the offerings and sacrifices and the dedication of the priesthood. Only after the dedication of the tabernacle and the priesthood were Moses and Aaron able to enter the tent (tabernacle) where God's glory dwelt (Lev 9:23). Moses received the instructions for the offerings and sacrifices from the "Tent of Meeting" outside the camp, but their purpose was to make the other "Tent of Meeting," the tabernacle, accessible. Thus, though here at the opening of this section the "Tent of Meeting" refers to the tent set up outside the camp, in the following chapters the expression "Tent of Meeting" refers to the tabernacle.

a. Burnt Offering (1:3–17)

These instructions deal with three types of burnt offerings which could be brought by "anyone" to the tabernacle: (1) those from the herd (vv. 3–9); (2) those from the flock (vv. 10–13); and (3) those from the birds (vv. 14–17). The offering was presented at the entrance of the Tent of Meeting (the tabernacle), where the offerer would lay his hand on the head of the offering, and, if it were then accepted, it would "make atonement for him" (v. 4). If the animal was from the herd or flock, the offerer would slaughter and prepare it and the priest would bring it and its blood to the altar, where it would be completely burned. If the offering was a bird, it would be given over to the priests, who would prepare it on the altar.

The priests' responsibilities are further outlined in 6:8–13 (MT 1–6). The burnt offering would lay on the altar throughout the night with the fire still burning. In the morning, the priest, properly dressed and consecrated, would remove the ashes and place them beside the altar while he changed his clothing. The priest would then take the ashes outside the camp to a ceremonially clean disposal site.

> **Command #63**, Lev 1:2, The procedure of the burnt offering: "When any of you brings an offering to the Lord."

b. Grain Offering (2:1–16)

A grain (or meal) offering was an offering of flour presented in any number of ways: fresh, baked, fried on a griddle, or cooked in a pan. The offering was brought to the priest, who then took a small portion of it to burn on the altar. The rest was taken to be used by the priests. The grain offering could not contain leaven (yeast) but was to be seasoned with salt.

> **Command #67**, Lev 2:1, The procedure of the meal (grain) offering: "When one brings a meal offering to the Lord."
>
> **Command #62**, Lev 2:13, Offerings must be salted: "Upon all your offerings you must offer salt."
>
> **Prohibition #98**, Lev 2:11, One must not offer yeast or honey on the altar: "You are not to burn any yeast or honey in an offering."
>
> **Prohibition #99**, Lev 2:13, One must not offer anything unsalted on the altar: "Season all your grain offerings with salt."

According to 6:14–18 (MT 7–11), the priests were to burn the portion of the grain offering on the altar with incense. The rest they could eat as their portion. It was to be eaten without leaven (yeast) and could only be eaten by a "male descendant of Aaron" in the courtyard of the tabernacle.

c. Peace Offering (3:1–17)

Unlike the burnt offering, in which the whole offering is consumed by fire, in the peace offering only the "fat portions" and the blood are burned. The rest of the animal was prepared and eaten by the priests and the offerer. The present passage gives only the instructions regarding the offering of the "fat portions." Instructions regarding the eating of the remaining portions are given in 7:11–36.

> **Command #66**, Lev 3:1, The procedure of the peace offering: "If his offering is a peace offering."

The central issue in the handling of the peace offering is that none of the "fat portions" or the blood was to be consumed (3:17). The various uses of the peace offering are not discussed in chapter 3.

In 7:12, 16, it is assumed that a peace offering would be given "as an expression of thankfulness" (v. 12), as a result of a vow (v. 16), or as a freewill offering (v. 16). The meat, the remainder of the offering after the "fat portions" were removed, could be eaten by anyone who was ceremonially clean (v. 19). The breast belonged to Aaron and his sons, and the right leg belonged to the priest who offered the blood of that sacrifice at the altar.

d. Sin Offering (4:1–5:13)

The purpose of the sin offering was to atone for unintentionally breaking one of the commandments given by God (4:20, 26, 31, 35). Different forms of offerings and procedures were required, depending on the status or identity of the offender. For example, a sin offering for the high priest (v. 3) or for the community as a whole (v. 13) required a young bull, whereas for an individual (v. 27) or a leader (v. 22) in the community a goat or lamb was required. A poor person (v. 7) was required to bring only two doves or two young pigeons (5:7). If one was unable to afford even this simple offering, a sin offering could be made of a tenth of an ephah of fine flour (5:11).

As with the burnt offering, one brought the appropriate sin offering to the tabernacle, laid his hands on the animal, and slaughtered it. The priest took the blood and sprinkled it on the altar. As with the peace offering, the "fat portions" were burned on the altar. When a priest was involved in the sin, either in the role of high priest or simply as a member of the community, the remainder of the sacrificial animal was carried outside the camp and burned on the ash heap where the ashes of the burnt offering were dumped (4:12, 21; 6:30 [MT 23]). In cases where the officiating priest was not involved in the sin, however, the meat of the animal was not burned on the ash heap but was given to the priest to eat (6:26, 29 [MT 19, 22]; 7:7).

> **Commands relating to the sin offering:**
> **Command #68**, Lev 4:13, If the congregation of Israel err in a decision, they must bring an offering: "If all the congregation of Israel err."
> **Command #69**, Lev 4:27, If a single individual errs unintentionally, he must bring a sin offering: "If one individual sins unintentionally."
> **Command #72**, Lev 5:1–11, The offering of varying cost: "If he cannot afford a lamb, he is to bring two doves or two young pigeons."

Command #178, Lev 5:1, A witness must testify: "If a person sins because he does not speak up when he hears a public charge to testify . . . he will be held responsible."

Prohibitions relating to the sin offering:

Prohibition #112, Lev 5:8, One must not sever the head of a sacrificial bird: "He is to wring its head from its neck, not severing it."

Prohibition #102, Lev 5:11, One must not use olive oil in a sin offering: "He must not put oil or incense on it, because it is a sin offering."

Prohibition #103, Lev 5:11, One must not use incense in a sin offering: "He must not put oil or incense on it, because it is a sin offering."

e. Guilt Offering (5:14–6:7 [MT 5:14–26])

The guilt offering provided for the restitution of a wrong (5:16a; 6:5 [MT 5:24]) along with atonement for the wrong itself (5:16b, 18; 6:7 [MT 5:26]). When restitution was made, the proper value was determined and a fifth (5:16; 6:5 [MT 5:24]) of that was added to the repayment. The atonement in each case was the offering of a ram (5:15; 6:6 [MT 5:25]). (See Nu 5:5–10.) The procedure for the slaughter and presentation of the guilt offering is described in 7:1–10.

Command #71, Lev 5:15, The actual guilt offering for various sins: "When a person commits a violation and sins unintentionally."

Command #118, Lev 5:16, Restitution to the temple for neglected dues: "He must make restitution for what he has failed to do."

Command #70, Lev 5:17–18, A sin offering that hangs in doubt: "If a person sins and does what is forbidden in any of the Lord's commands."

Command #194, Lev 5:23 (EVV 6:4), Stolen property must be returned: "He shall return the stolen property."

2. Sacrificial Instructions Pertaining to Priests (6:8–7:38 [MT 6:1–7:38])

a. Burnt Offering (6:8–13 [MT 1–6])

The burnt offering would lay on the altar throughout the night with the fire still burning. In the morning, the priest, properly dressed and consecrated, would remove the ashes and place them beside the altar while he changed his clothing. The priest would then take the ashes outside the camp to a ceremonially clean disposal site. (See comments above on 1:3–17.)

Command #30, Lev 6:3 (EVV 10), Priests are to remove ashes daily from the altar: "The priest shall put on his linen clothes."

Command #29, Lev 6:6 (EVV 13), One must keep the fire burning upon the altar: "The continual fire shall burn upon the altar."

Prohibition #81, Lev 6:6 (EVV 13), The fire on the altar must not be extinguished: "The fire must be kept burning on the altar continuously."

b. Grain Offering (6:14–23 [MT 7–16])

The priests were to burn a designated portion of the grain (meal) offering on the altar with incense. The rest they could eat as their portion. It was to be eaten without leaven (yeast) and could only be eaten by a "male descendant of Aaron" in the courtyard of the tabernacle. (See comments above on 2:1–16.)

The grain offering was also the offering to be given on the day that the high priest was anointed (6:20 [MT 13]). It was prepared by the "son who was to succeed him as anointed priest." Unlike the usual grain offering, this particular offering was burned completely because it was an offering of a priest (6:23 [MT 16]).

> **Command #88**, Lev 6:9 (EVV 16), The priests are to eat the remainder of the meal (grain) offering: "The remainder from the meal offering Aaron and his sons shall eat."
>
> **Command #40**, Lev 6:13 (EVV 20), The high priest is to present a meal offering twice daily: "This is the gift of Aaron and his sons."
>
> **Prohibition #124**, Lev 6:10 (EVV 17), The remains of the meal offering must not contain leaven: "It must not be baked with yeast."
>
> **Prohibition #138**, Lev 6:16 (EVV 23), The meal offering of a priest must not be eaten: "Every grain offering of a priest shall be burned completely; it must not be eaten."

c. Sin Offering (6:24–30 [MT 18–23])

Much has already been recorded regarding the sin offering (4:1–5:13), though this section clears up some important points. It was earlier implicit but is here made explicit that the meat of the animals offered by individuals and leaders was to be eaten by the priests who performed the sacrifice (6:26, 29 [MT 19, 22]). Furthermore, a sin offering carried out as part of the cleansing of the tabernacle could not be eaten by the priest (v. 30 [MT 23]). Thus the principle is established that the sin offering could be eaten by the priests as long as the offering had not been given in any way on behalf of the priests.

> **Command #64**, Lev 6:18 (EVV 25), The procedure of the sin offering: "This is the law of the sin offering."
>
> **Prohibition #139**, Lev 6:23 (EVV 30), The meat of the sin offering must not be eaten: "Any sin offering whose blood is brought into the Tent of Meeting to make atonement in the Holy Place must not be eaten; it must be burned."

d. Guilt Offering (7:1–10)

The nature and purpose of the guilt offering is described in 5:14–6:7 (MT 5:14–26). The present text gives the procedure for the slaughter and presentation of the offering. As part of the instructions, the high priest is told to keep the skin (עוֹר) of the sacrificed animal (7:8). Though the value this would have for the high priest and his family is obvious, the author may also want to call to mind the narrative of Genesis 3:21, where the Lord gave animal skins (עוֹר) to Adam and Eve. There are numerous attempts throughout the Pentateuch to associate God's earlier acts in the Garden with the covenant he made with Israel at Sinai.

> **Command #65**, Lev 7:1, The procedure of the guilt offering: "This is the law of the guilt offering."

e. Peace Offering (7:11–38)

In 7:12, 16, it is assumed that a peace (or fellowship) offering would be given "as an expression of thankfulness" (v. 12), as a result of a vow (v. 16), or as a freewill offering (v. 16). The meat, the remainder of the offering after the "fat portions" were removed, could be eaten by anyone who was ceremonially clean (v. 19). (See comments above on 3:1–17.)

Command #91, Lev 7:17, That which is left over from the offering on the third day must be burned: "That which was left over from the meat of the sacrifice shall be burned in fire on the third day."

Command #90, Lev 7:19, Consecrated things which have become unclean must be burned: "Meat which touches anything unclean."

Prohibition #132, Lev 7:18, One must not eat the meat of the fellowship (peace) offering on the third day: "If any meat of the fellowship offering is eaten on the third day it will not be accepted."

Prohibition #130, Lev 7:19, One must not eat any holy thing that has been profaned: "Meat that touches anything ceremonially unclean must not be eaten."

Prohibition #185, Lev 7:23, One must not eat fat of cattle, sheep, or goats: "Do not eat any of the fat of cattle, sheep, or goats."

Prohibition #184, Lev 7:26, One must not eat blood: "You must not eat the blood of any bird or animal."

The basic principle of eating the peace offering was that the fat and blood of the offering were devoted to God. It thus was "an offering by fire" to the Lord (7:25), and the eating of it was strictly forbidden. A second basic principle of the peace offering was that the priests were to have their share in the gifts. The breast belonged to Aaron and his sons, and the right leg belonged to the priest who offered the blood of that sacrifice at the altar.

B. Consecration of the Priests (8:1–9:24)

The instructions for the consecration of the priests for work in the tabernacle were given in Exodus 29:1–37. The execution of those instructions are carried out here in Leviticus 8 with little variation. In the retelling of the instructions, the writer is careful to label the various offerings according to the types of sacrifices described in the first part of the book. For example, the bull is consistently called "the bull of sin offering" (vv. 14–15), as in Exodus 29:14; the first ram is called "the ram for the burnt offering" (Lev 8:18), as in Exodus 29:18; and the second ram is called "the ram for the ordination" (Lev 8:22), as in Exodus 29:23. The writer underscores the priests' careful attention to detail by reminding the reader that all was done "according to what the Lord commanded Moses" (Lev 8:17, 22, 29).

After the seven days of consecration for the priests, Moses gathered Aaron, his sons, and the elders of Israel and instructed them to prepare for the appearance of the glory of the Lord at the tabernacle. This appears to be the same group who "saw" God at Mount Sinai in Exodus 24:9. The preparation consisted of presenting several of the kinds of offerings described at the beginning of the book. When Moses gave the instructions, they followed his word to the letter. The offerings were first given for Aaron and the priests and then for the people. At the conclusion, Moses and Aaron went into the Tent of Meeting (i.e., the tabernacle). In Exodus 40:35 Moses could not enter the Tent of Meeting (tabernacle) because of the glory of the Lord. Moses and Aaron could now go in because the sacrifices had been offered as the Lord had commanded. When they came out again, "they blessed the people" (Lev 9:23). The fire from before the Lord that consumed the burnt offering and the fat portions on the altar (v. 24) was a sign to all the people that God had accepted their offerings.

The pattern was hereby established: by means of the priests' proper entry into the tabernacle, the nation was blessed. The next chapter (Lev 10) gives a negative lesson of the same truth in the example of Nadab and Abihu: the blessing of God's people will come only through obedience to the divine pattern. In the narrative itself, the response of the people echoes God's acceptance of them: "When all the people saw it, they shouted for joy and fell facedown" (9:24).

Surprisingly, Aaron's offering of the goat for the people's sin offering (9:15–16) follows the instructions for the sin offering for a leader of the community, a male goat (4:22–26), rather than the sin offering for the whole community, a young bull (4:13–21), which one might have expected. The reason for this offering was apparently because the whole community had not specifically sinned; thus this offering was meant for any specific individual in the community who needed it.

In any event, since the requirements for either sin offering varied, Aaron's offering led to some difficulty, as we shall see in the next chapter (10:16–20). If the sin offering had been for the whole community, it should have been burned (4:21), which is, in fact, what happened (9:15; cf. 9:11). If it was a sin offering for an individual leader of the community, as the selection of a male goat indicates, parts of it should have been eaten by the priests. Since Aaron offered a goat, in the course of the narrative Moses was forced to confront Aaron for failing to eat the required parts (10:16–17).

C. Death of Nadab and Abihu (10:1–20)

Just as "the fire that came from before the LORD" had been a sign of God's approval of the dedication of the tabernacle and the priests in the previous chapter (9:24), so also "the fire that came from before the LORD" in this chapter (10:2) was a sign of God's disapproval. The writer's clear purpose in putting these two narratives together is to show the importance that God attached to obeying his commands. The reader is not told any details about the fire which the two sons of Aaron offered. Some have suggested that Moses' subsequent command that the sons of Aaron not drink wine or any fermented drink when they go into the tabernacle (Lev 10:9) gives a narrative clue that drunkenness may have been involved.[2] Such a view finds additional support from the similarities between this narrative and the earlier narrative of the drunkenness of Noah (Ge 9:20–29; see comments below on Lev 13 and 14). In any case, though it does not specifically describe their sin, the narrative shows unequivocally that the "unauthorized fire" which they offered before the Lord was wrong because it was "contrary to his command" (10:1). The purpose of the narrative is to show that the transgression of the sons of Aaron lay in their sin of disobedience.

Immediately after the incident, Mishael and Elzaphan, the sons of Aaron's uncle Uzziel, were summoned to carry the bodies of Nadab and Abihu out of the tabernacle. This was to ensure that Aaron and his other sons would not become defiled.

It is important to note that within the narrative, Moses himself has interpreted the severe judgment of Nadab and Abihu by laying down the

---

[2]See, e.g., Rashi, ad loc.

principle, "Among those who approach me [God] I will show myself holy. . . . I will be honored" (10:3). The purpose of the instructions for sacrifice and work at the altar, which have been outlined in detail in the previous chapters, was to provide a means of treating God as holy and honoring him before all the people. Thus this narrative shows that behind the rebellious offering of Nadab and Abihu was a disobedient heart. They refused to come before him "as he had commanded." The narrative is similar in many respects to that found in Samuel's response to Saul in 1 Samuel 15:22: "Does the LORD delight in burnt offerings and sacrifices as much as in obeying the voice of the LORD? To obey is better than sacrifice, and to heed is better than the fat of rams." (Cf. the sons of Eli in 1Sa 2:12–17.)

> **Prohibition #163**, Lev 10:6, Priests must not enter the temple with long hair: "Do not let your hair become unkempt."
>
> **Prohibition #164**, Lev 10:6, Priests must not enter the temple with torn clothes: "Do not tear you clothes."
>
> **Prohibition #165**, Lev 10:7, Priests must not leave the courtyard during the temple service: "Do not leave the entrance to the Tent of Meeting or you will die."
>
> **Prohibition #73**, Lev 10:9–11, One must not enter the temple (M. to teach the Torah) while in a state of intoxication: "You and your sons are not to drink wine or other fermented drink whenever you enter into the Tent of Meeting."

Within the course of the narrative itself, a question of the interpretation of the law arises. What should have been the procedure for Aaron's sons in carrying out the sin offering on this day of dedication? As Moses was reviewing the various offerings given at this dedication (10:12–15), he could not find the part of the sin offering that Aaron and his sons were to have eaten (v. 16). When he found that these parts had been burned and not eaten, as 9:15 suggests had been the case, he grew angry with Aaron (10:16b). According to Moses, the requirements of 6:26 (MT 19) should have been met and thus Aaron's sons should have eaten the offering (10:17). Though the burning of the offering might have been justified on the grounds that it was a sin offering for the people (cf. 9:15; 4:21), Moses apparently based his judgment on the fact that a goat, not a bull, was offered, which made it an offering that should have been eaten (6:26 [MT 19]). Moreover, Moses appealed to the ruling in 6:30 (MT 23), which prohibited eating the sin offering only if the blood had been taken into the Tent of Meeting (10:18), which in this case had not happened (9:15).

In his response, Aaron did not contest Moses' explanation of the regulations. Rather, he appealed to the events of that day, which, he argued, had rendered he and his sons unfit for eating the holy food. Although the narrative does not explicitly state it, the "things" that had happened on that day were apparently the death of Nadab and Abihu. But why did their death make Aaron and his sons unfit for holy food? The concern for ritual purity had already been taken care of when Mishael and Elzaphan were summoned to carry the dead bodies out of the tabernacle (10:4). There was, then, no danger that Aaron and his sons were ritually unclean because they had touched dead bodies.

Thus Aaron's defense does not fall back on another law. It rather appears simply to follow his own line of reasoning. When he saw the events of this day, Aaron concluded that a mourner should not take part in a sacrificial meal. The narrative is quick to point out that when Moses heard of Aaron's decision, he approved of it ("he was satisfied," 10:20). Interestingly enough, later, in Deuteronomy 26:14, this same ruling appears as part of the checks on ritual purity—a mourner was considered unclean. Thus, by means of this narrative, Aaron the high priest is presented as one who is capable of making a correct and just legal decision. He can legitimately distinguish the clean from the unclean (10:10–11).

The overall lesson of this narrative plays an important role in delineating the ongoing responsibility of Aaron's priesthood: discerning between the holy and the profane, the clean and the unclean (cf. Hag 2:11–12; Mal 2:7). In verses 10 and 11, Moses had further instructed Aaron that he and his sons were to have a lasting ordinance "to distinguish between the holy and the common, between the unclean and the clean" and "to teach the Israelites all the decrees that the LORD has given them through Moses." In the chapters that follow, Moses will list in great detail just these kinds of distinctions between the holy and the common, the unclean and the clean (e.g., 11:47).

In this narrative, then, we see Aaron actually doing the kind of thing that the sons of Aaron were to be responsible for throughout Israel's history. Even more importantly, we see that he had Moses' approval. Moreover, in the subsequent chapters of Leviticus we see the kinds of decisions that were to be made. The narrative of Aaron's decision, then, provides a fitting introduction to the purity laws which follow in the next chapters.

D. Laws of Purity and Impurity (11:1–15:33)

1. Regulations Concerning Animals, Birds, Water Creatures, and Creeping Things (11:1–46)

This chapter contains a selected list of creatures that divides each type of creature into various classes of purity. According to the final verse in the chapter, the decisive question was whether a class of animals was unclean or clean. The goal of the distinctions was to determine whether an animal could be eaten. The notion of uncleanness and cleanness is specifically applied in this chapter to the question of holiness. Violating any of the regulations relating to clean and unclean animals rendered one unclean (i.e., profane or common, 11:44–45), and thus unable to enter into community worship (12:4). The purpose of the chapter is to tie the concept of holiness to God's own example of holiness (11:45).

That some animals were clean and others were unclean does not imply that some animals are, in themselves, dirty. At the opening of the Pentateuch, for example, in the account of Creation, God saw all the animals he had created, and at that time he said that they were all "good" (Ge 1:21). This divine assessment of all creatures included even those animals called "detestable" here in Leviticus.

Looking at the larger arrangement of the chapter, we see that it contains regulations concerning four major groups of animals: land animals, birds or flying creatures, water animals, and "small creeping things." This is the same general classification of animal life found in the Genesis Creation account. The distribution of the regulations, however, does not always fall neatly into these four groups. The principle of distribution throughout the chapter is governed not only by the type of animal group but also by the type of impurity incurred. For example, the first category (vv. 1–8) concerns matters of eating and touching certain animals, the result of which is "uncleanness." The second group (vv. 9–23) concerns various types of animals that are considered "detestable" and consequently cannot be eaten. The third group (vv. 24–40) concerns the carcasses of animals of various types; if one touches their carcasses, one must wash and one is rendered unclean until evening. The fourth group (vv. 41–42) treats all small creeping land creatures as "detestable."

a. First Category: Concerning General Land Animals and Cleanliness (11:1–8)

What may be eaten (vv. 2–3): "You may eat any animal that has a split hoof completely divided and that chews the cud."

What may not be eaten (vv. 4–8): Animals that "only chew the cud or only have a split hoof" (camel, rock badger, and rabbit); animals that "chew the cud but do not have a split hoof" (pig); animals that "have a split hoof completely divided, but do not chew the cud."

b. Second Category: Concerning Detestable Things and Eating (11:9–23)

(1) Water Animals (11:9–12)

What may be eaten (v. 9): "Of all the creatures living in the water of the seas and the streams, you may eat any that have fins and scales."

What may not be eaten (vv. 10–12): "But all creatures in the seas or streams that do not have fins and scales. . . . you must not eat their meat."

(2) Flying Creatures (11:13–23)

What may not be eaten (vv. 13–20): This section contains a selected list of twenty-one (7 x 3) flying creatures—the eagle, the vulture, the black vulture, the red kite, any kind of black kite, any kind of raven, the horned owl, the screech owl, the gull, any kind of hawk, the little owl, the cormorant, the great owl, the white owl, the desert owl, the osprey, the stork, any kind of heron, the hoopoe, the bat, and all flying insects.

What may be eaten (vv. 21–23): Creeping flying creatures that have jointed legs and that hop—locust, katydid, cricket, grasshopper.

c. Third Category: Concerning Creatures and Temporary Uncleanness (11:24–40)

The following creatures, if touched, require the washing of clothes, and one remains unclean until evening: General land animals (v. 26): "Every animal that has a split hoof not completely divided or that does not chew the cud"; animals that walk on four legs and have paws (vv. 27–28); creeping animals (vv. 29–38): the weasel, rat, great lizard, gecko, monitor lizard, wall lizard, skink, and chameleon; clean animals that die (vv. 39–40)

d. Fourth Category: Concerning Detestable Things (11:41–42)

Every creature creeping upon the ground, on its belly, on four legs, or on many legs is detestable.

Commands relating to eating:

Command #149, Lev 11:2, Examination of animals for eating: "These are the animals you shall eat."

Command #96, Lev 11:8, One who touches a carcass is unclean: "You shall not touch their carcass."

Command #152, Lev 11:9, Examination of fish for eating: "This you may eat from all which is in the waters."

Command #151, Lev 11:21, Examination of locusts for eating: "Those that have jointed legs for hopping."

Command #97, Lev 11:29–31, The eight types of creeping things are unclean: "This is what is unclean."

Command #98, Lev 11:34, Food and drink becomes unclean when in contact with an unclean object: "All kinds of food which comes into contact with water is unclean."

Prohibitions relating to eating:

Prohibition #173, Lev 11:11, One must not eat unclean fish: "And since you are to detest them, you must not eat their meat."

Prohibition #174, Lev 11:13, One must not eat unclean birds: "These are the birds you are to detest and not eat because they are detestable."

Prohibition #176, Lev 11:41, One must not eat unclean creeping things that creep on the ground: "Every creature that moves about on the ground is detestable; it is not to be eaten."

Prohibition #178, Lev 11:42, One must not eat worms: "You are not to eat any creature that moves about on the ground, whether it moves on its belly or walks on all fours or on many feet; it is detestable."

Prohibition #179, Lev 11:43, One must not eat any detestable creature: "Do not defile yourselves by any of these creatures."

Prohibition #177, Lev 11:44, One must not eat creatures that move upon the ground (reptiles): "Do not make yourselves unclean by any creature that moves about on the ground."

2. Purification Relating to Childbirth (12:1–8)

This short chapter may seem at first glance to have been arbitrarily selected and placed here. It concerns only the case of purification related to a woman in childbirth. We should ask ourselves, however, why the author has chosen to place this specific topic at this point in the narrative. Perhaps its apparent arbitrariness belies its significance. Though this chapter contains only one regulation, it plays a strategic role in relationship to the surrounding texts. It is precisely in this regulation regarding childbirth that an explanation is given to the overall meaning of the notion of impurity throughout this whole section of legal texts. This narrative tells us that as long as the woman was unclean, "she must not touch anything sacred or go to the sanctuary" (12:4). This statement defines impurity with respect to the sanctuary (the tabernacle) and, more importantly, in terms of one's acceptability within the worshiping community. Impurity is not defined in terms of a vague notion of taboo but in terms of acceptance or restriction from worship. The sense of impurity is thus defined with respect to the goal of the covenant and the goal of Creation (cf. the commentary above on Ge 2:15), that is, the worship of God. Being in a state of impurity meant not being allowed to worship God in the community assembly. As the man and woman were cast off from God's presence in the Garden (Ge 3:24–25), so the one who is unclean cannot come before God in his sanctuary.

Thus, by placing this specific regulation in the midst of the general regulations dealing with impurities, the writer has provided a key to the notion of cleanness and uncleanness found throughout the rest of the book. Uncleanness was not a vague notion of guilt or a mere ostracism from the everyday life of the community. Uncleanness meant one was barred from the worship life of the covenant community. Uncleanness meant separation from the sacred and the tabernacle.

The Hebrew word translated "becomes pregnant" in the NIV is unusual. It is not the word one would expect in Hebrew to denote becoming pregnant. It is used only here and in the first chapter of Genesis (Ge 1:11–12, "plants bearing seed"). Why would such an unusual expression be used here? The answer may lie in the fact that the word means literally, "she produces a seed." Its use here may then give a clue to the reason that the author has, by means of this narrative, focused on the need for the woman's purification in childbirth.

First, the verbal link in the use of the term *seed* in this chapter (the woman "produces a seed") and the Creation account in Genesis 1 ("plants bearing seed") supports the long-acknowledged observation that this section of Leviticus follows remarkably closely the pattern of the Creation account in Genesis. In Genesis 1, for example, God distinguishes the good from the evil in his new creation. After each new act of creation God says, "It is good." In a similar way, in these chapters of Leviticus, God distinguishes the clean from the unclean. Just as he distinguished the "good" for humanity in creation, so now God distinguishes the "clean" for humanity in the covenant. Moreover, the order God follows in creation—dealing first with the animals, birds, sea creatures, and creeping things, and then with humanity—is the same order he follows here—dealing first with the animals, birds, and sea creatures, and then with humanity (Lev 11–12).[3] The author is clearly intent on our seeing a similar pattern in God's overall purpose and work.

Second, the use of the term *seed* in Leviticus 12:2 and the notion of childbirth may also allude to the promised "seed" of the woman in Genesis 3:15 as well as to the curse in Genesis 3:16: "I will greatly increase your pains in childbearing." There can be no doubt that the author has focused our attention on the central role of childbirth in fulfilling God's plan of blessing since the beginning chapters of Genesis. In Genesis 1:28, the first divine blessing of humankind is centered on the woman's role in childbirth: "Be fruitful and multiply and fill the land." After the Fall, the curse as well as the blessing centers on the woman and her childbearing: the curse, "I will greatly increase your pains in childbearing" (Ge 3:16), as well as the blessing, "[The woman's seed] will crush your [the serpent's] head and you will strike his heel" (Ge 3:15). Throughout the patriarchal narratives the promised "seed" lies at the center of the hope of blessing (e.g., Ge 12:1–3).

In the beginning narratives of Exodus the hope of God's fulfilling his promise of blessing finds its deepest expression in the narrative of Moses' birth. It should be no surprise, then, to find that God's provision of blessing

---

[3]See Rashi, ad loc.

for Israel in the covenant at Sinai also contains an echo of the hope that is centered in childbirth. In the later biblical narratives as well as in the Prophetic Books, the future fulfillment of God's promised blessing continues to be centered in the joy and expectation of childbirth (e.g., Isa 7:14; Mic 5:1–2).

Thus in the present narrative it may be that childbirth has been singled out in the discussion of purification because of its close association in the Pentateuch with both the blessing and the curse. It may be of interest to note that in 2 Timothy 2:15, when Paul alludes to Genesis 3:15, he links it specifically to the need of the woman to "remain in holiness." These are the same two themes linked in the present chapter.

The close association between the narrative themes of Genesis and the structure and arrangement of the present chapters in Leviticus which take up these same themes suggests that more links may be found in the next several chapters. Since the next topic in the Genesis narratives after the Fall is God's provision (עוֹר, "skin") for man's nakedness (עֵירֻם), it is significant that the next section in the Leviticus narratives also deals with the need for purification of the "skin [עוֹר] of the flesh." We can thus see the makings of a larger strategy at work in the pentateuchal narratives, one linking God's first work of Creation with his present work of covenant. Just as in the Fall God's good creation became contaminated with evil, so also provision must be made to distinguish the pure and the impure in the covenant community. The spread of impurity in the covenant community after the incident of the golden calf is described by means of the analogy with the spread of sin in God's good creation after the Fall.

> **Command #100**, Lev 12:2, A woman who has recently given birth is unclean: "A woman who becomes pregnant and gives birth."
>
> **Command #76**, Lev 12:6, The offering after childbirth: "And when the days of her cleanliness for the son or daughter are complete, she shall bring a yearling lamb."
>
> **Prohibition #129**, Lev 12:4, An unclean person must not eat of the holy things: "She must not touch anything sacred."

3. Regulations Relating to Skin Diseases (13:1–14:57)

As is common in these collections of regulations, the description of the contents and purpose of the collection is placed at the end (14:56–57). There, the contents of the chapter are described as "the instruction for all skin diseases, that for scabs, for clothing, for houses, raised spots, scabs, and bright spots" (v. 56). Its statement of purpose is "to teach the distinction between unclean and clean" (v. 57). The various tests for skin disease are enumerated first, and then the cleansing procedures are described.

The first section deals with the various examinations for skin disease (13:1–46) and the detection of such diseases on one's clothing (vv. 47–59). When a skin disease was detected, there was no provision for healing it. Rather, the diseased person was required to "wear torn clothes, let his hair be unkempt, cover the lower part of his face, and cry out, 'Unclean! Unclean!'" (v. 45). That person was to live alone "outside the camp" (v. 46). When clothing was found to be infected, it was either washed and reexamined (v. 54) or destroyed (vv. 52, 57; see Nu 5:1–4).

In the preceding sections we have tried to show that the purification regulations intentionally followed the sequential pattern established in the early chapters of Genesis. The apparent purpose of that pattern was to show that the spread of ritual defilement retraced the spread of sin in the beginning. Or, from the viewpoint of the Genesis narratives, its purpose was to show that humankind's original sin was a form of cultic contamination. Thus, as human skin was the focus of guilt and shame in the beginning, so now diseases of the skin provide an occasion to demonstrate the need for human cleansing. In other words, just as the effects of the first sin were immediately displayed in human skin ("And their eyes were opened and they knew that they were naked," Ge 3:7), so the writer uses the graphic horror of skin diseases found in these texts to depict the human state of uncleanness before a holy God.

Along similar lines, it is significant that in the Genesis narratives the first man and woman, once they had sinned, suffered the same consequences for their contamination as the unclean person in Leviticus. According to the regulations in Leviticus, if one were found to be unclean, "As long as he has the infection he remains unclean. He must live alone; he must live outside the camp" (13:46). In the same way, the Genesis narratives show that when Adam (and Eve) sinned, "the LORD God banished him from the Garden of Eden to work the ground from which he had been taken. And he drove Adam out" (Ge 3:23–24). Like the unclean person in Leviticus, they had to live "outside the camp." The notion of the contamination of clothing (Lev 13:47–58) also has an interesting analogy in the attempt of Adam and Eve to make clothing to cover their nakedness in the Garden (Ge 3:7), as well as in God's subsequent provision of clothing when they left the Garden (3:20).

As will become apparent below, in the further parallels between these levitical laws and the Genesis narratives, the writer sees that the Flood and Noah's sacrifice played an important role in the cleansing of humankind and in the preparation for God's covenant. We will see that the author continues to align these Levitical laws with the patterns of the Genesis narratives to reveal God's plan in the covenant stipulations within the context of his larger plan in Creation. It could hardly be coincidental that the narratives dealing with the "cleansing" of the skin diseases with water show close parallels with events and ideas in the biblical account of the Flood.

The next unit of text in the present narrative (Lev 14:1–53) deals with provisions for cleansing from the diseases enumerated in the preceding passage. This "cleansing" was a procedure for pronouncing that one had been healed. It did not provide for the healing of the disease. The text does not explain how one could be healed; it only explains how healed skin could be recognized. First the provisions for cleansing diseases of the flesh are given (vv. 1–32), and then those for cleansing diseases from the house (vv. 33–53). Both procedures are similar and follow the same pattern for pronouncing an object clean (cf. vv. 3–7 with vv. 48–53).

Cleansing a person who has been healed of a disease (14:4–7)	*Cleansing a house which has been cleared of disease (14:49–53)*
1. Two clean birds, cedar wood, scarlet yarn, and hyssop.	1. Two birds, cedar wood, scarlet yarn, and hyssop.

2.	One bird killed over fresh water in a clay pot. Live bird is dipped in blood of slain bird with the cedar wood, scarlet yarn, and hyssop over the fresh water.	2.	One bird killed over fresh water in a clay pot. Live bird is dipped in blood of slain bird and water with the cedar wood, scarlet yarn, and hyssop.
3.	One to be cleansed is sprinkled seven times with blood.	3.	Sprinkle blood and water over the house seven times.
4.	Live bird is released over the open field.	4.	Live bird is released over the open field.

The primary procedure for clearing a house of infection was, first, to close the house for seven days, and, second, if that did not remove the disease, the soiled stones of the house were removed and destroyed "outside the city," and then the house was to be replastered (vv. 38–42). In the case of skin disease, the provisions for cleansing assumed at the start that the one to be cleansed had already been healed (v. 3). Like the soiled stones of the contaminated house, however, the diseased person must remain unclean and live "outside the camp" (13:46).

Though quite similar, the two ceremonies have a major difference in their treatment of that which was found to be diseased. For example, while there is no provision for healing the skin diseases, there is a provision for clearing a house of infection.

An important difference between a contaminated person and a contaminated house was that there were offerings and sacrifices for the one healed of skin disease but not for the house that had been cleansed. It is understandable that sacrifices would not be offered for a house.

As we have suggested earlier, several features of the Flood narrative in Genesis have parallels in the present text of Leviticus. Some of these parallels are listed below. The significance of the parallels lies in the way they reveal the purpose and intention of the author. A strategy can be seen in the way he has laid out these texts as well as in the materials he has chosen to use. By following the patterns of the early narratives of Genesis, the author is able to show God's purpose in giving Israel these covenant regulations. They are God's way of effecting in the everyday life of his people the same goals and purposes he has for humankind. Sin and its contamination of worship and fellowship with God must be dealt with in God's way. As the Flood was once necessary to cleanse God's good creation from the evil that had contaminated it, so the ritual washings were a necessary part of checking the spread of sin and its results in the covenant community.

Flood Story (Genesis)	*Purification (Leviticus)*
1. The waters of the Flood were the means whereby God cleansed the land of "all flesh" that had "corrupted his way" (Ge 6:12)	The primary means of cleansing diseased flesh in these Levitical laws was water. Reference to the use of water occurs seven times in this passage (14:5, 6, 8, 9, 50, 51, 52).
2. The ark (תבה) was plastered (כפר) with pitch (כפר) inside (מבית) and out (מחוץ) (Ge 6:14).	The house (הבית) was plastered (טח), with clay (עפר) after the soiled material was removed inside (מבית) and taken out (מחוץ) of the city (Lev 14:41–42).

3. Noah waited at the door of the ark for seven days (Ge 7:4, 10).

The priest was to wait at the door of the house for seven days (Lev 14:38).

The house was atoned for (כפר) (Lev 14:53).

4. Noah, in the ark, waited for the bird for two sets of sevens (Ge 8:10, 12).

The one to be cleansed waited for two series of sevens (14:7–8).

5. Two birds were sent out of the ark. One, the raven, flew out over the water, and the other, a dove, flew over the dry land (Ge 8:7–9). The raven was an unclean bird (Lev 11:15) and the dove was clean.

Two "clean birds" were taken. One was slain "over water" and the other was released "over the face of the field." The slain bird, a sin offering (Lev 14:52), takes away the uncleanness; the other bird goes free.

6. A sacrifice was offered at the conclusion (Ge 6:20).

A sacrifice was offered at the conclusion (Lev 14:10, 21).

7. Noah offered a "clean animal" and a "clean bird' on the altar (Ge 8:20).

The one to be cleansed offered a male lamb and two doves on the altar (Lev 14:21–22).

8. Noah was given dietary regulations (Ge 9:3) and warned about consuming the blood (Ge 9:4).

Dietary regulations have been given (Lev 11), along with strict warning about consuming the blood (Lev 17; cf. 7:26).

9. God established a covenant with Noah (Ge 9:9).

God established a covenant with Israel (Lev 26:44).

10. The sign of the covenant was the rainbow in the clouds (Ge 9:14–15).

The sign of God's presence in the covenant was the cloud over the atonement cover (Lev 16:2).

11. Noah drank wine (יין) and became drunk (שכר) and lay naked in his tent (Ge 9:21).

Aaron and his sons were warned not to drink wine (יין) or fermented drink (שכר) when they went into the Tent of Meeting (Lev 10:9).

12. Noah's two sons, Ham and Canaan, were cursed (Ge 9:24–25).

Aaron's two sons, Nadab and Abihu, were cursed (Lev 10:1).

13. Noah's son "Ham, the father of Canaan, saw his father's nakedness" (Ge 9:22).

Lev 18:7, "Do not uncover the nakedness of you father." The whole of this chapter deals with problems of uncovering nakedness, which is called the defilement of the Canaanites (Lev 18:24–30).

14. At Babylon (בבל from בלל), God's concern was that "nothing they plan [זמם] to do will be impossible for them" (Ge 11:6). The verb זמם is used here and in Dt 19:19.

The holiness laws in Lev 18–20 are intended to ensure that there would be no "wickedness" (זמה from זמם, Lev 18:17; 19:29; 20:14) or "confusion" (תבל from בלל, Lev 18:23; 20:12) in the land. The nouns זמה (from זמם) and תבל (from בלל) are used only here in the Pentateuch.

15. Abram married Sarai, his half-sister (Ge 11:29; 20:12).

The holiness laws prohibited marriage to one's half-sister (Lev 18:11; 20:17).

Commands relating to skin diseases:
Command #101, Lev 13:3, A leper is unclean: "It is an infectious skin disease."

Command #112, Lev 13:45, A leper must be made conspicuous: "The person with such an infectious disease must wear torn clothes."

Command #102, Lev 13:51, A leprous garment is unclean: "It is a destructive mildew."

Command #110, Lev 14:2, Procedure for cleansing of leprosy: "This shall be the law of leprosy."

Command #111, Lev 14:9, Shaving the head of the leper: "On the seventh day, he must shave off all his hair."

Command #77, Lev 14:10, The offering of a leper who was cleansed: "On the eighth day he shall take two lambs."

Command #103, Lev 14:44, The house of a leper is unclean: "If the mildew has spread in the house."

Prohibitions relating to skin diseases:

Prohibition #307, Lev 13:33, One must not shave a leprous sore: "He must be shaved except for the diseased area."

4. Discharges Causing Uncleanness (15:1–33)

An outline and summary of the contents of this chapter is given in the final verses of the chapter: "These are the regulations for one with a discharge—for anyone made unclean by an emission of semen, for a woman in her monthly period, for a man or a woman with a discharge, and for a man who lies with a woman who is ceremonially unclean" (vv. 32–33).

The chapter begins with the basic premise of the regulations: "When anyone has a bodily discharge, the discharge is unclean" (v. 2). There are two major sections. The first deals with regulations concerning a man with a discharge (vv. 3–18). This section begins with a description of the nature of the discharge (vv. 4–12), and then follows with instructions for cleansing the discharge (vv. 13–18). The second section has regulations dealing with a woman with a discharge (15:19–30). This section also consists of two parts: the description of the woman's discharge (vv. 19–27), and instructions for cleansing the discharge (vv. 28–30). The instructions for cleansing are the same for the man and the woman. They are to wait seven days after the discharge has ceased. Then they are to wash their clothes and themselves with fresh water. On the eighth day, they are to offer two doves or pigeons at the Tent of Meeting. One is a sin offering and the other a burnt offering.

The chapter ends with an important reminder of the purpose of the purity laws. The Lord told Moses that the ceremonial purity of the Israelite community must be maintained so that "they will not die in their uncleanness for defiling my dwelling place, which is among them" (v. 31). In other words, these various conditions were not to be avoided because they were inherently evil, but because they disqualified one from participation in the worship of the covenant community.

Command #104, Lev 15:2, A man with a flow is unclean: "When any man has a bodily discharge."

Command #74, Lev 15:13–15, The offering of a man healed from a flow: "When a man with a flow is clean from his flow, on the eighth day he shall give two doves."

Command #105, Lev 15:16, A man with an emission of semen is unclean: "When a man has an emission of semen."

Command #109, Lev 15:16, Observance of cleansing in water: "He shall wash in water."

Command #99, Lev 15:19, A woman in menstruation is unclean: "The impurity of her monthly period."

Command #106, Lev 15:19, A woman with a flow is unclean: "When a woman has her regular flow of blood."

Command #75, Lev 15:28–29, The offering of a woman healed from a flow: "When she is clean from her flow."

E. Day of Atonement (16:1–34)

Once a year, on the tenth day of the seventh month, a Sabbath was proclaimed and atonement was made for the sins of the whole nation. This was the Day of Atonement. The heart of the ceremony was the time when the high priest laid his hands on a live goat and confessed all the sins of the nation (v. 21). The goat was then allowed to wander away from the camp and into the wilderness. Israel's sins were thus carried away. This was a lasting ordinance for Israel: "Atonement was made once a year for all the sins of the Israelites" (v. 34).

As a prelude to the instructions for this great day, the author recalls the tragic fate of Aaron's two sons, Nadab and Abihu (v. 1). Thus the fire that had consumed them served as a vivid reminder that God must be approached with utmost reverence and holiness at the tabernacle. The priests could not enter the tabernacle at their own whim; they had to enter properly. God's presence was "behind the curtain in front of the atonement cover on the ark," and any improper entry into the tent would result in death (v. 2).

The procedure for the celebration of the Day of Atonement consisted first of the consecration of the high priest (vv. 3–4). The high priest, Aaron, in linen garments (not his regular garments; cf. vv. 23–24), was to take a young bull and a ram for himself, and two male goats and a ram for the Israelite community. First, he offered the bull as his own sin offering. The bull was slaughtered, and some of the blood was taken "behind the curtain," where it was sprinkled "on the front of the atonement cover" (vv. 11–14). Incense was placed on the "fire before the LORD" (viz., the burning coals carried into the Holy of Holies by the priest's censer, v. 12), and its smoke covered the atonement plate and shielded the high priest. Then he took the two goats for the community. One goat was marked by lot as belonging to the Lord and the other was a "scapegoat."

The goat belonging to the Lord was then offered as a sin offering for the people, and its blood was taken "behind the curtain and sprinkled on the atonement cover" (v. 15). The purpose of this sin offering was to make "atonement for the Most Holy Place and the Tent of Meeting because of the uncleanness and rebellion of the Israelites" (v. 16). Then blood from the bull and the first goat was sprinkled on the horns of the altar to cleanse the altar.

The second goat was preserved to make atonement by sending it into the wilderness bearing the sins of the nation. The high priest laid his hands on the goat, confessed all of Israel's sins, and sent the goat away. The goat was said to "carry away the sins" of the people (v. 22). The man who led the goat out (v. 21) then washed his clothes and bathed before coming back into the camp (v. 26).

The high priest then changed into his regular priestly garments and sacrificed the second ram for a burnt offering for himself and the community's ram for a burnt offering for them. The bull and goat used for the sin offering were taken outside the camp and completely burned. The man assigned to burn them washed his clothes and bathed before coming back into the camp.

> **Command #49**, Lev 16:1ff., The service (*Avodah*) of the Day of Atonement. All the duties of this day are considered one command.
>
> **Command #164**, Lev 16:29, Fasting on the 10th of Tishri (Yom Kippur): "On the 10th day of the 7th month you must deny yourselves."
>
> **Command #165**, Lev 16:29, Resting on the 10th of Tishri (Yom Kippur): "And not do any work" (cf. Lev 16:31, "A Sabbath of rest it is to you.")
>
> **Prohibition #68**, Lev 16:2, The high priest must not enter the Holy Place at will: "Tell your brother Aaron not to come whenever he chooses into the Most Holy Place."

F. Warnings Against Improper Actions (17:1–16)

This chapter gives four specific warnings against improper actions. The first concerns slaughtering animals for sacrifices in places other than the Tent of Meeting (vv. 2–9). Some have maintained that this was a prohibition not just of sacrifices but of any kind of animal slaughter and that the prohibition was limited only to the time that Israel was in the wilderness.[4] However, verse 5, which refers to the killing of animals in verses 3–4, specifically speaks of sacrifices made to the Lord. It should also be noted as well that later in this same chapter (v. 13), provision is made for animals slain in hunting. Such a provision suggests that slaying animals for food was permissible; hence only slaughtering for sacrifice was expressly prohibited. Moreover, in verse 7 the prohibition is called an "eternal ordinance," which would rule out its limitation to the time of the wilderness sojourn. Furthermore, Deuteronomy 12:15 appears to be a clarification of this law, and it restates the provision that mere slaughtering of animals could be done anywhere. What Deuteronomy specifically prohibited was carrying out any kind of sacrifice apart from the central altar (see commentary on Dt 12:1–32).

The second warning found in this chapter forbids eating an animal with its blood (Lev 17:10–12). Third, eating a game animal with its blood is forbidden (vv. 13–14). Fourth, this chapter forbids eating an animal killed by a wild animal (vv. 15–16).

> **Command #147**, Lev 17:13, Covering the blood of animals and birds: "He shall pour out its blood and cover it with dust."
>
> **Prohibition #90**, Lev 17:3–4, One must not slaughter animals outside the temple: "Any Israelite who sacrifices an ox . . . instead of bringing it to the Tent of Meeting."

The writer's purpose in including the short text of verses 1–9 at this point in the narrative is to demonstrate the motive behind the strict rules regulating worship which are found throughout the following sections of the Pentateuch. The writer himself tells us, concerning the rules he gave, "This is so the Israelites will bring to the LORD the sacrifices they are now making in

---

[4]See Keil, *Pentateuch*, 2:408; Wenham, *Leviticus*, 241.

the open fields" (v. 5). Moreover, "They must no longer offer any of their sacrifices to the goat idols to whom they prostitute themselves" (v. 7). Thus, according to the plan of the narrative, the accumulation of laws regulating holiness has its motive in the prevention of further idolatry among the people. Just as the narrative about the incident of the golden calf revealed the imminent danger of Israel's falling into idolatry, so the present narrative demonstrates the ongoing threat. These two narratives play an important role in the composition of this part of the Pentateuch.

We have already seen that the legislation describing Israel's priestly worship in the reinstituted Sinai covenant (Ex 35–Lev 16) was prefaced by the narrative of the golden calf (Ex 32). The intent of the narrative was to show the need for further regulations in Israel's worship. Idolatry was a real threat, and so specific regulations were needed to prevent it. Here, in Leviticus 17, at the close of that large section of priestly laws, the writer has attached another short narrative dealing with a similar problem. Once again the threat of idolatry can be seen in Israel's practice of sacrificing to the "goat idols." The two narratives showing the threat of idolatry bracket the detailed legislation dealing with the office of the priest—legislation primarily directed toward preventing further idolatry. The narratives provide the priestly legislation with two vivid examples of Israel's falling away after "other gods." Thus, the writer provides justification for the legislation itself. The chart below shows the role of the two narratives, Exodus 32 and Leviticus 17, within the larger structure of the Pentateuch.

Covenant at Sinai Ex 19–31	Golden Calf Ex 32	Covenant Reestablished Ex 33–34	Office of Priest Ex 35–Lev 16	Goat Idols Lev 17

A further observation can be made regarding the larger structure of the arrangement of these laws. It has long been recognized that Leviticus 17 plays an important role with respect to the collection of laws that follows it, Leviticus 18–26. In modern biblical scholarship this collection of laws is known as the Holiness Code. The most recent tendency in scholarship, however, has been to discount the notion that the whole of Leviticus 18–26 represents a discernible unit. Rather, it appears to be made up of smaller sections of laws. Characteristic of the first collection of laws that follow (Lev 18–20) is that they relate to the life of the average individual and not to that of the priests. Its purpose is to show how God's law regulates the everyday life of the individual Israelite. Most would agree that chapter 17 forms the introduction to the laws that follow (Lev 18–26). From the perspective of the larger structure of the Pentateuch, however, one can see an even greater purpose for the narrative of Leviticus 17.

If we compare the two accounts of Israel's idolatry, Exodus 32 and Leviticus 17, we see that each has a specific point of view. The incident of the golden calf clearly centers on the role of Aaron the priest. Though the people instigated the building of the idol, and Aaron made an attempt to blame them (Ex 32:22–23), it is clear from the narrative that the calf idol was constructed through the leadership of Aaron the priest. Throughout the narrative in Exodus 32 the writer is careful to show that it was Aaron who led the people and made the idol. Within the narrative Moses himself acknowledged that Aaron led the people in this great sin (v. 21). Thus Israel's first idol came through the leadership of Aaron the priest. It is fitting, then, that the narrative of the golden calf should serve as the prologue to the laws that relate specifically to the office of the priest (Ex 35–Lev 16).

In Leviticus 17 the threat of idolatry came solely from the Israelite people. The actual problem was that the people were sacrificing "in the open fields" and not with the priests at the Tent of Meeting (vv. 5, 7). Unlike the situation with the golden calf, in this narrative the priest stood over against the people in the major line of defense against idolatry. Such a view of the role of the priesthood is appropriate to the structure and thematic development of the Pentateuch. By this time in the narrative strategy the priests had been consecrated and were now being shown as following the regulations given in Exodus 35–Leviticus 16. This narrative (Lev 17:1–9) shows that those regulations have had their effect on the priests, and consequently they now stood against the idolatry of the people. As far as the flow of narrative in the Pentateuch is concerned, the incident of the golden calf was behind the priests, but the problem of idolatry remained—not as a threat to the priesthood but now to the people at large.

God's people had now begun to sacrifice to the "goat idols." The text does not explain in detail the nature of the offerings to the "goat idols," but it does make clear that this was a form of false worship that led them away from the worship of God prescribed in the Sinai covenant. As in the case of the golden calf, the people were following after idols. The narrative in Leviticus 17:1–9 also shows that more regulations were still needed, not so much for the priests as for the people. More laws were need to deal with the everyday life of the people, to ensure that they remained holy and faithful to God. Thus Leviticus 17 plays a strategic role as a prologue to the laws that follow (Lev 18–26); it shows the necessity for this set of laws dealing with the everyday life of the people of God.

In the light of the role of the two idolatry narratives (Ex 32 and Lev 17), it is significant that within the two narratives the priests were involved with an image of a "calf" and the people with that of a "goat." This is important because within the Levitical laws, the "calf" and the "goat" have already played a significant role. In the regulations governing the consecration of the priests, for example, the sin offering required for a priest was precisely that of a "young bull" (פַּר בֶּן בָּקָר, Ex 29:1–14; Lev 4:3). We should note that in the initial statement of the regulations, the Hebrew text does not use "calf" (עֵגֶל) but rather "young bull" (פַּר בֶּן בָּקָר, Ex 29:1). When Aaron and the priests were consecrated in Leviticus 9:1–14, however, the sin offering was specifically called within the narrative a "calf" (עֵגֶל בֶּן בָּקָר), which recalls the vocabulary of the golden calf. For the writer of the Pentateuch, then, the incident of the golden calf (עֵגֶל) appears to have provided a particularly apt lesson in the importance of guiding the priests in their leadership of Israel's worship. The sin offering of the priests contained a reminder of the great sin of the priests.

In the same way that the golden calf incident served to introduce laws which governed the priests, the incident of the "goat idols" (Lev 17:7) provided an apt introduction to the laws intended to govern the common people. It should further be noted that in the Levitical laws, apart from the "young bull" required for the priest, the sin offering required a "male goat" for a leader of the people or a "female goat" for an individual of the community (4:22–31). It is fitting therefore that the narrative in Leviticus 17:2–9 portrays the people as guilty of sacrificing and prostituting themselves to "goats"(v. 7).[5]

Thus as the narrative of the golden calf was a fitting introduction to the laws governing the priests, so the present narrative of the "goat idols" provides a fitting introduction to the laws governing the people themselves. The following chart shows the larger structural arrangement of the material.

Golden Calf Ex 32	Priestly Laws (Calf Sin Offering) Ex 35–Lev 16	Goat Idols Lev 17	Everyday Laws (Goat Sin Offering) Lev 18–26

A basic principle of the rite of sacrifice is uncovered in 17:11: "For the life of a creature is in the blood, and I have given it to you to make atonement for yourselves on the altar; it is the blood that makes atonement for one's life." When the blood was drained from a sacrificial animal, its life was drained out and it died. Consequently, though the blood was the life of the animal, when it was shed it signified the loss of life and hence the animal's death. The death of the sacrificial animal "made atonement" in the sacrifice. The curse of death recounted in Genesis 2:17 and 3:19 lies at the foundation of the sacrificial atonement. Sin had brought the penalty of death to humankind. The death of the animal offered in sacrifice took the place of the death of the one offering the sacrifice. It was a substitution. In God's grace the offering of a substitute atoned for Israel's sins. In the NT, the meaning of Christ's death on the cross is grounded in this view of the sacrifice (Mt 20:28; 26:28; Eph 1:7; Col 1:20).

II. HOLINESS IN THE LIFE OF THE PEOPLE (18:1–27:34)

This section contains material concerned with the description and necessary instructions on how Israel was to become a holy nation—a nation set apart to God.

A. The Conduct of God's People (18:1–20:27)

As has been shown above, several features of this passage parallel the last two brief narratives of the primeval history in Genesis (9:20–27 and 11:1–9). In Genesis 9:20–27, Noah's son Ham looked upon his father's nakedness; consequently, the Canaanites, descendants of Ham, were cursed. So also Leviticus 18:7 warns not to "look upon your father's nakedness," lest you be defiled like the inhabitants of the land of Canaan (18:24–28). Note also an earlier parallel between the following two texts: Noah "drank wine and became drunk [הַיַּיִן וַיִּשְׁכָּר] in his tent" (Ge 9:21), whereas Leviticus 10:9 forbade Aaron and his sons to "drink wine or other fermented drink [יַיִן וְשֵׁכָר] in the Tent of Meeting." The result was that Noah's two sons, Ham

---

[5]The use of the plural "goats" is apparently intended to show that both male and female goats were used.

and Canaan, were cursed (Ge 9:24–24), as were Aaron's two sons, Nadab and Abihu (Lev 10:1ff.).

Genesis 11:1–9, the narrative of the building of Babylon, parallels certain features of Leviticus 18–20. In the building of Babylon (בבל from בלל), God confused the people's language and dispersed the city's inhabitants because, he said, "nothing they plan [זמם] to do will be impossible for them" (v. 6). The context of Genesis 11 offers little explanation of the meaning of their "plan" (זמם). Much is left unstated. The verb *plan* is used elsewhere in the Pentateuch only in Deuteronomy 19:19. In the holiness laws in Leviticus 18–20, however, the noun form of this word (זמה) occurs as part of the explanation of the purpose of personal holiness. By means of these laws, the Israelites were to ensure that there would be no "wickedness" (זמה from זמם, Lev 18:17; 19:29; 20:14) or "confusion" (תבל from בלל, 18:23; 20:12) in the land. The nouns זמה (from זמם) and תבל (from בלל) are used only here in the Pentateuch. A link is thus established and a parallel is drawn between the evils of Babylon and those of Canaan. The purpose of the narrative is to warn the reader not to become like Babylon or Canaan. Like the Israelites, the readers were not to be "mixed" with Babylon and Canaan.

1. Introduction (18:1–5)

This new segment of laws is given a formal introduction that clearly sets forth the purpose of the laws. The laws represented a way of life distinct from the "acts of Egypt" and the "acts of Canaan" (v. 3). They were God's "judgments," just as Exodus 20–23 were called God's "judgments." Israel was to "keep" them by "walking in them" (Lev 18:4). In reading this collection of laws in the Pentateuch, we should remember that it is only a selection of Israel's laws and as such plays an important narrative function within the larger structure of the book. The author has intentionally chosen these laws and has put them here as part of his larger strategy and purpose in writing the Pentateuch.

For Israel the result of keeping these laws was "life" (18:5): "Keep my decrees and laws, for the one who obeys them will live by them." When Ezekiel quotes this passage (Eze 20:11), he gives the notion of "life" the same sense that it has in the early chapters of Genesis—physical life as well as God's blessing of eternal life. Ezekiel sees Israel's time in the wilderness as a time of rebellion and failure to obey these laws. Consequently, he argues, Israel did not "live"; that is, the whole rebellious generation died in the wilderness and did not enter the Promised Land. "Yet the people of Israel rebelled against me in the desert. They did not follow my decrees but rejected my laws—although the one who obeys them will live by them. . . . So I said I would pour out my wrath on them and destroy them in the desert" (Eze 20:13–14). Though he goes on to show that God was compassionate to Israel and did not utterly destroy them, Ezekiel is clear in his understanding that "to live" means here "to live and to enjoy God's covenant blessings in the Promised Land." Thus Ezekiel correctly reflects the author's meaning in these narratives.

2. Defilements of the Canaanites (18:6–30)

The clue to the meaning of this segment of narrative is given at the close of the list of defilements. The laws are intended to distinguish the Israelites from the inhabitants of the land that they were about to possess: "Do not defile yourselves in any of these ways, because this is how the nations that I am going to drive out before you became defiled" (18:24). Various types of unlawful sexual relations are prohibited.

1. Family members (18:6–18). It is presupposed that the Israelites would not marry among the Canaanites (cf. Dt 7:3);[6] thus strict regulations on marriage within their own people were primarily what was necessary. A basic rule is stated in Leviticus 18:6: "No one is to approach any close relative to have sexual relations." The list below summarizes the prohibited and omitted relationships within a family.[7]

Prohibited:	Omitted
Mother	Mother's sister's daughter (cousin)
Mother's sister (aunt)	Mother's brother's daughter (cousin)
Mother's brother's wife (aunt)	Father's sister's daughter (cousin)
Sister	Father's brother's daughter (cousin)
Father's sister (aunt)	Daughter
Father's brother's wife (aunt)	
Brother's wife (sister-in-law)	
Son's wife (daughter-in-law)	
Granddaughter	
Stepmother	
Stepsister	
Stepdaughter	
Stepgranddaughter	

Prohibitions relating to sexual relations:

Prohibition #353, Lev 18:6, One must not have (M. close contact with or) a sexual relationship with any close relative: "No one is to approach any close relative to have sexual relations."

Prohibition #330, Lev 18:7, One must not have a sexual relationship with one's mother: "Do not dishonor your father by having sexual relations with your mother."

Prohibition #351, Lev 18:7, One must not commit an act of homosexuality with one's father: "Do not uncover the nakedness of your father."

Prohibition #331, Lev 18:8, One must not have a sexual relationship with one's stepmother: "Do not have sexual relations with your father's wife."

Prohibition #332, Lev 18:9, One must not have a sexual relationship with one's sister: "Do not have sexual relations with your sister."

Prohibition #334, Lev 18:10, One must not have a sexual relationship with the daughter of one's son: "Do not have sexual relations with your son's daughter."

Prohibition #335, Lev 18:10, One must not have a sexual relationship with one's daughter's daughter: "Do not have sexual relations with your daughter's daughter."

Prohibition #336, Lev 18:10 (M. One must not have a sexual relationship with one's daughter: This is not explicitly stated in the Torah, but is implied from the fact that such relationships are forbidden with one's daughter's daughter.)

---

[6]See Wenham, *Leviticus*, 253.
[7]See ibid., 254.

Prohibition #333, Lev 18:11, One must not have a sexual relationship with one's stepsister: "Do not have sexual relations with the daughter of your father's wife, born to your father."

Prohibition #340, Lev 18:12, One must not have a sexual relationship with one's father's sister: "Do not have sexual relations with your father's sister."

Prohibition #341, Lev 18:13, One must not have a sexual relationship with one's mother's sister: "Do not have sexual relations with your mother's sister."

Prohibition #342, Lev 18:14, One must not have a sexual relationship with the wife of the brother of one's father: "Do not dishonor your father's brother by approaching his wife to have sexual relations."

Prohibition #352, Lev 18:14, One must not commit an act of homosexuality with one's uncle: "Do not uncover the nakedness of your father's brother."

Prohibition #343, Lev 18:15, One must not have a sexual relationship with one's son's wife: "Do not have sexual relations with your daughter-in-law."

Prohibition #344, Lev 18:16, One must not have a sexual relationship with one's brother's wife: "Do not have sexual relations with your brother's wife."

Prohibition #337, Lev 18:17, One must not have a sexual relationship with a woman and her daughter: "Do not have sexual relations with both a woman and her daughter."

Prohibition #338, Lev 18:17, One must not have a sexual relationship with a woman and her son's daughter: "Do not have sexual relations with . . . her son's daughter."

Prohibition #339, Lev 18:17, One must not have a sexual relationship with a woman and her daughter's daughter: "Do not have sexual relations with . . . her daughter's daughter."

Prohibition #345, Lev 18:18, One must not have a sexual relationship with one's wife's sister while one's wife is still living: "Do not take your wife's sister as a rival wife and have sexual relations with her while your wife is living."

It is notable that according to this passage, when Abram married Sarai, his half-sister (Ge 11:29; 20:12), he violated the law that prohibited marriage to one's half-sister (Lev 18:11; 20:17). Also Amram, the father of Moses and Aaron, married his father's sister (Ex 6:20). Both these men, of course, lived before these laws were given, and hence their lives show the temporary and historically particular application of many of these laws. Though the author tells us that Abraham "kept the Law" (Ge 26:5), he means that Abraham lived a life of faith, and hence it could be said about him that he fulfilled the ultimate purpose of the Law.

2. During monthly period (18:19)

Prohibition #346, Lev 18:19, One must not have a sexual relationship with a menstruating woman: "Do not approach a woman to have sexual relations during the uncleanness of her monthly period."

3. Neighbor's wife (18:20)

Prohibition #347, Lev 18:20, One must not have a sexual relationship with the wife of another: "Do not have sexual relations with your neighbor's wife."

4. Giving children to Molech (18:21)

Prohibition #7, Lev 18:21, One must not offer children to Molech: "Do not give any of your children to be sacrificed to Molech."

5. Homosexuality (18:22)

Prohibition #350, Lev 18:22, One must not commit an act of homosexuality: "Do not lie with a man as one lies with a woman."

6. Bestiality (18:23)

Prohibition #348, Lev 18:23, A man must not have a sexual relationship with an animal: "Do not have sexual relations with an animal."

Prohibition #349, Lev 18:23, A woman must not have a sexual relationship with an animal: "A woman must not present herself to an animal to have sexual relations with it."

3. Statutes and Judgments (19:1–37)

a. Holiness Precepts (19:1–18)

This section is introduced with the admonition, "You shall be holy because I am holy." It consists of a list of twenty-one (3 x 7) laws. These laws are broken up into smaller units by the sevenfold repetition of the phrase "I am the LORD (your God)" (19:3, 4, 10, 12, 14, 16, 18).

21 Laws (7 x 3)

1	2	3	4	5	6	7
"I am the LORD your God"	"I am the LORD your God"	"I am the LORD your God"	"I am the LORD"	"I am the LORD"	"I am the LORD"	"I am the LORD"
19:3	19:4	19:10	19:12	19:14	19:16	19:18

The twenty-one laws in this section are:
1. Respect for parents (19:3)
2. Keep the Sabbath (19:3)
3. Prohibition of idolatry (19:4)
4. Procedure for peace offering (19:5–8)
5. Procedure for gleaning the field (19:9)
6. Procedure for gleaning the orchard (19:10)
7. Prohibition of stealing (19:11)
8. Prohibition of lying (19:11)
9. Prohibition of deception of a friend (19:11)
10. Prohibition of false oath (19:12)
11. Prohibition of oppressing one's neighbor (19:13)
12. Prohibition of robbery (19:13)
13. Swift payment of wages (19:13)
14. Respect for the deaf (19:14)
15. Respect for the blind (19:14)
16. Respect for God (19:14)
17. Fairness in judgments (19:15)
18. Prohibition of slander (19:16)
19. Respect for one's neighbor (19:16)
20. Openness in human relationships (19:17)
21. Love your neighbor (19:18)

Commands relating to holiness:

Command #211, Lev 19:3, You must fear your mother and your father: "Each of you must respect his mother and father."

Command #120, Lev 19:9, One must leave the corners of the field: "Do not reap the edges of your field."

Command #121, Lev 19:9, One must leave the gleanings of the field: "Do not gather the gleanings."

Command #123, Lev 19:10, One must leave the broken-off bunches of grapes: "Do not take the bunches of grapes that have broken off. Leave them."

Command #124, Lev 19:10, One must not glean the grapes: "Do not glean your orchard."

Command #108, Lev 19:13, Observance of the water of cleansing: "Because the water of cleansing has not been sprinkled on him he is unclean."

Command #177, Lev 19:15, Judges must be impartial: "In righteousness you shall judge your neighbor."

Command #205, Lev 19:17, You must correct the sinner: "Rebuke your neighbor frankly so you will not share in his guilt."

Command #206, Lev 19:18, You must love others as yourself: "Love your neighbor as yourself."

Prohibitions relating to holiness:

Prohibition #3, Lev 19:4, One must not make idols: "You shall not make gods of molten metal."

Prohibition #10, Lev 19:4, One must not follow after idolatry: "Do not turn to idolatry."

Prohibition #131, Lev 19:6-8, One must not eat sacrificial meat left over its limit: "It shall be eaten on the day you sacrifice it or on the next day; anything left over until the third day must be burned up."

Prohibition #211, Lev 19:9, One must not gather the grain that falls in harvest: "Do not . . . gather the gleanings of your harvest."

Prohibition #212, Lev 19:10, One must not pick one's vineyard a second time (M. to harvest the misformed clusters of grapes): "Do not go over your vineyard a second time."

Prohibition #213, Lev 19:10, One must not gather the grapes that fall during harvest: "Do not . . . pick up the grapes that have fallen."

Prohibition #244, Lev 19:11, Stealing (M. property) is prohibited: "You shall not steal [M. property]."

Prohibition #248, Lev 19:11, One must not lie (M. deny receipt of a loan or deposit): "Do not lie."

Prohibition #249, Lev 19:11, One must not deceive (M. swear falsely): "Do not deceive [M. swear falsely to] one another."

Prohibition #61, Lev 19:12, One must not break an oath made in God's name: "Do not swear falsely by my name."

Prohibition #238, Lev 19:13, One must not delay payment of wages: "Do not hold back the wages of a hired man overnight."

Prohibition #245, Lev 19:13, Robbery (M. by violence) is prohibited: "You shall not rob [M. by violence]."

Prohibition #247, Lev 19:13, One must not defraud another: "Do not defraud your neighbor."

Prohibition #299, Lev 19:14, One must not mislead another person with bad advice: "Do not put a stumbling block in front of the blind."

Prohibition #317, Lev 19:14, One must not curse the deaf (M. any Israelite): "Do not curse the deaf."

Prohibition #273, Lev 19:15, One must not pervert justice: "Do not pervert justice."

Prohibition #275, Lev 19:15, A judge must not be partial: "Do not show favoritism to the wealthy."

Prohibition #277, Lev 19:15, A judge must not favor the poor: "Do not show partiality to the poor."

Prohibition #297, Lev 19:16, One must not refuse to save another from danger: "You shall not stand [M. by] upon the blood of your friend."

Prohibition #301, Lev 19:16, One should not spread slander: "Do not go about spreading slander among your people."

Prohibition #302, Lev 19:17, One should not harbor hatred in his heart: "Do not hate your brother in your heart."

Prohibition #303, Lev 19:17, One should not fail to correct (M. shame) his neighbor: "Rebuke your neighbor frankly so you will not share in his guilt."

Prohibition #304, Lev 19:18, One must not seek revenge: "Do not seek revenge."

Prohibition #305, Lev 19:18, One must not bear a grudge: "Do not bear a grudge."

b. Statutes and Judgments (19:19–37)

This section is introduced with the admonition "You shall keep my statutes" (v. 19a) and concludes with a similar admonition, "You shall keep all my statutes and all my judgments" (v. 37a), and the statement "I am the LORD" (19:37b). Like the preceding section of laws, it consists of a list of twenty-one (3 x 7) laws. These laws also are broken up into smaller units by a sevenfold repetition of the phrase "I am the LORD (your God)" (19:25, 28, 30, 31, 32, 34, 36).

21 Laws (7 x 3)

1	2	3	4	5	6	7
"I am the LORD your God"	"I am the LORD"	"I am the LORD"	"I am the LORD"	"I am the LORD"	"I am the LORD your God"	"I am the LORD your God"
19:25	19:28	19:30	19:31	19:32	19:34	19:36

The Twenty-one laws in this section are:
1. Prohibition of mixed breeding (19:19)
2. Prohibition of mixed sowing (19:19)
3. Prohibition of mixed weaving (19:19)
4. Procedure for handling offense of sexual relationship with a slave (19:20–22)
5. Procedure for planting fruit trees (19:23–25)
6. Prohibition of eating blood (19:26)
7. Prohibition of divination (19:26)

8. Prohibition of sorcery (19:26)
9. Prohibition of cutting side locks (19:27)
10. Prohibition of trimming one's beard (19:27)
11. Prohibition of body incisions (19:28)
12. Prohibition of tattoos (19:28)
13. Prohibition of making one's daughter a prostitute (19:29)
14. Prohibition of prostitution in the land (19:29)
15. Keep the Sabbath (19:30)
16. Reverence for God's sanctuary (19:30)
17. Prohibition of mediums and spiritualists (19:31)
18. Respect for the aged (19:32)
19. Reverence for God (19:32)
20. Love the sojourner (19:33–34)
21. Honesty in standards (19:35–36)

Commands:

Command #119, Lev 19:24, The fourth year's growth of fruit is holy to the Lord: "In the fourth year all its fruit will be holy."

Command #21, Lev 19:30, One must fear (i.e., respect) the temple: "My holy place you shall fear."

Command #209, Lev 19:32, You must respect the wise: "Rise in the presence of the aged, show respect for the elderly, and revere your God."

Command #208, Lev 19:36, You must have correct weights and measures: "Use honest scales and weights."

Prohibitions:

Prohibition #215, Lev 19:19, One must not sow two kinds of seeds together: "Do not plant your field with two kinds of seed."

Prohibition #217, Lev 19:19, One must not mate two kinds of animals: "Do not mate different kinds of animals."

Prohibition #192, Lev 19:23, One must not eat uncircumcised fruit: "When you enter the land and plant any kind of fruit tree, regard its fruit as forbidden [Hebrew: uncircumcised]. For three years you are to consider it forbidden; it must not be eaten."

Prohibition #31, Lev 19:26, One must not practice divination: "Do not practice divination."

Prohibition #195, Lev 19:26, One must not eat meat upon blood (M. "upon blood" means "that which brings blood[shed], thus, "be gluttonous and drunken"): "Do not eat any meat upon the blood."

Prohibition #43, Lev 19:27, One must not cut the hair on the side of your head: "Do not cut the hair on the side of your head."

Prohibition #44, Lev 19:27, One must not cut one's beard: "Do not . . . clip off the edges of your beard."

Prohibition #41, Lev 19:28, One must not tattoo oneself: "Do not put tattoo marks on yourself."

Prohibition #8, Lev 19:31, One must not practice necromancy: "Do not turn to mediums."

Prohibition #9, Lev 19:31, One must not enquire of familiar spirits: "or seek out spiritists."

Prohibition #271, Lev 19:35, One must not defraud with weights and measures: "Do not use dishonest standards."

We have seen several times before that a close and meaningful relationship exists between the laws in the Pentateuch and the early narratives in Genesis. There may also be a similar relationship between the procedures outlined for planting fruit trees in this narrative and the account of Creation in Genesis 1. According to the provisions of the law in this chapter, when fruit trees were planted, they were not to be eaten for four years. They were to remain untouched for three years; on the fourth year they were holy to the Lord. On the fifth year their fruit could be eaten. In the Genesis account of Creation, God created fruit trees for human beings on the third day (Ge 1:11–12, 29) but there was not yet a human being to eat from them. Taking the pattern of "days" in Genesis 1 to correspond to a pattern of "years" in the present text, we see that human beings were created on the sixth day, the day when their food, the fruit trees, would be holy. Counting from the third day on, the sixth day would be the fourth day for the trees. On the next day, the Sabbath, they could eat from the fruit. The Sabbath would be the fifth day for the trees. Thus the writer portrayed God as following the pattern of the Torah in the work of creation.

4. Holiness Laws (20:1–27)

This selection of laws consists of fourteen (7 x 2) laws, concluded by an extended appeal for holiness on the part of the nation when they take possession of the land of Canaan (vv. 22–26). After the conclusion, one of the laws, the prohibition of mediums and spiritists (v. 6), is restated (v. 27). The repetition of this law was perhaps motivated by the emphasis the prohibition received later in the Deuteronomic laws (cf. Dt 18:14–22).

14 (7 x 2) Laws

1	2	B E H O L Y	3	4	5	6	7	8	9	10	11	12	13	14	B E H O L Y	2

1. Prohibition of offering one's child to Molech (20:2–5)
2. Prohibition of mediums and spiritists (20:6)
Be holy because I am the Lord your God (20:7)
Keep my statutes, I the Lord am making you holy (20:8)
3. Prohibition of cursing one's parents (20:9)
4. Prohibition of adultery (20:10; cf. Nu 5:11–31)
5. Prohibition of sexual relations with one's father's wife (20:11)
6. Prohibition of sexual relations with one's daughter-in-law (20:12)
7. Prohibition of homosexuality (20:13)
8. Prohibition of marriage to a woman and her daughter (20:14)
9. Prohibition of male bestiality (20:15)
10. Prohibition of female bestiality (20:16)
11. Prohibition of sexual relations with one's sister (20:17)
12. Prohibition of sexual relations during a woman's period (20:18)
13. Prohibition of sexual relations with one's aunt (20:19–20)

14. Prohibition of marriage to one's brother's wife (20:21)
Keep all my decrees and laws and follow them (20:22)
You must not live according to the customs of other nations (20:23–24)
You must distinguish between clean and unclean (20:25)
Be holy because I the Lord am holy (20:26)
15. Prohibition of mediums and spiritists (20:27)

Command #228, Lev 20:14, Capital punishment: "Both he and they must be burned with fire."

Prohibition #30, Lev 20:23, One must not walk in the ways of idolaters: "You shall not walk in the ways of the nations."

B. The Condition of Priests within the Community (21:1–22:33)

1. Regulations for Priests: First List (21:1–15)

The list has a brief introduction (v. 1) and ends with the introduction to the next list (v. 16). There are fourteen (7 x 2) laws in the list.

14 (7 x 2) Laws

1	2	3	4	5	6	7	8	9	10	11	12	13	14

1. A priest may become unclean for a close relative's death (21:1–3)
2. A priest may not become unclean for a relative by marriage (21:4)
3. Priests may not shave their heads (21:5)
4. Priests may not shave the ends of their beards (21:5)
5. Priests may not cut themselves (21:5–6)
6. Priests may not marry a prostitute (21:7a)
7. Priests may not marry a divorced woman (21:7b–8)
8. The daughter of a priest may not be a prostitute (21:9)
9. The high priest may not let his hair be unkempt or tear his clothes (21:10)
10. The high priest may not enter a place where there is a dead body (21:11)
11. The high priest may not leave the sanctuary or desecrate it (21:12)
12. The high priest must marry a virgin (21:13)
13. The high priest may not marry a widow, divorcee, or prostitute (21:14)
14. The high priest may not defile his seed among his people (21:15).

Commands relating to priests:
Command #37, Lev 21:2–3, Priests should become unclean for certain close relatives: "for them he shall be unclean."
Command #32, Lev 21:8, Give honor to the priests: "And you shall treat him as holy because he brings the bread of your God near."
Command #38, Lev 21:13, High priest should marry a virgin: "And he shall marry a woman in her virginity."

Prohibitions relating to priests:

Prohibition #166, Lev 21:1, A priest should not become unclean except for a close relative: "A priest must not make himself ceremonially unclean for any of his people who die, except for a close relative."

Prohibition #76, Lev 21:6, Priests must not profane God's name: "And must not profane the name of their God."

Prohibition #158, Lev 21:7, A priest must not marry a harlot: "They must not marry women defiled by prostitution."

Prohibition #159, Lev 21:7, A priest must not marry a defiled woman: "They must not marry . . . defiled women."

Prohibition #160, Lev 21:7, A priest must not marry a divorced woman: "They must not marry . . . divorced women."

Prohibition #167, Lev 21:11, The high priest must not become unclean for any reason: "He must not enter a place where there is a dead body."

Prohibition #168, Lev 21:11, The high priest must not become unclean in any way: "He must not make himself unclean, even for his father or mother."

Prohibition #161, Lev 21:14, A priest must not marry a widow: "He must not marry a widow."

Prohibition #162, Lev 21:15, A priest must not take a widow as a concubine: "So he will not defile his offspring among his people."

2. Regulations for Priests: Second List (21:16–24)

This list is introduced by the expression "And the LORD spoke to Moses saying, Speak to Aaron" (v. 16), and is concluded by the expression "And Moses spoke to Aaron" (v. 24). There are fourteen (7 x 2) laws in the list.

14 (7 x 2) Laws

1	2	3	4	5	6	7	8	9	10	11	12	13	14

1. A priest shall not be blind (21:18)
2. A priest shall not be lame (21:18)
3. A priest shall not be disfigured (21:18)
4. A priest shall not be deformed (21:18)
5. A priest shall not have a crippled foot (21:19)
6. A priest shall not have a crippled hand (21:19)
7. A priest shall not be hunchbacked (21:20)
8. A priest shall not be dwarfed (21:20)
9. A priest shall not have an eye defect (21:20)
10. A priest shall not have festering sores (21:20)
11. A priest shall not have running sores (21:20)
12. A priest shall not have damaged testicles (21:20)
13. Such a priest may eat the most holy food (21:22)
14. Such a priest may not go behind the curtain or approach the altar (21:23).

Prohibition #70, Lev 21:17, A priest with a physical blemish must not serve in the temple: "For the generations to come none of your descendants who has a defect may come near to offer."

Prohibition #71, Lev 21:18, A priest with a temporary physical blemish must not serve in the temple until the blemish is passed: "No man who has any defect may come near."

Prohibition #69, Lev 21:23, A priest with a physical blemish must not enter the temple: "Yet because of his defect, he must not go near the curtain or approach the altar."

3. Regulations for Priests: Third List (22:1–33)

a. Things that Profane a Priest (22:1–9)

Between a short introduction (vv. 1–2) and conclusion (v. 9), a selection of seven laws is given as examples of things which profane a priest.

7 Laws

1	2	3	4	5	6	7

The seven laws dealing with things that profane a priest are:
1. An infectious skin disease (22:4)
2. A bodily discharge (22:4)
3. Touching something defiled by a corpse (22:4)
4. An emission of semen (22:4)
5. Touching any unclean thing (22:5)
6. Eating something found dead (22:8)
7. Eating something torn by a wild animal (22:8)

Prohibition #75, Lev 22:2, Unclean priests must not serve in the temple: "Let Aaron and his sons be scrupulous about the sacred offerings."

Prohibition #136, Lev 22:4, The heave offering must not be eaten by an unclean priest: "If a descendant of Aaron has an infectious skin disease or a bodily discharge, he may not eat the sacred offerings."

b. Persons Not Authorized to Eat the Sacred Offering (22:10–15)

A selection of seven laws describes those unauthorized to eat the sacred offering. The basic principle was, "No one outside a priest's family may eat the sacred offering" (v. 10). This principle is repeated on either side of the list of seven laws (vv. 10, 13b). A brief statement regarding restitution for accidental eating of an offering is appended (vv. 14–16).

7 Laws

1	2	3	4	5	6	7

1. A priest's guest may not eat the offering (22:10)
2. A hired worker of a priest may not eat the offering (22:10)
3. A priest's slave purchased with money may eat the offering (22:11).
4. A priest's slave born in his house may eat the offering (22:11)

5. A priest's daughter who marries a nonpriest may not eat the offering (22:12)
6. A priest's widowed, childless daughter who returns to his house may eat the offering (22:13)
7. A priest's divorced, childless daughter who returns to his house may eat the offering (22:13)

Prohibition #133, Lev 22:10, The heave (wave) offering must not be eaten by a nonpriest: "No one outside a priest's family may eat the sacred offering."

Prohibition #134, Lev 22:10, The heave offering must not be eaten by a priest's guest or hired worker: "Nor may the guest of a priest or his hired worker eat it."

Prohibition #135, Lev 22:10, The heave offering must not be eaten by an uncircumcised person: This is not stated in the Torah but is derived by a complicated legal argument. We have included it here for completeness.

Prohibition #137, Lev 22:12, The daughter of a priest who is married to a nonpriest cannot eat of holy things: "If a priest's daughter marries anyone other than a priest, she may not eat of any of the sacred contributions."

Prohibition #153, Lev 22:15, One must not eat untithed produce: "The priests must not desecrate the sacred offerings the Israelites present to the Lord by allowing them to eat the sacred offerings."

c. Priestly Offerings (22:17–25)

A selection of seven laws pertaining to the offerings of the priests is given. The principle is stated at the conclusion: these offerings "will not be accepted on your behalf, because they are deformed and have defects" (v. 25).

7 Laws

1	2	3	4	5	6	7

The seven laws dealing with priestly offerings are:
1. A gift for a burnt offering must be a male without defect (22:18)
2. An animal with a defect is not acceptable (22:20)
3. A gift for a peace offering must be without defect (22:21)
4. An offering should not be an animal that is either blind, injured, maimed, or has warts or festering or running sores (22:22)
5. An ox with a defect may be presented as a freewill offering but not in fulfillment of a vow (22:23)
6. An animal whose testicles are bruised, crushed, torn, or cut may not be offered (22:24)
7. Offerings from foreign lands are not acceptable (22:25).

Command #61, Lev 22:21, Sacrificial animals must be without blemish: "It must be without blemish to be acceptable."

Prohibition #91, Lev 22:20, One must not sanctify a blemished animal: "Do not bring near anything with a defect."

Prohibition #97, Lev 22:21, One must not cause a blemish on a sacrificial animal: "It must be without defect or blemish."

Prohibition #92, Lev 22:22, One must not sacrifice a blemished animal: "Do not offer to the Lord the blind."

Prohibition #94, Lev 22:22, One must not burn with fire a blemished animal: "Do not place any of these on the altar as an offering made to the Lord by fire."

Prohibition #93, Lev 22:24, One must not sprinkle blood on a blemished animal: "Do not offer to the Lord an animal whose testicles are bruised, crushed, torn, or cut."

Prohibition #361, Lev 22:24, Castration is forbidden: "You must not offer to the Lord an animal whose testicles are bruised, crushed, torn, or cut. You must not do this in your own land."

Prohibition #96, Lev 22:25, One must not sacrifice to the Lord that which was offered by a foreigner: "And you must not accept such animals from the hand of a foreigner and offer them."

d. Time Periods of Offerings (22:26–33)

A selection of seven laws is given regarding time intervals of sacrifices.

7 Laws

1	2	3	4	5	6	7

The seven laws dealing with time periods of offerings are:
1. A newborn calf is to remain with its mother 7 days (22:27)
2. A newborn lamb is to remain with its mother 7 days (22:27)
3. A newborn goat is to remain with its mother 7 days (22:27)
4. A cow and a calf are not to be sacrificed on the same day (22:28)
5. A sheep and a lamb are not to be sacrificed on the same day (22:28)
6. A thank offering is to be sacrificed in an acceptable way (22:29)
7. A thank offering is to be eaten in one day, not to be left over until morning (22:30)

Command #60, Lev 22:27, Sacrificial animals must be eight days old or more: "And it shall be seven days with its mother."

Command #9, Lev 22:32, One must sanctify the name of God: "I will be sanctified in the midst of the sons of Israel."

Prohibition #101, Lev 22:28, One must not kill an animal and its young in one day: "Do not slaughter a cow or sheep and its young on the same day."

Prohibition #120, Lev 22:30, No part of the thanksgiving offering is to be left till morning: "It must be eaten that same day; leave none of it till morning."

Prohibition #63, Lev 22:32, One must not profane the Lord's name: "Do not profane my holy name."

C. The Calendar of the Religious Seasons (23:1–24:23)

1. Seasonal Events (23:1–44)

Seven special seasons of the year (מוֹעֲדִים) are enumerated. The section has a clearly defined introduction (vv. 1–2), which is repeated at the conclusion (v. 44)

7 Feasts

1	2	3	4	5	6	7

1. The Sabbath (23:3; cf. Nu 28:1–8)
2. The Passover and Unleavened Bread (Lev 23:4–8; cf. Nu 28:16–25)
3. The Firstfruits (Lev 23:9–14)
4. The Feast of Weeks (Lev 23:15–22; cf. Nu 28:26–31)
5. The Feast of Trumpets (Lev 23:23–25; cf. Nu 29:1–6)
6. The Day of Atonement (Lev 23:26–32; cf. Nu 29:7–11)
7. The Feast of Tabernacles (Lev 23:33–43; cf. Nu 29:12–40)

These feasts appear on the yearly calendar as follows:

Biblical Month (Babylonian, modern names)

1. Abib (Nisan, March/April)
   - 10th—Passover lamb chosen
   - 14th—Passover lamb slain in the evening
   - 15th—Feast of Unleavened Bread
   - 16th—Offering of Firstfruits of the Harvest
   - 21th—Conclusion of Feast of Unleavened Bread
2. Ziv (Iyar, April/May)
   - 14th—Second Passover lamb slain (see Nu 9:1–14)
3. Sivan (May/June)
   - 6th—Feast of Weeks (Feast of Pentecost)
4. Not mentioned (Tammuz, June/July)
5. Not mentioned (Ab, July/August)
6. Elul (August/September)
7. Ethanim (Tishri, September/October)
   - 1st—Feast of Trumpets
   - 10th—Day of Atonement
   - 15th—Feast of Tabernacles (Sukkoth, Booths)
8. Bul (Marcheshvan, October/November)
9. Kislev (November/December) (25th—Hanukkah)
10. Tebet (December/January)
11. Shebat (January/February)
12. Adar (February/March) (14th—Purim)
13. Adar Sheni (extra month added every second or third year)

Commands:

Command #44, Lev 23:10, A meal offering of a sheaf of barley on the sixteenth day of Nisan, the second day of Passover: "You shall bring the sheaf."

Command #161, Lev 23:15, Count from the gathering of the first sheaf forty-nine days: "You shall count from the morrow of the Sabbath."

Command #46, Lev 23:17, One must bring two loaves of bread as a wave (heave) offering: "From your dwellings you shall bring bread for the wave offering."

Command #162, Lev 23:21, Rest from work on holy days: "And you shall call in that very day a holy convocation."

Command #163, Lev 23:24, Rest on the first day of Tishri (Rosh Hashanah): "The first day of the month shall be a Sabbath to you."

Command #166, Lev 23:35, Resting on the first day of Sukkoth (Tabernacles): "On the first day it shall be a holy convocation."

Command #43, Lev 23:36, An additional gift (*musaf*) is to be offered on each of the seven days of Passover: "Seven days you shall offer fire to the Lord."

Command #167, Lev 23:36, Resting on the eighth day of Sukkoth (Tabernacles): "On the eight day it shall be a holy convocation."

Command #169, Lev 23:40, Take choice fruit and rejoice seven days: "You shall take for yourselves on the first day."

Command #168, Lev 23:42, Dwelling in booths seven days of Sukkoth (Tabernacles): "In booths you shall dwell seven days."

Prohibitions:

Prohibition #189, Lev 23:14, One must not eat bread made of new grain: "You must not eat any bread, or roasted or new grain."

Prohibition #190, Lev 23:14, One must not eat roasted new grain: "You must not eat any . . . roasted . . . grain."

Prohibition #191, Lev 23:14, One must not eat raw new grain: "You must not eat any . . . new grain."

Prohibition #325, Lev 23:21, One must not work on the Feast of Weeks: "Do no regular work."

Prohibition #210, Lev 23:22, One must not reap the whole of one's field: "Do not reap to the very edges of your field."

Prohibition #326, Lev 23:25, One must not work on the first day of the year (Rosh Hashanah): "Do no regular work."

Prohibition #329, Lev 23:28, One must not work on the Day of Atonement: "Do not work on that day."

Prohibition #196, Lev 23:29, One must not eat anything (fast) on the Day of Atonement: "Anyone who does not deny himself on that day must be cut off from his people."

Prohibition #327, Lev 23:35, One must not work on the first day of the Feast of Tabernacles: "On the first day . . . do no work at all on these days."

Prohibition #328, Lev 23:36, One must not work on the eighth day of the Feast of Tabernacles: "On the eighth day . . . do no regular work."

2. Continual Offerings (24:1–9)

Two continual offerings are enumerated: the burning of oil in the golden lampstand (vv. 1–4) and preparation of the twelve loaves of bread on the golden table (vv. 5–9). The bread was a regular part of the share of Aaron and his sons. They were to eat it within the tabernacle ("in a holy place").

3. A Blasphemer Stoned and Lex Talionis (24:10–23)

Embedded in the narrative about the stoning of a blasphemer is a reminder of the penalty for murder. The emphasis of the narrative is that the "whole congregation" was responsible for stoning the blasphemer (v. 14). This may be the reason why there is a reminder of the penalty for murder (lex talionis) just at this point in the narrative. The narrative thus sets up a contrast between the whole congregation's acting to take the life of a blasphemer and a single individual's (acting as an individual) taking "the life of a human being" (v. 17). Thus the writer has made an important distinction between capital punishment and murder. Capital punishment was an act of the whole community, whereas murder was an individual act.

> **Prohibition #60**, Lev 24:16, One must not blaspheme God's name: "Anyone who blasphemes the name of the Lord must be put to death."

D. The Sabbath and Jubilee Years (25:1–55)

At the close of the narratives dealing with God's speaking to Israel at Sinai, the writer recalls the setting of the giving of the Law: "The LORD said to Moses on Mount Sinai" (25:1; cf. 7:38). We, the readers, are thus being reappraised of the fact that all these laws were given by God to Moses. This reminder plays an important role in the evaluation of these laws as the expression of the will of God.

The central theme of this last set of instructions is that of restoration. Israel's life was to be governed by a pattern of seven-year periods, Sabbath years. After seven periods of seven years, in the Year of Jubilee, there was to be total restoration for God's people. "By the appointment of the year of jubilee, the disturbance and confusion of the divinely appointed relations, which had been introduced in the course of time through the inconstancy of all human or earthly things, were to be removed by the appointment of the year of jubilee, and the kingdom of Israel to be brought back to its original condition."[8]

1. Sabbath Year (25:1–7)

As had already been commanded (Ex 23:10–11), when the people entered the land they were to work it (sow and reap) for six years and eat its produce. On the seventh year, however, they were to leave the land fallow, that is, neither sow seed nor reap what might grow there from the previous year's crops. The owner of the land would not carry out an organized sowing and harvest. All the people of the land, rich and poor alike, were simply to live off the land: "Whatever the land yields during the sabbath year will be food for you" (Lev 25:6). This provision was especially intended for the "poor of the people" (Ex 23:11). It was to be their year of plenty.

In its overall plan, the Sabbath year was to be a replication of God's provisions for humankind in the Garden of Eden. When God created human beings and put them into the Garden, they were not to work for their livelihood but were to worship (see comments above on Ge 2:15). So also in the Sabbath year, each person was to share equally in all the good of God's provision (Lev 25:6). In the Garden, God provided for the man and woman an eternal rest (cf. Gen 2:9, the Tree of Life; 3:22b) and time of worship, the Sabbath (Gen 2:3). The Sabbath year was a foretaste of that time of rest and worship. Here, as on many other occasions, the writer has envisioned Israel's possession of the "good land" promised to them as a return to the Garden of Eden.

If Leviticus 25:20–22, which is clearly speaking only of the Jubilee Year, can be used to shed light on the Sabbath year, then each sixth year—if the people were obedient—God would provide an abundant harvest that would

---

[8]See Keil, *Pentateuch*, 2:455.

last through the next year. It would be much like the manna in the wilderness that God gave in extra abundance on the sixth day to last through the seventh. Verse 6, however, appears to argue against an analogy with the Jubilee Year in that it states that "whatever the land yields during the Sabbath year" was to be food for everyone. Thus it was only on the Jubilee Year and not on each sixth year that an extra abundance was given to last through the years of Sabbath. It would have been necessary to have an extra-abundant crop for the Jubilee year since two years of Sabbath were celebrated back-to-back in the Jubilee. The first was the regular Sabbath year (49th year) and the second was the Year of Jubilee (50th year).

Prohibitions relating to the seventh year:

Prohibition #220, Lev 25:4, One must not sow the ground in the seventh year: "In the seventh year the land is to have a Sabbath of rest. . . . Do not sow your fields."

Prohibition #221, Lev 25:4, One must not prune trees in the seventh year: "In the seventh year the land is to have a Sabbath of rest. . . . Do not prune your vineyards."

Prohibition #222, Lev 25:5, One must not reap a harvest in the seventh year: "Do not reap what grows of itself."

Prohibition #223, Lev 25:5, One must not harvest grapes in the seventh year: "Do not harvest grapes of your untended vines."

2. Jubilee Year (25:8–55)

Every seven Sabbath years, Israel was to proclaim a special Sabbath, a Jubilee Year. The basic idea of the Jubilee Year was to set aside the fiftieth year as a holy year in which total restoration of land, property, and debts was made. If the nation was obedient to God's laws, he would bless them and increase the produce of their land so that they would have enough to live through not only the Sabbath year, which was the forty-ninth year, but also the Jubilee Year, the fiftieth. God said, "I will send you such a blessing in the sixth year that the land will yield enough for three years" (v. 21). The three years would last from the end of the harvest in the preceding year to the harvest after the Jubilee Year. The first year would be the Sabbath Year preceding the Jubilee Year, the forty-ninth year. The second year would be the fiftieth year, the Jubilee Year. The third year would be the next year from the time of sowing until the harvest actually came in.

The term *Jubilee* (*yôḇēl*), meaning "shout," is related by a wordplay to the Hebrew term for "ram's horn" (*yôḇēl*). The sound of the ram's horn or trumpet (*šôp̄ār*, 25:9) signaled the beginning of the holiday (*yôḇēl*). On the fiftieth year, the tenth day of the seventh month, on the Day of Atonement, the ram's horn was to be sounded and the Jubilee Year was proclaimed (v. 9).

All reckoning of the value of property and real estate was made relative to the time of the Jubilee Year. The value was determined by how many years remained before the property would be released to its original owner (v. 15).

a. Real Estate (25:8–34)

In the Jubilee Year, all property that had been bought or sold since the last Jubilee would revert back to its original owner. Thus the land could not be sold permanently (v. 23). The reason given for this restriction was that all the land belonged to the Lord; the people of Israel were considered "tenants" on God's land (v. 23).

The Jubilee Year provision had two important exceptions. First, houses in walled cities could be sold permanently if the right of redemption had been forfeited by waiting one year (v. 29–31). Thus houses and property in the countryside and in unwalled cities were considered part of God's land and could not be sold permanently.

The second exception had to do with the property of the Levites. In a walled city that was a "Levitical town"—that is, a town set apart for the inheritance of the Levites (Nu 35:1–8)—property would be returned in the Jubilee Year (Lev 25:32–34).

Commands:

Command #140, Lev 25:8, Counting the Jubilee years (fiftieth year): "Count off seven sabbaths."

Command #137, Lev 25:9, Blowing of *shofar* on Yom Kippur to set Hebrew slaves free: "Then have the trumpet sounded."

Command #136, Lev 25:10, Sanctify the fiftieth year: "Consecrate the fiftieth year."

Command #245, Lev 25:14, Judgments involving sales: "If you sell land to one of your countrymen or buy any from him."

Command #138, Lev 25:24, Property returned in the fiftieth year: "Throughout the country that you hold as a possession you must provide for the redemption of the land."

Command #139, Lev 25:29–30, Redemption of property sold in a walled city: "If a man sells a house in a walled city."

Prohibitions:

Prohibition #224, Lev 25:11, One must not work the ground in the Jubilee Year: "The fiftieth year shall be a jubilee for you; do not sow."

Prohibition #225, Lev 25:11, One must not reap what grows of itself: "The fiftieth year shall be a jubilee for you; . . . do not reap what grows of itself."

Prohibition #226, Lev 25:11, One must not harvest fruit: "The fiftieth year shall be a jubilee for you; . . . do not harvest the untended vines."

Prohibition #250, Lev 25:14, One must not deceive another in business transactions: "If you sell land to one of your countrymen or buy any from him, do not take advantage of each other."

Prohibition #251, Lev 25:17, One must not take advantage (M. mislead verbally) of another: "Do not take advantage of each other."

Prohibition #227, Lev 25:23, One must not sell one's inheritance: "The land must not be sold permanently."

Prohibition #228, Lev 25:33, The Levitical lands must not be changed: "The pastureland belonging to their towns must not be sold."

b. Debt (25:35–55)

The Jubilee Year had three primary concerns with respect to incurring debt. First, Israelites were to lend money without interest to fellow Israelites in need (vv. 35–38). Such a provision would ensure that an Israelite would not loose his place among God's people. Second, a fellow Israelite could not be purchased as a slave. He could be hired as a worker but would be released in the Jubilee Year. Slaves were to come from non-Israelite people (vv. 39–46). In Exodus 21:1–6 (cf. Dt 15:12–18) an Israelite (Hebrew) servant could forego his freedom and remain with his master *forever* if he chose to do so. Since the meaning of the term *forever* in Hebrew need not always be "as long as he lives" but may imply only "a long time" (cf. 1Sa 1:22), it appears likely that the Hebrew servant could go free in the Jubilee Year if he desired. Third, an Israelite could not be taken as a slave by a non-Israelite. He could be hired as a worker but was to be released in the Jubilee Year (Lev 25:47–53).

> **Command #235**, Lev 25:46, Treatment of alien slaves: "You can will them to your children as inherited property."
>
> **Prohibition #235**, Lev 25:37, One must not lend money to another Israelite on interest: "You must not lend him money at interest or sell him food at a profit."
>
> **Prohibition #257**, Lev 25:39, One must not make an Israelite work as a slave: "Do not make him work as a slave."
>
> **Prohibition #258**, Lev 25:42, One must not sell an Israelite as a slave: "They must not be sold as slaves."
>
> **Prohibition #259**, Lev 25:43, One must not treat an Israelite worker cruelly: "Do not rule over them ruthlessly."
>
> **Prohibition #260**, Lev 25:53, One must not allow a foreigner to treat an Israelite worker cruelly: "You must see to it that his owner does not rule over him ruthlessly."

E. Final Conditions of the Covenant (26:1–46)

1. Introduction (26:1–2)

The repetition of the term *covenant* in this chapter shows that the author intends it as a summary of the conditions for the covenant reestablished after the incident of the golden calf. Thus, as has been the form throughout God's address to Israel on Mount Sinai, the statement of the conditions of the covenant is prefaced by a reminder of two central laws: the prohibition of idolatry (v. 1) and the call to observe the Sabbath (v. 2). It was through idolatry that Israel first broke the covenant at Sinai. By contrast the Sabbath was to be a sign of Israel's covenant relationship with God.

> **Prohibition #12**, Lev 26:1, One must not set up a stone for worship: "Do not place a carved stone in your land."

2. General Statement of Purpose (26:3–13)

If Israel obeyed God's "statutes and commandments," they would live with great blessing in the Promised Land. The description given here of life in the land is reminiscent of God's original blessing in the Garden of Eden. The Lord said, "You will eat all the food you want and live in safety in your land [cf. Ge 1:29]. . . . I will remove savage beasts from the land [cf. Ge 1:26]. . . . I will make you fruitful and multiply you [cf. Ge 1:28]. . . . I will put my dwelling place among you [cf. Ge 2:8]. . . . I will walk among you [cf. Ge 3:8] and be your God, and you will be my people" (Lev 26:5–12).

3. Warning of Results of Disobedience (26:14-39)

If Israel rejected God's "statutes and commandments," they would experience divine punishment (vv. 14-31), their land would be destroyed (v. 32), and they would be sent into exile (vv. 33-39).

4. Hope for the Future (26:40-45)

If Israel repented and humbled themselves, God would remember his covenant with the fathers (Abraham, Isaac, and Jacob) and his promise of the land, and he would not break his covenant with them. When Israel was in Egypt and was humbled under the hand of Pharaoh, God remembered his covenant with Abraham and delivered them (Ex 2:24). Similarly, in the future when Israel would humble themselves, God would remember his covenant and deliver his people.

F. Vows and Tithes (27:1-34)

Just as the whole of the giving of the Law at Sinai began with ten commandments, so it now ends with a list of ten laws. The content of the ten laws deals with the process of payment of vows and tithes made to the Lord.

1. Persons Dedicated to the Lord (27:1-8)

One specific type of vow is dealt with here: the vow that allowed for payment with a substitute. In this vow, one gave one's own worth in money to the Lord. The law in the present narrative does not relate to the vow so much as to the process of reckoning one's own value in money.

Command #114, Lev 27:2-8, Procedure of dedicating equivalent personal value: "If anyone makes a special vow to dedicate persons to the Lord."

2. Animals Dedicated to the Lord (27:9-13)

The concern in this law is with the status of an animal vowed in dedication to the Lord. Once an acceptable animal had been vowed, it could not be exchanged for a lesser animal. It was holy and remained so.

If the animal was unclean and thus not acceptable for an offering, the priest was to set its value apparently according to the current rate. It could then be reclaimed at one-fifth more value.

Command #87, Lev 27:10, An animal exchanged for an offering is holy: "It and his exchange are holy."

Command #115, Lev 27:12, Procedure of dedicating equivalent value of an animal: "The priest shall evaluate it."

Prohibition #106, Lev 27:10, One must not substitute sacrifices: "He must not exchange it or substitute a good one for a bad one."

3. Houses Dedicated to the Lord (27:14-15)

This law describes the procedure for dedicating one's house to the Lord and then buying it back. When the house was vowed, the priest set its value and it could be bought back for one-fifth more money.

Command #116, Lev 27:14, Procedure of dedicating equivalent value of a house: "If a man dedicates his house."

4. Inherited Land Dedicated to the Lord (27:16–21)

When inherited land was dedicated by a vow, the priest set the value based on the amount of produce of the land and the time remaining before the land would revert back to its owner in the Jubilee Year. This land, once vowed, was redeemable; that is, it could be repurchased by the one who gave it as a vow. If the land was not redeemed, however, in the Jubilee Year the land would be deeded over to the priests.

Command #117, Lev 27:16, Procedure of dedicating equivalent value of a field: "If a man dedicates to the Lord part of his family land."

5. Purchased Land Dedicated to the Lord (27:22–25)

Land which one purchased could be dedicated to the Lord by a vow. Its value would be reckoned by the priest and paid by the one making the vow. In the Jubilee Year the land would revert to the original owner.

6. Prohibition of Dedication of Firstborn Animals (27:26–27)

Since the firstborn was already dedicated to the Lord (Ex 13), it could not be given as a vow.

Prohibition #107, Lev 27:26, One must not substitute one category of offering for another: "No one may dedicate the firstborn of an animal, since the firstborn already belongs to the Lord."

7. Procedure for Total Devotion to the Lord (27:28)

A heightened form of vow was called a devotion (ḥērem). In this vow the person or thing devoted was given completely and without reservation to the Lord. Such a vow could not be reversed or substituted by a payment.

Command #145, Lev 27:28, Distinctions in the ḥērem (special vow): "Surely everything which one devotes to the Lord."

Prohibition #110, Lev 27:28, One must not sell a devoted thing: "But nothing that a man owes and devotes to the Lord . . . may be sold."

Prohibition #111, Lev 27:28, One must not redeem a devoted thing: "But nothing that a man owes and devotes to the Lord . . . may be redeemed."

8. Procedure for Total Devotion of a Person to the Lord (27:29)

This law represents a special instance of the previous total devotion. Under the law given at Mount Sinai, it was possible for one to commit an apostasy punishable by death, as in Exodus 22:20, "Whoever sacrifices to any god other than the LORD must be destroyed." Such a total devotion was irrevocable and could not be substituted by a payment.

9. Procedure for Tithes from the Produce of the Land (27:30–31)

A tithe, that is, a tenth, of the produce of the land was given to the Lord. In the present provision, one could repurchase the tithe by paying a price of one-fifth more value for it.

Command #127, Lev 27:30, Give the tithe of the produce of the land to the Levites: "All the tithe of the land belongs to the Lord."

10. Procedure for Tithes from the Livestock (27:32–34)

A tenth of the livestock was given to the Lord. No provision was given for repurchasing this gift. The institution of the tithe was already established in Israel (cf. Ge 14:20; 28:20–22). In this passage the tithe is said to belong to the Lord. Later, Numbers 18:8–32 explains the purpose and use of the tithe. It was to be the means of support for the priests and the Levites at the sanctuary. It was given to the Levites for their work at the tabernacle (Nu 18:21).

> **Command #78**, Lev 27:32, The tithe of one's cattle: "All the tithe of the herd or flock."
>
> **Command #87**, Lev 27:33, An animal exchanged for an offering is holy: "It and his exchange are holy."
>
> **Prohibition #109**, Lev 27:32, One must not sell the tithe of animals: "The entire tithe of the herd and flock . . . will be holy."

This section concludes briefly with the statement that "these are the commandments which the LORD commanded Moses [to give] to the Israelites on Mount Sinai" (27:34).

Chapter 4

NUMBERS

NAME

Traditionally, Numbers has been treated as an independent book. As is the case with the other books in the Pentateuch, Numbers is not really a separate book but only a section of the larger work. The traditional Hebrew title of Numbers is "And he spoke" or "In the wilderness" because these are the first words of what was considered the book of Numbers. The English title "Numbers" comes from the LXX and Vulgate and is based on the "numbering," or census, of the people in the first chapters (and in chap. 26).

STRUCTURE

The order of the material as it is arranged in the book is not strictly chronological.

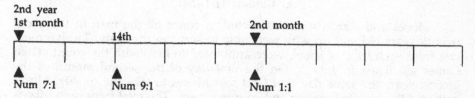

For example, Numbers 1:1 situates the events of the book on the first day of the second month of the second year after the Exodus from Egypt. Numbers 7:1 reverts back to the time of the setting up of the tabernacle, that is, the first day of the first month of the second year (Ex 40:17). In Numbers

9:1–5, however, the time period of the material is that of the Passover celebration on the fourteenth day of the first month of the second year. Thus the arrangement of the book is as much topical as it is chronological.

Within the larger structure of the Pentateuch, however, most of the narrative exhibits a chronological order. The events recorded fall into the time of the last days at Sinai and the period of Israel's sojourn in the wilderness. Within this larger time frame, the primary dividing point of the book is Numbers 14:45, the account of the destruction and defeat of disobedient Israel in the hill country of the Amalekites. Thus the book has two main divisions, chapters 1–14 and 15–36, falling on either side of the account of Israel's failure to believe in God.

The location of the events recorded in the early chapters of the book is the Sinai Desert. The people had encamped before Mount Sinai and set up the tabernacle. Moses had received the laws with the covenant, and plans were now being laid to leave Sinai and return to the Promised Land.

After the tabernacle had been set up, a census was taken to determine who would serve in the military. Israel's army totaled 603,550 men (Nu 1:46). Much of the material in these early chapters of Numbers is devoted to the details of the census and the arrangement of the tribes for battle. The primary purpose of the author's inclusion of this material in the Pentateuch appears to be to give the reader a full and accurate picture of the scale of operations and necessary preparations for Israel's return to the land. In some respects this material can be seen as an attempt to justify the scope of the laws given in the Pentateuch. It is clear, at least, that the picture given here of the size and state of the nation helps show why so many detailed regulations were necessary.

Moreover, within the narratives of the Pentateuch there is a noticeable contrast between the orderly movement of the tribes from Sinai, as is shown in the present text, and the picture of the people "running wild" in the account of the golden calf (Ex 32:25). Thus the narrative shows that the laws God gave to Israel at Sinai, which are listed between these two accounts, were necessary and had a salutary effect on the people. The emphasis on the size and number of the nation, then, is intended to stress the value and importance of the Law.

I. THE CENSUS AND THE ORGANIZATION
OF THE PEOPLE (1:1–2:34)

A. Census (1:1–54)

Moses and Aaron were instructed to count all the men in the camp twenty years old and up who were able to serve in the army. Twelve men, one from each tribe of Israel, were appointed to help with the count. Their names are listed in 1:5–15. On the first day of the second month of the second year, the same day that God told Moses to take the census, Moses gathered the people together and counted them. The total from each tribe is listed in the remainder of chapter 1.

Reuben:	46,500
Simeon:	59,300

Gad:	45,650
Judah:	74,600
Issachar:	54,400
Zebulun:	57,400
Ephraim:	40,500
Manasseh:	32,200
Benjamin:	35,400
Dan:	62,700
Asher:	41,500
Naphtali:	53,400
Total:	603,550

The census did not count the Levites, the men of the tribe of Levi, including Moses and Aaron. Their task—to keep charge of the tabernacle and Israel's worship—was distinct from that of the rest of the Israelites, and thus they conducted their own census in Numbers 3:15 and 4:34–49. The purpose of setting the Levites apart and arranging them around the tabernacle was so that "wrath will not fall on the Israelite community" (1:53; see comments on the theology of the tabernacle in the Excursus on "The Tabernacle-Temple Complex" at Ex 24).

B. Arrangement of the Tribal Camps (2:1–34)

The tribes were arranged in orderly fashion around the tabernacle. According to 2:34, their arrangement in camp was also the same order in which they were to travel.

If the list in this chapter is compared with that of the first chapter, it becomes evident that the arrangement of the tribes around the tabernacle served to highlight the importance and centrality of the tribe of Judah. As in Jacob's prophecy to his twelve sons (Ge 49:1–27), Judah has already gained the ascendancy over the other tribes. Even though Reuben was the firstborn, Judah was the tribe through which the royal son would be born who would bring redemption to God's people (see comments above on Ge 49). Moreover, the Genesis narratives devote much attention to the notion of "the east," a theme that also appears important in the arrangement of the tribes. After the Fall, Adam and Eve, and then Cain, were cast out of God's good land "toward the east" (3:24; 4:16). Furthermore, Babylon was built in the east (Ge 11:2), and Sodom was "east" of the Promised Land (13:11). Throughout these narratives the hope is developed that God's redemption would come from the east and that this redemption would be a time of restoration of God's original blessing and gift of the land in Creation. Thus, God's first act of preparing the land—when he said, "Let there be light" (1:3)—used the imagery of the sunrise in the east as a figure of the future redemption. Moreover, God's garden was planted for humankind "in the east" of Eden (2:8), and it was there that God intended to pour out his blessing on them.

Throughout the pentateuchal narratives, then, the concept of moving "eastward" plays an important role as a reminder of the Paradise Lost—the garden in the east of Eden—and a reminder of the hope for a return to God's blessing "from of the east"—the place of waiting in the wilderness. It was not without purpose, then, that the arrangement of the tribes around the tabernacle should reflect the same imagery of hope and redemption.

The order and position of the tribes was as follows:

On the east, toward the sunrise—Total: 186,400
Judah: 74,600
Issachar: 54,400
Zebulun: 57,400

On the south—Total: 151,450
Reuben: 46,500
Simeon: 59,300
Gad: 45,650

In the middle was the Tent of Meeting and the tribe of Levi. When Israel began to travel, the camp of the Levites was to set out from here, "in the middle of the camps," in the same order as they were encamped (Nu 2:17). Gershon camped on the west (3:23), Kohath on the south (3:29), Merari on the north (3:35), and the priests (Moses, Aaron, and his sons) on the east (3:38).

On the west—Total: 108,100
Ephraim: 40,500
Manasseh: 32,200
Benjamin: 35,400

On the north—Total: 157,600
Dan: 62,700
Asher: 41,500
Naphtali: 53,400

II. THE LEVITES (3:1–4:49)

The identity and duties of the tribe of Levi are covered in detail in these chapters. The writer begins by recounting the events that led to the death of two of Aaron's four sons, Nadab (the firstborn) and Abihu (see Lev 10). In a way similar to the replacement of Reuben (the firstborn) and Simeon by Judah and Levi in the family of Jacob (Ge 49:2–7), Aaron's firstborn, Nadab, and his brother Abihu were replaced by Eleazar and Ithamar. The priesthood had already been firmly rooted in the family of Aaron (Ex 29:9). Thus, henceforth, the priests who served at the tabernacle could only be from the families of Eleazar and Ithamar (Nu 3:10). It is important to note the special prominence given to Moses and Aaron and the priests. They were to camp on the east side of the tabernacle, like Judah, "toward the sunrise" (3:38; cf. 2:3; see commentary above on Nu 2:11–34).

In addition to the sons of Aaron, the Lord appointed the rest of the tribe of Levi to help the priests in the service at the tabernacle (3:7–8). The sons of Levi are identified specifically as the descendants of Levi's three sons, Gershon, Kohath, and Merari. Moses and Aaron are also included in this

The Order of the Travels (2:1–34; 10:11–28; 11:33; Jos 3:3)

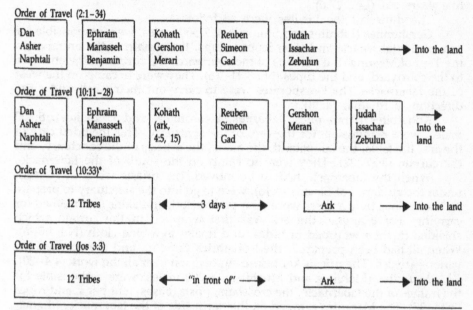

Order of Travel (2:1–34)

| Dan Asher Naphtali | Ephraim Manasseh Benjamin | Kohath Gershon Merari | Reuben Simeon Gad | Judah Issachar Zebulun | ⟶ Into the land |

Order of Travel (10:11–28)

| Dan Asher Naphtali | Ephraim Manasseh Benjamin | Kohath (ark, 4:5, 15) | Reuben Simeon Gad | Gershon Merari | Judah Issachar Zebulun | ⟶ Into the land |

Order of Travel (10:33)*

| 12 Tribes | ◀——3 days——▶ | Ark | ⟶ Into the land |

Order of Travel (Jos 3:3)

| 12 Tribes | ◀—— "in front of" ——▶ | Ark | ⟶ Into the land |

*The NIV renders "three days' journey" as "during those three days," which gives the impression that the order of 10:33 was only a temporary measure for finding a place to rest.

group since they were of the family of Kohath (Ex 6:18–20). Aaron's son Eleazar, a priest, was the chief leader of the Levites.

Three previous incidents in Israel's history led to God's selection of the Levites as his servants in the work of the tabernacle. First, Simeon and Levi had been rejected from participation with the tribes of Israel because with their "swords of violence" they killed men in anger (Ge 49:5–6). This is apparently a reference to their revenge of the rape of their sister Dinah (Ge 34:25). Second, the members of the family of Levi had rallied behind Moses and the Lord after the incident of the golden calf (Ex 32:26). On that occasion, we are told, the Lord chose the tribe of Levi for himself (Ex 32:29). Third, God had a claim to every Israelite firstborn who had been "passed over" in the Exodus (Ex 13:1–2, 11–13). God's claim on the firstborn of Israel was apparently intended at the start to be the means of establishing the priesthood in Israel (see comments above on Ex 13:1–2). Every firstborn son was to be a priest. Because of the Levites' faithfulness at the time of the golden calf, however, God now moved to relinquish his right to all firstborn Israelite males and put in their place the tribe of Levi (Nu 3:11–13). Once again, it is evident that the sin of the golden calf marked a decisive change in Israel's relationship with God in the Sinai covenant.

The substitution of Levites for the firstborn Israelite males was carried out by means of a census. First, a census of the Levites was taken. Its total was 22,000. Then, all firstborn males among the Israelites were listed by name. That list totaled 22,273. This surplus of 273 firstborn Israelites was then replaced by the payment of a redemption price—five shekels each. That price was the value set for the redemption of a child between one month and five years old (Lev 27:6).

The duties of the Levites were as follows:

Gershonites (Libnites and Shimeites), 7,500 males, were responsible for care of the tabernacle and tent, its coverings, the curtain at the entrance to the Tent of Meeting, the curtains of the courtyard, the curtain at the entrance to the courtyard, and the ropes (Nu 3:21–26). They were to camp on the west of the tabernacle. The Gershonites were to carry out their work under the direction of Ithamar (4:28).

Kohathites (Amramites, Izharites, Hebronites, and Uzzielites), 8,600 males, were responsible for the care of the sanctuary. This included care of the ark, the table, the lampstand, the altars, the articles of the sanctuary, and the curtain (3:27–32). They were to camp on the south of the tabernacle.

When the tabernacle had to be moved, the priests (sons of Aaron), under the guidance of Eleazar (4:16), were to go into the sanctuary to prepare it. The various holy articles were wrapped in cloth and skins and readied for carrying. For example, the ark was first wrapped in the curtain which shielded it, then wrapped in hides, and finally in a blue cloth (Nu 4:5–6). When all had been prepared, the Kohathites came in, and they carried the various articles. The priests kept close supervision over all the work (4:4–20).

Merarites (Mahlites and Mushites), 6,200 males, were responsible for the frames of the tabernacle, the crossbars, posts, bases, tent pegs, and ropes (3:33–37). The Merarites camped on the north side of the tabernacle. Ithamar directed the work of the Merarites as well as the Gershonites in the tabernacle (4:33).

At the conclusion of the instructions given for the Levites and their work with the tabernacle, Moses and Aaron counted the able-bodied men from the three Levitical families. The Kohathites numbered 2,750, the Gershonites 2,630, and the Merarites 3,200 (4:34–45). The total number of Levites from thirty to fifty years old was 8,580 (4:48).

Excursus: The Priests and the Levites

As descendants of the twelve sons of Jacob, the Israelites divided naturally into twelve tribal units. Because both of Joseph's sons, Ephraim and Manasseh, were given equal status (Ge 48:5), the number of tribes became thirteen. The number of tribal units was kept at twelve, however, by giving one tribe, the descendants of Levi, a special status among the other tribes. They were to be the mediators, set apart for holy work and worship at the tabernacle. Out of this selection of the tribe of Levi, three priestly groups were created within the covenant nation: the Levites, the priests, and the high priest.

In general, one may describe the duties of the Levites, together with that of the priests, as "performing the service of the sanctuary" (Nu 1:53).

The distinction between the Levites (all descendants of Levi) and the priests (only the descendants of Aaron) was based on the responsibilities given to each group. The priests were responsible for serving at the altar (18:7). The Levites were to attend to the general care of the tabernacle (3:25–39).

The clearest example of the distinction between the Levites and the priests can be seen in the narrative of Korah's rebellion (Nu 16). Korah (the son of Izhar and thus not of the house of Aaron, the son of Amram) was unwilling to accept the limitations of the Levites. He objected to the Aaronic priesthood's special privileges on the grounds that, in his opinion, the whole congregation was holy, not just the Aaronic priests (v. 3). But God demonstrated that even the Levites were to be considered "laymen" (v. 40 [MT 17:5]) in comparison to the special role of the priests from the house of Aaron.

The specific duties of the three Levitical families are outlined in Numbers 4. This passage gives only the duties of the Levites during the wilderness period. The book of Deuteronomy, however, describes the duties of the priests and Levites for the time period after the conquest of the land. At that time there would not have been as great a need for transporting the tabernacle; thus Deuteronomy lays less stress on the distinction between the Levites and the priests.

The priesthood was the strict prerogative of the house of Aaron (Nu 3:10; 16:1–50 [MT 16:1–17:15]). In the narrative of Korah's rebellion (Nu 16), God demonstrated his choice of Aaron's house by causing his staff, and not the others, to blossom and sprout ripe almonds (17:8 [MT 23]).

The duty of the priests was to represent the people before the Lord (Dt 18:5) in the sanctuary. This responsibility is distinct from that of the prophets, who represented the Lord to the people (Dt 18:9). As representatives of the people before Yahweh, the priests were to "carry the guilt of the people" (Nu 18:1). They were to do this by carrying out their duties as prescribed in the Law (Torah).

A second and equally important duty of the priests was to instruct and interpret the laws given by Moses (Lev 10:11; cf. Mal 2:7).

The specific duties of the high priest related primarily to the Day of Atonement (Lev 16) and the use of the Urim and Thummim (Ex 28:30; Lev 8:8). Though we know very little from the biblical text about the purpose and use of the Urim and Thummim (the words in Hebrew mean "lights and perfections"), it appears that they were used as a way of determining the will of God for the people (see 1Sa 28:6: "When Saul inquired of the LORD, the LORD did not answer him, either by dreams or by Urim or by prophets").

Leviticus 16 describes in detail the role of the high priest on the Day of Atonement. On that day he represented in the sanctuary before the LORD not only the priesthood but also all the people: "And he shall make atonement for the holy place, because of the impurities of the sons of Israel, and because of their transgressions, in regard to all their sins. . . . Then Aaron shall lay both of his hands on the head of the live goat, and confess over it all the iniquities of the sons of Israel, and all their transgressions in regard to all their sins. . . . He shall make atonement for the priests and for all the people of the assembly" (Lev 16:16–21).

III. HOLINESS AMONG THE PEOPLE (5:1–6:27)

The focus of the writer now turns from the priests and the Levites and their holiness to that of the individual Israelites in the camp. They also were to be part of the holy nation (Ex 19:5). In this section of the Pentateuch, by means of a series of regulations and selected narratives, the writer demonstrates the importance of the total commitment of all the people to the requirements of the Sinai Covenant.

A. The Purity of the Camp (5:1–4)

In Leviticus 13–15 Moses had instructed the priests in the examination and identification of diseases. When a skin disease was detected, there was no provision for healing the disease. The diseased person was required to "wear torn clothes, let his hair be unkempt, cover the lower part of his face, and cry out, 'Unclean! Unclean!'" (13:45). That person was to live alone "outside the camp" (13:46). Now, as the previous laws have their effect and the camp becomes progressively purer, we are shown that Moses' commands were, in fact, being carried out. The purpose of the writer is to show that at this point in the narrative, Israel's leaders, Moses and Aaron, were following God's will and the people were following them obediently. This theme will not continue long, however. The narrative will soon turn a corner and begin to show that the people quickly deviated from God's way and, with their leaders, Moses and Aaron, failed to continue to trust in God.

> **Command #31**, Nu 5:2, Remove unclean (leprous/flow) from the camp: "And they shall send out of the camp all the leprous and those that have a flow."
>
> **Prohibition #77**, Nu 5:3, No unclean person can enter the camp: "So they will not defile their camp." (M. takes "camp" to be "camp of God's presence," hence the temple. Thus this law is different from Prohibition #78, Dt 23:11 [EVV 10].)

B. Treachery Against Others and God (5:5–10)

Moses had given Israel the guilt offering as a means of making restitution for an offense against another Israelite (Lev 5:14–6:7 [MT 5:14–26]). The narrative here recalls that law in order to demonstrate the wrongfulness of acting treacherously against one's neighbor (Nu 5:6). In describing this offense of a man or woman against a member of the community, the narrative specifically calls such an offense "a treacherous act against the LORD" (Nu 5:6; NIV "unfaithful to the LORD"). Furthermore, the writer has included a special case of this offense (v. 8) as an example to show that the act of treachery was committed not only against one's neighbor but against the Lord as well. The example is that of the victim of a treacherous act who could not be found and hence the restitution could not be made. This example shows, however, that even in the case where the man or woman who had been wronged was not to be found, the restitution was still to be made to the Lord by giving the necessary compensation to the priests. Thus, though the one wronged, in a human sense, could not be recompensed, this example shows that God had also been wronged and must also be recompensed. The point is clear—wrongs committed against God's people were considered wrongs committed against God himself.

> **Command #73**, Nu 5:6–7, Confession of sin before God and repentance: "That person must confess the sin."

C. The Law of Jealousy (5:11–31)

The case of the jealous husband is a curious one that raises many questions about the nature of social relationships in ancient Israel. This passage, however, does not give enough information to allow even a sketchy reconstruction of the details of this ritual. Since the text has given us so little information, we should be careful not to read too much into the practice described here, especially on the basis of magical practices in primitive cultures from our own day or from the ancient world. Rather, we should attempt to understand what the writer has given us, not what has been left out. We should also note that the writer of the Pentateuch seems little interested in such details and more concerned with the larger theocratic lesson embodied in this specific law. In other words, this particular case law is included here because it gives another illustration of God's personal involvement in the restitution for the sin of the nation. Within God's covenant with Israel, there could be no hidden sin among God's people nor any hidden suspicion of sin.

In the previous case (5:5–10), when a man or a woman wronged another member of the community, they were to "confess the sin" and make restitution. But what happened when there was no confession? What happened when there was only suspicion and "no witnesses" (v. 13)? Did this mean that sin could be allowed to fester in the hearts of the community and go undetected? The law of jealousy shows that through the role of the priest, God was actively at work in the nation and that no sin of any sort could be tolerated among God's holy people.

> **Command #223**, Nu 5:15–27, Test of woman suspected of adultery: "Then he is to take his wife to the priest."
>
> **Prohibition #104**, Nu 5:15, One must not use olive oil in the jealousy offering: "He must not pour oil on it."
>
> **Prohibition #105**, Nu 5:15, One must not use incense in the jealousy offering: "He must not put incense on it."

D. The Nazirite (6:1–21)

Little is known today regarding the origin and practice of the Nazirite vow in ancient Israel. The text offers few clues. This type of vow was apparently already in common practice at the time that Moses received these instructions. The instruction Moses received was intended to regulate the practice of the vow, not to establish it. Though we know very little about the practice of this vow among the Israelites, it is relatively clear why the writer includes the provision for the vow at this point in the narrative. This law specifically shows that there were provisions not just for the priest but for all members of God's people to commit themselves wholly to God. Complete holiness was not the sole prerogative of the priesthood or the Levites. The Nazirite vow shows that even laypersons, men and women in everyday walks of life, could enter into a state of complete devotion to God. Thus this segment of text teaches that any person in God's nation could be totally committed to holiness.

The Nazirite vow entailed abstention from three things for a specified length of time. One abstained from drinking wine or fermented drink (vv. 3–4), cutting one's hair (v. 5), and contact with a dead body (vv. 6–7). At the conclusion of the vow, certain offerings were required (vv. 13–20). An important provision was made for the Nazirite who, because of an emergency situation, had broken the vow (vv. 9–12). In other words, there was the recognition that some things in life superseded the requirements of the vow. If someone died suddenly in one's presence, for example, the vow could be temporarily suspended (v. 9). After the emergency had passed, there were provisions for completing the vow (vv. 10–12ff).

The Nazirite's abstention from wine and strong drink is part of a larger picture in the Pentateuch of the association of strong drink with neglect for God's Law. For example, the priests were expressly prohibited from drinking wine and strong drink when they entered the Tent of Meeting (Lev 10:8). The implication of this specific context is that it would impair their judgment in distinguishing "between the unclean and the clean" (10:10). Since that warning was given in the same chapter as the account of the death of Nadab and Abihu, it is often assumed that wine and strong drink played a part in their offer of "strange fire" before the Lord. That assumption, at least, would be consistent with other texts in the Pentateuch that show wine as the cause of neglect and folly that ultimately leads to a curse. For example, Noah's nakedness in his tent and the subsequent curse of the descendants of Canaan was a result of his drinking wine (Ge 9:20–27). Moreover, the incestuous origin of the Ammonites and Moabites was the result of Lot's drunkenness from wine (Ge 19:32–38). The role of the Ammonites and Moabites as Israel's enemies is well established in the book of Numbers when they hired Balaam to curse God's people (Nu 22:1–3). They were ultimately barred from participation in Israel's worship assembly (Dt 23:3).

The view of the potentially disastrous consequences of wine and strong drink found in these texts appears also to have influenced the later prophets in their assessment of the effects of wine. For example, Habakkuk envisions wine as the ultimate source of the downfall of the world powers that rise up against God's people (Hab 2:5). In the book of Proverbs, King Lemuel's mother states precisely the view represented by the writer of the Pentateuch: "It is not for kings, Lemuel, to drink wine or to crave strong drink, lest they drink and forget what the law decrees" (Pr 31:4–5). In the view of Proverbs wine and strong drink are only for those "who are perishing" and "who are in anguish" (Pr 31:6).

> **Command #92**, Nu 6:5, A Nazirite must let his hair grow: "He must let the hair of his head grow long."
>
> **Command #93**, Nu 6:13, At the end of his vow, the Nazirite must shave his hair and bring his offerings: "When the period of his separation is over." (Cf. Nu 6:18, "The Nazirite must shave off the hair that he dedicated.")
>
> **Prohibition #202**, Nu 6:3, A Nazirite must not drink wine or strong drink: "He must abstain from wine and other fermented drink and must not drink vinegar made from wine or from other fermented drink."
>
> **Prohibition #203**, Nu 6:3, A Nazirite must not eat fresh grapes: "He must not. . . eat grapes."
>
> **Prohibition #204**, Nu 6:3, A Nazirite must not eat dried grapes: "He must not. . . eat dried grapes."
>
> **Prohibition #205**, Nu 6:4, A Nazirite must not eat grape seeds: "He must not. . . eat even the seeds."
>
> **Prohibition #206**, Nu 6:4, A Nazirite must not eat grape skins: "He must not. . . eat even the seeds or skins."

Prohibition #209, Nu 6:5, A Nazirite must not shave his head: "No razor may be used on his head."

Prohibition #208, Nu 6:6, A Nazirite must not enter a tent in which there is a dead body: "He shall not go into [M. a tent where there is] a dead body."

Prohibition #207, Nu 6:7, A Nazirite must not become unclean for the dead: "Even if his own father or mother or brother or sister dies, he must not make himself ceremonially unclean on account of them."

E. Priestly Blessing (6:22–27)

At the close of this section dealing with the holiness of the people, the writer has attached an account of the priestly blessing. On either side of the blessing, its purpose is explained: "This is how you are to bless the Israelites" (vv. 23, 27). By placing this text at this point in the narrative, the writer shows that a central task of the priests was to be a source of blessing for God's people. Moreover, the text shows that the people were to find their blessing only in the priesthood, not apart from it. The holiness and blessing of the people depend on their recognition of the divine sanction of the priesthood.

Command #26, Nu 6:23, Priests must bless Israel: "Thus you shall bless the sons of Israel."

IV. DEDICATION OF THE TABERNACLE (7:1–9:23)

A. Dedication of the Altar (7:1–89)

The narrative (7:1) reestablishes the time as that of the erection of the tabernacle in Exodus 40:1, the first day of the first month of the second year. The purpose of this section of narrative is to show that as the people had been generous in giving to the construction of the tabernacle (Ex 35:4–29), now they showed the same generosity in its dedication. The writer goes to great lengths to show that the whole nation gave sacrificially to the work of God.

The order of the gifts is the same as the appointment of the tribal leaders in chapter 2. Judah leads the list, as is consistent with the centrality of this tribe in the perspective of the writer (cf. Ge 49:8–12; see comments above on Nu 2:1–34).

At the end of this long description of the dedication offerings for the altar, the writer has inserted a note about the fulfilled promise of God (7:89). In Exodus 25:22 the plan and purpose of the atonement cover had been given to Moses along with the promise that God would speak with Moses from this place. Exodus 35:9 gave an account of the making of the cover, but the writer has intentionally delayed any mention of the fulfillment of God's promise to speak with Moses "between the two cherubim" until the completion of the dedication of the altar.

Command #34, Nu 7:9, Priests are to carry the ark on their shoulders: "The priests shall carry the ark upon their shoulders."

B. Lighting the Golden Lampstand (8:1–4)

Exodus 25:32–40 recorded the instructions for making the golden lampstand, and Exodus 37:17–24 recorded a report of its completion. The account of the completion of the lampstand is given in almost verbatim terms to that of the instructions. Neither of these texts, however, mentions the lighting of the lamp. The writer has waited until now to tell us that, as part of the dedication of the tabernacle, the lamps were lit.[1]

C. Dedication of the Levites (8:5–26)

In chapters 3 and 4 the Levites were set apart to help the priests in the work of the tabernacle. It is recounted there that the priests were to replace the firstborn as those dedicated to serve before the Lord. At this point in the narrative, however, the Levites had not yet been consecrated for this work as the priests had been in Leviticus 8. Thus the writer includes here an account of their dedication as part of the overall description of the dedication of the tabernacle.

What is particularly striking about the dedication of the Levites in this narrative is the role that the whole congregation plays in the process. Unlike the consecration of the priests, in which the people merely looked on (Lev 8:3–4), the Israelite people here play a central role in the dedication of the Levites by laying their hands on them during their consecration (Nu 8:10).

The purpose of the narrative is to show, first, that God instructed Moses on how the Levites were to be consecrated (vv. 5–19), and then that the instructions were faithfully carried out (vv. 20–26).

D. Passover (9:1–14)

The Passover was celebrated on the fourteenth day of the first month of the second year, as Moses had commanded (Ex 12). According to this passage, however, an unanticipated problem arose. Some men were not able to partake of the celebration because they were unclean, and they requested that they be allowed to participate. The purpose of the narrative here is to show the reader something about the way the laws were carried out among the people. Moses' response to this new situation demonstrates the way many of the laws in ancient Israel were carried out. Thus, as we see in this text, exceptions to specific laws were taken directly to God's representative for a decision (9:8). When the Israelites realized a need for a further ruling, they took their request to Moses and he then went before the Lord. As it turns out, God answers by confirming the people's request. A second celebration, just like the first, was allowed for those who were not able to participate in the first Passover because they were ceremonially unclean. The purpose of including this segment of narrative was perhaps to show that God's laws were not arbitrary and unreasonable. The Israelites themselves even played a part in their formulation.

> **Command #57**, Nu 9:11, Whoever was prohibited from slaughtering the first Passover lamb should slaughter the second Passover: "In the second month at twilight they shall do it."
>
> **Command #58**, Nu 9:11, The meat of the second Passover should be eaten on the night of the 15th of Iyar with matzo upon the bitter herbs: "Upon the matzo and bitter herbs they shall eat it." (Cf. Ex 12:8.)

---

[1] The NIV renders the expression "to light the lamps" as "to set up the lamps," and thus obscures the writer's point."

Prohibition #122, Nu 9:12, One must not break the bone of the second Passover lamb: "They must not . . . break any of the bones."

Prohibition #119, Nu 9:13 (EVV 12), No part of the second Passover lamb is to be left till morning: "They must not leave any of it till morning."

E. God's Leading in the Wilderness (9:15–23)

This section repeats what was said in Exodus 40:34–38 in order to show the similarity of pattern in God's leading Israel. As God led them to Sinai by the pillar of cloud by day and fire by night (Ex 13:21–22), so now he has begun to lead them into the Promised Land. The writer is intent on showing that at this point in their walk with the Lord, Israel was obedient and followed the Lord's guidance. The writer's concern to make this point can be seen in that seven times in this brief narrative, it is said that they "obeyed the commandment of the Lord" and thus traveled when the cloud lifted from the tabernacle and moved (9:18, 20, 23; cf. Ex 17:1).

V. DEPARTURE FROM SINAI (10:1–12:16)

A. Silver Trumpets (10:1–10)

As the people prepared to leave Sinai and travel to the Promised Land, a series of trumpet calls was sounded for the sons of Aaron to help lead the people on their march through the wilderness. As the people followed the cloud which led them through the wilderness, the blasts of the trumpet kept the order in their ranks.

Command #59, Nu 10:10, Trumpets should be sounded at sacred times with offerings: "And in the day which you rejoice you shall sound the trumpets."

The tribe of Judah, those dwelling on the east (2:3), moved out at the first blast. The rest of the tribes followed in order at each successive call of the trumpet.

The impression that this narrative intends to give is that of an orderly and obedient departure from Sinai. The picture is a far cry from the scene which Moses saw when he first returned from the mountain and found the nation celebrating before the golden calf: "the people were running wild and Aaron had let them get out of control and so become a laughingstock to their enemies" (Ex 32:25). In other words, the author is trying to make a point with this narrative. He shows that after the incident of the golden calf the Mosaic Law was able to bring order and obedience to the nation. The Law, necessitated by the disobedience of the people, was having its effect on them.

To this point in the narrative, at least, all seemed to be working well. As the narrative continues to unfold, however, it becomes apparent that the giving of the Law had not resulted in any fundamental change in the ways of the people. What lay ahead was not an unsullied path to the Promised Land but a progressively worsening series of failures—both of the people and of their leaders. Something more than the Law was needed if the people were to follow God's will.

B. Departure from Sinai (10:11–36)

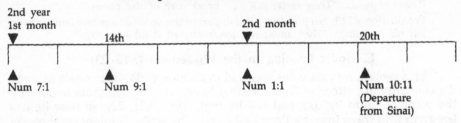

The departure was on the twentieth day of the second month of the second year (10:11). According to 9:11, they also celebrated the Feast of Unleavened Bread in the second month; thus they would have departed on the day before the last Sabbath of the feast (Ex 12:18). Israel's departure from Sinai to the Wilderness of Paran occurred just as planned. As the cloud lifted up from the tabernacle, the people followed it according to the order of the tribes described in numbers 2. Judah went first and the other tribes followed. The priests and Levites carried the tabernacle and its equipment. Rather than follow the group from the south side of the tabernacle (Reuben, Simeon, and Gad, as in 2:10–17), however, the priests and Levites followed the first group (Judah, Issachar, and Zebulun, 11:14–18). According to 10:33, the ark went out before them.

Hobab son of Reuel was the father-in-law (10:29–32) of Moses (see Jdg 4:11, NIV margin).[2] According to Exodus 3:1 he was also called Jethro. Reuel may have been a tribal name or, as is more likely, Reuel was the patriarch of Jethro's tribe and hence the father of Jethro. Thus in Exodus 2:18–21, because Moses was not yet married into the family, Reuel spoke in behalf of his son Jethro. After Moses married into the tribe and family (Ex 3:1), Jethro became the patriarch of the newly created branch of the tribe, and thus Moses henceforth dealt with Jethro, his actual father-in-law, the son of Reuel. Thus, according to the present narrative, Moses asked Hobab (Jethro) to remain with Israel because he, being a native of the region, knew the desert well and could help find suitable campsites.

We have attempted above to read all the various accounts of the family of Moses' wife in a way that harmonizes their content. There are also various accounts of Israel's journey through the wilderness. They were led by a cloud (Nu 9:15–23), by the priests who carried the ark (10:33), and now here, by Hobab (v. 31). If the Pentateuch is to be read as a completed whole, which we are now attempting to do, it seems likely that these various versions of the story should also be read in such a way that their content is understood harmonistically. In the final form of the Pentateuch the writer would surely have expected them to be read coherently, even if some explanation of their differences was necessary.

A possible implication of such a composite reading of all the narratives in Numbers is that Israel's path through the wilderness was guided by three distinct means. The cloud guided them (9:15–23); the ark guided them (10:33); and Hobab, Moses' father-in-law, guided them (v. 31). According to earlier instructions regarding their travel in the wilderness, however, the

---

[2]The lexical meaning of the Hebrew term ḥōṯēn is father-in-law, not brother-in-law.

Kohathites, who were to carry the ark, traveled (4:5) "in the middle of the camps" (2:17). It is thus difficult to see how the ark could have been out in front of the whole congregation if those who carried it were in the middle of the camp. The translators of the NIV and the KJV suggest by their translation "a distance of three days" (10:33) that the guidance of the ark was only a temporary measure. They translate here simply "during those three days," which means the time when the nation first departed from Sinai.[3] That translation would solve the problem in a convenient way; but, unfortunately, as is generally acknowledged, such a rendering does not suit the Hebrew text. This is especially shown to be true in the light of the fact that in Joshua's day the ark was still out in front of the people (Jos 3:1–6).

Part of the solution to the difficulty lies in recognizing that it is by no means certain that Hobab guided the Israelites in the wilderness as Moses had requested. We should note that in the account of Moses' request to Hobab, the narrative ends before we have heard Hobab's second and final reply. We should not assume that Hobab conceded to Moses' request; the narrative does not warrant that conclusion. In his first reply to Moses, Hobab states his intention quite clearly: "No, I will not go; I am going back to my own land and my own people." That Moses continued to press Hobab should not be taken as an indication in the narrative that Hobab afterward conceded. Moreover, the previous narrative states explicitly that, in their journeys through the wilderness, Israel followed the cloud that remained over the tent. It does not say that they followed Hobab—it says that they followed the cloud. Such an indication within the narrative itself cautions strongly against the conclusion that Hobab eventually conceded to Moses' request and went along with Moses and the people. While it is true that Hobab's descendants later took part with Judah in the conquest of portions of the land (Jdg 1:16), the biblical writer makes no attempt to associate this with Hobab's guidance of the people in the wilderness.[4] It seems reasonable to conclude, then, that Hobab went back to his home and did not accompany the Israelites in the wilderness. This assessment of the implication of the narrative is further confirmed from the similarity between the present narrative and two other narratives dealing with the separation of family members and specifically a son-in-law from his father-in-law (Ex 4:18, 24–26; and Ge 31:55–32:32; see comments on Nu 11:1–3 below). In each of these

---

[3]The NIV renders the verse: "The ark of the covenant of the LORD went before them during those three days to find them a place to rest" (Nu 10:33). The phrase "a journey of three days" is thus rendered "during those three days" in order to make it appear to be only a temporary measure for finding a place to rest. This helps resolve the difficulty of the Kohathites carrying the ark between the Reuben group and the Ephraim group in 11:11–28 and the Tent being "in the middle of the camps" in 2:17. Compare other translations: RSV, NASB: "three days' journey"; JPS: "a distance of three days"; KJV, Geneva: "in the three days' journey"; Luther: "und die lade des bunds der HERRN zog vor ihnen her drey tag-reise"; Rashi: "it traveled in front of them a distance of three days' journey."

[4]Targum Onkelos reads Moses' statement to Hobab as a comment about Israel's time in the wilderness during past days: "You know how we were camping in the wilderness, and the mighty deeds which were done to us you have seen with your own eyes." See also the LXX: "You were with us in the wilderness, and you will be an elder among us."

instances, the fact that the father-in-law was not taken along but rather was left behind plays a significant role in the narrative strategy. The larger family is left behind. Thus, according to this larger biblical pattern Moses also likely parted ways with his father-in-law.

Moreover, the earlier instructions in the Numbers narrative regarding the position of the Kohathites within the order of travel (Nu 2:10–17; 11:14–18) does not preclude the possibility that those who actually carried the ark went ahead of the whole congregation. In point of fact, though the earlier narratives say that the Kohathites carried the ark, it does not say specifically that the ark was carried in the rank and file of the Kohathites. In Joshua 3:3, for example, the ark is carried ahead of the people among the priests, hence not among the Kohathites.

Thus it is possible to read the narratives as a coherent whole—the Kohathites carried the articles of the Tent of Meeting "in the middle of the camps" (Nu 2:17). They—that is, some of the Kohathites—carried the ark ahead of the people "a journey of three days" (10:33), and the people followed as God (Dt 1:32–33) led them through the wilderness by means of the cloud (Nu 9:15–23). Hobab (Jethro, Ex 3:1), Moses' father-in-law (Jdg 4:11), did not lead the people in the wilderness; rather, in spite of Moses' attempts to persuade him to remain, he went back to his own people (Nu 10:30). His descendants later joined with Judah in taking possession of part of the land (Jdg 1:16).

The "three days' journey" (Nu 10:33) recalls the "three days' journey" requested by the Israelites in the Exodus from Egypt (Ex 3:18), the "three days' journey" from the Red Sea (Ex 15:22), and the "three days" to Moriah (Ge 22:4).

C. Fire from the Lord (11:1–3)

It will be remembered that in Exodus 4:18, when Moses left both Sinai and his father-in-law to return to his people, he was mysteriously met by the Lord who, because Moses had not circumcised his son, sought to kill him (Ex 4:24–26). His wife, Zipporah, intervened and the Lord quickly relented. In a curious repetition of this event, as Israel now left Sinai and again parted company with Moses' father-in-law, the Lord sent fire from above to destroy the outskirts of the camp.[5] As in Exodus 4:25, where Moses' wife had interceded and stayed the hand of God, so here Moses interceded and the Lord relented. A similar incident is also found in Genesis 32:22–32, where Jacob, after he had parted from his father-in-law (Ge 31:55), wrestled with God before entering into the land. These narratives are clearly similar and as such appear to have a similar purpose within the overall plan of the author. They represent a turning point in the flow of events. If we may argue from the effect these narratives have on the sense of the narratives, their purpose is to cast a foreboding mood over the course of those events being depicted or about to be depicted. They show that all is not well, and hence they stir up an anticipation that something worse is yet to happen.

It is significant to note, then, that at the beginning of each of those large narrative segments of the Pentateuch which deal with Israel's departure en route to the Promised Land, we see them come face-to-face with God and the

---

[5]Also compare the incident of the "fire from heaven" in Ge 19.

threat of his sudden wrath. In each case God threatens to put an immediate end to their venture, but also in each case God's action is averted and they are allowed to go on their way so much the wiser (if not wearier) for their encounter.

D. Manna and the Spirit of God (11:4–35)

The present narrative is complex. Unlike most of the narratives in the Pentateuch, it does not focus on a single topic or subject but incorporates several distinct narratives and topics. It begins with the people's complaint about manna in the wilderness and their yearning to return to Egypt, where they imagine they could enjoy a variety of good foods in abundance (11:4–9). The narrative then turns to Moses' discourse with God regarding the complaint of the people and God's response in promising to send his Spirit upon the select seventy elders (vv. 10–17). In the following narrative, God adds to his promise to care for Israel the further word that the people's desire for the food of Egypt would not only be fulfilled but it would be fulfilled to such an extent that it would actually have the effect of a curse for them ("until it comes out of your nostrils and you loathe it," vv. 18–20).

Moses' response (vv. 21–23), one of amazement, is then followed in the narrative by a lengthy report of God's sending his Spirit upon the seventy elders (vv. 24–30). At the close of the passage, God sends the people food in the form of quail, but as they are gathering the quail, this blessing suddenly becomes an ironic punishment for those who had complained (vv. 31–34).

Note the curious reversal at the conclusion of the story. The Lord had said earlier in the narrative that those who complained against his good provisions would eat meat, "not one day or twenty days but for a whole month," until it came out of their nostrils (v. 19). At the conclusion of the story, however, it does not happen just this way. Instead, those who had complained were destroyed "while the meat was still between their teeth" (v. 33).

That the whole passage is to be considered a single unit of narrative is clear from the fact that the name given to the place of destruction at the end (Kibroth Hattaavah, v. 34) is a wordplay on the "desire" (*mit'awwîm*) of the people for food at the beginning (v. 4, *hit'awwû*). Furthermore, the whole narrative is connected internally with numerous wordplays. For example, the Lord sent "his Spirit" (*rûaḥ*) upon the seventy elders (v. 25), and then "a wind" (*rûaḥ*) went out from the Lord (v. 31).

It is important to seek out the central theme in such a complex narrative. What is the writer intending to teach in weaving the various aspects of these events together into one continuous account?

The central purpose of the narrative appears to be to show the failure of Moses' office as mediator for the people. By means of the various parts of this narrative, the kind of leadership exhibited by Moses is placed alongside the role of the Spirit of God. The ideal leadership of God's people is shown in the example of the seventy elders. It is especially important to note that this lesson comes from the lips of Moses himself. It is Moses who tells God: "I cannot carry all these people by myself; the burden is too heavy for me" (v. 14), and it is God who responds by sending his Spirit upon the seventy elders. Curiously enough, when Joshua complained that two men who were not part of the selected group of seventy had also received the Spirit, Moses replied: "I wish that all the LORD's people were prophets and that the LORD would put his Spirit on them!" (v. 29). In other words, this narrative shows that Moses longed for a much different type of community than the one formed under the Law at Sinai. He longed for a community led not by a person like himself but a community guided by God's Spirit.

The view expressed by Moses in this narrative is precisely that of the later Israelite prophets in their description of the new covenant. For example, Jeremiah looked forward to a time when the whole nation would have the Law written not on tablets of stone but on the hearts of the people, "from the least to the greatest" (Jer 31:31–34). In their visions Joel and Ezekiel wrote of the fulfillment of Moses' ideal in the "last days" when God would pour out his Spirit on "all flesh" (Joel 2:28 [MT 3:1]) and put his Spirit in the human heart (Eze 36:22–27). Then, at last, according to these prophets, God's people would walk in his ways and keep his commandments (Eze 11:20). The same view is also developed further by Moses himself in Deuteronomy 30:6. In the future, after God's people had been dispersed throughout all the nations, God would gather them back into the land, circumcise their hearts, and cause them to walk in his ways.

Thus, within the Pentateuch itself Moses' role and the leadership he represents seem to change. The shortcomings were becoming obvious and the failure of the people increasingly transparent. Consequently, as the narrative continues to unfold, a different type of rule, more akin to the kind of leadership seen in the Spirit-controlled office of the prophet, begins to emerge.

In view of what we have just said, however, it is important to note that in the next chapter (Nu 12:1–16), the issue of Moses' leadership is directly raised and contrasted with the kind of leadership provided by priests and prophets. Also, in chapter 16 the question of Moses' leadership is still an issue to the writer of the Pentateuch.

E. Miriam and Aaron Oppose Moses (12:1–16)

The narrative of Miriam and Aaron's opposition to the leadership of Moses is brief and leaves many details unexplained. Its meaning, however, is clear from its relation to the previous chapter. In the previous chapter, the kind of leadership exemplified in Moses is put into question by the initiation of a new type of leadership, the leadership of elders who are led by the Spirit. In that narrative, Moses himself even insinuated the superiority of this new form of leadership in saying, "Would that all the LORD's people were prophets" (11:29). In this way, the narrative manages to raise important questions about the role of a leader like Moses. Does this mean that Moses' leadership was no better in God's eyes than that of other prophets like Miriam (see Ex 15:20)? Was Moses' role as leader not superior to that of the high priest, Aaron? The purpose of this chapter, then, is to vindicate Moses' divinely given leadership and to brush aside any further suggestion that, because of the establishment of other forms of authority, the type of leadership epitomized in Moses was no longer valid.

This vindication of Moses at the end of their sojourn in the wilderness is the same as that given to the people at the beginning. In the present narrative, the sign of Moses' leadership was Miriam's "leprosy, which was white as snow" (Nu 12:10). Similarly, one of the first signs given to vindicate

God's election of Moses as leader of his people was the sign of "leprosy, white as snow" (Ex 4:6). In the initial narratives dealing with the work of Moses, Moses himself doubted his calling and consequently became a leper. Here, however, it is Miriam who doubts and thus becomes a leper. We should also note that the other sign given to vindicate the role of Moses in the earlier narrative was the serpent that came from Moses' rod (Ex 4:3). So also here, when Moses' authority is further questioned by the people at the end of their time in the wilderness (Nu 21:5), God responds by sending serpents against them (21:6).

Moses Vindicated				Moses Vindicated	
Snakes Ex 4:3	Leprosy Ex 4:6	Wilderness Narratives	Leprosy Nu 12:10	Snakes Nu 21:6

As God's words to Aaron and Miriam show, God did speak to prophets like Miriam, but not in the same way as he spoke to Moses. Moses the mediator was not a mere prophet—he was God's servant. God spoke to him not in visions and dreams, but "face to face" (12:6–8).

Miriam was "confined outside the camp" for seven days (5:2–4), as Leviticus 13:4 required of one with an infectious skin disease (Nu 5:2–4). Note that in the narrative portrayal of this incident we see that Moses waited for Miriam "from afar," as she once waited for him "from afar" in the bulrushes (Ex 2:4).[6]

VI. THE DEFEAT OF THE FIRST GENERATION (13:1–14:45)

This rather large section of narrative introduces an important element in the development of God's covenant with Israel: the theme of the faithfulness of God in keeping the covenant and the unfaithfulness of humans in not trusting him. This is particularly notable in the account of the sending of the spies (Nu 13–14). The same theme recurs in the account of Moses' giving water from the rock to the people (Nu 20:1–13).

Following the account of the people's failure to believe in God in chapters 13 and 14, the writer has attached a further and rather large set of laws dealing with sacrifice and the priesthood (15:1–19:22). Thus, as has been the case throughout the earlier parts of the Pentateuch, after an account of Israel's unbelief, more laws are added within the narrative. Just as after the account of the failure of the people in the incident of the golden calf (Ex 32), so now in the present narrative the laws are added as a response to the failure of the people to trust God. Thus the structure and strategy of the narrative support Paul's assessment of the giving of the Law: "What, then, was the purpose of the law? It was added because of transgressions until the Seed to whom the promise referred had come. . . . Before this faith came, we were held prisoners by the law, locked up until faith should be revealed" (Gal 3:19–23). In the same way we can see that in the narratives of the Pentateuch, after the account of Israel's failure to believe God, more laws are added.

---

[6]See Rashi, ad loc.

Israel's Unbelief (Nu 13–14)	Laws (Nu 15–19)	Moses' Unbelief (Nu 20)

A. Spying Out the Land of Canaan (13:1–25)

God instructed Moses to send spies from each of the tribes into the land (Nu 13:2). The overall picture of this event in the Pentateuch suggests that the situation was actually more complex than is reported here. Moses sent twelve spies into the Negev and hill country (v. 17) to "see what the land is like, and whether the people who live in it are strong or weak, whether they are few or many" (v. 18). The spies spent forty days in the land and returned to Moses at Kadesh (Kadesh Barnea, Dt 1:19) with fruit they had gathered from the land. According to Deuteronomy 1:22–23, the people had first requested that spies be sent out after Moses challenged them to take the land (see the comments below on Dt 1:19–46 for a fuller discussion of this question).

B. Report of the Spies (13:26–33)

The report of the spies was that the land was filled with "milk and honey" and that the descendants of Anak occupied strongly fortified cities (Nu 13:28). The spies also gave an "evil report" (v. 32): "we are not able to go up against the people, for they are too strong for us" (v. 31). Of the twelve spies, only Joshua and Caleb were in favor of trusting God for his help in taking the land (v. 30; 14:6–7).

C. Unbelief of the People (14:1–12)

The narrative continues by showing that in the midst of the crying of the people, Yahweh spoke to Moses in the Tent of Meeting: "How long will this people spurn me? And how long will they not believe in me, despite all the signs which I have performed in their midst?" (vv. 11–12). It is essential to note that, within the narrative itself, the Lord calls their fearful response to the spies' report an act of "unbelief." Thus the writer is careful to point out that the people's failure at this important time in the wilderness was a failure to believe. The people certainly failed in many aspects, but the writer points specifically to, and takes great care to draw out, their failure to believe God. Thus this passage intends to show that the people failed to inherit the Promised Land and hence died in the wilderness without inheriting the blessing, not so much for a specific act of disobedience or for fear of the battles that lay ahead, but rather for the simple fact of their unbelief. They failed to trust in God.

Because of their lack of faith, the Lord said to Moses: "I will smite them with pestilence and dispossess them, and I will make you into a nation greater and mightier than they" (Nu 14:12). God was prepared to judge them severely for their lack of faith.

D. Moses' Intercession (14:13–19)

But as has happened before in the pentateuchal narratives (e.g., Ex 32:11–13), Moses interceded for Israel and replied to the Lord that his rejection of this people in the wilderness would have a lasting effect on the nations around them who had heard of what he had done in Egypt. Israel had broken their covenant with the Lord and he could have rightfully cast them off. But the Lord was gracious to them, "slow to anger and abundant in loyal love" (Nu 14:18; cf. Ex 33:9).

E. The People Are Judged (14:20–38)

God heard Moses' plea on behalf of the people. Though Israel proved unfaithful, God remained faithful and gracious. The result of Israel's lack of faith was nevertheless severe. Except for Joshua and Caleb, that whole generation who did not believe died in the wilderness (Nu 14:29); that is, that generation was to dwell in the wilderness for forty years until they had died (v. 33; see comments below on Dt 1:46).

F. Presumption of the People (14:39–45)

At the close of the narrative the writer recounts the aborted attempt of the people to take the land without the help of the Lord. The purpose of the narrative is to show the reverse side of their unbelief. Not only did they fail to trust God to give them the land, but in desperation they attempted to take it on their own. Their unbelief is manifest by their attempts to gain God's blessings without him.

In Numbers 14:25, the Lord told Moses to "turn back tomorrow and set out toward the desert along the route to the Red Sea." When Moses told this to the people (v. 39), they refused to obey the Lord, and "early the next morning they went up toward the high hill country" to take the land of Canaan (vv. 39–40). This direction was the opposite of where God had told them to go. Moses saw this as "disobeying the LORD's command" (v. 41). When this same event is recounted in Deuteronomy 1:34–46, the Lord says Israel disobeyed (v. 43) his command to go "out toward the desert along the route of the Red Sea" (v. 40), and thus they were defeated (v. 44); after returning from the defeat (v. 45), they dwelt in Kadesh many days (v. 46). Note that it is not recorded here that Israel left Kadesh. In Numbers 20:1 they are in Kadesh, so it may be that they spent the thirty-eight years there. The reference to Kadesh in Numbers 20:1, however, may also refer to a second journey there (cf. Dt 1:46 and the commentary on it below).

VII. LAWS GIVEN DURING AND AT THE CLOSE OF THE THIRTY-EIGHT YEARS (15:1–19:22)

A. Seven Laws (15:1–36)

The section consists of a selected list of seven laws, the last of which is the penalty for a "defiant sin." The list is followed by a narrative example of a "defiant sin,"—the willful disregard of God's Sabbath law among the people. At the conclusion of the section, the law regarding the wearing of tassels was placed after this example of the neglect of God's Law because the "tassels" were to serve as reminders to keep the Law.

The seven laws are:
1. Requirements for grain offerings with one lamb (vv. 3–5)
2. Requirements for grain offerings with a ram (vv. 6–7)
3. Requirements for grain offerings with a young bull (vv. 8–16);
4. Offering of a cake from the first of the ground meal (vv. 17–21)
5. Offering for the unintentional sin of the whole community (vv. 22–26)
6. Offering for the unintentional sin of an individual (vv. 27–29)
7. Penalty for a defiant sin (vv. 30–31)

Command #133, Nu 15:20, Offering of the first of the dough: "Present a cake from the first of your ground meal."

The laws regarding meal offerings are not those of Leviticus 2, which were offered separately as a gift, but are here introduced for the first time and are to be offered along with either a burnt offering or a peace offering.

In the case of the man caught gathering wood on the Sabbath (Nu 15:32–36), it should be noted that Moses did not immediately put the offender to death, as was stipulated in Exodus 31:14 and 35:2. Rather, he put him away "because it was unclear what was to be done to him" (Nu 15:34). Since the punishment of death for "doing work" (Ex 35:2) or "profaning the Sabbath" (Ex 31:14) had already been given to Moses by this point in the narrative, his uncertainty must have been regarding either the exact type of death penalty[7] or whether gathering wood constituted "work." Interestingly enough, the Lord's answer spoke to both questions: "The man must die. The whole assembly must stone him outside the camp" (Nu 15:35).

At three other places in the pentateuchal narratives it was necessary for Moses to enquire of God for a solution to a difficult legal problem. First, in Leviticus 24:10–23, an Israelite with an Egyptian father blasphemed the Lord's name, and "they put him in custody until the will of the LORD should be made clear to them." The present narrative bears remarkable similarity to that passage. Second, in Numbers 9:7–8, the issue of whether those who were ceremonially unclean could delay their Passover celebration was turned over to the Lord for clarification. Moses said, "Wait until I find out what the LORD commands concerning you." Third, the case of Zelophehad's daughters and their right to inheritance was "brought before the LORD" for a decision in Numbers 27:1–11. The purpose of these narratives is to show that God's will is not expressed in a once-for-all way. In Israel's ongoing relationship with God, he continued to make his will known to them, and they continued to play a part in the process.

B. Tassels (15:37–41)

The account of the command to make tassels for their garments demonstrates the underlying purpose of many of the laws given to Israel. These tassels were to remind the Israelites of the need to trust God and obey his commands. In many other ways, as well, God provided reminders for his people. The very minutiae of the laws of the Torah themselves were a continual reminder that in every area of life God's people were to trust him

---

[7]See Rashi, ad loc.

and obey his Word. The sense of texts such as these was clearly felt in later biblical interpretation, as the following quotation shows.

> The holy one, blessed be he, put nothing in the world, but that he gave with it a commandment to Israel. When they went out to plow, [he said] "You shall not plow with an ox and an ass together (Deut 12:10). When they went out to sow, [he said] "You shall not sow with two kinds of seed" (Lev 19:19). When they went out to reap, [he said] "You shall not wholly reap the corner of the field" (Lev 19:9). When they kneaded their bread, [he said] "Of the first of your dough you shall offer a cake" (Num 15:20). When they slaughtered [an animal], [he said] "You shall give to the priest, the shoulder and the two cheeks" (Deut 18:3). When they found a bird's nest, [he said] "You shall send away the mother" (Deut 22:6–7). When they caught wild animals or birds, [he said] "He shall pour out its blood and cover it with dust" (Lev 17:13). When they planted a fruit tree, [he said] "You shall treat it as uncircumcised. . ." (Lev 19:23). When a son was born, [he said] "The foreskin of his flesh shall be circumcised" (Lev 12:2). When they buried the dead, [he said] "You shall not cut yourselves" (Deut 14:1). When they shaved, [he said] "You shall not round the corner of your head" (Lev 19:27). When they built a house, [he said] "You shall make a parapet" (Deut 22:8) and "You shall write them on the posts" (Deut 6:9). When they clothed themselves, [he said] "You shall make tassels" (Num 15:28).[8]

There is an intentional selection behind the collections of laws found throughout the Pentateuch. The purpose of that selection appears clear enough. In reading through these laws we can readily see that God is concerned about every detail of human life. Nothing is too small or unimportant. It all has to be made available and dedicated to him.

Command #14, Nu 15:38, One must attach tassels to one's garments: "You are to make tassels on the corners of your garments."

Prohibition #47, Nu 15:39, One must not have impure thoughts or sights: "And not prostitute yourselves by going after the lusts of your own hearts and eyes."

C. Rebellion and Reaffirmation (16:1–18:32)

Several narratives now follow which have in view specifically the role of Aaron and the priests. Also central to each of the narratives is the idea of a growing rebellion and dissatisfaction among the people of the covenant nation. As the laws increase and the constraints grow, the people seem less willing or less capable of following them. At this point in the narrative we see that the whole order of the priesthood is thrown open to direct confrontation. God's Word revealed at Sinai, which at first seemed so final and authoritative, is now being challenged on every side.

In the first narrative, 16:1–40 (MT 16:1–17:5), the Levites instigate an organized opposition to the authority of Aaron and the priests. They contend that in claiming the unique right and responsibility to represent the people before God, Moses and Aaron had "gone too far" (v. 3). Their argument against Moses and Aaron was based on the premise that "the whole community is holy, every one of them, and the LORD is with them" (v. 3).

---

[8]Hizquni, ad loc.

Thus they asked, "Why then do you set yourselves above the LORD's assembly?" It was no longer the "rabble" (11:4), that is, the "mixed multitude," that stood behind Israel's disobedience. It was now those from the tribe of Levi itself, the very tribe set apart, consecrated, and made ceremonially clean only a few chapters earlier in the narrative (8:5–26). This was probably not the first time and certainly not the last that God's servants would not be content with the ministries given them and would presumptuously seek more status and power. God had established the house of Aaron—his sons and their descendants—as the priests among his people. They alone could officiate in the tabernacle (3:10). This role was given to Aaron's house as the expression of God's will at Sinai. However, the Levites had also been set apart for work in the tabernacle. Their responsibilities were laid out in Numbers 3 and 4. Hence the Levites' attempt to obtain the rights and duties of the priesthood, which the present narrative portrays, was a direct affront to God's will as revealed already in Scripture. That Moses was fully aware of this fact is shown in the narrative by his response to the Levites: "You have gone too far!" (16:8).

According to the narrative, God told Aaron to gather the bronze censers of the rebellious Levites and to overlay the altar with their metal. This was to be a "sign" to all Israel "that no one except a descendant of Aaron should come to burn incense before the LORD, or he would become like Korah and his followers" (16:40 [MT 17:5]).

To show that the rebellion of the Levites was not an isolated act but represented the mood of the whole community, the writer places immediately after this narrative an account of the opposition of the "whole Israelite community" (vv. 41–50 [MT 17:6–15]). This narrative shows that rather than having felt contrition and repentance, the people grumbled at the Lord's punishment of the rebellious Levites. Their response is portrayed here in a way similar to Cain's anger when he perceived that his offering was not acceptable to God (Ge 4:5). From the writer's point of view, their actions speak for their inner thoughts and feelings, just as Cain's killing of Abel revealed what was in his heart.

As the narrative concludes, ironically, it is the intercession of Aaron and his priesthood that ultimately saves the lives of the people in the ensuing plague. Aaron "made atonement for them" (Nu 16:47 [MT 17:12]), and he "stood between the living and the dead, and the plague stopped" (v. 48 [MT 17:13]).

As a continual reminder of the special office of priest and the importance of the house of Aaron, God gave Israel another "sign"—Aaron's budding staff (17:10 [MT 25]). The point of the sign was to remind the people of the death of those who had tried to usurp the place of Aaron and his family and go near to God in the tabernacle on their own. As the last two verses of chapter 17 show, the Israelites learned the lesson well. When they saw Aaron's budding staff, they said to Moses: "We will die! We are lost, we are all lost! Anyone who even comes near the tabernacle of the LORD will die" (vv. 12–13 [MT 27–28]). Their lament ends with a question: "Are we all going to die?" (v. 13b [MT 28b]).

The response of the people at the conclusion of this narrative is much the same as those who stood at the foot of Mount Sinai when God made his presence known in a great display of fire and earthquakes (Ex 20:19). On that occasion, the people were afraid to go near to God. Moses was therefore appointed a mediator for the people. In much the same way, in the present narrative the people's fear of going near to God leads to a reaffirmation of the priesthood of Aaron and his sons in the immediately following narrative. The difference between the narratives is that it is not Moses but Aaron who now steps into the limelight as the mediator of God's people.

Much of the material covered in chapter 18, dealing with the roles of and provisions for the priests and the Levites, has already been given in Numbers 2–3 and Leviticus 6. What is unique in the repetition of the material in the present chapter is that this narrative does not mention Moses in the instructions to the priests. Whereas earlier the Lord had spoken to Moses as well as to Aaron about the priest's duties, here he speaks only to Aaron and his sons. It should be noted that Moses is not again addressed until Numbers 18:25. At that point the focus of the writer returns to the Levites. What is to be made of the writer's exclusion of Moses in these matters that relate so closely to the duties of the priests? Why is Moses so conspicuously left out of the picture? The answer perhaps lies in the author's desire to tell us something about the role of Moses as leader of God's people. His role is not limited to the work of a priest. Aaron is shown here assuming most of that responsibility. In the view of the writer, then, it appears that the role of Moses was becoming more distinct from the office of priest. Thus the writer attempts to show that Moses' role as mediator of the covenant, already well established throughout these narratives, was not merely a priestly one. There is a concern to show that he also functioned in the role of prophet as well as king, two themes that will receive further development in the book of Deuteronomy (Dt 18:15; 33:5). Hence as the picture of Moses develops within the Pentateuch, it more closely resembles the future messianic ruler, who is anticipated already in the Pentateuch as a prophet, a priest, and a king.

The distinct roles of the priests and Levites are restated in Numbers 18:1–7.

> **Command #22**, Nu 18:4, Priests are to care for the temple always: "You and your sons with you before the tent of testimony."
>
> **Prohibition #72**, Nu 18:3, The priests and Levites must not do each other's work: "They [the Levites] must not go near the furnishings of the sanctuary or the altar, or both they and you will die."
>
> **Prohibition #74**, Nu 18:4, Strangers must not serve in the temple: "No outsider may come near."
>
> **Prohibition #67**, Nu 18:5, One must not be slack in taking care of the temple: "You shall keep the service of the temple."
>
> **Prohibition #108**, Nu 18:17, One must not redeem the firstborn of a clean animal: "But you must not redeem the firstborn of an ox, a sheep, or a goat; they are holy."

The provisions for the priests (18:8–20) and those for the Levites (vv. 21–32) follow. The Levites were to be supported by the payment of a tithe (v. 21). They in turn were to support the priests by paying a tithe of what was given to them (v. 28). The responsibility of giving a tithe, a tenth of one's produce, had already been commanded for all the people in Leviticus 27:30–33. At that point it was said only that the tithe belonged to the Lord.

The present passage adds considerably to our understanding of the purpose of the tithe: it is to be given to the Levites for their work at the tabernacle.

Command #23, Nu 18:23, Levites alone are to serve in the temple: "It is the Levites alone who are to do the work in the holy place."

Command #129, Nu 18:26, The Levites are to give a tithe to the priests: "Say to the Levites, 'When you take a tithe from the Israelites.'"

D. Water of Cleansing (19:1–22)

At first sight one may see little connection between the material in chapter 18 and that in chapter 19. Chapter 18 deals with the support of the priest and Levites, whereas chapter 19 deals with the ritual of the red heifer. Though both texts concern the rites and responsibilities of the priests, little else seems to connect them. It should be noted, however, that chapter 18 concludes with a warning about the consequences of sin and defilement, that is, death (v. 32). The fact that sin, defilement, and death are the central themes of the ritual of the red heifer suggests that the author intentionally links these two chapters by means of the statement of these themes given in verse 32.

In chapter 19, provision is given for the preparation of the "water of cleansing" (vv. 1–10). Following this passage are two examples of the use of this water: purification from contact with a dead body (vv. 11–13) and purification after being in the same tent with a dead body (vv. 14–22). Later, in 31:19–23, the "water of cleansing" is prescribed for those who had been in battle and had thus come into contact with the dead. In each of these contexts the use of the "water of cleansing" was specifically for purification from association or contact with the dead. Thus, though the present passage does not specify its purpose, it is generally assumed that the "water of cleansing" was a special provision of purification for all persons, Levites and laypersons alike, who had come into contact with the dead.

The procedure for preparing the water called for a "red heifer" or "red cow" without any blemish. The cow was never to have been yoked. It was to be taken outside the camp and slaughtered, and some of its blood was sprinkled "toward the tabernacle." Note that the cow was not to be slaughtered by the high priest (Aaron), but by the priest (his son, Eleazar; 19:3). Nor was the slaughter to be carried out at the altar in the tabernacle, as would have been usual for a sin offering. Rather, it was to be taken outside the camp and killed there. This fact has led many to argue that the red heifer was not slain as a sin offering. It is clear from the text, however, that it was a sin offering. Twice in this very passage it is called a sin offering (19:9, 17).[9] Hence we must leave open our understanding of the slaughter of the red heifer to include the possibility that the writer conceives of it as a sin offering, albeit a peculiar type. Indeed, the writer of the book of Hebrews groups this offering together with the "goats and bulls" of the sin offering (9:13), and thus he too seems to understand it to be such.

---

[9]In 19:9, the NIV implies that the "water of cleansing," rather than the heifer itself, was "for purification from sin"; but as the Hebrew text clearly states in 19:17, the heifer was "for purification from sin."

Command #113, Nu 19:2–9, Procedure of the red heifer: "This is the statute of the law."

Much has been postulated about the meaning of specific details of this ritual. For example, some interpret the "red" of the heifer to represent human sinfulness, as in Isaiah 1:18: "Though your sins are like scarlet, they shall be as white as snow." Others see the red color of the heifer to represent the blood of the sacrifice. Yet others argue that the red represents "humanity" (the Hebrew word for "red," *'dm*, is like the word for "humanity," *'dm*), and they apply it to Christ's suffering for sinful humanity. Since the passage itself does not explain these details, it is best not to read too much into the narrative. The writer appears content to give us only a general description of the ritual. It might be more helpful to ask why so much is omitted from this narrative rather than to attempt to fill in the passage with unwarranted suppositions. After all, what we are interested in here is why the author puts this account of the red heifer in the narrative at this point. This is quite a different question than the meaning the ritual may have had to Israel in the wilderness. Our question is what the narrative means to the reader of the Pentateuch, not what the ritual meant to Israel.

Within the immediate context of the chapter and the larger context of the Pentateuch as a whole, there are significant clues to the narrative meaning of the red heifer ritual. That is, we can explain why the author has included it here. It is important to note that the description of the ritual itself, 19:1–10, is further elaborated and explained by the two examples of its use given in 19:11–22. The two central features of the ritual are the "ashes" (vv. 9–10) of the heifer and the "water of cleansing" (v. 9) over which they are sprinkled. When the ritual is applied to a specific situation in the following passage, however, the "ashes" of the red heifer are not called "ashes" but the "dust" of the heifer (v. 17; NIV, however, renders it "ashes" and thus covers over the distinct clues in the text). Moreover, the "water" is not called merely "water" but rather "living water" (v. 17; NIV "fresh water"). Thus the "dust" of the heifer was sprinkled over the "living water." Admittedly, this may appear to be only a small change in terminology from the earlier descriptions; but, nonetheless, it is by no means an insignificant difference.

By means of these two modifications, the author of the Pentateuch has elevated the rather obscure ritual of the red heifer to a much higher thematic plane, so that the ritual now reflects the contrast between the "dust" of the heifer and the water of "life." By being elevated to this level, the narrative is brought into alignment with other central narratives in the Pentateuch. Specifically, the notion of the "dust" of the heifer and the water of "life" provide a specific link to the narrative of the Fall in Genesis 3, for the terms *dust* and *life* are the two key terms of the Fall narrative (Ge 3:19, 24). By linking these two texts, one can see that in the present form of the narrative the ashes of the heifer come to exemplify the "return to dust"—that which characterized humanity's fall in Genesis 3.

The writer's concern for the ritual of the red heifer at this point in the narrative, then, finds its roots in the earliest narratives of Genesis where death itself is viewed as the ultimate defilement of God's good creation. As such his point appears to be to show that just as in the beginning, so now among God's covenant people, death is the arch enemy. Just as death was alien to God's good creation, so also it is alien to all that God had intended in the covenant. God's people were not to linger over the bodies of the dead. One could not even remain in the same tent with the dead. The focus of the covenant was the blessing of life, not the curse of death. Within the larger message presented in the Pentateuch, the perennial need for cleansing from death exemplified in the red heifer ritual was to be another reminder of the necessity of dealing with the problem of sin.

It is hardly coincidental that the purification of the people after the incident of the golden calf (Ex 32:20) also shows a marked similarity with the procedures outlined for the red heifer.

> **Command #107**, Nu 19:14, A corpse is unclean: "This is the law of a man who dies in a tent."

VIII. TRAVEL FROM KADESH TO THE BORDER OF CANAAN (20:1-21:35)

It was now the first month of their last year in the wilderness. The Israelites had been wandering in the wilderness of Paran (Nu 13:3; 14:32-33) for forty years (see the comments above on Nu 14:39-45 and below on Dt 1:46). They are now encamped at Kadesh (20:1). By the end of these next two chapters (22:1), Israel will have reached their final destination in their travels in the Pentateuch, that is, the "plains of Moab" (cf. 33:49).

The death of Miriam is mentioned at the end of the first verse (20:1b). The writer thus wants us to know that she died while the Israelites were in Kadesh in the fortieth year of their stay in the wilderness. Though this is only a brief note, it is significant because it serves as a reminder that she did not enter the Promised Land with the new generation. Miriam, the prophetess, the sister of Moses, also died in the wilderness.

At the end of this chapter is a report of the death of her brother Aaron. Thus the narrative shows that not even Aaron, the high priest, was allowed to enter into the Promised Land. According to Numbers 33:38, Aaron died on the first day of the fifth month of the fortieth year after the Exodus from Egypt.

The central concern of this chapter, however, is the reminder that Moses himself was not allowed to enter the Promised Land. What had happened to the people because of their unbelief in chapter 14 was now being repeated in Israel's leadership—Miriam, Aaron, and Moses were to die in the wilderness, not able to enjoy the blessings of the Sinai covenant, the gift of God's good land.

A. Water from the Rock (20:1-13)

Though we often focus on Moses' action in this narrative as a means of determining just how and why he was denied the blessing of entering the Promised Land, it is important to note that the writer focuses instead on Moses' heart. A careful reading of the text reveals that the author has deliberately withheld the details of Moses' failure. Commentators have traditionally and sometimes ingeniously attempted to describe more precisely just what Moses and Aaron did to warrant God's displeasure. Some suppose Moses' act of unbelief was manifest in his striking the rock rather than speaking to it as God had instructed. Others, recognizing that the narrative does not condemn Moses or Aaron for this and that on other occasions God had actually called for them to strike a rock to produce water (Ex 17:6), suggest that Moses erred in striking the rock "twice," thus showing his anger and impatience. Still others argue that Moses' failure lay either in his speaking harshly to the people ("You rebellious ones") or in his attempt to take credit for the miracle by saying, "Must we [and not God] bring you water out of this rock?" Moses, they say, intended to have the people believe it was he and Aaron, rather than the Lord, who had brought about this work.

The fundamental problem with each of these explanations is that they go beyond what is given in the narrative itself and thus miss an important feature of the narrative. It should be noted that just at the point in the narrative where the writer could have described the actual misdeed of Moses and Aaron, the narrative is interrupted by a word from the Lord. When he spoke to Moses and Aaron, the Lord did not say that what they had done was wrong but rather, and simply, that they had acted in unbelief: "Because you did not believe [NIV 'trust'] in me to treat me as holy before the Israelites, neither of you will bring this community into the land I have given them" (20:12). The Lord's words in this narrative allow us to see that the underlying problem was the failure of Moses and Aaron to believe in the Lord and thus to treat him as holy before the people.

The writer no doubt wanted the reader of this narrative to get the larger message about the incident recorded here. He was not greatly interested that we know the details of this or that act of Moses and Aaron which led to God's punishing their unbelief. Indeed, one could reasonably argue that beyond this lack of faith Moses and Aaron had not done anything specifically wrong in this narrative. Their error was wholly a matter of their lack of faith in God. In some respects the narrative is like that of Cain and Abel's offerings (Ge 4:1–7), where we read simply that God accepted Abel's offering but not Cain's. The writer does not dwell on the nature of either offering but rather goes right to the heart of the question—to the Lord's evaluation of the offerers rather than the offerings. Thus this narrative also gives us a clear statement from God as to why Moses and Aaron could not enter the land. Put simply, they did not believe.

Failure to enjoy God's promises was the result of unbelief. At this point in the narrative the writer shows that it was not a failure to keep the law that led to their death in the wilderness. On the contrary, just as the people had failed to believe God and trust in him in chapter 14, so also Moses and Aaron were lacking in faith.

B. Edom Denied Israel Passage (20:14–21)

A coherent sequence in the events of Numbers 20:14–21:4 is difficult to obtain from this narrative (omitted in Dt 2:1–8). It may be that the series of events is not listed in chronological order. Though it is not of decisive moment in the interpretation of this passage, it is important to see how the text can be understood to harmonize. We will try briefly to reconstruct the sequence of events that are here gathered together.

Five distinct events must be related. First, Israel sent messengers to Edom to request permission to pass through their land (Nu 20:14–18).

Second, Israel as a whole came to the borders of Edom to make a second request to pass through Edom on the road, but this too was denied (vv. 19–21). After being denied passage through Edom this second time, Israel turned away, presumably to go to the Promised Land on an alternate route. Third, Israel left Kadesh and came to Mount Hor, where Aaron died (vv. 22–29). Fourth, Israel fought with Arad and decimated their cities (21:1–3). Fifth, Israel left Mount Hor and went around Edom by the "way of the sea" on their way to the land.

When the events are listed in the order that they occur in the text, as we have done above, chronological questions arise. According to 20:14–21, Israel left Kadesh to come to Edom and then left Edom to go to the land. After this, however, in Nu 20:22a, it is recounted that Israel left Kadesh and traveled to Mount Hor. Thus, after they have already left Kadesh, they appear to be back in Kadesh, where they again left for Mount Hor (v. 22b). The events of verses 23–29, including Aaron's death, took place at Mount Hor. The text does not give the time and place of their battle with Arad (21:1–3), but it appears to have occurred before Israel left Mount Hor (21:4). When they left Mount Hor, Israel traveled around Edom by the "way of the Red Sea" (21:4). This appears to be the same event recounted in 20:21, where Israel left the border of Edom to travel on their way to the land.

There are at least two plausible ways to reconcile these events. According to 20:14–18, Moses sent messengers to Edom while the Israelites were still at Kadesh. Kadesh is considered to be "a city on the edge of" Edom. When the Israelites asked for permission to pass through their land, the Edomites refused the request and did not let Israel travel through their land. The Israelites, made a second request to pass through the Edomite territory (vv. 19–21). That the request was made by "the Israelites" rather than "messengers" (v. 14a) is usually taken to mean that the Israelites, as a whole, were poised on Edom's borders ready to pass through. On the first request, Moses had sent messengers (v. 14a); but now the whole nation had left Kadesh and come to the border of Edom. The narrative in 20:19–21, then, assumes that Israel had left Kadesh en route to Edom and beyond, namely, to the Promised Land.

From references later in this same narrative, it appears that they were now camped at Mount Hor (Nu 21:4). When they failed again to gain permission to pass through Edom, the text says simply that the Israelites turned "away from them" (20:21b). The common assumption is that they left Edom to travel around it en route to the land. This view accords with 21:4, which recounts that Israel left Mount Hor to travel "around Edom." After leaving Mount Hor, they traveled around Edom by way of the "Red [Reed] Sea" (21:4). It is generally supposed, then, that by the time of the second request to pass through Edom (20:19–20) Israel had left Kadesh and had reached Mount Hor. Since Israel departed from Mount Hor (21:4) after the battle with Arad (21:1–3), it appears that that battle preceded Edom's second refusal to let Israel pass through their land (20:19–21). The sequence of events would be as follows:

1. While living in Kadesh: Moses sent messengers to Edom (20:14–18)
2. Israel departed from Kadesh (20:22a)
3. Israel arrived at Mount Hor (20:22b)
   Battle with Arad (21:1–3)

The Israelites made a second request to Edom and were turned away at the border of Edom (20:19–21)

4. Israel departed from Mount Hor to go around Edom by way of the Red Sea (21:4; 20:21b)

There is, however, another way to resolve the difficulties of this text. We may suppose that not the whole nation but only the messengers whom Moses originally sent in 20:14 returned the second time to request permission from Edom (20:19–20). When Edom again refused Israel's request, the messengers returned to Kadesh, from where the Israelites then departed and came to Mount Hor (20:22). Although the text does not state this explicitly, one may infer it from the fact that 20:22 seems clearly to assume that Israel was still at Kadesh.

An important clue in the text of 20:22 further supports this assumption. Numbers 20:19 states simply that "the Israelites" spoke to the Edomites. Verse 22 speaks further of "the Israelites," but now identifies them as "the whole congregation." Though the issue is by no means certain, this later identification in verse 22 of "the Israelites" with "the whole congregation" suggests that only at that point in the narrative (v. 22) did the whole people come into view, and thus the original group which spoke a second time to the Edomites in verse 19 was not the entire population but only the messengers who spoke for the people. While at Mount Hor, Israel fought with Arad (21:1–3) after which they departed from Mount Hor to go around Edom (21:4). Thus the sequence of events could be:

1. While living in Kadesh:
   Moses sent messengers to Edom (20:14–18)
   The Israelites made a second request to Edom still by means of messengers, who were turned away at the border of Edom (20:19–21; 20:21b)
2. Israel departed from Kadesh (20:22a)
3. Israel arrived at Mount Hor (20:22b)
   Battle with Arad (21:1–3)
4. Israel departed from Mount Hor to go around Edom by way of the Red Sea (21:4)

It is difficult to decide which of these two explanations is more probable. There is no reason why we should insist that the narratives must be arranged in strictly chronological order. As we will see below, the author is also concerned to establish patterns in these narrated events, and that concern sometimes causes him to link events out of their chronological order.

A close reading of these narratives shows that the pattern in the account of Israel's failure to believe (Nu 14) is repeated in this account of Moses' unbelief. The complaints of the people (14:1–4; 20:2–5) lead the Lord to conclude that Israel (14:11) and Moses (20:12) are lacking in faith. Moreover, both narratives are followed by an account of Israel's aborted attempt to gain immediate entrance into the Promised Land. In chapter 14, it was Israel's defeat by the Amalekites (14:40–45), and in the present passage it is Edom's refusal to let Israel pass through their land (20:14–21). In these various ways, the author seems intent on showing the similarities between Israel's failure of faith and that of Moses. Both failed to believe God and hence could not go into the land.

Complaint of People (14:1-4)	Israel's lack of faith (14:11)	Defeat by Amalekites (14:40-45)

Complaint of people (20:2-5)	Moses' lack of faith (20:12)	Defeat by Edomites (20:14)

C. Death of Aaron (20:22-29)

Surprisingly little is written of Aaron's death. The account of his death appears to foreshadow the death of Moses. They were guilty of the same sin, failure to trust the Lord (20:12), although here, unlike in Nu 20:12, their sin is called "rebellion" (20:24; cf. Dt 32:48–50). Just as Moses would be commanded by the Lord to go to the top of a mountain and die (Nu 27:12; Dt 32:48–50; 34:5), so here Aaron was told to go up to Mount Hor and there to die. Just before the report of his death, however, is a brief account of the investiture of the new high priest, Eleazar, the son of Aaron. In the same way, before the death of Moses, Joshua was installed as the new leader to take his place (Nu 27:18–23; Dt 34:9). These two new leaders, Joshua and Eleazar, were to take the place of those older leaders who were not permitted to enter into the Promised Land.

The priesthood of Eleazar and his family was to have a long succession throughout the remainder of Israelite history in the Bible. The descendants of Eleazar, Zadok and his sons (the Zadokites, 1Ch 24:3), were priests during the time of Solomon's kingdom, and they continued not only throughout the biblical period but also beyond that to the time of the Maccabees.

During the time of the judges, however, the office of priest was occupied by the house of Eli (1Sa 1:1–4:22). The biblical writers do not explain when or how the priesthood had been taken from the house of Eleazar and given to Eli's house. The narrative in 1 Samuel is clear that Israel suffered greatly during this time, and hence we may conclude that the writer did not approve of the replacement of the house of Eleazar by the house of Eli. The narrative emphasizes that the priests, Eli's sons Hophni and Phinehas, had abused the privileges of the office of the priesthood: "This sin of the young men was very great in the LORD's sight, for they were treating the LORD's offering with contempt" (1Sa 2:12–17). During the time of their priesthood, God had little dealings with Israel: "In those days, the word of the LORD was rare" (1Sa 3:1). An unnamed prophet proclaimed harsh words against Eli and his house and foretold not only their destruction but also the establishment of a more faithful line of priests (1Sa 2:27–36). Eventually, the tabernacle was destroyed and the ark of the covenant captured, and Eli's priesthood was abolished (1Sa 4:1–22).

In a graphic picture of the departure of God's glory from the nation because of the failure of Eli's priesthood, the narrative of 1 Samuel ends the account of the fall of the house of Eli with the naming of the heir apparent to his priesthood. When Eli received word that the ark had been captured, the narrative tells us he fell over backward, broke his neck, and died. The writer adds the seemingly incidental fact that Eli was a "heavy man" (1Sa 4:18). But we should note that the word *heavy* in Hebrew (*kābēd*) is closely related to the word *glory* (*kābôd*), and thus this particular fact provides the key to the whole narrative. When Eli's daughter-in-law heard the news, she, being pregnant, gave birth to a son and "named him 'Ichabod,' saying 'The glory has departed from Israel'" (1Sa 4:19–21). Thus the only surviving member of the house of Eli was marked by his ignominious name, "Where is the glory?"

In the structure of the present narratives in Numbers one can see a further pattern which anticipates and parallels the narrative events of the establishment of the Davidic kingship in 1 Samuel. As has been noted above, immediately before the narrative account of the establishment of the kingship in 1 Samuel, the author inserts a series of narratives that record the reestablishment of the proper priesthood from the family of Eleazar. There is thus a concern to return to the themes and events of Numbers 20–21. Furthermore, in the Balaam narratives which follow (Nu 22–24), the focus is upon the coming king who would reign over Israel's enemies and bring about God's judgment on them for their treatment of Israel (cf. Nu 24:9). The description of the coming king is remarkably similar to that of David. One of the last descriptions of the king who was to come was that he would bring an end to the Amalekites (24:20), who were Israel's "first" enemies (14:45) but who would "come to ruin at last" (24:20). In the narratives of 1 Samuel it was the failure of Saul to carry out God's judgment against the Amalekites that marked his rejection as the true king (1Sa 15:1–26). Specifically, Saul spared Agag, the Amalekite king (1Sa 15:9), whereas in Balaam's prophecy the true king was to be exalted over Agag (Nu 24:7). These pentateuchal narratives, then, appear deliberately to foreshadow the time of the establishment of the Davidic kingship. It will become clear at the end of the Balaam oracles, however, that the time of the fulfillment of these prophecies in Numbers looks far beyond David's own kingdom (see Nu 24:22–24). David is only an example of the kind of king who is yet to come.

The topic of the establishment of the priesthood of Eleazar in Numbers 20 is taken up again after the account of Balaam and his prophecies in the narrative of the zeal of Eleazar's son, Phinehas (Nu 25).

Anointing of Aaron's son Eleazar: Priest (Nu 20)	Balaam's Oracles: King (Nu 22–24)	Selection of Eleazar's son Phinehas: Priest (Nu 25)

Prophecy of the future priest: 1Sa 2:35	David the king: 1Sa 15–2 Samuel	Fulfillment of prophecy: priest (2Sa 8:17) 2Ki 2:35

D. Arad Destroyed (21:1–3)

The present narrative appears to have been shaped by its relationship to the events recorded in Exodus 17. The two narratives are conspicuously similar. In Exodus 17, the people murmured over lack of water, and Moses gave them water from the rock (Ex 17:1–7). They were attacked by the Amalekites but went on to defeat them miraculously while Moses held up his hands (in prayer?). So also in the present narrative, after an account of Israel's murmuring and of gaining water from the rock (Nu 20:1–13), Israel was attacked but miraculously went on to defeat the Canaanites because of Israel's prayer (21:1–3).

The mention of the place-name Hormah at the conclusion of the account of the defeat of the Canaanites ("They completely destroyed them . . . so the place was named Hormah," 21:3) provides a literary link with the earlier account of Israel's defeat at the hand of the Amalekites and Canaanites: "They beat them down all the way to Hormah" (14:45). Thus at the beginning of Israel's time in the wilderness they are opposed by the Amalekites living in the land of Canaan (Ex 17), and at the end of their time there they are opposed again by the Canaanites (Nu 21). The parallels between the two narratives suggest an intentional identification of the Amalekites in the Exodus narratives and the Canaanites here in Numbers 21:1–3. The structure of the narrative thus parallels Balaam's vision of the fate of the Amalekites: "Amalek was first among the nations, but he will come to ruin at last" (24:20). As is often the case in biblical narrative, the poetic section (24:20) provides a thematic expression of the intent of the narratives. Amalek was the first nation to bring destruction upon Israel, but, as can be seen proleptically in the parallels inherent in the present narrative, in the end they too would be brought to destruction.

E. The Bronze Serpent (21:4–9)

Here again the narratives of the Pentateuch appear to follow a larger pattern by which events at the beginning of Israel's sojourn are repeated at the close. Earlier, in the book of Exodus, when Moses went before Israel to announce that God was about to deliver them out of Egypt, Moses was given a sign to test and strengthen the people's faith. The sign was the snake that came from his staff (Ex 4:3, 30).[10] In the present narrative, now at the end of their sojourn in the wilderness, Israel again complained against God and Moses for bringing them out of Egypt. As at the beginning in Exodus 4, God gave Israel a similar sign, a snake on a staff. The purpose of such parallels is to underscore the basic themes of the book. In both narratives, the writer emphasizes the necessity of the people's response of faith in the sign. They must look to the sign in faith before they can be delivered (Ex 4:30–31; Nu 21:8). The NT writers appear to have been sensitive to these same themes. For example, in the Gospel of John, Jesus aptly applied the lesson of faith found in these narratives to the salvation brought about by his own death on the cross (John 3:14–15).

Some have thought it unusual that God would command Moses to make an image of a snake as a sign of Israel's faith, since earlier in the Pentateuch God had forbidden them to make a "likeness of anything in heaven above or upon the earth below" (Ex 20:4).[11] It is clear, however, that the image commanded in this passage was not intended as an idol to be worshiped, whereas the prohibition of making images was directed at idols, images representing God or gods.

Some have pointed out that God's command to Moses in 21:8 did not specifically say he was to make an image of the "snakes"; rather, he was to

---

[10]There is a possible link between the two passage in the wordplay on "and he ran from it" (וינס), Ex 4:3, and "put it on a pole" (נס), Nu 21:8.

[11]See Michael Walter, *Harmonia Biblica* (Nüremberg, 1696), 197.

make an image of the "fire" (NIV, however, translates "fire" as "snake" and overlooks this important detail). In verse 9, however, Moses made a "bronze snake." God had told him to make an image of the fire, but he made an image of a snake. What should we, as readers, make of this difference? Is this a significant difference which should be brought to bear on the sense of the narrative? Or is it merely an unrelated detail? Did God intend Moses to make an image of the "snakes" or did Moses go too far? Should he merely have made an image of the "fire"? We should note that at a later time in Israel's history, during the period of the kings, the people had begun to offer incense to this same image and had given it a name, "Nehushtan" (2Ki 18:4). It is also listed along with other idolatrous objects of worship that King Hezekiah had destroyed. It appears, then, that on the one hand Moses' bronze serpent was misunderstood by later generations as a venerable object of sorts. On the other hand, God honored the object when it was put up before the people and they looked to it in faith. The text thus treats the "bronze serpent" which Moses made in an ambivalent way. According to a strict reading of the text, the actual image of a "snake" was not specifically commanded by God but was Moses' own doing. Nevertheless, God honored the people's faith when they looked to it for healing. The bronze serpent, then, is in this respect analogous to Gideon's gold ephod which later generations worshiped and which "became a snare to Gideon and his family" (Jdg 8:27).

Furthermore, it should be noted that God did not instruct Moses concerning the exact material he was to use in making the image. Moses apparently chose on his own to make the snake of bronze. Some early interpreters argued that Moses chose bronze as the material for the image merely because in Hebrew the term for "bronze" was similar to the term for "snake."[12] In any event, the narrative appears intent on shifting a good deal of the responsibility for the details of the bronze serpent onto Moses' shoulders.

F. Journey to Moab (21:10–20)

A brief itinerary shows that the Israelites moved around Edom and into the territory of Moab. The writer has also included a selection from a book called the "Book of the Wars of the Lord." This book is not known apart from this one reference to it. The selection, though incomplete in its present, excerpted form, was apparently given to verify that the Arnon River was the border of Moab. The land of Moab is the central focus of the next several chapters of Numbers.

The apparent purpose of telling us, the readers, that the excerpt is from the "Book of the Wars of the Lord" was to provide a context for those details that are included in the short saying which follows. For example, that the saying is about the Lord's wars helps us appreciate the cryptic allusions in the saying to an occupation of the Moabite cities by an unnamed aggressor. If read in the context of a war, the boundaries listed are portrayed as conquered territory.

---

[12]See, e.g., Rashi, ad loc.

G. Defeat of Sihon (21:21–32; cf. Dt 2:24–37)

Only the bare facts of the battle and its causes are noted here. (See comments below on Dt 2:24–37 for a comparison of this account of the battle with Sihon with that in Deuteronomy.) Fortunately, the poetic sayings in the remainder of the narrative (e.g., 21:26–30) include further details to fill in the sketchy picture introduced here. These sayings focus on the previous military conquests of Sihon when he defeated Moab and captured their territory: "Heshbon was the city of Sihon king of the Amorites, who had fought against the former king of Moab and had taken from him all his land as far as the Arnon" (21:26). By means of such "historical notes," the writer shows a concern to justify Israel's conquest of the area that formerly belonged to Moab. They tell us that the land once occupied by Moab was now, at the time of the Israelite conquest, in the hands of the Amorites. What was the purpose of making this point? According to God's instructions, the territory belonging to the Moabites was not to be disturbed by the conquering Israelites because the Moabites were the descendants of Lot (Dt 2:9). What now belonged to the Amorites, however, had been promised to Israel and was theirs for the taking.

These short notes provide the necessary introduction to the account of Balaam which follows (Nu 22–24). The Moabite king Balak hired Balaam to curse Israel. But God would overturn Balaam's curse so that it resulted in Israel's blessing. The case could perhaps have been made that Israel had unfairly taken Moab's land and thus Balak was justified in hiring Balaam. These notes, however, show that such is not the case. Moab had already lost control of these areas to the Amorites, whom Israel had been chosen to dispossess (Ge 15:16–21). Israel had thus rightly taken them as their own.

H. The Defeat of Og (21:33–35; cf. Dt 3:1–11)

This brief narrative of the defeat of the king of Bashan shows that what God had done for Israel in the past, with their defeat of Sihon, he would continue to do with the rest of Israel's enemies. This purpose is stated directly by the Lord himself in 21:34: "Do not be afraid of him, for I have handed him over to you, with his whole army and his land. Do to him what you did to Sihon king of the Amorites, who reigned in Heshbon."

The importance of making this point here in the course of the narrative is that it provides an interpretive context for the events in the more detailed story which follows. Here we learn that Israel's victories are from the hand of God. The next two chapters teach the same lesson, but first they contrast God's assessment of Israel's victories with that of the king of Moab. As chapter 21 shows, Israel was now a present threat to Moab. Chapter 22 opens by reassuring us that their king, Balak, is well aware of the threat: "Now Balak son of Zippor saw all that Israel had done to the Amorites, and Moab was terrified." Balak's assessment of the cause of the threat, however, is quite different from God's assessment, which is expressed here. In the subsequent narratives, Balak resorts to magic and incantations in his attempt to defeat God's people, but his attempt shows only that such means are futile against the plans of a sovereign God.

IX. BALAAM (22:1–24:25)

The Balaam narratives have long puzzled readers of the Bible. The primary enigma centers on Balaam himself. As a historical character, he fits quite well among other ancient Near Eastern religious figures. There are, in fact, ancient inscriptions relating to the sayings of this same Balaam.[13] As a biblical character, however, Balaam appears to be neither fish nor fowl. He was not an Israelite (22:5), yet he appeared to know God (22:8), and God spoke through him (24:2–4, 15–16). He practiced magic and incantations (24:1) and eventually led Israel into apostasy (31:16). In the end he was killed by the Israelites in their destruction of the Midianites (31:8).

In spite of the fact that we know so little about the man, the narratives dealing with Balaam play a strategic role in the overall message of the Pentateuch. Their placement at this point in the book is part of the writer's plan to develop a central theological thesis. The first planks of this thesis were laid down already in Genesis 1, where the writer shows that at the center of God's purpose in creating humankind was his desire to bless them. Immediately after creating the man and the woman, God blessed them and said, "Be fruitful and multiply and fill the land" (Ge 1:28). Even after they fell away from God's protective care in the Garden of Eden, God let it be known that his plan for their blessing would not be thwarted by this act of disobedience. God promised that he would provide a means for restoring the blessing: a future "seed" who would one day come and crush the head of the serpent (Ge 3:15). God's original intention for humanity was blessing and his continual concern for them has been the same. When God chose Abraham as the channel of the promised "seed" (Ge 12:1–3), his express purpose was to bless Abraham and all the nations of the earth through this "seed." Like his original intent for Adam in the beginning, God's intent for Abraham was that he would become a great people and enjoy God's good land. When God's people were on the verge of entering into Egyptian bondage, God further elaborated his promise to Abraham by giving the patriarch Jacob a prophecy about one of his sons, Judah (Ge 49:8–12). Through the family of Judah, one would come who would be a king and restore God's blessing to Israel and all the nations. As God had forewarned Abraham (Ge 15:13–16), however, his people would first undergo a time of bondage and oppression. God also promised that after four generations Abraham's "seed" would return to the land (when the sin of the Amorites had reached its full measure, Ge 15:16) and again enjoy his blessing.

With this background in mind, we can now appreciate the plan of the writer of the Pentateuch and his concentration on the prophecies of Balaam. Underlying the narratives which tell the story of Balaam is the author's interest in the promise God had made to Abraham. According to that promise, those who bless his seed will be blessed and those who curse his seed will be cursed. Thus the narrative of the present chapter of Numbers opens with an account of Balak's dread of the great numbers of Israel. Balak, the king of Moab, had hired Balaam to curse the seed of Abraham, but as the story unfolds, God permitted him only to bless them. In spite of the nations'

---

[13]See Jean Hoftijzer and G. van der Kooij, *Aramaic Texts from Deir 'Alla* (Leiden: Brill, 1976).

attempts to curse God's people, all that could ultimately happen is their blessing. Through Balaam the seed of Abraham is blessed and the seed of Moab is cursed (Nu 24:17).

As is often the case in these biblical narratives, one story parallels another. Here the Balaam story, which lies at the close of Israel's sojourn in the wilderness, parallels many of the events and ideas of the story of Pharaoh at the beginning of the book of Exodus. Both men, Pharaoh and Balak, were kings of large and powerful nations which represented a major obstacle to Israel's entering the Promised Land. Israel was a threat to these nations only because God kept his promise to the fathers and had given them great increase in numbers. Pharaoh instigated plans to afflict Israel because he saw that they had become "much too numerous" (Ex 1:9). Within the narrative, Pharaoh's words merely reiterate the description of the narrator given two verses earlier: "The Israelites were fruitful and multiplied greatly and became exceedingly numerous" (Ex 1:7).

Moreover, as the narrator puts it, Pharaoh's plans were an attempt to stop Israel from returning to their land (Ex 1:10); that is, his plan was to block the very blessing which God had promised to Abraham (Ge 15:16)—enjoyment of the Promised Land. Thus, what the writer attempts to show is that the promise to Abraham—"I will make you into a great nation" (Ge 12:2)—and the blessing of humankind—"Be fruitful and multiply and fill the land" (Ge 1:28; 15:16)—were beginning to be fulfilled in Israel's sojourn in Egypt, and the nations were set on thwarting that promise. Like Pharaoh's plans, Balak's plans in Numbers were also motivated by the fact that Israel had become "too numerous" (Nu 22:6; NIV "too powerful"). Also like Pharaoh, Balak was intent on keeping the Israelites out of the land (22:6).

In the early narratives of Exodus, Pharaoh made three attempts to counteract the blessing and hence to decrease the number of God's people. He put slave masters over the Israelites to oppress them (Ex 1:11–14); he commanded the Hebrew midwives to kill the male children (vv. 15–21); and he commanded that every male child be thrown into the Nile (v. 22). Yet as the narrative unfolds, on each occasion God intervened and Pharaoh's plan was turned into a blessing. Whatever the particular scheme of the Egyptians, Israel increased all the more. Moreover, within the structure of the story unfolding in the narrative, it was as a result of Pharaoh's third plan, that of casting the male children into the Nile, that the writer was able to introduce the announcement of the birth of God's chosen deliverer, Moses. This narrative is remarkably similar to the present ones which deal with Balaam.

Like Pharaoh before him, Balak also made three attempts to thwart God's blessing for Israel (23:1–12, 13–26; 23:27–24:9), and each attempt was turned into a blessing (23:11–12, 25–26; 24:10–11). It should be noted that though Balaam gave more than three oracles, the writer has arranged the oracles into three attempts to curse Israel. Balak himself reflects the writer's interest when he says, "I summoned you to curse my enemies, but you have blessed them these three times" (24:10). As in the case of Pharaoh's three attempts, after Balak's third attempt the author turns to the question of the birth of God's chosen deliverer, the prophecy of the star that was to arise out of Jacob (24:12–25).

An interesting implication of the parallels presented here between the account of the birth of Moses in Exodus 2 and the announcement of the "star" to arise from the family of Jacob in Numbers 24 is that Moses thus appears to be portrayed in these narratives as a prototype of the "star of Jacob." Such a view of Moses is consistent with the fact that elsewhere in the Pentateuch Moses is cast as a figure of the coming king (Dt 33:5) and prophet (Dt 18 and 34). This is also consistent with the fact that later biblical writers often saw in Moses a picture of the future Messiah (e.g., Hos 2:2).

In view of this larger attempt by the author to portray events at the beginning of Israel's sojourn in the wilderness as parallel to similar events at the end, it is not surprising to find that Balaam's first three oracles are thematically parallel to Pharaoh's three attempts to suppress God's blessing of Israel in Egypt, and that his last oracle focuses on the coming of a deliverer. The account of Pharaoh's first attempt (Ex 1:11–14) is intended to show that "the more they were oppressed, the more they multiplied and spread" (Ex 1:12). In his first oracle Balaam focused precisely on this point: "How can I curse those whom God has not cursed?" (Nu 22:8), and he concluded by stressing the phenomenal growth of God's people: "Who can count the dust of Jacob or number the fourth part of Israel?" (22:10).

In Pharaoh's second attempt to thwart God's blessing the midwives, who feared God and disobeyed Pharaoh's command, express the central idea of the short narrative: "The Hebrew women are not like Egyptian women; they are vigorous and give birth before the midwives arrive" (Ex 1:19). To be sure, their words were a ruse to cover their disobeying Pharaoh's orders; nevertheless, they find an echo in the theme of Balaam's second oracle, Israel's mighty strength: "God brought them out of Egypt; they have the strength of a wild ox. . . . The people rise like a lioness; they rouse themselves like a lion" (Nu 24:8). It may be of interest to note that Pharaoh's plans were stymied by the apparent deception of the Hebrew midwives and that in Balaam's second oracle he states, "God is not a man, that he should lie" (Nu 23:19).

The third and last attempt of Pharaoh to thwart God's blessing, the order to cast all male children into the Nile (Ex 1:22), also finds an interesting parallel in Balaam's third oracle. In an ironic reversal of the evil intended by Pharaoh's order to cast the seed of Abraham into the river, Balaam's third oracle uses the well-watered gardens that spread out along the banks of a river to speak of the abundance of Israel's "seed." A literal reading of Balaam's remark in Numbers 24:7 is "Their seed is in the abundant waters" (the NIV paraphrases as "their seed will have abundant water"). Thus what was once the intended means for the destruction of the promised seed, that is, the "abundant waters," has now become the poetic image of God's faithfulness to his promise.

Other features in the verbal texture of the two narratives suggest that the above parallels are part of the author's conscious intention. For example, the story line of both passages is guided by the same verbal pattern in the use of the Hebrew term for *heavy* (כבד). The narrative of Pharaoh's opposition to releasing the Israelites is guided by the recurring reference to the "hardening" of his heart (Ex 7:14; 8:11, 28; 9:7, 34; 10:1). At the climax of the story, by means of a wordplay on the notion of hardening Pharaoh's heart, the Lord says, "I will gain glory for myself through Pharaoh" (Ex 14:4). It should be noted here that in Hebrew, the word for *glory* (כבד) has the same root as that for *harden* (כבד). Moreover, the story of Balaam is clearly guided

1. Israel a mighty nation (Ex 1:9) (רב עצום)	Exodus–Wilderness (Ex 16–Nu 21)	1. Israel a mighty nation (Nu 22:3, 6) (רב עצום)
2. Pharaoh "hardened" כבד		2. Balaam "honored" כבד

by Balak's promise to "reward" him richly if he would curse Israel (Nu 22:17, 37; 24:11). Again, the Hebrew root is the same as that for "to harden" and "to glory." The two narratives, then, are linked at the thematic, structural, and verbal levels.

Special messianic importance has been attached to the last oracles of Balaam, Numbers 24:1–24. It should first be noted that the author separates these oracles from the earlier ones by the introduction he gives them. Compare, for example, the simple introduction to Numbers 23:7 and 18, "Then Balaam uttered his oracle," with the additional statements in Numbers 24:3 and 15, "and he uttered his oracle: The oracle of Balaam son of Beor, the oracle of one whose eye sees clearly, the oracle of one who hears the words of God, who sees a vision from the Almighty, who falls prostrate, and whose eyes are opened." Moreover, the two sets of oracles make numerous allusions to each other and have many parallels. For example, what is said about Israel's past in Numbers 23 is repeated in Numbers 24, but here it describes the work of a future king. This parallel structure is not always appreciated in the English translations, which tend to render the singular forms in chapter 24 as plurals. Nevertheless, in the Hebrew text the writer has been careful to distinguish the two sets of oracles. In Numbers 23:22, for example, Balaam, looking back at the great salvific event of the Exodus, says of Israel: "God brought them [plural] out of Egypt; they have the strength of a wild ox." It is clear from Numbers 23:24 that Balaam is speaking about the people of Israel and the exodus from Egypt. In 24:8, however, Balaam repeats the same line and applies it, using singular forms, to the king he has introduced in 24:7: "God brought him [singular] out of Egypt; he has the strength of a wild ox."

The writer's purpose appears to be to view the reign of the future king in terms taken from God's great acts of salvation in the past. The future is going to be like the past. What God did for Israel in the past is seen as a type of what he will do for them in the future when he sends his promised king.

Not only do Balaam's final oracles allude to his own earlier ones, but also in speaking of the future king, Balaam alludes to and even quotes the earlier poetic sections in the Pentateuch. In the oracles of Balaam, then, we find the central messianic themes of the Pentateuch restated and expanded. For example, in Numbers 24:9, Balaam says of the future king about whom he gives his oracle: "Like a lion he [singular] crouches and lies down, like a lioness—who dares to rouse him [singular]?" This entire section of Balaam's oracle is a quotation of Jacob's prophecy of the king who will come from the tribe of Judah: "Like a lion he crouches and lies down, like a lioness—who dares to rouse him?" (Ge 49:9). When Balaam says of this future king, "Those who bless you will be blessed and those who curse you will be cursed," he clearly applies to this future king the blessing to the seed of Isaac: "Those who curse you will be cursed and those who bless you will be blessed" (Ge 27:29), and that of Abraham: "I will bless those who bless you, and whoever curses you I will curse" (Ge 12:3). Finally, Balaam's description of the future victory of the coming king, "He will crush the foreheads of Moab and the skulls of all the sons of Sheth" (Nu 24:17), draws heavily on God's words of promise and judgment spoken to the serpent in Genesis 3:15: "I will put enmity between you and the woman and between your seed and hers; he will crush your head."

Since the medieval period, it has been debated whether Balaam's prophecy should be taken as a reference to the reign of David, the greatest king of the house of Judah, or to the Messiah, also to be from the house of Judah and David. Most would agree, however, that from the vantage point of Balaam, the oracle is about one who was yet to come, be it David or the Messiah. In Balaam's own words: "I see him, but not now; I behold him, but he is not near" (Nu 24:17).

We should, however, also raise the question: Does the writer of the Pentateuch understand these oracles of Balaam to refer to David or to someone else in the more distant future? An answer to this question is provided in the oracle that concludes this section, Numbers 24:23–24. In this oracle the victory of the future king is extended to cover the defeat of "Asshur and Eber" (probably Babylon) at the hands of the Kittim (probably the Romans). Moreover, in the end, even the Kittim "will come to ruin" (v. 24) "when God does this" (v. 23). From the standpoint of later biblical history, the events alluded to here extend far beyond the reign of the historical David. It is difficult in this context not to think of texts like Genesis 10:2–4, where the Kittim are associated with nations such as Magog, Tubal, Media, and Meshech, nations which figure prominently in the later prophetic books (e.g., Eze 38:2–3), and of Daniel 11:30, where the Kittim are again mentioned in reference to the last great battle. In any case, this last oracle of Balaam appears to place the scope of his oracles too far in the future to be a reference to the reign of David.[14]

X. THE ESTABLISHMENT OF NEW LEADERSHIP IN ISRAEL: THE PRIESTS AND THE PROPHET (25:1–27:23)

A. The Failure of the Old Leaders: Moab Seduces Israel (25:1–18)

Though the introduction focuses on the daughters of Moab, the central narrative is about a Midianite woman, Cozbi, who led the people away from

---

[14]It is of interest that the tendency of biblical criticism is to understand the oracle eschatologically and hence to see it as a late addition to the Pentateuch. E.g., H. Holzinger, *Numeri*, Kurzer Hand-Commentar zum Alten Testament (Tübingen: Mohr [Siebeck], 1903), 125, dates the oracle to the first half of the 2d century B.C. The fact that it is eschatological, however, does not necessitate our reading it as a late addition, unless we rule out the possibility of true prophecy in the Bible.

the Lord (25:6, 14, 15, 18). Moreover, in the later narrative (chap. 31), Midian is also held responsible for the actions of this chapter. According to Numbers 31:16, the whole of this incident was brought about by the counsel of Balaam.

The events of the narrative are situated in Shittim. Shittim (25:1) was located on the plains of Moab. It was the last campsite of the Israelites before entering into the land. Joshua sent the spies from here into Jericho (Jos 2:1).

As is often the case in the Bible, the account of God's act of salvation is immediately followed by that of the people's apostasy. In this case, "the men began to indulge in sexual immorality with the Moabite women" (25:1), and this led to their following after the Moabite gods. The parallels and contrasts between this narrative and the book of Ruth suggest that both texts are dealing with similar ideas. In fact, the picture of Ruth provides an excellent counterexample to that of the men of Israel in this episode. Ruth the Moabitess married an Israelite man and forsook her nation's gods to follow the Lord. For this she was given an inheritance in Israel. In this respect she is also like the daughters of Zelophehad in the next chapters of Numbers who also gained an inheritance among the men of Israel (Nu 27:1–11).

Amid this time of apostasy, the writer points to a specific incident which shows not only the horrible conditions among the Israelites but also the need for new forms of leadership. When a Midianite woman, Cozbi (25:15), was taken into the tent of an Israelite man before the eyes of Moses and the whole congregation, there was much distress but little action. In this narrative, Moses is remarkably ineffective in the face of a blatant transgression (v. 6). The day was saved, however, by the decisive action of one from the next generation of priests, Phinehas, the grandson of Aaron. Through his zeal for the Lord, he stayed God's judgment, and the house of Phinehas was rewarded with a lasting "covenant of priesthood" (v. 13).

B. Second Census (26:1–65)

The brief narrative introduction to this census locates it in the plains of Moab (26:3), where they had camped just before the incident with Balak and Balaam (22:1).

The list shows a great deal of intentional selection and structure.[15] The purpose of going over the new census is stated at the end of the chapter. None of the earlier generation had survived except Joshua and Caleb, who were allowed to possess the land (26:64–65). Thus the text refers here to the Lord's words of judgment in Numbers 14:22–24. Within the whole Pentateuch are many narrative examples of the fulfillment of God's word. This text is one of them. What God had said in Numbers 14:22–24 is shown to have been fulfilled. The purpose of such narratives is to show that God's word is sure and certain. What he has promised, he will do. The writer is thus building a case about God. He shows in these narratives that God is faithful

---

[15]A total of 75 names is given. This number may be related to the 70 nations listed in Ge 10 and the 70 sons of Jacob who went down into Egypt in Ge 46. In both of those passages there is textual uncertainty whether the final number in the lists was 70 or 75. It is fortunately not necessary to resolve this question in order to see the point of the numbers. This list is not intended to be complete; rather, the numerical totals were understood in general terms. The number 70 or 75 expresses the idea that all the sons of Jacob were counted.

in both judgment and salvation. Joseph's words echo throughout these passages: "The matter has been firmly decided by God, and God will do it soon" (Ge 41:32).

On three occasions in the midst of this list of names and numbers (Nu 26:8–11, 19, 33), the writers turns his attention away from the mere listing of names to mention a brief biographical fact. These comments have at least one feature in common—they deal with the situation of the continuance of a family line in spite of the death of the head of the family. For example, the mention of the rebellion of Dathan and Abiram (26:8–11) explains that the house of Korah did not die out when Korah and the others were destroyed. Earlier, in Numbers 16:32, it may have been possible to say that Korah and "all his men" were destroyed in the earthquake and fire, but the note here goes on further to explain that his "sons" survived. By reminding the reader of the large-scale destruction of the house of Korah, this note also provides an explanation why the number of the men of Reuben, who were among those of Korah's rebellion, was smaller in this census (cf. Nu 1:21; Dt 33:6).

The second note, that Er and Onan "died in the land of the Canaan" (Nu 26:19), draws a connection between these two disobedient sons of Judah and the disobedient generation of Israelites who died in the wilderness (cf. 26:65). This note, however, also explains that the house of Shelah survived and was reckoned in the census, even though the earlier narratives (Ge 38) do not mention his descendants.

The third note, the mention of Zelophehad (26:33), prepares the way for the account of the request of Zelophehad's daughters for continuance of the rights of their father (27:1–11). Here, the house of Zelophehad is already noted as continuing through his daughters after his death.

As this list shows, Moses, Aaron, and Miriam were of the house of Levi. The names of the father and mother of Moses were not given in the account of his birth in Exodus 2:1. From the present passage some have supposed that the mother and father of Moses were Jochebed and Amram. Verse 59, however, appears to have telescoped several generations into a simple expression of the lineage of Moses: "The name of the wife of Amram was Jochebed, the daughter of Levi, whom she [Levi's wife] bore to Levi in Egypt, and she [Jochebed] bore to Amram Aaron, Moses, and Miriam their sister." The NIV translates this verse somewhat differently, but the translation offered above represents the Hebrew more literally. This verse, then, does not state specifically when Jochebed and Amram lived, but only that they were from the house of Levi and that Moses, Aaron, and Miriam were born into their lineage. Since during the time of Moses the "Amramites" (i.e., those of the house of Amram) apparently numbered in the hundreds if not thousands (Nu 3:28), it is more likely that the unnamed Levite father and mother of Moses in Exodus 2:1 were only distant relatives of Amram and Jochebed. This explanation finds support in Exodus 6:18–20, which states that Amram is one of the sons of Levi and that Jochebed bore "to him [Amram] Aaron and Moses." It is also possible, but not likely, however, that there were two Amrams, one of the progenitor of the "Amramites" of Numbers 3:28, and the other the husband of Jochebed and father of Moses.[16]

---

[16]See Keil, *Pentateuch*, 1:470.

Instructions for the parceling out of the land by lot are given in Numbers 26:52–56.

C. Zelophehad's Daughters (27:1–11)

The previous chapter stated that the line of Korah did not die out (26:11), even though earlier 16:32 had said "all of Korah's men" had been swallowed by the earthquake. This raises the question: How could the line be preserved if there were no men to receive their father's name? The present narrative about the daughters of Zelophehad appears to raise this issue intentionally in order to speak precisely to the question. In this narrative we are shown how it was possible to preserve a lineage in the absence of sons. According to the ruling in 27:8, the property rights and family name were to go to the daughters if there were no sons in the family. If there were no daughters, however, the rights were to go to one of the brothers. If there was no brother to receive the inheritance, then the family rights were to go to the uncle or nearest of kin. A close relationship between the situation of Zelophehad's daughters and the question of the survival of the line of Korah is further implied in the fact that the daughters themselves raise the example of Korah's death in the wilderness and compare their father's death with it. Though he was not of the congregation of Korah, like him their father died in the wilderness because of sin (27:3). Behind the seemingly miscellaneous collection of narratives in this section of the Pentateuch, then, there appears to be a conscious attempt to deal with the larger issue of the survival of the priestly line. Even in the midst of God's judgment, a remnant of the house of Korah is saved.

Command #248, Nu 27:8, Judgments involving inheritance: "If a man dies and leaves no son."

D. Joshua Appointed Successor to Moses (27:12–23)

In the comments on Numbers 20:22–29, we drew attention to the similarities between the death of Moses and the death of Aaron, as well as the connections between the installation of Eleazar as priest and the fall of the house of Eli in 1 Samuel. There appear to be similar connections between the present narrative and future events. The portrayal of Moses' passing his authority (splendor or majesty) over to Joshua and Joshua's reception of the Spirit is noticeably similar to the transition of prophetic office from Elijah to Elisha in 2 Kings 2:7–15. It appears that the writer of the book of Kings has intentionally worked some of these themes into his narrative to draw out the comparison. For example, Elijah, like Moses at the Red Sea, divided the waters of the Jordan with his mantle (2Ki 2:8). After Elijah had been taken away and the Spirit which was upon him had come upon Elisha, Elisha then parted the same waters of the Jordan (2Ki 2:14). This follows the pattern of Moses and Joshua. After the glory of Moses had come upon Joshua, a man in whom dwelt the Spirit, he also went on to divide the waters of the Jordan as Moses had divided the Red Sea (Jos 3:7: "And the LORD said to Joshua, 'Today I will begin to exalt you in the eyes of all Israel, so they may know that I am with you as I was with Moses' "). In modeling the Elijah and Elisha narratives after the pentateuchal narratives, the writer of Kings correctly followed their lead. The type of leadership exhibited by Moses and Joshua is the same as that of Elijah and Elisha. It is a leadership that is guided by the Spirit of God.

In Deuteronomy 18:14–22 we will see that the office of the prophet in later Israel was patterned after God's work in Moses: "The LORD your God will raise up for you a prophet like me from among your own brothers. You must listen to him." Thus the succession of Moses and Joshua is cast as a succession of the prophetic office guided by the Spirit of God. It became a model even for the succession of prophets at a later period. In the light of the emphasis on the work of the prophetic Spirit in this section, it is interesting and appropriate that Moses refers to God in this passage as "the God of spirits" (Nu 27:16). This section is repeated almost verbatim in Deuteronomy 32:48–52.

The close of the chapter (Nu 27:21) describes the relationship between the offices of priest and (prophetic) leader. The priest, Eleazar, was to enquire of the Lord by means of the Urim. The (prophetic) leader, Joshua, was to follow his advice.

XI. REGULAR CELEBRATIONS (28:1–29:40 [MT 30:1])

The writer is aware that the instructions for the regular celebrations in Israel's worship calendar have thus far been mentioned at various points in the previous narratives but that he still needs to gather these together into a summary statement and specify the nature of their additional offerings. Thus a description of the regular offerings for each time of celebration now follows. These offerings were to be given in addition to those required for each special feast.

The present list is drawn up primarily from the calendar of feasts in Leviticus 23. There is no mention of the celebration of the "firstfruits" (Lev 23:9–14) in this passage. The offering to be made on that occasion is already specified in Leviticus 23:12, so perhaps there was no need to repeat it here. We should note that other celebrations are repeated in this passage even though they do not have special offerings (e.g., the Passover) and that other celebrations which had special offerings are added here for the first time. Such cases indicate a desire to make this a comprehensive list. The fact that the "firstfruits" has been omitted, however, suggests that though the writer is striving for a comprehensive listing he avoids a merely redundant repetition of Leviticus 23. Since both a description of the "firstfruits" and its offerings had already been specified in Leviticus 23, there was no reason to repeat it here.

The effect of the present description is cumulative; that is, there is a daily offering for each day of the year, a Sabbath offering for each Sabbath, an offering for the first day of each month, and offerings for each of the special feast days. On any one of the appropriate days, each offering was given in its turn. Thus, for example, on each Sabbath, not only were the Sabbath offerings presented but also the daily offerings.

It may also be important that this list is given after the account of the death of the old generation and the conclusion of the new census. Thus, for the new generation who were now being called on to move into the Promised Land, the religious duties are reiterated. Though the Passover was celebrated at the time of the Exodus (Ex 12) and the next year (Nu 9:1–2), according to Joshua 9:5–8, some if not all of the religious duties of the people were not kept during the years in the wilderness. There would have been a need, therefore, for a summary of past requirements for the new generation.

A. Daily Offerings (28:1–8)

These provisions were given in Exodus 29:38–42 and are repeated here for completeness, apparently because they had not been mentioned in Leviticus 23.

> Command # 39, Nu 28:3, Two yearling lambs presented to the Lord daily (*Tamid*): "You are to present to the Lord: two lambs a year old without defect, as a regular burnt offering each day."

B. Sabbath Offerings (28:9–10)

Observance of the Sabbath rest was grounded in Creation when God himself "rested" from all his work (Ge 2:2–3). The Sabbath was prescribed as part of the Decalogue in Exodus 20:8–11 and was included as part of the regular celebrations in Leviticus 23:3. Leviticus 23 makes no mention of the need to present offerings on this day. The description of a specific offering for this day is mentioned here for the first time (cf. Eze 46:1–5).

> Command #41, Nu 28:9, An additional gift (*musaf*) is to be offered every Sabbath: "Two yearling lambs."

C. Monthly Offerings (28:11–15)

The instructions for regular worship in Leviticus 23 do not mention setting apart the "first of the month" or new moon as a special day. Numbers 10:10, however, does mention the "first of the month" as a time set apart for celebration by the blowing of trumpets. Its inclusion here further shows that the earlier list in Leviticus is selective and that the present list is intended to be comprehensive.

> Command #42, Nu 28:11, An additional gift is to be offered every month: "At the beginning of your months."

D. Yearly Celebrations (28:16–29:40)

1. Passover and Unleavened Bread (28:16–25)

The Passover was briefly described in Leviticus 23:5–8, which recounted only that an offering of "fire" (Lev 23:8) was to be presented to the Lord for each of the seven days of the Feast of Unleavened Bread. In the present passage, however, the nature of this "fire offering" is described (Nu 28:19–22). It should be noted that there was no need to list the Passover here since no specific offerings are given for that day. The offerings mentioned here are only for the seven days of the Unleavened Bread.[17] This again shows that the writer's purpose was to be comprehensive in his description of the prescribed calendar of worship.

2. Feast of Weeks (28:26–31; cf. Dt 16:9–12)

At the end of fifty days after the time of the "firstfruits" the Feast of Weeks was celebrated. In Leviticus 23:18 this feast already called for the

---

[17]See Holzinger, *Numeri*, 143.

offering of seven lambs, a bull, and two rams. What then is the purpose of the offerings listed here? Are they the same offerings, or are they additional offerings for the Feast of Weeks? As this passage is traditionally interpreted, the offerings described here (two bulls, a ram, and seven lambs) were to be given in addition to those noted in Leviticus 23.

A helpful summary of the traditional interpretation of this passage is found in Maimonides' *Mishneh Torah*:

> In the fiftieth day from the numbering of the sheaves is the Feast of Weeks (Ex 34:22) and it is a solemn assembly. This day they offer more, like the additional offerings on the New Moon feast, that is, two bulls, a ram and seven lambs. All of them are burnt offerings. Also a goat for a sin offering. These are the offerings spoken of in Numbers 28:26, 27, and 30. They are in addition to that of the daily offerings. They still must bring more for this day, that is, a meal offering in two loaves, and they must bring with the two loaves a bull, two rams, and seven lambs (all burnt offerings) and a goat for a sin offering and two lambs for peace offerings. These are those spoken of in Leviticus 23. So there are to be offered on this day, over and above the two daily offerings, three bulls, three rams, and fourteen lambs, twenty animals in all for burnt offerings. Also two goats for sin offerings, which are eaten, and two lambs for peace offerings, which are eaten.[18]

Some believe there is a textual confusion between the two descriptions of this feast in Leviticus and Numbers. According to A. Noordtzij, the offerings given in Numbers have been erroneously brought over into the Leviticus passage.[19] There is, however, no textual evidence for this assumption.

> **Command #45**, Nu 28:26–27, An additional gift is to be given fifty days from the offering of the sheaf, i.e., on Shavuot (Feast of Weeks): "On the day of the firstfruits when they bring their offering."

3. Feast of Trumpets (29:1–6)

The Feast of Trumpets, celebrated on the first day of the seventh month, is mentioned in Leviticus 23:23–25 as a time of special remembrance. The offerings for that day are listed here. In later Judaism, probably soon after the destruction of the second temple (A.D. 70), this feast was celebrated as Rosh Hashanah, the New Year's Day feast. In the Bible, however, it is never called a New Year's Day feast because during the biblical period the New Year began in March/April, the month of Abib (Ex 12:2). There was early precedent, however, for taking the "seventh month" (Tishri) as the month of the New Year since this was apparently the custom in Israel before the time of the Exodus (cf. Ex 23:16). The mention of the New Year in Ezekiel 40:1 is most likely to Nisan, the month of the Exodus from Egypt.

> **Command #47**, Nu 29:1–2, An additional gift is to be given on Rosh Hashanah (1st of Tishri): "On the seventh month, on the first day of the month, you shall make a burnt offering."

---

[18]Maimonides, *Tamidin*, 8.1.

[19]A. Noordtzij, *Numbers*, Bible Student's Commentary, trans. Ed van der Maas (Grand Rapids: Zondervan, 1983), 236.

Command #170, Nu 29:1, One must hear the *shofar* on the first day of Tishri (Rosh Hashanah): "A day of trumpet sounding it shall be to you."

4. Day of Atonement (29:7–11)

Instructions for the celebration of the Day of Atonement on the tenth day of the seventh month are recorded in Leviticus 23:27–32. The "atonement" offerings are described in Leviticus 16. In the present chapter the writer lists only the offerings prescribed in addition to those of Leviticus 16. It is noteworthy that, as with the offerings for the other feasts, in addition to those offerings mentioned in Leviticus, the Day of Atonement was to have its own sin offering of a male goat (Nu 29:11). "On Atonement day, they offered an addition according to the addition of the beginning of the year, a bull and a ram. This ram is called the people's ram. Also offered were seven lambs, all of them for burnt offerings, and a goat for a sin offering, and it was eaten at evening. Moreover (according to Lev 16:9–10), the congregation offered a goat for a sin offering, which was burnt, and another goat, which was sent away for a scapegoat."[20]

> **Command #48**, Nu 29:7–8, An additional gift is to be given on the Day of Atonement (10th of Tishri): "On the tenth of the seventh month you shall offer a burnt offering, fire to the Lord."

5. Feast of Tabernacles (29:12–38)

The Feast of Tabernacles is described in Leviticus 23:33–43. It was to be celebrated on the fifteenth day of the seventh month (Tishri). In this passage it is called only "the festival," which suggests that it was a well-known and important yearly celebration. According to Leviticus 23:39 it was to mark the time of the "ingathering" or harvest of crops and thus corresponds roughly to our Thanksgiving Day. The present chapter is devoted only to the special offerings for the eight days of its celebration. The sheer volume of the required offerings and sacrifices (13 bulls, 2 rams, and 14 lambs on the first day) suggests that this was considered the grandest of the early feast days. On each successive day of the feast, one less bull is offered. Thus a total of seventy bulls are offered, and on the seventh day of the feast, seven bulls are offered.

> The sacred number 7 is very prominent. . . . Note the accumulation of special occasions in the 7th month, and the special character (implied by the special offerings) of the 1st day of that month, the seven-day duration of each of the two great festivals in the 1st and 7th month respectively (28:17; 29:12); and, further, that the descending numerical series of bullocks required for the autumn (7th month) feast yields the total 70, and that thus the total number of victims offered on the seven days of this feast is 7 x 7 x 2 lambs, 7 x 7 rams, 7 x 10 bullocks, 7 goats.[21]

> **Command #50**, Nu 29:13, An additional offering is to be given for the Feast of Sukkoth (Tabernacles): "And you shall bring a burnt offering."

---

[20]Maimonides, *Tamidin*, 10.12.

[21]G. B. Gray, *A Critical and Exegetical Commentary on Numbers*, ICC (Edinburgh: T. & T. Clark, 1903), 406–7.

Command #51, Nu 29:36, An additional offering is to be given for the eighth day of the Feast of Sukkoth (Tabernacles): "And you shall offer a burnt offering."

XII. VOWS FOR MEN AND WOMEN (30:1–16 [MT 2–17])

The arrangement and placement of this passage on vows at this point in the text is motivated by the mention of "vows" in the previous section, Numbers 29:39.[22] It focuses on the relationship between husbands and wives as well as fathers and daughters and thus augments that which has been previously given on vows (Lev 27; Nu 6:1–21).

Command #95, Num 30:3 (EVV 2), One must not break a vow: "He must not break his word but must do everything he said." (M. Only a judge can annul a vow in accordance with the law: "and he must not break his own word"— implying someone else, a judge, can break his word.)

Prohibition #157, Nu 30:3 (EVV 2), One must not break his word: "He must not break his word."

The section begins with a general statement of obligation in making vows: When a man made a vow, he was bound by it (30:2). It then goes on to assert that a man was also responsible for vows made by women in his household. If he heard a woman in his own household make a vow, his daughter or his wife, he could nullify the vow by speaking out. If he did not speak out, the vow was left to stand. In the case of a widow or a divorced woman (i.e., where there was no father or husband in the household), the word of the woman alone sufficed (30:9).

The assumed culpability of Adam in Genesis 3 may stem from the principle behind this law. In 3:6, Adam's wife makes a rash decision in his presence: "She took from the tree and ate and gave it to her husband who was with her." In view of this passage in Numbers, Adam's silence in the narrative makes him culpable for his wife's action.

XIII. BATTLE WITH THE MIDIANITES (31:1–54)

The narrative now returns to the sin of the people at Baal Peor (Nu 25). At the close of chapter 25, the Lord had instructed Moses to smite the Midianites for the cunning allurement of the Israelites by Cozbi, the daughter of a Midianite leader (vv. 6–15). Just as Phinehas was responsible for putting an end to the people's apostasy in chapter 25, so here he was called upon here to carry out the revenge on the Midianites. In the ensuing battle, the 12,000 Israelite soldiers, under the command of Phinehas, killed "every man," including the five kings of Midian and Balaam son of Beor.

By saving the women and children of Midian, the Israelite officers renewed the old threat of mixing with Canaanite women and thus forsaking the Lord. Hence they inadvertently returned to the dangerous conditions of chapter 25. This time it was Moses, not Phinehas, who rose to the occasion and dealt forcibly with the problem. Moses' harsh solution is explained by a reference to the plague which struck 24,000 people during the previous

---

[22]See Holzinger, *Numeri*, 146.

apostasy with the Moabite and Midianite women (31:16). The command that the army must ritually cleanse themselves after the battle (on the third and seventh days) is based on the instructions requiring cleansing after touching a corpse (19:16–21). Such a command is also commensurate with the fact that their mission was one of carrying out the divine wrath upon the Midianites (cf. 25:16–17).

The "statute of the law that the LORD gave Moses," which Eleazar referred to in 31:21, is not found elsewhere in the Pentateuch, though a part of what he commands (the water of cleansing) is given in Numbers 19. This shows either that the laws included in the Pentateuch are selective (i.e., not every law given to Moses was included), or that any law given by a priest may be called a "statute of the law that the LORD gave Moses" (cf. Dt 33:10). The former alternative appears more likely because the text expressly states that the statute was one that the Lord gave "to Moses."

XIV. THE TRANSJORDAN TRIBES (32:1–42)

This narrative provides a contrast between the earlier generation of Israelites who died in the wilderness and the new generation that was about to enter the land. The contrast comes as a result of Moses' misunderstanding the request for land by the tribes of Reuben and Gad. Moses at first interpreted their request to remain on the far side of the Jordan as a source of "discouragement" to the people, just as the bad report of the spies had been in Numbers 13. The willingness of these tribes to fight for the rest of the nation, however, shows that Moses was mistaken and that this generation was quite different from the one that had refused to enter the land.

The "half tribe" of Manasseh is not mentioned along with Reuben and Gad at the beginning of the narrative. They are mentioned for the first time only in 32:33, when Moses parcels out the territory of the Transjordan. To clarify their also being allotted a portion of the area of the Transjordan, the writer concludes the narrative with an account of the conquests of the sons of Manasseh in this region (vv. 39–42). We should note that the tribe of Manasseh was allotted Gilead (v. 40), although Reuben and Gad had requested the land of Gilead (v. 1). This could imply that the initial request of Reuben and Gad included the allotment of Manasseh. Thus in the present narrative it appears that Gilead was given both to Reuben (v. 1) and to Manasseh (v. 40). This difficulty is later explained: Half of Gilead went to the tribes of Reuben and half to Manasseh (Dt 3:12–13; cf. Jos 13:24–31). Apparently, the region of Gilead was not a specific location but a broad area of land in the central Transjordan.[23]

XV. ISRAEL'S CAMPS IN THE WILDERNESS (33:1–49)

The list of encampments in the wilderness begins with the Israelites' departure from Rameses on the fifteenth day of the first month and concludes with their encampment on the "plains of Moab," where they have been since Numbers 22:1. Between Rameses and the plains of Moab there are

---

[23]Cf. Carl G. Rasmussen, NIV Atlas of the Bible (Grand Rapids: Zondervan, 1989), 101.

forty encampments, perhaps literarily reflecting the forty years spent in the wilderness. If Rameses and the plains of Moab are counted, the number is forty-two. In either case the list is selective, since some sites recorded earlier are not included (e.g., Shur, Taberah, and Hormah, as well as those sites mentioned in Nu 21:11–13, 16–19). Many of these sites are known only from this list.[24]

Within the list of encampments are two short narratives that focus on the work of Moses (vv. 2–3) and Aaron (vv. 38–39). In these two segments are found the only dates for Israel's journeys (vv. 3, 38b), marking the beginning and end of the forty-year period in the wilderness. Both narratives have the same comment that Moses (v. 2) and Aaron (v. 38) obeyed "the command of the LORD." Thus one of the purposes of this list within the larger strategy of the book appears to be to give a brief review of the work of these two great leaders. God used them and their obedience to lead the people in the wilderness for the forty years. That the positive side of their work is stressed can be seen from the fact that when Aaron's death is recorded here, there is no mention of the rebellion of Moses and Aaron, a theme often stressed in other references to their deaths (cf. Nu 20:24). In fact, in this passage Aaron's death is portrayed as his last act of obedience: "At the LORD's command Aaron the priest went up Mount Hor and died" (33:38).

XVI. PREPARATION FOR POSSESSION OF THE PROMISED LAND
(33:50–36:13)

A. Division of the Land (33:50–34:29)

1. Instructions to Drive Out All the Canaanites (33:50–56)

In this passage, the author is careful to point out that Israel's possession of the land was an act of obedience to God's will. God was Lord of the land. He had created it "in the beginning" (Ge 1:1). He still owned it, and he "would give it to whomever was pleasing in his sight" (Jer 27:5). This passage attempts to show that the people of Israel were not taking the land for their own gain but were acting as God's agents in punishing the idolatrous Canaanites. Thus they were to destroy all Canaanite idols and places of worship when they entered the land, and they were not to allow the Canaanites to remain among them. It is important to note that if Israel failed to obey God—which proved to be the case—they too were to be the objects of God's punishment. The Lord's last words have an ominous tone: "Then I will do to you what I plan to do to them" (Nu 33:56).

Joshua gave a similar warning to the nation of Israel after their initial success at taking the land (Jos 23:12), but even in his day God's command had not been carried out. The Gibeonites deceived Israel into making a covenant with them, "So Joshua saved them from the Israelites, and they did not kill them" (Jos 9:26). Later biblical writers looked back to the failure of Israel to carry out this command as a central cause of their apostasy: "They did not destroy the peoples as the LORD had commanded them, but they mingled with the nations and adopted their customs. They worshiped their idols, which became a snare to them. They sacrificed their sons and their

---

[24]See Gray, *Numbers*, 444.

daughters to demons. They shed innocent blood, the blood of their sons and daughters, whom they sacrificed to the idols of Canaan and the land was desecrated by their blood" (Ps 106:34–39).

2. Description of the Borders of the Land (34:1–15)

Besides the obvious geographical markers, such as the Mediterranean Sea, many of the sites noted in this chapter are not identifiable today. A general outline of the area, however, can be obtained by following the natural boundaries of the land itself.[25] It is important to note that the boundaries, drawn here by reference to key geopolitical sites, were never fully realized during Israel's subsequent history. For example, western boundaries of the Israelite nation never extended as far as the Mediterranean Sea; "it always lay some distance back from the coast."[26] We should thus understand this list as a set of outside perimeters within which Israel was free to occupy territory.

The principal concern of the writer is not, however, the exact identification of all these sites. After all, the author does not intend the reader of the Pentateuch to go out and take these cities. Rather, his purpose is to show the work of God in allotting the land to his people. God is portrayed elsewhere in the Pentateuch as one who apportions the boundaries of all the nations (Ge 10; Dt 32:8), and here he is shown doing the same for his own people. The land is a gift from God and Israel is to receive it with gratitude.

3. List of Leaders Responsible for Dividing the Land (34:16–29)

The first three names in this list are well known from the previous narratives: Joshua, Eleazar, and Caleb. The rest of the names are new. These men thus represent the new generation that was to take possession of the land. Each of the men is given the title "prince," which here means tribal representative. The order of the tribes reflected in this list is: Judah, Simeon, Benjamin, Dan, Manasseh, Ephraim, Zebulon, Issachar, Asher, and Naphtali. This order differs from that of the tribes in Numbers 1 and 7, but follows somewhat the order of the allotment of the land in Joshua 19. The two tribes of Reuben and Gad are omitted since the focus is only on the region west of the Jordan.

B. Cities for the Levites (35:1–8)

A total of forty-eight cities were to be given to the tribe of Levi, that is, the Levites. Each lot was approximately 207 acres and consisted of a town and pasture.[27] Six of these sites were to be cities of refuge. These instructions were carried out under Joshua's allotment of the land. Joshua 21 gives a list of these cities. Reference to the Levitical cities can be found during the later period of the monarchy (2Ch 31:15) as well as after the return from Babylonian captivity (Ezr 2:70). In the years before the Captivity, the prophet Jeremiah, who was from a priestly family, lived in Anathoth, one of the Levitical cities mentioned in Joshua 21:18.

---

[25]See Barry J. Beitzel, *The Moody Atlas of Bible Lands* (Chicago: Moody, 1985), 9.
[26]Gray, *Numbers*, 453.
[27]Ibid., 464.

Cities of Refuge

The idea of providing cities of refuge (Jos 20:1-9) for capital offenses is rooted in the tension between customary tribal law (retaliation or revenge, in which the blood relative is obligated to execute vengeance) and civil law (carried out less personally by an assembly according to a standard code of justice).

Blood feuds are usually associated with nomadic groups; legal procedures, with villages and towns. Israel, a society in the process of sedentarization, found it necessary to adopt an intermediate step regulating manslaughter, so that an innocent person would not be killed before standing trial. Absolution was possible only by being cleared by his hometown assembly, and by the eventual death of the high priest, which freed the offender from ritual pollution.

• Kedesh

• Acco

• Golan

• Dor

Beth Shan•

• Ramoth

Shechem•

Peniel

Gezer

• Gibeon

• Bezer

Heshbon

Hebron•

The six cities of refuge are shown in bold type.

Beersheba•

Miles 10 5 0   10   20
Kms 10 5 0   10   20   30

Taken from THE NIV STUDY BIBLE. Copyright © 1985 by The Zondervan Corporation. Used by permission.

Command #183, Nu 35:2, Levitical cities: "Give the Levites towns to live in."

C. Cities of Refuge (35:9–34; cf. Dt 19:1–14)

After enumerating the provision for the cities of refuge, the writer inserts a rather comprehensive description of the laws governing their use. As one can see in the specifications given, the cities were to provide a shelter for anyone who committed a homicide. The natural assumption was that a close relative of a homicide victim would seek to avenge his death; thus provision was made to prevent this vengeance. Once the innocent "manslayer" had found a safe haven, a trial was to ensue. If it could be determined that he had intentionally slain the victim, it was to be ruled a capital offense, and he was to be put to death. If the death was ruled accidental, he was to remain under the protection of the city of refuge "until the death of the high priest" (35:25).

At the conclusion of the legislation, the underlying basis of this law is given: "Do not defile the land where you live and where I dwell, for I, the LORD, dwell among the Israelites" (35:34). In fact, this principle was the basis of much of Israel's law. As has often been remarked, the uniqueness of biblical law lies in the fact that it represents the will of a personal God who graciously dwells among his own people.

Command #225, Nu 35:25, You must exile the accidental manslayer: "The assembly must protect the one accused of murder."

Prohibition #292, Nu 35:12, One must not be executed without a trial: "A person accused of murder may not die before he stands trial before the assembly."

Prohibition #291, Nu 35:30, One must not be put to death on the testimony of one witness (M. a witness must not act as judge): "No one is to be put to death on the testimony of only one witness."

Prohibition #295, Nu 35:31, One must not take a ransom from a murderer: "You must not take a ransom for the life of a murderer guilty of death."

Prohibition #296, Nu 35:32, One must not take a ransom from a manslayer: "Do not accept a ransom for anyone who has fled to a city of refuge and so allow him to go back and live on his own land before the death of the high priest."

D. Inheritance of Zelophehad's Daughters (36:1–13)

The issue raised here stems from the decision regarding female inheritance in Numbers 27. The problem and its solution are clear from the text. In order to prevent a tribe's loss of allotted inheritance in the event that it goes to a woman who then marries into another tribe, an additional stipulation was added to the ruling of chapter 27. The women of any tribe who have inherited property as a result of the ruling in chapter 27 cannot then marry into another tribe. Such a rule would ensure that a tribe's inheritance would not be taken into the inheritance of another tribe.

The reason this passage is placed here rather than with chapter 27 is twofold. First, it concerns the issue of tribal allotments, which is the focus of these last chapters of Numbers. Second, it is customary for large sections of the Hebrew Bible, including whole books, to conclude on a positive note. Thus the last words of this section provide an appropriate conclusion for the whole: "So Zelophehad's daughters did as the LORD commanded Moses . . . and their inheritance remained in their father's clan and tribe" (36:10–12). In this way these women provide a positive parting view of God's laws and the well-being of the people when they are carried out.[28]

---

[28]See Ronald B. Allen and Kenneth L. Barker, note on Nu 36:10 in *The NIV Study Bible* (Grand Rapids: Zondervan, 1985), 242.

Chapter 5

DEUTERONOMY

$\mathbf{W}$e should remember that Deuteronomy is not a separate book but an integral part of the whole Pentateuch. Very early in tradition, however, it was regarded as a book.

The traditional Hebrew name, "These are the words," is taken from the first words. The English name, Deuteronomy, is taken from the Greek rendering of Deuteronomy 17:18, where the phrase "copy of the Law" was read as "a second Law" (δευτερονόμιον). Though this was a misreading of the verse, the name Deuteronomy continued to be used because this section of the Pentateuch gives the impression of being a "second Law," since much of the material it contains has already been recorded in the earlier sections of the Pentateuch. For example, the Decalogue, which is found in Exodus 20, is repeated in Deuteronomy 5. But one must not be left with the impression that the earlier material is repeated in merely a redundant way. The key to understanding this repetition is Moses' statement of purpose in 1:5: "to expound this Law." Deuteronomy thus is an explanation of the Law, not merely a repetition of it. In many ways it is helpful to think of this section as a commentary on the earlier passages of the Pentateuch.

I. INTRODUCTION (1:1–5)

The opening section gives the setting of this part of the Pentateuch and its purpose. This section consists of a collection of public addresses given by Moses to "all Israel." These public addresses are the last words Moses spoke to the people as they were preparing to enter the Promised Land. The location of the addresses in the narrative is the "Transjordan" area, where the people are gathered after their forty years in the wilderness.

The purpose of the book, as given in the preamble, is "to expound the Law" (1:5). After the military struggles to gain the Transjordan, Moses devoted himself to the task of making the Law of God clear to the people (cf. Dt 27:8; Hab 2:2). The book of Deuteronomy is the result of that work. It is an attempt to make the sense and purpose of the Law (Torah) clear to the people as they entered the land. It was to be their guide to the Law while living in the land.

The English term *Law*, which is used to describe the book of Deuteronomy, translates the Hebrew word *Torah*. Unfortunately, the English term often carries the negative meaning of strict prohibition. The Hebrew word *Torah*, however, is primarily positive. It is not so much prohibition as "instruction." Thus we should see here a reference to the divine instruction which Moses now gave to the people as they prepared to enter the land. It is instruction in God's will. It is intended to tell them how they should live in God's land. In view of this, one should not think of Deuteronomy as a book of laws but as that which reveals and explains the will of God.

At the close of this book, when Moses presented this Torah to the people, he represented it as God's way of restoring to them the divine view of "good and evil" which was lost in the Garden of Eden: "See, I set before you today life and prosperity [Hebrew: 'life, namely, the good'], death and destruction [Hebrew: 'death, namely, the evil']. For I command you today to love the LORD your God, to walk in his ways, and to keep his commands, decrees, and laws; then you will live and increase, and the LORD your God will bless you in the land you are entering to possess" (Dt 30:15–16). What the man and woman lost in the Garden is now restored to them in the Torah, namely, God's plan for their good.

II. HISTORICAL REVIEW OF THE EARLIER NARRATIVES (1:6–3:29)

Moses introduces his explanation of the Law with a historical review of God's gracious acts. The account begins with Israel's departure from Sinai (cf. Nu 10:11). It does not go back to the events at Sinai nor those of the Exodus from Egypt, though in Deuteronomy 1:30 Moses mentions the events in Egypt as something his listeners would recall. Moreover, the events of Mount Sinai will be taken up in detail in chapters 9–10, and those of the Exodus in chapter 11. They are thus treated in reverse order to their occurrence in the earlier parts of the Pentateuch.

It should be pointed out here that when Moses reflects on the past, he does so, with few exceptions (see below), on the basis of the account of the past already written in the preceding narratives. Moses' view of the past is a "scriptural view." He does not recount events which were not recorded earlier. In other words, he does not assume a knowledge of Israel's history that is independent of the biblical account itself. His focus is on those events already present in the mind of the readers of the Pentateuch. It is important to note this focus because it shows that his audience is not merely those Israelites whom Moses was addressing at a particular time on the plains of Moab. His audience is anyone who has read the earlier portions of the Pentateuch! In this way one can see that Moses' audience, and hence the audience of the Pentateuch, is always the contemporary reader. He is not addressing only those in the past. He speaks directly to the contemporary reader as well.

An interesting confirmation of this feature of the Pentateuch can be found in a few examples in Deuteronomy which do refer to events not recorded earlier in the Pentateuch. For example, in 2:5, 9, 19 the writer mentions that the Lord had given certain sections of land to the descendants of Esau (v. 5), the Moabites (v. 9), and the Ammonites (v. 19). Since none of these events was recorded earlier in the Pentateuch, the writer gives a brief historical account of the events leading up to God's giving these nations their inheritance (vv. 10–12, 20–23). In other words, when relevant historical information is missing, the writer of the Pentateuch supplies the reader with an account of just those events. The writer does not assume that his readers have or would know such information, and thus he supplies it when needed.

The reason Moses' speech focuses here only on the most recent events is that they concern the new generation which is to take possession of the Promised Land. Thus in telling the earlier events, Moses' desire is to cast light on the situation of his own listeners (and that of the readers). They are the new generation. Their forefathers had all died in the wilderness. It is now their task to take up where those before them had failed. Though the narrative is about past events, the events are recounted in order to demonstrate that they are not simply about the "past" but rather about the "beginning" of God's new work. The past is not something that is done and over with; the past is rather the beginning of the future. Throughout the narrative the stress is on the new beginnings of God's acts. The past is prologue to the future. Throughout the narrative the call is for the people to take the land promised to their forefathers.

A. Departure from Sinai (1:6–8; cf. Nu 10–20)

The speech begins by giving the basis of God's dealings with Israel—the promise of the land which God made to the fathers, Abraham, Isaac, and Jacob. It should be noted that the boundaries of the land are those of the original promise in Genesis 15:18–19.

B. Appointment of Leaders (1:9–18; cf. Ex 18; Nu 11)

In this section Moses refers to the narrative in Exodus 18:13–26 (cf. Nu 11:16, 24). In that narrative, Moses, on the advice of his father-in-law, had appointed experienced officials to help in the administration of the nation. One of the central purposes of that narrative was to show that the need for additional leaders in Israel stemmed from God's faithfulness in blessing the nation (cf. Ge 12:2; 15:5; Ex 1:7; Nu 23:10). Note that when Moses retells the events in the present narrative he does not follow the chronological order of the earlier narrative in the Pentateuch but rather inserts a parenthetical narrative from Exodus. The events recorded here in Deuteronomy 1:9–18 (the appointment of leaders) occur in the earlier Exodus narratives (Ex 18:13–26), prior to those events in verses 6–8 (Moses' call to leave Mount Sinai, see Nu 10:11). Consequently, after this parenthetical section about the appointment of leaders (1:9–18), the narrative returns to an account of Israel's leaving Mount Sinai (Horeb) (1:19–46), thus picking up the events from 1:6–8.

Prohibition #276, Dt 1:17, A judge must not be afraid of anyone: "Do not be afraid of anyone."

Prohibition #284, Dt 1:17, A judge should not show partiality in judgment (M. a person who is not learned in the Torah should not be appointed as a judge): "Do not show partiality in judging."

C. The Spies and Israel's Rebellion (1:19–46; cf. Nu 13–14)

This section resumes the events of 1:6–8: the people have left Mount Sinai (Horeb) and are en route to the "hill country of the Amorites" (1:19). They camped at Kadesh Barnea (Wilderness of Paran, Kadesh, Nu 12:16; 13:26). The same events are recounted in Numbers 13. However, Moses tells the events somewhat differently here than in Numbers. Here the people ask to send spies in response to Moses' call to take the land, and Moses approves. In Numbers 13, however, it is the Lord who commands that the spies be sent. This difference is usually explained by merging the two accounts in the following way: When challenged by Moses to take the land (Dt 1:20–21), the people, because of their lack of faith, requested that spies be sent first (v. 22). Moses, who approved their plan (v. 23a), took their request to the Lord (which the text does not mention). The Lord also approved their plan and commanded Moses to appoint the spies (Nu 13:1–2). The Samaritan Pentateuch, an early version of the Hebrew Bible, adds the verses in Deuteronomy 1:20–23a to the beginning of Numbers 13:1, and thus reads the story in this way:

> [Dt 1:20–23a] And Moses said to the sons of Israel, "You have come to the hill country of the Ammorites which the LORD our God has given to us. See now, the LORD your God has put before you the land. Go up and take possession of it as the LORD the God of your fathers has promised to you. Do not be afraid and do not tremble." And they drew near to Moses and said, "Let us send men before us and let them search out the land for us and bring us back a word regarding the way we should go up and about the cities against which we are going." And the matter seemed good to Moses. [Nu 13:1–2] And the LORD said to Moses, "Send men out and let them spy out the land."

Though this is surely not the original text, there are reasonable grounds for assuming that it reflects the original intention behind the final shape of the Pentateuch. Throughout the Pentateuch the writer has supplied numerous comments to bring the final work to a harmonious completion. It is thus unlikely that such a glaring difference would have survived the final composition had it not been understood along lines similar to that of the explanation given above. There is, in fact, some warrant for seeing such a harmonization already in the present form of Numbers. Rashi argued, for example, that the Hebrew syntax of Numbers 13:2 (שְׁלַח־לְךָ) could be read: "As you wish, go ahead and send men to spy out the land," thus presupposing the version of the story given in Deuteronomy 1:19–46.

It is important to note how Moses heightens the foolishness of Israel's failure to trust God by picturing God's care for them as that of a father caring for his son (1:31). As is common in Deuteronomy, lessons are brought home with much more vivid imagery, and sin is depicted not merely as evil but also as the height of folly. These narratives thus prepare the way for Moses' sermon at the close of this section (Dt 4) where he will argue that following the Torah is "wisdom" (Dt 4:6). Hence he can depict sin here as foolishness.

The failure of the people to take the land at the beginning of their sojourn in the wilderness is explained here the same way as in Numbers 13–14, they "did not believe" (Dt 1:32; "did not trust" in NIV; cf. Nu 14:11). This is one of the few times in the Pentateuch when the reader is given an inside look at Israel's actions.

The syntax of Deuteronomy 1:37 suggests that Moses added this reference to his own failure to trust God parenthetically in this section, even though it happened much later (Nu 20). Syntactically, the remark breaks into the Lord's discourse.

In Deuteronomy 1:39 Moses refers first to the people's fear that their "little ones who do not know good and evil" would be taken as spoils of war, and then he refers to God's promise that they would see the Promised Land (Nu 14:31). His reason for stressing that part of the previous narratives in Numbers lies in the fact that now, forty years later, as they stand on the banks of the Jordan preparing to go into the land, the present generation to whom he is speaking were those "little ones." By describing them as those who "do not know good and evil," Moses draws an important connection between entering the Promised Land and the original story of humankind in the Garden of Eden. It is as though Moses wants to show that this new generation is now in much the same position as the first man and woman in the Garden. They "did not know good and evil" and thus had to depend on God to provide for them. As in Deuteronomy 1:31, the picture of God is that of a father or parent providing for his child (cf. Dt 32:6). The Torah which Moses gives to the people is the means whereby God provides for their good (cf. Dt 30:15–16).

A recurring theme in these narratives is the Lord's promise to "fight for" his people. The purpose of stressing this theme is to encourage this new generation to trust God to do for them what he has done for those who have gone before them.

The Israelites came to Kadesh Barnea after leaving Mount Sinai (1:19). After their defeat at the hands of the Amorites (Amalekites and Canaanites), they returned to Kadesh (1:45) and, according to 1:46, dwelt in Kadesh "many days." In the next verse (2:1), they wandered in the hill country of Seir "many days," then traveled beyond Seir (2:8) to Moab and across the Zered Valley (2:13; Nu 21:12). The total time from their stay in Kadesh to their arrival in the Zered Valley was thirty-eight years (Dt 2:14). Since, according to Numbers 20:1, the Israelites were dwelling in Kadesh at the end of the forty years (cf. Nu 20:28—Aaron died, apparently shortly after leaving Kadesh—and Nu 33:38—Aaron died in the 40th year after the Exodus), it is generally supposed either that they dwelt in Kadesh throughout the thirty-eight years or that they, having left Kadesh after their defeat at the hands of the Amalekites (Nu 14), they returned a second time to Kadesh. It should be pointed out, however, that though the Lord had told them to leave Kadesh (Nu 14:25), there is no mention of their doing so (see the commentary above on Nu 14:39–45). The fact that Deuteronomy 1:43–46 states that they disobeyed the Lord and "went up to the hill country," and that they "returned" after the battle and "dwelt in Kadesh many days," suggests that the thirty-eight years were spent in Kadesh. We should not forget that, according to the narrative, the site of Kadesh was geographically adjacent to Seir (Nu 20:16).

Excursus: The Chronology and Location of the Thirty-eight Years

The text is not clear with respect to the sequence of events of Israel's sojourn in Kadesh during the thirty-eight years. Critical scholarship attempts to explain the various versions of the sojourn (in Nu 14; Dt 1–2; and Jdg 11:16–18) in terms of conflicting documents used in the composition of the Pentateuch. Below we have listed S. R. Driver's reconstruction of the two documents (J and D) and their accounts of Israel's sojourn in the wilderness.[1] From our perspective, Driver has stressed the differences in the various accounts at the expense of the similarities. Thus we have also listed the various ways that traditional harmonistic exegesis has explained the sojourn at Kadesh.[2]

1. Critical View (Driver)

a. JE: Numbers 14; Judges 11:16–18

"If the present narrative of JE in Numbers be *complete*, the 38 years in the wilderness will have been spent at Kadesh: nothing is said of the Israelites moving elsewhere; and the circuit round Edom (Nu. 21:4) will have taken place at the close of this period, merely in order to enable the Israelites to reach the E(ast) side of Jordan."[3]

1. The Israelites were commanded to "turn back into the wilderness by the way to the Red Sea" (Nu 14:25), but it is not stated whether they did so after their defeat.
2. The Israelites were still dwelling in Kadesh in the fortieth year (Nu 20:1, 16).
3. The Israelites requested permission to pass through the Edomite territory and were denied (Nu 20:14–21a).
4. The Israelites turned aside and traveled from Kadesh to Mount Hor (Nu 20:22), where Aaron died (Nu 20:23–29).
5. The Israelites left Mount Hor and proceeded "by the way to the Red Sea to compass the land of Edom" (Nu 21:4).
6. The Israelites reached the wilderness on the east side of Moab (Nu 21:13).

b. Dt.: Deuteronomy 1–2

"The 38 years of the wanderings are occupied entirely with circling about Mount Seir."[4]

1. The Israelites were commanded to "turn back into the wilderness by the way to the Red Sea" (Dt 1:40).

---

[1]S. R. Driver, *A Critical and Exegetical Commentary on Deuteronomy*, ICC (Edinburgh: T. & T. Clark, 1895), 32–33.

[2]C. F. Keil, *Pentateuch*, 3:277–97; Robert Jamieson, A. R. Fausset, and David Brown, *A Commentary Critical, Experimental and Practical on the Old and New Testament* (Grand Rapids: Eerdmans, repr. 1945); Carl G. Rasmussen, *NIV Atlas of the Bible* (Grand Rapids: Zondervan, 1989), 91.

[3]Driver, *Deuteronomy*, 32.

[4]Ibid.

2. After their defeat the Israelites dwelt in Kadesh "many days" (Dt 1:46).

3. In obedience to 1:40, the Israelites "turn back to the wilderness by the way to the Red Sea and compass Mount Seir many days" (Dt 2:1).

4. After "enough" time, the Israelites were told to "turn northward" (Dt 2:2b) and along the east border of Edom (2:8), arriving at Zered on the border of Moab thirty-eight years after leaving Kadesh (2:13–14).

2. Wandering from Kadesh and Back (Keil, Jamieson, Rasmussen)

1. The Israelites were commanded to "turn back into the wilderness by the way to the Red Sea" (Nu 14:25), and they refused.

2. After their defeat, the Israelites dwelt in Kadesh "many days," which amounted to a short period of time (Dt 1:46).

3. In obedience to Deuteronomy 1:40 (= Nu 14:25), the Israelites turned southward to the wilderness by the way to the Red Sea and compassed Mount Seir "many days," which amounted to 38 years (Dt 2:1).

4. At the close of this thirty-eight-year period, the Israelites went northward a second time to Kadesh (Nu 20:1, 16).

5. The Israelites requested permission to pass through the Edomite territory and were denied (Nu 20:14–21a).

6. The Israelites turned aside and traveled from Kadesh to Mount Hor (Nu 20:22), where Aaron died (Nu 20:23–29).

7. The Israelites left Mount Hor and proceeded "by the way to the Red Sea to compass the land of Edom" (Nu 21:4–5).

8. After "enough" time, the Israelites were told to "turn northward" (Dt 2:2b), and they did so along the east border of Edom (Dt 2:8) and arrived at Zered on the border of Moab thirty-eight years after first leaving Kadesh (Dt 2:13–14; Nu 21:13). At this time they passed Edom on the east and could gain passage through their land because they were on their weak side.

3. Ainsworth

1. The Israelites were commanded to "turn back into the wilderness by the way to the Red Sea" (Nu 14:25), and they refused for a time. Later, they obeyed (Dt 2:1).

2. After their defeat the Israelites dwelt in Kadesh Barnea "many days," which amounted to a short period of time (Dt 1:46).

3. After that short time, in obedience to 1:40 (= Nu 14:25), the Israelites turned southward to the wilderness by the way to the Red Sea and compassed Mount Seir "many days" (Dt 1:46; 2:1).[5] The "many days" here are the thirty-eight years the Israelites were in the wilderness (Dt 1:22–23; 2:14)[6] The Israelites requested permission to pass through Edomite territory but were denied (Nu 20:14–21a). The Edomites still required Israel to buy supplies from them as they passed by (Dt 2:28–29).

4. At the close of the forty-year period, Israel dwelt in Kadesh (Nu 20:1), which was a different Kadesh from Kadesh Barnea where the spies

[5]Henry Ainsworth, *Annotations upon the Five Bookes of Moses* (London: M. Parsons, 1639), "Numbers," 86, 125.
[6]Ibid., 125.

were sent out (Nu 13–14).[7] This was a site in the Wilderness of Sin where Israel came after Ezion-geber (Nu 33:36; Jdg 11:16).

5. The Israelites turned aside and traveled from Kadesh to Mount Hor (Nu 20:22; 33:37), where Aaron died (Nu 20:23–29).

6. The Israelites returned back from Ezion-geber toward Canaan "by the way of the spies" (Nu 21:1).[8] There they defeated the Canaanite cities (Nu 21:1–3).

7. The Israelites left Mount Hor and proceeded "by the way to the Red Sea to compass the land of Edom" (Nu 21:4–5).

8. After "enough" time, the Israelites were told to "turn northward" (Dt 2:2b) a second time (Nu 21:1), and they did so, this time along the east border of Edom (Dt 2:8), and arrived at Zered on the border of Moab thirty-eight years after first leaving Kadesh (Dt 2:13–14; Nu 21:13).

4. Beitzel

1. The Israelites were commanded to "turn back into the wilderness by the way to the Red Sea" (Nu 14:25), but it is not stated whether they did so after their defeat.

2. The Israelites were still dwelling in Kadesh in the fortieth year (Nu 20:1, 16).[9]

3. The Israelites requested permission to pass through the Edomite territory but were denied (Nu 20:14–21a).

4. The Israelites turned aside and traveled from Kadesh to Mount Hor (Nu 20:22), where Aaron died (Nu 20:23–29).

5. The Israelites left Mount Hor and proceeded "by the way to the Red Sea to compass the land of Edom" (Nu 21:4; Dt 2:8).

6. The Israelites reached the wilderness on the east side of Moab (Nu 21:13; 33:45–49).

D. Passing Through the Transjordan Wilderness
(2:1–23; cf. Nu 21; 32–35)

The events of Israel's thirty-eight years in the wilderness are repeated by reminding the Israelites why the Edomite, Moabite, and Ammonite territories were not taken. These three nations were related to the Israelites and their history through the patriarchal narratives. In regard to these nations God had said, "I will not give you portions of their land because I have given [their portion] to them as an inheritance" (2:5, 9, 19; cf. 19:14). Though it may sound as if these words refer to specific events or statements in the patriarchal narratives, they do not appear to do so. Rather, here for the first time we learn that God has granted these nations an inheritance, along with that of Israel. (The promise of Deir to Esau may, however, be an allusion to Ge 27:39 and 36:8.)

---

[7]Hizquni: "This is not the Kadesh whereof it is said, and you dwelt in Kadesh many days (Deut 1:46), for that Kadesh is El-Paran (Gen 14:6) and is called Kadesh Barnea, and from there the spies were sent out, but this Kadesh in Num 20 is in the wilderness of Sin, in the border of the land of Edom" (*Commentary on the Torah* [Hebrew] [Jerusalem: Mossad Harav Kook, 1988], 480).

[8]Targum Onkelos, ad loc.. Ainsworth, "Numbers," 131.

[9]Barry J. Beitzel, *The Moody Atlas of Bible Lands* (Chicago: Moody Press, 1985), 93.

In the absence of specific evidence from the earlier patriarchal narratives that the Lord had given these lands to these nations, the text supplies its own examples of how these nations had been granted possession of their lands (Dt 2:10–12, 20–23). They took possession of their lands just as the Lord had granted Israel its land—by defeating the former inhabitants and dwelling there in their place. We should note that these comments attribute the inheritance of these nations specifically to the work of the Lord: "The LORD destroyed them from before the Ammonites. . . . The LORD had done the same for the descendants of Esau" (2:21b–22a). It has been suggested that these verses must be later additions to the text since they refer to God's giving Israel its inheritance as something already past.[10] Though that may be the case, it is also possible that this text is intended to be understood as the writing of Moses and that the mention of God's having given Israel its inheritance refers only to those sections of the Transjordan which God had already given to Israel.[11] We should view these short narratives, then, as giving the reader important and relevant background information to understand the text properly. They show that God was also at work in the events of history of the other nations on behalf of his own chosen people.

It is interesting that Numbers 24:17–19 describes the future king to reign in Israel as one who will defeat the Moabites and the sons of Sheth and take possession of Edom. His kingdom will include those nations not yet given to Israel.

This section emphasizes that the whole of the previous generation died during this time (Dt 2:15–16). As such it plays an important role in the narrative by turning the reader's attention to the present generation. It is this generation that Moses now addresses in Deuteronomy.

Though Deuteronomy omits the denial of Israel's request to pass through Edom (Nu 20:14–21), the narrative presupposes it. Moses recounts that they spent "many days going around the hill country of Seir," and that after a time, the Lord instructed them to turn north and go past Edom (the descendants of Esau) and not provoke them to war (Dt 2:1–8).

E. Conquest of the Transjordan (2:24–3:11; cf. Nu 21)

1. Defeat of Sihon (2:24–37)

When Moses retells the story of the conquest of the land of King Sihon, he makes several significant additions to the earlier account in Numbers 21. He first shows, by paraphrasing the account in Numbers 21:21, that Israel's request to pass through Sihon's land was made on the best of terms. It was an offering of peace to the king (Dt 2:26), not an act of war. He adds that Israel had originally offered to buy supplies from Sihon (2:28), something not mentioned in the Numbers account. Furthermore, the additional material in Deuteronomy shows that Israel's intention was not to take Sihon's land as

---

[10]"Ea verba a Samuele aut alio propheta addita sunt ad historiam Mose," Johannes Coccejus, *Opera Omnia Theologica, Exegetica, Didactica, Polemica, Philologica* (Amsterdam: Blaev, 1701), 1:186.

[11]This is supported by the Hebrew syntax. The perfect is used for those lands already taken (2:12) and the participle for those lands yet to be taken from the point of view of the speaker (2:29).

their possession; they wanted only to pass through his land on their way to the Promised Land (2:29). This is perhaps because Numbers 21:26 shows that the land of Sihon belonged to the Moabites and thus was not given to Israel (Dt 2:9). (See comments above on Nu 21:21–32). Most importantly, however, Moses' words here show that God had other intentions. The Lord hardened Sihon's spirit and his heart so that he would resist Israel. This was the first act of God in delivering the land into Israel's hands (Dt 2:30–31), and it is remarkably similar to God's first act of delivering Israel from Egypt (Ex 7:3).

Thus in Deuteronomy Moses sees beyond the events previously recorded in Numbers to their underlying significance. God was at work in these events and he was bringing about his purposes. Such a stress on the work of God behind Israel's actions helps account for the severity of Israel's actions in taking this land: "At that time we took all his towns and completely destroyed them—men, women, and children" (Dt 2:34), a feature of the battle not mentioned in Numbers. The Bible is clear that Israel was acting on God's behalf and that the destruction they wreaked on those in the land was the result of divine wrath on those people's sins (Ge 15:16). As Moses will go on to show in this book, Israel itself was not exempt from the same divine judgment (Dt 27–28) and was later to experience a similar fate (30:1).

This event thus marked the beginning of the work of God in giving Israel their inheritance. Coupled with the idea of the passing of the previous generation, the theme of these earlier narratives, is that of the "new work" that God was now beginning with the present generation: "This day I will begin" (2:25). The key terms in this section center on the idea of the new beginnings (2:25, 31; 3:23).

2. Defeat of Og (3:1–11)

Moses repeats the account of the defeat of Og from Numbers 21:33–35 with one significant additional remark: "So the LORD our God also gave Og king of Bashan into our hands" (3:3). This remark stresses the theme of the earlier narrative account of Sihon's defeat. In the present speech, Moses clearly wants to reiterate that the defeat of Og was the Lord's work. Israel's success was not of their own making. This message could not be lost on those who listened to Moses on that day, nor does the author of the Pentateuch intend it to be lost on those who read his book.

Verses 6–11 go beyond the earlier account of this battle in Numbers (Nu 21:33–35) to stress the obedience and success of Israel in taking the Transjordan as well as the considerable size of the kingdom of Og. As was the case with the kingdom of Sihon, the whole of the kingdom of Og was destroyed. (On the severity of Israel's actions, see the comments above on Dt 2:24–37.)

F. Transjordan Given to Reuben and Gad (3:12–20)

Recalling events from Numbers 32, Moses reiterates the division of the land among Reuben, Gad, and Manasseh. He adds a historical note about Jair's conquest of part of this land, which had been recounted in Numbers 32:41. The Numbers passage had not specified that the region Jair took was considered part of the territory of Bashan, thus leaving the possible misimpression that Jair had taken the land of Gilead. When recounted again here, the text adds specifically that Jair's conquest was in Bashan and thus a part of the land given to the tribe of Manasseh (Dt 3:13). Later biblical writers identified Bashan and Gilead in such a way that Gilead appears as a more general area within which Bashan was situated (e.g., Jdg 10:4; cf. 1Ki 4:13; Jos 13:30). There was apparently another individual by the name Jair in the time of the Judges (see Jdg 10:3–4).

As Moses here looks back on the first stages of the conquest, he views the plan of God for this people from a new perspective. Whereas in his earlier description he had stressed Israel's role in their taking the land (Nu 32), he now views this event from the perspective of the Lord's giving Israel rest (Dt 3:20). Moses would again use the term *rest* to portray Israel's entry into the Promised Land as a time of rest and enjoyment of God's blessing (Dt 12:10). This theme is clearly reminiscent of God's original intention of the "rest" (נוח) enjoyed in the Garden of Eden (Ge 2:1–3 [שׁבת], 15 [נוח]). The conquest of the land is viewed as a return to God's blessing in Eden.

G. Joshua Replaces Moses (3:21–29)

As he continues his opening speech, Moses adds two important details regarding the events he has been recounting that were not mentioned in the earlier account. The first is the reminder of the encouragement he had given to Joshua: "Do not be afraid of them; the LORD your God himself will fight for you" (3:21–22). The importance of adding this element to the narrative is clearly to provide the same encouragement for the readers. As Moses speaks to Joshua, he also intends the reader to get the message. The second additional element is Moses' prayer for clemency and permission to go into the Promised Land (Dt 3:23–25). Though the request was denied, Moses was allowed to see the land from the top of Mount Pisgah.

These two short narratives provide an important bridge to the subsequent books in the OT canon (cf. Jos 1:8–9). The central theme of the book of Joshua is grounded in these two speeches of Moses.

III. MOSES' SPEECH: CALL TO OBEDIENCE (4:1–40)

Having surveyed past events leading up to this moment, Moses is now to part ways with the people and to allow Joshua to take them into the land. He thus turns to explain the Law that they are to take with them. He would not enter the land and guide the people in God's Law, so he now gives them his explanation of the Law to use in his absence. His central purpose in this section is to draw out the chief ideas of the Sinai narratives, Exodus 19–33.

A. The Torah Is Wisdom (4:1–14)

As frequently happens in Deuteronomy, Moses focuses on only a few central ideas taken from the previous narratives. His purpose is to give a general summary. First he turns to the issue of obedience to the will of God. This he explains within the context of "wisdom." What other nations sought in attempting to gain wisdom, Israel had found in the revelation of the will of God at Sinai. Just as in Exodus 33:16 God's presence distinguished Israel from all the nations, so here it is divine wisdom given in the Torah that singles them out. Moses reminds Israel that the great display of God's power in the giving of the Law at Sinai (cf. Ex 20:18–19) was to underscore the basic foundation of their wisdom—the fear of the Lord (cf. Ex 20:20). As is frequently repeated in Scripture, "the fear of the LORD is the beginning of wisdom" (Ps 111:10).

B. Warning Against Idolatry (4:15–24)

The second central idea that Moses stresses in this introduction is the warning against idolatry. Just as Israel had easily slipped into idolatry, even while at Mount Sinai (Ex 32), so Moses is careful to warn them of the ever-present danger of further apostasy. It should be recalled that the warning against idolatry is the first of the Ten Commandments (Ex 20:2–6) and the first command in the Covenant Code (Ex 20:23a). Referring to their failure to trust God in the wilderness (Nu 20), for a second time Moses here lays the responsibility of past failure on the shoulders of the people: "The LORD was angry with me because of you" (v. 21; cf. 3:26). In the Numbers passage it is clear that ultimately Moses was denied entry into the Promised Land because he (and Aaron) "did not believe" (Nu 20:12). Here in Deuteronomy, however, he reminds the people that it was their own murmuring and complaints that provided the occasion for his unbelief (Nu 20:3–6). Moses is not simply justifying his actions, nor is he seeking merely to cast the blame on the people. He seems rather to be laying a basis for reiterating a lesson found throughout the earlier narratives: even though Israel has had godly leadership (e.g., Moses or Joshua), if the people failed to trust God, that leadership would be to no avail. Thus he warns them sternly: "Watch yourselves lest you forget the covenant of the LORD your God" (Dt 4:23).

C. The Exile (4:25–31)

In the same breath that he warns the people of the impending exile, Moses encourages the people by the reminder of God's great mercy. In no uncertain terms, Moses warns the Israelites that if they persisted in idolatry, they would be taken off the land and scattered among all the nations in exile. But in the midst of his description of the exile (4:25–28), Moses turns his attention to Israel's return from exile. When Israel returns to the Lord, the Lord will return them to the land promised to the fathers (vv. 29–31). Moses here expresses the same ideas underlying the narratives dealing with Israel's first foray into idolatry, the golden calf (Ex 32). In that narrative, God was angry with Israel and was ready to cast them off, but Moses intervened and the Lord showed himself to be long-suffering and forgiving (Ex 33:19).

D. God's Presence with Israel (4:32–40)

Just as in Exodus 33:15 the presence of God among his people marked them as a unique nation, so in the present narrative Moses returns to the theme of God's presence to underscore his mercy. Has there ever been a people who has heard the voice of the one true God speaking with them in their midst (Dt 4:32–33)? Moses here refers to God's speaking with Israel at Sinai (Ex 19–20). Has there ever been a people among whom God has displayed great signs and wonders and delivered them in mighty wars (Dt 4:34)? Moses here refers to God's delivering Israel from the Egyptians (Ex 4–12). God did all this for Israel because he loved them and had chosen them as far back as the time of the patriarchs (Dt 4:37–38).

Why does Moses again stress God's love and mercy? Because it is the basis of the call for obedience (Dt 4:39–40). Moses' speech is punctuated with the call for a wholehearted obedience to the will of God.

It is not without purpose that at this point in the speech Moses refers to the patriarchs (Dt 4:37). Throughout the Pentateuch the patriarchs, particularly Abraham, are used as examples of what it means to "keep God's laws" (Ge 26:5). Thus when the Pentateuch calls for obedience to God's "statutes and commandments," it should be remembered that the foremost example of one who kept these "statutes and commandments" is Abraham (Ge 26:5), a man who lived by faith (15:6). Thus from the perspective of the whole Pentateuch, the reader is here being called upon to live a life like Abraham, a man of faith. Faith is thus seen as the means of "keeping the Law." (See the Introduction above for further discussion of this theme in the Pentateuch.)

IV. CITIES OF REFUGE (4:41–43)

This section of text is actually a narrative insertion in the midst of Moses' speech. It deals with the allotment of cities of refuge to the tribes on the east side of the Jordan (cf. Nu 35:6, 9–34). Since the topic of the cities of refuge is treated in detail in Deuteronomy 19, it is curious that mention of it should be made here. There is, however, some justification for its being included here. Moses has been rehearsing the events dealing with the conquest of the area east of the Jordan. It is appropriate, then, to turn immediately to the legislation specifically relevant to that conquest.

There is more to it than this, however. If this were the only reason, we would have expected it to be placed in chapter 3, which narrates the conquest of the east Jordan territory. A further explanation is that since this narrative deals specifically with the question of the "manslayer," it is appropriate that it is inserted immediately before the restatement of the Ten Commandments. In being placed here, then, within the context of the book, it provides a helpful qualification of the otherwise unqualified prohibition, "You shall not kill" (Dt 5:17). Thus the narrative plays an important role in providing an interpretive context for the law dealing with capital punishment.

V. GIVING OF THE LAW (4:44–5:33 [MT 30])

A. The Setting of the Law (4:44–49)

Much of what has already been recounted in chapters 1–3 is here repeated in summary form. We should note that it is cast in the form of a narration about Moses and is not a part of Moses' own discourse. The repetition found here is thus part of the book's composition and not part of Moses' speech to the people. As such this short summary plays an important role in guiding the reader through the book. Its purpose is to distinguish between the introductory material of the first three chapters and the exposition of the Law itself in the subsequent chapters.

B. Introduction to the Law: The Covenant at Sinai (5:1–5)

After the narrative introduction (4:44–49), Moses now provides a rhetorical introduction which supplies a context for his repetition of the

earlier laws. He is particularly intent on driving home the point that the
covenant made with Israel at Sinai was the immediate responsibility of the
present generation. It was not a covenant made to earlier generations ("our
fathers") but to those of the present generation who had stood at the foot of
Mount Sinai and heard the voice of God. From the previous narratives in
Deuteronomy and in the Pentateuch, we know that this generation of
Israelites were still children when the original covenant was given at Sinai.
Nevertheless, Moses treats them rightfully as those who were present and
who still had a vivid recollection of God's power. It should be noted that
according to Deuteronomy 11:2ff., this generation (as children) saw God's
glory in Egypt and in the wilderness but their children did not. The first
generation in Egypt and the second, their children (the present generation),
saw the great displays of God's glory. The next generation (the third),
however, did not. The importance of placing this reminder at this stage in
the narrative can be seen in the fact that the motivation given for the
prohibition of idolatry in the next section is its threat to the children of "the
third and fourth generation" (5:9).

This generation of Israelites is thus reminded that the Ten Commandments which follow have as their primary goal to preserve the worship of
God throughout the future generations.

On the relationship of this passage to Exodus 19–20, see the comments
above on Exodus 19:16–25.

C. The Ten Commandments (5:6–22 [MT 19])

The Ten Commandments are repeated here to provide the context for
the discussion which follows: Moses' explication of the Law. This passage is,
as it were, the text for Moses' sermon which follows. The Ten Commandments are repeated almost verbatim from Exodus 20:1–17. As is true of most
texts in Scripture, however, the same material is here found in a different
context, and thus its sense may vary slightly from its earlier statement. This
shift in meaning is, of course, facilitated by the fact that the wording of some
of these ten laws differs from that of Exodus. In any event, we should not
merely suppose that these important laws were repeated without purpose.
We should seek to understand them in their new context of Moses' speech in
Deuteronomy.

First, the introductory words, "I am the LORD your God who brought
you up out of Egypt," are the same as in Exodus, even though in the forty
years that had intervened, the LORD had done many more things for Israel.
Though Deuteronomy 1–3 has updated God's acts of grace and mercy
toward his people, the beginning call to obedience is still the one great act of
deliverance of the people from Egypt.

Second, the prohibition of idolatry, which marks the opening of the
commandments in both Exodus and Deuteronomy, takes on a more realistic
tone in its present context in Deuteronomy. The preceding narratives of
Exodus and Numbers have stressed Israel's continual backsliding into
idolatry. After such narratives, the relevance of the prohibition of idolatry is
not difficult to appreciate. Furthermore, the visitation of God's punishment
on the "third and fourth generation" (5:9) takes on new meaning when
spoken to the "second" generation, as is the case here in Deuteronomy (see
comments above on Dt 5:1–5). Thus this second generation was being called

upon to teach God's ways to the third generation (cf. Dt 6:2). The context of Deuteronomy, then, provides a concrete basis for understanding these divine warnings. "The things revealed belong to us and to our children forever" (Dt 29:29 [MT 28]).

Third, the concept of rest on the seventh day is extended in Deuteronomy to include one's whole household and servants. Israel is to remember their time of service in Egypt and thus treat their own servants like themselves. The rest called for in Exodus could have been applied in only a limited way, but it is here made to apply in the most general way to everyone. In the same way, the reason for the Sabbath is now stated to be God's deliverance of the people from Egypt, rather than God's rest at Creation. Thus God's special acts of deliverance are moved to the center of Israel's attention in the motivation given for keeping the Law.

Fourth, the phrase "that it may go well with you" is added to the commandment regarding honoring one's parents (5:16). Though a seemingly minor addition, it shows that merely dwelling in the land was not God's ultimate goal for his people. He wanted their living in the land to be "good" as well. This addition is consistent with the overall perspective of Deuteronomy that the land which God is giving to Israel is the "good land" which they are to enjoy.

In this way the author of the Pentateuch is able to tie together the themes of God's "good land" in the early chapters of Genesis with Israel's enjoyment of the land in the conquest. In the conquest of the land, Israel is thus shown returning to God's "good land" created and prepared for them since the beginning.

Fifth, the numbering of the Ten Commandments in Exodus and Deuteronomy is problematic (see the introductory comments above on Ex 20:1–17). Though it is not clearly reflected in the NIV, the Hebrew form of the last commandment (Dt 5:21 [MT 18]), separates it into two distinct commandments. In the Hebrew text, the conjunction *waw*, "and," is added to the last five statements, thus separating them into distinct and discrete utterances: "You shall not covet your neighbor's wife" *and* "You shall not set your desire on your neighbor's house. . . ." Moreover, whereas Exodus 20:14 uses the same word *desire* for both statements, Deuteronomy 5:21 (MT 18) distinguishes the vocabulary of the two commandments. Finally, the object of the "desire" which is prohibited in the two commands in Exodus 20:14 is reversed in Deuteronomy 5:21 (MT 18). As stated in Exodus 20:14, first the desire of "a neighbor's house" is prohibited and then follow a list of items that are further prohibited: "a neighbor's wife, servant, female servant, and finally all that belongs to your neighbor." In Exodus 20:14, the list of items could be understood as an enumeration of that which is meant in the phrase "your neighbor's house." Is the neighbor's wife considered merely a part of his property? The text in Exodus is ambiguous. In Deuteronomy 5:21 (MT 18), however, the text is clear: the neighbor's wife is not part of his property. The objects of both commandments are reversed. The first prohibition is specifically stated to be desiring (חמד) "your neighbor's wife." This is followed by the more general prohibition of desiring (אוה) "your neighbor's house," followed by the same list as in Exodus 20:14: "his servant, female servant, . . . and all that belongs to him." The only change in this specific list is that the term *neighbor's wife* has been replaced by the term *his field*.

Deuteronomy 5:21 (MT 18), then, is clearly to be read as two distinct prohibitions. The first is, "You should not desire your neighbor's wife," and the second is, "You should not desire your neighbor's property." Consequently, the ambiguity of Exodus 20:14 is clarified in Deuteronomy. The net effect of the sense given to these last two commandments in Deuteronomy is that the prohibition of desiring one's "neighbor's wife" is made more distinct from that of desiring his property. There is thus no possibility of understanding the neighbor's wife as his property. The wife is considered quite distinct from his property. If the Exodus passage had been ambiguous on this point, all doubt is removed in Deuteronomy.

The question of the status of the female servant, which still remains somewhat ambiguous in this passage, is later treated in Deuteronomy 15:12–18 (MT 17).

> **Prohibition #347**, Lev 18:20, One must not have a sexual relationship with the wife of another: "Do not have sexual relations with your neighbor's wife." Cf. Ex 20:14; Dt 5:17 (EVV 18), "You shall not commit adultery."
>
> **Prohibition #266**, Dt 5:18 (EVV 21), One must not even desire another's possessions: "You shall not set your desire on your neighbor's house."

D. Moses Appointed as Mediator (5:23–33 [MT 20–30])

Referring back to the response of the people at Sinai in Exodus 20:18–21, Moses recounts and expounds on their fear at hearing God's voice and on his consequent role as mediator between God and the people. In this text, the fear of the people is seen as a positive sign. The purpose of their fear was to provoke them to seek after God and to turn away from idols. It is stressed here because within the context of Deuteronomy, "fear" is central to the concept of divine wisdom. The Lord's words in 5:29 (MT 26), however, show that the fear exhibited at Sinai was not yet the kind of fear that would produce obedience: The Lord said, "Oh, that their hearts would be inclined to fear me and keep all my commands always." The narrative in Exodus 20 is clear that the Lord's words expressed only a wish. The subsequent narratives in Exodus and Numbers further demonstrate that their fear was of a different kind. Nevertheless, Moses returns in this narrative to the notice of the fear of the people at Sinai because in the following exhortation the "fear of the LORD" is the foundation for obedience to the will of God (e.g., 6:2). Once again the reference to events in the earlier pentateuchal narratives serves as an introduction to the subsequent list of laws.

VI. GENERAL PRINCIPLES OF LAW (6:1–11:32)

In the speeches of Moses which follow, there appears to be a conscious effort to develop the central ideas of the first sections of the Ten Commandments that are given in chapter 5—wholehearted worship of God and forsaking idols.

A. Explication of the First Section of the First Commandment: Fear God and Keep His Commandments (6:1–25)

Fear (i.e., a deeply felt respect for the Lord) is to be taught to all generations as the basis for godly living and obedience. The result of obedience is blessing—living long and well in the land. The notion of blessing stressed here is that of Genesis 1:28: "Be fruitful, multiply, and fill the land." God's covenant with Israel was to be the fulfillment of God's original purposes in Creation. The book of Joshua will show that though there were initial successes, the people ultimately were not able to keep the covenant and hence did not fully enjoy its blessings.

Ironically, the fear of God which produces obedience is here called "love"—"You shall love the LORD your God with all your heart" (Dt 6:5). It is thus clear that the "fear of the LORD" which Moses has in mind is not that which flees from his presence but that which longs to do his will. It is a fear that produces not obeisance but obedience, not worry but worship (6:13). The central concern of Moses in this section is clearly the propensity of the people to fall into idolatry. Hence, what he stresses beyond the need for love and reverence is the absolute "oneness" of God. There are no "other gods" beside him.

Thus Moses begins his exhortation with a summation of one of the most central ideas in all of Scripture: "Hear, O Israel: The LORD our God, the LORD is one." This statement, called the "Shema" in later Jewish tradition, is considered the second of the 613 laws of the Torah. Jesus referred to it as the "first" of all the commandments (Mk 12:29). Much discussion has focused on the meaning of the phrase "the LORD is one" in this verse. The sense of the phrase becomes quite clear if read in the light of the strict prohibition of idolatry and polytheism in the present text of Deuteronomy. The intent of the phrase is to give a clear statement of the principle of monotheism, that is, that there is one God and only one God who exists. It thus has also been translated, "The LORD is our God, the LORD alone."[12] It is important to note, however, that the stress on the uniqueness of God over against the worship of false idols is not stated in such a way as to exclude the equally important notion of the divine Trinity. The word used for "one" in this passage does not mean "singleness" but "unity." The same word is used in Genesis 2:24, where the husband and wife in marriage are said to be "one flesh." Thus, while this verse is intended as a clear and concise statement of monotheism, it does not address or exclude the concept of the Trinity.

> **Command #2**, Dt 6:4, One must believe that God is one: "Hear, O Israel."
>
> **Command #3**, Dt 6:5, One must love God: "You shall love the Lord your God."
>
> **Command #10**, Dt 6:7, One must recite the *Shema* each morning: "And you shall speak them."
>
> **Command #11**, Dt 6:7, One must teach the Torah: "And you shall teach them to your sons."
>
> **Command #12**, Dt 6:8, One must bind *tefillin* on the head: "And they shall be bands between your eyes."
>
> **Command #13**, Dt 6:8, One must bind *tefillin* on the hand: "You shall bind them for signs upon your hands."
>
> **Command #15**, Dt 6:9, One must fix a *mezuzah* on the door: "You shall write them upon the doorpost of your house."
>
> **Command #4**, Dt 6:13, One must fear God: "You shall fear the Lord your God."

---

[12]*Tanakh: The Holy Scriptures. The New JPS Translation According to the Traditional Hebrew Text* (Philadelphia: Jewish Publication Society, 1988), 284.

Command #7, Dt 6:13, One must swear by the name of God: "And you shall swear by his name." (Cf. Dt 10:20.)

Command #64, Dt 6:16, One must not try the Lord: "Do not test the Lord your God."

B. Explication of the Second Section of the First Commandment: Separation from the Gods of Other Nations (7:1–26)

This passage weaves together sections of Exodus (19:1–7; 23:20–33) as a means of elaborating on the importance of separation from the nations. The references to the first commandment are quite clear. Israel is called to forsake any possibility of following after the idols of the nations and to remember the only God who keeps "his covenant of love to a thousand generations of those who love him" (Dt 7:9). In this section Moses appears intent on stressing the notion that separation from the gods of other nations necessarily entails separation from the nations themselves: "Make no treaty with them, and show them no mercy. Do not intermarry with them" (7:2–3). Moses' statements in these texts, which sound severe on the face of it, should be read in the light of the narratives of Rahab and Ruth—both Canaanite women who married into the families of Israel (Jos 6:25 and the book of Ruth; note also the narrative of the conversion of the gentile sailors and Ninevites in the book of Jonah). Moses' concern is with the effect of joining in marriage and treaties with the Canaanites, who practice idolatry, "for they will turn your sons away from following me to serve other gods" (Dt 7:4). Thus he is not speaking of those Canaanites who actually forsook their idols and followed the Lord. Furthermore, Moses also seems intent on stressing the fact that separation from these pagan gods also entails a refusal to allow the practice of their religion in their midst: "Break down their altars, smash their sacred stones" (7:5).

Command #185, Dt 7:5, Remove idolatry from your midst: "Break down their altars."

Prohibition #48, Dt 7:2, One must not make a covenant with the Canaanites: "Make no treaty with them."

Prohibition #50, Dt 7:2, One must show no mercy to idolaters: "Show them no mercy."

Prohibition #52, Dt 7:3, One must not intermarry with idolaters: "Do not intermarry with them."

Moses traces the underlying concern for Israel's worship of God back to their election. Israel was God's "treasured possession" (7:6). They were unique among the nations, just as God was unique among the false idols. He alone was God, and Israel alone was his chosen people. Lest their be any reason for Israel's pride to gain a foothold, however, Moses quickly adds: "The LORD did not set his affection on you and choose you because you were more numerous than other people, for you were the fewest of all peoples" (7:7). The basis of God's election of Israel was God's love, not Israel's greatness (7:8).

The fact that the total conquest of the land would not be quick has already been anticipated in Exodus 23:27–33. Both here and in Exodus the reason given is the same. God would not allow them to destroy the land totally until they had grown to sufficient size to care for it adequately.

Nevertheless, when Israel went in to take the land, it was promised that the defeat of the people of the land would be "quick" (Dt 4:26; 9:3). We know from later books of the Bible (e.g., Joshua) that Israel fought against and quickly defeated the enemy, although some areas remained unconquered for generations (cf. Jos 15:63).

> **Prohibition #58**, Dt 7:21, One must not fear the enemy: "Do not be terrified by them."
>
> **Prohibition #22**, Dt 7:25, One must not covet the value of idols: "Do not covet the silver and gold on them [idols]."
>
> **Prohibition #25**, Dt 7:26, One must not use anything associated with idolatry: "You shall not bring the abomination into your house."

C. Warning Against Forgetting the Lord (8:1–20)

In this section, Moses first recalls God's provision for the people during their sojourn of forty years in the wilderness. This time of forty years is considered a time of affliction and testing, "to know what was in your heart, whether you would keep his commands" (8:2). As in Exodus, the gift of manna is viewed here as one of God's tests to see "whether they will follow [his] instructions" (Ex 16:4). The manna is presented here as a test similar to that of the Tree of Knowledge of Good and Evil in the Garden (Ge 2:16–17). It is fitting therefore that in this section Moses also describes the Promised Land and the blessings of the people living there in terms reminiscent of the Garden of Eden in Genesis: "So that you may live and increase and enter and possess the land . . . [8:1; cf. Ge 1:28]. For the LORD your God is bringing you into a good land—a land with streams and pools of water" (8:7; cf. Ge 1:9–10; 2:10–14). Just as the Genesis narratives used God's act of providing clothing for Adam and Eve to demonstrate his care for humankind after they were cast out of the Garden (Ge 3:21), so God's care for Israel in the wilderness is pictured here in his providing for their clothing (Dt 8:4). Moreover, the same picture of God as a loving father, which permeates the early chapters of Genesis (see comments above on Ge 1), is recalled again here: "As a man disciplines his son, so the LORD your God disciplines you" (Dt 8:5; cf. 32:6).

If Moses is intentionally linking the manna and the Tree of Knowledge of Good and Evil, then it is all the more significant that in this text he also links the manna with the Word of God: "Man does not live on bread alone but on every word that comes from the mouth of the LORD" (8:3). Throughout these allusions to past events, Moses carefully weaves earlier narratives together with those at the close of the book. In this passage, then, the story of God's sending the manna becomes a picture of the first test of humanity in the Garden, that is, the Tree of Knowledge of Good and Evil. The manna is God's way of testing Israel in the wilderness just as the Tree was God's way of testing the man and woman in the Garden. Since the manna is also identified with God's Word, a further association between God's word and the Tree of Knowledge of Good and Evil may also be implied. What was lost in the Garden is being restored in the Torah, the word of God. Thus near the close of the book (Dt 30:15), Moses depicts the Torah as a return to the Tree of Knowledge of Good and Evil: "See, I put before you today life, the good, and death, the evil." Obedience to the Torah is seen as the key to enjoying once again the blessings of the good land and of avoiding the curse of death (8:20).

> **Command #19**, Dt 8:10, One must give a blessing after eating: "And you shall eat and be satisfied and bless the Lord your God."

D. Illustrations from Israel's Past (9:1–10:11)

Moses now uses his illustrations from the past to support his central lesson that Israel should live a life of constant vigilance before God. He turns first to the incident of the golden calf recorded in Exodus 32. The earlier rehearsals of past events had focused on God's faithfulness. The present illustrations focus on Israel's failure and faithlessness. They come primarily from Exodus and thus move further back in time than the earlier historical introduction found in Deuteronomy (Dt 1–3) ,which began by recounting events from the book of Numbers.

1. Introduction (9:1–6)

Moses begins with a reminder of what the previous pentateuchal narratives have repeatedly stressed—Israel's possession of the land was not a reward given them on account of their own righteousness. The land was to be taken from the other nations "because of their wickedness" (9:5). It was to be given to Israel "to accomplish what he swore to [their] fathers, to Abraham, Isaac, and Jacob," that is, as a fulfillment of God's promise to the fathers (9:6). We should remember that a central part of the promise to the fathers was that "all the peoples on earth will be blessed through you" (Ge 12:3). Thus, in terms of God's ultimate purposes, God's driving the nations out of the land and giving it to Israel was part of God's ongoing plan to bring blessing to all nations, including, ironically, those who were now being driven out of the land.

In this speech, Moses leaves the people (and the reader) with a clear understanding that possession of the land was based on God's grace, not Israel's own righteousness (9:6). He thus anticipates the views of the later prophets, who based their hope in the future on God's faithfulness to his promises and not on the righteousness of "a stiff-necked people" (9:6b). For example, Ezekiel looked beyond the judgment of God on his people to a future time when God would fulfill his promises to the fathers "for the sake of [his] holy name, which [Israel] had profaned among the nations" (Eze 36:22). At that time, says God through Ezekiel, "the nations will know that I am the LORD . . . when I show myself holy through you before their eyes" (Eze 36:23). It is significant, then, that in the narrative here in Deuteronomy 9, Moses closes his account of the incident of the golden calf by recounting his prayer not only for the people of Israel but also on behalf of the nations who had heard of God's dealings with his people (9:26–29).

2. The Golden Calf (9:7–21)

In retelling the story of Sinai and Israel's breach of covenant in making an idol of the golden calf, Moses lays the same stress on how quickly the people fell into idolatry. As the Lord told Moses: "Your people whom you brought out of Egypt have become corrupt. They have turned away quickly from what I commanded them and have made a cast idol for themselves"

(9:12). His purpose is to emphasize the importance of constant vigilance. The people's heart can turn away from God when it is least expected. Certainly their standing at the foot of Mount Sinai while the prohibitions of idolatry were being written on the stone tablets was not a likely place for instigating the worship of the golden calf. Nevertheless, it happened then, thus serving as a cogent warning of how quickly and unexpectedly the heart of the people can go astray.

Moses also alludes to other places in the Torah where Israel's failure to trust God was manifest: Taberah, Massah, and Kibroth Hattaavah (9:22), and then he turns briefly to Kadesh Barnea (vv. 23–24). God's words to Israel at Kadesh Barnea are important in this context because they express the central themes of the whole Pentateuch. At Kadesh, Israel rebelled against the will of God and hence did not put their faith in him. This reference to Israel's lack of "faith" (NIV "trust") is central to the argument of the Pentateuch. For the writer, the motivation for Israel's actions goes far deeper than mere "disobedience" to the Law. Their disobedience was a disobedience symptomatic of a lack of faith. Unlike Abraham, a man of faith (Ge 15:6), to whom these texts repeatedly allude, the people of Israel were unable or unwilling to walk with God in simple faith. This was Israel's chronic source of failure. Moses thus returns to the theme of faith and simple trust in God throughout these writings.

Returning to the incident at Sinai, Moses recounts his prayer in behalf of the people (Dt 9:25–29). Within this text, Moses' prayer serves as a general statement of his concern for the people throughout the whole forty years in the wilderness. It is significant that Moses' prayer does not stress their "righteousness" but rather God's righteousness: "Remember your servants Abraham, Isaac, and Jacob. Overlook the stubbornness of this people, their wickedness and their sin" (9:27). Moreover, God's concerns for all the nations, a principal part of the Abrahamic covenant (Ge 12:3), can also be seen in Moses' words: "Otherwise, the country from which you brought us will say, 'Because the LORD was not able to take them into the land he had promised them'" (9:28). The prayer of Moses, then, becomes a means for the writer to turn our attention to the promises to Abraham and to view the present warnings from that broader perspective.

3. New Tablets at Sinai (10:1–5)

In order to show that the Lord heard the prayer of Moses and reestablished the covenant with them, Moses further recounts the making of two new tablets for the Ten Commandments. When repeating these events, already recorded in Exodus 34, Moses adds a detail not specifically mentioned earlier. He says that in addition to the stone tablets he also made a wooden box in which to keep them. This wooden box, or ark, is either the same as the ark of the covenant which Bezalel made for the tabernacle (Ex 37:1–2) and in which the tablets were eventually placed (40:20), or it is a different and temporary storage box for the tablets. Those who attempt to understand this wooden box as the ark of the covenant commonly suppose that Moses' narrative does not follow a strict chronology. If read in a strictly chronological order, it would appear that Bezalel made the ark of the covenant after Moses had been given the new tablets (37:1–2). The ark for the stone tablets, however, appears to have been made before Moses went up the mountain to receive the new tablets (Dt 10:3a).

However, it is not necessary to resort to such an expediency in order to identify this wooden box with the ark of the covenant. It is possible to understand Moses to say here that before he went up the mountain to receive the new tablets, he began work on the wooden box; that is, according to Exodus 25:10, he had instructed Bezalel how to make it. After he returned from the mountain, Bezalel completed the ark (37:1) and the new tablets were placed inside it (40:20). It should be noted that the text of Deuteronomy 10:1–6 does not say specifically that Moses took the wooden box with him onto the mountain. It says only that he took the stone tablets with him and that upon returning from the mountain he placed them in the ark. It is possible, then, to read the text chronologically and to understand this wooden box to be the ark of the covenant.

We should note that the parenthetical mention of the ark of the covenant in the following section (Dt 10:6–9) further suggests that the writer intends the reader to identify the wooden ark in this passage with the ark of the covenant. Thus some such understanding of the "ark" as that proposed above was apparently a part of the author's own reading of these narratives.

4. Parenthesis: Itinerary in the Wilderness (10:6–9)

Moses is concerned to show that the priesthood of Aaron and the Levites was also restored after the incident of the golden calf (cf. Dt 9:20). He thus inserts this parenthetical narrative into the account of the events at Sinai. The narrative recounts God's establishment of the house of Levi as priests before the Lord.

5. Conclusion: Dismissal from Mount Sinai (10:10–11)

At the conclusion of his speech, Moses states what his previous words have already suggested. God was gracious to the people; that is, "It was not his will to destroy [them]" (10:10). Furthermore, God intended his people to enjoy the blessings of his promises to the fathers. God's past dealings with Israel has now become the basis for their trust and obedience in the present.

E. Admonition to Fear the Lord (10:12–22)

Moses here drives home the lesson of the preceding narrative. Israel is called upon to fear God, walk in his ways, love him, and serve him with a whole heart. These are the central ideas not only of Deuteronomy but of the whole Pentateuch in its final shape. Thus the writer gives full expression here to his central concerns. Because of God's grace and love for Israel, Israel was to be gracious and kind to others. In view of their immediate past, for Israel to follow in God's ways would mean a fundamental change of heart. Such a change of heart, envisioned by Moses for his people, is described as "circumcision of the heart" (10:16), an idea he will return to in 30:6, where his focus extends far beyond the present events and this immediate generation (cf. 30:1ff.). The ideas Moses appears to be working with here and in chapter 30 are remarkably similar to those of the new covenant promises in the later prophets (e.g., Jer 31:31–34 and Eze 36:22–27). This is merely one more example of the frequent convergence of the message of the Pentateuch and that of the Prophets.

Command #207, Dt 10:19, You must love the sojourners: "You are to love those who are aliens."

Command #6, Dt 10:20, One must cling to God: "And to him you shall cling."

F. Conclusion: Call to Love God and Obey His Will (11:1–32)

Thus far Moses has given an introduction to the collection of laws and judgments which follow in this book. His purpose has been to set forth two clear alternatives. Either Israel must obey the will of God and love him with all their heart, or they cannot continue to enjoy his blessings.

Here at the conclusion of the introduction to the collection of laws, Moses recalls what these people had seen God do to the Egyptians "with their own eyes" (11:7). He appears to want to emphasize that it was they "and not their children" who saw the mighty works of God. If we remember the larger context of the Pentateuch, we will recall that Moses is here addressing the "new generation," those whose parents had died in the wilderness. Thus those in this generation were only children themselves when they saw God's mighty acts. In fact, it was this generation who were the "firstborn" children whose lives were delivered in the night of the Exodus (Ex 12:21).

Having reminded them of their own participation in God's work, Moses turns to the responsibility given them as parents and guardians of the next generation, their children, who had not witnessed "with their own eyes" the great acts of God. For that generation, and for all subsequent ones, God's great acts were not to be seen "with their own eyes," as had been the case for the first generation, but were to be "seen" now in the words of Scripture. It was to be in Moses' words here in the Pentateuch that the acts of God would be put before the eyes of their children: "Fix these words of mine in your hearts and minds . . . teach them to your children, talking about them when you sit at home and when you walk along the road" (Dt 11:18–19). The first priority is thus given to Scripture as the means of teaching the greatness and grace of God.

As a final means for driving home the importance of obedience and trust in God, Moses gives instructions for a ceremony which the people were to carry out when they entered the land (11:29–32). They were to read the curses and blessings of the covenant on Mount Gerizim and Mount Ebal (see 27:1–14). This ceremony was initiated under Joshua (Jos 8:33).

VII. INSTRUCTIONS FOR LIFE IN THE NEW LAND (12:1–26:19)

A. Instructions for the Life of Worship (12:1–16:17)

1. Central Place of Worship (12:1–32 [MT 12:1–13:1])

Moses begins by repeating his instructions (see 7:5) regarding what to do with the false worship centers after Israel had taken possession of the land of the Canaanites. They were to "destroy them completely" (Dt. 12:2).

Command #185, Dt 12:2, Remove idolatry from your midst: "Destroy completely all the places."

Command #83, Dt 12:5, Animals to be used as offerings must be offered at the earliest opportunity: "You shall come there and you shall bring them there."

Prohibition #65, Dt 12:4, One must not erase God's name from houses of worship: "You must not do thus to the Lord your God."

Furthermore, Israel was to worship the Lord at a single, central place of worship. Not just any site would do (v. 13); only that site chosen by the Lord himself (v. 14). Little is known about the location of this site before the time of David (cf. 1Sa 1–4), but since David's time, the site of Israel's worship was Jerusalem (2Sa 6–7).

Command #84, Dt 12:14, Offerings are to be given at the temple only: "There you shall bring your burnt offerings and do them there."

Prohibition #89, Dt 12:13, One must not offer sacrifices outside the temple: "Be careful not to sacrifice your burnt offerings anywhere you please."

The provision in Deuteronomy 12:15–25 that animals may be slaughtered for food at any place in the land is a continuation and clarification of the provision in Leviticus 17:1–7. In Leviticus the slaughtering of animals for sacrifice could be done only at the Tent of Meeting. That provision implied, but did not specifically state, that the slaughter of animals merely for food could take place anywhere. The present passage in Deuteronomy makes this point explicit: "You may slaughter your animals in any of your towns and eat as much of the meat as you want" (12:15). In so doing, the question of offering sacrifices other than at the one sanctuary chosen by the Lord was also clarified. Thus, this passage stresses that all sacrifices must be carried out at the one central sanctuary.

The present text, then, draws a clear distinction between slaughtering animals for food and slaughtering animals for sacrifice. That distinction was already implicit in the earlier laws of Leviticus 17, although it had not been specifically stated.

Command #86, Dt 12:15, Redemption of consecrated things that have been blemished: "Surely in every place you desire you may slaughter and eat the meat."

Command #146, Dt 12:21, Slaughtering animals: "You may slaughter animals from the herds and flocks."

Command #85, Dt 12:26, Offerings from outside the land are also to be brought to the temple: "Take your consecrated things and whatever you have vowed to give and go to the place."

Prohibition #141, Dt 12:17, One must not eat the second tithe of grain outside Jerusalem: "You must not eat in your own towns the tithe of grain."

Prohibition #142, Dt 12:17, One must not consume the second tithe of wine outside Jerusalem: "You must not consume in your own towns the tithe of . . . new wine."

Prohibition #143, Dt 12:17, One must not consume the second tithe of oil outside Jerusalem: "You must not consume in your own towns the tithe of oil."

Prohibition #144, Dt 12:17, One must not eat the second tithe of the firstborn outside Jerusalem: "You must not eat in your own towns the tithe of the firstborn."

Prohibition #145, Dt 12:17, The priests must not eat the sin and guilt offerings outside the temple (viz., in your own towns): "You must not eat the firstborn of your herds and flocks in your own towns." (M. derives this interpretation from the fact that "herds and flocks" are mentioned in Scripture only in reference to the sin and guilt offerings.)

Prohibition #146, Dt 12:17, The priest must not eat the meat of the burnt offerings: "You must not eat in your own towns . . . what you have vowed to give." (M. derives burnt offerings from vows.)

Prohibition #147, Dt 12:17, The priest must not eat the lighter sacrifices before the blood is sprinkled: "You must not eat in your own towns . . . your freewill offerings." (M. derives "before the blood is sprinkled" from "freewill offerings.")

Prohibition #149, Dt 12:17, A priest may not eat the firstfruits outside the temple: "You must not eat in your own towns . . . special gifts." (M. derives "firstfruits" from "special gifts.")

Prohibition #229, Dt 12:19, One must not forsake the support of the Levites: "Be careful not to neglect the Levites as long as you live in your land."

Prohibition #182, Dt 12:23, One must not eat a body part taken from a living animal: "You must not eat the life with the meat."

The chapter ends with an oft-repeated warning against following after the gods of the nations (12:29–32 [MT 12:29–13:1]) and thus provides an appropriate introduction to the next chapter.

Prohibition #313, Dt 13:1 (EVV 12:32), One must not add to the law: "Do not add to it."

Prohibition #314, Dt 13:1 (EVV 12:32), One must not change the law: "Do not add to it."

2. Warning against Those Who Entice Others to Follow "Other Gods" (13:1–18 [MT 2–19])

Three illustrations of possible temptations to follow other gods are enumerated. Moses' point is to teach that under no circumstances are they to forsake the Lord and follow other gods. If a prophet or dreamer, even one whose predictions may come true, suggests that the people forsake the Lord by following other gods, his words are not to be heeded (13:1–5 [MT 2–6]). According to 18:21–22, if a prophet's word comes true, it is a sign that this person is a true prophet. Thus, even though such signs may vouch for the word of a prophet, if he attempts to persuade others to follow false gods, his words are to be rejected and he is to be put to death. This is the same penalty as that for the false prophet in 18:20.

If someone from one's own family entices them to follow other gods, he or she is to be rejected (13:6–11 [MT 7–12]). The penalty is death, as in the previous example. Finally, if an entire city is found to have forsaken the Lord and followed other gods, that city was to be completely destroyed (13:12–18 [MT 13–19]).

Command #179, Dt 13:15 (EVV 14), A witness should be closely examined: "You must inquire, probe, and investigate it thoroughly."

Command #186, Dt 13:17 (EVV 16), Destroy an idolatrous city: "You shall burn the city with fire."

Prohibition #28, Dt 13:3–4 (EVV 2–3), One must not listen to a false prophet: "You must not listen to the words of that prophet."

Prohibition #17, Dt 13:9 (EVV 8), One must not desire one who seeks to persuade others to follow idols: "Do not yield to him."

Prohibition #18, Dt 13:9 (EVV 8), One must not listen to one who seeks to persuade others to follow idols: "Do not listen to him."

Prohibition #19, Dt 13:9 (evv 8), One must not pity one who seeks to persuade others to follow idols: "Let not your eye pity him."

Prohibition #20, Dt 13:9 (evv 8), One must not spare one who seeks to persuade others to follow idols: "Do not spare him."

Prohibition #21, Dt 13:9 (evv 8), One must not hide one who seeks to persuade others to follow idols: "Do not hide him."

Prohibition #16, Dt 13:12 (evv 11), One must not seek to persuade another Israelite to follow idols: "And no one among you will do such an evil thing again."

Prohibition #23, Dt 13:17 (evv 16), One must not rebuild that which has been destroyed because of idolatry: "It is to remain a ruin forever."

Prohibition #24, Dt 13:18 (evv 17), One must not gain wealth from that which has been destroyed because of idolatry: "None of those condemned things shall be found in your hands."

3. The Purity of the People (14:1–21)

A selection of regulations is placed here to show the measures that must be taken to maintain the holiness of the people. The repeated purpose of these regulations is to show that Israel was "a people holy to the LORD [their] God" (14:2, 21).

The first regulation is that Israel was not to "cut themselves" or "shave the front of their head" as a sign of mourning for the dead (14:1). A similar prohibition is found in Leviticus 19:28 and 21:5.

Prohibition #45, Dt 14:1, One must not cut oneself for the dead: "Do not cut yourself . . . for the dead."

Prohibition # 171, Dt 14:1, One must not shave the head for the dead: "Do not . . . shave the front of your heads for the dead."

Second, a summary of clean and unclean animals is listed (14:3–20). This list is drawn from Leviticus 11:2–23. A comparison of the two lists shows that the present list is a summary of Leviticus and to some extent also an explanation. For example, on the one hand, in cases where the Leviticus passage describes only the kinds of clean animals that can be eaten, without giving examples (Lev 11:3), Deuteronomy lists specific examples (Dt 14:4–5). On the other hand, when Leviticus gives examples (Lev 11:21–23), Deuteronomy lists only the general regulation (Dt 14:20).

Command #150, Dt 14:11, Examination of birds for eating: "Every clean bird you may eat."

Prohibition #140, Dt 14:3, Consecrated animals which have become blemished must not be eaten: "Do not eat any destestable thing."

Prohibition #172, Dt 14:7, One must not eat unclean animals: "This is what you must not eat."

Prohibition #175, Dt 14:19, One must not eat unclean creeping things that fly: "All flying insects that swarm are unclean to you; do not eat them."

Third, the prohibition of eating from a carcass is repeated from Exodus 22:31 and Leviticus 17:15–16. In the present passage, however, such meat from a carcass can be given to the "alien in the gates" (Dt 14:21). However, since the Leviticus passage prohibits both the Israelite and the "alien" (גר) from eating the meat of a carcass, it appears that the present passage has a different sort of "outsider" (גר) in mind. We can only suppose it is an "alien" (גר) or outsider that has not joined with Israel in the covenant, that is, one who is not a member of the "holy people" (v. 21a). He is further identified in this passage by being associated with the "strangers" (נכרי).

> **Prohibition #180**, Dt 14:21, One must not eat an animal that has died of a natural death: "Do not eat anything you find already dead."

Fourth, the prohibition of boiling a kid in its mother's milk is repeated from Exodus 23:19 and 34:26.

4. Tithes (14:22–29)

A tithe is one-tenth of one's produce, whether grain, fruit, oil, cattle, or sheep. It is closely associated with the giving of "firstfruits" in Exodus 22:28. In Deuteronomy 12:6–8 Moses had commanded the people to bring their tithes and "firstlings of the herd" to the sanctuary and to celebrate a joyous feast in thanksgiving for the Lord's blessings. Here he explains in more detail the procedures they were to follow.

Instructions regarding a tithe have already been given in Leviticus 27:30–33 and Numbers 18:21–32. That tithe, usually called the "first tithe," was to be given for the support of the Levites, who in turn gave a tenth of it to the priests. According to the present passage, a "second tithe" was also to be given by each Israelite "in order to teach the fear of the Lord" (Dt 14:23). This tithe was to be given out of the remainder of the produce after the first tithe had been given to the Levites. A family celebration which included the Levites was to be held out of this tithe. If one lived too far away to bring his tithe to the sanctuary, he was to sell his tithe and purchase food and drink for the celebration when he arrived (14:24–27).

Every third year the tithe was to be given to the needy (cf. 26:12). Since the Levites are also mentioned here (14:28–29), this is probably a general statement that includes not only the tithe spoken of here, the "second tithe," but also that in Numbers 18. Thus the Levites are to have their customary tithe and the needy are to partake of this "second" tithe.[13]

According to Exodus 23:10–11, during the seventh year the land was to be "unplowed and unused" and available for the needy among the people. Thus, in a cycle of seven years, for the first two years the tithe was eaten by the owner of the land, in the third and sixth years it was given to the needy, in the fourth and fifth years it was eaten by the owner again, and in the seventh year the whole of the land was left for the needy.

> **Command #128**, Dt 14:22, The second tithe: "Set aside a tenth of all."
>
> **Command #130**, Dt 14:28, Tithe for the poor on the third and sixth years instead of the second tithe: "At the end of three years you shall bring out."

5. Care for the Poor (15:1–18)

a. The Year for Release of Debts (15:1–6)

The present passage is a further exposition of the Sabbath year release recorded in Exodus 23:10 and Leviticus 25:2–7. The premise of the exposition offered here is that if the land was left unused in the Sabbath year, the

---

[13]See Rashi, ad loc.

landowner would not have money to pay his debts. To alleviate this hardship on the landowner, the debts were to be released for one year during this time. The sense of the word *release* is not "to cancel," as may be suggested in some English translations (e.g., NIV), but rather "to postpone." The debt was postponed for a year.[14] This provision was not intended for the "foreigner" (Dt 15:3); it applied only to those who lived permanently in the land. The "foreigner" was one who stayed only temporarily in the land. Such a one was not a "sojourner," that is, a non-Israelite who had come to live permanently in the land.[15]

In verses 4–5 Moses interjects an explanation and thus qualifies his discussion of the "poor" in the land. He reminds the people that if they obey the Lord, they would have no need of laws dealing with the poor because God would so bless them that there would be no poor in the land. They would have such abundance that they would be the creditors of many nations. In reality, however, Israel would not obey (cf. Dt 31:29), and there would be poor in the land.

> **Command #141**, Dt 15:3, The release of all debts: "You must cancel any debt."
>
> **Command #142**, Dt 15:3, Debts of foreigners may be exacted: "You may require payment from a foreigner."
>
> **Prohibition #230**, Dt 15:2, One must not demand payment of a loan after the seventh year: "Every creditor shall cancel the loan he has made to his fellow Israelite."

b. Help for the One in Need (15:7–11)

The ideal is that there be no poor in the land; hence Moses ensures that in the event that there were those in need, the Israelites would generously provide for them out of their own abundance. Moses' concern is motivated by the realization expressed in verse 11 that there will always be those in need. Out of the blessings of some, the needs of others were to be met, and thus there would be no poor in the land.

> **Command #195**, Dt 15:8, Give to the poor: "You shall open your hand."
>
> **Prohibition #232**, Dt 15:7, One must not deny help to the poor: "Do not be hardhearted or tightfisted toward your poor brother."
>
> **Prohibition #231**, Dt 15:9, One must not refuse a loan to the poor because of the approaching seventh year: "Be careful not to harbor this thought: 'The seventh year . . . is near,' so that you do not show ill will toward your needy brother and give him nothing."

c. Law of Service (15:12–18)

According to Leviticus 25:39, an Israelite could sell himself to another Israelite as a hired worker if he could not pay his debts. In the light of such a provision, there was a need for a ruling regarding the length of such service. The ruling itself is repeated from Exodus 21:2–7 with some further explanations. The length of service was not to exceed six years. In the Exodus passage the law is stated only in terms of male servants, whereas here in Deuteronomy the provision is enlarged to include female servants

---

[14]See Keil, *Pentateuch*, 3:370.
[15]See Driver, *Deuteronomy*, 175.

and their rights. Moses thus draws out of the earlier provision a further application. (Cf. the discussion above of Dt 5:21 for a similar treatment of earlier laws.)

> **Command #196**, Dt 15:14, A freed Hebrew slave must be given gifts: "Supply him liberally."
>
> **Prohibition #233**, Dt 15:13, One must not send a poor Hebrew slave away empty-handed: "When you release him, do not send him away empty-handed."

6. Firstborn Animals (15:19–23)

Laws regarding the firstborn have been given in Exodus 13:11–16; 22:29–30; and Numbers 18:15–18. In the last-mentioned text, the firstlings were to be given to the priests as gifts to be eaten by them. In Deuteronomy 12:6–7 the firstlings are included in a list of offerings to be brought to the central worship site and eaten in a joyous convocation. The present text further specifies the regulations regarding the firstlings among the cattle and sheep. They were not to be worked or sheared like the other animals. Only those without blemish were to be brought to the place of worship and eaten by all the people. Since they were given specifically to the priests (Nu 18:15–19), we may presume that the priests shared the gift with all those present at the celebration.

> **Prohibition #113**, Dt 15:19, One must not work a consecrated animal: "Do not put the firstborn of your oxen to work."
>
> **Prohibition #114**, Dt 15:19, One must not shear a consecrated animal: "Do not shear the firstborn of your sheep."

7. Feasts (16:1–17)

Moses now discusses the feasts during which the people were to appear before the Lord at the central worship site.

a. Passover (16:1–8)

Reference to the Feast of Passover is made on numerous occasions in the Pentateuch (see Ex 12:1–49; 23:18; 34:25; Lev 23:5; Nu 9:1–14; 28:16). Since several offerings were given during the time of this feast, Moses refers generally to the sacrifice of "an animal from your flock or herd." The offering of the Passover itself was to be only a lamb (Ex 12:5). However, additional offerings were also to be made during the Passover and the subsequent seven days of the Feast of Unleavened Bread (Nu 28:19–25). In addition to these offerings, which were mandatory, even more offerings could be given for the feasts. In Josiah's day, for example, the king provided an extra three thousand cattle from his own possessions for the Feast of Passover (cf. 2Ch 35:7–8). In later Jewish custom, these extra offerings for the feast were called the *Chagigah*, "feast offering."[16]

It is commonly held that in this passage yet another new aspect or additional feature of the Passover is given. Since here in Deuteronomy the worship of the Lord was being restricted to one site (repeated six times in this passage alone, vv. 2, 6, 7, 11, 15, 16), Passover could no longer be

---

[16]See Maimonides, *Korban Pesaḥ*, 10.12.

celebrated in each and every house (Ex 12:46) but only at the central place of worship (Dt 16:5–6). This restriction was, however, already anticipated in Exodus 40:17—the tabernacle was completed in time for the first celebration of Passover in the wilderness (see commentary on Ex 40:17–33).

According to Deuteronomy 16:7, the Israelites were to "boil" their offering "and eat" it at Passover. The NIV translation of 16:7, "Roast it and eat," conceals the fact that the Hebrew text says "boil" here, not "roast." There thus appears to be a conflict between the instructions here and those in Exodus 12:9: "Do not boil it [the Passover lamb]." The Passover lamb was to be roasted, not boiled. Since the Hebrew word used here can have the general sense of "to cook," the NIV's translation is possibly correct (cf. "And you shall cook and eat it" NASB). It seems difficult to accept, however, that the same Hebrew word in the same set of instructions would have such a divergence in meaning. It is possible that in this passage, that which was to be boiled was not the Passover lamb but rather the other offerings mentioned in verse 2 above. The Passover lamb was to be eaten "roasted and not boiled," as in Exodus; and, according to the present text, the additional offerings were to be "boiled and eaten." Thus in 2 Chronicles 35:13, Josiah appears to have followed both Deuteronomy and Exodus in "roasting" the Passover animals but "boiling" the "holy offerings," that is, the additional offerings for that day.

> **Prohibition #199**, Dt 16:3, One must not eat anything mixed with yeast after the middle of the fourteenth of Nisan (the day before Passover): "Do not eat it with yeast."
>
> **Prohibition #118**, Dt 16:4, One must not leave any portion of the Chagigah (festive offering), offered on the fourteenth, until the third day: "Do not let any of the meat you sacrifice on the evening of the first day remain until morning."

b. Feast of Weeks (16:9–12)

This feast day is referred to several times in the Pentateuch. It is also called the "Harvest Feast" (Ex 23:16) and the "Day of Firstfruits" (Nu 28:26). According to Deuteronomy 16:9, it is to begin seven weeks after "the sickle is put to the standing grain." Depending on the particular season, this day could vary. In Leviticus 23:15, however, the time of reckoning the seven weeks or "fifty days" (Pentecost) begins "on the next day" after the Sabbath. Early tradition has associated this day with the day after Passover (Targum Jerusalmi), i.e., the sixteenth of Nisan. The purpose of the feast was to celebrate God's deliverance of the people from bondage in Egypt. It was a time of remembrance. It should be noted that according to Acts 2, the "firstfruits of the Spirit" (Ro 8:23) were given on Pentecost.

c. Feast of Tabernacles or Booths (16:13–15)

This feast is also called the "Feast of Ingathering" and "Sukkoth" (Ex 23:16). Though not explained here in Deuteronomy, elsewhere (Lev 23:43) it is stated that the "booths" awere o commemorate the huts the Israelites lived in when they came out of Egypt. As with the other feasts, it was to be a time of great joy in remembrance.

> **Command #54**, Dt 16:14, One must rejoice during each festival: "You should rejoice in your festival."

d. Summary (16:16–17)

This summary is a repetition of Exodus 23:17. Here, however, Moses specifies that which has been the main point of this section of Deuteronomy—the feasts are to be celebrated only at the central place of worship.

B. Instruction for Leadership (16:18–18:22)

1. Judges (16:18–20)

In Deuteronomy 1:9–15 Moses recounted the occasion for the appointment of leaders for each of the tribes. These leaders are here called "judges and officials." The work of governing God's people was too much for one man (Moses). Thus these judges were to carry on the work of Moses within each of the tribes and families. According to 17:8–13 these legal officials were to be organized at a local level as well as at a higher level for appeals. It was thus similar to the modern appellate court system. A similar administration of the law was carried out during their time in the wilderness (Ex 18:21–23).

In the following passage a series of occasions is described in which the need for a judge may arise. This can be seen in Deuteronomy 17:9, where, after various situations are listed and summarized, the possible need for further "judgment" is still recognized. Thus the judge was to play an important role in implementing and enforcing the prohibitions listed below.

> **Command #176,** Dt 16:18, Appointment of judges and officials: "Appoint judges and officials for each of your tribes."

2. Prohibition of Wooden Asherah Poles and Pillars (16:21–22)

The Asherah poles and pillars have been mentioned in Deuteronomy 7:5 as accoutrements of Canaanite worship. They were to be destroyed when the Israelites moved into the land. In the present context the concern is that the central worship place not contain any trace of Canaanite worship.

> **Prohibition #13,** Dt 16:21, One must not set up trees in the temple: "Do not set up any wooden Asherah pole beside the altar."
> **Prohibition #11,** Dt 16:22, One must not build a pillar: "And do not erect a sacred stone."

3. Prohibition of Defective Sacrifice (17:1)

A defective sacrifice is here described as an "abomination" to the Lord. The description of the defects listed here is a summary of Leviticus 1:3, 10 and 22:17–26.

> **Prohibition #95,** Dt 17:1, One must not sacrifice to the Lord any blemished animal (M. takes this as a temporary blemish): "Do not sacrifice to the Lord your God an ox or sheep that has a defect."

4. Penalty for Worshiping Other Gods (17:2–7)

The penalty for worshiping other gods has been given already in Exodus 22:20: "Whoever sacrifices to any god other than the LORD must be destroyed." Here the implementation of the penalty is closely described and applied to "any man or woman." The penalty is the same as that for one who seduces another to worship idols (Dt 13:7–12).

5. Law Cases for the Priests and Judges (17:8–13)

The system of legal administration described here represents an implementation of that form of law established during their time in the wilderness (Ex 18:21–23; Dt 1:16–17; 19:17–18). There were judges at the local level throughout the land as well as centralized at the place of worship. Obedience to the law is here presented as obedience to the will of God. Violation of the law is seen as rebellion against God.

> **Command #174**, Dt 17:11, Obey the leaders: "Act according to the law they teach you."
>
> **Prohibition #312**, Dt 17:11, One must not rebel against those who teach the law (M. tradition): "Act according to the law they teach you and the decisions they give you."

6. The King (17:14–20)

The office of kingship has been anticipated in the Pentateuch since the Lord's promise to Abraham and his seed: "I will bless her [Sarah] so that she will be the mother of nations; kings of peoples will come from her" (Ge 17:16), and "Kings will come from you" (Ge 35:11; cf. 36:31). That this king would come from the tribe of Judah is clear from Genesis 49:9–12. At key moments in the Pentateuch reference is made to this king and the role he will play in bringing about God's promises to Israel (e.g., Nu 24:7; Dt 33:5).

The ideal set forth in this passage is that of a king who is obedient to the will of God, which he learns from reading the Torah (Dt 17:18–19). The result of his reading the Torah is his "fear of the LORD" and humility (vv. 9b–20). At a time when most kings were virtually illiterate, Israel was to have a king who could make his own copy of the Torah (v. 18b) and study it daily. The king was to be a scribe and scholar of Scripture. The picture of David, a writer of psalms, and Solomon, a writer of proverbs, is commensurate with this ideal.

The present passage anticipates the time when a king would be established over Israel and thus prescribes the kind of king they were to have. Central to the question of a king is that he is to be one whom the Lord himself shall choose (Dt 17:15). Just as Israel was only to worship God at the place which God would choose, so their king was to be chosen only by God. It is not difficult to see in these words the anticipation of King David, whose family God chose from among all the tribes (2Sa 7:18–24; Ps 78:70). Moreover, the warnings listed here regarding the dangers inherent in the kingship (e.g., "He must not take many wives") easily call to mind the downfall of Solomon, David's son ("He had seven hundred wives of royal birth and three hundred concubines," 1Ki 11:3).

Underlying these warnings is the larger issue that Israel was ultimately to look to God as their King and thus not put their trust in another human being. In other words, their request for a king should not arise out of a faltering faith in the Lord. We should note here that when the day came that Israel did request a king, God and his prophet Samuel saw in their request a veiled attempt to reject divine leadership (1Sa 8:6–9). The Lord himself said, "They have rejected me as their king" (1Sa 8:7).

> **Command #173**, Dt 17:15, Appointment of a king: "You shall set a king over you."

Command #17, Dt 17:18, The king must write for himself a copy of the Torah: "And when he sits upon the throne of his kingdom, he shall write for himself a copy of this Torah."

Prohibition #362, Dt 17:15, The king is to be from the house of Israel: "He must be from among your own brothers."

Prohibition #46, Dt 17:16, One must not return to Egypt to dwell: "You are not to go back that way again."

Prohibition #363, Dt 17:16, The king must not have many horses: "The king, moreover, must not acquire great numbers of horses."

Prohibition #364, Dt 17:17, The king must not have many wives: "He must not take many wives."

Prohibition #365, Dt 17:17, The king must not accumulate great wealth: "He must not accumulate large amounts of silver and gold."

7. Offerings for the Priests and Levites (18:1–8)

The role of the priests, having been chosen by God and separated as his servants, is briefly summarized here. Their support was to come from a prescribed portion of the offerings given to the Lord. From the animals offered they were to receive the shoulder, the jowls, and the inner parts. From the rest of the offerings they were to be given the firstfruits.

According to Leviticus 7:31–34, the priests were to receive a portion of the fellowship offering, that is, the breast and the right thigh of the animals offered. The portions for the priests described here in Deuteronomy, however, were probably to be taken from the additional offerings prescribed above in chapter 14. These were for the feasts that accompanied the celebration at the tabernacle.[17]

Command #143, Dt 18:3, The priest's share of an offering: "This is the judgment for the priest."

Command #126, Dt 18:4, Bring the great heave (wave) offering: "The firstfruits of your grain you shall give to him."

Command #144, Dt 18:4, The first of the fleece for the priest: "The first wool from the shearing of your sheep."

Command #36, Dt 18:6–8, Priests should do their duties in rotation: "If a Levite comes from one of your towns . . . he may minister in the name of the Lord his God like all his fellow Levites who serve there in the presence of the Lord. He is to share equally in their benefits."

Prohibition #169, Dt 18:1, The tribe of Levi must not have an inheritance in the dividing of the land: "The priests, who are Levites—indeed the whole tribe of Levi—are to have no allotment or inheritance with Israel."

Prohibition #170, Dt 18:1, The tribe of Levi must not take part in the spoils of war: "The priests, who are Levites—indeed the whole tribe of Levi—are to have no allotment or inheritance with Israel."

8. Detestable Practices (18:9–14)

Before introducing the office of the prophet, Moses here emphatically prohibits all other means of knowing the will of God. Israel was to have the office of the prophet as the means of knowing God's will; hence these other means must not be used to rival it.

---

[17]See Keil, *Pentateuch*, 3:390.

Prohibition #31, Dt 18:10, One must not practice divination (קסם): "Let no one be found among you who . . . practices divination."

Prohibition #32, Dt 18:10, One must not practice soothsaying: "Let no one be found among you who . . . practices soothsaying."

Prohibition #33, Dt 18:10–11, One must not practice divination (נחש): "Let no one be found among you who . . . practices divination." (Cf. #31, Lev 19:26.)

Prohibition #34, Dt 18:10–11, One must not practice sorcery: "Let no one be found among you who . . . practices sorcery."

Prohibition #35, Dt 18:10–11, One must not practice charms: "Let no one be found among you who . . . practices charms."

Prohibition #36, Dt 18:10–11, One must not consult spirits: "Let no one be found among you who . . . consults spirits."

Prohibition #37, Dt 18:10–11, One must not consult familiar spirits: "Let no one be found among you who . . . consults familiar spirits."

Prohibition #38, Dt 18:10–11, One must not practice necromancy: "Let no one be found among you who . . . practices necromancy."

9. The Prophet (18:15–22)

Abraham is called a prophet in Genesis 20:7, and the existence of prophets is presupposed in the Pentateuch (Ex 7:1; Nu 11:29; 12:6, Dt 13:2–3). The present text, however, is the first to discuss the office of the prophet.

The historical basis of the office is Israel's request for a mediator at Sinai (Ex 19:16–19; 20:19–21). Fearing to stand in God's presence, the people asked Moses to go before the Lord and return God's words to them. Thus the prophet was to be "like Moses." This suggests that the office of the prophet was to play an important role in the further history of God's dealings with Israel. Indeed, a major section of the OT canon is devoted to the work of the prophets (Isaiah–Malachi). The prophet was to be God's mouthpiece to the people. Just as Aaron spoke God's words to Moses and was thus called a prophet (Ex 7:1), so the prophet(s) whom the Lord would later raise up would speak to the people on God's behalf.

Because the prophet spoke on God's behalf, his words were to be taken as the final authority. For this reason, strict measures were taken to ensure that false prophets would not arise among the people to lead them away from the Lord. The simple test of a true prophet was whether his words came true. This suggests that an important role of the prophet was "foretelling" the future.

In the NT, this particular passage, Deuteronomy 18:18, is read in reference to the coming of the Messiah (Ac 3:22–23). It should be noted that even within the OT itself this passage was taken to refer to a specific individual and not merely to the succession of prophets who were to arise after Moses. In Deuteronomy 34:10, for example, the final words of the book recall the promise of Moses in 18:18 and look far into the future to a single individual for its fulfillment. Thus by the time the last verses of Deuteronomy were attached to the Pentateuch, these verses in Deuteronomy 18 were already being understood eschatologically and messianically.

Command #172, Dt 18:15, Obey the prophet: "The man who does not obey the words of the prophet which he speaks in my name."

Prohibition #26, Dt 18:20, One must not prophesy in the name of idols: "A prophet who speaks in the name of another god must be put to death."

Prohibition #27, Dt 18:20, One must not prophesy falsely: "A prophet who presumes to speak in my name anything I have not commanded him."

Prohibition #29, Dt 18:22, One must not fear the words of a false prophet: "Do not be afraid of him."

C. Instructions for Order (19:1–23:14)

1. Cities of Refuge (19:1–13)

According to Numbers 35:9–34, Israel was to establish six "cities of refuge" to prevent the escalation of blood revenge and provide the means for a fair trial in the case of a homicide. Three of these cities were to be east of the Jordan and the other three west of the Jordan. Deuteronomy 4:41–43 recounts the establishment of the first group, those cities east of the Jordan. The present passage looks only at the second group, the three cities west of the Jordan.

Verses 8–9 envision a third group of cities, but they were apparently never established. Because of Israel's continued disobedience, God never permanently increased their borders; thus the cities were not needed. Since these cities were not built during Israel's history, the question of the fulfillment of these words of Moses has attracted much attention among Christian and Jewish interpreters. Because the condition of Israel's obedience must be met (19:8–9) before the cities are built, it is often maintained that these cities will be built only when the Messiah comes.

Command #182, Dt 19:3, Six cities of refuge: "Build roads to them."

Prohibition #279, Dt 19:13, A judge should not have pity on the condemned: "Show him no pity."

2. Boundary Markers (19:14)

In the ancient world, territory was staked out by means of stones bearing inscriptions which identified the owner of the property. These could be easily moved with a corresponding gain or loss of property. The notion of secretly or forcefully moving a neighbor's boundary marker thus became a proverbial expression for treachery and rebellion (Job 24:1–2; Pr 22:28). Its use here in Deuteronomy probably carries this same sense; that is, it is a warning against violating any standard set up by "predecessors" and ordained by God.

The "predecessors" spoken of here are either Joshua and the elders, who cast lots for the various boundaries (Jos 13:6), or the patriarchs, such as Abraham (Ge 13:17) or Jacob (Ge 49), who, through their travels and encampments in the Genesis narratives, had already claimed and apportioned the land for their descendants. The term *predecessors* in Hebrew is general enough to allow even for a reference to God's work of apportioning boundaries for all of the nations: "When the Most High gave the nations their inheritance, when he divided all mankind, he set up boundaries for the peoples according to the numbers of the sons of Israel" (Dt 32:8; cf. 2:5, 9, 19). Even these boundaries should be observed and honored.

Prohibition #246, Dt 19:14, One must not move a boundary marker: "Do not move your neighbor's boundary stone . . . in the inheritance you receive in the land."

3. Witnesses (19:15–21)

According to Numbers 35:30 and Deuteronomy 17:6, more than one witness was required for a capital offense. The present passage (and 17:6) specifies that two or three witnesses were enough. But it also raises another issue. What happens when the witness is false? Here Moses appeals to a provision stated earlier (Dt 17:8–13): difficult cases were to be taken to the judges and priests at the central worship place. According to the present text, the accused and the suspected false witness were to stand before the Lord, and judges were to investigate thoroughly. This passage does not explain how or why the witness was suspected of being false. What is important, however, is that the text does not allow for merely counting witnesses. If there was any suspicion of falsehood, as in the case of contradictory testimony, further investigation was required rather than merely the addition of more witnesses. The underlying concern of this text is the prevention of collusion.

Command #180, Dt 19:19, A false witness shall be punished appropriately: "You shall do to him what he intended to do to his brother."

Prohibition #288, Dt 19:15, One must not pass judgment on the testimony of one witness alone: "One witness is not enough to convict a man accused of any crime or offense."

4. War (20:1–20)

These regulations governing the conduct of warfare are not found elsewhere in the Pentateuch. Curiously, however, when Abraham carried out an act of war, he appeared to follow these regulations in remarkable detail (see the commentary above on Ge 14). Moreover, Moses himself follows these rules in Dt 2:24–3:11. The central purpose of these instructions is to emphasize that Israel's warfare was not intended for foreign aggression or personal wealth (cf. Ge 14:21–24).

Israel was to follow two standards of warfare: one with nations "afar off" (Dt 20:10–15) and a different one with those nations whose land they were to inherit through God's promises to their fathers (20:16–20).

On the one hand, with offending nations "afar off," that is, not a part of the Promised Land, Israel was first to offer terms of peace. It is assumed that the cause of the warfare was just and hence Israel would have been justified in destroying the city. Thus Israel is to act mercifully with the offending nations. If, however, the terms of peace were not met, Israel was justified in waging war. This passage therefore allows for a just war with nations "afar off" but does not state the grounds for such a war. The effect of these regulations can be seen in 1 Kings 20:31, where Israel was known by their neighbors as a "merciful" people in warfare.

On the other hand, Israel was to take the Promised Land as a gift from the Lord. They were not to grow rich from its spoils. All the spoils were to be "completely destroyed" (20:17). In this way Israel would not grow rich from their wars and there would be no possibility of Israel's learning the "detestable worship" of the Canaanites.

These regulations emphasize that Israel had no need of a large standing army (Dt 17:16). The Lord would fight for his people, and they were to trust in his help. The whole of the army was to have complete trust in the Lord and was to act in complete obedience to his will. If there was any question about a person's wholehearted devotion to the Lord and to the task of war, he was to be taken out of the ranks and allowed to return home.

Just as this section looks back to Abraham as a successful example of fighting the Lord's battle, it also anticipates the disobedience of Achan, who "acted unfaithfully in regard to the devoted things" (Jos 7:1–26).

> **Command #191**, Dt 20:2, The priest must instruct the people in warfare: "When you are about to go into battle, the priest shall come forward."
>
> **Command #190**, Dt 20:12, Procedure for wars with the rest of the nations: "If they refuse to make peace."
>
> **Command #187**, Dt 20:17, Destruction of the seven Canaanite nations: "Completely destroy them."
>
> **Prohibition #49** Dt 20:16, One must not save the life of a Canaanite: "Do not leave alive anything that breathes."
>
> **Prohibition #57**, Dt 20:19, One must not destroy fruit trees in war: "When you lay siege to a city . . . do not destroy its trees."

5. Unsolved Murder (21:1–9)

This law is not given elsewhere in the Pentateuch. Its purpose is clear from the text. Whenever innocent blood was shed, it was the responsibility of the people to carry out justice and punish the offender (19:1–14). In the event that the guilty party was unknown, justice could not be adequately served, and thus the people were still held responsible. The present law, then, was the means whereby the people as a whole could settle a case of unsolved murder.

> **Command #181**, Dt 21:4, Ritual of breaking the heifer's neck: "They are to break the heifer's neck."
>
> **Prohibition #309**, Dt 21:4, One must not sow or work a valley that is to be used for the ritual of the red heifer: "A valley that has not been plowed or planted."

6. Treatment of Captive Women (21:10–14)

In warfare with nations that were "afar off," the Israelites were not to take the lives of the women and children when capturing a city (20:14). The present law ensures the well-being of those captured women by giving them protection against being sold into slavery. It also provides for the assimilation of the captive women into Israelite society by allowing marriage to them. This provision, however, raises a question, since marriage to Canaanite women has already been expressly forbidden (Dt 7:3).

The present passage does not mention the personal faith or religion of such a woman taken into the house of an Israelite. In view of the strict warnings against the dangers of foreign women leading Israel into idolatry and false religion (7:3–4), however, it seems reasonable to conclude that this case presumes that the women would accept Israel's covenant stipulations. In this sense, the law anticipates the case of Rahab, whom Joshua spared and who continued to "live among the Israelites" for the remainder of her life (Jos 6:25). The example of Rahab, however, may not specifically apply here,

since she was not from a nation "afar off" but was from one of the cities of
Canaan (Jericho).

> **Command #221**, Dt 21:11, Treatment of a female captive: "If you notice among
> the captives a beautiful woman."
> **Prohibition #263**, Dt 21:14, One must not sell a female captive: "You must not
> sell her."
> **Prohibition #264**, Dt 21:14, One must not treat a female captive as a slave: "You
> must not . . . treat her as a slave."

7. Right of the Firstborn (21:15–17)

This law is not mentioned elsewhere in the Pentateuch, though the
right of the "firstborn" is assumed throughout the pentateuchal narratives
(e.g., Ge 25:31; 49:3). The law is intended to protect the legitimate firstborn
son, even though his mother may not have been a favorite wife. Polygamy is
not sanctioned by this law; rather, its adverse effects are curtailed. The writer
of the Pentateuch has assumed the principle of monogamy since the
beginning (Ge 2:24). A double portion of inheritance was to be given to the
firstborn.

8. A Rebellious Son (21:18–21)

According to Leviticus 20:9, a son was to be put to death if he cursed his
father or mother; in Exodus 21:15, the same penalty was given to one who
attacked his father or mother. The present law generalizes the offense to
include any kind of refusal to obey and assumes the same stiff measures. The
law here in Deuteronomy, however, provides an additional safeguard. The
parents were required to bring the child before a council of the elders.
The council, not the parents, was required to decided the case and
administer the penalty.

The stated purpose of the law was to eliminate the evil influence of
such a child from among the people (Dt 21:21). Moreover, it was also to
provide a warning to parents and children alike of the consequences of
disobedience and rebellion. We should remember that laws such as this are
not being held up to the readers of the Pentateuch as examples of how they
should obey God and do his will. If we look at these laws and others like
them from the viewpoint of their literary role within the composition of the
Pentateuch, we see that they are put here as examples of what God required
of Israel under the Sinai covenant. We should be careful to remember that the
author of the Pentateuch has already presented Abraham as his one sterling
example of what it means to "keep the Law" (Ge 26:5). Abraham "kept the
Law" but did not have before him these "laws" of the Sinai covenant (see the
discussion in the Introduction above). In Abraham's life we see that faith and
trust in God are the author's answer to the question of what keeping the Law
is all about. In selecting these various laws from the Sinai covenant, the
author of the Pentateuch intends to give the readers a glimpse of life under
the covenant at Sinai. When reading texts like this one, one can easily agree
with Paul that such a law was a "yoke of bondage" (Gal 5:1). Even during OT
times, for those under the Sinai covenant, laws such as this would have been
difficult to enforce.

9. Various Laws (21:22–22:12)

a. Hanging (21:22–23)

After an execution, the body was permitted to hand on a tree as a public display of the consequences of disobedience. The body was not to remain on the tree overnight, however; it was to be properly buried on that same day.

> **Command #230**, Dt 21:22, Hanging the body of the executed: "If a man guilty of a capital offense is put to death and his body is hung on a tree."
> **Command #231**, Dt 21:23, The hanged must be buried on the same day they were killed: "You must not leave his body on the tree overnight."
> **Prohibition #66**, Dt 21:23, One must not allow a body to hang on a tree overnight: "You must not leave his body on the tree overnight."

b. Responsibility for Lost Property (22:1–4)

The general principle is laid down that one cannot hide one's eyes from an obvious need. It is one's duty to care for the lost property of a neighbor. The same duty was described in Exodus 23:4–5.

> **Command #204**, Dt 22:1, You must restore a lost animal to its owner: "If you see your brother's ox or sheep straying, do not ignore it but be sure to take it back to him."
> **Command #203**, Dt 22:4, You must help load a burden on a man or animal: "If you see your brother's donkey or his ox fallen on the road."
> **Prohibition #269**, Dt 22:3, One should not ignore a neighbor's lost article: "Do not ignore it."

c. Gender Distinctions (22:5)

This rule, found only here in the Pentateuch, is sufficiently general to forbid a man's wearing any item of feminine clothing or ornamentation or a woman's wearing any item of masculine clothing or ornamentation. The only reason given is that such a practice is an "abomination to the LORD."

> **Prohibition #39**, Dt 22:5, Women must not wear men's clothing: "A woman must not wear men's clothing."
> **Prohibition #40**, Dt 22:5, Men must not wear women's clothing: "Nor a man wear women's clothing."

d. Birds' Nests (22:6–7)

Most take this law, found only here in the Pentateuch, to be an example of the humanity and sense of fair play inherent in God's Law. It also shows that God cares for the least among his creation. He wants Israel to care not only for their neighbor's possessions but also for all his creatures.

> **Command #148**, Dt 22:7, Freeing the nest: "You shall set the bird free and take the chicks."
> **Prohibition #306**, Dt 22:6, One must not take the mother bird when taking the young birds: "You shall not take the mother with the young ones."

e. Parapet or Railing (22:8)

This law, found only here in the Pentateuch, is another example of the importance of looking out for one's neighbor. As with the earlier examples in this chapter, it also shows God's concern for seemingly insignificant details.

There appears to have been no area of life which did not come under the close scrutiny of God's will. Whether intended to do so or not, such laws leave a lasting impression that God's will pervades every area of human existence.

> **Command #184**, Dt 22:8, Remove hazards from your dwellings: "When you build a new house, make a parapet around your roof."
>
> **Prohibition #298**, Dt 22:8, One must not leave a dangerous trap in one's house: "Do not bring bloodshed into your house."

f. Prohibition of Mixing Natural Distinctions (22:9–11)

Breeding mixed cattle, sowing mixed crops, or sewing mixed threads was prohibited in Leviticus 19:19. In like manner, mixing two kinds of seed in an orchard, plowing with an ox and a donkey, and wearing mixed cloth are also prohibited here in Deuteronomy. In neither passage, however, is the prohibition specifically explained. The underlying assumption of the prohibition is that set forth in the Creation account of Genesis 1—God made everything "after its own kind," and thus any attempt to mix the created order is seen as a violation of his will.

> **Prohibition #193**, Dt 22:9, One must not eat the produce of mixed planting: "Do not plant two kinds of seed in your vineyard; if you do, not only the crops you plant but also the fruit of the vineyard will be defiled."
>
> **Prohibition #216**, Dt 22:9, One must not plant two kinds of seed in a vineyard (M. sow grain in a vineyard): "Do not plant two kinds of seed in your vineyard."
>
> **Prohibition #218**, Dt 22:10, One must not work two species of animals together: "Do not plow with an ox and a donkey yoked together."
>
> **Prohibition #42**, Dt 22:11, One must not wear clothing made of wool and linen mixed: "Do not weave clothes of wool and linen woven together."

g. Tassels (22:12)

The purpose of the tassels was explained in Numbers 15:39: "You will have these tassels to look at and so you will remember all the commands of the LORD, that you may obey them."

10. Marriage, Adultery, and Rape (22:13–30 [MT 22:13–23:1])

a. Proof of Virginity (22:13–21)

One who doubted the virginity of one's bride was to make a formal accusation to the "elders of the city," and her parents were to give proof of virginity. A wife was thus protected from any wantonness on the part of her husband. If the accusation was false, the husband was to pay a penalty. It is usually supposed that the proof consisted of a bloodstained cloth or clothing which the parents had kept since the night of the wedding. However, the text is not clear regarding the exact nature of the proof. We must keep in mind that there are many things in Scripture about which we know very little. The purpose of the writer was not to give the readers a full explication of the religious and social customs of ancient Israel but to give a general description of the requirements of living under the Sinai covenant. Passages such as this one, which gives only a general sketch of the actual requirements of the Law, show that the Pentateuch was not intended to be a manual of the Law. There are too many gaps for it to have functioned that way. The Pentateuch is ultimately more about the new covenant than the old. It looks forward to a time when the Torah will be written on a person's heart (as in Jer 31:31–34), and all will obey it by faith.

> **Command #219**, Dt 22:18–19, One who unjustly accuses his wife must be punished: "And the elders shall take the man and punish him."
>
> **Prohibition #359**, Dt 22:19, One who has slandered his wife must not divorce her: "He must not divorce her as long as he lives."

b. Adultery (22:22)

Though the terminology is different, the law prohibiting adultery in Leviticus 20:20 is restated here. Its purpose is further explained here by the addition of the phrase, "to purge the evil from among you."

c. Rape (22:23–29)

Various conditions are given for deciding the penalty for rape. The first cases (vv. 23–27) are those in which the young girl has already been "pledged to be married." In this case the young girl is considered as a married woman, and thus the penalty for adultery applies. The only question is whether both the young girl and the man consented. The second case (vv. 28–29) deals with the rape of a young girl who is not "pledged to be married" (cf. Ex 22:15–16). The law is clearly aimed at protecting the young girl and ensuring her continued welfare.

> **Command #229**, Dt 22:24, Capital punishment: "You shall take both of them to the gate of that town and stone them to death."
>
> **Command #218**, Dt 22:29, He who violates a virgin must marry her: "He must marry the girl."
>
> **Prohibition #294**, Dt 22:26, One must not punish one forced to do a crime: "Do nothing to the girl."
>
> **Prohibition #358**, Dt 22:29, One who has married a woman because he raped her must not divorce her: "He can never divorce her as long as he lives."

d. Marriage to a Stepmother (22:30 [MT 23:1])

Leviticus 18 forbids a number of interkinship marriages. The present text repeats only one: marriage to "the wife of one's father." This is generally taken to mean marriage to one's stepmother because in Leviticus 18:7–8 the same expression is used in opposition to "one's mother."

11. Exclusion from the Assembly (23:1–8 [MT 2–9])

Several conditions are enumerated which disqualify one from "entering the assembly of the LORD"—emasculation (23:1 [MT 2]), being the offspring of a forbidden marriage (v. 2 [MT 3]), being the offspring of Ammonites or Moabites (vv. 3–6 [MT 4–7]), and, to a lesser extent, being the offspring of Edomites and Egyptians (vv. 7–8 [MT 8–9]). It is not entirely clear what "entering the assembly" means in this passage. It may have the limited sense of exclusion from public service or marriage into an Israelite family; or, more generally, it may mean exclusion from Israel's covenant relationship with God altogether. In the light of the fact that other biblical texts state quite clearly that foreigners were to enjoy the same privileges in Israel's worship as native Israelites (e.g., Nu 15:15), a more limited interpretation of this passage is warranted. Those mentioned were probably prohibited from participation in public worship at the temple (La 1:10) or from marriage to Israelites. Deuteronomy 7:3 already stressed the threat of marriage to "foreigners": "for they will turn your sons away from following [the Lord] to serve other gods." The issue seems to be the threat of foreign influence in Israel's worship of God. Thus full participation of non-Israelites was accepted if they exhibited true faith in God. Isaiah 56:3–7 is quite clear that the eunuch and the foreigner who bind themselves to the Lord may have free access to worship at the temple. The book of Ruth provides a clear example of a believing Moabite who entered into the congregation of Israel (Ru 1:16) and was allowed to marry into the royal tribe of Judah (Ru 4:13).

In postexilic times, the stipulations of this section were used to exclude "foreign wives" from the membership in the community of Israel (Ne 13:1–3). According to Ezra 9:1–2 and Nehemiah 13:23–27, however, these "foreign wives" were excluded not merely on the basis of their national origin but also because they were leading the people away from God and "into sin" (Ne 13:26) to follow "their detestable practices" (Ezr 9:1).

> **Prohibition #360**, Dt 23:2 (evv 1), One who is a eunuch must not marry into the assembly of Israel: "No one who has been emasculated by crushing or cutting may enter the assembly of the Lord."
>
> **Prohibition #354**, Dt 23:3 (evv 2), One must not marry one born of a forbidden marriage (bastard): "No one born of a forbidden marriage may enter the assembly of the Lord."
>
> **Prohibition #53**, Dt 23:4 (evv 3), One must not allow an Israelite woman to marry an Ammonite or Moabite: "No Ammonite or Moabite or any of his descendants may enter the assembly of the Lord."
>
> **Prohibition #56**, Dt 23:7 (evv 6), One must not make a peace treaty with the Ammonite or Moabite: "Do not seek a treaty of friendship with them."
>
> **Prohibition #54**, Dt 23:8 (evv 7), One must not cast off the seed of Esau: "Do not abhor an Edomite."
>
> **Prohibition #55**, Dt 23:8 (evv 7), One must not cast off the Egyptians: "Do not abhor an Egyptian."

12. Uncleanness in the Battle Camp (23:9–14 [MT 10–15])

In Numbers 5:1–4 instructions were given for maintaining the purity of the whole of the Israelite camp. Here the concern is for the camps of Israel's armies during the time of battle.

> **Command #192**, Dt 23:14 (evv 13), Sanitation of the military camp: "As part of your equipment have something to dig with."
>
> **Command #193**, Dt 23:14 (evv 13), Soldiers must have necessary equipment: "As part of your equipment have something to dig with."
>
> **Prohibition #78**, Dt 23:11 (evv 10), No unclean person can remain in the camp: "If one of your men is unclean because of a nocturnal emission, he is to go outside the camp and stay there."

D. Miscellaneous Laws (23:15 [MT 16]–25:19)

At the close of this section, the author has selected twenty-one (7 x 3) sample laws to illustrate further the nature of the requirements of living under the Sinai covenant.

1. A fugitive slave (23:15–16 [MT 16–17]) is not to be turned over to his master.

> **Prohibition #254**, Dt 23:16 (EVV 15), One must not return an escaped slave to his master: "If a slave has taken refuge with you, do not hand him over to his master."

> **Prohibition #255**, Dt 23:17 (EVV 16), One must not take advantage of an escaped slave: "Let him live among you wherever he likes and in whatever town he chooses. Do not oppress him."

2. Shrine prostitution (23:17–18 [MT 18–19]) is forbidden.

> **Prohibition #355**, Dt 23:18 (EVV 17), One must not be a prostitute: "No Israelite man or woman is to become a shrine prostitute."

> **Prohibition #100**, Dt 23:19 (EVV 18), One must not offer an animal purchased as the wage of a harlot or as the price of a dog: "You must not bring the earnings of a female prostitute or of a male prostitute into the house of the Lord."

3. Lending money on interest (23:19–20 [MT 20–21]) to an Israelite was forbidden but was allowed to foreigners (cf. Ex 22:25 [MT 24]; Lev 25:36–37).

> **Command #198**, Dt 23:21 (EVV 20), Lend to the foreigner with interest: "You may charge a foreigner interest."

> **Prohibition #236**, Dt 23:20 (EVV 19), One must not borrow money from another Israelite on interest: "You may charge a foreigner interest, but not a brother Israelite."

4. Though vows (23:21–23 [MT 22–24]) were made voluntarily, they were to be promptly kept once made.

> **Command #94**, Dt 23:24 (EVV 23), One must keep his word: "You shall keep what comes out from your lips."

> **Prohibition #155**, Dt 23:22 (EVV 21), One must not delay payment of offerings: "If you make a vow to the Lord, do not be slow to pay it."

5. Farmers were to share their produce with the people of the land, but the people were not to profit from the farmer's generosity (23:24–25).

> **Command #201**, Dt 23:25–26 (EVV 24–25), A worker is allowed to eat produce while working: "If you enter your neighbor's vineyard."

> **Prohibition #268**, Dt 23:25 (EVV 24), One must not take more fruit than he can eat: "If you enter your neighbor's vineyard, you may eat all the grapes you want, but do not put any in your basket."

> **Prohibition #267**, Dt 23:26 (EVV 25), One must not harvest the grain of his neighbor: "If you enter your neighbor's grainfield, you may pick kernels with your hands, but you must not put a sickle to his standing grain."

6. Divorce (24:1–4) was permitted but restricted. The statement in 24:1–4 consists of two parts. The first part (vv. 1–3) states the conditions on which the second part (v. 4—the verdict) rests. The three primary conditions are: (1) if a man legally divorces his wife (v. 1), (2) if his wife then marries another man (v. 2), and (3) if the new husband then divorces her or dies

(v. 3). The verdict is that the woman cannot return to her first husband (v. 4). The apparent reason for this prohibition is that taking his former wife would entail the man's marrying a "defiled" woman and that would be an abomination to the Lord. "Thus the second marriage of a divorced woman was placed *implicite* upon a par with adultery, and some approach made towards the teaching of Christ concerning marriage: 'Whosoever shall marry her that is divorced, committeth adultery' (Matt. 5:32)."[18]

> **Command #213**, Dt 24:1, You must marry according to the law: "When a man marries a woman."
>
> **Command #222**, Dt 24:1, The divorce certificate: "And he writes her a certificate of divorce."
>
> **Prohibition #356**, Dt 24:4, One who is divorced must not marry her former husband: "Her first husband, who divorced her, is not allowed to marry her again."

7. During the first year of marriage, a man was not held responsible for military service or any other duty (24:5). He was to devote the first year of marriage to "bring happiness to the wife he has married."

> **Command #214**, Dt 24:5, You must stay with your new bride one year: "If a man has recently married, he must not be sent to war or have any other duty laid on him."
>
> **Prohibition #311**, Dt 24:5, One must not force a bridegroom to serve in the military during the first year of his marriage: "He must not be sent to war or have any other duty laid on him."

8. The millstones were not to be taken in pledge because a person's daily subsistence depended on them (24:6).

> **Prohibition #242**, Dt 24:6, One must not take a pledge from a person if he earns his living with it: "Do not take a pair of millstones—not even the upper one— as security for a debt, because that would be taking a man's livelihood as security."

9. Kidnapping was prohibited in Exodus 21:16. The prohibition is here repeated (Dt 24:7) with only slight elaboration. The focus of the current law is the kidnapping and selling of a fellow Israelite. The specific wording of the law is reminiscent of the story of Joseph, who was kidnapped and sold into slavery by his brothers (Ge 37:26–27; 40:15). In that narrative Judah's plan to save Joseph violates this law (37:26–27). It is interesting to note, however, that when the sale is carried out (37:28), the text is deliberately ambiguous about who actually "sold" Joseph to the Ishmaelites. The way the Hebrew text reads, it was not Joseph's brothers who sold him but the Midianites (37:28, 36) and the Ishmaelites (39:1). When Joseph retells the story (40:5; 45:4), however, he clearly implicates his brothers.

10. A brief further warning regarding the plague of leprosy (Dt 24:8–9) is then given. We should note that reference is made here to the earlier priestly teaching on the subject in Leviticus 13–14. No attempt is made to clarify it or update its content as is so often the case in Deuteronomy. It is as if at this point in the book, the author is content merely to refer the reader

---

[18]Keil, *Pentateuch*, 3:418.

back to previous sections of the Pentateuch. This is simply exhortation regarding previous instructions.

Prohibition #308, Dt 24:8, One must not remove or hide a leprous sore: "Watch closely the sore of leprosy."

11. Especially in lending money, God's people are to act righteously (24:10–13). An example of a righteous lender is one who does not forcefully exact payment and who allows a poor person to retain his pledge overnight if it is a necessity.

Command #199, Dt 24:10, Restore a pledge to its owner if he needs it: "Do not go into his house to get a pledge."
Prohibition #239, Dt 24:10, One must not take a pledge by violence: "Do not go into his house to get what he is offering as a pledge."
Prohibition #240, Dt 24:12, One must not keep a pledge from a poor person if he needs it: "If the man is poor, do not go to sleep with his pledge in your possession."

12. Wages are to be paid promptly to hired workers (24:14–15).

Command #200, Dt 24:15, Pay the worker his wages on time: "In his day you shall pay his wages."

13. Punishment for a crime was to be borne only by the offender (24:16). Family members were not held responsible for each other's crimes (cf. (Eze 18:1–4). This should not be read as a contradiction of Dt 5:9 (Ex 20:5): "for I, the LORD your God, am a jealous God, punishing the children for the sin of the fathers." The difference is that in the earlier passage (Dt 5:9), "children are linked to their parents by ties, physical and social, from which they cannot free themselves; and they suffer, not because they are *guilty* of their father's sins, but because by the self-acting operation of natural laws their fathers' sins entail disgrace or misfortune upon them."[19] Nevertheless, in the present passage "a law is prescribed for *human action*, and a principle is laid down for the administration of justice by the State: the family of a criminal is not to be punished judicially with him. . . . it is one thing that, in virtue of the physical and social conditions in which they live, children should suffer for their fathers' sins; it is another thing that, by the deliberate intervention of human authority, they should be punished for criminal acts which they have not committed."[20]

Prohibition #287, Dt 24:16, One must not give (or accept) testimony from a relative of the accused: "Fathers shall not be put to death for their children."

14. The administration of law should be carried out with equity for all members of society (24:17–18).

Prohibition #241, Dt 24:17, One must not take a pledge from a widow: "Do not . . . take the cloak of a widow as a pledge."
Prohibition #280, Dt 24:17, A judge should not pervert justice for strangers and orphans: "Do not deprive the alien or the fatherless of justice."

15. The practice of allowing the needy to glean in the field (Lev 19:9;

---

[19]Driver, *Deuteronomy*, 277.
[20]Ibid., 277–78.

23:22) is here grounded in remembrance of Israel's hard service in Egypt (Dt 24:19–22).

> **Command #122**, Dt 24:19, One must leave the forgotten sheaves: "When you are harvesting in the field and overlook a sheaf."
>
> **Prohibition #214**, Dt 24:19, One must not return to take a forgotten sheaf: "When you are harvesting in your field and you overlook a sheaf, do not go back to get it. Leave it for the alien."

16. Punishment for crimes committed was to be equably carried out in the presence of the judges (25:1–3) and was limited to forty stripes.

> **Command #224**, Dt 25:2, Punishment of flogging: "If the guilty man deserves to be beaten."
>
> **Prohibition #300**, Dt 25:2–3, One must not give the guilty more lashes than the crime deserves: "With the number of lashes his crime deserves."

17. A concrete example is given to illustrate a general principle (Dt 25:4). A worker should be allowed to enjoy the fruit of his own labor. Paul applied this principle to Christian service in 1 Corinthians 9:9–10.

> **Prohibition #219**, Dt 25:4, One must not prevent an animal from eating of its work: "Do not muzzle an ox while it is treading out the grain."

18. Levirate marriage (Dt 25:5–10) is described only here, though the earlier narratives presuppose it (e.g., Ge 38:8). Its purpose was to preserve the name of a deceased brother. The custom itself was an exception to the general law forbidding marriage with the wife of one's brother (Lev 18:16; 20:21).

> **Command #216**, Dt 25:5, Levirate marriage: "Her husband's brother shall take her and marry her."
>
> **Command #217**, Dt 25:9, *Halitzah* (removing the sandal of a brother-in-law): "His brother's widow shall go up to him in the presence of the elders, take off one of his sandals."
>
> **Prohibition #357**, Dt 25:5, A widowed sister-in-law must not marry any but her husband's brother: "His widow must not marry outside the family."

19. The consequence of the immodest act of Deuteronomy 25:11–12 is the only example of punishment by mutilation in the Pentateuch.[21]

> **Command #247**, Dt 25:12, You must rescue the one who is persecuted at all cost: "You shall cut off her hand. Show her no pity."
>
> **Prohibition #293**, Dt 25:12, One must not have pity on or spare a guilty party: "Show her no pity."

20. The weights and measures of trade are to be kept equably (25:13–16). The motive is not only the blessing of long life in the land but also the fact that "the LORD God detests anyone who does these things." (Cf. Leviticus 19:35.)

> **Prohibition #272**, Dt 25:13, One must not (M. even) possess inaccurate weights: "Do not have two differing weights in your bag."

---

[21]See Carl Steuernagel, *Das Deuteronomium*, Handkommentar zum Alten Testament (Göttingen: Vandenhoeck & Ruprecht, 1900), 92.

21. The admonition to remember the treachery of the Amalekites is repeated to this new generation (25:17-19) just as it was repeated to those who came out of Egypt (Ex 17:14). Particular importance is attached to the fate of the Amalekites in the Pentateuch, especially as a sign of God's faithfulness in fulfilling his promises. For example, Balaam's oracle of the future king in Israel (Nu 24:1-19) is followed by the reminder of the destruction of the Amalekites: "Amalek was first among the nations, but he will come to ruin at last" (Nu 24:20; cf. 1Ch 4:42-43).

> Command #189, Dt 25:17, Remember what the Amalekites did to Israel: "Remember what the Amalekites did to you."
>
> Command #188, Dt 25:19, Destruction of the memory of the Amalekites: "You shall blot out the memory of Amalek.
>
> Prohibition #59, Dt 25:19, One must not forget the evil done by the Amalekites: "You shall blot out the memory of the Amalekite from under heaven. Do not forget."

E. Two Ceremonies: Firstfruits and Tithes (26:1-15)

1. Firstfruits (26:1-11)

The Israelites were to give the first of the produce of the land to the Lord (Ex 23:9-14; 34:26; Lev 27:30-33; Nu 18:12-13), that is, to the priests as their inheritance (DT 18:3-8). The firstfruits were brought during the Feast of Harvest or Pentecost (Ex 34:22; Lev 23:15-17; Nu 28:26; Dt 16:9-10) and Passover (Lev 2:14; 23:10). The present passage, however, initiates a special ceremony to be carried out at this time in which a portion of the firstfruits was set apart in a basket and brought to the priest in acknowledgment of God's gift of the good land. Also at this time the rehearsal of God's gracious dealings with the fathers was spoken before the Lord (Dt 26:5-9). Thus in Deuteronomy, the purpose of the special feasts is extended to include "instruction and teaching."

> Command #132, Dt 26:5, Declaration must be said with offering of firstfruits: "Then you shall declare before the Lord."

2. Tithes (26:12-15)

According to Deuteronomy 14:28-29, each Israelite was to give a "second tithe," "in order to teach the fear of the LORD" (Dt 14:23). This tithe was to be given out of the remainder of the produce after the first tithe had been given to the Levites. A family celebration, which included the Levites, was held out of this tithe. Every third year the tithe was given to the needy (see 14:28-29). The present passage describes the prayer that was offered at the giving of this tithe. The prayer is not only an acknowledgment of payment of the tithe but also a confession of general obedience to the Lord and expectation of his blessing.

> Command #131, Dt 26:13, Declaration must be said with tithes: "Then you shall say to the Lord."
>
> Prohibition #150, Dt 26:14, One must not eat the second tithe while in a state of impurity: "Nor have I removed any of it while I was unclean."

Prohibition #151, Dt 26:14, One must not eat the second tithe while in a state of mourning: "I have not eaten any of the sacred portion while I was in mourning."

Prohibition #152, Dt 26:14, One must not use the second tithe redemption money for anything other than food and drink: "Nor have I offered any of it to the dead."

F. Conclusion (26:16–19)

Moses' concluding words hark back to the beginning of the covenant at Sinai in Exodus 19:5–6. If Israel obeys the covenant, they will be God's prized possession, and he will make them an exalted and holy nation.

VIII. THE COVENANT CEREMONY IN MOAB (27:1–28:68)

A. Instructions Regarding the Stones and Altar on Mount Ebal (27:1–10)

When the people enter the land they are here instructed to set up large stones on Mount Ebal (vv. 1–4) along with an altar for sacrifices, peace offerings, and a sacred meal (vv. 5–8). The stones were to be plastered over and prepared for writing. This was a common method for public monuments in ancient Canaan (cf. the Deir 'Alla texts).[22] These stones appear to be the same stones as those used for the altar (v. 8). The content of the writing is not specified, and it is difficult to surmise what it may have been. Some have suggested that only the Decalogue was written on the stones. Others have suggested that the writing consisted only of the blessings and curses of chapters 27–28. We cannot rule out the possibility that it may have been the whole of Deuteronomy. It is not likely, however, that it was the whole Pentateuch as we now have it. In Joshua 8:32, when this command was carried out, Joshua wrote upon the stones a "copy of the Law." The same expression is used as in Deuteronomy 17:18, where the king was to obtain a "copy of the Law" from the priests. The purpose of writing on the stones was to remind the people that it was important to obey the covenant and its laws.

The ceremony described in this text is reminiscent of the covenant ceremony in Exodus 24:4–8, where an altar was built with twelve stone pillars and God's words were written on the stone tablets and read before all the people. These instructions were fulfilled by Joshua and the people in Joshua 8:33–34.

B. Twelve Curses (27:11–26)

The people were to perform a further ceremony when they entered the land. It was to be held in the northern territory of the tribe of Manasseh near Shechem. There stood two mountains, Gerizim and Ebal. Half the tribes of Israel were to stand on Mount Gerizim (Simeon, Levi, Judah, Issachar, Joseph, and Benjamin) to recount the blessings of the covenant, and the other tribes were to stand on Mount Ebal (Reuben, Gad, Asher, Zebulun, Dan, and Naphtali) to recount the curses. The first set of curses, twelve in all,

---

[22]J. Hoftijzer and G. van der Kooij, *Aramaic Texts from Deir 'Alla* (Leiden: Brill, 1976), 23–28.

are recorded in 27:14–26. Curiously enough, the "blessings," which were to be recited on Mount Gerizim, are not recorded in the present passage. It is commonly held that the blessings have been omitted here to stress that Israel did not prove themselves obedient to the covenant and hence did not enjoy the blessings.

C. Blessings and Curses (28:1–68)

Immediately following the description of the covenant ceremony is another list of blessings and curses (vv. 2–14). These are not a continuation of the words which were to be recited at Ebal and Gerizim but are rather a further elaboration of the blessings and curses that would be incurred in the covenant. Joshua 8:34 implies, however, that these blessings and curses were also recited by the tribes at Ebal and Gerizim: "Joshua read all the words of the law—the blessings and the curses—just as it is written in the Book of the Law." If this "Book of the Law" is the same as our Pentateuch, then the blessings which they read on that occasion could only have been those of chapter 28, since, as we have seen above, no blessings are recorded in chapter 27.

Just as the curses were given more prominence in the ceremony of chapter 27, so the curses incurred by disobedience to the covenant are much more fully developed here. The perspective of the writer is that Israel will not prove faithful to the covenant (cf. Dt 31:16–18, 27) and will not enjoy the blessings of the covenant. Thus the curses receive much more attention in these sections than the blessings. The blessings are recorded in 28:1–14 and the second set of curses in 28:15–68.

The nature of the blessings is reminiscent of the blessing in the Garden of Eden—enjoyment of God's good land (Ge 1:28, "Be fruitful and multiply and fill the land"): "the fruit of your womb will be blessed, and the crops of your land, and the young of your livestock. . . . The LORD your God will bless you in the land he is giving you" (28:4, 8). The description of the curse is reminiscent of the curse after the Fall in the Genesis narratives—affliction and ultimately exile from God's land (Dt 28:36, 64–68). The description of the curse also anticipates the fate of the nation at the time of the Babylonian captivity (Jer 43:7; 52:1–27).

Command #8, Dt 28:9, One must imitate God: "And you shall walk in his ways."

IX. THE NEW COVENANT (29:1 [MT 28:69]–34:12)

A. Introduction (29:1 [MT 28:69])

It is not entirely correct to speak of a "renewal" of the covenant in this introductory verse. It states quite clearly that the covenant which Moses now speaks of is "in addition to the covenant he had made with them at Horeb [Sinai]." With these words, Moses deliberately sets up a contrast between the covenant at Sinai and the covenant he envisions for Israel in the future. The past has ended in Israel's failure to keep the covenant and to trust in God. However, there is hope for the future. It is to this hope that Moses now turns. Thus the content of the following chapter focuses clearly on the themes of the new covenant. It is no accident that it is precisely in these chapters that the NT writers see a prophetic message regarding faith and the coming of Christ (e.g., Ro 10:6–13).

B. Warnings Regarding the Covenant (29:2–28 [MT 1–27])

With a sober realism regarding Israel's failure to keep the covenant, Moses gives a final warning of the consequences of disobedience. In this section, the warnings appear designed not so much to call Israel to obedience as to lay before them the tragic consequences of their repeated failure. This is not just one more call for obedience. Deuteronomy already has plenty of such calls. It is rather the groundwork for a new work of God, which lies yet in the future and which will be described in chapter 30. It is the work of faith and obedience that flows from a new heart (30:6).

Moses begins with a review of Israel's complete failure to see and understand the work of God in their midst: "But to this day the LORD has not given you a mind that understands or eyes that see or ears that hear" (29:4 [MT 3]). This review covers the same lessons of the early chapters of Deuteronomy. It begins with God's work in Egypt and continues to the conquest of the Transjordan (vv. 2–8 [MT 1–7]). In this section, Moses further grounds the work of God in the promises made to the "fathers, Abraham, Isaac, and Jacob" (vv. 9–13 [MT 8–12]); thus he presupposes the lessons of the narratives of Genesis. As one example of this, Moses turns to the story of Sodom and Gomorrah (v. 23 [MT 22]). His treatment of that narrative is an interesting reversal of the themes found in Genesis. In Genesis, the account of the destruction of Sodom and Gomorrah was intended to show not only God's wrath against the wickedness of the pagan nations but also his salvation of the "righteous." The reminder that this same divine wrath could also be turned against his own disobedient people is a startling thought here at the close of the Pentateuch. It redefines, or at least clarifies, what the Genesis narrative means when it speaks of the "righteous." It was not enough to be God's own people, or even to be a member of the covenant. Something more is here called for. Initially in this chapter that "something more" is described negatively as "they went off and worshiped other gods" (v. 27 [MT 26]). The next chapter, however, stresses the positive side: "The LORD your God will circumcise your hearts and the hearts of your descendants, so that you may love him with all your heart and with all your soul and live" (30:6).

C. Conclusion (29:29 [MT 28])

Moses ends his opening remarks with a statement regarding the limits of God's revelation. The abruptness of the conclusion seems to correspond to the sense of this last statement. God's revelation has limits. God has not revealed the whole of his wisdom and knowledge, but he has revealed "the words of this law," and they are given to all generations. There is no end to the "secret mysteries" that human beings devise about God and his world. Moses, however, puts a halt to all of them here by simply pointing to God's great act of grace in revealing his will in the Torah.

Some have understood the "secret things" in this passage as "secret sins," and hence have seen in these remarks a limit to the kinds of sins for which human beings are to judge themselves.[23] But the passage suggests otherwise. The contrast with "that which is revealed," namely, the Scriptures, suggests that the "secret things" are simply that which God has not revealed in Scripture.

D. Future Blessing (30:1–20)

Before bringing the book to its conclusion, Moses takes a long look into the future of this people. He speaks of a time when Israel's disobedience would lead to their captivity in a foreign land. He has already anticipated this view of Israel's future in his previous words (e.g., 28:36, 64–68). However, he now looks beyond the destruction of that time of judgment to an even more distant time of restoration and redemption for Israel. At some point in the future, when Israel finds itself dispersed among all the nations, they will again turn to the Lord and the Lord will have compassion on them and restore them to the land (30:1–5).

At that time the Lord will give them a new heart, that is, a "circumcised heart" (30:6; cf. 10:16), and they will "love him with all [their] heart and with all [their] soul and they will live" (30:6). Moses apparently has in view the promise of the "new covenant" spoken of in Jeremiah 31:31–34 and Ezekiel 36:22–28. For these later prophets the hope still remained that in spite of their repeated failure, God's promises to the fathers would ultimately be fulfilled, and sometime in the future Israel would be restored both to the land and to the covenant.

In the time after the Babylonian captivity, when the Israelites were allowed to return to the land, much expectation arose regarding the fulfillment of this promise in Deuteronomy 30. For example, the words of Nehemiah's prayer (Ne 9) reflect his hope that in his own day, after the Babylonian captivity, the promise would be fulfilled. As the book of Nehemiah goes on to show, however, Nehemiah's hope was not realized, and the time of the return from Babylonian captivity was not to be the time of its fulfillment. In the NT, the example of Simeon (Lk 2:25) shows that at the time of Christ's coming, devout Israelites were still awaiting its fulfillment. Jesus himself was quite clear that these texts in Deuteronomy and the Prophets, as well as many other statements in Scripture, were to be understood as pointers to his coming (e.g., Lk 24:25–27).

In explaining the nature of the new covenant which he envisions in these chapters, Moses compares it to the covenant at Sinai (Dt 30:11–14). In the covenant given at Sinai, the Law was written on tablets of stone which Moses had to go up the mountain to receive and then take back to proclaim to the people. Thus when he says in the present chapter: "This commandment . . . is not up in heaven, so that you have to ask, 'Who will ascend into heaven to get it and proclaim it to us so we may obey it?' " he means that in the new covenant the Law would not be given again on tablets of stone but written on circumcised hearts (as in Eze 36:26). The view that Moses went "up to heaven" to receive the Law has already been expressed in Deuteronomy. At Sinai, for example, God spoke directly to the people "from heaven" (Dt 4:36). Moses' words here also reflect the words of the people at

---

[23]"Concealed acts concern the LORD our God" (*Tanakh: The Holy Scriptures* (Philadelphia: Jewish Publication Society, 1988), 322. This is also the view of Ibn Ezra (ad loc.).

Mount Sinai, "You [Moses] go near and listen to all that the LORD our GAod says. Then tell us whatever the LORD our God tells you" (5:27; cf. Ex 20:18–21).[24] Furthermore, his reference to "going across the sea to get [the commandment]" (30:13) also appears, in the larger context of the Pentateuch, to be an allusion to Moses' leading the people across the Red Sea and to Sinai. Thus in contrast to the giving of the Law in the Sinai covenant, in the covenant of which Moses speaks here, "the word is very near you; it is in your mouth and in your heart to do it" (v. 14). This is again very similar to the view of Jeremiah with respect to the new covenant (Jer 31:31). Much in keeping with the intent of the Pentateuch, Paul also understands the reference in this verse to the coming of Christ and the new covenant emphasis on "faith," i.e., messianically (Ro 10:6).

As the word "today" shows (Dt 30:15), at this point in the chapter the perspective and focus of Moses' words are no longer that of the future time after the captivity. This word brings us back to Moses and the people who are about to enter the land. Moses closes this section with several allusions to the first instance of the revelation of the will of God in the Scriptures, Adam in the Garden of Eden. His purpose is to draw a comparison between the first work of God in providing a "good land" for his people and the situation of Israel as they prepare to enter again into God's good land. Just as God had put "the Tree of Knowledge of Good and Evil" before the first man and woman in the Garden (Ge 2:9b) and had commanded them not to eat from it on pain of death (2:17), that is, being separated from the "Tree of Life" (Ge 3:22–24), so now Moses again presents to the people the choice of "good and evil" and "life and death" (Dt 30:16). Just as Adam and Eve were to depend on God's knowledge of "the good and the evil," so also in this covenant the people were to look to God's Torah as the pathway to the "good" and the means of regaining the "life" that was lost in the Fall (Ge 3:22–24). Just as the godly were described in the Genesis narratives as those who "walked with God" (3:8; 5:22–24; 6:9; 17:1), so also here, keeping the covenant and enjoying God's blessings are described as "walking in his ways" (Dt 30:16). Carefully choosing his words to reflect back on these earlier themes in the Pentateuch, Moses skillfully draws his book to a conclusion by returning to its central themes. He thus ends on the same note as he began—compare: "You will live and increase, and the LORD your God will bless you in the land you are entering to possess" (30:16) with: "Be fruitful, multiply, and fill the land" (Ge 1:28).

The tragedy latent in these final words of hope is that in the next chapter Moses will show that the future choice of God's people would not be for the good; rather, "they will forsake [the Lord] and break the covenant [he] made with them . . . [and] many disasters [evils] and difficulties will come upon them" (Dt 31:16–17). Their actions were thus foreshadowed in those of the first man and woman in the Garden (Ge 3:6–8). There is the tragedy of future failure lying behind all these expressions of hope.

---

[24]Targum Neofiti 1 represents an early interpretation of this verse that comes close to what we are suggesting: "The law is not in the heavens, that one should say, 'Would that we had one like Moses the prophet who would go up to heaven and fetch it. . . .'" Neofiti 1, ed. Alejandro Díez Macho (Madrid: Lansejo Superior de Investigaciones científicas, 1978), 5.255.

Command #94, Dt 30:3, One must keep his word: "According to all that goes out from his mouth he shall do."

E. Provisions for Maintaining the Leadership of Moses (31:1–29)

The work of Moses was to be maintained and continued in various ways after his death. The Lord himself was to go out before the people in battle with the Canaanites (31:3–6), and Joshua, in place of Moses, was to be their leader (31:1–8, 14–18, 23). Moses was to write down the Torah which God had given them and entrust it to the priests. The priests were to keep the Torah in (or beside; see comments above on Ex 16:34) the ark of the covenant, and it was to be read publicly every seven years during the Feast of Tabernacles (Dt 31:9–13, 24–27).

Command #16, Dt 31:12, One must assemble every seventh year to hear the Torah read: "Gather together the people, the men."

Furthermore, Moses was to write a song which was to serve as a continual reminder of the message of the Torah (vv. 19–22; 31:30–32:47).

Command #18, Dt 31:19, Each person must write for himself a copy of the Torah: "Write for yourselves this song."

This section stresses repeatedly the disobedience and failure of the people (vv. 16–18, 27–29). According to 31:29, it was because of the failure of the people that God commanded Moses to write his song. The song was to be a warning that "in the last days" ("in days to come," NIV) disaster would fall on God's people. It is important to see that the introduction of this poem clearly sets its context as "the last days." It is not about something that will happen in the immediate future, but rather something that will take place "at the end of the days" (באחרית הימים). It is not surprising then to find that this poem has no references to specific historical events. The description of the judgment of God on Israel and the nations is apocalyptic in scope and global in extent. Chapter 32 is another example of the way poetry is used in the Pentateuch to teach its major themes. In Genesis 49, Jacob's poetic "last words" provided a similar panoramic view of God's future work (הימים בחרית) in history. The poetry of Balaam in Numbers 24 is yet another example.

F. The Song of Moses (31:30–32:47)

The central theme of the poem is Israel's apostasy and God's threatening judgment. After a short introduction (vv. 1–7), the poem begins with a description of God's election of Israel (vv. 8–9) and his care for them from the time of the wilderness wanderings (vv. 10–12) to their possession and initial enjoyment of the blessings in the land (vv. 13–14). However, the poem turns quickly to Israel's presumptuous neglect of God's goodness and their apostasy (vv. 15–21a). Once again it is idolatry that turns their hearts from God. Following the description of Israel's apostasy, Moses gives a dramatic portrayal of God's future outpouring of wrath on his people (vv. 21b–27) and Israel's continuing blindness in the face of it (vv. 28–33). The emphasis on God's judgment of Israel raises the question of God's judgment of all the nations (vv. 34–38). The vengeance stored up against Israel (v. 34) is grounded in God's righteous vindication of the iniquity of all peoples (vv.

35–42). In the end, however, God's judgment of Israel and the nations leads to a broader understanding of the concept of the people of God—not just Israel but the nations as well are called to praise God as "his people" (v. 43).[25]

Moses closes his song with a reminder to the people to pay close attention to these words he has put before them and to teach them carefully to their children (32:45–47). These words are of central importance. They are the very life of the people as they now enter the Promised Land. Again it can be seen that the text portrays the Torah as God's gift of life to his people in much the same way as the Tree of Life was put into the midst of the Garden of Eden (Ge 2:8–17). Just as obedience to the Lord's command not to eat of the Tree of Knowledge of Good and Evil was the key to their access to the Tree of Life (Ge 2:16–17), so obedience to the Lord's command in the Torah was to be the key to Israel's "living long in the land" that God had prepared for them.

> Prohibition #194, Dt 32:38, One must not use wine offered to idols: It is said of idols, "they who drank the wine of their drink offerings."

G. God's Instructions to Moses to Die on Mount Nebo (32:48–52)

God's instructions to Moses are given here a second time (see Nu 27:12–14). In this passage the instructions are more detailed. The purpose of the repetition of God's words to Moses is not immediately clear, though we may suppose that it was to reestablish the general chronological sequence of events here at the close of the book. In this way, we are reminded that the whole of Deuteronomy has been intended to be read as a discourse between Moses and Israel. Thus here at its close, the line of events is taken up again from the narrative at the close of the book of Numbers. This section in Deuteronomy also anticipates the final chapter, which records the death of Moses. Moses' death was thus a fulfillment of God's words spoken in the present text. Those who hold to a Mosaic authorship of the whole Pentateuch usually see these last chapters as a supplementary addition.[26]

H. The Blessing of Moses (33:1–29)

The final words of Moses to the people are introduced as a "blessing." They begin with a brief introduction (vv. 2–5), and, after listing the blessings for each of the tribes of Israel (vv. 6–25), Simeon excluded,[27] they conclude with a summary (vv. 26–29).

1. Introduction (33:1–5)

Moses returns to the central theme of the Pentateuch—the appearance of God among his people that was initiated at Mount Sinai and continued

---

[25]The Hebrew text reads, "Rejoice, O nations, his people," thus designating "the nations" as "his people." The NIV and other English translations have amended the text to read, "Rejoice, O nations, *with* his people." There is no good textual reason to change the Hebrew text. The idea expressed that "the nations" are God's people is a theme also found in other parts of Scripture (cf. Ps 47:9 and Isa 19:24–25).

[26]See, e.g., Keil, *Pentateuch*, 3:492.

[27]Since the tribe of Levi is included in this list, the tribe of Simeon is excluded to maintain the number of twelve sons. See also commentary on Ge 49:5–7.

throughout their time in the wilderness. This was a time, Moses says in this passage, when God showed Israel his love and cared for them with his holy angels. Through the Law given them by Moses Israel received God's instruction. The *Law* here refers not to the laws given at Sinai but to the "Book of the Law" which Moses wrote down and gave to the people (31:24–26). The present text is probably appended to the Pentateuch as a whole, its purpose being to show the importance of this book as divine instruction. Thus the blessing of the tribe of Levi stresses the responsibility given to the Levites in 31:9–31 and 24–26 of guarding the "Book of the Law" and teaching it to Israel (33:10). Already with the Pentateuch there is a clear distinction between the laws given Israel at Sinai and the Law or Torah, which is represented by the Pentateuch itself.

Furthermore, Moses is here portrayed as a "king" among God's people. Though it is possible to argue that the "king" in 33:5 is meant to be understood as the Lord, the immediate context suggests strongly that it is Moses. This is important because the next chapter, Deuteronomy 34, views Moses as a prototype of the coming prophet who was promised in 18:15. Thus at the close of the Pentateuch, the two central messianic visions of the book—that of a coming king (Ge 49:10; Nu 24:7–9) and that of a prophet (Dt 18:15)—are united in the figure of Moses, the prophet-king. We should note that throughout the Pentateuch Moses also carries out the duties of priest. Thus in the figure of Moses, the Pentateuch is able to bring together the offices of prophet, priest, and king. The author is always careful to note, however, that Moses was not a priest of the house of Aaron. The Aaronic priesthood is of a different order than that pictured in the office of Moses. If we were looking for an analogy to Moses elsewhere in the Pentateuch, we need look no farther than the figure of Melchizedek, the priest-king from Salem. Thus as Melchizedek the priest-king blessed Abraham at the beginning of the patriarchal narratives: "God Most High, who delivered [מִגֵּן] your enemies into your hand" (Ge 14:19), so here Moses the priest-king blessed the Israelites at the conclusion: "He is your shield [מָגֵן]. . . . Your enemies will cower before you" (Dt 33:29).

2. Blessings (33:6–25)

The blessings of each of the individual tribes are similar in many respects to the words of Jacob in Genesis 49:1–27. Unlike Genesis 49, however, where Judah is the central figure, the present passage pays rather scant attention to the tribe of Judah and emphasizes instead the importance of Levi and Joseph. The Levites are given the role of teaching the Torah to all Israel (Dt 33:8–11), and the tribe of Joseph is pictured as enjoying the most abundant part of the land (vv. 13–17). The intention of the blessings is clearly to include the whole of Israel in God's blessing, both the tribes of the north, represented here in Joseph (Ephraim and Manasseh, 33:17), and the priests, the house of Levi, who are otherwise excluded from the inheritance of the land.

We should not think, however, that the importance of the tribe of Judah has been diminished in this blessing. On the contrary, by focusing on the centrality of the "king" among the tribes of Israel, the introduction to the blessing draws heavily on the earlier blessings which have stressed the role of Judah in God's future dealings with Israel (Ge 49:10; Nu 24:7–9).

3. Conclusion (33:26–29)

The final words of the blessing speak of the nation as a whole and of its enjoyment of God's good gift of the land. As we might expect, here at the end of the book, Moses pictures Israel's dwelling in the land as a reversal of the events of the early chapters of Genesis, when Adam and Eve were cast out of the Garden. Just as God had once "driven" (גרש) the man and woman from his "good land" (Ge 3:23) and "stationed" (שכן) cherubim to guard its entry, so he will again "drive" (גרש, Dt 33:27) the enemy from the "good land" and "station" (שכן, v. 28) Israel there to enjoy its blessings. In other words, the future that Moses envisions for the people of Israel is like that which God intended in the beginning.

I. The Death of Moses (34:1–12)

The account of Moses' death appears to have been added to the end of the Pentateuch long after the event. By the time this last chapter was written, the burial of Moses was so far in the past that the location of his grave was uncertain to the writer: "To this day no one knows where his grave is" (v. 6). Furthermore, a long succession of prophets has come and gone so that the writer can say, "Since then, no prophet has risen in Israel like Moses" (v. 10). Though added later, this chapter plays a major role in the interpretation of the Pentateuch in its final form.

The chapter provides the final statement regarding the Lord's refusal to allow Moses to enter the Promised Land. It thus links up with an important theme in the Pentateuch: Moses, who lived under the Law, was not allowed to enter into God's blessings because he failed "to believe" (Nu 20:12). According to this chapter, Moses did not die of old age—"his eyes were not weak nor his strength gone" (Dt 34:7). His death was punishment, just as the generation that died in the wilderness during the forty years was punished (Nu 14:22–23). That he was 120 years old may give the appearance that he died at a ripe old age, but one must remember that it was just this age that was set as a limit to human life after the Fall (Ge 6:3). From the perspective of the Pentateuch as a whole, Moses died young. He did not live the many centuries of the early patriarchs before the Flood. Thus at the close of the Pentateuch the life of Moses becomes the last example of the consequences of the Fall of the first man and woman. Like them, he was not allowed to enjoy the blessing of God's good land.

In contrast to its portrayal of Moses, this final chapter also portrays Joshua as the new leader, ready and able to take the people into the Promised Land in obedience to God's commands. What is stressed here is that Joshua was "filled with the spirit of wisdom" (34:9) and thus able to do the work of God. Like Joseph (Ge 41:37) and Bezalel (Ex 31:3), who were filled with "the Spirit of God," Joshua was able to do God's work successfully. Thus this last chapter of the Pentateuch returns to a central theme, begun already in the first chapter of Genesis: "and the Spirit of God hovered over the face of the deep" (Ge 1:2). It is the Spirit of God that is the means of doing the work of God. Even when God himself does his work of creation, it is by means of his Spirit. Such an emphasis on the role of God's Spirit is central to the later prophets' view of the new covenant (Eze 36:26).

Finally, this last chapter provides an important link to the books of the

Bible which follow by showing us that, long after the time of Moses, "the prophet like Moses" had not yet come (34:10). For example, it would otherwise be possible to read the book of Joshua and conclude that all the promises to Israel had been fulfilled in the successful conquest of the land under Joshua's leadership. Deuteronomy 34, however, warns us that there is still more to God's promises than that which lay immediately ahead in Israel's history. In this respect it anticipates further statements in Joshua (e.g., Jos 23:15–16) and Judges (Jdg 2:10–15) that show that the initial success of Israel under Joshua's leadership ended in failure, much as had been the case with Israel under Moses' leadership. We are thus invited to look beyond those events to the coming of someone else, one like Joshua, and also one like Moses. In other words, this final chapter picks up the theme of the coming Messiah, and using Moses as a type, it turns our gaze beyond the immediate historical events to the future work of God in fulfilling his promises to the fathers.

APPENDIX:
Summary of Maimonides'
List of the Laws in the Torah

In the twelfth century A.D. the Jewish philosopher and exegete Maimonides published a definitive list of the laws in the Pentateuch, the *Sepher Mitzvoth* (Book of the Commandments).[1] In this list Maimonides enumerated 613 distinct laws in the Pentateuch. Before Maimonides, the traditional number of laws in the Pentateuch was taken to be 611. This number equals the *gematria* value of the Hebrew word for "Law" (תורה).[2] Maimonides obtained his number by accepting the traditional count of 611 and interpreting the first statement of the Decalogue, "I am the LORD your God" (Ex 20:1), as a command to believe in the existence of God, and the *Shema* (Dt 6:4) as a command to believe that God is one. Of these 613 laws, Maimonides, following earlier tradition, distinguished 248 positive commands and 365 negative. He reckoned that since there were 248 distinct parts of the human body, one was to remember to obey God's positive commands with "all one's self," and since there were 365 days of the year, one was to remember not to disobey God's commands each day of the year. Since the time of Maimonides, his count of 613 laws has been accepted as the traditional number.

---

[1]*Sepher Mitzvoth*, ed. Mordecai J. Lev (Jerusalem: Mossad Harav Kook, 1990). I am dependent on the article "Commandments, the 613," in *Encyclopedia Judaica* for the subdivisions of the laws, and on Arias Montanus, *Liber Generationis et Regenerationis Adam* (Antwerp, 1593), for the rendering of some of the laws.

[2]*Gematria* is the practice of comparing words and their meaning by assigning numerical values to the Hebrew consonants.

Maimonides' list of laws has particularly lasting value in that it represents an attempt to state comprehensively the principles represented in the collection of pentateuchal laws. One sees quite clearly in Maimonides' list an attempt to comprehend the whole of the will of God expressed in these various laws in the Pentateuch. It is for this reason that we have thought it helpful to include Maimonides' list in this appendix. In cases where Maimonides has focused more on justifying later traditional law than on formulating the precise principle found in the biblical text, we have cast the law in the terms in which it is stated in the biblical text rather than the later law. In those cases we have included Maimonides' interpretation in parentheses and marked it with "M."

Though this expression of the meaning of the laws in the Pentateuch is an important part of the tradition surrounding the biblical text, no special theological or exegetical value is attached to it here. It does, however, represent a careful and sensitive reading of the text. As a part of this commentary its value lies in the example it gives of the way in which the pentateuchal laws can and have shaped the moral conscience of Judaism and Christianity. Christians through the ages have been fundamentally influenced in their understanding of biblical law by the particular statement of it found in Maimonides' list.[3]

Thus we have pointed out examples where Jesus and the NT writers take up or assume these same principles. The list is not intended to be exhaustive; the references to the NT are by no means complete. Moreover, we are not suggesting that in each case these particular commandments from the Torah were necessarily or consciously on the mind of NT writers. A close reading of the list, however, shows clearly how much of the moral and theological structure of the NT is based on Moses' teaching in the Torah.

COMMANDS

A. Commands relating to one's relationship with God:

1. Ex 20:1, One must believe that God is: "I am the Lord your God" (cf. Dt 5:6).

—Heb 11:6, "anyone who comes to [God] must believe that he exists."

2. Dt 6:4, One must believe that God is one: "Hear, O Israel."

—Ro 3:29, "Is God the God of Jews only? Is he not the God of Gentiles too? Yes, of Gentiles too, since there is only one God."

3. Dt 6:5, One must love God: "You shall love the Lord your God."

—Mt 22:35–38, "One of them, an expert in the law, tested him with this question: 'Teacher, which is the greatest commandment in the Law?' Jesus replied: 'Love the Lord your God with all your heart and with all your soul and with all your mind.' This is the first and greatest commandment."

4. Dt 6:13, One must fear God: "You shall fear the Lord your God."

---

[3]For an excellent discussion of the influence that Maimonides' interpretation of the pentateuchal laws in his *Mishneh Torah* has had on Christian theology and exegesis, see Aaron L. Katchen, *Christian Hebraists and Dutch Rabbis: Seventeenth Century Apologetics and the Study of Maimonides' Mishneh Torah*, Harvard University Center for Jewish Studies (Cambridge: Harvard Univ. Press, 1984).

—**Mt 10:28–29,** "Do not be afraid of those who kill the body but cannot kill the soul. Rather, be afraid of the one who can destroy both soul and body in hell."

5. **Ex 23:25,** One must worship God: "You shall worship the Lord your God." (Cf. Dt 6:13, "him you shall serve"; 11:13, "to serve him with all your heart"; 13:4 [EVV5], "and him you shall serve.")

—**Mt 4:10,** "Jesus said to him, 'Away from me, Satan! For it is written: 'Worship the Lord your God, and serve him only.'"

6. **Dt 10:20,** One must cling to God: "And to him you shall cling."

—**1Co 6:17,** "But he who unites himself with the Lord is one with him in spirit."

7. **Dt 6:13,** One must swear by the name of God: "And you shall swear by his name." (Cf. Dt 10:20.)

8. **Dt 28:9,** One must imitate God: "And you shall walk in his ways."

—**Eph 2:10,** "For we are his workmanship, created in Christ Jesus for good works, which God prepared beforehand, that we should walk in them" (RSV).

9. **Lev 22:32,** One must sanctify the name of God: "I will be sanctified in the midst of the sons of Israel."

—**1Pe 3:15,** "But sanctify Christ as Lord in your hearts" (NASB).

B. Commands relating to the study of the Torah:

10. **Dt 6:7,** One must recite the *Shema* each morning: "And you shall speak them."

11. **Dt 6:7,** One must teach the Torah: "And you shall teach them to your sons."

—**Col 3:16,** "Let the word of Christ dwell in you richly as you teach and admonish one another with all wisdom."

12. **Dt 6:8,** One must bind *tefillin* on the head: "And they shall be bands between your eyes."

13. **Dt 6:8,** One must bind *tefillin* on the hand: "You shall bind them for signs upon your hands."

14. **Nu 15:38,** One must attach tassels to one's garments: "You are to make tassels on the corners of your garments."

15. **Dt 6:9,** One must fix a *mezuzah* on the door: "You shall write them upon the doorpost of your house."

16. **Dt 31:12,** One must assemble every seventh year to hear the Torah read: "Gather together the people, the men."

17. **Dt 17:18,** The king must write for himself a copy of the Torah: "And when he sits upon the throne of his kingdom, he shall write for himself a copy of this Torah."

18. **Dt 31:19,** Each person must write for himself a copy of the Torah: "Write for yourselves this song."

19. **Dt 8:10,** One must give a blessing after eating: "And you shall eat and be satisfied and bless the Lord your God."

—**Luke 11:3,** "Give us each day our daily bread."

C. Commands relating to the temple:

20. Ex 25:8, To build a temple: "And they shall make for me a temple."

21. Lev 19:30, To fear (i.e., respect) the temple: "My holy place you shall fear."

—Mt 21:12, "Jesus entered the temple area and drove out all who were buying and selling there."

22. Nu 18:4, Priests are to care for the temple always: "You and your sons with you before the tent of testimony."

23. Nu 18:23, Levites alone to serve in the temple: "It is the Levites alone who are to do the work in the holy place."

24. Ex 30:19, Priests must wash before they serve in the temple: "And Aaron and his sons shall wash their hands and feet when they enter the Tent of Meeting."

25. Ex 27:21, Priests must light the candles in the temple: "And Aaron and his sons are to arrange it [the lamp] from evening until morning before the Lord."

26. Nu 6:23, Priests must bless Israel: "Thus you shall bless the sons of Israel."

27. Ex 25:30, Priests must set up the shewbread (bread of the Presence): "And you shall put the shewbread upon the table."

28. Ex 30:7, Priests must burn the incense on the golden altar: "Aaron must burn fragrant incense on the altar every morning when he tends the lamps."

29. Lev 6:6, To keep the fire burning upon the altar: "The continual fire shall burn upon the altar."

30. Lev 6:3, Priests are to remove ashes daily from the altar: "The priest shall put on his linen clothes."

31. Nu 5:2, Remove unclean (leprous/flow) from the camp: "And they shall send out of the camp all the leprous and those that have a flow."

32. Lev 21:8, Give honor to the priests: "And you shall treat him as holy because he brings the bread of your God near."

33. Ex 28:2, Priests are to wear special garments: "And they shall make holy garments for Aaron."

34. Nu 7:9, Priests are to carry the ark on their shoulders: "The priests shall carry the ark upon their shoulders."

35. Ex 30:31, Holy oil must be prepared: "This is to be my sacred anointing oil for the generations to come."

36. Dt 18:6–8, Priests should do their duties in rotation: "If a Levite comes from one of your towns . . . he may minister in the name of the Lord his God like all his fellow Levites who serve there in the presence of the Lord. He is to share equally in their benefits."

37. Lev 21:2–3, Priests should become unclean for certain close relatives: "For them he shall be unclean."

38. Lev 21:13, The high priest should marry a virgin: "And he shall marry a woman in her virginity."

D. Commands dealing with sacrifices:

39. Nu 28:3, Two yearling lambs presented to the Lord daily (Tamid): "You are to present to the Lord: two lambs a year old without defect, as a regular burnt offering each day."

40. Lev 6:13 (EVV 20), The high priest is to present a meal offering twice daily: "This is the gift of Aaron and his sons."

41. Nu 28:9, An additional gift (*musaf*) is to be offered every Sabbath: "Two yearling lambs."

42. Nu 28:11, An additional gift (*musaf*) is to be offered every month: "At the beginning of your months."

43. Lev 23:36, An additional gift (*musaf*) is to be offered on each of the seven days of Passover: "Seven days you shall offer fire to the Lord."

44. Lev 23:10, A meal offering of a sheaf of barley is to be given on the sixteenth day of Nisan, the second day of Passover: "You shall being the sheaf."

45. Nu 28:26–27, An additional gift (*musaf*) is to be given fifty days from the offering of the sheaf, i.e., on *Shavuot* (Feast of Weeks): "On the day of the firstfruits when they bring their offering."

46. Lev 23:17, One must bring two loaves of bread as a wave (heave) offering: "From your dwellings you shall bring bread for the wave offering."

47. Nu 29:1–2, An additional gift (*musaf*) is to be given on Rosh Hashanah (1st of Tishri): "On the seventh month, on the first day of the month, you shall make a burnt offering."

48. Nu 29:7–8, An additional gift (*musaf*) is to be given on the Day of Atonement (10th of Tishri): "On the tenth of the seventh month you shall offer a burnt offering, fire to the Lord."

49. Lev 16:1ff., The service (*Avodah*) of the Day of Atonement. All the duties of this day are considered one command.

50. Nu 29:13, An additional offering (*musaf*) is to be given for the Feast of Sukkoth (Tabernacles): "And you shall bring a burnt offering."

51. Nu 29:36, An additional offering (*musaf*) is to be given for the eighth day of the Feast of Sukkoth (Tabernacles): "And you shall offer a burnt offering."

52. Ex 23:14, Pilgrimage to the temple three times a year: "Three pilgrimages you shall make for me in a year."

53. Ex 34:23, One must appear during each of the three pilgrimages: "Three times in the year all your males must appear." (Cf. Dt 16:16.)

54. Dt 16:14, One must rejoice during each festival: "You should rejoice in your festival."

—Lk 13:10–17, "On a Sabbath Jesus was teaching in one of the synagogues . . . and all the people rejoiced at all the glorious things that were done by him."

55. Ex 12:6, One must slaughter the Passover lamb on the fourteenth of Nisan: "Until the fourteenth day of the month and then all the congregation of Israel shall slaughter it at twilight."

56. Ex 12:8, One must eat the roasted Passover lamb on the night of the fifteenth of Nisan according to the instructions (e.g., in one house, with matzo upon the bitter herbs): "And they shall eat the meat in that night, roasted with fire, and matzo upon the bitter herbs they shall eat it."

57. Nu 9:11, Whoever was prohibited from slaughtering the first Passover lamb should slaughter the second Passover lamb: "In the second month at twilight they shall do it."

58. Nu 9:11, The meat of the second Passover should be eaten on the night of

the fifteenth of Iyar with matzo upon the bitter herbs: "Upon the matzo and bitter herbs they shall eat it." (Cf. Ex 12:8.)

59. Nu 10:10, Trumpets should be sounded at sacred times with offerings: "And in the day which you rejoice you shall sound the trumpets."

60. Lev 22:27, Sacrificial animals must be eight days old or more: "And it shall be seven days with its mother."

61. Lev 22:21, Sacrificial animals must be without blemish: "It must be without blemish to be acceptable."

62. Lev 2:13, Offerings must be salted: "Upon all your offerings you must offer salt."

63. Lev 1:2, The procedure of the burnt offering: "When any of you brings an offering to the Lord."

64. Lev 6:18 (EVV 25), The procedure of the sin offering: "This is the law of the sin offering."

65. Lev 7:1, The procedure of the guilt offering: "This is the law of the guilt offering."

66. Lev 3:1, The procedure of the peace offering: "If his offering is a peace offering."

67. Lev 2:1, The procedure of the meal (grain) offering: "When one brings a meal offering to the Lord." (Cf. Lev 6:7, "This is the law of the meal offering.")

68. Lev 4:13, If the congregation of Israel err in a decision, they must bring an offering: "If all the congregation of Israel err."

69. Lev 4:27, If a single individual errs unintentionally he must bring a sin offering: "If one individual sins unintentionally."

70. Lev 5:17–18, A sin offering that hangs in doubt: "If a person sins and does what is forbidden in any of the Lord's commands."

71. Lev 5:15, The actual guilt offering for various sins: "When a person commits a violation and sins unintentionally."

72. Lev 5:1–11, The offering of varying cost: "If he cannot afford a lamb, he is to bring two doves or two young pigeons."

73. Nu 5:6–7, Confession of sin before God and repentance: "That person must confess the sin."

—Mt 5:22–23, "Therefore, if you are offering your gift at the altar and there remember that your brother has something against you, leave your gift there in front of the altar. First go and be reconciled to your brother; then come and offer your gift."

—Luke 19:8–9, "Zacchaeus stood up and said to the Lord, '. . . if I have cheated anybody out of anything, I will pay back four times the amount.' Jesus said to him, 'Today salvation has come to this house, because this man, too, is a son of Abraham.'"

74. Lev 15:13–15, The offering of a man healed from a flow: "When a man with a flow is clean from his flow, on the eighth day he shall give two doves."

75. Lev 15:28–29, The offering of a woman healed from a flow: "When she is clean from her flow."

76. Lev 12:6, The offering after childbirth: "And when the days of her cleanliness for the son or daughter is complete, she shall bring a yearling lamb."

77. Lev 14:10, The offering of a leper who was cleansed: "On the eighth day he shall take two lambs."

78. Lev 27:32, The tithe of one's cattle: "All the tithe of the herd or flock."

79. Ex 13:2, Sanctifying the firstborn males: "Sanctify to me all the firstborn males."

80. Ex 22:28, Redemption of firstborn sons: "The firstborn of your sons belongs to me." (Cf. Nu 18:15, "You shall redeem the firstborn of man.")

81. Ex 34:20, Redemption of a firstborn ass: "The firstborn of an ass you must redeem with a sheep."

82. Ex 13:13, One must break the neck of an ass if it is not redeemed: "If you do not redeem it [an ass] you must break its neck."

83. Dt 12:5, Animals to be used as offerings must be offered at the earliest opportunity: "You shall come there and you shall bring them there."

84. Dt 12:14, Offerings are to be given at the temple only: "There you shall bring your burnt offerings and do them there."

85. Dt 12:26, Offerings from outside the land are also to be brought to the temple: "Take your consecrated things and whatever you have vowed to give and go to the place."

86. Dt 12:15, Redemption of consecrated things that have been blemished: "Surely in every place you desire you may slaughter and eat the meat."

87. Lev 27:10, An animal exchanged for an offering is holy: "It and his exchange are holy." (Cf. Lev 27:33, An animal exchanged for an offering is holy: "It and his exchange are holy.")

88. Lev 6:9, The priests are to eat the remainder of the meal offering: "The remainder from the meal offering Aaron and his sons shall eat."

89. Ex 29:33, The priests are to eat the meat of the consecrated offerings (sin and guilt): "They shall eat that by which atonement was made for their ordination."

90. Lev 7:19, Consecrated things which have become unclean must be burned: "Meat which touches anything unclean."

91. Lev 7:17, That which is left over from the offering must be burned: "That which is left over from the meat of the sacrifice shall be burned in fire."

E. Commands dealing with vows:

92. Nu 6:5, A Nazirite must let his hair grow: "He must let the hair of his head grow long."

93. Nu 6:18, At the end of his vow, the Nazirite must shave his hair and bring his offerings: "The Nazirite must shave off the hair that he dedicated." (Cf. Nu 6:13, "When the period of his separation is over.")

94. Dt 23:24 (EVV 23), One must keep his word: "You shall keep what comes out from your lips." (Cf. Dt 30:3, One must keep his word: "According to all that goes out from his mouth he shall do.")

—Mt 5:33–37, "You have heard that it was said to the people long ago, 'Do not break your oath, but keep the oaths you have made to the Lord.' But I tell you, Do not swear at all. . . . Simply let your 'Yes' be 'Yes,' and your 'No,' 'No.'"

95. Nu 30:3 (EVV 2), One must not break a vow: "He must not break his word but must do everything he said." (M. Only a judge can annul a vow in accordance with

the law: "and he must not break his own word"—implying someone else, a judge, can break his word.)

F. Commands dealing with ritual purity:

96. Lev 11:8, One who touches a carcass is unclean: "You shall not touch their carcass."

97. Lev 11:29–31, The eight types of creeping things are unclean: "This is what is unclean."

98. Lev 11:34, Food and drink become unclean when in contact with an unclean object: "All kinds of food which come into contact with water are unclean."

99. Lev 15:19, A woman in menstruation is unclean: "The impurity of her monthly period."

100. Lev 12:2, A woman who has recently given birth is unclean: "A woman who becomes pregnant and gives birth."

101. Lev 13:3, A leper is unclean: "It is an infectious skin disease."

102. Lev 13:51, A leprous garment is unclean: "It is a destructive mildew."

103. Lev 14:44, The house of a leper is unclean: "If the mildew has spread in the house."

104. Lev 15:2, A man with a flow is unclean: "When any man has a bodily discharge."

105. Lev 15:16, A man with an emission of semen is unclean: "When a man has an emission of semen."

106. Lev 15:19, A woman with a flow is unclean: "When a woman has her regular flow of blood."

107. Nu 19:14, A corpse is unclean: "This is the law of a man who dies in a tent."

108. Lev 19:13, Observance of the water of cleansing: "Because the water of cleansing has not been sprinkled on him he is unclean." (Cf. Lev 19:21, "Anyone who touches the water of cleansing will be unclean till evening.")

109. Lev 15:16, Observance of cleansing in water: "He shall wash in water."

110. Lev 14:2, Procedure for cleansing of leprosy: "This shall be the law of leprosy." (Cf. Lev 14:49, "To purify the house.")

111. Lev 14:9, Shaving the head of the leper: "On the seventh day, he must shave off all his hair."

112. Lev 13:45, A leper must be made conspicuous: "The person with such an infectious disease must wear torn clothes."

113. Nu 19:2–9, Procedure of the red heifer: "This is the statute of the law."

G. Commands dealing with donations to the temple:

114. Lev 27:2–8, Procedure of dedicating equivalent personal value: "If anyone makes a special vow to dedicate persons to the Lord."

115. Lev 27:12, Procedure of dedicating equivalent value of an animal: "The priest shall evaluate it."

116. Lev 27:14, Procedure of dedicating equivalent value of a house: "If a man dedicates his house."

117. Lev 27:16, Procedure of dedicating equivalent value of a field: "If a man dedicates to the Lord part of his family land."

118. Lev 5:16, Restitution to the temple for neglected dues: "He must make restitution for what he has failed to do."

119. Lev 19:24, The fourth year's growth of fruit is holy to the Lord: "In the fourth year all its fruit will be holy."

120. Lev 19:9, One must leave the corners of the field: "Do not reap the edges of your field."

121. Lev 19:9, One must leave the gleanings of the field: "Do not gather the gleanings."

122. Dt 24:19, One must leave the forgotten sheaves: "When you are harvesting in the field and overlook a sheaf."

123. Lev 19:10, One must leave the broken-off bunches of grapes: "Do not take the bunches of grapes that have broken off. Leave them."

124. Lev 19:10, One must not glean the grapes: "Do not glean your orchard."

125. Ex 23:19, Bring firstfruits to the temple: "The firstfruits of your ground you must bring to the temple."

—**James 1:18**, "He chose to give us birth through the word of truth, that we might be a kind of firstfruits of all he created" (cf. Rev 14:4).

126. Dt 18:4, Bring the great heave (wave) offering: "The firstfruits of your grain you shall give to him."

127. Lev 27:30, Give the tithe of the produce of the land to the Levites: "All the tithe of the land belongs to the Lord." (Cf. Nu 18:24, "I give to the Levites as their inheritance the tithes.")

—**Mt 23:23**, "Woe to you, teachers of the law and Pharisees, you hypocrites! You give a tenth of your spices—mint, dill and cummin. But you have neglected the more important matters of the law— justice, mercy and faithfulness. You should have practiced the latter, without neglecting the former."

128. Dt 14:22, The second tithe: "Set aside a tenth of all."

129. Nu 18:26, The Levites are to give a tithe to the priests: "Say to the Levites, 'When you take a tithe from the Israelites.' "

130. Dt 14:28, Tithe for the poor on the third and sixth years instead of the second tithe: "At the end of three years you shall bring out."

131. Dt 26:13, Declaration must be said with tithes: "Then you shall say to the Lord."

132. Dt 26:5, Declaration must be said with offering of firstfruits: "Then you shall declare before the Lord."

133. Nu 15:20, Offering of the first of the dough: "Present a cake from the first of your ground meal."

H. Commands dealing with the Sabbath year:

134. Ex 23:11, In the seventh year the land belongs to all: "During the seventh year let the land lie unplowed and unused."

135. Ex 34:21, On the seventh year the ground is left fallow: "Even during the plowing season and harvest you must rest."

136. Lev 25:10, Sanctify the fiftieth year: "Consecrate the fiftieth year."

137. Lev 25:9, Blowing of *shofar* on Yom Kippur to set Hebrew slaves free: "Then have the trumpet sounded."

138. Lev 25:24, Property returned in fiftieth year: "Throughout the country that you hold as a possession you must provide for the redemption of the land."

139. Lev 25:29–30, Redemption of property sold in a walled city: "If a man sells a house in a walled city."

140. Lev 25:8, Counting the Jubilee years (50th year): "Count off seven sabbaths."

141. Dt 15:3, The release of all debts: "You must cancel any debt."

142. Dt 15:3, Debts of foreigners may be exacted: "You may require payment from a foreigner."

I. Commands dealing with slaughtering of animals:

143. Dt 18:3, The priest's share of an offering: "This is the judgment for the priest."

144. Dt 18:4, The first of the fleece for the priest: "The first wool from the shearing of your sheep."

145. Lev 27:28, Distinctions in the *ḥērem* (special vow): "Surely everything which one devotes to the Lord."

146. Dt 12:21, Slaughtering animals: "You may slaughter animals from the herds and flocks."

147. Lev 17:13, Covering the blood of animals and birds: "He shall pour out its blood and cover it with dust."

148. Dt 22:7, Freeing the nest: "You shall set the bird free and take the chicks."

149. Lev 11:2, Examination of animals for eating: "These are the animals you shall eat."

150. Dt 14:11, Examination of birds for eating: "Every clean bird you may eat."

151. Lev 11:21, Examination of locusts for eating: "Those that have jointed legs for hopping."

152. Lev 11:9, Examination of fish for eating: "This you may eat from all which is in the waters."

153. Ex 12:2, Sanctify and calculate the months of the year for the worship of God: "This month shall be to you the beginning of the months." (Cf. Dt 16:1, "Keep the month of Abib and make the Passover.")

J. Commands dealing with festivals:

154. Ex 23:12, Rest on the Sabbath: "On the seventh day you shall rest."

—Mark 2:27, "Then [Jesus] said to them, 'The Sabbath was made for man, not man for the Sabbath. So the Son of Man is Lord even of the Sabbath.'"

155. Ex 20:8, Sanctify the Sabbath: "Remember the day of Sabbath to sanctify it."

156. Ex 12:15, Remove all leaven (on the 14th of Nisan): "On the first day you shall remove the leaven from your houses."

157. Ex 13:8, Recounting the story of the Exodus (on the 15th of Nisan): "You shall declare to your son on that day."

—1Co 10:1–6, "For I do not want you to be ignorant of the fact, brothers, that our forefathers were all under the cloud and that they all passed through the sea. They were all baptized into Moses. . . . Now these things occurred as examples to keep us from setting our hearts on evil things as they did."

158. Ex 12:18, Eating matzo on the night of the fifteenth of Nisan: "In the evening you shall eat matzo."

159. Ex 12:16, Rest on the first day of Passover: "On the first day hold a sacred convocation."

160. Ex 12:16, Rest on the seventh day of Passover: "On the seventh day hold a sacred convocation."

161. Lev 23:15, Count from the gathering of the first sheaf forty-nine days: "You shall count from the morrow of the Sabbath."

162. Lev 23:21, Rest from work on holy days: "And you shall call in that very day a holy convocation."

—Heb 4:1–3, "Therefore, since the promise of entering his rest still stands, let us be careful that none of you be found to have fallen short of it. . . . Now we who have believed enter that rest."

163. Lev 23:24, Rest on the first day of Tishri (Rosh Hashanah): "The first day of the month shall be a Sabbath to you."

164. Lev 16:29, Fasting on the tenth of Tishri (Yom Kippur): "On the tenth day of the seventh month you must deny yourselves."

165. Lev 16:29, Resting on the tenth of Tishri (Yom Kippur): "And not do any work." (Cf. Lev 16:32, "A Sabbath of rest it is to you.")

166. Lev 23:35, Resting on the first day of Sukkoth (Tabernacles): "On the first day it shall be a holy convocation."

167. Lev 23:36, Resting on the eighth day of Sukkoth (Tabernacles): "In booths you shall dwell seven days."

168. Lev 23:42, Dwelling in booths for the seven days of Sukkoth (Tabernacles): "In booths you shall dwell seven days."

169. Lev 23:40, Take choice fruit and rejoice seven days: "You shall take for yourselves on the first day."

170. Nu 29:1, One must hear the *shofar* on the first day of Tishri (Rosh Hashanah): "A day of trumpet sounding it shall be to you."

K. Commands dealing with order in the community:

171. Ex 30:12–13, To give half a shekel every year to the temple: "Each one should pay to the Lord a ransom for his life."

172. Dt 18:15, Obey the prophet: "The man who does not obey the words of the prophet which he speaks in my name."

—Luke 16:31, "He said to him, 'If they do not listen to Moses and the Prophets, they will not be convinced even if someone rises from the dead.'"

173. Dt 17:15, Appointment of a king: "You shall set a king over you."

—Rev 19:11–16, "I saw heaven standing open and there before me was a

white horse, whose rider is called Faithful and True. . . . On his robe
and on his thigh he has this name written: KING OF KINGS AND LORD OF
LORDS."

174. Dt 17:11, Obey the leaders: "Act according to the law they teach you."

—Ac 4:19, "But Peter and John replied [to the Sanhedrin], 'Judge for
yourselves whether it is right in God's sight to obey you rather than
God.'"

175. Ex 23:2, Do not pervert justice by following the many: "Do not pervert
justice by siding with the crowd." (M. In judgments follow the many: "Incline after
the many.")

—Mt 27:24, "When Pilate saw that he was getting nowhere, but that
instead an uproar was starting, he took water and washed his hands in
front of the crowd, 'I am innocent of this man's blood,' he said, 'It is
your responsibility.'"

176. Dt 16:18, Appointment of judges and officials: "Appoint judges and
officials for each of your tribes."

177. Lev 19:15, Judges must be impartial: "In righteousness you shall judge
your neighbor."

—James 2:9, "If you show favoritism, you sin and are convicted by the
law as lawbreakers."

—1Ti 5:21, "I charge you, in the sight of God and Christ Jesus and the
elect angels, to keep these instructions without partiality, and to do
nothing out of favoritism."

178. Lev 5:1, A witness must testify: "If a person sins because he does not speak
up when he hears a public charge to testify . . . he will be held responsible."

—Mt 26:57–75, "Those who had arrested Jesus took him to Caiaphas, the
high priest, where the teachers of the law and the elders had
assembled. And Peter followed him at a distance. . . . Then [Peter]
began to call down curses on himself and he swore to them, 'I do not
know the man!'"

—James 4:17, "Anyone, then, who knows the good he ought to do and
does not do it, sins."

179. Dt 13:15 (EVV 14) A witness should be closely examined: "You must inquire,
probe, and investigate it thoroughly."

—Jn 7:52, "They replied, '. . . Look into it, and you will find that a
prophet does not come out of Galilee.'"

180. Dt 19:19, A false witness shall be punished appropriately: "You shall do to
him what he intended to do to his brother."

181. Dt 21:4, Ritual of breaking the heifer's neck: "They are to break the heifer's
neck."

182. Dt 19:3, Six cities of refuge: "Build roads to them."

183. Nu 35:2, Levitical cities: "Give the Levites towns to live in."

184. Dt 22:8, Remove hazards from your dwellings: "When you build a new
house, make a parapet around your roof."

L. Commands relating to idolatry:

185. Dt 12:2, Remove idolatry from your midst: "Destroy completely all the
places." (Cf. Dt 7:5, "Break down their altars.")

—1Co 10:14, "Therefore, my dear friends, flee from idolatry."

186. Dt 13:17 (EVV 16), Destroy an idolatrous city: "You shall burn the city with fire."

187. Dt 20:17, Destruction of the seven Canaanite nations: "Completely destroy them."

188. Dt 25:19, Destruction of the memory of the Amalekites: "You shall blot out the memory of Amalek."

189. Dt 25:17, Remember what the Amalekites did to Israel: "Remember what the Amalekites did to you."

M. Commands dealing with war:

190. Dt 20:12, Procedure for wars with the rest of the nations: "If they refuse to make peace."

191. Dt 20:2, The priest must instruct the people in warfare: "When you are about to go into battle, the priest shall come forward."

192. Dt 23:14 (EVV 13), Sanitation of the military camp: "As part of your equipment have something to dig with."

193. Dt 23:14 (EVV 13), Soldiers must have necessary equipment: "As part of your equipment have something to dig with."

N. Commands dealing with the social structure:

194. Lev 5:23 (EVV 6:4), Stolen property must be returned: "He shall return the stolen property."

195. Dt 15:8, Give to the poor: "You shall open your hand."

—Mt 19:21, "Jesus answered, 'If you want to be perfect, go, sell your possessions and give to the poor, and you will have treasure in heaven."

196. Dt 15:14, A freed Hebrew slave must be given gifts: "Supply him liberally."

197. Ex 22:24 (EVV 25), Lend to the poor without interest: "If you lend money to one of my people among you who is needy."

198. Dt 23:21 (EVV 20), Lend to the foreigner with interest: "You may charge a foreigner interest."

199. Dt 24:10, Restore a pledge to its owner if he needs it: "Do not go into his house to get a pledge."

200. Dt 24:15, Pay the worker his wages on time: "In his day you shall pay his wages."

—Mt 10:10, "For the worker is worth his keep."

201. Dt 23:25–26 (EVV 24–25), A worker is allowed to eat produce while working: "If you enter your neighbor's vineyard."

—Mt 12:1, "At that time Jesus went through the grainfields on the Sabbath. His disciples were hungry and began to pick some heads of grain and eat them."

202. Ex 23:5, You must help an overburdened donkey: "If you see the donkey of someone who hates you fallen down under its load."

—Lk 14:5, "Then he asked them, 'If one of you has a son [or donkey] or an ox that falls into a well on the Sabbath day, will you not immediately pull him out?'"

203. Dt 22:4, You must help load a burden on a man or animal: "If you see your brother's donkey or his ox fallen on the road."

—Mt 12:11, "He said to them, 'If any of you has a sheep and it falls into a pit on the Sabbath, will you not take hold of it and lift it out?'"

204. Dt 22:1, You must restore a lost animal to its owner: "If you see your brother's ox or sheep straying, do not ignore it but be sure to take it back to him."

205. Lev 19:17, You must correct the sinner: "Rebuke your neighbor frankly so you will not share in his guilt."

—Titus 1:13, "Therefore rebuke them sharply, so that they will be sound in the faith."

206. Lev 19:18, You must love others as yourself: "Love your neighbor as yourself."

—Gal 5:14, "The entire law is summed up in a single command: 'Love your neighbor as yourself.'"

207. Dt 10:19, You must love the sojourners: "You are to love those who are aliens."

—1Pe 4:9, "Offer hospitality to one another without grumbling."

208. Lev 19:36, You must have correct weights and measures: "Use honest scales and weights."

O. Commands relating to the family:

209. Lev 19:32, You must respect the wise: "Rise in the presence of the aged, show respect for the elderly, and revere your God."

—1Ti 5:1, "Do not rebuke an older man harshly, but exhort him as if he were your father."

210. Ex 20:12, You must honor your parents: "Honor your father and your mother."

—Mt 15:3-4, "Jesus replied, 'And why do you break the command of God for the sake of your tradition? For God said, 'Honor your father and mother.'"

—Eph 6:2, "Honor your father and mother."

211. Lev 19:3, You must fear your mother and your father: "Each of you must respect his mother and father."

—Eph (5:21) 6:1, "(Submit to one another out of fear of Christ. . .) Children, obey your parents in the Lord, for this is right."

212. Ge 1:28, You must be fruitful and multiply: "Be fruitful and multiply."

—Ac 17:26, "From one man he made every nation of men, that they should inhabit the whole earth."

213. Dt 24:1, You must marry according to the Law: "When a man marries a woman."

—Mt 19:4-5, " 'Have you not read,' he replied, 'that at the beginning the Creator made them male and female,' and said, 'For this reason a man will leave his father and mother and be united to his wife, and the two will become one flesh.'"

214. Dt 24:5, You must stay with your new bride one year: "If a man has recently married, he must not be sent to war or have any other duty laid on him."

—Mt 14:20, "Still another said, 'I just got married, so I cannot come.'"

215. Ge 17:10, Circumcision: "You must circumcise every male."

216. Dt 25:5, Levirate marriage: "Her husband's brother shall take her and marry her."

217. Dt 25:9, *Halitzah* (removing the sandal of a brother-in-law): "His brother's widow shall go up to him in the presence of the elders, take off one of his sandals."

218. Dt 22:29, He who violates a virgin must marry her: "He must marry the girl."

219. Dt 22:18–19, One who unjustly accuses his wife must be punished: "And the elders shall take the man and punish him."

220. Ex 22:15–23 (EVV 16–24), A seducer must be punished: "If a man seduces a virgin."

221. Dt 21:11, Treatment of a female captive: "If you notice among the captives a beautiful woman."

222. Dt 24:1, The divorce certificate: "And he writes her a certificate of divorce."

223. Nu 5:15–27, Test of woman suspected of adultery: "Then he is to take his wife to the priest."

P. Commands dealing with the administration of law:

224. Dt 25:2, Punishment of flogging: "If the guilty man deserves to be beaten."

—Ac 23:3, "Then Paul said to him, 'God will strike you, you white-washed wall! You sit there to judge me according to the law, yet you yourself violate the law by commanding that I be struck!'"

225. Nu 35:25, You must exile the accidental manslayer: "The assembly must protect the one accused of murder."

226. Ex 21:20, Capital punishment (M. with a sword): "He must be avenged."

—Mt 5:21, "Anyone who murders will be subject to judgment."

227. Ex 21:16, Capital punishment (M. with strangulation): "He must be put to death."

228. Lev 20:14, Capital punishment (M. by burning): "Both he and they must be burned with fire."

229. Dt 22:24, Capital punishment: "You shall take both of them to the gate of that town and stone them to death."

230. Dt 21:22, Hanging the body of the executed: "If a man guilty of a capital offense is put to death and his body is hung on a tree."

231. Dt 21:23, The hanged must be buried on the same day they were killed: "You must not leave his body on the tree overnight."

Q. Commands dealing with treatment of servants:

232. Ex 21:2, Treatment of Hebrew servants: "If you buy a Hebrew servant."

233. Ex 21:8, The master must marry his female Hebrew servant: "Her master who designated her for himself."

234. Ex 21:8, The master must redeem his female Hebrew servants: "He must let her be redeemed."

235. Lev 25:46, Treatment of alien servants: "You can will them to your children as inherited property."

R. General commands:

236. Ex 21:18, Injury caused by a person: "If men quarrel and one hits the other."

237. Ex 21:28, Injury caused by an animal: "If a bull gores a man or a woman to death."

238. Ex 21:33–34, Injury caused by a pit: "If a man uncovers a pit or digs one and fails to cover it."

239. Ex 21:37–22:3 (EVV 22:1–4), Punishment of robbers: "If a man steals an ox or a sheep."

240. Ex 22:4 (EVV 5), Punishment for trespassing: "If a man grazes his livestock in a field or vineyard and lets them stray."

241. Ex 22:5 (EVV 6), Punishment for arson: "If a fire breaks out."

242. Ex 22:6–8 (EVV 7–9), Punishment for a guardian (M. Unpaid) who steals: "If a man gives his neighbor silver or goods for safekeeping."

243. Ex 22:9–12 (EVV 10–13), Punishment for a guardian (M. paid) who steals: "If a man gives a donkey, an ox, a sheep."

244. Ex 22:13 (EVV 14), Punishment for loss of borrowed property: "If a man borrows an animal."

245. Lev 25:14, Judgments involving sales: "If you sell land to one of your countrymen or buy any from him."

246. Ex 22:8 (EVV 9), Judgments involving all matters of property: "In all cases of illegal possession."

247. Dt 25:12, You must rescue the one who is persecuted at all cost: "You shall cut off her hand. Show her no pity."

248. Nu 27:8, Judgments involving inheritance: "If a man dies and leaves no son."

PROHIBITIONS

A. Prohibitions relating to idolatry and false religion:

1. Ex 20:3, One must not believe in the existence of another god: "You shall have no other gods before me."

2. Ex 20:4, One must not make images to worship: "You shall not make for yourself an idol."

—Ac 15:20, "We [the Jerusalem council] should write to them [the Gentiles who are turning to God], telling them to abstain from the pollutions of idols."

—John 4:24, "God is spirit, and his worshipers must worship him in spirit and in truth."

3. Lev 19:4, One must not make idols: "You shall not make gods of molten metal."

4. Ex 20:20, One must not make forms of living creatures from wood or stone: "Do not make gods of silver or gold."

5. Ex 20:5, One must not bow down to idols: "You shall not bow down to them."

6. Ex 20:5, One must not worship idols: "You shall not bow down to them."

7. Lev 18:21, One must not offer children to Molech: "Do not give any of your children to be sacrificed to Molech."

8. Lev 19:31, One must not practice necromancy: "Do not turn to mediums."

9. Lev 19:31, One must not enquire of familiar spirits: "Or seek out spiritists."

10. Lev 19:4, One must not follow after idolatry: "Do not turn to idolatry."

11. Dt 16:22, One must not build a pillar: "And do not erect a sacred stone."

12. Lev 26:1, One must not set up a stone for worship: "Do not place a carved stone in your land."

13. Dt 16:21, One must not set up trees in the temple: "Do not set up any wooden Asherah pole beside the altar."

14. Ex 23:13, One must not swear by idols: "Do not invoke the names of other gods."

15. Ex 23:13, One must not seek to persuade another to follow idols: "Let it not be heard from your mouth."

16. Dt 13:12 (EVV 11), One must not seek to persuade another Israelite to follow idols: "And no one among you will do such an evil thing again."

17. Dt 13:9 (EVV 8), One must not desire one who seeks to persuade others to follow idols: "Do not yield to him."

18. Dt 13:9 (EVV 8), One must not listen to one who seeks to persuade others to follow idols: "Do not listen to him."

19. Dt 13:9 (EVV 8), One must not pity one who seeks to persuade others to follow idols: "Let not your eye pity him."

20. Dt 13:9 (EVV 8), One must not spare one who seeks to persuade others to follow idols: "Do not spare him."

21. Dt 13:9 (EVV 8), One must not hide one who seeks to persuade others to follow idols: "Do not hide him."

22. Dt 7:25, One must not covet the value of idols: "Do not covet the silver and gold on them [idols]."

23. Dt 13:17 (EVV 16), One must not rebuild that which has been destroyed because of idolatry: "It is to remain a ruin forever."

24. Dt 13:18 (EVV 17), One must not gain wealth from that which has been destroyed because of idolatry: "None of those condemned things shall be found in your hands."

25. Dt 7:26, One must not use anything associated with idolatry: "You shall not bring the abomination into your house."

26. Dt 18:20, One must not prophesy in the name of idols: "A prophet who speaks in the name of another god must be put to death."

27. Dt 18:20, One must not prophesy falsely: "A prophet who presumes to speak in my name anything I have not commanded him."

28. Dt 13:3-4, One must not listen to a false prophet: "You must not listen to the words of the prophet."

29. Dt 18:22, One must not fear the words of a false prophet: "Do not be afraid of him."

30. Lev 20:23, One must not walk in the ways of idolaters: "You shall not walk in the ways of the nations."

31. Lev 19:26, One must not practice divination (קסם): "Do not practice divination." (Cf. Dt 18:10, "Let no one be found among you who . . . practices divination.")

32. Dt 18:10, One must not practice soothsaying: "Let no one be found among you who . . . practices soothsaying."

33. Dt 18:10-11, One must not practice divination (נחם): "Let no one be found among you who . . . practices divination."

34. Dt 18:10-11, One must not practice sorcery: "Let no one be found among you who . . . practices sorcery."

35. Dt 18:10-11, One must not practice charms: "Let no one be found among you who . . . practices charms."

36. Dt 18:10-11, One must not consult spirits: "Let no one be found among you who . . . consults spirits."

37. Dt 18:10-11, One must not consult familiar spirits: "Let no one be found among you who . . . consults familiar spirits."

38. Dt 18:10-11, One must not practice necromancy: "Let no one be found among you who . . . practices necromancy."

39. Dt 22:5, Women must not wear men's clothing: "A woman must not wear men's clothing."

40. Dt 22:5, Men must not wear women's clothing: "Nor a man wear women's clothing."

—1Co 11:14-15, "Does not the very nature of things teach you that if a man has long hair, it is a disgrace to him, but that if a woman has long hair, it is her glory? For long hair is given to her as a covering."

41. Lev 19:28, One must not tattoo oneself: "Do not put tattoo marks on yourself."

42. Dt 22:11, One must not wear clothing made of wool and linen mixed: "Do not weave clothes of wool and linen woven together."

43. Lev 19:27, One must not cut the hair on the side of your head: "Do not cut the hair on the side of your head."

44. Lev 19:27, One must not cut your beard: "Do not . . . clip off the edges of your beard."

45. Dt 14:1, One must not cut oneself for the dead: "Do not cut yourself . . . for the dead." (Cf. Lev 19:28, "Do not cut yourself . . . for the dead.")

B. Prohibitions relating to historical events:

46. Dt 17:16, One must not return to Egypt to dwell: "You are not to go back that way again."

47. Nu 15:39, One must not have impure thoughts or sights: "And not prostitute yourselves by going after the lusts of your own hearts and eyes."

—**Mt 5:28**, "But I tell you that anyone who looks at a woman lustfully has already committed adultery with her in his heart."

48. Ex 23:32, One must not make a covenant with the Canaanites: "You shall not make a covenant with them." (Cf. Dt 7:2, "Make no treaty with them.")

49. Dt 20:16, One must not save the life of a Canaanite: "Do not leave alive anything that breathes."

50. Dt 7:2, One must show no mercy to idolaters: "Show them no mercy."

51. Ex 23:33, One must not allow idolaters to live in the land: "They shall not dwell in your land."

52. Dt 7:3, One must not intermarry with idolaters: "Do not intermarry with them."

53. Dt 23:4 (EVV 3), One must not allow an Israelite woman to marry an Ammonite or Moabite: "No Ammonite or Moabite or any of his descendants may enter the assembly of the Lord."

54. Dt 23:8 (EVV 7), One must not cast off the seed of Esau: "Do not abhor an Edomite."

55. Dt 23:8 (EVV 7), One must not cast off the Egyptians: "Do not abhor an Egyptian."

56. Dt 23:7 (EVV 6), One must not make a peace treaty with the Ammonite or Moabite: "Do not seek a treaty of friendship with them."

57. Dt 20:19, One must not destroy fruit trees in war: "When you lay siege to a city . . . do not destroy its trees."

58. Dt 7:21, One must not fear the enemy: "Do not be terrified by them."

59. Dt 25:19, One must not forget the evil done by the Amalekites: "You shall blot out the memory of the Amalekite from under heaven. Do not forget."

C. Prohibitions relating to blasphemy:

60. Lev 24:16, One must not blaspheme God's name: "Anyone who blasphemes the name of the Lord must be put to death." (Cf. Ex 22:27 [EVV 28] "Do not blaspheme God.")

—**Mt 12:36**, "But I tell you that men will have to give account on the day of judgment for every careless word they have spoken. For by your words you will be acquitted, and by your words you will be condemned."

61. Lev 19:12, One must not break an oath made in God's name: "Do not swear falsely by my name."

62. Ex 60:7, One must not take God's name in vain: "You shall not misuse the name of the Lord your God."

63. Lev 22:32, One must not profane the Lord's name: "Do not profane my holy name."

64. Dt 6:16, One must not try the Lord: "Do not test the Lord your God."

65. Dt 12:4, One must not erase God's name from houses of worship: "You must not do thus to the Lord your God."

66. Dt 21:23, One must not allow a body to hang on a tree overnight: "You must not leave his body on the tree overnight."

D. Prohibitions relating to the temple:

67. Nu 18:5, One must not be slack in taking care of the temple: "You shall keep the service of the temple."

68. Lev 16:2, The high priest must not enter the Holy Place at will: "Tell your brother Aaron not to come whenever he chooses into the Most Holy Place."

69. Lev 21:23, A priest with a physical blemish must not enter the temple: "Yet because of his defect, he must not go near the curtain or approach the altar."

70. Lev 21:17, A priest with a physical blemish must not serve in the temple: "For the generations to come none of your descendants who has a defect may come near to offer."

71. Lev 21:18, A priest with a temporary physical blemish must not serve in the temple until the blemish is passed: "No man who has any defect may come near."

72. Nu 18:3, The priests and Levites must not do each other's work: "They [the Levites] must not go near the furnishings of the sanctuary or the altar, or both they and you will die."

73. Lev 10:9–11, One must not enter the temple (M. to teach the Torah) while in a state of intoxication: "You and your sons are not to drink wine or other fermented drink whenever you enter into the Tent of Meeting."

74. Nu 18:4, Strangers must not serve in the temple: "No outsider may come near."

75. Lev 22:2, Unclean priests must not serve in the temple: "Let Aaron and his sons be scrupulous about the sacred offerings."

76. Lev 21:6, Priests must not profane God's name: "And must not profane the name of their God."

77. Nu 5:3, No unclean person can enter the camp: "So they will not defile their camp." (M. takes "camp" to be "camp of God's presence," hence, the temple. Thus this law is different from the next law, no. 78, Dt 23:11 [evv 10].)

78. Dt 23:11 (evv 10), No unclean person can remain in the camp: "If one of your men is unclean because of a nocturnal emission, he is to go outside the camp and stay there."

79. Ex 20:25, One must not make an altar of hewn stone: "Do not build it with hewn stones."

80. Ex 20:26, One must not make an altar with steps: "And do not go up to my altar on steps."

81. Lev 6:6 (evv 13), The fire on the altar must not be extinguished: "The fire must be kept burning on the altar continuously."

82. Ex 30:9, Only the prescribed incense must be burned on the gold altar in the temple: "Do not offer on this altar any other incense."

83. Ex 30:32, One must not make oil like that of the anointing oil: "Do not make any oil with the same formula."

84. Ex 30:32, The anointing oil is only for the high priest and the king: "Do not pour it on men's bodies."

85. Ex 30:37, One must not make other incense like that for the altar: "Do not make any incense with this formula for yourselves."

86. Ex 25:15, One must not remove the poles from the ark: "The poles are to remain in the rings of this ark." (Note 1Ki 8:8: "These poles were so long that their

ends could be seen from the Holy Place in front of the inner sanctuary, but not from outside the Holy Place; and they are still there today.")

87. Ex 28:28, One must not remove the breastpiece from the ephod: "The rings of the breastpiece are to be tied to the rings of the ephod with blue cord, connecting it to the waistband, so that the breastpiece will not swing out from the ephod."

88. Ex 28:32, One must make a tear in the coat of the high priest: "There shall be a woven edge like a collar around the opening so that it will not tear."

E. Prohibitions relating to sacrifices:

89. Dt 12:13, One must not offer sacrifices outside the temple: "Be careful not to sacrifice your burnt offerings anywhere you please."

90. Lev 17:3–4, One must not slaughter animals outside the temple: "Any Israelite who sacrifices an ox . . . instead of bringing it to the Tent of Meeting."

91. Lev 22:20, One must not sanctify a blemished animal: "Do not bring near anything with a defect."

92. Lev 22:22, One must not sacrifice a blemished animal: "Do not offer to the Lord the blind."

93. Lev 22:24, One must not sprinkle blood on a blemished animal: "Do not offer to the Lord an animal whose testicles are bruised, crushed, torn, or cut."

94. Lev 22:22, One must not burn with fire a blemished animal: "Do not place any of these on the altar as an offering made to the Lord by fire."

95. Dt 17:1, One must not sacrifice to the Lord any blemished animal (M. takes this as a temporary blemish): "Do not sacrifice to the Lord your God an ox or sheep that has a defect."

96. Lev 22:25, One must not sacrifice to the Lord that which was offered by a foreigner: "And you must not accept such animals from the hand of a foreigner and offer them."

97. Lev 22:21, One must not cause a blemish on a sacrificial animal: "It must be without defect or blemish."

98. Lev 2:11, One must not offer yeast or honey on the altar: "You are not to burn any yeast or honey in an offering."

99. Lev 2:13, One must not offer anything unsalted on the altar: "Season all your grain offerings with salt."

100. Dt 23:19 (EVV 18), One must not offer an animal purchased as the wage of a harlot or as the price of a dog: "You must not bring the earnings of a female prostitute or of a male prostitute into the house of the Lord."

101. Lev 22:28, One must not kill an animal and its young in one day: "Do not slaughter a cow or sheep and its young on the same day."

102. Lev 5:11, One must not use olive oil in a sin offering: "He must not put oil or incense on it, because it is a sin offering."

103. Lev 5:11, One must not use incense in a sin offering: "He must not put oil or incense on it, because it is a sin offering."

104. Nu 5:15, One must not use olive oil in the jealousy offering: "He must not pour oil on it."

105. Nu 5:15, One must not use incense in the jealousy offering: "He must not put incense on it."

106. Lev 27:10, One must not substitute sacrifices: "He must not exchange it or substitute a good one for a bad one."

107. Lev 27:26, One must not substitute one category of offering for another (e.g., offering a peace offering as a guilt offering): "No one may dedicate the firstborn of an animal, since the firstborn already belongs to the Lord."

108. Nu 18:17, One must not redeem the firstborn of a clean animal: "But you must not redeem the firstborn of an ox, a sheep, or a goat; they are holy."

109. Lev 27:33, One must not sell the tithe of animals: "The entire tithe of the herd and flock . . . will be holy."

110. Lev 27:28, One must not sell a devoted thing: "But nothing that a man owes and devotes to the Lord . . . may be sold."

111. Lev 27:28, One must not redeem a devoted thing: "But nothing that a man owes and devotes to the Lord . . . may be redeemed."

112. Lev 5:8, One must not sever the head of a sacrificial bird: "He is to wring its head from its neck, not severing it."

113. Dt 15:19, One must not work a consecrated animal: "Do not put the firstborn of your oxen to work."

114. Dt 15:19, One must not shear a consecrated animal: "Do not shear the firstborn of your sheep."

115. Ex 34:25, One must not slaughter the Passover lamb with yeast: "Do not offer the blood of a sacrifice to me along with anything containing yeast."

116. Ex 23:18, One must not let fat portions of an offering remain overnight: "The fat of my festival offerings must not be kept until morning."

117. Ex 12:10, The meat of the Passover must not be left till morning: "Do not leave any of it till morning."

118. Dt 16:4, One must not leave any portion of the Chagigah (festive offering), offered on the fourteenth, until the third day: "Do not let any of the meat you sacrifice on the evening of the first day remain until morning."

119. Nu 9:12, No part of the second Passover lamb is to be left till morning: "They must not leave any of it till morning."

120. Lev 22:30, No part of the thanksgiving offering is to be left till morning: "It must be eaten that same day; leave none of it till morning."

121. Ex 12:46, One must not break the bone of the Passover lamb: "Do not break any of the bones."

122. Nu 9:12, One must not break the bone of the second Passover lamb: "They must not . . . break any of the bones."

123. Ex 12:46, One must not carry the meat of the Passover lamb outside the house where it is being eaten: "Take none of the meat outside the house."

124. Lev 6:10 (EVV 17), The remains of the meal offering must not become leaven: "It must not be baked with yeast."

125. Ex 12:9, One must not eat the Passover lamb raw or boiled; it must be roasted: "Do not eat the meat raw or cooked in water, but roast it over the fire."

126. Ex 12:45, An alien must not be allowed to eat the Passover: "But a temporary resident and a hired worker may not eat of it."

127. Ex 12:48, An uncircumcised person must not be allowed to eat the

Passover: "An alien living among you who wants to celebrate the Lord's Passover must have all the males in his household circumcised; then he may take part."

128. Ex 12:43, A foreigner must not be allowed to eat the Passover: "No foreigner is to eat of it."

129. Lev 12:4, An unclean person must not eat of the holy things: "She must not touch anything sacred."

130. Lev 7:19, One must not eat any holy thing that has been profaned: "Meat that touches anything ceremonially unclean must not be eaten."

131. Lev 19:6–8, One must not eat sacrificial meat left over its limit: "It shall be eaten on the day you sacrifice it or on the next day; anything left over until the third day must be burned up."

132. Lev 7:18, One must not eat the meat of the fellowship (peace) offering on the third day: "If any meat of the fellowship offering is eaten on the third day it will not be accepted." (M. considers this prohibition to mean an offering presented with wrong intentions.)

133. Lev 22:10, The heave (wave) offering must not be eaten by a nonpriest: "No one outside a priest's family may eat the sacred offering."

134. Lev 22:10, The heave offering must not be eaten by a priest's guest or hired worker: "Nor may the guest of a priest or his hired worker eat it."

135. Lev 22:10, The heave offering must not be eaten by an uncircumcised person: This is not stated in the Torah but is derived by *gezerah sheva* (use of similar words or ideas in two distinct texts provides a link between those texts) from the fact that the uncircumcised cannot eat the Passover (Ex 12:48).

136. Lev 22:4, The heave offering must not be eaten by an unclean priest: "If a descendant of Aaron has an infectious skin disease or a bodily discharge, he may not eat the sacred offerings."

137. Lev 22:12, The daughter of a priest who is married to a nonpriest cannot eat of holy things: "If a priest's daughter marries anyone other than a priest, she may not eat of any of the sacred contributions."

138. Lev 6:16 (EVV 23), The meal offering of a priest must not be eaten: "Every grain offering of a priest shall be burned completely; it must not be eaten."

139. Lev 6:23 (EVV 30), The meat of the sin offering must not be eaten: "Any sin offering whose blood is brought into the Tent of Meeting to make atonement in the Holy Place must not be eaten; it must be burned."

140. Dt 14:3, Consecrated animals which have become blemished must not be eaten: "Do not eat any detestable thing."

141. Dt 12:17, One must not eat the second tithe of grain outside Jerusalem: "You must not eat in your own towns the tithe of grain."

142. Dt 12:17, One must not consume the second tithe of wine outside Jerusalem: "You must not consume in your own towns the tithe of . . . new wine."

143. Dt 12:17, One must not consume the second tithe of oil outside Jerusalem: "You must not consume in your own towns the tithe of oil."

144. Dt 12:17, One must not eat the second tithe of the firstborn outside Jerusalem: "You must not eat in your own towns the tithe of the firstborn."

145. Dt 12:17, The priests must not eat the sin and guilt offerings outside the temple (viz., in your own towns): "You must not eat the firstborn of your herds and flocks in your own towns." (M. derives this interpretation from the fact that "herds

and flocks" are mentioned in Scripture only in reference to the sin and guilt offerings.)

146. Dt 12:17, The priest must not eat the meat of the burnt offerings: "You must not eat in your own towns . . . what you have vowed to give." (M. derives burnt offerings from vows.)

147. Dt 12:17, The priest must not eat the lighter sacrifices before the blood is sprinkled: "You must not eat in your own towns . . . your freewill offerings." (M. derives "before the blood is sprinkled" from "freewill offerings.")

148. Ex 29:33, A nonpriest may not eat of the holiest sacrifices: "No one else may eat them because they are sacred."

149. Dt 12:17, A priest may not eat the firstfruits outside the temple: "You must not eat in your own towns . . . special gifts." (M. derives "firstfruits" from "special gifts.")

150. Dt 26:14, One must not eat the second tithe while in a state of impurity: "Nor have I removed any of it while I was unclean."

151. Dt 26:14, One must not eat the second tithe while in a state of mourning: "I have not eaten any of the sacred portion while I was in mourning."

152. Dt 26:14, One must not use the second tithe redemption money for anything other than food and drink: "Nor have I offered any of it to the dead."

153. Lev 22:15, One must not eat untithed produce: "The priests must not desecrate the sacred offerings the Israelites present to the Lord by allowing them to eat the sacred offerings."

154. Ex 22:28 (EVV 29), One must not change the order of separating the tithes: "Do not hold back offerings from your granaries or your vats."

155. Dt 23:22 (EVV 21), One must not delay payment of offerings: "If you make a vow to the Lord, do not be slow to pay it."

156. Ex 23:15, One must not go on a pilgrimage without an offering: "No one is to appear before me empty-handed."

157. Nu 30:3 (EVV 2), One must not break his word: "He must not break his word."

F. Prohibitions relating to the priests:

158. Lev 21:7, A priest must not marry a harlot: "They must not marry women defiled by prostitution."

159. Lev 21:7, A priest must not marry a defiled woman: "They must not marry . . . defiled women."

160. Lev 21:7, A priest must not marry a divorced woman: "They must not marry . . . divorced women."

161. Lev 21:14, A priest must not marry a widow: "He must not marry a widow."

162. Lev 21:15, A priest must not take a widow as a concubine: "So he will not defile his offspring among his people."

163. Lev 10:6, Priests must not enter the temple with long hair: "Do not let your hair become unkempt."

164. Lev 10:6, Priests must not enter the temple with torn clothes: "Do not tear your clothes."

165. Lev 10:7, Priests must not leave the courtyard during the temple service: "Do not leave the entrance to the Tent of Meeting or you will die."

166. Lev 21:1, A priest should not become unclean except for a close relative: "A priest must not make himself ceremonially unclean for any of his people who die, except for a close relative."

167. Lev 21:11, The high priest must not become unclean for any reason: "He must not enter a place where there is a dead body."

168. Lev 21:11, The high priest must not become unclean in any way: "He must not make himself unclean, even for his father or mother."

169. Dt 18:1, The tribe of Levi must not have an inheritance in the dividing of the land: "The priests, who are Levites—indeed, the whole tribe of Levi,—are to have no allotment or inheritance with Israel."

170. Dt 18:1, The tribe of Levi must not take part in the spoils of war: "The priests, who are Levites—indeed, the whole tribe of Levi—are to have no allotment or inheritance with Israel."

171. Dt 14:1, One must not shave the head for the dead: "Do not . . . shave the front of your heads for the dead."

G. Prohibitions relating to dietary laws:

172. Dt 14:7, One must not eat unclean animals: "This is what you must not eat."

173. Lev 11:11, One must not eat unclean fish: "And since you are to detest them, you must not eat their meat."

174. Lev 11:13, One must not eat unclean birds: "These are the birds you are to detest and not eat because they are detestable."

175. Dt 14:19, One must not eat unclean creeping things that fly: "All flying insects that swarm are unclean to you; do not eat them."

176. Lev 11:41, One must not eat unclean creeping things that creep on the ground: "Every creature that moves about on the ground is detestable; it is not to be eaten."

177. Lev 11:44, One must not eat creatures that move upon the ground (reptiles): "Do not make yourselves unclean by any creature that moves about on the ground."

178. Lev 11:42, One must not eat worms or wormlike creatures: "You are not to eat any creature that moves about on the ground, whether it moves on its belly or walks on all fours or on many feet; it is detestable."

179. Lev 11:43, One must not eat any detestable creature: "Do not defile yourselves by any of these creatures."

180. Dt 14:21, One must not eat an animal that has died of a natural death: "Do not eat anything you find already dead."

181. Ex 22:30 (EVV 31), One must not eat an animal that was killed by a predator: "Do not eat the meat of an animal torn by wild beast."

182. Dt 12:23, One must not eat a body part taken from a living animal: "You must not eat the life with the meat."

183. Ge 32:33 (EVV 32), One must not eat the sinew of the thigh: "The Israelites do not eat the tendon attached to the socket of the hip."

184. Lev 7:26, One must not eat blood: "You must not eat the blood of any bird or animal."

185. Lev 7:23, One must not eat fat of cattle, sheep, or goats: "Do not eat any of the fat of cattle, sheep, or goats."

186. Ex 23:19, One must not boil a young goat in its mother's milk (cook meat with milk): "Do not cook a young goat in its mother's milk."

187. Ex 34:26, One must not eat a young goat in its mother's milk (eat meat with milk): "Do not cook a young goat in its mother's milk."

188. Ex 21:28, One must not eat an ox that has been stoned: "And its meat must not be eaten."

189. Lev 23:14, One must not eat bread made of new grain: "You must not eat any bread, or roasted or new grain."

190. Lev 23:14, One must not eat roasted new grain: "You must not eat any . . . roasted . . . grain."

191. Lev 23:14, One must not eat raw new grain: "You must not eat any . . . new grain."

192. Lev 19:23, One must not eat uncircumcised fruit: "When you enter the land and plant any kind of fruit tree, regard its fruit as forbidden [Hebrew: uncircumcised]. For three years you are to consider it forbidden; it must not be eaten."

193. Dt 22:9, One must not eat the produce of mixed planting: "Do not plant two kinds of seed in your vineyard; if you do, not only the crops you plant but also the fruit of the vineyard will be defiled."

194. Dt 32:38, One must not use wine offered to idols: it is said of idols, "They who drank the wine of their drink offerings."

195. Lev 19:26, One must not eat meat upon blood (M. "upon blood" means "that which brings blood[shed], thus, "be gluttonous and drunken"): "Do not eat any meat upon the blood." (Cf. Dt 21:20, "He is a profligate and a drunkard.")

196. Lev 23:29, One must not eat anything (fast) on the Day of Atonement: "Anyone who does not deny himself on that day must be cut off from his people."

197. Ex 13:3, One must not eat yeast on the day of the Passover: "Commemorate this day, the day you came out of Egypt. . . . Eat nothing containing yeast."

198. Ex 12:20, One must not eat anything mixed with yeast on the day of the Passover: "Eat nothing made with yeast."

199. Dt 16:3, One must not eat anything mixed with yeast after the middle of the fourteenth of Nisan (the day before Passover): "Do not eat it with yeast."

200. Ex 13:7, No yeast must be seen during the celebration of the Passover: "Nothing with yeast in it is to be seen among you, nor shall any yeast be seen anywhere within your borders."

201. Ex 12:19, No yeast must be found in one's house during the celebration of the Passover: "For seven days no yeast is to be found in your houses."

H. Prohibitions relating to the Nazirite:

202. Nu 6:3, A Nazirite must not drink wine or strong drink: "He must abstain from wine and other fermented drink and must not drink vinegar made from wine or from other fermented drink."

203. Nu 6:3, A Nazirite must not eat fresh grapes: "He must not . . . eat grapes."

204. Nu 6:3, A Nazirite must not eat dried grapes: "He must not . . . eat dried grapes."

205. Nu 6:4, A Nazirite must not eat grape seeds: "He must not . . . eat even the seeds."

206. Nu 6:4, A Nazirite must not eat grape skins: "He must not . . . eat even the seeds or skins."

207. Nu 6:7, A Nazirite must not become unclean for the dead: "Even if his own father or mother or brother or sister dies, he must not make himself ceremonially unclean on account of them."

208. Nu 6:6, A Nazirite must not enter a tent in which there is a dead body: "He must not go in to [M. a tent where there is] a dead body."

209. Nu 6:5, A Nazirite must not shave his head: "No razor may be used on his head."

I. Prohibitions relating to agriculture:

210. Lev 23:22, One must not reap the whole of one's field: "Do not reap to the very edges of your field."

211. Lev 19:9, One must not gather the grain that falls in harvest: "Do not . . . gather the gleanings of your harvest."

212. Lev 19:10, One must not pick one's vineyard a second time (M. to harvest the misformed clusters of grapes): "Do not go over your vineyard a second time."

213. Lev 19:10, One must not gather the grapes that fall during harvest: "Do not . . . pick up the grapes that have fallen."

214. Dt 24:19, One must not return to take a forgotten sheaf: "When you are harvesting in your field and you overlook a sheaf, do not go back to get it. Leave it for the alien."

215. Lev 19:19, One must not sow two kinds of seeds together: " Do not plant your field with two kinds of seed."

—Mt 13:24–25, "Jesus told them another parable: 'The kingdom of heaven is like a man who sowed good seed in his field. But while everyone was sleeping, his enemy came and sowed weeds among the wheat, and went away.' "

216. Dt 22:9, One must not plant two kinds of seed in a vineyard (M. sow grain in a vineyard): "Do not plant two kinds of seed in your vineyard."

217. Lev 19:19, One must not mate two kinds of animals: "Do not mate different kinds of animals."

218. Dt 22:10, One must not work two species of animals together: "Do not plow with an ox and a donkey yoked together."

219. Dt 25:4, One must not prevent an animal from eating of its work: "Do not muzzle an ox while it is treading out the grain."

—1Co 9:9–10, "For it is written in the Law of Moses: 'Do not muzzle an ox while it is treading out the grain.' Surely he says this for us, doesn't he? Yes, this was written for us, because when the plowman plows and the thresher threshes, they ought to do so in the hope of sharing in the harvest."

—1Ti 5:17–18, "The elders who direct the affairs of the church well are worthy of double honor, especially those whose work is preaching and teaching. For the Scripture says, 'Do not muzzle the ox while it is treading out the grain.'"

220. Lev 25:4, One must not sow the ground in the seventh year: "In the seventh year the land is to have a sabbath of rest. . . . Do not sow your fields."

221. Lev 25:4, One must not prune trees in the seventh year: "In the seventh year the land is to have a sabbath of rest. . . . Do not prune your vineyards."

222. Lev 25:5, One must not reap a harvest in the seventh year: "Do not reap what grows of itself."

223. Lev 25:5, One must not harvest grapes in the seventh year: "Do not harvest grapes of your untended vines."

224. Lev 25:11, One must not work the ground in the Jubilee Year: "The fiftieth year shall be a jubilee for you; do not sow."

225. Lev 25:11, One must not reap what grows of itself: "The fiftieth year shall be a jubilee for you; . . . do not reap what grows of itself."

226. Lev 25:11, One must not harvest fruit: "The fiftieth year shall be a jubilee for you; . . . do not harvest the untended vines."

227. Lev 25:23, One must not sell one's inheritance: "The land must not be sold permanently."

228. Lev 25:33, The Levitical lands must not be changed: "The pastureland belonging to their towns must not be sold."

229. Dt 12:19, One must not forsake the support of the Levites: "Be careful not to neglect the Levites as long as you live in your land."

J. Prohibitions relating to business affairs:

230. Dt 15:2, One must not demand payment of a loan after the seventh year: "Every creditor shall cancel the loan he has made to his fellow Israelite."

231. Dt 15:9, One must not refuse a loan to the poor because of the approaching seventh year: "Be careful not to harbor this thought: 'The seventh year . . . is near,' so that you do not show ill will toward your needy brother and give him nothing."

232. Dt 15:7, One must not deny help to the poor: "Do not be hardhearted or tightfisted toward your poor brother."

233. Dt 15:13, One must not send a poor Hebrew slave away empty-handed: "When you release him, do not send him away empty-handed."

234. Ex 22:24 (EVV 25), One must not take interest from the needy: "If you lend money to one of my people among you who is in need, do not be like a moneylender."

235. Lev 25:37, One must not lend money to another Israelite on interest: "You must not lend him money at interest or sell him food at a profit."

236. Dt 23:20, One must not borrow money from another Israelite on interest: "You may charge a foreigner interest, but not a brother Israelite."

237. Ex 22:24 (EVV 25), One must not participate in agreements with the needy involving interest: "Charge him no interest."

238. Lev 19:13, One must not delay payment of wages: "Do not hold back the wages of a hired man overnight."

—Mt 20:8, "When evening came, the owner of the vineyard said to his foreman, 'Call the workers and pay them their wages.'"

239. Dt 24:10, One must not take a pledge by violence: "Do not go into his house to get what he is offering as a pledge."

240. Dt 24:12, One must not keep a pledge from a poor person if he needs it: "If the man is poor, do not go to sleep with his pledge in your possession."

241. Dt 24:17, One must not take a pledge from a widow: "Do not . . . take the cloak of a widow as a pledge."

242. Dt 24:6, One must not take a pledge from a person if he earns his living with it: "Do not take a pair of millstones—not even the upper one—as security for a debt, because that would be taking a man's livelihood as security."

243. Ex 20:13, Stealing (M. kidnapping) is prohibited: "You shall not steal [M. kidnap]."

—**Mt 19:18,** "Jesus replied, '. . . Do not steal.' "

244. Lev 19:11, Stealing (M. property) is prohibited: "You shall not steal [M. property]."

245. Lev 19:13, Robbery (M. by violence) is prohibited: "You shall not rob [M. by violence]."

246. Dt 19:14, One must not move a boundary marker: "Do not move your neighbor's boundary stone . . . in the inheritance you receive in the land."

247. Lev 19:13, One must not defraud another: "Do not defraud your neighbor."

—**Mk 10:19,** "Jesus answered, '. . . Do not defraud.' "

248. Lev 19:11, One must not lie (M. deny receipt of a loan or deposit): "Do not lie."

—**Col 3:9,** "Do not lie to each other."

249. Lev 19:11, One must not deceive (M. swear falsely): "Do not deceive (swear falsely) one another."

—**Mt 19:18,** "Jesus replied, '. . . Do not give false testimony.' "

250. Lev 25:14, One must not deceive another in business transactions: "If you sell land to one of your countrymen or buy any from him, do not take advantage of each other."

—**Eph 4:25,** "Therefore each of you must put off falsehood and speak
truthfully to his neighbor."

251. Lev 25:17, One must not take advantage of (M. mislead verbally) another: "Do not take advantage of each other."

252. Ex 22:20 (ᴇᴠᴠ 21), One must not take advantage of a foreigner (with words): "Do not mistreat an alien."

253. Ex 22:20 (ᴇᴠᴠ 21), One must not oppress a foreigner (M. in trade): "Do not oppress him."

254. Dt 23:16 (ᴇᴠᴠ 15), One must not return an escaped slave to his master: "If a slave has taken refuge with you, do not hand him over to his master."

—**Phm 12–16,** "I am sending him [Onesimus] . . . back to you. . . . no
longer as a slave, but as a dear brother."

255. Dt 23:17 (ᴇᴠᴠ 16), One must not take advantage of an escaped slave: "Let him live among you wherever he likes and in whatever town he chooses. Do not oppress him."

—**Phm 17,** "Welcome him as you would welcome me."

256. Ex 22:21 (EVV 22), One must not oppress the widow and orphan: "Do not take advantage of a widow or an orphan."

—Jas 1:27, "Religion that God our Father accepts as pure and faultless is this: to look after orphans and widows in their distress."

257. Lev 25:39, One must not make an Israelite work as a slave: "Do not make him work as a slave."

258. Lev 25:42, One must not sell an Israelite as a slave: "They must not be sold as slaves."

259. Lev 25:43, One must not treat an Israelite worker cruelly: "Do not rule over them ruthlessly."

260. Lev 25:53, One must not allow a foreigner to treat an Israelite worker cruelly: "You must see to it that his owner does not rule over him ruthlessly."

260. Lev 25:53, One must not allow a foreigner to treat an Israelite worker cruelly: "You must see to it that his owner does not rule over him ruthlessly."

261. Ex 21:8, One must not see his Hebrew maidservant: "He must let her be redeemed. He has no right to sell her to foreigners."

262. Ex 21:10, If one marries his Hebrew maidservant, he must not deprive her of food, clothing, or marital rights: "He must not deprive the first one of her food, clothing, and marital rights."

263. Dt 21:14, One must not sell a female captive: "You must not sell her."

264. Dt 21:14, One must not treat a female captive as a slave: "You must not . . . treat her as a slave."

265. Ex 20:17, One must not covet another's possessions: "You shall not covet your neighbor's house."

—Ro 13:9, "The commandments, 'Do not commit adultery,' 'Do not murder,' 'Do not steal,' 'Do not covet,' and whatever other commandment there may be, are summed up in this one rule: 'Love your neighbor as yourself.'"

266. Dt 5:18 (EVV 21), One must not even desire another's possessions: "You shall not set your desire on your neighbor's house."

—Lk 12:15, "Watch out! Be on your guard against all kinds of greed."

267. Dt 23:26 (EVV 25), One must not harvest the grain of his neighbor: "If you enter your neighbor's grainfield, you may pick kernels with your hands, but you must not put a sickle to his standing grain."

268. Dt 23:25 (EVV 24), One must not take more fruit than one can eat: "If you enter your neighbor's vineyard, you may eat all the grapes you want, but do not put any in your basket."

269. Dt 22:3, One should not ignore a neighbor's lost article: "Do not ignore it."

—Lk 14:5, "If one of you has a son [donkey] or an ox that falls into a well on the Sabbath day, will you not immediately pull him out?"

270. Ex 23:5, One should not refuse to help a man or animal who has collapsed under a heavy burden: "Do not leave it there; be sure you help him with it."

—Mt 12:11, "He said to them, 'If any of you has a sheep and it falls into a pit on the Sabbath, will you not take hold of it and lift it out?'"

271. Lev 19:35, One must not defraud with weights and measures: "Do not use dishonest standards."

272. Dt 25:13, One must not (M. even) possess inaccurate weights: "Do not have two differing weights in your bag."

K. Prohibitions relating to the administration of justice:

273. Lev 19:15, One must not pervert justice: "Do not pervert justice."

—Mt 27:19, "While Pilate was sitting on the judge's seat, his wife sent him this message: 'Do not have anything to do with that innocent man.'"

274. Ex 23:8, A judge must not accept a bribe in a decision: "Do not accept a bribe."

275. Lev 19:15, A judge must not be partial: "Do not show favoritism to the wealthy."

—Jas 2:3, "If you show special attention to the man wearing fine clothes and say, 'Here's a good seat for you,' but say to the poor man, 'You stand there' or 'Sit on the floor by my feet,' have you not discriminated among yourselves and become judges with evil thoughts?"

276. Dt 1:17, A judge must not be afraid of anyone: "Do not be afraid of anyone."

277. Lev 19:15, A judge must not favor the poor: "Do not show partiality to the poor." (Cf. Ex 23:3, "Do not show favoritism to a poor man in his lawsuit.")

278. Ex 23:6, A judge should not discriminate against the poor: "Do not deny justice to your poor people in their lawsuits."

279. Dt 19:13, A judge should not have pity on the condemned: "Show him no pity."

280. Dt 24:17, A judge should not pervert justice for strangers and orphans: "Do not deprive the alien or the fatherless of justice."

281. Ex 23:1, One should not spread false reports (M. it is forbidden to hear one litigant without the other being present): "Do not spread false reports."

282. Ex 23:2, A judge should not be persuaded by the crowd: "Do not follow the crowd in doing wrong."

—Mt 27:24, "When Pilate saw that he was getting nowhere, but that instead an uproar was starting, he took water and washed his hands in front of the crowd."

283. Ex 23:2, A judge should not pervert justice by siding with the crowd: "Do not pervert justice by siding with the crowd."

—Mt 27:25–26, "All the people answered, 'Let his blood be on us and on our children!' Then [Pilate] released Barabbas to them. But he had Jesus flogged, and handed him over to be crucified."

284. Dt 1:17, A judge should not show partiality in judgment (M. a person who is not learned in the Torah should not be appointed as a judge): "Do not show partiality in judging."

—Jn 7:50–51, "Nicodemus . . . asked, 'Does our law condemn anyone without first hearing him to find out what he is doing?'"

285. Ex 20:16, One must not give false testimony: "You shall not give false testimony against your neighbor."

—Ac 6:13, "They produced false witnesses, who testified, 'This fellow never stops speaking against this holy place and against the law.'"

286. Ex 23:1, One must not give false testimony for the guilty: "Do not help a wicked man by being a malicious witness."

287. Dt 24:16, One must not give (or accept) testimony from a relative of the accused: "Fathers shall not be put to death for their children."

288. Dt 19:15, One must not pass judgment on the testimony of one witness alone: "One witness is not enough to convict a man accused of any crime or offense."

—2Co 13:1, "This will be my third visit to you. 'Every matter must be established by the testimony of two or three witnesses.'"

—1Ti 5:21, "Do not entertain an accusation against an elder unless it is brought by two or three witnesses."

289. Ex 20:13, One must not murder another: "You shall not murder."

—1Pe 4:15, "But let none of you suffer as a murderer."

290. Ex 23:7, One must not punish an innocent or honest person (M. convict on the basis of circumstantial evidence alone): "Do not put to death an innocent or honest person."

—Mt 27:22–23, " 'What shall I do, then, with Jesus who is called Christ?' Pilate asked. They all answered, 'Crucify him!' 'Why? What crime has he committed?' asked Pilate."

291. Nu 35:30, One must not be put to death on the testimony of one witness (M. a witness must not act as judge): "No one is to be put to death on the testimony of only one witness."

—Mt 26:60–61, "The chief priests and the whole Sanhedrin were looking for false evidence against Jesus so that they could put him to death. But they did not find any, though many false witnesses came forward. Finally two came forward."

292. Nu 35:12, One must not be executed without a trial: "A person accused of murder may not die before he stands trial before the assembly."

—Mt 26:57, "Those who had arrested Jesus took him to Caiaphas, the high priest, where the teachers of the law and the elders had assembled."

293. Dt 25:12, One must not have pity on or spare a guilty party: "Show her no pity."

294. Dt 22:26, One must not punish one forced to do a crime: "Do nothing to the girl."

295. Nu 35:31, One must not take a ransom from a murderer: "You must not take a ransom for the life of a murderer guilty of death."

—Mt 27:15, "Now it was the governor's custom at the feast to release a prisoner chosen by the crowd."

296. Nu 35:32, One must not take a ransom from the manslayer: "Do not accept a ransom for anyone who has fled to a city of refuge and so allow him to go back and live on his own land before the death of the high priest."

297. Lev 19:16, One must not refuse to save another from danger: "You shall not stand [M. by] upon the blood of your friend."

—Lk 10:30–32, "In reply Jesus said: 'A man was going down from Jerusalem to Jericho, when he fell into the hands of robbers. They stripped him of his clothes, beat him, and went away, leaving him half dead. A priest happened to be going down the same road, and when he saw the man, he passed by on the other side. So too, a Levite. . . . '"

298. Dt 22:8, One must not leave a dangerous trap in one's house: "Do not bring bloodshed into your house."

299. Lev 19:14, One must not mislead another person with bad advice: "Do not put a stumbling block in front of the blind."

—**Ro 14:13**, "Make up your mind not to put any stumbling block or obstacle in your brother's way."

300. Dt 25:2–3, One must not give the guilty more lashes than the crime deserves: "With the number of lashes his crime deserves."

—**2Co 11:24**, "Five times I received from the Jews forty lashes minus one."

301. Lev 19:16, One should not spread slander: "Do not go about spreading slander among your people."

—**Ro 3:8**, "As we are being slanderously reported as saying and as some claim that we say."

302. Lev 19:17, One should not harbor hatred in his heart: "Do not hate your brother in your heart."

—**Mt 18:15**, "If your brother sins against you, go and show him his fault, just between the two of you. If he listens to you, you have won your brother over."

303. Lev 19:17, One should not fail to correct (M. shame) his neighbor: "Rebuke your neighbor frankly so you will not share in his guilt."

—**Lk 17:3**, "So watch yourselves. If your brother sins, rebuke him, and if he repents, forgive him."

304. Lev 19:18, One must not seek revenge: "Do not seek revenge."

—**Ro 12:19**, "Do not take revenge, my friends, but leave room for God's wrath."

305. Lev 19:18, One must not bear a grudge: "Do not bear a grudge."

306. Dt 22:6, One must not take the mother bird when taking the young birds: "You shall not take the mother with the young ones."

307. Lev 13:33, One must not shave a leprous sore: "He must be shaved except for the diseased area."

308. Dt 24:8, One must not remove or hide a leprous sore: "Watch closely the sore of leprosy."

309. Dt 21:4, One must not sow or work a valley that is to be used for the ritual of the red heifer: "A valley that has not been plowed or planted."

310. Ex 22:17, One must not allow a sorceress to live: "Do not allow a sorceress to live."

311. Dt 24:5, One must not force a bridegroom to serve in the military during the first year of his marriage: "He must not be sent to war or have any other duty laid on him."

312. Dt 17:11, One must not rebel against those who teach the law (M. tradition): "Act according to the law they teach you and the decisions they give you."

313. Dt 13:1 (ᴇᴠᴠ 12:32), One must not add to the law: "Do not add to it."

—**Mk 7:7**, "You have let go of the commands of God and are holding on to the traditions of men."

314. Dt 13:1 (ᴇᴠᴠ 12:32), One must not change the law: "Do not add to it."

—**Mt 5:18**, "I tell you the truth, until heaven and earth disappear, not the smallest letter, not the least stroke of a pen, will by any means disappear from the law until everything is accomplished."

315. Ex 22:27 (evv 28), One must not curse God (M. a judge): "Do not blaspheme God."

—1Ti 6:1, "So that God's name and our teaching may not be blasphemed."

316. Ex 22:27 (evv 28), One must not curse a ruler: "Do not curse the ruler of your people."

—Ac 23:4, "Those who were standing near Paul said, 'You dare to insult God's high priest?' Paul replied, 'Brothers, I did not realize that he was the high priest; for it is written: "Do not speak evil about the ruler of your people." ' "

317. Lev 19:14, One must not curse the deaf (M. any Israelite): "Do not curse the deaf."

318. Ex 21:17, One must not curse one's parents: "Anyone who curses his father or mother must be put to death."

—Ro 1:29–30, "They have become filled with every kind of wickedness . . . they disobey their parents."

319. Ex 21:15, One must not strike one's parents: "Anyone who strikes his father or mother must be put to death."

320. Ex 20:10, One must not work on the Sabbath: "You shall not do any work."

321. Ex 16:29, One must not travel on the Sabbath: "Everyone is to stay where he is on the seventh day; no one is to go out."

322. Ex 35:3, One must not light a fire (M. inflict punishment) on the Sabbath: "Do not light a fire in any of your dwellings."

323. Ex 12:16, One must not work on the first day of Passover: "On the first day . . . do no work at all on these days."

324. Ex 12:16, One must not work on the seventh day of Passover: "On the seventh day . . . do no work at all on these days."

325. Lev 23:21, One must not work on the Feast of Weeks: "Do no regular work."

326. Lev 23:25, One must not work on Rosh Hashanah: "Do no regular work."

327. Lev 23:35, One must not work on the first day of the Feast of Tabernacles: "On the first day . . . do no work at all on these days."

328. Lev 23:36, One must not work on the eighth day of the Feast of Sukkoth (Tabernacles): "On the eighth day . . . do no regular work."

329. Lev 23:28, One must not work on the Day of Atonement: "Do not work on that day."

L. Prohibitions relating to family relationships:

330. Lev 18:7, One must not have a sexual relationship with one's mother: "Do not dishonor your father by having sexual relations with your mother."

—1Co 5:1, "It is actually reported that there is sexual immorality among you, and of a kind that does not occur even among pagans: A man has his father's wife."

—1Co 6:18, "Flee from sexual immorality."

331. Lev 18:8, One must not have a sexual relationship with one's stepmother: "Do not have sexual relations with your father's wife."

332. Lev 18:9, One must not have a sexual relationship with one's sister: "Do not have sexual relations with your sister."

333. Lev 18:11, One must not have a sexual relationship with one's stepsister: "Do not have sexual relations with the daughter of your father's wife, born to your father."

334. Lev 18:10, One must not have a sexual relationship with the daughter of one's son: "Do not have sexual relations with your son's daughter."

335. Lev 18:10, One must not have a sexual relationship with one's daughter's daughter: "Do not have sexual relations with your daughter's daughter."

336. Lev 18:10 (M. One must not have a sexual relationship with one's daughter: This is not explicitly stated in the Torah, but is implied from the fact that such relationships are forbidden with one's daughter's daughter.)

337. Lev 18:17, One must not have a sexual relationship with a woman and her daughter: "Do not have sexual relations with both a woman and her daughter."

338. Lev 18:17, One must not have a sexual relationship with a woman and her son's daughter: "Do not have sexual relations with . . . her son's daughter."

339. Lev 18:17, One must not have a sexual relationship with a woman and her daughter's daughter: "Do not have sexual relations with . . . her daughter's daughter."

340. Lev 18:12, One must not have a sexual relationship with one's father's sister: "Do not have sexual relations with your father's sister."

341. Lev 18:13, One must not have a sexual relationship with one's mother's sister: "Do not have sexual relations with your mother's sister."

342. Lev 18:14, One must not have a sexual relationship with the wife of the brother of one's father: "Do not dishonor your father's brother by approaching his wife to have sexual relations."

343. Lev 18:15, One must not have a sexual relationship with one's son's wife: "Do not have sexual relations with your daughter-in-law."

344. Lev 18:16, One must not have a sexual relationship with one's brother's wife: "Do not have sexual relations with your brother's wife."

345. Lev 18:18, One must not have a sexual relationship with one's wife's sister while one's wife is still living: "Do not take your wife's sister as a rival wife and have sexual relations with her while your wife is living."

346. Lev 18:19, One must not have a sexual relationship with a menstruating woman: "Do not approach a woman to have sexual relations during the uncleanness of her monthly period."

347. Lev 18:20, One must not have a sexual relationship with the wife of another: " Do not have sexual relations with your neighbor's wife." (Cf. Ex 20:14; Dt 5:17 [EVV 18], "You shall not commit adultery.")

—**Mt 5:28,** "I tell you that anyone who looks at a woman lustfully has already committed adultery with her in his heart."

348. Lev 18:23, A man must not have a sexual relationship with an animal: "Do not have sexual relations with an animal."

349. Lev 18:23, A woman must not have a sexual relationship with an animal: "A woman must not present herself to an animal to have sexual relations with it."

350. Lev 18:22, One must not commit an act of homosexuality: "Do not lie with a man as one lies with a woman."

—Ro 1:26–27, "Because of this, God gave them over to shameful lusts. Even their women exchanged natural relations for unnatural ones. In the same way the men also abandoned natural relations with women and were inflamed with lust for one another. Men committed indecent acts with other men, and received in themselves the due penalty for their perversion."

351. Lev 18:7, One must not commit an act of homosexuality with one's father: "Do not uncover the nakedness of your father."

352. Lev 18:14, One must not commit an act of homosexuality with one's uncle: "Do not uncover the nakedness of your father's brother."

353. Lev 18:6, One must not have (M. close contact with or) a sexual relationship with any close relative: "No one is to approach any close relative to have sexual relations."

354. Dt 23:3 (evv 2), One must not marry one born of a forbidden marriage (bastard): "No one born of a forbidden marriage may enter the assembly of the Lord."

355. Dt 23:18 (evv 17), One must not be a prostitute: "No Israelite man or woman is to become a shrine prostitute."

356. Dt 24:4, One who is divorced must not marry her former husband: "Her first husband, who divorced her, is not allowed to marry her again."

—Lk 16:18, "Anyone who divorces his wife and marries another woman commits adultery, and the man who marries a divorced woman commits adultery."

357. Dt 25:5, A widowed sister-in-law must not marry any but her husband's brother: "His widow must not marry outside the family."

358. Dt 22:29, One who has married a woman because he raped her must not divorce her: "He can never divorce her as long as he lives."

359. Dt 22:19, One who has slandered his wife must not divorce her: "He must not divorce her as long as he lives."

360. Dt 23:2 (evv 1), One who is a eunuch must not marry into the assembly of Israel: "No one who has been emasculated by crushing or cutting may enter the assembly of the Lord."

361. Lev 22:24, Castration is forbidden: "You must not offer to the Lord an animal whose testicles are bruised, crushed, torn, or cut. You must not do this in your own land."

M. Prohibitions relating to the king:

362. Dt 17:15, The king is to be from the house of Israel: "He must be from among your own brothers."

363. Dt 17:16, The king must not have many horses: "The king, moreover, must not acquire great numbers of horses."

364. Dt 17:17, The king must not have many wives: "He must not take many wives."

365. Dt 17:17, The king must not accumulate great wealth: "He must not accumulate large amounts of silver and gold."

LIST OF WORKS CONSULTED

Ainsworth, Henry. *Annotations upon the Five Books of Moses*. London: M. Parsons, 1639.

Allen, Ronald B., and Kenneth L. Barker. "Numbers." In *The NIV Study Bible.*" Ed. Kenneth L. Barker. Grand Rapids: Zondervan, 1985.

Andersen, Francis I. *The Sentence in Biblical Hebrew*. The Hague: Mouton Publishers, 1980.

Augustine, Saint. *The City of God Against the Pagans*. Ed. Philip Levine. Loeb Classical Library. Cambridge: Harvard Univ. Press, 1966.

Die Babylonische Talmud. Ed. Lazarus Goldschmidt. Berlin: Jüdischer Verlag, 1930.

Bacher, Wilhelm. *Die Exegetische Terminologie der Jüdischen Traditionsliteratur*. Hildesheim: Georg Olms, 1965.

Barth, Karl. *Church Dogmatics*. New York: Scribner, 1956.

Beitzel, Barry J. "Exodus 3:14 and the Divine Name: A Case of Biblical Paronomasia." *TrinJ*, n.s., 1 (1980) 5–20.

———. *The Moody Atlas of Bible Lands*. Chicago: Moody Press, 1985.

Bertholet, Alfred. *Leviticus*. Tübingen: J. C. B. Mohr (Paul Siebeck), 1901.

Blum, Erhard, *Die Komposition der Vätergeschichte*. Neukirchen-Vluyn: Neukirchener, 1984.

———. *Studien zur Komposition des Pentateuch*. BZAW 189. Berlin: de Gruyter, 1990.

Böklen, Ernst. *Die Verwandtschaft der jüdisch-christlichen mit der Parsischen Eschatologie*. Göttingen: Vandenhoeck K. Ruprecht, 1902.

Brekelmans, C. "Die sogenannten deuteronomischen Elemente in Genesis bei Numeri. Ein Beitrag zur Vorgeschichte des Deuteronomiums." *VTSup* 15 (Leiden: Brill, 1966) 90–96.

Calvin, John. *Commentaries on the First Book of Moses Called Genesis*. Trans. John King. Grand Rapids: Baker, repr. 1979.

———. *Commentaries on the Four Last Books of Moses Arranged in the Form of a Harmony*. Trans. Charles William Bingham. Grand Rapids: Baker, 1979.

Carson, D. A. "Redaction Criticism: On the Legitimacy and Illegitimacy of a Literary Tool." In *Scripture and Truth*, ed. D. A. Carson and John Woodbridge (Grand Rapids: Zondervan, 1983) 119–42.

_____. "Matthew." *EBC* , ed. Frank E. Gaebelein. Grand Rapids: Zondervan, 1984) 8:3–599.

Caspari, Wilhelm. "Heimat und Soziale Wirkung des alttestamentlichen Bundesbuches." *ZDMG* 83 (1929) 97–110.

Cassuto, U. *A Commentary on the Book of Exodus.* Trans. Israel Abrahams. Jerusalem: Magnes, 1967.

_____. *A Commentary on the Book of Genesis.* Part 1: *From Adam to Noah.* Trans. Israel Abrahams. Jerusalem: Magnes, 1972.

Cazelles, Henri. "L'auteur du code de l'alliance." *RB* 52 (1945) 173–91.

Charles, R. H., ed. *The Apocrypha and Pseudepigrapha of the Old Testament in English.* 2 vols. Oxford: Clarendon, 1913.

Coccejus, J. *Opera Omnia Theologica, Exegetica, Didactica, Polemica, Philologica, Divisa in Decem Volumina.* Amsterdam: P. et J. Blaev, 1701.

De Beaugrade, Robert, and Wolfgang Dressler. *Introduction to Text Linguistics.* London: Longman, 1981.

Delitzsch, F. *A New Commentary on Genesis.* Edinburgh: T. & T. Clark, 1888.

Diestel, L. *Geschichte des Alten Testaments in der christliche Kirche.* Jena: Mauke's Verlag, 1869.

Driver, S. R. *A Critical and Exegetical Commentary on Deuteronomy.* ICC. Edinburgh: T. & T. Clark, 1895.

Eichrodt, Wlater. *Theology of the Old Testament.* Trans. J. A. Baker. 2 vols. OTL. Philadelphia: Westminster, 1961.

Eissfeldt, Otto. *The Old Testament: An Introduction*, trans. P. R. Ackroyd. New York: Harper & Row, 1965.

_____. *Hexateuch-Synopse, Die Erzählung der fünf Bücher Mose und des Buches Josua mit dem Anfange des Richerbuches.* Darmstadt: Wissenschaftliche Buchgesellschaft, 1973.

Encyclopaedia Biblica. 8 vols. Jerusalem: Bialik Institute, 1955–1956.

Fishbane, Michael. *Biblical Interpretation in Ancient Israel.* Oxford: Clarendon, 1985.

Flacius, Matthias. *Clavis Scripturae seu de Sermone Sacrarum Literarum, plurimas generales Regulas continentis, Altera Pars.* Leipzig, 1695 (1st ed., 1567).

Fohrer, Georg. *Introduction to the Old Testament.* Trans. D. E. Green. Nashville: Abingdon, 1968.

_____. *Exegese des Alten Testaments.* Heidelberg: Quelle & Meyer, 1983.

Frei, Hans W. *The Eclipse of Biblical Narrative: A Study in Eighteenth and Nineteenth Century Hermeneutics.* New Haven: Yale Univ. Press, 1974.

Gerhard, Johann. *Locorum Theologicorum cum pro adstruenda veritate, tum pro destruends quorumuis contradicentium falsitate, per theses nervose, solide et copiose explicatorum.* In *De Scriptura sacra* (Geneva, 1639).

Ginzberg, Louis. *The Legends of the Jews.* 7 vols. Philadelphia: Jewish Publication Society, 1968.

Goldschmidt, L. *Der Babylonische Talmud.* 12 vols. Berlin: Jüdischer Verlag, 1930.

Gray, George Buchanan. *A Critical and Exegetical Commentary on Numbers.* ICC. Edinburgh: T. & T. Clark, 1903.

Gressmann, Hugo. *Mose und seine Zeit, ein Kommentar zu den Mose-Sagen.* Göttingen: Vandenhoeck & Ruprecht, 1913.

Gross, W. "Syntaktische Erscheinungen am Anfang althebräischer Erzählungen: Hintergrund und Vordergrund." *VTSup* 32 (Leiden: Brill, 1981) 131–45.

Gulich, Elisabeth, and Wolfgang Raible. "Überlegungen zu einer makrostrukturellen Textanalyse: J. Thurber, The Lover and His Lass." In *Untersuchungen in Texttheorie* (Göttingen: Vandenhoeck & Ruprecht, 1977) 132–75.

Gunkel, Hermann. *Genesis übersetz und erklärt.* 9th ed. Göttingen: Vandenhoeck & Ruprecht, 1977).

Harrison, R. K. *Introduction to the Old Testament.* Grand Rapids: Eerdmans, 1969.

Hatturim, Baal. *Chumash* (Hebrew). New York: Philipp Feldheim, 1967.

Hayes, William C. *Cambridge Ancient History*. 3d ed. Cambridge: Cambridge Univ. Press, 1973.

Heppe, Heinrich. *Die Dogmatik der evangelisch-reformierten Kirche*. Neukirchen: Neukirchener, 1935.

Hirsch, Emanuel. *Geschichte der neuern evangelischen Theologie im Zusammenhang mit den allgemeinen Bewegungen des europäischen Denkens*, 5 vols. Gütersloh: Bertelsmann, 1949.

Hizquni. *Commentary on the Torah* (Hebrew). Jerusalem: Mossad Harav Kook, 1988.

Hoftijzer, J., and G. van der Kooij. *Aramaic Texts from Deir 'Alla*. Leiden: Brill, 1976.

Holzinger, H. *Einleitung in den Hexateuch*. Freiburg: Mohr [Siebeck], 1893.

_____. *Numeri*. Kurzer Hand-Commentar zum Alten Testament. Tübingen: J. C. B. Mohr [Paul Siebeck], 1903.

Ibn Ezra. *Torat Chaim Chumash* (Hebrew). Ed. M. L. Gesinlinburg. Jerusalem: Mossad Harav Kook, 1986.

Jacob, Benno. *Das erste Buch der Tora, Genesis*. Berlin: Schocken, 1934.

Jamieson, Robert, A. R. Fausset, and David Brown. *A Commentary Critical, Experimental and Practical on the Old and New Testaments*. 3 vols. (Grand Rapids: Eerdmans, 1945.

Josephus, Flavius. *Works*. Trans. H. St. J. Thackeray, Loeb Classical Library, 9 vols. Cambridge: Harvard Univ. Press, repr. 1966.

Kahnis, Karl F. A. *Die lutherische Dogmatik historisch-genetisch dargestellt*. Leipzig: Dorffling and Franke, 1874.

Kaiser, Walter, Jr. *Toward Old Testament Ethics*. Grand Rapids: Zondervan, 1983.

_____. "Exodus." *EBC*, ed. Frank E. Gaebelein (Grand Rapids: Zondervan, 1990) 2:287–497.

Katchen, Aaron L. *Christian Hebraists and Dutch Rabbis: Seventeenth Century Apologetics and the Study of Maimonides' Mishneh Torah*. Harvard University Center for Jewish Studies. Cambridge: Harvard Univ. Press, 1984.

Kautsch, E. *Gesenius' Hebrew Grammar*. Trans. and rev. A. E. Cowley. Oxford: Clarendon, 1910.

Keeney, Bradford P. *Aesthetics of Change, New York: Guilford, 1983*.

Keil, C. F., and F. Delitzsch. *The Pentateuch*. 3 vols. Grand Rapids: Eerdmans, 1971 (repr.).

Kitchen, K. A. "Magic and Sorcery." In *New Bible Dictionary*, ed. J. D. Douglas (Grand Rapids: Eerdmans, 1962) 766-71.

_____. "Plagues of Egypt." In *New Bible Dictionary*, ed. J. D. Douglas (Grand Rapids: Eerdmans, 1962) 1001–1003.

Knierim, Rolf P. "The Composition of the Pentateuch." In *SBL 1985 Seminar Papers* (Atlanta: Scholars Press, 1987) 393–415.

Knudtzon, J. A. *Die El-Amarna-Tafeln*. Aalen: Otto Zeller, 1964.

Koehler, Ludwig, and Walter Baumgartner. *Hebräisches und Aramäisches Lexikon zum alten Testament*. Leiden: Brill, 1974.

König, Eduard. *Die Genesis: Eingeleitet, übersetzt und erklärt*. Gütersloh: Bertelsmann, 1919.

Kraus, F. R. "Ein Zentrales Problem des Altmesopotamischen Rechtes: Was Ist der Codex Hammu-rabi?" *Genava* 8 (1960) 283–96.

Kraus, Hans-Joachim. *Die Biblische Theologie: Ihre Geschichte und Problematik*. Neukirchen: Neukirchener, 1970.

Lev, Mordecai J., ed. *Sepher Mitzvoth* (Hebrew). Jerusalem: Mossad Harav Kook, 1990.

Levy, Jacob. *Chaldäisches Wörterbuch über die Targumim*. 2 vols. Leipzig: Baumgärtner's Buchhandlung, 1881.

Lohmeyer, Ernst. *Das Evangelium des Matthäus*. Kritisch-exegetischer Kommentar über das Neue Testament. Göttingen: Vandenhoeck & Ruprecht, 1962.

Macho, Alejandro Diez, ed. *Neophyti I Targum Palestinense MS de la Biblioteca Vaticana*. 5 vols. Madrid: Consejo Superior de Investigaciones Cientificas, 1968+.

Maimonides. *Sepher Mitzvoth* (Hebrew). Ed. Mordecai J. Lev. Jerusalem: Mossad Harav Kook, 1990.

_____. *Mishneh Torah, Tefillin.* Trans. Philip Birnbaum. New York: Hebrew Publishing Co., 1967.

Mendenhall, George E. "Ancient Oriental and Biblical Law." In *The Biblical Archaeologist Reader,* ed. E. F. Campbell and David Noel Freedman (New York: Anchor Books, 1970: 3–24.

Mercerus, Johannes. *In Genesin Primum Mosis Librum, sic a Graecis Appellatum, Commentarius.* Genevae, 1598.

Midrash Rabbah. New York: KTAV, n.d.

Montanus, Arias. *Liber Generationis et Regenerationis Adam.* Antwerp, 1593.

Noordtzij, A. *Numbers.* Trans. Ed van der Maas. Bible Student's Commentary. Grand Rapids: Zondervan, 1983.

Oberforcher, Robert. *Die Flutprologe als kompositions-schlüssel der biblischen Urgeschichte.* Innsbruck: Tyrolia, 1981.

O'Donovan, O. M. T. "Towards an Interpretation of Biblical Ethics." *Tyndale Bulletin* 27 (1976) 54–78.

Oeming, Manfred. "Bedeutung und Funktionen von 'Fiktionen' in der alttestamentlichen Geschichtsschreibung." *EvT* 44 (1984) 254–66.

Pearson, J., A. Scattergood, F. Gouldman, and R. Pearson, eds. *Critici Sacri: Annotata Doctissimorum Virorum in Vetus ac Novum Testamentum.* Amsterdam, 1698.

Philippi, Friedrich A. *Kirchliche Glaubenslehre.* 5 vols. Gütersloh: C. Bertelsmann, 1883.

Philo, Judeus. *Works.* Trans. F. H. Colson, Loeb Classical Library 10 vols. Cambridge: Harvard Univ. Press, repr. 1966.

Pictet, Benedict. *Theologia Christiana Ex puris S. S. Literarum Fontibus hausta.* Langerak, 1723.

Pol, Matthius. *Synopsis Criticorum Aliorumque Sacrae Scripturae Interpretum.* 5 vols. Utrecht: Leusden, 1684.

Procksch, Otto. *Die Genesis übersetzt und erklärt.* KAT. Leipzig: A. Deichert, 1913.

Quenstedt, J. A. *Theologia Didactico-polemica sive Systema Theologicum.* Wittenberg, 1685.

Rambam. *The Commentary of Rambam on the Torah* (Hebrew). Ed. H. D. Shual. Jerusalem: Mossad Harav Kook, 1984.

Rashi. *Torah Chaim Chumash.* 2 vols. Jerusalem: Mossad Harav Kook, 1987.

_____. *Commentary on the Torah* (Hebrew). Ed. Chaim Dov Shual. Jerusalem: Mossad Harav Kook, 1988.

Rasmussen, Carl G. *NIV Atlas of the Bible.* Grand Rapids: Zondervan, 1989.

Realencyklopädie für protestantische Theologie und Kirche, 3d ed., 24 vols. Leipzig: J. C. Hinrichs'sche, 1904ff.

Rendtorff, Rolf. *Das überlieferungsgeschichtliche Problem des Pentateuch.* BZAW 147. Berlin: de Gruyter, 1977.

Rivetus, Andreas. *Isagoge.* Lugdunus, 1627.

_____. *Opera Theologica.* Rotterdam, 1651.

Rohnert, W. *Die Dogmatik der evangelisch-lutherischen Kirche.* Leipzig: Hellmuth Wollermann, 1902.

Sailhamer, John. "Exegetical Notes: Genesis 1:1–2:4a." *TrinJ* 5, no. 1 (1984) 73–82.

_____. "A Database Approach to the Analysis of Hebrew Narrative." *MAARAV* 5–6 (Spring 1990) 319–35.

_____. "Genesis." In *EBC,* ed. Frank E. Gaebelein (Grand Rapids: Zondervan, 1990) 2:3–284.

_____. "The Mosaic Law and the Theology of the Pentateuch." *WTJ* 53 (Fall 1991) 241–61.

Sasson, J. M. "Wordplay in the OT." In *IDBS,* ed. Keith Crim (Nashville: Abingdon, 1976) 968–70.

Schmid, Heinrich. *The Doctrinal Theology of the Evangelical Lutheran Church*. Minneapolis: Augsburg, n.d.

Schmidt, Hans-Christoph. "Redaktion des Pentateuch im Geiste der Prophetie, Beobachtungen zur Bedeutung der 'Glaubens'-Thematik innerhalb der Theologie des Pentateuch." *VT* 2 (1983) 170–89.

Schmidt, Siegfried J. "Towards a Pragmatic Interpretation of Fictionality." In *Pragmatics of Language and Literature*, ed. T. A. van Dijk (Amsterdam: North-Holland Publishing Co., 1976) 161–78.

—————. *Text theorie, Probleme einer Linguistik der sprachlichen Kommunikation*. Uni-Taschenbücher 202. Munich: Wilhelm Fink, 1976.

Schmidt, Werner H. *Old Testament Introduction*. Trans. Matthew J. O'Connell. New York: Crossroad, 1984.

Schmitt, Armin. "Interpretation der Genesis aus hellenistischem Geist." *ZAW* 86 (1974) 137–63.

Schmitt, Hans-Christoph. "Redaktion des Pentateuch im Geiste der Prophetie." *VT* 2 (1982) 170–89.

Seforno. *Torat Chaim Chumash* (Hebrew). Jerusalem: Mossad Harav Kook, 1987.

Sekine, Masao. "Vom Verstehen der Heilsgeschichte: Das Grundproblem der alttestamentlichen Theologie." *ZAW* 75 (1963) 145–54.

Sperber, A., ed. *The Bible in Aramaic*. 4 vols. Leiden: Brill, 1959–1968.

Stadelmann, Helge. ed. *Epochen der Heilsgeschichte, Beiträge zur Förderung heilsgeschichtlicher Theologie*. Wuppertal: R. Brockhaus, 1984.

—————. *Grundlinien eines bibeltreuen Schriftverständnisses*. Wuppertal: R. Brockhaus, 1985.

—————, ed. *Glaube und Geschichte, Heilsgeschichte als Thema der Theologie*. Giessen: Brunnen, 1986.

Sternberg, Meir. *The Poetics of Biblical Narrative, Ideological Literature and the Drama of Reading*. Bloomington: Indiana Univ. Press, 1985.

Steuernagel, Carl. *Das Deuteronomium*. Handkommentar zum Alten Testament. Göttingen: Vandenhoeck & Ruprecht, 1900.

Strack, H. L., and Paul Billerbeck. *Kommentar zum Neuen Testament aus Talmud und Midrasch*. 6 vols. Munich: C. H. Beck'sche, 1926.

Strack, H. L., and G. Stemberger. *Introduction to the Talmud and Midrash*. Trans. M. Bockmuehl. Edinburgh: T. & T. Clark, 1991.

Swete, Henry Barclay. *An Introduction to the Old Testament in Greek*. New York: KTAV, 1968.

Tanakh: The Holy Scriptures. The New JPS Translation According to the Traditional Hebrew Text. Philadelphia: Jewish Publication Society, 1988.

Turrettini, Franciscus. *Institutio Theologiae Elencticae*. New York, 1847.

Ussher, James. *Annales Veteris Testamenti*. London, 1650.

Von Rad, Gerhard. *Genesis*. Trans. John H. Marks. OTL. Philadelphia: Westminster, 1961.

Vos, G. *Biblical Theology: Old and New Testaments*. Grand Rapids: Eerdmans, 1948, repr. 1980.

Walter, Michael. *Harmonia Biblica*. Nüremberg, 1969.

—————. *Harmonia Totius s. Scripturae*. Argentorate: Eberhard Zetzner, 1927.

Warfield, Benjamin B. *Revelation and Inspiration*. Oxford: Oxford Univ. Press, 1927; repr. Grand Rapids: Baker, 1981.

Welch, Adam. *Deuteronomy, The Framework to the Code*. London: J. Clarke, 1932.

Wenham, Gordon J. *The Book of Leviticus*. NICOT. Grand Rapids: Eerdmans, 1979.

—————. "Sanctuary Symbolism in the Garden of Eden Story." *Proceedings of the World Congress of Jewish Studies* 9 (1986) 19–25.

Westermann, Claus. *Theologie des Alten Testaments in Grundzügen*. Göttingen: Vandenhoeck & Ruprecht, 1978.

—————. *Genesis*. Trans. John J. Scullion. 3 vols. Minneapolis: Augsburg, 1984–86.

White, Hayden. "The Value of Narrativity in the Representation of Reality." *Critical Inquiry* 7 (1980) 5–27.

Wohlenberg, Gustav. *Der erste und zeite Petrusbrief und der Judasbrief*. Leipzig: A. Deichert, 1915.

Yalkut Shemoni (Hebrew). Jerusalem, 1960.

Zöckler, O. "Schöpfung." *RE*, 3d edition (Gotha: Verlag von rudolf Besser, 1866) 20:735-36.

Zorell, Franciscus. *Lexicon Hebraicum et Aramaicum Veteris Testament*. Rome: Pontificium Institutum Biblicum, 1968.